Childhood and Adolescence

Childhood and Adolescence
Cross-Cultural Perspectives and Applications

Edited by

Uwe P. Gielen and Jaipaul Roopnarine

Advances in Applied Developmental Psychology, Number 23
Irving E. Sigel, Series Editor

Westport, Connecticut
London

Library of Congress Cataloging-in-Publication Data

Workshop on Childhood and Adolescence in Cross-Cultural Perspective (2000 : New
  York Academy of Sciences)
  Childhood and adolescence : cross-cultural perspectives and applications / edited by
  Uwe P. Gielen and Jaipaul Roopnarine.
      p. cm. — (Advances in applied developmental psychology ; no. 23)
      Includes bibliographical references and index.
      ISBN 1–56750–660–7 (alk. paper) — ISBN 1–56750–661–5 (pbk. : alk. paper)
      1. Childhood psychology—Cross-cultural studies—Congresses.   2. Adolescent
  psychology—Cross-cultural studies—Congresses.   3. Ethnopsychology—Congresses.
  I. Gielen, Uwe P. (Uwe Peter), 1940–   II. Roopnarine, Jaipaul L.   III. Title.   IV. Series.
  BF721.W67   2004
  155.4—dc22   2004042785

British Library Cataloguing in Publication Data is available.

Library of Congress Catalog Card Number: 2004042785
ISBN: 1–56750–660–7
        1–56750–661–5 (pbk.)

First published in 2004

Praeger Publishers, 88 Post Road West, Westport, CT 06881
An imprint of Greenwood Publishing Group, Inc.
www.praeger.com

Printed in the United States of America

The paper used in this book complies with the
Permanent Paper Standard issued by the National
Information Standards Organization (Z39.48–1984).

10 9 8 7 6 5 4 3 2 1

Contents

Foreword

T. S. Saraswathi

In 1996, in his foreword to the thought-provoking volume by Brad Shore, titled *Culture in Mind*, Jerome Bruner eloquently elucidated the concept of *meaning-making*. The ideas expressed therein have left a lasting impression on me. Meaning-making bridges culture as it exists outside the person and the neurological mechanism that is the biological endowment of man, contributing to the concept of culture in mind. The emphasis here is on a "cognitive view of culture and cultural view of mind" (Shore, 1996, p. 39). Socialization and enculturation act as mediators in the construction of this reality. Bruner refers to meaning-making as a process "without which human beings in every culture fall into terror. The product of meaning making is Reality" (1996, p. xv). Shore, in turn, elaborates the process of meaning-making as "twice born," first at the cultural level in terms of "the communal or canonical meaning of something or act or utterance, and then the idiosyncratic meaning *for* some individual or some occasion" (Bruner, 1996, p. xv).

The chapters in *Childhood and Adolescence: Cross-Cultural Perspectives and Applications*, edited by Uwe P. Gielen and Jaipaul Roopnarine, present clinching evidence of the interplay of divergent cultural beliefs and practices, with the process of meaning-making influenced by varied individual experiences both within and across cultures. They facilitate the understanding of how specific ecocultural factors contribute to the construction of varied realities and a range of acceptable or adaptive human expressions of a wide range of psychological characteristics. As stated by Chen and Kaspar, in their chapter "Cross-Cultural Research on Childhood," "The dialectic between culture and development requires the investigation of cultural influences on the child from a developmental perspective. . . . [T]he relations between the child and culture are interactional and dynamic. Children are active participants in constructing and creating their cultural environment" (pp. 69–70).

making successful school and peer adjustments, three- to four-year-old children living in a Central Africa foraging society and weaning themselves from their mothers, Mayan elementary schoolchildren teaching their younger siblings the ins and outs of their culture, boys and girls soaking up the gender roles of their society in an almost osmosis-like fashion, teenagers in developing countries becoming increasingly savvy about the steadily spreading and changing global teenage culture, war-traumatized youngsters surviving in an Ethiopian refugee camp, and adolescents and their friendships among the Ijo of Nigeria. Perusing such a diversity of lives, the reader cannot but arrive at a more global, holistic, differentiated, down-to-earth, and culturally informed conception of human development than may be found in mainstream textbooks.

Preparing this volume has been a pleasure because so many people supported our efforts. We would like to thank the New York Academy of Sciences and, especially, the members of its Psychology Section Advisory Board for supporting and hosting the workshop that provided the original inspiration for the book. Natasha Carty, Monica Cupen, Petra Bernard, Oksana Chumachenko, and Oraine Ramoo contributed their considerable typing, proofreading, and computer skills while helping to prepare the book manuscript. St. Francis College, through the Institute for International and Cross-Cultural Psychology, provided much appreciated institutional and financial support. And above all, we as editors would like to extend our sincere thanks to each of the authors, without whose contributions this volume would not exist.

We express appreciation to the University Seminars at Columbia University for assistance in the preparation of the manuscript for publication. Material drawn from this work was presented to the University Seminar on Moral Education.

We dedicate this book to the children of this world.

That daily life practices in settings such as the family, the playground, and the school act as vital agencies in meaning-making is highlighted in Bornstein, Haynes, Pascual, and Painter's chapter, "Competence and Satisfaction in Parenting Young Children," and in contributions by Fuligni, in "The Adaptation and Accultura-tion of Children from Immigrant Families," and Jia, in "The Acquisition of English and Maintenance of First Language by Immigrant Children and Adolescents in North America." The co-construction of the meaning of cultural practices in the interactions between the socializing agent(s) and the child/adolescent draws at-tention to the dynamic nature of culture and adaptation.

The three chapters in Part V, on adaptation of immigrant children in the United States, focus singularly on the dynamics of acculturation. They comple-ment the cross-cultural perspective adopted by the other chapters that examine cultural universals or relativism. The aspects of acculturation experiences re-viewed here relate specifically to second-language learning (English), retention of first language, and schooling and education. The chapters point out that second-language learning and first-language retention are complex phenomena involving several factors. Some of the contributing factors include parents, rea-sons for migration, socioeconomic status, level of education, and significantly, parental ethnotheories or beliefs and practices related to disciplinary practices and education. These are examined in their interaction with factors such as the prestige of the first language in the host country, age of introduction of the sec-ond language, and the receptivity of parents, teachers, and children with respect to the retention of the first language. The reviews highlight most clearly that culture is not a monolithic, stable entity but a dynamic product of a socio-historical context. The aspects of acculturation selected for review in Part V lend themselves to investigating both the process and the outcomes of acculturation (Berry & Sam, 1997) together with factors associated with both the immigrants and the host cultures (as elaborated in Ogbu, 1994). The factors buffer or exac-erbate the stress experienced. More significantly, they draw attention to the dy-namic quality of culture-in-mind and the process of cultural construction with implications for other aspects of culture-mind interaction.

A second major theme that emerges across chapters is the significance of *al-ternative pathways to development*. Gielen sets the stage for elucidating this theme in his lucid and provocative introduction, titled aptly as an "opinionated" his-torical introduction! Instead of searching for the elusive psychic unity or the much debated psychological universals, almost all the chapters illustrate that optimal human development cannot and should not be examined against the single template of the Western model of child development. I am particularly pleased with the contribution by Robert LeVine, whose evolutionary theory of child development has often conveyed a misleading impression of cultural pro-gression that optimizes the Western model of man with emphasis on focused, dyadic, face-to-face, verbal interaction. LeVine makes a strong case for child-rearing and child development that is ecoculturally adaptive.

In a similar vein, Maynard's chapter, on sibling relationship, takes a broad anthropological perspective and examines the cultural construction of the meaning of sibling relations in the majority world, with large families, many siblings, a hierarchical family structure, and prescriptive role obligations. In my own country, in the northern half of India, the culturally prescribed obligation of the siblings to each other is reiterated through the annual festival of Rakhi, wherein the sisters ceremonially tie a decorative thread on their brothers' wrists, pledging their bond of affection, and seek the support and protection of brothers throughout life (even after marriage and the establishment of one's own conjugal family). What is more, the sibling relationship is not confined only to those who share genes but also includes those related as cousins or only through ties of friendship and affection, thereby expanding the kinship network of social support. Again, it is not a question of personal choice as it is in the West, but a cultural practice embedded in the idea of interdependence and the concept of duty and dharma.

The concept of divergent realities also finds expression in Gibbons's and Arnett's chapters on adolescence in a global perspective, Aptekar's description of children and adolescents growing up in difficult circumstances, and Best's analysis of gender differences. The sociohistorical and ecocultural factors that contribute to the cultural construction of adolescence and alternative pathways to their development have received detailed attention in the book *World Youth: Adolescence in Eight Regions of the Globe*, edited by Brown, Larson, and Saraswathi (2002).

Childhood and Adolescence: Cross-Cultural Perspectives and Applications will effectively complement the existing texts in cross-cultural psychology (such as those by Berry, Poortinga, Segall, & Dasen [1992]; Segall, Dasen, Berry, & Poortinga [1999]; Adler & Gielen [2001]; and Gardiner & Kosmitzki [2004]). It will serve to illustrate to young scholars the process of making meaning in divergent realities and the consequent alternate pathways to development. This book also carries the significant and implicit message that knowledge in the field itself is a cultural construction whose horizons expand with an expanding culture-inclusive vision, situated in sociohistorical time and ecocultural space. What is revealed across the chapters is that the field has come a long way from the "culture-free" and "culture-fair" approaches of a value-neutral "scientific" psychology, to its current stand of "culture in mind" (Cole, 1996; Shore, 1996) and culture-inclusive psychology (Valsiner, 1989). The lucid introduction by Gielen should serve to temper the contemporary hostile agendas that exist in the field, which lead to artificial divides and act at times as deterrents to progress in knowledge construction in the discipline.

REFERENCES

Adler, L. L., & Gielen, U. P. (Eds.). (2001). *Cross-Cultural topics in psychology* (2nd ed.). Westport, CT: Greenwood.

Berry, J. W., Poortinga, Y. H., Segall, M. H., & Dasen, P. R. (1992). *Cross-cultural psychology. Research and applications*. New York: Cambridge University Press.

Berry, J. W., & Sam, D. L. (1997). Acculturation and adaptation. In J. W. Berry, M. H. Segall, & C. Kagitcibasi (Eds.), *Handbook of cross-cultural psychology*, Vol. 3, *Social behavior and applications* (pp. 291–326). Boston: Allyn & Bacon.

Brown, B., Larson, R., & Saraswathi, T. S. (Eds.). (2002). *World youth: Adolescence in eight regions of the globe*. London: Cambridge University Press.

Bruner, J. (1996). Foreword to B. Shore (Ed.), *Culture in mind* (pp. xiv–xvii). New York: Oxford University Press.

Cole, M. (1996). *Cultural psychology: A once and future discipline*. Cambridge: Belknap Press of Harvard University Press.

Gardiner, H. W., & Kosmitzki, C. (2004). *Lives across cultures: Cross-cultural human development* (3rd ed.). Boston: Allyn & Bacon.

Ogbu, J. U. (1994). From cultural differences to differences in cultural frame of reference. In P. Greenfield & R. Cocking (Eds.), *Cross-cultural roots of minority child development* (pp. 365–391). Hillsdale, NJ: Erlbaum.

Segall, M. H., Dasen, P. R., Berry, J. W., & Poortinga, Y. H. (1999). *Human development in global perspective: An introduction to cross-cultural psychology*. Boston: Allyn & Bacon.

Shore, B. (1996). *Culture in mind*. New York: Oxford University Press.

Valsiner, J. (1989). *Child development in cultural context*. Toronto: Hogrefe & Huber.

Introduction

Uwe P. Gielen and Jaipaul Roopnarine

During the last twenty years there has been a rapidly growing research interest in child and adolescent development across cultures. It is the purpose of *Childhood and Adolescence* to present an overview of some of the most recent and challenging work in this area. This volume includes the contributions of a diverse group of psychologists and anthropologists who share the conviction that a comprehensive understanding of human development requires a contextual approach in which cultural factors play a prominent role. Their contributions describe and analyze the socioemotional and sociocognitive development of children and adolescents in a wide variety of cultural settings spread throughout the world. The volume is about the lives of the more than two billion children and teenagers who, in just a few years, will grow into young women and men ready to shape the future for us all.

Many of the chapters included in this volume are of an integrative nature while others focus on applied issues. The contributors were asked to analyze an area of cross-cultural research falling within the purview of their expertise, while reflecting on their own research programs in the wider context of related studies conducted by other authors. Thus the reader will gain an overview of specific cross-cultural research topics, including worldwide changes in children's lives, parent-child relationships, sibling relationships, gender roles, and adolescence in the industrialized and the developing worlds, as refracted through the eyes of leading contributors to the scientific literature. In contrast, the chapters are less centered on broad disciplinary and well-known debates such as those between cultural and cross-cultural psychologists, cultural and psychological anthropologists, or anthropologists and psychologists. The volume's predominant focus is on substantive contributions in the context of medium-range theories and hypotheses rather than on arcane epistemological, theoretical, or methodological debates.

This volume is intended to be read by psychologists, cultural and psychological anthropologists, educators, and advanced undergraduate and graduate students interested in cross-cultural contributions to the study of childhood and adolescence. The book should be of interest to both teachers and researchers.

The idea of developing this book arose in connection with the Workshop on Childhood and Adolescence in Cross-Cultural Perspective, which was held at the New York Academy of Sciences on October 27–28, 2000. Uwe P. Gielen served as organizer and chair of the workshop, with Thomas M. Achenbach, Lewis Aptekar, Marc H. Bornstein, Xinyin Chen, Florence L. Denmark, Andrew Fuligni, Harry Gardiner, Judith L. Gibbons, Barry Hewlett, Gisela Jia, Violet Kaspar, Robert A. LeVine, Margot Nadien, Jaipaul Roopnarine, and Dinesh Sharma presenting papers and chairing various sessions.

After the meeting, we asked the participants to expand their workshop presentations in light of the discussions that had taken place during the event. In addition, we solicited further contributions from scholars who are well-known for their creative work in cross-cultural developmental psychology and anthropology. The contributors include many leading figures who have shaped recent research and theories in the field. In addition, we are pleased to include chapters from several promising younger scholars whose work is bound to shape emerging trends in developmental cross-cultural research.

The systematic cross-cultural study of childhood and adolescence is a relatively recent endeavor, sponsored by two originally rather reluctant parents, namely developmental psychology and cultural anthropology. During the first ninety years of its existence, from about 1880 to 1970, developmental psychology showed little interest in the systematic cross-cultural study of human development. Instead, psychologists attempted to delineate (supposedly) universal trajectories of development as well as a variety of general mechanisms of learning and information processing. The overwhelming majority of their research studies were conducted in the United States, Canada, and Europe, with a few studies from non-Western cultures thrown in to make the intellectual meal appear a bit more exotic. Culture as a crucial shaping influence on development was largely overlooked. The cultural anthropologists, in turn, spent their time attempting to understand a wide variety of mostly non-Western cultures. As part of their efforts, they were eager to grasp the "natives' point of view," but employed adults rather than children as informants because it seemed obvious to them that adults were better informed about their own culture than were children. Neither developmental psychologists nor anthropologists saw human development as a transformative process in which cultural forces constantly interact with biological and psychological forces to create a rich diversity of "biopsychosociocultural" entities.

The scarcity of systematic cross-cultural research on children and adolescents came under critical scrutiny in the 1980s and 1990s, when public opinion in the United States and Western Europe began to be swayed by multiculturalism, and the forces of globalization were making themselves felt in a pervasive manner. This led an increasing number of social scientists to conceptualize diverse developmental trajectories for minority group members, immigrants, and representatives of the mainstream culture. Others began to pay increasing attention to the development of children and adolescents in non-Western societies, including both postindustrial countries such as Japan as well as many countries located in the developing world. In addition, numerous social scientists in the non-Western world have begun to study human development as it takes place in their own cultures, finding that Western approaches and research results can be quite unsatisfactory. As a result, they increasingly favor indigenous, more emically oriented theoretical frameworks, methods, and research goals.

In the face of ever-accelerating global change, the developmental scenarios proposed by the founders of the field of developmental psychology, such as Preyer, Freud, Gesell, Piaget, and others, now appear too static, too homogeneous, too Euro-American, too "white," too middle-class, too male, and too monocultural. In response to these developments, a variety of research projects on culturally diverse groups of children and adolescents have been initiated, with some of them being widely regarded as constituting the cutting edge of research on socioemotional development. This volume takes stock of some of these research efforts and hopes to provide the reader with a map for related future endeavors.

ORGANIZATION OF THE BOOK

It is the purpose of this book to present an overview of selected areas of research in the field of cross-cultural human development together with specific examples of such research. The chapters have been prepared by some of the main contributors to the scientific literature in the belief that productive researchers are best able to convey to the reader the intellectual background, purposes, scope, intricacies, and main findings of ongoing research projects. The volume is divided into six parts, an epilogue, and a selected bibliography. Each of the parts contains several chapters revolving around related questions, topics, and issues of concern. At the same time, the respective authors have adopted a broad variety of theoretical perspectives and methodological approaches. Taken together, these subjects represent much of the richness, complexity, intellectual fervor, and theoretical tensions of the newly emerging field.

Part I: Worldwide Perspectives on Childhood and Adolescence

The first part of the book contains four broadly conceived chapters that set the stage for the contributions to follow. How did the cross-cultural study of human development evolve and what are some of the main assumptions that have guided the field in recent years? These are the two questions posed by Uwe P. Gielen in his chapter, "The Cross-Cultural Study of Human Development: An Opinionated Historical Introduction." He points out that the field has traditionally adopted a double identity. On the one hand, cross-cultural comparisons have been used to test the general validity of leading developmental theories, such as those proposed by G. Stanley Hall, Jean Piaget, Lev S. Vygotsky, Lawrence Kohlberg, and John Bowlby. On the other hand, cross-cultural developmental psychology has evolved into a field with its very own problems and methodological concerns revolving around the study of the cultural nature of mind and behavior. Gielen reviews the history of the field by focusing on some early and highly speculative evolutionary theorizing, Margaret Mead's contrasting emphasis on cultural relativism, the lasting legacies left by the contributions of Piaget, Kohlberg, and Vygotsky, and the recent return of neo-evolutionary approaches, including those proposed by John Bowlby and his student, Mary D. S. Ainsworth.

Guided by a synthetic approach, Gielen then introduces ten assumptions that can be said to structure modern cross-cultural inquiries into the nature of human development. These assumptions favor the multidisciplinary study of socioemotional and cognitive development with the help of a whole array of methodologies mostly created by psychologists and anthropologists. These two fields, in turn, have favored rather different ways of studying human development across cultures.

Gielen concludes that only a combination of anthropological and psychological approaches, together with additional contributions from fields such as demography, sociology, and biology, can create a comprehensive, balanced, and valid picture of human development in all its complexities around the world. In contrast to this approach, mainstream developmental psychology is said to remain in many ways myopic and ethnocentric.

Chen and Kaspar, in their chapter, "Cross-Cultural Research on Childhood," discuss cross-cultural research on children's play, peer interactions, academic achievement, family conditions including parental childrearing practices, and their socioemotional adjustment and maladjustment. Given Chen's extensive involvement in comparative research on the socioemotional development of Chinese and North American children, the authors are especially interested in comparisons between East Asian and Western children.

Like many other cross-cultural developmental psychologists, Chen and Kaspar adopt a socioecological approach when comparing and integrating the results of the available research literature. They regard patterns of social communication and interaction as intermediate links between the shaping influence of culture and the socioemotional and sociocognitive development of children. Cultural belief systems, for instance, shape "developmental niches" within which the development of children can unfold.

Consider, for instance, children's play. On the one hand, children's play behavior in many societies tends to follow a developmental trajectory advancing from sensorimotor forms of play in infancy to the more complex forms of sociodramatic play found among preschool and elementary school-age children. On the other hand, cultures differ widely in the degree to which children's play is encouraged—ranging from severely penalizing play, as is practiced among the Sinai Bedouin Arabs, to systematically encouraging play as part of modern "child-centered" forms of education, as is prevalent in many Western countries.

Similarly, East Asian cultures tend to encourage children's and adolescents' persistent focus on educational tasks, whereas American children are more likely to come under the sway of competing ideologies emphasizing alternative activities such as sports, dating, having fun, and risk-taking behavior. Different cultures, then, are likely to promote different pathways for their members in response to varying ecological, economic, historical, and other social conditions.

Gielen and Chumachenko, in their chapter, "All the World's Children: The Impact of Global Demographic Trends and Economic Disparities," provide us with an overview of the world's 2.15 billion children under the age of eighteen by examining worldwide economic and demographic trends. Their analysis points to striking differences in children's environments between the poorer and the richer countries as manifested by divergent fertility and mortality data, rapid declines in family size and family stability, changing gender roles, the emergence of adolescence and adolescent subcultures in the wealthier nations, and the importance of child labor in the poor countries and prolonged schooling in the rich countries. After analyzing pertinent information about ten representative nations located around the globe, the authors introduce us to twenty worldwide trends that, in their opinion, will continue to shape childrearing conditions in the foreseeable future. Throughout their essay they stress the pervasive and long-term impact of material conditions on children's well-being and life chances, in contrast to more "culturologically" oriented approaches that emphasize the importance of different cultural belief systems. The thrust of their chapter is to discuss children's lives rather than to arrive at a theory designed to trace children's development through a series of stages.

Daniel A. Wagner, one of the world's leading literacy experts, presents a broad overview of literacy acquisition in his chapter, "Literacy Development in Global Perspective: A Research and Policy Approach." He points out that in the past, literacy was often transmitted in families and religious institutions, but today the development and maintenance of a nationwide schooling system is the universal ambition of nations located around the world.

For most children in today's world, going to school and achieving literacy is a central task. Whereas in industrialized countries schooling is almost universal and begins around the age of six, in the poor and developing nations the acquisition of literacy may also take place in adolescence and even adulthood.

Moreover, close to 1 billion youth remain illiterate (to various degrees), and they live mostly in the developing world.

Wagner reviews the past and present context of literacy, discusses various controversies revolving around the question of how best to define literacy, outlines global policies and policy debates centering on literacy learning in children, youth, and adults, surveys the literature on literacy acquisition from a developmental point of view, and examines questions of literacy instruction for various age groups. Throughout his chapter, Wagner adopts a global point of view and emphasizes the practical and policy-oriented aspects of research on literacy acquisition: in the modern world, being literate is a must for everybody, and those youngsters kept out of school for economic, political, or gender-related reasons will see their chances for a satisfactory future life sharply diminished.

Taken together, the four chapters in Part I set the stage for the later chapters. They paint a broad picture of some of the main theoretical approaches, substantive and methodological assumptions, worldwide findings, and selected applications to be found in historical and modern cross-cultural research on childhood and adolescence. The interplay between culture and human development is examined from a variety of perspectives, most of which emphasize a socioecological framework for the study of children's material circumstances, socioemotional and identity development, family interactions, peer relationships, educational adjustment, and successes and failures in the light of difficult social and environmental circumstances. Because cross-cultural research has multiplied in recent years, it is becoming possible for the first time in history to sketch a globally constructed and reasonably realistic picture of how children and adolescents develop, learn, adjust, thrive, and suffer in their increasingly multicultural environments.

Part II: Childcare and Parenting

The three contributions to Part II are united by a shared focus on childcare and parent-child relationships. These are investigated within the context of specific empirical studies conducted in a variety of cultural and ecological settings. While Fouts compares the weaning practices of Central African foragers and farmers from the viewpoint of evolutionary theory, LeVine uses the findings of a multidisciplinary study conducted among the Gusii of Kenya to critically evaluate the universalistic claims of American childrearing experts, and Bornstein and colleagues compare how American and Argentinean mothers feel about their childrearing activities. The respective samples employed in these studies, then, are meant to represent a foraging society, two traditional agricultural societies, and two modern industrialized societies.

Young anthropologist Hillary N. Fouts, in her chapter, "Social Contexts of Weaning: The Importance of Cross-Cultural Studies," points out that humans have spent approximately 99 percent of their existence living as hunter-gatherers, and most of the remaining 1 percent as traditional agriculturalists. It should consequently be of great interest to compare hunter-gatherers and agriculturalists, such as the Bofi of Central Africa, with respect to basic cultural practices such as weaning, and to analyze its social and emotional components. More specifically, she reviews in her chapter some comparative studies of weaning age, adult-versus child-led weaning, and the caregiving environments of weaning as seen from the point of view of her own African research and of evolutionary theory.

The Bofi foragers and farmers, who reside in the northern Congo Basin rainforest, lend themselves to cross-cultural comparison because they share similar natural ecologies and speak the same language, but nevertheless depend on different subsistence economies. The economies, in turn, are connected to divergent childcare and cultural practices. The two groups and their situation constitute, so to speak, a natural experiment elucidating the influence of subsistence economies upon childrearing and weaning practices.

Whereas the foragers have adopted lenient childrearing practices, support the psychological independence of their children, and wean their children around age three to four, the farmers use tougher, more fear-oriented childrearing methods, encourage obedience and conformity in their children, and wean their children at age one to two. Interestingly, the weaning among the foragers is often initiated by the children themselves rather than their mothers, whereas in the farming communities it is the mothers who forcefully induce the weaning. Fouts discusses some of these behavioral patterns within their broader sociocultural contexts and asks how evolutionary theory might be able to explain the observed cross-cultural differences.

In the United States, many child development experts educate the public that there is now a "science" of early childhood development that provides information about what infants and young children require for their healthy and happy development: consistent, warm, and loving care, sustained stimulation through visual engagements and verbal interaction, adult supervision, frequent praise rather than recurrent criticism, parental efforts to further the children's sense of self-esteem and self-efficacy, and a social environment conducive to active exploration and to development of a sense of appropriate independence. Implicitly or explicitly, the claim is made that these psychosocial requirements are the optimal conditions for children worldwide.

Disagreeing with this idea is prominent psychological anthropologist Robert A. LeVine in his chapter, "Challenging Expert Knowledge: Findings from an African Study of Infant Care and Development." Based on an extensive, multidisciplinary earlier study of Gusii mothers in Kenya, their infants, and their infant care practices, LeVine argues that these mothers follow a very different cultural script or parental ethnotheory. It is connected, in part, to their ecological adaptation and to the fact that in the mid-1970s, the average married Gusii mother bore nine or ten children.

While Gusii mothers are sensitive to infant distress signals, they place little importance on initiating verbal interactions with their infants. As controlling and restrictive disciplinarians little inclined to express positive emotions, they delegate many caretaking chores to the child's older siblings, who soon become the central figures in its socialization process. Yet there is little evidence that such a "deviant" childrearing environment leads to serious mental health problems or cognitive impoverishment.

For LeVine, the lesson deriving from the findings of his earlier African study—and numerous other studies—is clear. Many of the recommendations promoted by American "experts" for developmentally appropriate and "scientifically" based childrearing practices are merely a reflection of the practices preferred by upper-middle-class Americans. The recommendations are driven at least as much by ideology as by science. Whether implicitly or explicitly, the recommendations denigrate alternative practices such as those followed by the Gusii mothers—yet again ignoring the lessons of cultural relativism.

How does culture influence the feelings and perceptions that mothers have about their childrearing activities? In their chapter, "Competence and Satisfaction in Parenting Young Children: An Ecological, Multivariate Comparison of Expressions and Sources of Self-Evaluation in the United States and Argentina," the international research team of Marc H. Bornstein, O. Maurice Haynes, Liliana Pascual, and Kathleen Painter report on a comparative study conducted with 112 American and Argentinean first-time mothers of twenty-month-old infants. In it, they focus on a broad array of possible influences on the mothers' feelings of competence and satisfaction. These include cultural, socio-demographic, and maternal personological characteristics together with child gender and linguistic performance.

In both countries, the mothers' sense of competence and of satisfaction with their parental activities proved to be largely independent of each other. Furthermore, less socially anxious mothers who enjoyed a wider familial network of social support saw themselves as more competent in their childrearing activities. For the Argentinean mothers, social support from their husbands also proved important in maintaining their sense of competence. The mothers' sense of satisfaction, however, was especially responsive to the social support they received from relatives other than spouse, mother, and mother-in-law.

In general, the optimistic American mothers perceived themselves as being both more competent and more satisfied with their parenting activities. In contrast, the Argentinean mothers appeared to have internalized a greater sense of uncertainty, self-doubt, and hesitancy. In this context, it is important to keep in mind that contemporary Argentinean middle-class society has been exposed to considerable economic and political instability in recent years. Furthermore, Argentina lacks a public healthcare system ready to provide support and guidance to young mothers. However, cultural differences between the two Ameri-

can societies proved to be of considerable importance in accounting for the results of this well-controlled study.

Part III: Two Themes in Children's Lives: Gender Roles and Siblings

The contributions to the third part of the book revolve around two fundamental themes in children's lives: the significance of gender roles and the importance of sibling relationships. In all known societies, children are socialized
into different gender roles that, in turn, shape their identity and opportunities
throughout the life cycle. Furthermore, in traditional societies, at least, the large
majority of children grow up together with siblings with whom they are expected
to maintain lifelong bonds and alliances.

Together with her former mentor and coworker, John E. Williams, Deborah L.
Best, a past president of the International Association for Cross-Cultural Psychology, has been known for her worldwide investigations of gender-linked stereotypes
and self-perceptions. It does not come as a surprise, therefore, that in her wide-
ranging chapter, "Gender Roles in Childhood and Adolescence," she arrives at the
conclusion that pancultural similarities in sex and gender greatly outweigh the
cultural differences that are found.

Best reviews a variety of prominent perspectives in the worldwide study of
gender roles and gender differences. Some of these emphasize biological aspects,
beginning with the fact that in all human societies modal sex differences in
physical characteristics can be found. Other approaches concern themselves with
the "psychosociocultural" aspects of gender, such as gender identity, gender roles,
gender-role ideology, gender stereotypes, gender differences, cross-cultural socialization practices regarding girls and boys, cultural practices that influence the
behavior of females and males, sociocultural change in gender roles, and so on.
These topics are the special focus of Best's chapter.

A variety of theories have been advanced to explain the ubiquitous presence
of gender roles and gender differences around the world as well as cross-cultural
variations in gender-linked cultural practices. These include various versions of
evolutionary theory, social role theory, social learning theory, cognitive stage
theories, and gender schema theories. As is so often the case in psychology, each
of these theories is able to account for some of the findings contained in the
cross-cultural literature, but none by itself is able to provide a convincing and
comprehensive account of them.

In many societies of the past and the present, large families have been and
are the norm. In sub-Saharan Africa, for instance, popular pronatalist ideologies emphasize that large numbers of children are a blessing, since they will contribute to a family's economic strength, political power, and spiritual continuity
across generations. In such societies, older siblings play an essential role in the
upbringing of children and adolescents. While the parents are involved in

economic and other activities to ensure the survival of the family, children—
and especially girls at a young age—are expected to care for their younger siblings, socialize them, and guide them on their developmental path toward
becoming responsible members of society.

Young cultural psychologist Ashley E. Maynard, in her chapter, "Sibling Interactions," emphasizes that the study of sibling relationships in non-Western cultures has added to our understanding of the role that siblings play as guides for
each other in internalizing cultural practices. Frequently, they provide critical
social support and help to shape the social and emotional development, cognitive development, language socialization, and play activities of their brothers and
sisters. In her account, Maynard emphasizes the usefulness of the ecocultural
approach that sees childrearing and development as a cultural project in the
context of a society's surrounding ecology.

A considerable number of studies have suggested that siblings may play an
important role in the younger child's understanding and sociocognitive appropriation of the adult world. In play, for instance, and guided by their siblings,
young children frequently reproduce selected features of the adult world and
anticipate some of their future roles in that world. Many socially useful skills and
behaviors such as social perspective taking, linguistic and listening skills, understanding and sympathizing with others' emotional states, taking care of others,
and understanding complex, hierarchically ordered social roles inside and outside the family may be developed in the context of sibling interactions.

Part IV: Adolescents in the Global Village

As children progress through the life stages, developing into adolescents and
then young adults, their life perspectives become more future-oriented. This is
certainly the case for many youths in the developing nations. Frequently, they
must face a very limited repertoire of economic and social alternatives, which
are offered by societies undergoing pervasive social change (see Gielen &
Chumachenko, this volume).

Spanning a number of years, the former president of the Society for Cross-
Cultural Research, Judith L. Gibbons, has conducted comparative research on
adolescents in the developing world. These adolescents experience different
economic and sociocultural circumstances depending on their country of residence, gender, rural versus urban residence, access to or lack of schooling, family responsibilities, and so on. A central focus of her chapter concerns adolescents'
daily activities, their well-being, and their social relations with family members,
peers, and friends. Compared to their peers in the industrialized world, adolescents in the developing world are especially likely to fulfill family responsibilities such as performing household chores and caring for siblings. At the same
time, they are less likely to receive a secondary education—if any education at

all. This is especially true for girls, who are likely to be socialized into a way of life where the early assumption of family responsibilities and hard work is the norm. Given this situation, it is not surprising that, especially among the poorest, their scores are lower on scales of psychological well-being, when compared to their counterparts in more affluent countries. They are, however, more likely to develop a sense of shared identity and interconnectedness with their immediate social world in contrast to a sense of independence and self-reliance, which is highly regarded in the United States and Western Europe.

During the late twentieth century, rapid social and cultural changes reached even the most remote geographic areas. A global teenage culture began to attract youngsters living in nations or areas as distant from each other as Papua New Guinea, Egypt, and Terra del Fuego. This culture is important because youth worldwide must prepare themselves for a world social climate that, in some sense, is in its earliest stages of development.

Given this situation, what changes will the twenty-first century bring to teenagers around the world? Jeffrey Jensen Arnett, author of the first truly culturally and cross-culturally oriented psychology textbook on adolescence, asks this question in his chapter, "Adolescence in the Twenty-First Century: A Worldwide Survey." He examines the prospects for adolescents in six regions of the world: sub-Saharan Africa, northern Africa and the Middle East, India, Asia, South America, and the West. For each region, he identifies a small number of issues likely to be central to the lives of adolescents in the new century.

Of all the world's major regions, sub-Saharan Africa is the most disadvantaged in terms of per capita income, life expectancy, prevalence of diseases, and many other indicators of life quality. Consequently, Arnett identifies chronic poverty, war, and HIV/AIDS as three crucial problems likely to impact negatively on the lives of many teenagers who reside in this region of the world. In contrast, three key issues in the future lives of North African and Middle Eastern youngsters are likely to be the continued strength of Islam, patriarchal family relationships, and the general subordination of women. For multicultural India, Arnett emphasizes the alternative of school versus work, the tradition of early arranged marriages, the lingering caste system, and the rights of women as fundamental issues likely to confront twenty-first-century teenagers.

East Asia was the first non-Western region of the world to successfully follow the Western path of industrialization. In this context—but also building upon indigenous Confucian value systems—East Asian youngsters will probably continue to experience intense pressures to succeed in demanding educational systems. In addition, they will be expected to follow some of the traditions of filial piety that have been creating the cohesiveness of East Asian families for centuries. Conflicts about the rights of women and one's right to select one or more romantic partners are also likely to be of major importance in the lives of many future East Asian adolescents and youth.

In contrast to most East Asian countries, many Latin American countries suffered from political and economic instability in the later part of the twentieth century, leading to high rates of unemployment, especially among the youth. Arnett, however, believes that the prospects for young people in Latin America are likely to improve in the new century. Reduced birthrates, improved education, and more legitimate forms of government should mean that many Latin American youngsters would be able to compete successfully in the increasingly information-based global economy. The same should be even truer for young people in the West, although Arnett believes that for them, the principal issues of the twenty-first century will revolve around questions of education, unemployment, immigration, and health-compromising behaviors such as homicide, reckless driving, cigarette smoking, and so on.

Part V: The Adaptation of Immigrant Children in the United States

The three chapters in Part V focus on the psychosocial and linguistic adaptation and acculturation of immigrant children and adolescents to a dynamic multicultural society. In this context and for convenience sake, a distinction may be drawn between the respective concerns of "multicultural psychology" and "cross-cultural psychology." Multicultural psychology is interested in group differences of a predominantly domestic nature. Questions of bicultural identity, majority-minority relationships, political struggles for power, and the integration of immigrants into mainstream society are typical issues raised by multicultural psychologists. In contrast, cross-cultural psychologists frequently wish to compare the nature of psychological processes between members of different cultural groups and nations located around the world.

In the United States, children with immigrant parents represent about one-fifth of all children. In his chapter, "The Adaptation and Acculturation of Children from Immigrant Families," Andrew J. Fuligni asks how well these children are faring given that they frequently come from cultural backgrounds quite different from those of "mainstream" children. His research-based answer to this question is indeed surprising: many of these children prove to be better off in terms of their overall psychological adjustment and school achievement than their American-born peers. Such a finding is quite remarkable given that immigrant children must often face steep hurdles in terms of cultural and linguistic adjustments, together with serious economic problems. Similarly, both first-generation and second-generation adolescents from immigrant families are engaged in fewer delinquent and violent acts, are less likely to abuse drugs and alcohol, and rarely miss school because of emotional or health problems.

Fuligni reviews a variety of explanations for these remarkable findings and suggests that in order to arrive at better explanations, there is a need for large-scale, longitudinal studies of a variety of children from immigrant backgrounds.

Furthermore, such studies need to include control groups of native-born children and their families to understand more clearly why most groups of immigrant children and adolescents in the United States (with the exception of some
groups from Latin American backgrounds) are more academically and socio-
culturally adjusted. What role do selection factors involved in emigration play
in this context? To what aspects of American society do immigrant children and
their children adapt—or fail to adapt? What influence do family ethos and emphasis on academic achievement exert on the psychological and academic
adjustment and acculturation of immigrant children when compared to nonimmigrant children and adolescents? To this we may add a question not asked
by Fuligni: How do American findings on immigrant children compare with findings of studies on immigrant children in other societies?

Whereas Fuligni's contribution focuses on immigrant children in general, the
team of Jaipaul Roopnarine, Pauline F. Bynoe, and Ronald Singh explores a variety of factors tied to the schooling of children of English-speaking Caribbean
immigrants in the United States. In this context, they discuss families who have
migrated from countries such as Barbados, Belize, Grenada, Guyana, Jamaica,
Trinidad and Tobago, and various other islands of the eastern Caribbean. The
authors' special focus is on New York City, where more than 50 percent of all
non-Hispanic African Caribbeans reside. Half of all children in public schools
are the offspring of such families.

Roopnarine, Bynoe, and Singh are especially interested in the beliefs, goals,
and educational processes both within the Caribbean family and within New
York public schools that exert an influence on the education and educational
achievements of young children from Caribbean backgrounds. Because these are
"children and families of color" who often reside in crowded ethnic enclaves
within a dynamic multicultural society, questions of educational, occupational,
and housing discrimination play an important role in their lives.

The authors review a variety of parent-child relationships and adjustment patterns together with parental childrearing styles and patterns of parental support
for their children's education. In this context, they suggest that there may be a
mismatch between the rather strict and authoritarian, homework-oriented childrearing styles favored by so many Caribbean parents, and the more liberal, child-
centered approaches favored by most American primary school teachers. In this
context, the authors develop a theoretical scheme designed to account for the
sometimes uneasy alliances between Caribbean parents and the teachers of their
children. Comparable to LeVine's skepticism expressed in his earlier chapter,
Roopnarine and colleagues doubt whether the "developmentally appropriate practices" favored by most American mainstream child experts and teachers are always
culturally appropriate in the context of minority child education.

One of the major hurdles facing immigrant children is the learning of a
new language and, perhaps, maintaining one's native language. The hurdle is

especially difficult for children from non-Western backgrounds, since their native language will most likely be organized around principles quite different from those governing the English language. In addition, the process of acquiring a new language is typically intertwined with intensive exposure to a new culture, one's development into a bicultural person, choosing new friends and perhaps giving up old ones, exposure to and a choice of new reading materials, movies, and favorite songs, and defining one's identity in new and more complex ways. For immigrant children, learning a new language is part and parcel of an acculturation process during which cognitive, affective, and identity issues become interwoven in intricate ways.

Chinese American psychologist Gisela Jia considers some of these processes in her chapter, "The Acquisition of English and Maintenance of First Language by Immigrant Children and Adolescents in North America." In it she notes that from the late 1960s to the late 1980s, many second-language acquisition studies were guided by Lenneberg's biologically oriented "critical period hypothesis." He suggested in 1967 that there is a critical period for language acquisition that is dependent on a variety of genetically preprogrammed interactions of various aspects of brain maturation, influencing both first- and second-language acquisition. More recently, however, researchers such as Jia have identified a number of cultural and psychological factors that uniquely predict English proficiency independent of the arrival date of immigrants. Years of education in the host country, the English proficiency of family members, a variety of motivational and attitudinal variables, similarities or lack of similarities between the first and the second language, identification with the host culture, and a variety of other cognitive, social, and cultural factors jointly shape the course of the second-language acquisition. Proficiency in the new language, in turn, is likely to exert a strong effect on the cultural identity of children and adolescents and influences their choice of friends and reading materials.

The three chapters in Part V demonstrate the complexity of the study of children and adolescents from immigrant backgrounds. Age of arrival in the new country, linguistic proficiency, adaptation to new school environments, family factors, the interaction between one's family and the larger society, the response of the host society to immigrant families and their children, the cultural distance between the original society and the new society, and many other factors influence the children's identity development, school performance, and psychosocial and cultural adjustment. Given that global rates of migration have increased in recent years, it is imperative that the sociocultural context of immigrant children be studied, not only in the United States but also from a comparative point of view in other nations worldwide. To the culturally aware psychologist, such studies can exert a special kind of fascination because they repeatedly remind him or her how intricately intertwined psychosocial, cultural, and biological processes really are.

Part VI: Difficult Adjustments

In many parts of the world, a large number of children have to live in very difficult circumstances. These include civil war, extreme poverty, malnutrition, prostitution, excessive labor, destructive family circumstances, being orphaned through disease and wars, and living in the streets. Counseling psychologist Lewis Aptekar has for many years worked with such children and youngsters in Latin America, Africa, and elsewhere. His chapter, "The Changing Developmental Dynamics of Children in Particularly Difficult Circumstances: Examples of Street and War-Traumatized Children," is based both on his own experiences as well as on a provocative review of the pertinent research literature. Some of the findings analyzed by him may come as a surprise to the reader. A study of street children in Guatemala and Colombia, for instance, concluded that they were often better off than their siblings who remained at home. However, there are far fewer girls on the streets than boys, and they often have difficult relationships with their families of origin, while their male counterparts typically do not.

In the first part of his review, Aptekar discusses developmental differences among street children, gender differences, differences between street children living in the developing and the developed world, adolescents traumatized by war, and gender differences among war-traumatized boys and girls. Subsequently, the author focuses on those problems researchers must confront when collecting data about street children and war-traumatized adolescents. Additional topics discussed by him include problems in supplying mental health services to such children and the frequent necessity of having to make excruciating moral choices when working with them. Aptekar's chapter is bound to challenge some preconceived notions that we readers might have about the nature and situation of street and war-traumatized children and adolescents. At the same time, it includes vivid examples that will stay in the attentive reader's mind for a long time.

Cross-cultural psychologists and especially anthropologists frequently emphasize differences in cultural meanings—after all, if these did not exist, cross-cultural researchers would be out of a job! In contrast to this pattern, Thomas M. Achenbach, in his chapter, "Cross-Cultural Perspectives on Development Psychopathology," focuses on a variety of cross-culturally *similar* psychopathological syndromes. Children around the world share a variety of problems such as being withdrawn, presenting certain somatic complaints, being anxious and depressed, creating social problems, suffering from thought problems, finding it difficult to focus their attention, manifesting a variety of delinquent behaviors, and displaying aggressive behavior.

Achenbach's "Empirically Based Paradigm for Assessment and Taxonomy" has generated assessment instruments that have already been translated into sixty-one languages and generated more than 5,000 published studies. In addition, a variety of developmental assessment instruments are available for completion by parents, teachers, caregivers, direct observers, psychometrists, clinical interviewers, and the children themselves. Cross-culturally similar syndromes appear when these instruments are factor analyzed. The author introduces some examples of the instruments and subsequently reviews some representative findings based on them. For instance, longitudinal studies spanning recent decades have shown that American children suffer increasingly from some of the problems delineated above, while Dutch children showed only small increases in the same time frame.

Achenbach's approach suggests that children's psychopathology can be assessed in reliable and valid ways in a great diversity of cultural settings. Not surprisingly, this paradigm has already been found useful for a variety of practical purposes such as epidemiological research, longitudinal studies, training mental health workers, evaluating treatment outcomes, and assessing immigrants and refugees in numerous cultures. At the same time, his research center is now in the possession of an incomparable databank that can be employed to compare the results of new studies against a vast array of cross-cultural data on children's psychopathology.

Epilogue

One of the most experienced cross-cultural human development researchers is Harry Gardiner, who has participated in the creation of cross-cultural psychology since its beginnings in the early 1970s. In his concluding chapter, "Cross-Cultural Study of Human Development: Following the Yellow Brick Road in Search of New Approaches for the Twenty-First Century," he comments briefly on the origins of research on cross-cultural development, points to its relationships with other social sciences, summarizes some present trends in the field, and considers its possible future.

He emphasizes the advantages of an ecocultural, thoroughly contextual, and interdisciplinary approach and suggests that the time has come to "give cross-cultural psychology and anthropology away" by applying them to pressing social policy issues. Surely this is an appropriate conclusion for the many contributions contained in this volume, which have throughout emphasized that the cross-cultural study of human development has coalesced into a vital field of scientific study incorporating important suggestions and implications for improving the lives of children and adolescents around the globe.

CONCLUDING REMARKS AND A WORD OF THANKS

Throughout the book, the reader will encounter descriptions of children and adolescents from diverse sociocultural backgrounds: Chinese boys and girls

PART I

Worldwide Perspectives on Childhood and Adolescence

The Cross-Cultural Study of Human Development: An Opinionated Historical Introduction

Uwe P. Gielen

Our new global society requires a new global science of human development.

Pema ("Lotus Blossom") is an eleven-year-old girl living in Stok Village, perched high up in the Western Himalayas, which dominate the district of Ladakh, India. Like most inhabitants of the village, her family follows the tenets of Tibetan Buddhism, which give significance and meaning to their lives. The family includes herself, her younger brother, her mother, her "older father" and "younger father" (two brothers married to the same wife), as well as her paternal grandparents. The family is poor and owns a few small fields planted with barley together with some goats, sheep, and *dzo* (the offspring of a yak and a cow). While Pema loves skipping down to the small village school in the morning, on many days her parents tell her that she must instead guard some of the family's animals that are grazing in the meadows glittering in the sunshine high above the village. She feels lonely up there in the mountains and at times scared, too, although she otherwise lives in a very peaceful society. Pema feels that her parents care deeply for her, but family survival comes first, and so she remains separated from her playmates on too many days. While little psychological and anthropological research has been carried out on children in Ladakh, the few existing studies do suggest that in spite of her poverty, Pema is likely to grow up into a reasonably happy, mild-mannered, and caring young woman (Gielen, 2001; Norberg-Hodge, 1994).

Many thousands of miles away, in the middle-sized German town of Giessen, sixteen-year-old Holger is living together with his older brother, his mother, and his well-paid father, who has been drifting away from the family after an extended series of marital squabbles. The boy tries to isolate himself from the tensions in his home by getting lost in cyberspace, playing endless games on his computer, and fanatically following the ups and downs of his favorite soccer team, Eintracht Frankfurt. His school performance has recently taken a downward course for reasons he does not fully understand, although his godfather tries to give him good advice and protect him from the impact of his father's verbal attacks. The father fears for the future of his son, but also feels guilty because he suspects that his own behavior lies behind some of the psychological problems Holger is experiencing. Holger has a good relationship with his brother, Peter—but Peter is preoccupied with his upcoming *Abitur Prüfungen* (baccalaureate examinations), the results of which will determine which university, if any, he will be allowed to attend.

It is not too difficult for most of us to appreciate and understand Holger's family situation, his preoccupations, his inner tensions, and his ways of dealing with them. But Pema's life presents a puzzle to us: after all, we do not send eleven-year-old girls up the mountains to spend many of their days taking care of goats and sheep; we do not know families where two brothers are married to the same wife; and we are unfamiliar with the many invisible *lha* (deities, spirits) whose protective yet dangerous powers Pema and her family sense all around them. There are so many questions we might ask about her development as it unfolds within the context of her village society: What effects do her responsibilities have on her social, emotional, and cognitive development? In what ways do her parents' Buddhist beliefs influence their childrearing practices, and how do these practices in turn influence Pema's psychosocial adjustment? What might gender roles be like in a society that practices fraternal polyandry? Do her parents periodically remove her from school because she is a girl rather than a boy? Would it be sensible to ask Pema to respond to some of Kohlberg's moral dilemmas, or would they have to be reshaped completely? Are there any children in Ladakh who suffer from attention deficit disorders or the various other psychological problems commonly encountered in Western societies such as Germany? What is adolescence like in a society where some children are expected to work from an early age? Could it be true that there is no "adolescence" at all for poor girls who marry early? How will the pervasive social change Ladakh is now undergoing influence Pema's development? Are the prevailing psychosocial conditions in Ladakh in any way similar to those in other parts of India, other agricultural societies, preindustrial Europe, or other Buddhist societies? If, by accident, Pema and Holger meet (this is not impossible, since quite a few German tourists visit Ladakh each year), what would they see in each other, either in their first encounter or after a more extended series of interactions?

Cultural and psychological anthropologists have for many years asserted that humankind shares a fundamental psychic unity while simultaneously endorsing the notion of cultural relativism, with its claim that belief systems, attitudes, perceptions, feelings, and behaviors tend to differ radically from one society to the next. Following a related train of thought, a prominent team of psychological anthropologists and cultural psychologists recently titled its theoretical review chapter as follows: "The Cultural Psychology of Development: One Mind, Many Mentalities" (Shweder, Goodnow, Hatano, LeVine, Markus, & Miller, 1998). However, such seemingly contradictory statements mean little unless they are redeemed by convincing evidence demonstrating how the abstraction "one mind" can be reconciled with the more concrete evidence for "many mentalities," and how the vague idea of "psychic unity" fits together with the apparently contradictory idea of "cultural relativism." Applied to the developmental changes that Pema and Holger are undergoing, this means that psychological anthropologists would have to demonstrate that, whereas their radically different lives are unfolding in two highly divergent socioecologies, similar psychological processes and developmental principles are at work in both cases. To demonstrate such similarities and to unveil general developmental principles at work in different cultures may turn out to be the ultimate challenge for cross-cultural developmental research, rather than the much simpler demonstration that developmental trajectories vary from one cultural context to the next.

To see the lives of children and adolescents such as Pema and Holger in comparative perspective, to search for similarities and differences in their life trajectories, to understand holistically their development-in-ecological-and-sociocultural-context, to investigate how proximate and distal causes—as mediated by the nested developmental niches within which human growth takes place—shape the unfolding of their lives: this is the complex but fascinating task cross-cultural developmental psychologists and psychological anthropologists have set for themselves. In this endeavor, they are helped by representatives from many other disciplines, including demographers who summarize human life cycles with the aid of dry but powerful statistics (e.g., Gielen & Chumachenko, this volume); sociologists who are apt to conceptualize human development as occurring within the framework of social structures; historians who inform us that in former times, Western childhood was of a quite different nature than it is now; epidemiologists who provide data useful for a better understanding of physical and psychosocial maldevelopments; ethologists who emphasize adaptive, biologically based response systems; evolutionary psychologists and anthropologists who see human development from a cross-species as well as cross-cultural point of view; and so many others.

Traditionally, cross-cultural developmental psychology has adopted a double identity. On the one hand, cross-cultural comparisons represent a useful and necessary methodological tool to test the general validity of just about any developmental theory, whether it be the cognitive-developmental theories of Kohlberg and Piaget, the sociohistorical theory of Vygotsky, theories of socioemotional development such as those proposed by Erikson, Freud, and Rohner, evolutionary theories such as Bowlby's attachment theory, developmental theories of psychopathology such as that depicted by Achenbach in this volume, or theories on gender roles such as those analyzed by Best in this volume. On the other hand, cross-cultural developmental psychology constitutes a field with its very own problems and questions: Why do shy children fare so much better in China than in the United States of America? Are the major forms of child psychopathology similar or dissimilar around the world? Is adolescence a universal phenomenon, or is it relative to time and place? How do immigrant children and adolescents adapt to their new cultural environments? What does bilingualism tell us about the nature of language development in general? Is it true that culture and mind make each other up? The attempts to answer these and many other questions of a related kind constitute the field of cross-cultural human development.

A BRIEF HISTORY OF CROSS-CULTURAL HUMAN DEVELOPMENT STUDIES

The cross-cultural study of human development as a recognized field of study with its own definite identity is no more than twenty-five years old. By 1975–1980, a critical mass of studies investigating the psychological development of children and adolescents in a variety of non-Western and Western societies had accumulated. Quite a few of these were reviewed in R. H. Munroe, R. L. Munroe, and B. B. Whiting's *Handbook of Cross-Cultural Human Development* (1981), the first comprehensive survey of the field. In addition, the six-volume *Handbook of Cross-Cultural Psychology* included a volume titled *Developmental Psychology* (1981), coedited by Triandis and Heron. Together with two brief introductory textbooks written respectively by Munroe and Munroe (1975) and by Werner (1979), these handbook volumes announced to the social sciences community that a comprehensive developmental psychology could not be built merely on the study of North American and European "mainstream" children and adolescents, but that instead a thorough understanding of human development in a rich diversity of socioecological conditions was needed for this purpose.

It would take at least another decade, however, before this message began to sink in, so that today, for instance, publishers systematically encourage authors of mainstream developmental psychology textbooks to include in their accounts research conducted in non-Western societies. One suspects that the main impetus for this evolution did not derive so much from developments within the field as from a growing awareness that Western societies, and together with them our students, are becoming ever more multicultural in character. In addition, colleagues in countries as far apart as India, Mexico, China, and Cameroon have been complaining loudly that American children and adolescents are hardly representative of the world's children and adolescents, but that instead they merely constitute a small and in many ways unrepresentative minority. After all, more than 86 percent of all children and adolescents live in the so-called developing world, and more of them live in India alone than in Western Europe and the United States combined (Gielen & Chumachenko, this volume).

It may be useful in this context to recapitulate briefly how cross-cultural human development studies evolved during the twentieth century, especially since a systematic historical account of these efforts is currently unavailable. In the late nineteenth and early twentieth centuries, Darwin's evolutionary theory dominated Anglo-Saxon scientific thinking in both anthropology and psychology. Spurred by the dubious pronouncements of Social Darwinism, these immature disciplines were seduced by evolutionary considerations and a kind of rough analogical thinking to postulate close parallels between phylogenetic and ontogenetic development (Jahoda, 2000; Jahoda & Lewis, 1988/1989). While anthropologists developed evolutionary schemes tracing the development of humanity from a stage of "savagery" to the stage of "barbarism" and then on to the stage of "civilization," psychologists such as G. S. Hall claimed that in their development, children in civilized society recapitulate the evolution of humankind from its primitive protohuman origins to the complexities of contemporary English and American society (Hall, 1904). Children and adolescents in non-Western societies, in turn, were studied only very rarely. However, it was widely assumed that adolescents in many African and other "primitive" societies suffered from "arrested development"—due, perhaps, to the debilitating influence of sexual preoccupations, as well as racial differences (e.g., Kidd, 1906/1969). Ethnocentric beliefs in the moral and racial superiority of one's own society went hand in hand with unbridled speculation and a general paucity of detailed observational studies. While the more extreme forms of this approach had become discredited by the 1930s, milder versions of it have left distinct traces in the works of Freud, Jung, and Vygotsky, to cite but a few prominent psychologists still influential today.

Margaret Mead, the Culture and Personality School, and Cultural Relativism

While very few systematic studies of children and adolescents were conducted among nonliterate people during the 1920s and 1930s, these years saw the rising influence of German-American anthropologist Franz Boas (a former student of Wilhelm Wundt), together with his students Margaret Mead and Ruth Benedict. They argued that "the growing child is systematically patterned [by his culture] in every detail, in posture as well as in gesture, in tempo as well as in speech, in his way of thinking, in his capacity to feel as well as in the forms which his feeling takes and that only by an understanding of the extent and internal relationships of any of these systems of socialization can the psychologist operate usefully with 'the Zuñi child' or 'the Arapesh child'" (Mead, 1954, p. 737). Mead's views, in particular, exerted not only an enormous influence on American anthropology and the educated American public, but she was also viewed by psychologists as the foremost expert on the "psychology of primitive children." In this context, she was invited to write survey chapters on this topic in several editions of the leading handbook of child psychology of the day (Mead, 1931, 1954). In the chapters, she saw it as her mission to convince psychologists that they must assimilate "the more recent findings of ethnologists which stress that a fully acculturated member of a living culture differs in *every respect*, and *systematically*, from members of any other culture" (Mead, 1954, p. 737, emphases added).

Mead (1901–1978) first achieved scientific and public fame through the publication of her book *Coming of Age in Samoa* (1928). To this day, it remains one of her most frequently read but also most controversial books (Freeman, 1983). Written in a convincing literary style, she reports in it the results of her six-month investigation of sixty-seven girls living in several villages in Western Samoa. For the first time, a professionally trained anthropologist (though still a graduate student) was systematically testing a major psychological hypothesis about the very nature of adolescence among a group of non-Western young girls, and did so for comparative purposes. Mead wished to know whether adolescence is "naturally" (that is, mainly because of biological reasons) a period of *Sturm und Drang* ("Storm and Stress"), or whether the turmoil of adolescence results mainly from cultural influences. Both explicitly and implicitly, she was pitting culture against biology, sexual repression against sexual freedom, the power of instincts against the power of learning, competitive American society against easygoing Polynesian society, and fast-moving, modern civilization against more slowly moving, traditional village society. Based on her observations, she concluded that Samoan girls live in a casual society supporting diffuse socioemotional bonds, where premarital sexual relationships are widely accepted and sexual jealousies are uncommon. In her view, adolescence in Samoa lacked the typically Western qualities of rebelliousness, emotional conflict, restlessness, confusion, and inner and interpersonal uproar. Consequently, adolescence must be a product of culture much more than a product of biology.

Many years later, Australian anthropologist Freeman (1983) would launch a strident attack on Mead's observations regarding Samoan society and the teenage girls living in it. In contrast to Mead, he emphasized the importance of virginity for the girls, the frequency of rape, suicides, other aggressive or self-destructive behavior, especially among young men, and many other phenomena indicating that adolescence in Samoa is, and presumably was in prior decades, quite stressful. Mead, he asserted, had been misled by her inexperience, her limited command of the Samoan language, her credulity, and above all by her belief in the doctrine of cultural determinism to see what she expected and wanted to see.

While some of Freeman's assertions and criticisms were too sweeping, there is little doubt that Mead's observations do not constitute decisive evidence in favor of her theoretical ideas. She did, however, ask precisely the right kinds of questions about how to test Hall's theory and more generally, any other developmental theory. (For a recent treatment of the Storm and Stress theory of adolescence, see Arnett, 1999.)

While Mead and her friend Benedict were not completely consistent adherents to the doctrine of cultural relativism, they did more than anybody else to popularize it among American cultural anthropologists and the public at large. Mead, for instance, followed up her study in Samoa with studies of young children among the Manus of the Admiralty Islands north of New Guinea (Mead, 1930), claiming that contrary to Piaget's universalistic theory of cognitive development, the children displayed little if any animistic thinking. Furthermore, after having investigated sex roles and temperamental differences between the sexes among three contrasting societies in New Guinea, she concluded that "many, if not all, of the personality traits which we have called masculine or feminine are as lightly linked to sex as are the clothing, the manners, and the form of head-dress that a society at a given period assigns to either sex" (Mead, 1935/1963, p. 280). Later she would argue that her book had been misunderstood and that in it, she did not postulate a complete absence of innate sex differences in regard to temperament and personality. Many passages in her book, however, would seem to imply just that—and this is how her often feminist readers understood her.

Subsequent studies of Mead's contrasting three societies—the Arapesh, Mundugumor, and Tschambuli—have led the investigators to sharply contrasting conclusions. Mead's supposedly gentle and nurturant Arapesh men, for instance, were actually involved in many homicides (Tuzin, 1977), and those supposedly emotional, fickle, gossipy, artsy, somewhat effeminate Tschambuli men were in fact "unemployed head hunters" who, contrary to Mead's description, dominated their wives (Gewertz, 1981). Some of Mead's relativistic conclusions have proven just too pat, and her interpretations of her field observations are sometimes surprisingly far off the mark. Nevertheless, her influence on American cultural anthropology and the public was enormous during her lifetime.

Under the influence of Benedict and Mead, cultural relativism became the reigning doctrine of American cultural anthropology. As such, it entered an alliance with the environmentalism that formed the center of the academically predominant learning theories of Hull, Spence, Tolman, Guthrie, Miller, Dollard, and Skinner. Miller and Dollard (1941), for instance, claimed that it was the job of psychologists to study the *mechanisms* on which all learning is based, whereas anthropologists should investigate the culturally variable *content* that a child is expected to learn. In other words, the learning theorist can tell us *how* we learn and the cultural anthropologist *what* we learn. This statement implies that the major learning mechanisms such as classical conditioning, operant conditioning, and observational learning are universal in character, whereas the norms, values, beliefs, and behaviors children are expected to acquire are relative to their respective cultures.

The long-term result of this suggested professional division of labor was indeed ironic: American psychology soon became a monocultural enterprise paying lip service to the importance of culture while ignoring it in practice (Gielen, 1994). Miller and Dollard's suggestion had become a handy recipe for professional compartmentalization that most American psychologists were very happy to follow. This trend was strengthened in the years after World War II, when American psychologists began to see themselves as the undisputed leaders of international psychology. Most of them ignored the resurrection of psychology in central Europe, its alternative visions, and the progress that it was making elsewhere around the globe. Even today, far too few American psychologists consult foreign professional journals on a regular basis even when these journals are published in English (Gielen, 1994).

In the 1970s and 1980s, the Culture and Personality school of thought began to lose influence in American academic circles for a number of reasons. Grand theories in general, and Freudian theory in particular, seemingly had not fulfilled their promise and began to be considered as premature. For instance, many representatives of the Culture and Personality school had claimed that they could discern "modal personalities" or "national characters" among the peoples they studied. But empirical data tended to show otherwise: even in relatively small-scale societies a considerable variety of personalities could be found. Likewise, many attempts to link specific early childrearing practices such as length of breast-feeding, weaning procedures, swaddling, and strictness of toilet training to adult character structures proved inconclusive (e.g., Orlansky, 1949), although Freudian theorists had predicted just such links. Finally, psychoanalytically inclined anthropologists seemed unable to develop reliable and reasonably objective methods of measurement and interpretation. In hindsight and in spite of its achievements (Barnouw, 1985), the Culture and Personality approach must be considered a magnificent failure. The rising skepticism about the methodological adequacy of the approach, in particular, would lead John W. M. Whiting, Irvin Child, William Lambert, and Beatrice B. Whiting to adopt a much more behavioristic approach, which culminated in the Six Cultures project.

The Whitings and the Six Cultures Project

In the early 1950s, several scholars began to plan a systematic series of childrearing studies in several carefully selected societies based on a unified handbook for fieldworkers by Whiting, Child, and Lambert (1966). The handbook emphasized the importance of structured behavioral observations and interviews, while the more "Freudian" and projective Child Thematic Apperception Test was only occasionally used. Six field research teams applied this approach to systematically chosen samples of mothers and three- to ten-year-old children among the Gusii (Kenya), Okinawans (Japan), Mixtecan Indians (Mexico), Rajputs (India), inhabitants of Tarong (Philippines), and New Englanders (United States). A central focus of these studies comprised nine behavior systems, including succorance, nurturance, self-reliance, achievement, responsibility, obedience, dominance, sociability, and aggression. The results of these studies were published and analyzed in a series of influential volumes, including those by Whiting (1963), Minturn and Lambert (1964), Whiting and Whiting (1975), and B. B. Whiting and Edwards (1988).

The Six Cultures project represented a major step forward in the comparative study of human development. For the first time, it became possible to compare, in a quantitative fashion, systematically structured behavioral observations of carefully selected samples of children across a number of predominantly non-Western cultures rather than engaging in ad hoc and post facto comparisons. The Whitings and their students analyzed and compared mothers' caretaking practices as well as children's age trends, gender differences, and behavior patterns among children living in different family arrangements and socioecological settings. To this day, their findings rank among the more solidly established in the comparative literature on human development. At the same time, the Whitings trained a generation of students who have made, and continue to make, numerous contributions to the field. They typically kept their respect for empirical observations and generalizations at a time when many American cultural anthropologists were becoming increasingly enthralled by the much more subjectivist, relativistic, nonquantitative, and politicized perspectives of postmodernism (d'Andrade, 2000).

Beginning in the early 1980s, Beatrice and John Whiting initiated and coordinated a project titled "Adolescence in a Changing World." The project originally included seven teams of anthropologists who, based on a shared methodological approach, returned to their field sites to investigate adolescence as part of several rapidly changing societies. So far, reasonably detailed reports about adolescence in five cultural groups have resulted from this effort together with a special issue of *Ethos* (Schlegel, 1995; for summaries and analyses of the results of this project, see Dasen, 2000; Whiting & Whiting, 1991; and Gibbons, this volume).

The joint project included studies of adolescents in an Australian Aboriginal community (Burbank, 1988), two Ijo communities in Nigeria (Hollos & Leis, 1989), a settlement of Inuits in Canada (Condon, 1988), a periurban Kikuyu community in Kenya (Worthman & Whiting, 1987), and a small town in Morocco (Davis & Davis, 1989). Taken together, these studies have provided us with a rich picture of the emergence of adolescence in five widely separated communities undergoing rapid social change. A broad variety of issues is discussed in the various reports. These include adolescent sexuality, mate selection, the balance between adolescent autonomy and relatedness, circumcision, gender differences, generation gaps, parental influences and control, sociocultural continuities and discontinuities, the effects of introducing modern schooling and mass media produced outside the community on the adolescents and their parents, and many other issues. Seen as a whole, the studies represented a major step forward in our understanding of the nature of adolescence in developing societies. Methodologically speaking, they suggest that striking a flexible balance between following standardized investigative procedures and providing a complex, sensitive, but less standardized ethnographic account of community practices can produce rich results.

Jean Piaget's Cognitive-Developmental Approach

While the Whitings were attempting to move psychological anthropology away from its excessive emphasis on Freudian theories and interpretive methods in favor of a more objective, measurement-oriented behavioristic approach, another kind of revolution was underway in American developmental psychology. Influenced by Chomsky's devastating critique (1959) of Skinner's *Verbal Behavior* (1957), the growth of psycholinguistics, and new approaches to the study of memory, perception, and thinking, American psychology was becoming more cognitivistic in nature. A crucial role in this process was played by the American psychologists' rediscovery of the works, respectively, of Swiss epistemologist Piaget (1896–1980) and Soviet psychologist and educator Vygotsky (1896–1934), both of whom had rejected behaviorism and its conditioning paradigms in favor of a more interactional view emphasizing the intricacies of mental development. An important role in this historical rediscovery process was played by the work of Lawrence Kohlberg (1927–1987), who—taking into account Baldwin, Cooley, and Mead's theories about the social origins of the self as a consequence of social role-taking—extended Piaget's stage model to the study of perspective- and social role-taking, moral reasoning, and gender identity development.

Piaget's central contribution to developmental psychology is his detailed model of cognitive transformations that are said to arise out of the child's active engagement with his or her environment. These transformations follow an inner developmental logic of differentiation and hierarchical integration quite different in character from the piecemeal acquisition of behavior emphasized by behavioristic learning theories.

According to cognitive-developmental theory, mental structures arise out of the interaction between the maturing organism and the physical and social environment. In this view, the structures are neither simply "wired" into the organism nor are they "hammered" into it through mechanistic learning processes or through cultural indoctrination. Rather, the growing child constructs step-by-step a picture of reality that reflects, simultaneously, universal properties of the world as well as emerging "categories of experience" such as quantity, substantiality, causality, space, time, and logical relations of inclusion, implication, and so on (Kohlberg, 1969/1984, pp. 8–18). Both Piaget and Kohlberg were cognitive constructivists, although they eschewed the more extreme and relativistic assertions of social constructivism that serve as the underpinning of postmodern thinking.

Piaget had originally created his universalistic four-stage model of cognitive development without much regard for cross-cultural considerations. Influenced in part by Mead's insistence on the cultural specificity of mental functioning, he somewhat reluctantly supported in his later years the effort to test his model cross-culturally (Piaget, 1966). In spite of these inauspicious beginnings, many hundreds of studies have in recent decades been conducted in a broad range of cultures to support, or throw into doubt, the validity of his epistemological approach (for summaries of this research, see Dasen & Heron, 1981; Segall, Dasen, Berry, & Poortinga, 1999). Although cognitive development is almost certainly not as stagelike as Piaget had originally postulated, his theory has in general survived the cross-cultural testing process rather well: many aspects of the first three stages of development, usually evolving in the same sequence though at varying ages, can be found in a wide range of cultures. In contrast, the last stage of formal operations is much more culturally and individually variable. At the same time, the mostly nonsocial type of intelligence assessed by Piagetian tests may not be appreciated in some nontechnological cultures. The Baoulé of the Ivory Coast, for instance, value instead a form of social intelligence and wisdom that is not easily measured by existing psychological tests but is somehow recognized by them (Dasen, Dembele, Ettien, Kabran, Kamagate, Koffi, & N'Guessan, 1985). In this context, one may speculate that in contrast to Baoulé society, modern industrial societies place a special emphasis on cognitive sophistication, because this emphasis helps them to reproduce themselves and thrive in the midst of a highly competitive and technologically oriented global environment.

Lawrence Kohlberg: Sociomoral Reasoning Follows a Universal Trajectory

By the 1950s and early 1960s, cultural relativism had conquered American anthropology and sociology at a time when various versions of behavioristic and social learning theories predominated in American (though not in European) academic psychology. Applied to the cross-cultural study of human development, this historical evolution meant that processes of enculturation and socialization were seen as the central phenomena needing explanation. By enculturation, anthropologists such as Herskovitz (1948, pp. 39–42) meant that children and adolescents learn—often nonconsciously—the values, norms, and contents of their culture and make them their own. In a related fashion, most psychologists were convinced that through the process of socialization, children and adolescents acquire the set of values, norms, and behavior patterns that are customary and prescribed in their respective cultures and subcultures. The growing individual was believed to internalize group norms because of positive and negative sanctions by others, learning by reinforcement, imitation, and observation, and perhaps also through a more "Freudian" process of identification with authority figures such as parents and teachers. While society was seen as molding most children and adolescents into whatever shape it deems desirable, psychopaths and other deviants were considered examples of a failed socialization and enculturation process.

In contrast to these theories, Piaget and his follower Kohlberg insisted that children live in worlds of their own that differ qualitatively from those of adults. Furthermore, they stated that children's worlds are repeatedly transformed in a process of cognitive growth that follows its own inherent logic of differentiation and integration rather than being structured by the learning mechanisms emphasized by behaviorists and social learning theorists. By applying this way of thinking to the process of moral reasoning development, Kohlberg (1969/1984) undermined the implicit and explicit consensus of American psychologists and anthropologists about the very nature of socialization and enculturation. He opposed both cultural relativism (i.e., the empirical claim that morality does *in fact* differ radically from society to society) and moral relativism (i.e., the normative belief that given the cultural specificity of moral norms, social scientists *should not* judge other societies by the culturally arbitrary standards of their own society). Instead, he postulated that moral reasoning everywhere follows a sequence of stages that culminates in principled forms of moral reasoning about universal problems of justice. As in Piaget's theory, the sequence of stages is said to be universal although the speed of development and the final stage of attainment may vary from society to society and from individual to individual.

Kohlberg assumes that universal categories of social experience evolve as the growing child interacts with others based on the process of social role-taking. In all societies, social interaction and communication are said to be based on the growing awareness "that the other is in some way like the self and that the other knows or is responsive to the self in a system of complementary expectations" (Kohlberg, 1969/1984, p. 9). Complementary expectations, in turn, are conceptualized through universal mental operations such as approving, blaming, assigning rights, duties, and obligations, making "should" statements, and making references to values, ideals, and norms. With increasing experience, the growing child and adolescent learn to coordinate these mental operations in an ever more differentiated and integrated fashion. This process, in turn, is assumed to give rise to developmentally ordered stages of moral reasoning whose general structures do not directly derive from cultural indoctrination, but rather from the child and adolescent's efforts to make sense out of his or her social experience. Nevertheless, culture and individual experience are both expected to shape much of the specific content of moral judgments. They also provide facilitating or constraining conditions for the developmental process.

In response to Kohlberg's theory, various critics of his theory (e.g., Dien, 1982; Gilligan, 1982; Vine, 1986) soon began to argue that Kohlberg's stages of moral reasoning, and above all the more advanced stages of principled reasoning, incorporate fundamental Western, male, and social-class biases. In the critics' view, Kohlberg's emphasis on moral autonomy as the endpoint of development reflects an ideological, male-oriented preoccupation with the modern Western themes of autonomy and individualism, thus making his theory ethnocentric and sexist in nature.

Following the rather casual publication of Kohlberg's initially collected cross-cultural data as part of a theoretical chapter in 1969, more than 100 studies have investigated whether the development of moral reasoning does indeed follow the sequence suggested by him. The studies have been conducted in a broad variety of cultures and have employed a variety of methods including his own interview method, Rest's Defining Issues Test (1986), Lind's Moralisches Urteil Test (1986), and others. The studies have generally validated the existence and developmental properties of the preconventional (stages 1 and 2) and conventional (stages 3 and 4) levels of moral reasoning, but the cross-cultural evidence for the post-conventional, principled forms of moral reasoning has been weaker (e.g., Eckensberger & Zimba, 1997; Gielen, 1996; Rest, Narvaez, Bebeau, & Thoma, 1999; Snarey, 1985). However, after surveying a series of studies applying the Defining Issues Test mostly to high school and university students in fourteen countries, Gielen and Markoulis (2001) concluded that postconventional forms of moral reasoning are both recognized and preferred by many older East Asian students, and that postconventional forms of moral reasoning and moral autonomy were already present in the classical philosophical traditions of China, Greece, and India some 2,500 years ago. Criticizing Kohlberg's critics, they draw a clear dividing line between the notion of moral autonomy (which the studies indicate exists just as much in collectivistic societies such as Taiwan or Israeli kibbutzim as in Western individualistic societies such as the United States of America) and rugged individualism (which constitutes a culturally variable ideology). In addition, their survey revealed few systematic gender differences. Their conclusions are directly at variance with many of the criticisms of Kohlberg's theory noted above.

Although there exists considerable cross-cultural support for Kohlberg's structural stage theory and it is regularly cited in developmental psychology textbooks, he remained an outsider to much of cross-cultural psychology. For instance, textbooks of cross-cultural psychology frequently treat his theory and the cross-cultural evidence supporting it in a perfunctory way (e.g., Segall et al., 1999) or ignore it altogether (e.g., Brislin, 2000). This is hardly surprising, since deep down most cross-cultural researchers remain convinced that cross-cultural variations in moral norms outweigh whatever developmental similarities might exist—if any. In contrast to this situation, Vygotsky's theory has found many Western followers in recent decades.

Lev S. Vygotsky: A Marxist Cultural-Historical Theory

There are few stories as strange in the history of Western (and especially American) psychology as the resurrection of the ideas of Vygotsky (1896–1934), which began in the 1960s and continues to this day. Vygotsky, who began his life in the same year as Piaget but died forty-six years before him, became a significant force in Soviet psychology following his move to Moscow in 1924. There he formed a group of talented psychologists around him, including Luria, Leontiev, Bozhovich, Zaporoshets, and others. When Stalin began to impose an increasingly orthodox Marxist-Leninist ideology in the early 1930s, he became a kind of persona non grata for his Marxist colleagues and died in political and personal isolation in 1934.

Vygotsky argued that the development of all higher cognitive processes and functions is by nature social and all social development has a cognitive basis. The social basis of higher cognitive processes, in turn, is intertwined with the economic conditions prevailing in a given society. In this context, Vygotsky and Luria (1930/1993) developed a threefold Marxist vision bringing together phylogenetic, sociohistorical, and ontogenetic development. Internalized symbolic signs are said to mediate between environment and behavior, so that these "psychological tools" structure all higher mental processes including attention, memory, intentional behavior, self-control, developmentally appropriate learning, and so on. A fundamental part of this process is the interiorization of speech, which occurs in the context of social communication. According to the theory, children's development is shaped through a process of social guidance whereby parents, teachers, older siblings, and others help them accomplish new and relatively difficult actions that they will later be able to complete by themselves. Culture plays a central role in this developmental process since it provides the symbolic means by which it takes place.

Endorsing the Marxist theory of societal evolution, Vygotsky prepared and, in 1931 and 1932, Luria organized two psychological expeditions to Soviet Central Asia. They hoped to validate Vygotsky's hypothesis that the political-economic and social-cognitive dimensions of human existence are intertwined, with economic factors providing the lead for subsequent psychological transformation. Comparing traditional, mostly illiterate Muslim peasants and agropastoralists with better educated members of collectivistic *kolkhozes*, Luria's interviews seemed to show, for instance, that the illiterate traditionalists were unable (or unwilling?) to solve simple syllogisms or to engage in counter-factual thinking. However, because Vygotsky and Luria were sharply criticized in the

Soviet Union for their cross-cultural and "cross-historical" interpretations of the expeditions' results, these were in the main published many years later (Luria, 1974, 1976).

Vygotsky's ideas have played a central role in the recent flowering of cultural psychology in the West. American psychologists such as Cole (a personal student of Luria), Greenfield, Rogoff, Wertsch, and many others have appropriated and elaborated on Vygotsky's central insights by (re)introducing his paradigm into developmental psychology and by providing considerable cross-cultural evidence for notions such as zone of proximal development, guided learning, social co-construction, mediated learning, scaffolding, and so on (see, e.g., Cole, 1996; Rogoff, 1990; in addition, Maynard, this volume, provides examples of guided learning processes among siblings). It is not exaggerated to say that Vygotsky's sociocognitive vision of learning and development has generated more excitement among modern American cultural psychologists than any other theoretical paradigm.

When American psychologists began to appropriate Vygotsky's ideas beginning in the 1960s, they conveniently shoved aside the Marxist basis of his theorizing. One could never guess from most American textbook discussions, for instance, that Marxist educator Vygotsky developed and used his notion of a zone of proximal development in order to lend support to the proclaimed goal of Soviet education: to create the new Soviet Man. Similarly, Luria's expedition to Central Asia occurred in the context of Russian-Soviet expansionism and colonialism accompanied by mass starvation, mass murder, and an utterly brutal process of forcing hapless peasants to join collectivistic *kolkhozes*—or to starve and die. Luria, however, convinced himself that these bloody political developments meant, above all, social, political, and cognitive progress (Gielen & Jeshmaridian, 1999; Luria, 1979).

The highly selective appropriation of Vygotsky's ideas by American developmental psychologists has frequently shorn them of their historical, political, and cross-cultural context. His Marxist ideas in general, and his tendency to perceive distinct parallels between historical and ontogenetic development in particular, have been widely ignored since they are incompatible with the ahistorical, individualistic ideological framework implicitly or explicitly favored by most American developmental psychologists. There hangs a fine mist of irony over this process of appropriation, since the very same psychologists have also insisted on the crucial importance of sociocultural context in one's understanding of the development of children, adolescents, and everybody else (Gardiner & Kozmitzki, 2002; see also Gardiner's chapter in this volume). Yet, what could be more noncontextual than the reception of Vygotsky's ideas among so many Western developmental psychologists?

It is instructive to compare the respective roles of Piaget, Kohlberg, and Vygotsky in the evolution of cross-cultural developmental psychology. Piaget's central image of the child was that of an autonomous small scientist who, through his or her physical and mental actions upon the world and the feedback he or she receives from it, gradually develops an increasingly complex, differentiated, structured, and integrated way of interpreting the world. Accordingly, cultural and social influences on this developmental process are just this: they are influences speeding it up or slowing it down rather than being a constituent part of it. Kohlberg added to this theory his conception of an evolving, increasingly co-ordinated process of social role-taking together with a co-evolving self. However, cultural belief systems played only a limited role in his account, since it represents a social rather than a cultural theory. Unlike Kohlberg, however, few cross-cultural psychologists seem to be aware that evolving processes of social role-taking, although constituting a necessary and fundamental basis of *all* human societies, cannot be reduced to the internalization of cultural norms. They do not understand that a hole yawns at the center of their theories of social development.

While cross-cultural investigations have played an important role in exploring the general validity of Piaget's and Kohlberg's theories, they have done little to redefine them in an essential way. In this sense, one may argue that many of these cross-cultural investigations exhibit a certain kind of theoretical sterility: they are icing on the cake, but not the cake itself. In comparison to these scientific endeavors, the followers of Vygotsky have introduced greater theoretical innovation and added more flesh to his theories. I suspect that this is true for two reasons. On the one hand, culture plays a more central role in Vygotsky's theory than it does in Piaget's or Kohlberg's theories. On the other hand, Vygotsky wrote his major works in a mere ten years, which, as a consequence, tend to be of a sketchy and preliminary nature. Consequently, in order to arrive at a more detailed picture of sociocognitive development, Vygotsky's followers have had to tease out and further develop the implications of his overall approach—a creative task that continues to engage their attention to this day.

Together, Piaget, Kohlberg, and Vygotsky helped to move American developmental psychology away from its excessive reliance on traditional learning theories that had created the misleading image of the newborn infant as an "empty organism." Instead of perceiving children as being molded, in a one-directional way, by society and its socialization agents, modern theorists view children as active co-constructors of their own development. Equipped with a specific temperament, a range of incipient competencies, evolving modules of the mind, and a repertoire of proximity-seeking behaviors, young children, according to the newer theories, actively elicit from their caretakers a variety of caretaking behaviors in tune with evolutionary demands, which are then executed according to various culturally shaped scripts.

Together with the linguist Noam Chomsky, Piaget, Kohlberg, and Vygotsky, each in his own way, were descendants of the Enlightenment period. As such, they assigned in their theories primary importance to cognition, rationality, active information processing, and conscious, goal-directed behavior. This placed them in direct opposition to the irrational accounts of both Freud and the learning theorists. Freud, in particular, emphasized unconscious motivation and the emotions in his stark portrayal of human nature. While Freud and his followers have steadily lost ground in academic psychology because of the serious methodological shortcomings of their approach, a new family of irrational theories has emerged in the recent cross-cultural literature on human development. These are the neo-evolutionary theories, which claim that humans, like other animals, are the mostly unwitting "servants" of their genes. The genes program them to pursue inclusive fitness as the ultimate goal in life—or else face extinction in the next generation.

THE RETURN OF EVOLUTIONARY THEORY AND THE RISE OF NEO-EVOLUTIONARY APPROACHES

As noted previously, Darwinian theories have exerted an enormous influence on the development of Anglo-Saxon psychology, sociology, anthropology, and comparative research. At the same time, they have also evoked considerable resistance. Mead's cultural relativism, for instance, ignores the forces of biological evolution and differentiation. Her insistence that gender roles and gender differences derive overwhelmingly from culture rather than from biology provides a good example. It places her in direct contradiction to Darwinian and neo-Darwinian theories of sexual selection and to the cross-cultural evidence on gender differences and gender roles that has accumulated after her earlier research was published (Best, this volume).

The resistance against evolutionary theories was in part fueled by liberal scholars' repugnance toward the pronouncements of Social Darwinism, which favored conservative ideologies supporting Western imperialism, racialism, capitalist exploitation, opposition to social welfare legislation, and the general notion that the progress of humankind should not be held up by misguided compassion for the weak, the poor, and those who fall by the wayside in the struggle for survival. Social Darwinism offered far too many pseudoscientific moral rationalizations justifying why the powerful should rule and exploit the powerless, and why the big fish should be allowed to eat the little fish, preferably without the useless and "progress-inhibiting" pangs of guilt. Many American robber barons, for instance, embraced this account because it helped them to feel better about their dark deeds: not only was God (supposedly) on their side, but sociocultural evolution was as well. How wonderful!

Throughout the twentieth century, however, scientific evolutionary theory progressed greatly and, in the 1960s and 1970s, began to be applied to human development in more subtle and convincing ways than had been true before. These changes were initially fueled by important advances in evolutionary biology such as those made by Smith (1964), Hamilton (1964), Trivers (1972), Wilson (1975, 1978), and Dawkins (1976). In addition, European ethologists such as Lorenz (1981), Tinbergen (1951), and Eibl-Eibesfeldt (1989) emphasized the value of naturalistic field observations of animal and human behavior as well as the importance of cross-species comparisons for a biologically and evolutionary theory–oriented understanding of human adaptation. Most recently, evolutionary psychologists such as Buss (1989, 1995) and Daly and Wilson (1988), researchers working in the area of evolutionary ecology including Konner (1982) and Blurton-Jones (1993), and evolutionary cultural anthropologists such as Durham (1992) have shown how neo-evolutionary theory can throw light on many aspects of human development in a variety of socio-ecological conditions.

As a relatively early example of this new kind of evolutionary theorizing, we may cite Bowlby's influential attachment theory (1982). Influenced by psychoanalytic considerations, studies pointing to the detrimental effects of infant care in some orphanages, Lorenz's demonstration of the phenomenon of "imprinting" among various birds, and Harlow's classic research (e.g., Harlow & Zimmerman, 1959) on the effects of early social deprivation on rhesus monkeys, Bowlby proposed that over the long course of human evolution, children must have evolved powerful attachment behaviors so that they would stay close to their caretakers and be protected from predators and other sources of harm. This notion meant, among other things, that we can understand behavior only by considering its "environment of adaptedness," which, in the case of humans, refers mostly to the environment they encountered during the course of many thousands of years as hunters and gatherers.

The child's attachment behaviors include all those gestures and signals serving to maintain proximity to their caretaker(s): smiling, babbling, grasping, following, sucking, crying, and so on. After an initial phase of indiscriminate responsiveness to a variety of humans, the child's attachment behaviors become increasingly focused on a particular person—most often, the baby's mother. When separated from her, the baby displays signs of separation anxiety and, in the presence of strangers, stranger anxiety.

Bowlby's theory was taken up by his research assistant, Mary D. S. Ainsworth, who in the early 1950s made careful naturalistic observations of attachment behaviors among young children living in several villages in the vicinity of Kampala, Uganda (Ainsworth, 1967). Furthermore, she also explored the possibility that babies may develop specific attachment styles while using the mother as a secure base from which to explore. In later studies in the United States, she developed a specific behavioral test to study children's attachment behavior, the Strange Situation (Ainsworth, Bell, & Stanton, 1971).

Bowlby's evolutionary theorizing and Ainsworth's cross-cultural and methodological explorations have stimulated a great amount of subsequent research (Cassidy & Shaver, 1999). Later cross-cultural research, for instance, has demonstrated considerable cross-cultural variation in the frequency and nature of children's attachment reactions (IJzendoorn & Kroonenburg, 1988; IJzendoorn & Sagi, 1999). These appear to result, in part, from differing ecological conditions that favor certain cultural values. These, in turn, are translated into different parental childrearing practices, which may be expected to lead to different reactions of children in the Strange Situation. In addition, the Strange Situation has different meanings in dissimilar cultures, thus making cross-cultural differences difficult to interpret.

Although Bowlby's original formulations had been more or less culture-blind (LeVine, Dixon, LeVine, Richman, Leiderman, Keefer, & Brazelton, 1994; see also LeVine, this volume), evolutionary theorizing and cross-cultural research on human development can be natural allies: for several decades now, researchers inspired by evolutionary theory have conducted cross-cultural investigations of infant behavior, childrearing practices of mothers and fathers, birth spacing and weaning (Fouts, this volume), parental investment in children, child abuse and infanticide, gender differences (e.g., Best, this volume), sexual jealousies, adolescent preferences for mates, adolescent behavior, relationships between kin, altruism, murder, and numerous other topics in a broad variety of cultures. In this context, neo-evolutionary theorists have already proposed hundreds of specific hypotheses that have been, or should be, tested cross-culturally.

Many of the investigations instigated by evolutionary theory are based on a paradigm that differs significantly from the alternative paradigms adopted by many cross-cultural developmental psychologists (Bjorklund & Pellegrini, 2002). For instance, evolutionary theorists usually take the general validity of the principles of natural selection, inclusive fitness, and so on, for granted, whereas most psychologists know only too well that their preferred paradigm is merely one among several equally plausible paradigms. While evolutionary theorists emphasize the lasting influence of distal but powerful (and frequently nonobvious) causes working themselves out over numerous generations, psychologists tend to focus on more obvious proximate causes. It should be added that according to evolutionary theory, natural selection functions as the final, long-term arbiter of behavioral tendencies and evolved behavioral adaptations, but these functions may be fulfilled through a variety of proximate mechanisms.

Whereas many evolutionary theorists favor "hard" observational methods and data focused on concrete behaviors in their functional contexts (e.g., Fouts, this volume), cross-cultural psychologists more often employ questionnaires designed to elicit culturally meaningful descriptions and self-descriptions of thoughts, feelings, and behaviors. Additionally, evolutionary theorists believe that there is a general human nature that manifests itself in all cultures and includes many selfish tendencies. From the point of view of evolutionary theory, infanticide, murder, rape, male competition for status, constantly shifting balances between agonistic and cooperative behaviors, conflicts between parents and their offspring, "politically incorrect" behavioral sex differences, and many other "evolved behaviors" may be expected to occur under certain circumstances in all societies. In contrast, cultural anthropologists and psychologists (together with their more ideologically inclined allies, the feminists and Marxists), tend to believe that humans are above all shaped by sociocultural conditions that, in principle, can be ameliorated in the service of societal progress. In the view of some evolutionary theorists (and others), however, cultural anthropologists and psychologists have tended to overlook some of the harsher aspects of life in non-Western societies because they do not wish to be accused of the mortal academic sin of ethnocentrism (Edgerton, 1992). From the point of view of neo-Darwinian theorists, many postmodern studies, in particular, intermingle fact and interpretation to such an extent that their validity must remain in doubt.

Neo-evolutionary theorists have a very long way to go before they can be said to provide a comprehensive and convincing account of ontogenetic development in the context of gene-culture coevolution. Nevertheless, it seems likely to me that a successful and general future theory of cross-cultural human development will need to be embedded in, or at least strongly influenced by, evolutionary considerations. Such a reconciliation between seemingly contradictory perspectives will be made easier by the fact that some of the newer evolutionary theories are increasingly paying attention to the nature of cultural transmission (e.g., Blackmore, 1999) and to interactions between ecological conditions, biological mechanisms, and cultural mechanisms. There is much room in neo-Darwinian theories of human development for behavioral plasticity together with both inter-individual and cross-cultural diversity, as long as it is understood that such diversity is ultimately grounded in past and present evolutionary adaptations to frequently shifting ecological conditions. In the encounter between evolutionary theory and culture theory, both approaches are bound to reemerge in substantially altered forms.

There is, nevertheless, something surrealistic about the recent debates surrounding neo-Darwinian theories. Just when women's fertility levels in almost all industrialized societies have declined to extremely low levels never before seen in history (see Gielen & Chumachenko, this volume), we are told that as humans we are genetically programmed to maximize our "inclusive fitness."

It is difficult to see how the many childless and "child-poor" couples and singles practicing their modern lifestyles can be said to pursue such strategies. Instead, it appears that the enticements of rich industrialized societies act at cross-purposes with the "evolutionary imperative" emphasized by neo-Darwinian theories.

Be that as it may, our long-term goal as cross-cultural developmentalists should be to create an overall, vertically integrated theory that simultaneously takes into account several levels of biological distal and proximate causes, psychological processes, sociocultural forces, ecological conditions, and their mutual inter-actions. At present, however, we are far from understanding what such a comprehensive and integrated theory might look like.

ADDITIONAL HISTORICAL CONTRIBUTIONS

The foregoing brief review of some highlights in the history of cross-cultural human development research has neglected numerous creative contributions to the field. Because of space constraints, we can mention here only a few of them. These include Erikson's suggestive and cross-culturally fruitful formulation (1963) of ego-identity development throughout the human life cycle; Rohner's investigations (1975, 1986) of parental acceptance and rejection across a broad variety of cultures based on a considerable variety of methods; McClelland's inventive cross-cultural investigations (1961) of achievement and power motivation; LeVine's broadly integrative approach (1970; LeVine et al., 1994) to the study of childcare, personality, and culture; Cole and colleagues' important studies (1971) of the cultural context of learning and thinking; Bronfenbrenner's influential model (1979) of the ecology of human development; Berry's emphasis (1976) on seeing human adaptation and differentiation in relationship to ecological factors; Super and Harkness's cross-culturally fruitful notion (1986) of a "developmental niche"; Stevenson, Stigler, and Lee's widely cited cross-national comparisons (e.g., Stevenson & Lee, 1990; Stevenson & Stigler, 1992) of children's performance on mathematics and other tests in East Asia and the United States of America; Hofstede's (1980) and Triandis's (1995) delineations of broad cross-cultural dimensions such as collectivism-individualism, together with the idea that these notions can be applied to cross-culturally shaped developmental scripts (e.g., Greenfield & Cocking, 1994); Kagitçibasi's effort (1996) to conceptualize family systems and human development in an integrative way; and so many other efforts.

In recent decades, the field of cross-cultural human development has profited from the rise of psychology in many non-Western countries. In Asia, for instance, there exists now a critical mass of psychologists in India (e.g., Saraswathi & Kaur,

1993), Japan (e.g., Gielen & Naito, 1999), and Hong Kong (e.g., Bond, 1996). Other important areas include Mexico, South Africa, and to some extent the Arab countries. Although developmental research in non-Western and semi-Western countries is not necessarily comparative in nature, indigenous psychologists are, implicitly or explicitly, confronted with the question of whether the theoretical principles and findings of mainstream Western developmental psychology are applicable in their respective countries. Although the present volume does not focus on the international scene in developmental psychology, a few representative works containing significant material about child and adolescent development in non-Western cultures may be cited. These include Shwalb and Shwalb (1996) for Japan; Lau (1997) for Chinese societies; Kakar (1978/1981), Saraswathi (1999), and Saraswathi and Kaur (1993) for India; Suvannathat, Bhanthumnavin, Bhuapirom, and Keats (1985) for Thailand; Nsamenang (1992) for sub-Saharan Africa; and Ahmed and Gielen (1998) for the Arab world.

Today, the cross-cultural study of human development is a thriving enterprise in which no single discipline, theoretical approach, or methodology predominates. Furthermore, there exists now an international community of developmental researchers located on several continents that can more easily cooperate in comparative investigations than ever before, thanks to modern means of communication. In addition, a group of psychologists and other social scientists such as Berry, Fuligni, Jia, Neto, Ogbu, Phinney, Portes, Roopnarine, Rumbaut, Silbereisen, Schmitz, Suárez-Orozco, and Waters have shown a special research interest in the psychological development of immigrant children and adolescents, together with a preference for cross-cultural comparisons (see in this context the respective contributions by Fuligni; Jia; and Roopnarine, Bynoe, & Singh in this volume).

Table 1.1 presents a brief overview of some of the writings that have helped to shape the history of the field of cross-cultural human development. Given the focus of this volume, the table is restricted to studies of childhood and adolescence although the field's extension to the whole life cycle represents an important modern development (e.g., Comunian & Gielen, 2000; Gardiner & Kozmitzki, 2002). In addition, the table omits writings on the history of childhood (e.g., Ariès, 1965; Hawes & Hiner, 1991) as well as comparative primate studies (e.g., Pereira & Fairbanks, 1993), although both areas of research are of considerable relevance to the field. Finally, the table omits the numerous hologeistic studies that have played an important role in the history of psychological anthropology (see, e.g., Williams, 1983, table 6-4, which lists sixty-five conclusions reached through the use of the holocultural method of the study of socialization).

Table 1.1
Some Milestones in the Cross-Cultural Study of Childhood and Adolescence

Authors and Publications	Year	Comments
D. Kidd, *Savage Childhood*	1906	Pioneering work describing the Bantu children of South Africa.
A. Van Gennep, *Les Rites de Passage*	1909	Classic work providing analytic framework for the study of life-cycle rituals.
M. Mead, *Coming of Age in Samoa: A Psychological Study of Primitive Youth*	1928	First, though controversial, study of nonwestern female adolescents testing the Storm and Stress theory–and finding it wanting.
M. Mead, *Growing up in New Guinea: A Comparative Study of Primitive Education*	1930	Analyzes the upbringing of children of the Admiralty Islands. Mead restudied the Manus 25 years later and found them extraordinarily changed.
M. Fortes, "Social and psychological aspects of education in Taleland"	1938	British social anthropologist describes informal education and parent-child relationships in an African society.
E. H. Erikson, *Childhood and Society*	1950, 1963	Outlines his eight-stage model of ego-identity development throughout the life-cycle together with sensitive biographies and analyses of childhood in different cultures.
D. C. McClelland, *The Achieving Society*	1961	Relates emphasis on achievement themes in children's readers to later national economic development across the world. Unique approach that has found few recent successors.
B. B. Whiting (Ed.), *Six Cultures: Studies of Child Rearing*	1963	Part of the Six Cultures project which moved the field of psychological anthropology toward a more systematic, measurement-oriented approach.
M. D. S. Ainsworth, *Infancy in Uganda: Infant Care and the Growth of Love*	1967	Suggested that Bowlby's attachment theory holds true in Uganda. Helped to create a new area of cross-cultural research shaped both by ethological and psychoanalytic notions.
L. Kohlberg, "Stage and sequence"	1969/ 1984	Most important chapter on social development written by a psychologist during the last 50 years. It outlines the universalistic basis of the cognitive-developmental approach and includes some cross-cultural data.
U. Bronfenbrenner, *Two Worlds of Childhood: U.S. and U.S.S.R.*	1970	Classic comparison of childhood in an individualistic and a more collectivistic society based on social learning theory.
M. Cole, J. Gay, J. Glick, & D. Sharp, *The Cultural Context of Learning and Thinking*	1971	Performance on cognitive tests frequently depends more on situational factors than on underlying differences in cognitive competence.
D. G. Freedman, *Human Infancy: An Evolutionary Perspective*	1974	Helped to reintroduce evolutionary considerations to the cross-cultural study of infants.
B. B. Whiting & J. W. P. Whiting, *Children of Six Cultures*	1975	Central publication of the Six Cultures project.
W. H. Holtzman, R. Diaz-Guerrero, & J. D. Swartz, *Personality development in Two Cultures: A Cross-Cultural Longitudinal Study of Children in Mexico and the United States*	1975	Multi-method comparative study of personality development.
R. L. Munroe & R. H. Munroe, *Cross-Cultural Human Development*	1975	First textbook on cross-cultural developmental research; it was reprinted in 1994 with a new foreword.
S. Kakar, *The Inner World: A Psychoanalytic Study of Childhood and Society in India*	1978	Psychoanalytic exploration of (mostly male) Indian childhood patterns; emphasizes boys' "maternal enthrallment" and its psychological consequences. See also Sharma & Gielen (2000).
P. R. Dasen, B. Inhelder, M. Lavallée, & J. Retschitzki, *Naissance du l'Intelligence chez l'Enfant Baoulé de Côte d'Ivoire*	1978	Influential monograph on Piagetian research in an African society. Numerous other studies on Piagetian stages in nonwestern societies have appeared, before and since.

(continued)

Table 1.1 (Continued)

U. Bronfenbrenner, *The Ecology of Human Development*	1979	Influential model delineating the contexts within which children and others develop.
R. H. Munroe, R. L. Munroe, & B. B. Whiting (Eds.), *Handbook of Cross-Cultural Human Development*	1981	First comprehensive handbook integrating anthropological and psychological research on cross-cultural human development.
H. C. Triandis & A. Heron (Eds.), *Developmental Psychology* (Vol. 4 of *Handbook of Cross-Cultural Psychology*)	1981	One of six volumes of the first handbook of cross-cultural psychology edited by H. C. Triandis. Less comprehensive and integrative than Munroe, Munroe, & Whiting (1981)
V. Barnouw, *Culture and Personality* (4th ed.)	1985	Best available summary of the methods and achievements of the Culture and Personality approach.
J. Snarey, "Cross-cultural validity of socio-moral development: A critical review of Kohlbergian research"	1985	Well-integrated assessment of cross-cultural studies suggesting that stages 1 through 4 can be found in many societies, but principled moral reasoning is absent in small-scale cultures.
C. Suvannathat, D. Bhanthumnavin, L. Bhuapirom, & D. M. Keats (Eds.), *Handbook of Asian Child Development and Child Rearing Practices*	1985	Broad survey of child development studies by a team of mostly Thai researchers: Chapters cite mostly American studies, though.
C. Super & S. Harkness, "The developmental niche"	1986	Classic article outlining the three aspects of a "developmental niche." Outlines a socioecological approach.
B. B. Whiting, J. W. M. Whiting, V. Burbank, R. G. Condon, D. A. Davis, S. S. Davis, M. Hollos, P. E. Leis, C. M. Worthman, et al.: Adolescence in a Changing World project	1987-1989	Joint project focusing on adolescence among Australian Aborigines, Ijos, Inuits, Kikuyus, Moroccans, etc.
B. B. Whiting & C. P. Edwards, Children of Different Worlds: *The Formation of Social Behavior*	1988	Broadly conceived, integrative volume on cross-cultural development based, in part, on the Six Cultures project.
B. Bril & H. Lehalle, *Le Développement Psychologique: Est-il Universelle?*	1988	First overview of cross-cultural psychological research on human development in the French language.
D. Offer, E. Ostrov, K. I. Howard, & R. Atkinson, *The Teenage World: Adolescents' Self-Image in Ten Countries*	1988	Found that self-conceptions of teenagers are more similar than dissimilar across ten nations. Most teenagers have positive rather than conflictual self-images.
G. Trommsdorff (Ed.), *Sozialisation im Kulturvergleich*	1989	The contributors to this German publication discuss culture-comparative approaches to socialization.
J. Tobin, D. Wu, & D. Davidson, *Preschool in Three Cultures*	1989	Introduces innovative cross-cultural methodology using videotaping of preschool classrooms in East Asian cultures and the United States.
J. Valsiner, *Human Development and Culture: The Social Nature of Personality and its Study*	1989	Trained in Russian and Central European psychology, the cultural psychologist Valsiner develops in this, and his many other books, a sociohistorical perspective on personality development. See also Valsiner (2000).
I. Eibl-Eibesfeldt, *Human Ethology*	1989	Major survey of the ethological approach including cross-cultural data.
M. Cole & S. R. Cole, *The Development of Children* (1st–5th ed.)	1989-2004	Major child development textbook by leading cultural psychologist. Good integration of cross-cultural viewpoint with biological and psychological perspectives.
H. W. Stevenson & S. Y. Lee, "Contexts of achievement: A study of American, Chinese, and Japanese children"	1990	Thorough study exploring why Chinese and Japanese children and adolescents perform better on mathematics and other tests than their American peers.

Table 1.1 (Continued)

D. Gilmore, *Manhood in the Making: Cultural Concepts of Masculinity*	1990	Discusses gender expectations for adolescent boys in a variety of traditional, nonindustrialized societies.
A. Schlegel & H. Barry, *Adolescence: An Anthropological Inquiry*	1991	Important hologeistic worldwide survey of adolescence. Finds that some form of adolescence is universal.
B. Hewlett, *Intimate Fathers: The Nature and Context of Aka Pygmy Paternal Infant Care*	1991	Among the Aka pygmies, a central African group of hunters/gatherers, fathers are heavily involved in infant care.
A. B. Nsamenang, *Human Development in Cultural Context: A Third World Perspective*	1992	Cameroonian scholar emphasizes contextual viewpoint and the contributions that indigenous researchers can make.
T. S. Saraswathi & B. Kaur (Eds.), *Human Development and Family Studies in India*	1993	Edited volume by India's leading developmental psychologist. See also Saraswathi (1999).
P. M. Greenfield & R. R. Cocking (Eds.), *Cross-Cultural Roots of Minority Child Development*	1994	Well-integrated chapters discuss minority children both from multi-cultural (within the USA) and cross-cultural perspectives. Emphasis on contrast between collectivistic and individualistic developmental scripts.
R. A. LeVine, S. Dixon, S. LeVine, A. Richman, P. H. Leiderman, C. H. Keefer, & T. B. Brazelton, *Child Care and Culture: Lessons from Africa*	1994	Major interdisciplinary project among the Gusii (Kenya): Child care in a high-fertility, polygynous African Society.
K. Hurrelmann (Ed.), *International Handbook of Adolescence*	1994	Summarizes research on adolescence in 31 countries from around the world.
D. W. Shwalb & J. Shwalb (Eds.), *Japanese Childrearing: Two Generations of Scholarship*	1996	Biographically and historically oriented accounts by senior scholars and responses by junior scholars discuss 50 years of research on Japanese childrearing, often in comparison to Chinese and American childrearing.
S. Harkness & C. M. Super (Eds.), *Parents' Cultural Belief Systems: Their Origins, Experiences, and Consequences*	1996	The contributors examine parental belief systems and their implications for childrearing and child development in numerous cultures.
C. Suárez-Orozco & M. Suárez-Orozco, *Transformations: Migration, Family Life and Achievement Motivation among Latino Adolescents*	1996	Monograph about large-scale project focusing on the educational and psychosocial adjustment of Latino immigrant adolescents in the United States.
Ç. Kagitçibasi, *Family and Human Development Across Cultures: A View from the Other Side*	1996	Turkish psychologist develops her contextual-developmental-functional approach to child development in the context of families. She emphasizes that interdependence and independence must be balanced in self-development.
J. W. Berry, P. R. Dasen, & T. S. Saraswathi (Eds.), *Basic Processes and Human Development* (Vol. 2 of *Handbook of Cross-Cultural Psychology*)	1997	One of three volumes of the leading cross-cultural psychology handbook, it reflects the recent rise of cultural psychology approaches.
S. Lau (Ed.), *Growing up the Chinese Way: Chinese Child and Adolescent Development*	1997	Convenient summary of Chinese developmental research which has burgeoned in recent years.
R. A. Ahmed & U. P. Gielen (Eds.), *Psychology in the Arab Countries*	1998	First survey of Arab psychology including research on human development.
K. H. Rubin (Guest Editor), *Special Issue: Social and Emotional Development: A Cross-Cultural Perspective* (Developmental Psychology)	1998	This special issue includes cross-cultural studies of emotional development, parenting and parent-child relationships, social cognition and social relationships, and social and emotional adjustment and maladjustment.
H. W. Gardiner, (J. Mutter), & C. Kosmitzki, *Lives Across Cultures: Cross-Cultural Human Development* (two editions)	1998/ 2002	Easy-to-read, standard psychology textbook reviewing cross-cultural studies of the human life cycle.

(continued)

Table 1.1 (Continued)

C. Beckwith & A. Fisher, *African Ceremonies*, Vols. 1-2	1999	Both volumes contain stunning photographs documenting African life-cycle and other rituals in numerous societies. Some of the rituals are now being abandoned.
G. Weisfeld, *Evolutionary Principles of Human Adolescence*	1999	Joins evolutionary and ethological perspectives with cross-cultural and cross-species studies to arrive at a universalistic theory of adolescence.
A. L. Comunian & U. P. Gielen (Eds.), *International Perspectives on Human Development*	2000	Broadly conceived volume; includes theoretical and empirical papers by international cast of contributors emphasizing cross-cultural and integrative perspectives on the human life-cycle.
J. J. Arnett, *Adolescence and Emerging Adulthood: A Cultural Approach*	2001	First comprehensive psychology textbook on adolescence to consistently adopt a cultural point of view.
D.F. Bjorklund & A.D. Pellegrini, *The Origins of Developmental Psychology.*	2002	Applies the basic principles of Darwinian evolution to explain human development.
B. B. Brown, R. Larson, & T. S. Saraswathi (Eds.), *The World's Youth: Adolescence in Eight Regions of the Globe*	2002	Broad survey depicting the overall psychological situation of adolescents in eight major regions of the world.
H. Keller, Y. H. Poortinga, & A. Schölmerich (Eds.), *Between Biology and Culture: Perspectives on Ontogenetic Development*	2002	Promising volume outlining new perspectives on the interplay between biology and culture in relationship to ontogenetic development.
T. S. Saraswathi (Ed.), *Cross-Cultural Perspectives in Human Development: Theory, Research and Practice*	2003	Leading IACCP members and others outline a variety of theoretical positions and discuss interventions in India, Turkey and elsewhere.
U. P. Gielen & J. L. Roopnarine (Eds.), *Childhood and Adolescence: Cross-Cultural Perspectives and Applications*	2004	Prominent group of scholars review cross-cultural research together with studies of immigrant children and adolescents from a variety of theoretical positions.

TEN GENERAL ASSUMPTIONS STRUCTURING PRESENT-DAY CROSS-CULTURAL INVESTIGATIONS OF HUMAN DEVELOPMENT

As the field of cross-cultural human development studies matured and a wide variety of researchers and theoreticians began to introduce broadly based evidence from a large range of societies, many members of the scientific community began to endorse a number of general assumptions about the nature of the field. Because these assumptions form the tacit background for the present book, a brief summary of them may prove helpful:

1. Human development is the outcome of a continuous interaction between long-term evolutionary forces, evolved general and individual biological predispositions, complex psychological processes, changing physical environments, changing social forces, and intricate cultural belief systems. Biological evolution and sociocultural evolution proceed in an intertwined fashion and provide the general conditions under which individual lives evolve over time. Development results from multiple causes, operating through multiple, highly complex processes, at multiple levels, and these are frequently connected to each other through feedback loops. Consequently, no single sovereign theory is likely to be able to explain cross-cultural human development in all of its intricacies. Instead,

human development must be analyzed in multiple ways at different levels of complexity.

2. Cultural forces are ubiquitous, complex, evolving, intertwined with economic, social-class, technological, and ecological conditions, and not rarely contradictory in nature. In order to understand their ongoing role in the process of human development, the "variable" of culture must be broken up. However, culture is not simply an external variable influencing the functioning of the mind and the expression of behavior, but rather, culture, mind, and behavior "make each other up." Such a perspective is especially favored by cultural psychologists (e.g., Shweder et al., 1998).

3. In light of the foregoing, cultural determinism and cultural relativism as well as biological determinism constitute outdated points of view that do not adequately take into account the interaction among biological predispositions, mental processes, behavioral tendencies, (physical) environmental forces, and evolving sociocultural conditions. Similarly, the *analytic* distinction between nature and nurture should not be reified (taken to be a real phenomenon), since all behavior is performed by biological organisms acting and developing in some kind of physical and sociocultural environment. Best, for instance, outlines in her chapter how the interaction between biological and sociocultural factors has been conceived in cross-cultural theories and empirical studies of gender differences and gender roles.

4. Human development in all its variety can only be understood in cross-cultural perspective, if representatives of different disciplines contribute their special perspectives and methodologies to the joint enterprise. The more problem-centered a research project, the more likely it is that multidisciplinary cooperation does in fact take place rather than remaining only a theoretical ideal. However, at present, no graduate program exists that trains its students systematically and simultaneously in the different disciplines, viewpoints, and methodologies needed to give an adequate account of cross-cultural human development. The establishment of such programs is long overdue and will probably require the cooperation among researchers from different institutions.

5. In a general way, conclusions reached by researchers about the nature of cross-cultural human adaptation and development should be compatible with evolutionary theory. This does not mean, however, that all or even most specific evolutionary hypotheses are necessarily true, since human development is influenced by numerous, and often contradictory, biological, psychological, and sociocultural factors. The balance between enabling and constraining forces is not easily summarized by a ready set of theoretical generalizations derived from evolutionary theory—or from any other theory, for that matter.

There exist at present three groups of modern evolutionary theorists, each of which has tended to approach human development from a different angle (Smith, 2000). For instance, a number of scholars have conducted quantitative behavioral studies of infants, children, and childcare among foragers, pastoralists, and horticulturalists (e.g., Fouts, this volume; Hewlett, 1991; Konner, 1977). A second group of researchers, who identify themselves as evolutionary psychologists, has attempted to identify universal "modules" or "mental organs" of the mind, such as a module for language (Pinker, 1994). These are thought to have evolved during Bowlby's "environment of evolutionary adaptation" (1969). Finally, a group of evolutionary cultural anthropologists has focused on the evolutionary nature of culture and cultural diversity together with an attempt to try to apply the notion of "selection mechanisms" to cultural inheritance systems (e.g., Blackmore, 1999). These three groups have already made valuable if sometimes controversial contributions to the cross-cultural study of human development, each in its own way.

6. Cross-cultural development researchers should not depend on a single methodology. In many research situations, a multimethod approach sometimes called triangulation (e.g., Cournoyer, 2000; Holtzman, Diaz-Guerrero, & Swartz, 1975; Rohner, 1986) is optimal, since it can tell us to what extent a phenomenon is "created" by a specific method, and to what extent a phenomenon can be considered robust in nature by manifesting itself across a variety of methods. Although from a theoretical point of view, many researchers favor a multimethod approach, for practical reasons this often remains an ideal rather than becoming a routine aspect of the research process. In this context, multidisciplinary approaches may be considered especially fruitful since members of different disciplines naturally tend to favor, and are competent in applying, a variety of methods and techniques.

7. Anthropologists and psychologists sometimes distinguish between "emic" and "etic" perspectives in the study of behavior. The emic viewpoint emphasizes the understanding of behavior within a given cultural framework of meanings, whereas the etic viewpoint interprets behavior within a framework of scientific concepts that frequently originate outside a given culture. Explicitly or implicitly, researchers guided by evolutionary approaches as well as mainstream psychologists have tended to favor etic forms of theorizing. In contrast, many cultural anthropologists, cultural psychologists, and researchers favoring indigenous approaches emphasize the advantages of an emic perspective. It should be added, however, that the traditional focus of many cultural anthropologists on unique, deterministic, self-existing cultural configurations not anchored in psychological processes is largely incompatible with the viewpoint adopted by many contributors to this volume.

Like many other analytic distinctions in the social sciences, the dichotomy between "emic" and "etic" viewpoints can be misleading. While investigating development within a given culture, all researchers must pay at least some attention to an (emic) understanding of the point of view of their respondents. At the same time, all scientific cross-cultural comparisons must by necessity rely on observations and responses that can be classified according to some scientific system of meaning more or less external to the respondents (Triandis, 2000). Although sometimes advocated, a consistently emic approach is neither possible nor desirable since it would imprison the researcher in a unique, never-to-be-repeated framework of meanings relative to time and place. Similarly, an exclusive emphasis on "indigenous psychologies" would soon prove self-defeating: since there exist thousands of different cultures and subcultures in this world, such an effort would result in thousands of separate psychologies united by little more than the term "psychology." The outcome of the effort would be an epistemological nightmare.

8. Much has been made of the fact that the social sciences in general, and cross-cultural theories and research on human development in particular, originated in the West, where to this day one can find the majority of active researchers and theoreticians. Emphasizing this, Canadian cross-cultural psychologist Berry found the discipline of mainstream psychology "so culture-bound and culture-blind that . . . it should not be employed as it is" (1983, p. 449). Such an observation is not entirely wrong but it is also not that helpful. The fact that a given scientific theory originated in a particular cultural context cannot tell us how valid or scientifically useful it is. To accuse, for instance, psychology of a Western bias is of limited value since Western psychologists have produced a rich variety of contradictory theories, none of which can be said to represent "the" Western outlook. Indeed, there may be no such thing as a "Western" theory, nor have non-Western social scientists been able to develop truly different theories from those created by American and European researchers. Indeed, disciplinary boundaries have often proven more difficult to cross than cultural boundaries between investigators who, though coming from different cultural backgrounds, are pursuing shared research goals. Professional tunnel vision, excessive attachment to one's favorite scientific theory in the face of contradictory evidence, a restrictive methodological outlook, and unwillingness to face the ostracism consequent to one's contradicting basic ideas and assumptions fashionable in one's academic-political milieu tend to create greater impediments to scientific progress in the social sciences than cross-cultural differences between investigators.

From a more pragmatic perspective, however, the increasing importance of non-Western researchers in the social sciences can only be welcomed. Often, they have access to culturally varied research populations as well as bringing with them a different set of research priorities. Many of them function in a bicultural or multicultural mode on a daily basis, since they are surrounded by their local culture while also participating in the larger, mostly English-speaking community of international scientists. Having been trained at Western universities—or, alternatively, at local universities following the Western model of scientific training—they experience in themselves those cultural tensions that both liberate and alienate them from their local sociocultural contexts. This process can serve as a powerful catalyst for cultural insights that may be hidden from Western researchers who may be too embedded in their own culture to see it, or other cultures, clearly.

Concerning the cross-cultural study of human development, then, the field will do well to follow Mao Tse-Tung's slogan (though not his execution of it): "Let a Thousand Flowers Bloom."

9. It is widely understood by modern cross-cultural researchers that intragroup differences in psychological functioning are frequently more pronounced than intergroup differences. In other words, even if a psychological researcher finds clear statistical differences between the means of two contrasting cultural samples, the overlap between the two groups may nevertheless be large.

In contrast to this understanding, earlier representatives of the Personality and Culture school such as Mead tended to overemphasize the homogeneity of the cultures they studied, thereby consistently underestimating psychological variation among its members. For Mead and for Benedict, the concept of culture had almost assumed the characteristics of an ideal Platonic form, and they considered as "deviants" those (supposedly) few members not living up to its ideals (as they understood them). At the same time, Mead also asserted that (as previously discussed) all members of a given culture are fundamentally different from all members of all other cultures. In a somewhat similar vein, many proponents of national character and modal personality studies, whether implicitly or explicitly, have mistakenly assumed that most members of a given society are molded by it into a single—or perhaps a very few—predominant personality type(s). This assumption, it may be added, also entails important implications for the question of whether the study of cross-cultural differences or similarities is more important: whereas theorists and researchers interested in cross-cultural differences tend to "level" within-group differences and "sharpen" between-group differences, those interested in similarities between cultural groups tend to downplay between-group differences in their search for common human proclivities.

10. A considerable (though not unlimited) variety of childrearing strategies is appropriate for rearing competent children, adolescents, and adults who are able to function successfully in the ecological conditions both surrounding, and being created by, their societies (Chen & Kaspar, this volume). Furthermore, as societies change, formerly adaptive childrearing strategies may grow maladaptive. In such a situation, parents must increasingly educate children and adolescents for a world that does not yet exist and which they cannot fully comprehend. The children and adolescents, in turn, need to internalize knowledge and ways of behaving that increasingly derive from peer group contact, schools, and other institutions outside the home. Consequently, the "developmental niches" of adolescents living in traditional agricultural societies and those residing in modern information societies tend to be of a different nature (Arnett, Gibbons,

Gielen & Chumachenko, all in this volume). Traditional societies tend to convey relatively unitary worldviews and forms of knowledge to their youngsters, whereas rapidly changing modern societies can only transmit preliminary, fragmentary, and sometimes contradictory messages, forms of knowledge, and skills to their future generations.

The appropriateness of specific childrearing strategies needs to be evaluated in the context of the socioecological conditions to which a group must adapt (Fouts, this volume). For instance, the authoritative, child-centered, self-esteem-promoting childrearing strategies favored by most American developmental textbook writers are probably much more adaptive for a fast changing, individualistic, postmodern society with small families than for a traditional, agricultural society based on large, polygynous families (LeVine, this volume). Similarly, a societal emphasis on childrearing strategies promoting the development of interpersonal sensitivity, emotional warmth, tender-minded concern for outgroup members, and responsive obedience would be ill suited for the many horticultural, nomadic, and agricultural societies of the past (and sometimes present) that had to survive under conditions of permanent warfare and intertribal or intercity hostility (e.g., many Amazonian Indians, American Plains Indians, nomads inhabiting the Arab Peninsula, the Pashtun/Pathan of Afghanistan and Pakistan, precolonial New Guinea, neighbors of the Aztec empire, classical Greek city-states). Unfortunately, childrearing methods and personality development have been insufficiently studied in such societies (for an example, see Lindholm, 1998).

CROSS-CULTURAL PSYCHOLOGISTS AND PSYCHOLOGICAL AND CULTURAL ANTHROPOLOGISTS

We have seen that the cross-cultural study of human development prospers when an interdisciplinary team of researchers applies a variety of theoretical approaches and methods to systematically selected and culturally varied samples of respondents. While this ideal is rarely realized in full, it may be useful in the context of this volume to take a look at the two disciplines that in recent years have contributed the most to the cross-cultural study of human development: cross-cultural psychology and cultural/psychological anthropology. Historically, the anthropologists came first, but in recent years, the number of active cross-cultural psychologists has easily surpassed the number of cultural/psychological anthropologists active in the field. This situation is, for instance, reflected among the membership of the Society for Cross-Cultural Research: whereas psychological anthropologists—especially those associated with the perspective of Beatrice and John Whiting—were once dominant in this association, nowadays psychologists make up about 60 percent of its membership. In contrast, a shrinking and aging group of quantitatively oriented cross-cultural anthropologists feels increasingly marginalized in their profession by those anthropologists advocating more qualitative and postmodern perspectives (d'Andrade, 2000). In contrast to this situation, cross-cultural and multicultural psychologists have increased their numbers while intensifying their impact on mainstream psychology, especially during the last two decades.

Table 1.2 presents an ideal-type comparison between the respective approaches of cross-cultural psychologists and cultural/psychological anthropologists. It should be understood that the contrasting comparisons do not point to absolute differences between the two disciplines but rather to tendencies underlying many but by no means all investigations. Furthermore, the present essay tends to downplay differences between psychological and cultural anthropologists, between cultural psychologists and cross-cultural psychologists, and between cross-cultural psychologists and anthropologists, in the interest of arriving at a synthetic overview of the cross-cultural study of ontogenetic development.

American psychologists have traditionally emphasized experimentation as the royal road to knowledge followed by quantifiable observations and questionnaire responses. In their view, it should be the central purpose of scientific investigation to understand relationships between variables as specified by specific hypotheses. The hypotheses typically center on questions designed to elucidate the nature of major psychological processes designated as learning, memory, cognition, perception, emotion, development, personality dimensions, personality dynamics, and so on. To test the hypotheses, specific samples of research participants are drawn, participants who, for the sake of convenience rather than for theoretical reasons, are most often selected from captive populations such as nurseries and preschools, schools, colleges and universities, inmates of old-age homes, and so on. Research participants are most often characterized according to general categories such as age, gender, ethnic or cultural group, social-class background of their family, and so on.

In practice, a major proportion of the available cross-cultural psychological literature has compared "Western" samples (especially Americans) with "non-Western" samples, with the latter frequently including students from East Asian countries. These are often said to represent a "collectivistic" culture whereas, in contrast, American students are meant to represent the mind-set of persons living in individualistic cultures. The Americans are frequently—and falsely—designated as representatives of "the" West, whereas East Asian students are often—and falsely—considered to be typical representatives of (the whole of) Asia. In this context, little attention tends to be paid to the fact that a broad variety of ways of life can be found in Asia, ranging from that of Muslim peasants in Turkmenistan to the contrasting lifeways of Siberian nomads, Tibetan hermits in the Himalayas, Russian gangsters, gun-wielding tribesmen from Afghanistan, Indian computer experts, Balinese temple dancers, and hip coeds from Tokyo. Similarly, "the" West includes, in reality, quite varied cultural traditions and populations such as Portuguese small-town businessmen, conservative church-

Table 1.2
Some Idealized Differences Between Cultural Anthropologists and Cross-Cultural Psychologists

	Cross-Cultural Psychologists	Cultural/Psychological Anthropologists
Purpose of the investigation	To understand relationships between variables	To understand small-scale cultures, subcultures, or major institutions; some quantitative investigations
Range of problems investigated	Psychological processes suggested by current theories of perception, memory, cognitive development, emotional expression, language development, personality dimensions and dynamics, etc.	Broad range of everyday behaviors held together by cultural worldviews, values, societal institutions, ecological conditions
Most frequently studied populations	Captive populations in schools, colleges, universities, etc. located in large-scale literate societies	Villagers, foragers, people living in neighborhoods or organizations (e.g., hospitals)
Main focus of professional training	Experimental procedures and statistical techniques, survey techniques, quantitative observation methods based on category systems	Creation of holistic ethnographies, interview schedules, disciplined observation of common behaviors
Nature of data	Quantitative, supplanted by some qualitative observations	Qualitative observations together with some quantitative supportive data; observations of everyday behaviors and events
Time framework for data collection	Often only 30-90 minutes per respondent	9-24 months
Sampling procedures	Large, systematically selected samples categorized by age, gender, SES, cultural membership, etc.	Small number of (sometimes psychologically marginal) informants, small underspecified selection of respondents, household survey data
Concern for cultural context of investigation	Low to moderate	Central to investigation
Concern for economic context of investigation	Frequently lacking or tangential to investigation	Modes of production, economic basis of group under investigation are part of the "big picture"
Common methodological criticisms of field	Behaviors torn out of cultural context; trivial conclusions because they are based on small range of investigated problems and responses; too much reliance on formal questionnaires and verbal reports rather than observations of day-to-day behaviors; methodologies too artificial and supporting false sense of precision	Insufficient delineation of underlying psychological processes; poor sampling procedures, lack of quantitative data; interpretations too subjective and based on non-repeatable data collection procedures

going wives of Greek farmers, Swedish reindeer herders, Dutch prostitutes, Swiss bankers, English "soccer hooligans," and many others who may little resemble American students in their opinions, behaviors, feelings, and identities. In addition, Latin American societies such as Argentina and Chile are just as "Western" as Canada or the United States of America (e.g., see Bornstein et al., this volume). The implicit or explicit tendency of many American and non-American social scientists to treat American society as "the" model Western society reflects its hegemony in the military, economic, linguistic, mass media, and social science areas, but it nevertheless constitutes poor scientific practice that encourages stereotypical thinking among social scientists and their readers.

Nonliterate populations, lower-class respondents, villagers depending on agriculture, representatives of foraging cultures, mature working adults, aging housewives, and so on, are much less frequently selected for cross-cultural investigation. While recent investigators have tended to show an increased concern for the respondents' cultural context, only a limited number of investigations report observations of daily behavior in natural settings. Instead, much of cross-cultural psychology has become a kind of comparative-study-of-responses-to-questionnaires-by-university-students-from-various-nations. *The field relies too much on students' reports about their own and other people's behavior rather than studying the behavior itself.* In Lewis Aptekar's chapter in this volume, the reader will encounter a lucid discussion of why questionnaire-oriented methodologies are, for instance, inappropriate for the study of street children. Many street children are masters at presenting themselves in different ways to different researchers in an attempt to solicit their material support. Could it not be true that other children and adolescents are similarly concerned with presenting themselves in the "right" light to those researchers pursuing them with questionnaires?

In contrast to the analytic and quantitative research paradigm underlying most investigations by cross-cultural psychologists, cultural and psychological anthropologists have tended to emphasize a more contextual, qualitative approach to the study of culturally defined groups and the psychological processes occurring in those individuals making them up. The participant observation of everyday behaviors based on empathic role-taking as well as the drawing of inferences about underlying worldviews and other culturally constituted meaning systems remains at the center of many anthropological investigations. Anthropologists are also far more likely to study villagers, foragers, and nonliterate or semiliterate populations than most psychologists, whose continued preference for questionnaire-based methodologies rules out the employment of nonliterate and semiliterate populations in their studies, anyway.

My comparison of "the" cultural anthropology approach with "the" cross-cultural psychology approach suggests that a combination of the two ways of doing social science should prove productive, especially since the respective strengths of the two approaches might compensate for some of their corresponding weaknesses. There has, indeed, been some mutual recognition of this possibility. However, a comparison between recent articles published in two typical journals—*Ethos*, as the house journal of the Society for Psychological Anthropology, and the *International Journal of Behavioral Development*, as the official publication of the psychology-oriented International Society for the Study of Behavioral Development—demonstrates that the two disciplines continue to favor distinctive methodological approaches. Nevertheless, increased cross-disciplinary collaboration and integration would almost certainly make it more likely that a more balanced, complex, and realistic understanding of human development emerges from our investigations. We hope that this volume will contribute toward this goal. It contains mostly contributions by cross-cultural psychologists who, however, are well aware of parallel developments in psychological anthropology.

CONCLUSION

In this chapter I have reviewed some of the tasks of cross-cultural developmental psychologists and anthropologists. In addition, I have discussed the history of cross-cultural developmental research, identified some of its underlying assumptions and methodological principles, and compared approaches respectively taken by anthropologists and by psychologists.

While cross-cultural human development is a relatively new field of scientific study, it is remarkable that the contributions in this volume arrive at a good many sound conclusions opposed to those expressed in many developmental psychology textbooks, by professional psychologists, or by the general public. For instance, conventional wisdom tells us that parents are the main socializing agents of children, an assumed "fact" that, indeed, forms the taken-for-granted cornerstone of orthodox psychoanalysis with its emphasis on the Oedipus complex. Yet this premise cannot be accurate, states Maynard, since in many cultures siblings are more important socialization agents than parents. The research conducted by Fouts on Bofi farming families and by LeVine on Gusii polygamous farming families reinforces this conclusion. There are many more examples discussed in the following chapters that demonstrate that cross-cultural developmental psychology can free us from ethnocentric blinders, throw into doubt theories at variance with the prevailing psychocultural conditions in many non-Western societies, redefine what is important in human development, and ultimately help us gain a more comprehensive and less biased understanding of the human condition. This is certainly an appropriate goal for the new century, in which cross-cultural misunderstandings are likely to have serious, even deadly, consequences for children, adolescents, and adults alike.

Although the field of cross-cultural developmental research has a short history, it is becoming increasingly clear that it will be long lasting. In the past, American and European researchers argued that the study of (mostly mainstream) children and adolescents in their respective countries will one day result in a comprehensive and universally valid theory of human development—such notions have been debunked. Rather, in order to develop such a theory, it is necessary to trace and compare the developmental trajectories of children, adolescents, and adults in a broad spectrum of ecological and sociocultural settings around the globe. Such a path has been taken by the contributors to this volume, as is demonstrated in the following chapters.

NOTE

A small section of this paper previously appeared as: Gielen, U. P., & Jeshmaridian, S. (1999). Lev S. Vygotsky: The man and the era. *International Journal of Group Tensions*, 28 (3–4), 273–301. Copyright © 1999 Kluwer/Plenum Publisher.

REFERENCES

Ahmed, R. A., & Gielen, U. P. (Eds.). (1998). *Psychology in the Arab countries*. Menoufia, Egypt: Menoufia University Press.

Ainsworth, M. D. S. (1967). *Infancy in Uganda: Infant care and the growth of love*. Baltimore: Johns Hopkins University Press.

Ainsworth, M. D. S., Bell, S. M. V., & Stanton, D. J. (1971). Individual differences in Strange-Situation behaviour of one-year-olds. In H. R. Schaffer (Ed.), *The origins of human social relations* (pp. 17–57). New York: Academic Press.

Ariès, P. (1965). *Centuries of childhood*. New York: Random House.

Arnett, J. J. (1999). Adolescent storm and stress reconsidered. *American Psychologist, 54*, 317–326.

———. (2001). *Adolescence and emerging adulthood: A cultural approach*. Upper Saddle River, NJ: Prentice-Hall.

Barnouw, V. (1985). *Culture and personality* (4th ed.). Homewood, IL: Dorsey Press.

Beckwith, C., & Fisher A. (1999). *African ceremonies*. Vols.1–2. New York: Abrams.

Berry, J. W. (1976). *Human ecology and cognitive style*. Beverly Hills, CA: Sage.

———. (1983). The sociogenesis of social sciences: An analysis of the cultural relativity of social psychology. In B. Bain (Ed.), *The sociogenesis of language and human conduct* (pp. 449–458). New York: Plenum.

Berry, J. W., Dasen, P. R., & Saraswathi, T. S. (Eds.). (1997). *Handbook of cross-cultural psychology* (2nd ed.). Vol. 2, *Basic processes and human development*. Boston: Allyn & Bacon.

Bjorklund, D. F., & Pellegrini, A. D. (2002). *The origins of human nature: Evolutionary developmental psychology*. Washington, DC: American Psychological Association.

Blackmore, S. (1999). *The meme machine*. Oxford: Oxford University Press.

Blurton-Jones, N. G. (1993). The lives of hunter-gather children: Effects of parental behavior and parental reproductive strategy. In M. E. Pereira & L. A. Fairbanks (Eds.), *Juvenile primates* (pp. 309–326). New York: Oxford University Press.

Bond, M. (Ed.). (1996). *The handbook of Chinese psychology*. Hong Kong: Oxford University Press.

Bowlby, J. (1969). *Attachment and loss.* Vol. 1, *Attachment.* New York: Basic Books.

———. (1982). *Attachment and loss.* Vol. 1, *Attachment* (2nd ed.). New York: Basic Books.

Bril, B., & Lehalle, H. (1998). *Le développement psychologique est-il universel? Approches interculturelles* [Psychological development: Is it universal? Intercultural approaches]. Paris: Presses Universitaires de France.

Brislin, R. (2000). *Understanding culture's influence on behavior* (2nd ed.). Fort Worth: Harcourt.

Bronfenbrenner, U. (1970). *Two worlds of childhood: U.S. and U.S.S.R.* New York: Russell Sage.

———. (1979). *The ecology of human development: Experiments by nature and design.* Cambridge, MA: Harvard University Press.

Brown, B. B., Larson, R., & Saraswathi, T. S. (Eds.). (2002). *The world's youth: Adolescence in eight regions of the globe.* New York: Cambridge University Press.

Burbank, V. (1988). *Aboriginal adolescence: Maidenhood in an Australian Aboriginal community.* New Brunswick, NJ: Rutgers University Press.

Buss, D. M. (1989). Sex differences in human mate preferences: Evolutionary hypothesis tested in thirty-seven cultures. *Behavioral and Brain Sciences, 12,* 1–49.

———. (1995). *The evolution of desire: Strategies of human mating.* New York: Basic Books.

Cassidy, J., & Shaver, P. R. (Eds.). (1999). *Handbook of attachment.* New York: Guilford Press.

Chomsky, N. (1959). [Review of *Verbal Behavior* by B. F. Skinner]. *Language, 35,* 26–58.

Cohen, A. R. (1999). *A history of children.* Westport, CT: Greenwood Press.

Cole, M. (1996). *Cultural psychology: A once and future discipline.* Cambridge, MA: Belknap Press.

Cole, M., & Cole, S. R. (2004). *The development of children* (5th ed.). New York: Worth.

Cole, M., Gay, J., Glick, J., & Sharp, D. (1971). *The cultural context of learning and thinking.* New York: Basic Books.

Comunian, A. L., & Gielen, U. P. (2000). *International perspectives on human development.* Lengerich, Germany: Pabst Science.

Condon, R. G. (1988). *Inuit youths: Growth and change in the Canadian Artic.* New Brunswick, NJ: Rutgers University Press.

Cournoyer, D. E. (2000). Universalist research: Examples drawn from the methods and findings of Parental Acceptance/Rejection Theory. In A. L. Comunian & U. P. Gielen (Eds.), *International perspectives on human development* (pp. 213–232). Lengerich, Germany: Pabst Science.

Daly, M., & Wilson, M. (1988). *Homicide.* New York: Aldine de Gruyter.

d'Andrade, R. (2000). The sad story of anthropology, 1950–1999. *Cross-Cultural Research, 34* (3), 219–232.

Dasen, P. R. (2000). Rapid social change and the turmoil of adolescence: A cross-cultural perspective. In J. L. Gibbons & U. P. Gielen (Eds.), Adolescence in international and cross-cultural perspective. Special issue, *International Journal of Group Tensions, 29* (1–2), 17–49.

Dasen, P. R., Dembele, B., Ettien, K., Kabran, K., Kamagate, D., Koffi, D. A., & N'Guessan, A. (1985). Ngoulèlê: L'intelligence chez les Baoulé [N'goulèlê: Intelligence among the Baoulé]. *Archives de Psychologie, 53,* 293–324.

Dasen, P. R., & Heron, A. (1981). Cross-cultural tests of Piaget's theory. In H. C. Triandis

& A. Heron (Eds.), *Handbook of cross-cultural psychology*, Vol. 4, *Developmental psychology* (pp. 295–342). Boston: Allyn & Bacon.

Dasen, P. R., Inhelder, B., Lavalle, M., & Retschitzki, J. (1978). *Naissance du l'intelligence chez l'enfant Baoulé de Côte d'Ivoire* [The birth of intelligence in the Baoulé child of the Ivory Coast]. Berne: Hans Huber.

Davis, S. S., & Davis, D. A. (1989). *Adolescence in a Moroccan town: Making social sense*. New Brunswick, NJ: Rutgers University Press.

Dawkins, R. (1976). *The selfish gene*. Oxford: Oxford University Press.

Dien, D. S. (1982). A Chinese perspective on Kohlberg's theory of moral development. *Developmental Review, 2*, 331–341.

Durham, W. H. (1992). *Coevolution: Genes, culture, and human diversity*. Palo Alto, CA: Stanford University Press.

Eckensberger, L. H., & Zimba, R. (1997). The development of moral judgment. In J. W. Berry, P. R. Dasen, & T. S. Saraswathi (Eds.), *Handbook of cross-cultural psychology*, Vol. 2, *Basic processes and human development* (pp. 299–338). Needham Heights, MA: Allyn & Bacon.

Edgerton, R. B. (1992). *Sick societies: Challenging the myth of primitive harmony*. New York: Free Press.

Eibl-Eibesfeldt, I. (1989). *Human ethology*. New York: Aldine de Gruyter.

Erikson, E. H. (1963). *Childhood and society* (2nd ed.). New York: Norton.

Fortes, M. (1938). Social and psychological aspects of education in Taleland. Supplement to *Africa, 2* (4).

Freedman, D. G. (1974). *Human infancy: An evolutionary perspective*. Hillsdale, NJ: Erlbaum.

Freeman, D. (1983). *Margaret Mead and Samoa: The making and unmaking of an anthropological myth*. Cambridge, MA: Harvard University Press.

Gardiner, H. W., & Kozmitzki, C. (2002). *Lives across cultures: Cross-cultural human development* (2nd ed.). Boston: Allyn & Bacon.

Gewertz, D. (1981). A historical reconsideration of female dominance among the Chambri of Papua New Guinea. *American Ethnologist, 8*, 94–106.

Gibbons, J. L., & Gielen, U. P. (Eds.). (2000). Adolescence in international and cross-cultural perspective. Special issue, *International Journal of Group Tensions, 29* (2).

Gielen, U. P. (1994). American mainstream psychology and its relationship to international and cross-cultural psychology. In A. L. Comunian & U. P. Gielen (Eds.), *Advancing psychology and its applications: International perspectives* (pp. 26–40). Milan: FrancoAngeli.

———. (1996). Moral reasoning in cross-cultural perspective: A review of Kohlbergian research. *World Psychology, 2* (3–4), i–viii, 265–496.

———. (2001). Some themes in the ethos of Buddhist Ladakh. In P. Kaplanian (Ed.), *Ladakh Himalaya Occidental ethnologie, écologie* (pp. 115–126). Paris: Author.

Gielen, U. P., & Jeshmaridian, S. S. (1999). Lev S. Vygotsky: The man and the era. *International Journal of Group Tensions, 28* (3–4), 273–301.

Gielen, U. P., & Markoulis, D. C. (2001). Preference for principled moral reasoning: A developmental and cross-cultural perspective. In L. L. Adler & U. P. Gielen (Eds.), *Cross-cultural topics in psychology* (2nd ed., pp. 81–101). Westport, CT: Praeger.

Gielen, U. P., & Naito, T. (1999). Teaching perspectives on cross-cultural psychology and Japanese society. *International Journal of Group Tensions, 28* (3–4), 319–344.

Gilligan, C. (1982). *In a different voice: Psychology theory and women's development.* Cambridge, MA: Harvard University Press.

Gilmore, D. (1990). *Manhood in the making: Cultural concepts of masculinity.* New Haven: Yale University Press.

Göncü, R. (Ed.). (1999). *Children's engagement in the world: Sociocultural perspectives.* Cambridge, MA: Cambridge University Press.

Greenfield, P. M., & Cocking, R. R. (Eds.). (1994). *Cross-cultural roots of minority child development.* Hillsdale, NJ: Erlbaum.

Hall, G. S. (1904). *Adolescence.* New York: Appleton.

Hamilton, W. D. (1964). The genetical evolution of social behavior. *Journal of Theoretical Behavior, 7,* 1–52.

Harkness, S., & Super, C. M. (Eds.). (1996). *Parents' cultural belief systems: Their origins, experiences and consequences.* New York: Guilford Press.

Harlow, H. W., & Zimmerman, R. (1959). Affectional responses in the infant monkey. *Science, 130,* 421–432.

Hawes, J. M., & Hiner, N. R. (Eds.). (1991). *Children in historical and comparative perspective.* Westport, CT: Greenwood Press.

Herskovitz, M. J. (1948). *Man and his works: The science of cultural anthropology.* New York: Knopf.

Hewlett, B. (1991). *Intimate fathers: The nature and context of Aka pygmy paternal infant care.* Ann Arbor: University of Michigan Press.

Hofstede, G. (1980). *Culture's consequences: International differences in work-related values.* Beverly Hills, CA: Sage.

Hollos, M., & Leis, P. E. (1989). *Becoming Nigerian in Ijo society.* New Brunswick, NJ: Rutgers University Press.

Holtzman, W. H., Diaz-Guerrero, R., & Swartz, J. D. (1975). *Personality development in two cultures: A cross-cultural longitudinal study of school children in Mexico and the United States.* Austin: University of Texas Press.

Hurrelmann, K. (Ed.). (1994). *International handbook of adolescence.* Westport, CT: Greenwood Press.

IJzendoorn, M. H. van, & Kroonenberg, P. M. (1988). Cross-cultural patterns of attachment: A meta-analysis of the Strange Situation. *Child Development, 59,* 147–156.

IJzendoorn, M. H. van, & Sagi, A. (1999). Cross-cultural patterns of attachment. In J. Cassidy & P. R. Shaver (Eds.), *Handbook of attachment: Theory, research, and clinical applications* (pp. 713–734). New York: Guilford Press.

Jahoda, G. (2000). On the prehistory of cross-cultured development research. In A. L. Comunian & U. P. Gielen (Eds.), *International perspectives on human development* (pp. 5–17). Lengerich, Germany: Pabst Science.

Jahoda, G., & Lewis, I. M. (1988/1989). Introduction: Child development in psychology and anthropology. In G. Jahoda & I. M. Lewis (Eds.), *Acquiring culture: Cross cultural studies in child development* (pp. 1–34). London: Routledge.

Kagitçibasi, Ç. (1996). *Family and human development across cultures: A view from the other side.* Mahwah, NJ: Erlbaum.

Kakar, S. (1978/1981). *The inner world: A psychoanalytic study of childhood and society in India.* Delhi: Oxford University Press.

Keller, H., Poortinga, Y. H., & Schölmerich, A. (Eds.). (in press). *Between biology and culture: Perspectives on ontogenetic development.* Cambridge, UK: Cambridge University Press.

Kidd, D. (1906/1969). *Savage childhood.* New York: Negro Universities Press.

Kohlberg, L. (1969/1984). Stage and sequence. In *The psychology of moral development: The nature and validity of moral stages* (pp. 7–169). Cambridge, MA: Harper.

Konner, M. J. (1977). Infancy among the Kalahari Desert San. In P. H. Leiderman, S. R. Tulkin, & A. Rosenfeld (Eds.), *Culture and infancy* (pp. 287–328). New York: Academic Press.

———. (1982). *The tangled wing: Biological constraints on the human spirit.* New York: Holt, Rinehart, & Winston.

Larson, R. W., & Verma, S. (1999). How children and adolescents spend time across the world: Work, play, and developmental opportunities. *Psychological Bulletin, 25,* 701–736.

Lau, S. (Ed.). (1997). *Growing up the Chinese way: Chinese child and adolescent development.* Hong Kong: Chinese University Press.

LeVine, R. A. (1970). Cross-cultural study in child psychology. In P. Mussen (Ed.), *Carmichael's manual of child psychology* (3rd ed., Vol. 2, pp. 559–612). New York: Wiley.

LeVine, R. A., Dixon, S., LeVine, S., Richman, A., Leiderman, P. H., Keefer, C. H., & Brazelton, T. B. (1994). *Child care and culture: Lessons from Africa.* Cambridge: Cambridge University Press.

Lind, G. (1986). Cultural differences in moral judgment competence? A study of West and East European university students. *Behavior Science Research, 20* (1–4), 208–225.

Lindholm, C. (1998). The Swat Pukhtun family as a political training ground. In R. J. Castillo (Ed.), *Meanings of madness* (pp. 40–44). Pacific Grove: Brooks/Cole.

Lorenz, K. (1981). *The foundations of ethology.* New York: Touchstone Books (Simon & Schuster).

Luria, A. R. (1974). *Ob istoricheskom razvitii poznavatel'nykh protssesov* [Historical development of cognitive processes]. Moscow: Nanka.

———. (1976). *Cognitive and development: Its cultural and social foundations.* Cambridge, MA: Harvard University Press.

———. (1979). *The making of a mind: A personal account of Soviet psychology.* Cambridge, MA: Harvard University Press.

McClelland, D. C. (1961). *The achieving society.* New York: Van Nostrand.

Mead, M. (1928). *Coming of age in Samoa.* New York: Morrow.

———. (1930). *Growing up in New Guinea: A comparative study of primitive education.* New York: Morrow.

———. (1931). The primitive child. In C. Murchison (Ed.), *A handbook of child psychology* (pp. 669–687). Worcester: Clark University Press.

———. (1935/1963). *Sex and temperament in three primitive societies.* New York: Morrow Quill.

———. (1954). Research on primitive children. In L. Carmichael (Ed.), *Manual of child psychology* (2nd ed., pp. 735–780). New York: Wiley.

Miller, N. E., & Dollard, J. (1941). *Social learning and imitation*. New Haven: Yale University Press.

Minturn, L., & Lambert, W. (1964). *Mothers of six cultures: Antecedents of child rearing*. New York: Wiley.

Munroe, R. H., Munroe, R. L., & Whiting, B. B. (1981). *Handbook of cross-cultural human development*. New York: Garland STPM Press.

Munroe, R. L., & Munroe, R. H. (1975). *Cross-cultural human development*. Prospect Heights, IL: Waveland Press.

Norberg-Hodge, H., with Russell, H. (1994). Birth and childrearing in Zangskar. In J. Crook & H. Osmaston (Eds.), *Himalayan Buddhist villages: Environment, resources, society, and religious life in Zangskar, Ladakh* (pp. 519–532). Bristol, UK: University of Bristol.

Nsamenang, A. B. (1992). *Human development in cultural context: A Third World perspective*. Newbury Park, CA: Sage.

Offer, D., Ostrov, E., Howard, K. I., & Atkinson, R. (1988). *The teenage world: Adolescents' self-image in ten countries*. New York: Plenum Medical.

Orlansky, H. (1949). Infant care and personality. *Psychological Bulletin, 46*, 1–48.

Pereira, M. E., & Fairbanks, L. A. (Eds.). (1993). *Juvenile primates*. New York: Oxford University Press.

Piaget, J. (1966). Nécessité et signification des recherches comparatives en psychologie génétique [Need and significance of cross-cultural studies in genetic psychology]. *International Journal of Psychology, 1*, 3–13.

Pinker, S. (1994). *The language instinct*. New York: Harper/Perennial.

Rest, J. (1986). *Manual for the Defining Issues Test: An objective test of moral development* (3rd ed.). Minneapolis: Center for the Study of Ethical Development, University of Minnesota.

Rest, J., Narvaez, D., Bebeau, M. J., & Thoma, S. J. (1999). *Postconventional moral thinking: A neo-Kohlbergian approach*. Mahwah, NJ: Erlbaum.

Rogoff, B. (1990). *Apprenticeship in thinking: Cognitive development in social context*. New York: Oxford University Press.

Rohner, R. P. (1975). *They love me, they love me not: A worldwide study of the effects of parental acceptance and rejection*. New Haven: HRAF Press.

———. (1986). *The warmth dimension*. Beverly Hills, CA: Sage.

Rubin, K. H. (Ed.). (1998). Social and emotional development: A cross-cultural perspective. Special issue, *Developmental Psychology, 34* (4).

Saraswathi, T. S. (Ed.). (1999). *Culture, socialization, and human development: Theory, research, and applications in India*. New Delhi: Sage.

———. (2003). *Cross-cultural perspectives in human development: Theory, research, and practice*. New Delhi: Sage.

Saraswathi, T. S., & Kaur, B. (Eds.). (1993). *Human development and family studies in India*. New Delhi: Sage.

Schlegel, A. (1995). Introduction. Special issue on adolescence, *Ethos, 23*, 3–14.

Schlegel, A., & Barry, H. (1991). *Adolescence: An anthropological inquiry*. New York: Free Press.

Segall, M. H., Dasen, P. R., Berry, J. W., & Poortinga, Y. H. (1999). *Human behavior in global perspective* (2nd ed.). Boston: Allyn & Bacon.

Sharma, D., & Gielen, U. P. (Eds.). (2000). Childhood and sociocultural change in India: A reinterpretation of Sudhir Kakar's work. Special issue, *International Journal of Group Tensions*, 29 (3–4).

Shwalb, D. W., & Shwalb, B. (Eds.). (1996). *Japanese childrearing: Two generations of scholarship*. New York: Guilford.

Shweder, R. A., Goodnow, J., Hatano, G., LeVine, R. A., Markus, H., & Miller, P. (1998). The cultural psychology of development: One mind, many mentalities. In W. Damon (Ed.), *Handbook of child psychology* (5th ed.), Vol. 1 (R. M. Lerner, Ed.), *Theoretical models of human development* (pp. 865–937). New York: Wiley.

Skinner, B. F. (1957). *Verbal behavior*. New York: Appleton.

Smith, E. A. (2000). Three styles in the evolutionary study of human behavior. In L. Cronk, N. Chagnon, & W. Irons (Eds.), *Adaptation and human behavior* (pp. 27–46). New York: Aldine.

Smith, J. M. (1964). Group selection and kin selection. *Nature, 201*, 1145–1147.

Snarey, J. (1985). Cross-cultural universality of socio-moral development: A critical review of Kohlbergian research. *Psychological Bulletin, 97*, 202–232.

Stevenson, H. W., & Lee, S. Y. (1990). Contexts of achievement: A study of American, Chinese, and Japanese children. *Monographs of the Society for Research in Child Development, 55*.

Stevenson, H. W., & Stigler, J. (1992). *The learning gap: Why our schools are failing and what we can learn from Japanese and Chinese education*. New York: Summit Books.

Suárez-Orozco, C., & Suárez-Orozco, M. (1995). *Transformations: Migration, family life, and achievement motivation among Latino Adolescents*. Palo Alto, CA: Stanford University Press.

Super, C., & Harkness, S. (1986). The developmental niche: A conceptualization of the interface of child and culture. *International Journal of Behavioral Development, 9*, 545–570.

Suvannathat, C., Bhanthumnavin, D., Bhuapirom, L., & Keats, D. M. (Eds.). (1985). *Handbook of Asian child development and child rearing practices*. Bangkok: Burapasilpa Press.

Tinbergen, N. (1951). *The study of instinct*. Oxford: Clarendon Press.

Tobin, J. J., Wu, D. Y. H., & Davidson, D. H. (1989). *Preschool in three cultures: Japan, China, and the United States*. New Haven: Yale University Press.

Triandis, H. C. (1995). *Individualism and collectivism*. Boulder, CO: Westview.

———. (2000). Cross-cultural versus cultural psychology: A synthesis. In A. L. Comunian & U. P. Gielen (Eds.), *International perspectives on human development* (pp. 81–95). Lengerich, Germany: Pabst Science.

Triandis, H. C., & Heron, A. (1981). *Handbook of cross-cultural psychology*. Vol. 4, *Developmental psychology*. Boston: Allyn & Bacon.

Trivers, R. L. (1972). Parental investment and sexual selection. In B. Campbell (Ed.), *Sexual selection and the descent of man* (pp. 136–179). Chicago: Aldine de Gruyter.

Trommsdorff, G. (Ed.). (1989). *Sozialisation in Kulturvergleich* [Socialization in cross-cultural comparison]. Stuttgart: F. Enke Vlg.

Tuzin, D. F. (1977). *The Ilahita Arapesh*. Berkeley: University of California Press.

Valsiner, J. (1989). *Human development and culture: The social nature of personality and its study*. Lexington, MA: Lexington Books.

————. (2000). *Culture and human development*. London: Sage.

Van der Veer, R., & Valsiner, J. (1991). *Understanding Vygotsky: A quest for synthesis*. Cambridge, MA: Basil Blackwell.

Van Gennep, A. (1909). *Les rites de passage [The rites of passage]*. Paris: Libraire Critique Emile Nourry.

Vine, I. (1986). Moral maturity in socio-cultural perspective: Are Kohlberg's stages universal? In S. Mogdil & C. Mogdil (Eds.), *Lawrence Kohlberg: Consensus and controversy* (pp. 431–450). London: Falmer Press.

Vygotsky, L. S., & Luria, A. R. (1930/1993). *Studies on the history of behavior: Ape, primitive, and child*. (Victor I. Golod & Jane E. Knox, Eds. and Trans.). Hillsdale, NJ: Erlbaum.

Weisfeld, G. (1999). *Evolutionary principles of human adolescence*. New York: Basic Books.

Werner, E. E. (1979). *Cross-cultural child development: A view from Planet Earth*. Monterey, CA: Brooks/Cole.

Whiting, B. B. (Ed.). (1963). *Six cultures: Studies of childrearing*. New York: Wiley.

Whiting, B. B., & Edwards, C. P. (1988). *Children of different worlds: The formation of social behavior*. Cambridge, MA: Harvard University Press.

Whiting, B. B., & Whiting, J. W. M. (1975). *Children of six cultures: A psycho-cultural analysis*. Cambridge, MA: Harvard University Press.

————. (1991). Preindustrial world, Adolescence in. In R. A. Lerner & A. C. Petersen (Eds.), *Encyclopedia of adolescence* (Vol. 2, pp. 814–829). New York: Garland.

Whiting, J. W. M., Child, I. L., & Lambert, W. W. (1966). *Field guide for a study of socialization*. New York: Wiley.

Williams, J. E., & Best, D. L. (1982/1990). *Measuring sex stereotypes: A multination study* (rev. ed., 1990). Newbury Park, CA: Sage.

Williams, T. R. (1983). *Socialization*. Englewood Cliffs, NJ: Prentice-Hall.

Wilson, E. D. (1975). *Sociobiology: The new synthesis*. Cambridge, MA: Belknap Press.

————. (1978). *On human nature*. Cambridge, MA: Belknap Press.

Worthman, C. M., & Whiting, J. W. M (1987). Social change in adolescent sexual behavior, mate selection, and pre-marital pregnancy rates in a Kikuyu community. *Ethos, 15*, 145–165.

CHAPTER 2

Cross-Cultural Research on Childhood

Xinyin Chen and Violet Kaspar

In human development, childhood is a critical period, ranging approximately from ages two to twelve in most cultures, during which the child gradually learns to enter the social world outside of the family. Extensive contacts and interactions with peers may be a major part of social life throughout childhood. While most children get along with peers and enjoy social activities, some children may find it difficult to get involved in positive interactions with peers, and appear to be distressed by the challenges of peer group activities. Among the latter group, some children may be socially wary, anxious, and inhibited, and consequently withdraw from the group, and others may develop negative attitudes and affect toward others and exhibit hostile and aggressive behaviors. Whether a child moves along with, away from, or against the world may predict later social and cognitive functioning (e.g., Caspi, Elder, & Bem, 1987, 1988; Chen, Rubin, & Li, 1995c).

In most contemporary societies, children start to receive formal education in school at six or seven years of age (Thomas, 1988). From that time on, although social interactions and relationships are still important, academic achievement may become a primary, and even critical in some cultures, task in their life. Academic difficulties and failure may lead to not only lower educational attainment but also emotional and psychological problems.

In this chapter, we will discuss cross-cultural research on children's play and peer interactions, school achievement, and emotional and behavioral functioning and problems. Given the significance of familial socialization influences during the childhood period, we will describe and discuss some relevant cross-cultural studies concerning the relations between family, particularly parenting, and child social and academic functioning. It should be noted that cross-cultural psychological research has traditionally been focused on children's performance on cognitive tasks such as IQ testing and Piagetian conservation tasks (Cole, 1992). In the past two decades, however, largely due to the influences of sociologists' and cultural anthropologists' conceptual and empirical work on childhood (Super & Harkness, 1986; Whiting & Edwards, 1988), many developmental researchers have been interested in children's actual life experiences and adjustment problems in different cultures. This chapter reflects this recent trend in cross-cultural research on childhood.

CULTURAL INVOLVEMENT IN CHILD DEVELOPMENT: SOME GENERAL COMMENTS

Many cross-cultural researchers now agree that it may not be appropriate to ask which behaviors are universal and which are culturally specific, because all behaviors are probably both, at different levels (Harkness & Super, 1995). It may be more interesting to examine how cultural factors are involved in the organization of developmental "niches" in which human cognitive and social growth occur. It has been proposed that social communications and interactions may constitute the interface between culture and individual development (Hinde, 1987). According to a sociocultural perspective (Vygotsky, 1978), for example, interpersonal interactions, including play in childhood, serve an important function in the mediation of cultural influences on the development of human higher psychological functioning. Vygotsky's notion of the "zone of proximal development" indicates that the child's active participation in social interactions plays an important role in the processes by which the culture and the individual "shape" each other in the course of human development. Although Vygotsky's theory focuses mostly on vertical relationships (e.g., adult-child), it has been found that, with increasing age, child-peer interactions play increasingly important roles in social and cognitive adjustment (Hinde, Perret-Clermont, & Stevenson-Hinde, 1985).

Culture not only provides a context for social interactions and development but also imparts meanings to specific actions by providing a frame of reference for social judgment and evaluation (Bornstein, 1995), which serve as a basis for social acceptance and rejection, and regulate children's behaviors in social situations. Thus, whereas it is interesting to examine cross-cultural similarities and differences in the prevalence and variance of certain behaviors such as aggression across cultures, it is important to investigate the meaning of the behavior in the culture. Chen (2000a) has suggested that the significance, function, and cultural meaning of individual characteristics and behaviors should be examined and understood from a broad, contextual perspective, in terms of their connections with concurrent interpersonal and socioecological conditions as well as developmental antecedents and outcomes.

On the other hand, cultural influences on children's social and cognitive functioning may occur in a developmental context. Regardless of the culture, for example, some common developmental tasks and requirements in socialization, such as learning to understand and respond appropriately to social and cultural standards and acquiring personal independence (Kagan, 1981; Whiting & Edwards, 1988), may lead to cross-culturally similar patterns in human development. The view of interactions between cultural context and developmental factors may help us understand complex processes through which children with certain dispositional features grow in the context of various culturally constructed socioecological settings.

CHILDREN'S PLAY AND PEER INTERACTIONS

Play is a predominant social activity in early and middle childhood in most but not all societies (Roopnarine, Johnson, & Hooper, 1994). In Western cultures, it has been demonstrated that play is important for socioemotional, cognitive, and personality development (e.g., for a comprehensive review, see Creasey, Jarvis, & Berk, 1998; and Rubin, Fein, & Vandenburg, 1983). During social interactions in play, children learn the norms for appropriate social behaviors and social skills for interpersonal communication, emotional regulation, and coping with frustrations, which are obviously important for later social adjustment.

The significance of play for social, emotional, and cognitive development has been neglected in many cultures. For example, in traditional Chinese culture, play is considered an appropriate activity only for children below age four or five years, because they don't understand things yet ("Bo Dong Shi" in Mandarin). It is believed that children above age five or six should work and receive formal training in more "serious" fields. Children who spend much time on play are usually regarded as socially immature and irresponsible. Similar attitudes toward children's play have been reported in other cultures such as Japan, India, Kenya, and Mayan societies (Gaskins & Goncu, 1992; Roopnarine et al., 1994; Whiting & Edwards, 1988). Relative to their age-mates in North America and Western Europe, children in these cultures generally spend less time on play because they are expected to help adults with a large number of household chores and work outside the home, and/or because play is regarded as a waste of time. Extremely negative attitudes toward play exist in some culture groups such as the Sinai Bedouin Arabs (Ariel & Sever, 1980), in which children who engage in play may be severely penalized.

Largely due to the influences of Western ideology, children's social and emotional functioning, including the significance of play, has recently received increasing attention from both professionals and the public in non-Western countries. In some places in Taiwan and Korea, for example, early educational agents such as preschools and kindergartens have integrated play as a part of their program. Research on children's play and peer interactions in these cultures, although still rare, has increased in the past decade.

While cultural anthropologists are mainly interested in the forms, contents, and meanings of children's play in different cultures (e.g., Harkness & Super, 1983; Salter, 1978; Whiting & Whiting, 1975), developmental psychologists have paid more attention to children's behaviors and emotional reactions in play activities. Based on Piaget's cognitive stage theory, researchers (Howes, 1988; Smilansky, 1968) identified several levels of play behavior that vary in terms of cognitive complexity from functional (simple aimless motor activities), exploratory (examining an object to obtain information), constructive (constructing or creating something), to dramatic/pretend play (forms of pretense). Another dimension that is often examined in the study of children's play is social participation, which typically ranges from solitary (the child plays apart from other children), parallel (the child plays beside but not with other children), to associative/group (the child plays and shares with others) levels (Parten, 1932). A good example of integrating the two dimensions of play behavior is reflected in Rubin's *Play Observation Scale* (1989), in which cognitive categories such as functional and constructive plays are nested in three levels of social participation (solitary, parallel, and group). In addition to the major cognitive and social categories, researchers often include some other types of behavioral and emotional features in play research such as unoccupied behavior, onlooker, aggression, conversation, and positive and negative affect (e.g., Howes, 1988; Rubin, 1982). Indexes of behavioral patterns that reflect underlying psychological constructs such as social withdrawal, sociability, and hostility may be derived from aggregating similar specific play behaviors (e.g., Asendorpf, 1991; Coplan et al., 1994).

Cross-cultural research on children's play behavior (e.g., Farver & Howes, 1988; Farver, Kim, & Lee, 1995; Liddell & Kruger, 1987, 1989; Martini, 1994; Pan, 1994; Prosser, Hutt, Hutt, Mahindadasa, & Goonetilleke, 1986) has been largely based on Western conceptualizations of play behavior (Parten, 1932; Rubin et al., 1983). In general, the results indicate that children in different cultures may display different behavioral styles. Culture-specific play behaviors have been found to be mainly related to the organization and structure of the setting in which children engage in social interactions, which may or may not be related to cultural conventions; and cultural norms, values, and expectations of appropriate behaviors in the society. Nevertheless, cross-cultural research has revealed some similar patterns of development, typically from solitary sensorimotor behavior to sociodramatic behavior, in children's play across cultures.

Setting Conditions, Play Behavior, and Social Interactions

Social and ecological setting conditions, as one of the important developmental niches (Super & Harkness, 1986), have been found to affect how children typically behave and interact in play. For example, in a study of children's play behavior in Korean preschools in the United States (Farver, Kim, & Lee, 1995), it was found that, compared with Anglo-American children, Korean American children displayed more passive-solitary and parallel play behaviors. In contrast, Anglo-American children appeared to be more sophisticated in the forms and levels of play, as indicated by higher frequencies of social play and pretend play. Similar results regarding parallel play as the predominant form of social behavior have been reported in preschoolers in Korea in an earlier study (Tieszen, 1979). Farver and colleagues (1995) argued that these results might be due to the highly structured daily schedule in the Korean American preschool, which in turn might be related to the traditionally high expectations of academic performance in Korean culture. Indeed, it was noted that the Korean American setting had few, if any, materials available for pretend play and that few opportunities were provided for the children to interact socially with each other. Consistent with Farver and colleagues' results (1995), children in some other cultures such as Maya (Gaskins, 1991) and Bedouin Arab (Ariel & Sever, 1980) have been found to engage in little sociodramatic play. Setting conditions including lack of toys and devices for pretend play also have been noticed as one of the salient contributing factors.

How might the lack of sociodramatic play in the non-Western cultures affect social and cognitive development? In North American culture, the ability to engage in the elaborate form of pretense is considered a representation of mastery of important social skills to promote sharing and the coordination of decontextualized and substitutive activities (Rubin, Bukowski, & Parker, 1998). Moreover, it has been argued that the experience of sociodramatic play serves developmental functions and is associated with social perspective-taking skills, communication skills, and mature interpersonal competence (e.g., Connolly, Doyle, & Reznick, 1988; Garvey, 1990; Singer & Singer, 1990). In an experimental study in Guyana, South America, Taharally (1991) found that when a group of four- and five-year-old children were provided with play materials designed to stimulate fantasy play such as dress-up clothes, they scored significantly higher than the control group in later language production tests. Nevertheless, there is no clear evidence for a negative impact of low levels of sociodramatic behavior in Korean, Mayan, or other non-Western cultures on social and cognitive development. It may be premature and imprudent to generalize the findings based on a limited number of cultures.

In contrast to cultures in which play and peer interactions are restricted and controlled, children in the Bamenda Grassfields of Northwest Cameroon engage in extensive "free" play and peer interactions without overt adult intervention (Nsamenang & Lamb, 1993). This socioecological setting provides opportunities for children to learn socially acceptable and expected behaviors and interactional styles from their peer "coparticipants." It was found that children under such circumstance displayed sophisticated social skills in peer collaboration and cooperation and developed a high level of perspective-taking ability and collective responsibility (Nsamenang, 1992).

The influences of socioecological settings on children's social behavior in peer interactions may be clearly illustrated in Israeli kibbutz children (Levy-Shiff & Hoffman, 1985; Regev, Beit-Hallahmi, & Sharabany, 1980; Rosenthal, 1991). As the result of a communal movement that began seventy years ago, kibbutz children are raised from early years by "trained" caregivers in collective day care centers, rather than by parents at home. Rosenthal (1991) found that, compared with their urban counterparts raised at home, kibbutz children raised in day care centers were more involved in associative-dramatic play and showed less unoccupied, aimless behaviors. Moreover, it was found that kibbutz nursery school children engaged in relatively less functional play and more coordinated and prosocial behaviors in the peer group. However, it has been reported that kibbutz children are less affectively involved with peers and less skillful in solving social and affective problems. Similar results were reported by Levy-Shiff and Hoffman (1985). It was found that kibbutz preschoolers engaged in more frequent coordinated play and were less competitive in group situations than were urban preschoolers. In regard to affective characteristics, kibbutz children were found to express positive affect less frequently toward their peers than their urban counterparts. Consistent with these findings, Shapira and Madson (1974) found that kibbutz children were more cooperative and less competitive than children raised at home. It has been argued that "the intensive social nature of the environment of kibbutz children supports their acquisition of advanced social skills, whereas the complicated socioemotional nature of their experience in communal sleeping underlies their affective behaviors and style" (Aviezer, IJzendoorn, Sagi, & Schuengel, 1994, p. 112).

Social Norms and Social Behavior

Relatively low affective response in social interactions has also been reported for Asian children. Farver and colleagues (1995) found that Korean children rarely expressed positive affect in play; their affect was mainly categorized as "neutral." Similar results were obtained for Indonesian children (Farver & Howes, 1988) and Chinese children (Pan, 1994). It was found, for example, that Indonesian children clearly showed less positive affect toward each other than American children in peer interactions. When Indonesian children initiated play, their partners were less likely to respond with smiling, accepting the toy, or verbally accepting the invitation, compared to American children. Whereas low affective reactions in kibbutz children may be largely due to their experiences in communal rearing settings, explanations for the lack of dramatic affective expression in social interactions in Asian children often focus on cultural factors.

It has been suggested that the neutral affect displayed by Korean, Indonesian, and Chinese children is considered appropriate in those Asian cultures in which children are encouraged to hide their feelings (Farver & Howes, 1988; Farver et al., 1995). Indeed, in both Confucian and Taoist philosophies, psychologically healthy and socially mature and sophisticated individuals are described as emotionally "stable" and unresponsive to social and environmental events (Chen & Swartzman, 2001).

Similar to the results found in Israeli kibbutz children, low levels of positive affect in the Asian children do not imply that they would necessarily have low frequencies of cooperative or prosocial behaviors in peer interactions. It was found that Korean American children tended to be more cooperative and less aggressive in play than Anglo-American children (Farver et al., 1995). Low levels of aggression and high levels of cooperation have also been reported for Japanese and Chinese children (e.g., Friedman et al., 1994; Orlick, Zhou, & Partington, 1990). According to Farver and colleagues (1995), high frequencies of prosocial behavior among many Asian children may be a reflection of the culture's emphasis on group harmony and cooperation.

Therefore, cross-cultural differences in social behaviors may be due to environmental conditions and constraints such as availability of toys and kibbutz childrearing settings, and at the same time, related to culture-specific values and expectations of certain behaviors. Behaviors that are highly valued in one culture may not be regarded likewise in others. As well, some behaviors that are considered negative in one culture may be acceptable in other cultures. These arguments have been supported by the findings of cross-cultural research on children's social functioning and peer acceptance and rejection (e.g., Casiglia, Lo Coco, & Zappulla, 1998; Chen, Rubin, & Sun, 1992; Krispin, Sternberg, & Lamb, 1992).

In Western cultures, it has been found that prosocial, cooperative, and friendly behaviors are positively associated with and predictive of peer acceptance (e.g., Gottmen, 1983; Rubin, Chen, & Hymel, 1993). In contrast, aggression-disruption and shyness-social inhibition have been found to be related to peer rejection or isolation (e.g., Rubin, Chen, McDougall, Bowker, & McKinnon, 1995). In a series of cross-cultural studies concerning children's peer interactions and relationships (Chen et al., 1992; Chen et al., 1995c; Chen, Rubin, Li, & Li, 1999), it has been found, in both Chinese and North American children, that prosocial and sociable behavior is both encouraged and associated with peer acceptance and other indexes of social adjustment, whereas disruptive and aggressive behavior is related to social problems, including peer rejection. Unlike in Western cultures, where shy, sensitive, and inhibited behavior is considered socially incompetent and immature, this behavior is positively valued in Chinese culture. Behavioral restraint and inhibition are regarded as indicators of mastery, maturity, and accomplishment in traditional Confucian philosophy.

Indeed, it has been found that, whereas shy and withdrawn children have difficulties in peer interactions in North America, shy-inhibited children in China are popular and adjust well to their social environment (Chen et al., 1992; Chen, Rubin, & Li, 1995a). Moreover, shyness and social inhibition in early and middle childhood have been found to predict social adaptation in late childhood and adolescence (Chen et al., 1995c; Chen et al., 1999).

Chen (2000b) has recently proposed two distinct dimensions of social functioning, social initiative and self-control, as fundamental systems that may account for individual behavioral styles in social interactions. According to this model, social initiative or level of social participation represents the tendency to initiate and maintain social interaction, whereas self-control or self-regulation serves to regulate or modulate behavioral and emotional reactivity in order to perform in social situations in an appropriate manner. Different types of social functioning, such as prosocial-sociable behavior (high social initiative and high self-control), shyness-sensitivity (low social initiative and high self-control), aggression-disruption (high social initiative and low self-control), and internalizing problems (low initiative and low self-control), may be formed on the basis of the two dimensions.

Cross-cultural differences have been found in children's initiative and self-regulation in social situations. It has been reported, for example, that Chinese, Indonesian, Thai, and Korean children have a lower level of social initiative in novel situations than do their North American counterparts (Chan & Eysenck, 1981; Chen et al., 1998; Farver & Howes, 1988; Mizuta, Zahn-Waxler, Cole, & Hirma, 1996). It has also been found that Chinese children obtain significantly higher scores on measures of voluntary, committed control of behavior than their Canadian counterparts (Chen, 1999). Moreover, as required by socialization goals (e.g., self-reliance, autonomy, and assertive social skills in Western cultures, conformity and interdependence in collectivistic cultures), social initiative and self-control may be valued and emphasized differently across cultures. Empirical findings indicate that child social reactivity and self-control are associated with different parental childrearing attitudes in Chinese and North American cultures (e.g., Chen et al., 1998). Specifically, reactive and inhibited behavior is positively associated with parental disappointment and rejection in Canada, but with parental warmth and acceptance in China. In addition, in early childhood, Chinese parents expect a higher level, or more mature form, of self-regulation in children than do North American parents. When a child displays a form of self-control that is maintained by external, situational factors, Canadian parents are likely to express satisfied and accepting attitudes toward the child. However, Chinese parents are clearly disappointed and frustrated and tend to use high power strategies and punitive practices in parenting.

Developmental Patterns

Regardless of differences in children's social behaviors across cultures, some similar patterns of development of social behavior have been reported. In a study conducted in two ordinary kindergartens in Taiwan (Pan, 1994), it was found that, as for their American counterparts, age was negatively associated with functional and solitary behaviors in play, and positively associated with constructive and parallel and group play. Thus, with age, children were less likely to display aimless and isolated behaviors and more likely to engage in social and constructive play. This developmental trend also has been found in other cultures such as Korea (Tieszen, 1979, 1982) and South Africa (Liddell, Kvalsvig, Strydom, Qotyana, & Shabalala, 1993). In a short-term longitudinal study, Levy-Shiff and Hoffman (1989) found, in a sample of Israeli preschoolers in Tel Aviv, that socially immature behaviors, such as unoccupied and onlooker behaviors in play, predicted later social and emotional maladjustment as assessed by teachers. Similarly, children's physical aggression in peer interactions predicted later socioemotional problems. In addition, it was found that positive affect was predictive of social functioning. These results were virtually the same as those reported in Western children (e.g., Rubin et al., 1995). Interestingly, Levy-Shiff and Hoffman (1989) found that although onlooker and unoccupied behaviors predicted maladjustment, passive-solitary behavior was not significantly associated with later problems. Similar results have been found recently in North American children (Coplan et al., 1994). In short, some cross-culturally similar patterns concerning social development have been found in studies of children's play and peer interactions. Nevertheless, research on children's social interactions from a developmental perspective has been so scarce in non-Western cultures that any conclusion concerning general patterns must be drawn with great caution.

ACADEMIC ACHIEVEMENT

Academic achievement is an important task for most school-age children in contemporary societies. Pressure on children to excel academically may be particularly pronounced in some developing countries. Due to limited opportunities to receive a higher education, academic competition in the school is usually strong in these countries. In some Asian countries such as China, children start to learn academic subject matters such as reading and mathematics even in preschool and kindergarten. Numerous studies have been carried out in the past decade concerning academic achievement among children across nations and cultures (e.g., Arbeiter, 1984; Bacon & Ichikawa, 1988; Garden, 1987; Lapointe, Mead, & Philips, 1989; McKnight et al., 1987; Ninio, 1990; Ramist & Arbeiter, 1984; Stevenson et al., 1990). Among them, comparative research conducted by Stevenson and his colleagues on Asian and American children is most influential and has received controversial responses from the academic community and the public.

Since the early 1980s, Stevenson and his international collaborators have systematically compared children's performance in mathematics and reading in the United States, Japan, Taiwan, and the People's Republic of China. In their studies, random samples of children in each country were administered achievement tests in reading and mathematics, which were developed by the researchers specifically for the cross-cultural project. The findings were striking: Asian children consistently outperformed their North American peers in various academic areas. Moreover, these differences emerged as early as kindergarten and persisted throughout elementary and high schools (e.g., Stevenson, Chen, & Lee, 1993).

School and Family Conditions and Academic Achievement

How can the remarkable differences between American and Asian children in academic achievement be explained? It has been argued that better performance of Asian children in academic achievement may be related to their superiority in intelligence and cognitive abilities (e.g., Lynn, 1977, 1982). According to Stevenson (Stevenson et al., 1985; Stevenson et al., 1990), however, cross-cultural differences in academic achievement cannot be accounted for by cognitive abilities because children in Japan, China, and the United States do not differ in general level of intellectual functioning when socioeconomic background is controlled, and when children are tested with culturally appropriate materials (Stevenson et al., 1985). Although children in these countries perform differently on specific cognitive tasks such as coding, perceptual speed, auditory memory, serial memory for words, and serial memory for numbers, the patterns of differences were not consistent with the variations in academic achievement. To search for factors that may be responsible for academic excellence in Chinese and Japanese children, researchers have examined curriculum, instructional strategies, school schedules and activities, family involvement, and achievement-related cultural beliefs in these countries (e.g., Au & Harachiewica, 1986; Stevenson et al., 1990; Stigler, Lee, Lucker, & Stevenson, 1982).

School is obviously a major source of influence on children's academic achievement. It has been found, for example, that children in Japan and Taiwan spend more time in school each day than American children. Moreover, Asian students spend a higher proportion of school time on academic work than American students. Classroom activities are highly structured and organized, and students are required to concentrate intensely on academic work in Asian schools. Teachers in Japanese and Chinese schools are better prepared for and organized in their classroom management and instruction. In addition, it has been noted that there are rich extracurricular activities, mostly academic, in

Chinese and Japanese schools from kindergarten to high school, which are relatively uncommon in American schools (Stevenson et al., 1990).

There also are remarkable differences among American, Japanese, and Chinese families with regard to financial status, living conditions, parental education and occupation, and family structure and organization. However, these cross-cultural differences have proved to account for little cross-cultural variance in academic achievement. For example, although Chinese children perform better than their American age-mates in academic areas, most Chinese parents, in both urban and rural areas, have an educational level of high school or below. Moreover, financial and living conditions in Chinese families are generally poorer than those in North America. Researchers have found that familial factors that may be associated with overall high level of academic achievement in China and Japan mainly include parental beliefs in effects of effort and encouragement of optimal performance in children, and parental monitoring of children's academic activities. While American parents believe that academic achievement is largely determined by innate abilities, Chinese and Japanese parents believe that it is mainly based on diligence and effort. As a result, East Asian parents constantly push their children to study hard. It was also found that compared with American parents, East Asian parents keep closer contact with the school and pay more attention to their children's academic performance (Hess, Azuma, Kashiwagi, Holloway, & Wenegrat, 1987; Stevenson et al., 1990). While the mother may assume primary responsibility for assisting children with their schoolwork in Japan and the United States, the whole Chinese family is involved in children's academic work.

Beliefs, Motivation, and Academic Achievement

In addition to school environment and family involvement, motivation has been found to play a major role in academic achievement in Chinese and Japanese children. For example, it has been found that, compared with their American peers, Asian children hold higher standards and expectations for academic achievement (Stevenson et al., 1990). Interestingly, American children tend to have more positive self-perceptions of their academic competence; they are more likely to think they are good at academic subjects, to like schoolwork, and to find it more interesting and less difficult (Chen & Stevenson, 1995). These findings seem to suggest that positive self-perceptions and evaluations of academic competence may lead to low achievement motivation and lack of diligence, as described in a Chinese adage "Modesty makes one go forward."

Researchers have recently found that Asian American children have significantly higher average scores in achievement tests than Caucasian American classmates who attend the same type of schools in the United States (Dornbusch, Ritter, Leiderman, Roberts, & Fraleigh, 1987; Steinberg, Dornbusch, & Brown,

1992). It has been reported also, however, that Asian American children have lower scores on achievement tests than their peers in Asian countries (Chen & Stevenson, 1995). The findings concerning achievement-related beliefs and behaviors have indicated that Asian American children stand between Caucasian American children and the Asian children. For example, standards for academic achievement held by Asian American children are higher than those held by Caucasian American children, but lower than those held by Chinese and Japanese children. The modification of academic motivation, beliefs, and practices in the processes of acculturation in Asian American children clearly demonstrates the important role of cultural factors in academic achievement (see also Fuligni, this volume).

Academic Achievement and Psychological Functioning

Although Asian children perform better than their American counterparts in academic achievement, it is often believed that children in the Asian countries may suffer from the high pressure for achievement and consequently develop psychopathological problems such as anxiety and depression. Indeed, in many Asian cultures, including China, Korea, and Japan, children are pressured by parents, teachers, relatives, and peers to perform optimally in school. Children who fail to achieve the standards of the significant adult group are often considered problematic and abnormal (Wu & Tseng, 1985), and sometimes receive humiliation in public situations in the school and harsh punishment at home. Malicious incidents such as child and adolescent suicide due to academic pressure and failure have been reported in the media (e.g., "China Youth Daily," July 14, 1994). According to Stevenson and his associates (Crystal et al., 1994), however, no significant differences have been found among Chinese, Japanese, and American children on indexes of social and psychological problems, including academic anxiety and depression.

Further investigation is clearly needed on this issue. Cross-cultural comparisons on overall level of psychological distress may not be an appropriate approach because it does not provide information on the relative contributions of academic problems and other difficulties, such as family problems, to the development of psychopathological symptoms. It may be more important to examine the relations between social and emotional functioning and academic achievement at both the intercultural and intracultural levels. Indeed, in our recent studies (Chen et al., 1995a; Chen, Rubin, & Li, 1995b), it has been found that academic achievement is associated with self-reported distress such as depression in Chinese children. Nevertheless, we have also found that family resources, including parental acceptance and harmonious relationships, may buffer the negative effects of academic difficulties on the development of depressive symptoms. Specifically, academic difficulties are predictive of later depression only for children from families in which parents are rejecting of the child, and parents have a conflictual relationship. Children who have academic problems but are accepted by their parents and live in a harmonious family environment are not depressed in later years. Thus, parental acceptance and positive family relationships serve as a protective factor which "buffers" children who have academic difficulties from developing depressive and other psychopathological symptoms.

In summary, cross-cultural research has revealed that children across cultures, including Asia and North America, may not achieve at the same pace on academic subject matters such as reading and mathematics. It has been argued that cross-cultural differences in academic achievement may reflect the cultural imposition of selected values on members, especially less mature members of the society (Hatano, 1990). Particular emphasis on academic achievement in Asian and some other cultures constitutes an important social condition for children within the culture to acquire intellectual attainment as well as psychological well-being. The significance of academic achievement must be taken into account in cross-cultural studies of children's cognitive and socioemotional adjustment.

SOCIOEMOTIONAL ADJUSTMENT

It is now commonly acknowledged that cultural factors are involved in social, emotional, and behavioral adjustment. Due to diverse life circumstances, children across cultures and societies may experience different types of stress and possess different resources. Moreover, given specific cultural conventions and beliefs, children in different cultures may use different strategies to cope with stress. Finally, cultural norms and beliefs may influence how social and psychological adjustment and problems are defined and evaluated (Benedict, 1934). In short, culture determines, to a great extent, what normal and abnormal events children may be exposed to, and what risk and protective factors may exist in children's adaptive and maladaptive development.

Two models have been proposed concerning the cultural influences on children's social and emotional well-being (Weisz, Suwanlert, Chaiyasit, & Walter, 1987). First, the "suppression-facilitation" model indicates that cultural values and norms may directly affect the occurrence and prevalence of normal and abnormal behaviors. For example, in a culture that values and encourages violence and fierceness, such as the Yanomamo Indian society in Venezuela (Chagnon, 1983), it is not surprising that children are likely to display a high frequency and strong intensity of violent and aggressive behavior. Similarly, in many Eastern societies such as Thailand and China, in which dependent and restrained behavior is acceptable, children may exhibit a high level of social inhibition and passivity (e.g., Ho, 1986; Huntsinger & José, 1995). Second, according to the "threshold" model, culture influences adults' attitudes toward children's behavior. In a culture that prohibits aggression and disruption, individuals tend to have a low distress threshold for such behaviors. Consequently, occurrence of these behaviors will be least tolerated. This model has received empirical support from recent research conducted by Weisz, Chaiyasit, Weiss, Eastman, and Jackson (1995) among Thai and American children. It was found in this study that, according to observations, Thai children displayed a significantly lower level of externalizing problems, such as aggression in school settings, than American children. However, compared with American data, Thai teachers reported more aggressive and off-task problems among Thai children, a finding that reflects the teachers' expectations of low levels of aggression in the school. It is important to note that although the "suppression-facilitation" and the "threshold" models are not conceptually contradictory, they may predict different responses in adult reports of children's emotional and behavioral problems.

Cross-Cultural Research on Socioemotional Adjustment

In a large collaborative study in Beijing (China), Seoul (Korea), and Tokyo (Japan) (Matsura et al., 1993; Wang, Shen, Gu, Jia, & Zhan, 1988), using the Rutter Child Scales, researchers found some distinctive behavioral patterns in the Western Pacific region. For example, compared with the available Western data (e.g., Rutter, Cox, Tupling, Berger, & Yule, 1975), Asian parents reported that their children had more somatic complaints. It was also found that the rates of antisocial behavior in the Asian children, as reported by teachers and parents, were significantly lower than those in Western children. Among the three Asian countries, Chinese and Japanese children had lower antisocial-deviant scores than Korean children. Similar results concerning relatively fewer externalizing problems and more internalizing problems, particularly somatic complaints, in Chinese and Japanese children have been reported in other studies (e.g., Ekblad, 1990). It has been argued that in cultures that suppress expression of externalizing problems, children may "internalize" their emotional disturbance, which may, in turn, lead to psychosomatic problems such as headaches and stomach aches. This argument is consistent with the psychodynamic theory concerning the conversion of psychic distress in individuals under pressure to comply with strictly defined behavioral rules.

In our longitudinal project on children's social adjustment in the People's Republic of China (Chen, Rubin, Li, & Li, 1999), we collected CBCL (Child Behavior Checklist) data from both parents of a large sample of Chinese children. It was found that, compared with Western results (Achenbach, 1991; see also Achenbach, this volume), the externalizing scores, both on delinquency and aggression, for the Chinese children were significantly lower. In contrast, consistent with previous findings (e.g., Ekblad, 1990), the Chinese children had relatively high scores on somatic complaints. These cross-cultural differences were consistent across gender. In this study, we also asked the children to complete a self-report measure of depression (Child Depression Inventory [CDI], Kovacs, 1980–1981). It was found that the Chinese children tended to be more depressed than their Western counterparts (Chen et al., 1995b).

Weisz and his colleagues have conducted a series of studies, using the CBCL, in Thailand, Kenya, and Jamaica (Lambert, Weisz, & Knight, 1989; Weisz et al., 1987; Weisz et al., 1988). Consistent with findings in Chinese, Japanese, and Korean children, it was found that children in Thailand, Kenya, and Jamaica clearly displayed fewer externalizing behavioral problems than their age-mates in the United States. It was found also that Jamaican children and Embu children in Kenya were rated particularly high on overcontrolled problems mainly because of the numerous somatic problems reported.

Finally, Thomas H. Ollendick and his associates (e.g., Dong, Yang, & Ollendick, 1994) recently conducted, in large samples of children in the United States, Australia, the People's Republic of China, and Nigeria, a study of self-perceived fears related to failure and criticism, the unknown, minor injury and small animals, danger and death, and medical problems. It was first found that, in general, the African children endorsed fears at higher levels than Chinese children, who in turn reported higher levels of fear than Australian and American children. The latter two groups did not differ significantly. More interesting, it was found that Chinese children, both boys and girls, reported a high level of social-evaluative fears, which might be due to their concern of losing "face" in public, and that African children reported extremely high levels of fear related to physical safety, as evidenced by fears of snakes, guns, and deep water. The authors suggested that cultures that favor inhibition, obedience, and internalizing behaviors serve to increase levels of fears, which was consistent with the "suppression-facilitation" model (Weisz et al., 1987). Furthermore, it was suggested that broad cultural influences might interact with learning experiences in determining the development of specific patterns and types of fear in children (Dong et al., 1994).

Taken together, increasing evidence has indicated that children in North American individualistic cultures tend to display more behavioral problems of an externalizing nature than their counterparts in many Asian, African, and South American cultures. In contrast, in cultures where discipline, obedience, and emotional inhibition are encouraged, internalizing symptoms including feelings of depression and somatic complaints are relatively more common in children. Furthermore, interactions among cultural conventions, individual characteristics, and life experiences in development may create a variety of specific patterns of socioemotional adjustment and maladjustment in children. Next, we will discuss the effects of traumatic life experiences on the adjustment of children living in extremely adverse circumstances.

Children's Adjustment in Adverse Sociopolitical Circumstances

Children's psychological and social adjustment in extremely adverse socio-political circumstances has recently caught the attention of developmental psychologists (see Aptekar, this volume). In the past fifty years, many countries and areas have been involved in war and communal violence. As described by Rosenblatt (1983), in some places at war for a lengthy period, such as Lebanon and Cambodia, the children "have known nothing but war in their experiences" (p. 15). Experience of the death of family members, forced displacement of family or destruction of home, and witnessing of killing and death are perhaps common to children in these places. Although the findings concerning adolescents' and adults' socioemotional adjustment and problems in such situations are inconsistent, evidence has clearly demonstrated negative effects of adverse political conditions on the functioning of children (e.g., Leavitt & Fox, 1993). The particular consequences of massive exposure to war and violence on children may be due to their relatively low level of cognitive ability to understand the situation, lack of social capacity in coping with the stress, poor communication skills in the expression of their experiences and feelings of frustration, and egocentrism in causal attributions of disasters (Jensen & Shaw, 1993).

It has been found that children in conditions of war and political violence display both externalizing problems such as aggressive, antisocial, and destructive behaviors, hostility, and resentment (e.g., Leavitt & Fox, 1993), and internalizing symptoms including exhibition of nervous and regressive behaviors, fear, sadness, depression, feelings of helplessness, sleep disturbance and nightmares, and somatic complaints (e.g., Zivcic, 1993). Moreover, the negative effects of exposure to traumatic events on children's functioning and adjustment tend to persist even years after the immediate experiences. For example, in a study of Cambodian children, ages six to twelve years, who experienced separation from family, forced labor, and starvation, and witnessed many deaths, Kinzie, Sack, Angell, and Manson (1986) found that approximately 50 percent of the children manifested posttraumatic stress disorder and prolonged depressive symptoms four years after leaving Cambodia. Follow-up studies (Kinzie, Sack, Angell, Clarke, & Ben, 1989; Sack et al., 1993) revealed that the emotional problems were also highly prevalent seven years later, and still existed ten years after the immediate experiences were over. The high prevalence of externalizing and internalizing problems have been reported in children in other areas at war and violence, including Croatia (Rumboldt, Rumboldt, & Pesenti, 1994; Zivcic, 1993), South Africa (Dawes, 1990; Liddell, Kvalsvig, Qotyana, & Shabalala, 1994), the Middle East (Chimienti, Nasr, & Khalifeh, 1989; Kostelny & Garbarino, 1994; Punamaki, 1987, 1988), and Northern Ireland (Cairns, 1987; Toner, 1994). Nevertheless, it has been found that personal factors, including child temperamental characteristics, cognitive competence, and coping styles; availability of support systems, including a stable relationship with at least one parent or other reference person; and community support may mediate and moderate the negative impact of adverse circumstances on the child (e.g., Jensen & Shaw, 1993; see also Aptekar, this volume).

Problems and Suggestions

It is important to note that most cross-cultural studies of children's socio-emotional adjustment have been conducted using Western-based measures such as the CBCL. Moreover, the initial conceptualization of social and behavioral problems, such as the broad-band categorization of externalizing versus internalizing problems, has been based on Western, particularly North American, cultures and research (for international data, see Achenbach, this volume). Given the role of cultural values and norms and life experiences in determining how children perceive, express, and cope with social and personal distress, research on children's adjustment processes and outcomes without a contextual perspective may have limited validity. For example, we have found that the distinction between externalizing and internalizing problems as formulated in the Western literature (Achenbach & Edelbrock, 1981) is quite unclear in Chinese children. The overlap or comorbidity among internalizing symptoms, conduct disorder, and academic problems in Chinese children is sometimes so high that the different categories may be neither conceptually meaningful nor empirically useful. Children who display externalizing problems such as acting out and aggression often have academic difficulties in school and feel lonely, depressed, and worthless at the same time. In contrast, interestingly, children who exhibit socially withdrawn and inhibited behaviors, which are typical indicators of internalizing problems in Western literature, often adjust well to the social and school environment and are *less* likely than their counterparts to feel depressed and distressed in China (Chen et al., 1995a). Thus, negative internalizing experiences such as feelings of depression, loneliness and insecurity, on the one hand, and behavioral reticence and inhibition, on the other hand, may reflect different constructs.

In addition, by using Western-based constructs and methodology in research in other cultures, we may focus on phenomena and dimensions that are not relevant to children in these cultures. At the same time, we may overlook or neglect important social and behavioral issues in these cultures. Cross-cultural researchers should be sensitive to these issues in the future. Finally, it is important to examine cultural involvement in the developmental origins, ontogeny, and outcomes of children's social and emotional adjustment and maladjustment. Cross-cultural longitudinal studies are required to achieve this goal.

PARENTING AND FAMILY INFLUENCES

Developmental and cross-cultural theorists and researchers have long been interested in family influences on child social and cognitive functioning (e.g.,

Sears, Maccoby, & Levin, 1957). The general consensus is that family, as a primary socialization agent, plays a critical role in the development of individuals' adaptive and maladaptive functioning. This belief has been supported by the results of numerous empirical studies concerning the associations among parenting practices, family organization and family socioecological conditions, and child adaptive and maladaptive functioning in various settings (for comprehensive reviews, see Bornstein, 1991, 1995; Collins, Maccoby, Steinberg, Hetherington, & Bornstein, 2000; and Parke & Buriel, 1998), although different opinions still exist (e.g., Harris, 1995).

Among family variables, childrearing ideologies and practices compose a central theme in the cross-cultural study of childhood (e.g., Bornstein, 1994; Lamb, Hwang, & Broberg, 1989; Maccoby & Martin, 1983; Parke & Buriel, 1998). Several explanations for cross-cultural variations in childrearing have been suggested. First, an anthropological perspective proposes that differential susceptibility to threats to the survival of children accounts for the variability in childrearing practices (LeVine, 1974). Alternatively, it has been suggested that parental desires to engender the values and attitudes necessary for becoming a competent adult, able to fulfill expected roles in his or her respective culture, may be related to different childrearing practices across cultures (Hoffman, 1987). It has also been argued that cross-cultural differences in childrearing attitudes and behaviors may reflect variability in beliefs pertaining to children's characteristics and to the world in general (Super & Harkness, 1986).

Cross-Cultural Differences in Childrearing Ideologies

Researchers are interested in parental ideologies concerning childrearing because they may provide useful information regarding the explanation of different parenting behaviors across cultures. Moreover, it is a reasonable assumption that parental cognitions, ideas, and beliefs serve a mediating function in processes of cultural influences on parental attitudes and behaviors toward the child (Goodnow, 1995). Indeed, it has been found that parents in different cultures have different expectations and goals concerning childrearing and that socialization goals are associated with parental judgment and evaluation of normal and abnormal child behaviors (Hess, Kashiwagi, Azuma, Price, & Dixon, 1980). In traditional Chinese cultures, for example, "filial piety" is a Confucian doctrine dictating that children pledge obedience and reverence to parents (e.g., Hsu, 1981). Chinese parents, in turn, are responsible for "governing" (i.e., teaching, disciplining) their children, and are held accountable for their children's failures. While individualistic values are emphasized in Western cultures, with children being socialized to be independent and self-assertive (Hess et al., 1980), Chinese children are socialized to be self-disciplined, well-mannered, mutually dependent, and concerned with the collective (e.g., Chiu, 1987; Ho & Kang, 1984).

Cross-cultural differences in parenting ideology may be illustrated also in different values concerning child autonomy in collectivistic and individualistic cultures. A sense of autonomy is considered crucial to adaptive development in many Western cultures (Maccoby & Martin, 1983), but might not bear such significance to the adaptive development of children raised in other cultures. Indeed, there is little emphasis on socializing children to be autonomous in Japanese culture (Befu, 1986; Lebra, 1976; Rothbaum, Pott, Azuma, Miyake, & Weisz, 2000). While American mothers are more likely than Japanese mothers to encourage in their children personal autonomy and assertiveness such as defending one's rights, Japanese mothers are more likely to socialize their children to be well-mannered and deferential to authority figures (Befu, 1986; Hess et al., 1980; Itoh & Taylor, 1981). Weisz, Rothbaum, and Blackburn (1984) argued that different emphases on autonomy might account for such cross-cultural differences as Japanese children showing more self-discipline and sensitivity to others and American children being more self-expressive.

Parental belief systems consist of a wide range of ideas, perceptions, values, and expectations concerning normative developmental processes, socialization goals, and parenting strategies (Goodnow, 1995). Cultural variations in parental beliefs and values are a major source of contribution to cross-cultural differences in parental attitudes, actions, and behaviors in childrearing (e.g., Harkness & Super, 1995). Nevertheless, it should be noted that the links between parental beliefs and behaviors typically range from weak to moderate in the Western literature (Sigel, McGillicuddy-DeLisi, & Goodnow, 1992). It is largely unknown how belief systems might be associated with childrearing practices at the cross-cultural level, because these two constructs have not been clearly differentiated in many cross-cultural studies.

Cross-Cultural Research on Childrearing Practices

In the Western psychological literature, research on parenting practices has focused mainly on dimensions of parental warmth and control. It has been argued that parental warmth constitutes social and emotional resources that allow children to explore their social and nonsocial environments (Bowlby, 1969). A lack of parental social and affective nourishment may impede the development of feelings of security, confidence, trust, and positive orientation toward others. Parental nurturant or hostile behaviors may also serve as a model for children (Bandura, 1978). Finally, parental warmth and affection have been found to influence the efficacy of other parenting techniques such as parental training and control practices (e.g., Baumrind, 1980). These latter parenting strategies may be effective in combination with affectionate and responsive attitudes, but may not work or even have adverse effects if based on indifferent and cold affect.

The interaction between parental warmth and control has been elaborated systematically by Baumrind (1971). According to Baumrind's postulations, the effects of parental control or demandingness are a function of parents' affect and attitudes toward the child. At the same time, the relations between warmth and child behavior may also be moderated by the degree of parental supervision and power assertion. The interaction of the two continua constitutes a widely referred-to fourfold scheme that includes authoritative (high warmth, high control), authoritarian (low warmth, high control), indulgent/permissive (high warmth, low control), and indifferent/uninvolved (low warmth, low control) parenting styles (Baumrind, 1971; Maccoby & Martin, 1983). Among the four parenting styles, authoritative parenting, based on positive affect and adequate control, has been found to be associated with adaptive and competent child functioning, such as mature moral reasoning and prosocial behavior, high self-esteem, peer acceptance, and academic achievement. In contrast, parents who provide insufficient or imbalanced responsiveness and control are likely to have children who display adjustment problems (e.g., Baumrind, 1991; Dornbusch, Ritter, Leiderman, Roberts, & Fraleigh, 1987; Eisenberg & Murphy, 1995; Hart, DeWolf, Wozniak, & Burts, 1992; Martin, 1975).

Although the role of parental behavior in child development is recognized in most societies (Whiting & Edwards, 1988), sociocultural influences on parental beliefs, values, and behaviors regarding childrearing pose a challenge to the conceptualization of basic tenets and implications of childrearing practices in cultural context. At minimum, it remains to be examined whether the Western-based notions of parenting dimensions and schemes such as parental warmth and control and their interactions can be generalized to other cultures.

It has been argued that regardless of diverse strategies in childrearing—including sleeping arrangement, customs of childcare, and training techniques (e.g., Whiting & Whiting, 1975)—parental warmth and acceptance versus neglect and rejection may represent the fundamental dimension of parenting and have cross-culturally universal meanings for children's social and cognitive adjustment (Rohner, 1975, 1986). This argument has received support from studies concerning relations between parental nurturance and indexes of child adjustment in various cultures (e.g., Chen & Rubin, 1994; Rohner & Pettengill, 1985). For example, Chen and his colleagues (e.g., Chen, Liu, & Li, 2000; Chen, Wu, Chen, Wang, & Cen, 2001; Chen & Rubin, 1994; Chen, Rubin, & Li, 1997) reported that, in accordance with findings in Western culture, parental warmth and acceptance positively predicted Chinese children's competent, prosocial behavior and school achievement. In contrast, parental rejection and neglect predicted children's maladaptive behaviors, such as aggression and hostility.

The adaptational meanings and significance of parental restrictiveness and control, however, are less clear. In Western cultures, parental strictness and lack of concern for a child's sense of autonomy have been considered indicative of a general rejection of, or hostility toward, the child (e.g., Rohner & Pettengill, 1985). In some other cultures such as China, however, parental strictness, enforcement, and even physical punishment may be regarded as indicating a positive orientation of care and involvement (Chao, 1994; Ho, 1986) and protection (Smith, 1987). Indeed, the childrearing practices of Chinese parents most closely approximate what has been termed, in Western culture, the "authoritarian" style (Chao, 1994; Chen et al., 1998; Chiu, 1987; Dornbusch et al., 1987; Lin & Fu, 1990). This is not surprising, given the emphasis on parental authority and the child's obedience in traditional Chinese culture.

Relatively high control and authoritarianism have also been found in Japanese (Trommsdorff, 1985), Korean (Rohner & Pettengill, 1985), and Israeli (Rosenthal & Zilkha, 1987) parents. For example, it has been reported that in comparison to American mothers, Israeli mothers used more authoritarian strategies in managing their child's behavior and displayed less expressive affect and less patience toward their children (Rosenthal & Zilkha, 1987). It has been argued that in collectivistic cultures, restrictive and authoritarian features, as reflected in parenting practices, may be a strategy for maintaining harmonious family functioning and societal stability (Lau & Cheung, 1987; see also Roopnarine, Bynoe, & Singh, this volume).

How do authoritarian and authoritative parenting practices influence children's functioning and adjustment in collectivistic cultures? Are the associations between these parenting styles and children's social and academic performance in these cultures similar to those reported in Western cultures? According to Chao (1994) and Steinberg and colleagues (1992), authoritarian and controlling parenting practices, regarded as acceptable in Asian cultures, may not be important for the development of Asian children. Our recent Chinese studies have demonstrated that authoritative parenting style is associated with positive parent-child relationships and child social and school adjustment, including peer acceptance, leadership, and academic achievement. In contrast, authoritarian parenting style among Chinese parents is associated with social and academic problems such as aggression, learning problems, and peer rejection (Chen, Dong, & Zhou, 1997; Chen, Liu, Li, Cen, & Chen, 2000). The results are virtually identical to what is proposed in Baumrind's theory (1971) and the findings in regard to Western children. Thus, it may be true that Chinese parents tend to be highly controlling and authoritarian, compared to North American parents. However, authoritative and authoritarian parenting styles may serve similar significance in child development. Given that coercive, power assertive, and prohibitive strategies may lead to the child's negative emotional and behavioral reactions such as fear, frustration, and anger, it is not difficult to understand that authoritarian parenting may be associated with social, behavioral, and academic problems. In contrast, since authoritative and rational parenting provides explanation, guidance, and communication of affect, it may help children develop feelings of confidence and security in the exploration of the world and positive parent-child relationships, which in turn may contribute to social and scholastic competence.

The Role of Family Socioecological Conditions

Evidence from cross-cultural research has indicated cultural involvement not only in family functioning and organization but also in the mediation and moderation of family influences on children. In a cross-cultural investigation of interactions among family functioning, culture, and affective symptomatology, for example, Keitner and colleagues found that although families with a depressed member were generally characterized as poor in overall functioning compared to families containing no depressed members, such dysfunctional environments were experienced differently in Hungarian and American families (Keitner, Fodor, Ryan, Miller, Bishop, & Epstein, 1991). Specifically, whereas American families reported difficulties in identifying and resolving problems, communicating in an articulate and direct manner, and involvement (i.e., overinvolved or lacking interest in the welfare of other family members), difficulties reported in Hungarian families were mainly in the domain of behavior control among family members, including preservation of appropriate standards of conduct and discipline in the family.

Cultural mediation of the effects of family conditions has been demonstrated also in our studies in China (Chen, Li, & Xu, 1993; Chen & Rubin, 1994; Chen et al., 1995a). In North America, although divorce is associated with child social and school maladjustment, it has been found that marital conflict may play an important role in this process (e.g., Emery, 1982). Researchers have noticed that many behavioral problems in children are present before the family experiences divorce. Moreover, children whose divorced parents continue to have conflicts after the divorce have more psychological difficulties than children whose parents are relatively conflict-free. The divorce rate in China is generally low (below 5 percent in 1980, 11.4 percent in 1995, and 13 percent in 1997; Ni, 2000), compared with that in North America. However, parental divorce, once it occurs, has significant and negative effects on children's socioemotional functioning and adjustment. It was found in China that children from divorced families were rated by teachers and peers as more aggressive-disruptive and less socially competent than their counterparts from intact families. Moreover, children from divorced families were more likely to be rejected by their peers, compared with children from intact families. Finally, it was found that children, particularly boys, from divorced families had more difficulties in academic achievement than their counterparts from intact families. In contrast, marital conflict has been found to have weak effects on children's functioning. Correlations between marital conflict and harmony and child behaviors were generally low and nonsignificant, with magnitudes ranging from the 0.10s to the 0.20s (Chen et al., 1993). Therefore, divorce, as a form of threat to the collective harmony, may cause significant damage to the family and lead to harmful consequences for family members, including children. However, extensive social support in the collectivistic society may constitute a social and psychological resource in coping with family conflict.

In addition to family social psychological conditions, family capital conditions such as financial status and living conditions may have culture-specific meanings in child development in Chinese culture. The Western literature has consistently indicated that family economic hardship may be related to parental stress and rejection and maladaptive behaviors in children (e.g., Conger et al., 1993; Lempers, Clark-Lempers, & Simons, 1989). It was found, however, that family capital resources, including income and housing conditions, were positively associated with social and behavioral problems, particularly of an externalizing nature, in China (Chen & Rubin, 1994). Children from families with good material conditions were more likely to display aggressive, impulsive, and undercontrolled behaviors than children from relatively poor families. These results are opposite to those typically found in Western societies (e.g., Lempers et al., 1989). It has been suggested that negative effects of family capital conditions in Chinese children may be related to social and cultural circumstance in China (Chen & Rubin, 1994). First, although most people live a life of low income and low consumption in China, some people have become richer in recent years by doing business in the "free market," working for extra hours beyond their regular work load, or having more than one job. It may simply be the case that parents who spend more time earning a relatively high income are less involved in childrearing. Consequently, children from these families are less likely to receive parental care and supervision and more likely to display deviant behaviors than others. This explanation is supported by the finding that family income was negatively correlated with parental reports of acceptance and involvement in childrearing. Second, it is possible that parents from poorer families are more likely to expect their children to succeed in the future and thus invest more time and energy in parenting. This explanation is consistent with a report that children from poor families were more mature in judging social and moral issues than those from relatively rich families in China (Chen, Zhu, Xu, Jing, & Xiang, 1990).

The Changing Context for Socialization

The emphasis on cross-cultural issues pertaining to socialization should not be taken to imply that the philosophies underlying childrearing practices sanctioned by parents from different cultures are unmalleable. In fact, it is the case that parental attitudes and family structure are flexible and influenced by the ever-changing context in which socialization occurs. Tamura and Lau (1992) have argued, for example, that cultural value systems have changed dramatically in postwar Japan, due to the influences of American culture and industrialization. In general, value systems have become more egalitarian and individualistic, and nuclear family structures have gained social sanction in postwar Japan. Also, rapid industrialization in Greece, a collectivist culture in which traditional hierarchical family roles are valued, is believed to underlie changes in attitudes about socially appropriate roles of family members (Georgas, 1991). The rapid political and economic changes in China in the past decades have been found to be related to changes in parental attitudes pertaining to the socialization of children (Chen, 2000a; Lee & Zhan, 1991). Finally, expanding global migration and high technology for communication in contemporary societies have weakened cultural boundaries and modified the social and ecological environment of socialization. As demonstrated in a number of studies on immigrant populations (e.g., Chen & Stevenson, 1995; Chiu, 1987), exposure and adjustment to different cultures may lead to dramatic changes in the mode of family life, including the processes of socialization and development of the child.

CONCLUSION

Cross-cultural psychological research on childhood has revealed multiple pathways along which cultural factors contribute to human cognitive and socioemotional development. First, and consistent with Whiting and Edwards's argument (1988), culture may affect child activities and behaviors through the organization of the physical and social settings of daily life. Second, social and cultural norms, values, and conventions may direct and regulate the child's behavior through the process of social evaluation. During childhood and preadolescence, due to children's particular need for peer integration and intimacy, peer evaluation and social acceptance in the peer group may play a critical role in the mediation of cultural influences on individual functioning. Third, in the process of socialization, culturally shaped parental belief systems and parenting practices may mediate and moderate children's acquisition of cultural messages. Finally, formal training in educational institutions such as the school constitutes another important channel for the transmission of human knowledge and cultural values from adults to children in contemporary societies.

In this chapter, we have discussed how culture may be involved in children's social, emotional, and academic adjustment and maladjustment. Our focus has been not only on cultural influences on the occurrence and prevalence of child behavioral characteristics, but also on their "meanings" in cultural context. Moreover, we believe that cultural effects on child functioning and their adaptational significance may be constrained by developmental factors. The dialectic between culture and development requires the investigation of cultural influences on the child from a developmental perspective. It should be noted also that although most psychologists are interested mainly in cultural influences on child development and socialization, the relations between the child and culture are interactional and dynamic. Children are active participants in constructing and creating their cultural environment.

Despite the rich literature on the role of culturally organized environments in human development, research on children's cognitive, social, and emotional functioning from cultural and cross-cultural perspectives has mostly been descriptive and unsystematic. Furthermore, cross-cultural studies of childhood have been plagued by theoretical or methodological problems and limitations, including ethnocentric conceptualizations, lack of culturally appropriate terminology, poor psychometric quality of research procedures, and inadequate representiveness of diverse populations. Nevertheless, cross-cultural developmental research has clearly demonstrated its strengths not only in evaluating the generalizability or constraints of Euro-American based developmental theories and findings, but also in investigating culture-related developmental phenomena. Some findings of cross-cultural studies of childhood (e.g., Chen et al., 1992; Chen et al., 1998; Stevenson et al., 1990; Weisz et al., 1987) have already been integrated into descriptions of human social, emotional, and cognitive development and into the "mainstream" construction and modification of developmental theories. More important, research on childhood in different cultures has been growing rapidly, in both quantity and quality, in recent years. As a result, many developmental theorists and researchers have now realized that child development and socialization are complex phenomena that cannot be understood completely and accurately without taking cultural factors into account.

NOTE

Preparation of the chapter was supported by grants from the Social Sciences and Humanities Research Council of Canada, a William T. Grant Faculty Scholars Award, and a Canadian Institutes of Health Research Health Career Award.

REFERENCES

Achenbach, T. M. (1991). *Manual for the Child Behavior Checklist 14–18 and 1991 Profile*. Burlington: University of Vermont Press.

Achenbach, T. M., & Edelbrock, C. (1981). Behavioral problems and competencies reported by parents of normal and disturbed children aged four through sixteen. *Monographs of the Society for Research in Child Development*, 46 (serial no. 188).

Arbeiter, S. (1984). *Profiles: College-bound seniors, 1984*. New York: College Entrance Examination Board.

Ariel, S., & Sever, I. (1980). Play in the desert and play in the town: On play activities of Bedouin Arab children. In H. B. Schwartzman (Ed.), *Play and culture* (pp. 164–175). West Point, NY: Leisure Press.

Asendorpf, J. (1991). Development of inhibited children's coping with unfamiliarity. *Child Development*, *62*, 1460–1474.

Au, T. K., & Harachiewica, J. M. (1986). The effects of perceived parental expectations on Chinese children's mathematics performance. *Merrill-Palmer Quarterly*, *32*, 383–392.

Aviezer, O., IJzendoorn, M. H. van, Sagi, A., & Schuengel, C. (1994). "Children of the dream" revisited: Seventy years of collective early child care in Israeli kibbutzim. *Psychological Bulletin*, *116*, 99–116.

Bacon, W. F., & Ichikawa, V. (1988). Maternal expectations, classroom experiences, and achievement among kindergarteners in the United States and Japan. *Human Development*, *31*, 378–383.

Bandura, A. (1978). The self-system in reciprocal determinism. *American Psychologist*, *33*, 344–358.

Baumrind, D. (1971). Current patterns of parental authority. *Developmental Psychology Monograph*, *4* (1, pt. 2), 1–103.

———. (1980). New directions in socialization research. *American Psychologist*, *35*, 639–652.

———. (1991). The influences of parenting style on adolescent competence and substance use. *Journal of Early Adolescence*, *11*, 56–95.

Befu, H. (1986). Social and cultural background for child development in Japan and the United States. In H. W. Stevenson, H. Azuma, & K. Hakuta (Eds.), *Child development and education in Japan* (pp. 13–27). San Francisco: Freeman.

Benedict, R. (1934). Anthropology and the abnormal. *Journal of General Psychology*, *10*, 59–82.

Bornstein, M. H. (1991). *Cultural approaches to parenting*. Hillsdale, NJ: Erlbaum.

———. (1994). Cross-cultural perspectives on parenting. In G. d'Ydewalle, P. Eelen, & P. Bertelson (Eds.), *International perspectives on psychological science*, Vol. 2, *State of the art lectures presented at the XXVth International Congress of Psychology, Brussels, 1991* (pp. 359–369). Hove, England: Erlbaum.

———. (1995). Form and function: Implications for studies of culture and human development. *Culture and Psychology*, *1* (1), 123–138.

Bowlby, J. (1969). *Attachment and loss*. Vol. 1. New York: Basic Books.

Cairns, E. (1987). *Caught in crossfire: Children and the Northern Ireland conflict*. Belfast: Appletree.

Casiglia, A. C., Lo Coco, A., & Zappulla, C. (1998). Aspects of social reputation and peer relationships in Italian children: A cross-cultural perspective. *Developmental Psychology*, *34*, 723–730.

Caspi, A., Elder, G. H., Jr., & Bem, D. J. (1987). Moving against the world: Life-course patterns of explosive children. *Developmental Psychology*, *23*, 308–313.

———. (1988). Moving away from the world: Life-course patterns of shy children. *Developmental Psychology*, *24*, 824–831.

Chagnon, N. A. (1983). *Yanomamo: The fierce people* (3rd ed.). New York: Holt, Rinehart, & Winston.

Chan, J., & Eysenck, S. B. G. (1981, August). National differences in personality: Hong Kong and England. Paper presented at the joint IACCP-ICP Asian Regional Meeting, National Taiwan University, Taipei.

Chao, R. K. (1994). Beyond parental control and authoritarian parenting styles: Understanding Chinese parenting through the cultural notion of training. *Child Development, 65,* 1111–1119.

Chen, C., & Stevenson, H. (1995). Motivation and mathematics achievement: A comparative study of Asian-American, Caucasian-American, and East Asian high school students. *Child Development, 66,* 1215–1234.

Chen, X. (1999, February). Self-control in Chinese and Canadian children. Paper presented at the annual meeting of the Society for Cross-Cultural Research, Santa Fe, NM.

———. (2000a). Growing up in a collectivistic culture: Socialization and socioemotional development in Chinese children. In A. L. Comunian & U. P. Gielen (Eds.), *International perspectives on human development* (pp. 331–353). Lengerich, Germany: Pabst Science.

———. (2000b). Social and emotional development in Chinese children and adolescents: A contextual cross-cultural perspective. In F. Columbus (Ed.), *Advances in psychology research* (Vol. 1, pp. 229–251). Huntington, NY: Nova Science.

Chen, X., Dong, Q., & Zhou, H. (1997). Authoritative and authoritarian parenting practices and social and school adjustment. *International Journal of Behavioral Development, 20,* 855–873.

Chen, X., Hastings, P., Rubin, K. H., Chen, H., Cen, G., & Stewart, S. L. (1998). Childrearing attitudes and behavioral inhibition in Chinese and Canadian toddlers: A cross-cultural study. *Developmental Psychology, 34,* 677–686.

Chen, X., Li, Z., & Xu, L. (1993, March). Social and school adjustment of children from divorced and high conflict intact families in China. Paper presented at the biennial conference of the Society for Research in Child Development (SRCD). New Orleans, LA.

Chen, X., Liu, M., & Li, D. (2000). Parental warmth, control, and indulgence and their relations to adjustment in Chinese children: A longitudinal study. *Journal of Family Psychology, 14,* 401–419.

Chen, X., Liu, M., Li, B., Cen, G., & Chen, H. (2000). Maternal authoritative and authoritarian attitudes and mother-child interactions and relationships in China. *International Journal of Behavioral Development, 24,* 119–126.

Chen, X., & Rubin, K. H. (1994). Family conditions, parental acceptance, and social competence and aggression in Chinese children. *Social Development, 3* (3), 269–290.

Chen, X., Rubin, K. H., & Li, B. (1995a). Depressed mood in Chinese children: Relations with school performance and family environment. *Journal of Consulting and Clinical Psychology, 63,* 938–947.

———. (1995b). Social and school adjustment of shy and aggressive children in China. *Development and Psychopathology, 7* (2), 337–349.

———. (1995c). Social functioning and adjustment in Chinese children: A longitudinal study. *Developmental Psychology, 31,* 531–539.

———. (1997). Maternal acceptance and social and school adjustment in Chinese children: A four-year longitudinal study. *Merrill-Palmer Quarterly, 43* (4), 663–681.

Chen, X., Rubin, K. H., Li, B., & Li. Z. (1999). Adolescent outcomes of social functioning in Chinese children. *International Journal of Behavioral Development, 23,* 199–223.

Chen, X., Rubin, K. H., & Sun, Y. (1992). Social reputation and peer relationships in Chinese and Canadian children: A cross-cultural study. *Child Development, 63,* 1336–1343.

Chen, X., & Swartzman, L. (2001). Health beliefs, attitudes, and experiences in Asian cultures. In S. S. Kazarian & D. R. Evans (Eds.), *Handbook of cultural health psychology* (pp. 389–410). New York: Academic Press.

Chen, X., Wu, H., Chen, H., Wang, L., & Cen, G. (2001). Parental affect, guidance, and power assertion and aggressive behavior in Chinese children. *Parenting: Science and Practice, 1,* 159–183.

Chen, X., Zhu, D., Xu, L., Jing, H., & Xiang, Y. (1990). The development of moral judgment among Chinese adolescents and its correlates [in Chinese]. *Psychological Science, 1,* 23–29.

Chimienti, G., Nasr, J. A., & Khalifeh, I. (1989). Children's reactions to war-related stress. *Social Psychiatry and Psychiatric Epidmiology, 24,* 282–287.

Chiu, L. H. (1987). Child-rearing attitudes of Chinese, Chinese-American, and Anglo-American mothers. *International Journal of Psychology, 22,* 409–419.

Cole, M. (1992). Culture in development. In M. H. Bornstein & M. E. Lamb (Eds.), *Developmental psychology: An advanced textbook* (pp. 731–789). Hillsdale, NJ: Erlbaum..

Collins, W. A., Maccoby, E. E., Steinberg, L., Hetherington, E. M., & Bornstein, M. H. (2000). Contemporary research on parenting. *American Psychologist, 55,* 218–232.

Conger, R. D., Conger, K. J., Elder Jr., G. H., Lorenz, F., Simons, R., & Whitbeck, L. (1993). Family economic stress and adjustment of early adolescent girls. *Developmental Psychology, 29,* 206–219.

Connolly, J. A., Doyle, A. B., & Reznick, E. (1988). Social pretend play and social interaction in preschoolers. *Journal of Applied Developmental Psychology, 9,* 301–313.

Coplan, R. J., Rubin, K. H., Fox, N., Calkins, S. D., & Stewart, S. L. (1994). Being alone, playing alone, and acting alone: Distinguishing among reticence and passive- and active-solitude in young children. *Child Development, 65,* 129–138.

Creasey, G. L., Jarvis, P. A., & Berk, L. E. (1998). Play and social competence. In O. N. Saracho, & B. Spodek (Eds.), *Multiple perspectives on play in early childhood education* (pp. 116–143). Albany: State University of New York Press.

Crystal, D. S., Chen, C., Fuligni, A. J., Hsu, C. C., Ko, H. J., Kitamura, S., & Kimura, S. (1994). Psychological maladjustment and academic achievement: A cross-cultural study of Japanese, Chinese, and American high school students. *Child Development, 65,* 738–753.

Dawes, A. (1990). The effects of political violence on children: A consideration of South African and related studies. *International Journal of Psychology, 25,* 13–31.

Dong, Q., Yang, B., & Ollendick, T. H. (1994). Fears in Chinese children and adolescents and their relations to anxiety and depression. *Journal of Child Psychology and Psychiatry, 35,* 351–363.

Dornbusch, S., Ritter, P., Leiderman, R., Roberts, D., & Fraleigh, M. (1987). The relation of parenting style to adolescent school performance. *Child Development, 58,* 1244–1257.

Eisenberg, N., & Murphy, B. (1995). Parenting and children's moral development. In

M. H. Bornstein (Ed.), *Handbook of parenting*, Vol. 4, *Applied and practical parenting* (pp. 227–258). Mahwah, NJ: Erlbaum.

Ekblad, S. (1990). The children's behaviour questionnaire for completion by parents and teachers in a Chinese sample. *Journal of Child Psychology and Psychiatry, 31*, 775–791.

Emery, R. E. (1982). Interparental conflict and the children of discord and divorce. *Psychological Bulletin, 92*, 310–330.

Farver, J. M., & Howes, C. (1988). Cultural differences in social interaction: A comparison of American and Indonesian children. *Journal of Cross-Cultural Psychology, 19*, 203–215.

Farver, J. M., Kim, Y. K., & Lee, Y. (1995). Cultural differences in Korean- and Anglo-American preschoolers' social interaction and play behaviors. *Child Development, 66*, 1088–1099.

Friedman, R. J., Zahn-Waxler, C., Mizuta, I., Cole, P. M., Hiruma, N., & Dominichi-Lake, P. (1994, July). Symbolic play patterns, narratives, and emotions: A comparison of Japanese and American preschool children. Poster presented at the biennial conference of the International Society for the Study of Behavioral Development (ISSBD), Amsterdam, Netherlands.

Garden, R. A. (1987). The second IEA mathematics study. *Comparative Education Review, 31*, 47–68.

Garvey, C. (1990). *Play*. Cambridge, MA: Harvard University Press.

Gaskins, S. (1991). Mayan exploratory play and development. *Dissertation Abstract International, 51*, 3590.

Gaskins, S., & Goncu, A. (1992). Cultural variation in play: A challenge to Piaget and Vygotsky. *Quarterly Newsletter of the Laboratory of Comparative Human Cognition, 14* (2), 31–35.

Georgas, J. (1991). Intrafamily acculturation of values in Greece. *Journal of Cross-Cultural Psychology, 22* (4), 445–457.

Goodnow, J. J. (1995). Parents' knowledge and expectations. In M. H. Bornstein (Ed.), *Handbook of parenting*, Vol. 3, *Status and social conditions of parenting* (pp. 305–332). Mahwah, NJ: Erlbaum.

Gottmen, J. M. (1983). How children become friends. *Monographs of the Society for Research in Child Development, 48* (3) (serial no. 201).

Harkness, S., & Super, C. M. (1983). The cultural construct of child development: A framework for the socialization of affect. *Ethos, 11*, 221–231.

———. (1995). Culture and parenting. In M. H. Bornstein (Ed.), *Handbook of parenting*, Vol. 2, *Biology and ecology of parenting* (pp. 211–234). Mahwah, NJ: Erlbaum.

Harris, J. R. (1995). Where is the child's environment? A group socialization theory of development. *Psychological Review, 102*, 458–489.

Hart, C. H., DeWolf, D. M., Wozniak, P., & Burts, D. (1992). Maternal and paternal disciplinary styles: Relations with preschoolers' playground behavioral orientations and peer status. *Child Development, 63*, 879–892.

Hatano, G. (1990). Toward the cultural psychology of mathematical cognition. In H. W. Stevenson, S. Lee, C. Chen, J. W. Stigler, C. Hsu, & S. Kitamura (Eds.), Contexts of achievement, *Monographs of the Society for Research in Child Development, 55* (serial no. 221).

Hess, R. D., Azuma, H., Kashiwagi, K., Holloway, S. D., & Wenegrat, A. (1987). Cultural variations in socialization for school achievement: Contrasts between Japan and the United States. *Journal of Applied Developmental Psychology, 8*, 421–440.

Hess, R. D., Kashiwagi, K., Azuma, H., Price, G. G., & Dixon, W. P. (1980). Maternal expectations for mastery of developmental tasks in Japan and the United States. *International Journal of Psychology, 15*, 259–271.

Hinde, R. A. (1987). *Individuals, relationships, and culture*. Cambridge: Cambridge University Press.

Hinde, R. A., Perret-Clermont, A., & Stevenson-Hinde, J. (1985). *Social relationships and cognitive development*. Oxford: Clarendon Press.

Ho, D. Y. F. (1986). Chinese pattern of socialization: A critical review. In M. H. Bond (Ed.), *The psychology of Chinese people* (pp. 1–37). New York: Oxford University Press.

Ho, D. Y. F., & Kang, T. K. (1984). Intergenerational comparisons of child-rearing attitudes and practices in Hong Kong. *Developmental Psychology, 20*, 1004–1016.

Hoffman, L. W. (1987). The value of children to parents and childrearing patterns. *Social Behavior, 2*, 123–141.

Howes, C. (1988). Peer interaction of young children. *Monographs for the Society of Research in Child Development, 53* (1) (serial no. 217).

Hsu, F. L. K. (1981). *Americans and Chinese: Passage to differences* (3rd ed.). Honolulu: University of Hawaii.

Huntsinger, C. S., & José, P. E. (1995). Chinese American and Caucasian American family interaction patterns in spatial rotation puzzle sulutions. *Merrill-Palmer Quarterly, 41*, 471–496.

Itoh, F., & Taylor, C. M. (1981). A comparison of childrearing expectations of parents in Japan and the United States. *Journal of Comparative Family Studies, 12*, 449–460.

Jensen, P. S., & Shaw, J. (1993). Children as victims of war: Current knowledge and future research needs. *Journal of American Academy of Child and Adolescent Psychiatry, 32* (4), 697–708.

Kagan, J. (1981). Universals in human development. In R. H. Munroe, R. L. Munroe, & B. B. Whiting (Eds.), *Handbook of cross-cultural human development* (pp. 53–62). New York: Garland STPM Press.

Keitner, G. I., Fodor, J., Ryan, C. E., Miller, I. W., Bishop, D. S., & Epstein, N. B. (1991). A cross-cultural study of major depression and family functioning. *Canadian Journal of Psychiatry, 36*, 254–259.

Kinzie, J. D., Sack, W. H., Angell, R. H., Clarke, G., & Ben, R. (1989). A three-year follow-up of Cambodian young people traumatized as children. *Journal of American Academy of Child and Adolescent Psychiatry, 28* (4), 501–504.

Kinzie, J. D., Sack, W. H., Angell, R. H., & Manson, S. (1986). The psychiatric effects of massive trauma on Cambodian children, Part 1: The children. *Journal of American Academy of Child and Adolescent Psychiatry, 25* (3), 370–376.

Kostelny, K., & Garbarino, J. (1994). Coping with the consequences of living in danger: The case of Palestinian children and youth. *International Journal of Behavioral Development, 17* (4), 595–611.

Kovacs, M. (1980–1981). Rating scales to assess depression in school-aged children. *Acta Paedopsychiatry, 46*, 305–315.

Krispin, O., Sternberg, K. J., & Lamb, M. E. (1992). The dimensions of peer evaluation in Israel: A cross-cultural perspective. *International Journal of Behavioral Development, 15* (3), 299–314.

Lamb, M. E., Hwang, C. P., & Broberg, A. (1989). Associations between parental agreement regarding child-rearing and the characteristics of families and children in Sweden. *International Society for the Study of Behavioral Development, 12*, 115–129.

Lambert, M. C., Weisz, J. R., & Knight, F. (1989). Over- and undercontrolled clinic referral problems of Jamaican and American children and adolescents: The culture-general and the culture-specific. *Journal of Consulting and Clinical Psychology, 57*, 467–472.

Lapointe, A. E., Mead, N. A., & Philips, G. W. (1989). *A world of differences*. Princeton, NJ: Educational Testing Service.

Lau, S., & Cheung, P. C. (1987). Relations between Chinese adolescents' perceptions of parental control and organization and their perception of parental warmth. *Developmental Psychology, 23* (5), 726–729.

Leavitt, L. A., & Fox, N. A. (1993). *The psychological effects of war and violence on children*. Hillsdale, NJ: Erlbaum.

Lebra, T. S. (1976). *Japanese patterns of behavior*. Honolulu: University of Hawaii.

Lee, L. C., & Zhan, G. Q. (1991). Political socialization and parental values in the People's Republic of China. *International Journal of Behavioral Development, 14* (4), 337–373.

Lempers, J. D., Clark-Lempers, D., & Simons, R. L. (1989). Economic hardship, parenting, and distress in adolescence. *Child Development, 60*, 138–151.

LeVine, R. A. (1974). Parental goals: A cross-cultural view. *Teachers College Record, 76* (2), 226–239.

Levy-Shiff, R., & Hoffman, M. A. (1985). Social behavior of urban and kibbutz preschool children in Israel. *Developmental Psychology, 21*, 1204–1205.

———. (1989). Social behavior as a predictor of adjustment among three-year-olds. *Journal of Clinical Child Psychology, 18*, 65–71.

Liddell, C., & Kruger, P. (1987). Activity and social behavior in a South African township nursery: Some effects of crowding. *Merrill-Palmer Quarterly, 33*, 195–211.

———. (1989). Activity and social behavior in a crowded South African township nursey: A follow-up study on the effects of crowding at home. *Merrill-Palmer Quarterly, 35*, 209–226.

Liddell, C., Kvalsvig, J., Qotyana, P., & Shabalala, A. (1994). Community violence and young South African children's involvement in aggression. *International Journal of Behavioral Development, 17* (4), 613–628.

Liddell, C., Kvalsvig, J., Strydom, N., Qotyana, P., & Shabalala, A. (1993). An observational study of five-year-old South African children in the year before school. *International Journal of Behavioral Development, 16* (4), 537–561.

Lin, C. C., & Fu, V. R. (1990). A comparison of child-rearing practices among Chinese, immigrant Chinese, and Caucasian-American parents. *Child Development, 61*, 429–433.

Lynn, R. (1977). The intelligence of the Japanese. *Bulletin of the British Psychological Society, 30,* 69–72.

———. (1982). IQ in Japan and the United States show a growing disparity. *Nature, 297,* 222–223.

Maccoby, E. E., & Martin, C. N. (1983). Socialization in the context of family: Parent-child interaction. In E. M. Hetherington (Ed.), *Handbook of child psychology,* Vol. 4, *Socialization, personality, and social development* (pp. 1–102). New York: Wiley.

Martin, B. (1975). Parent-child relations. In F. D. Horowitz (Ed.), *Review of child development research* (Vol. 4, pp. 463–540). Chicago: University of Chicago Press.

Martini, M. (1994). Peer interactions in Polynesia: A view from the Marquesas. In J. L. Roopnarine, J. E. Johnson, & F. H. Hooper (Eds.), *Children's play in diverse cultures* (pp. 73–103). Albany: State University of New York Press.

Matsura, M., Okubo, Y., Kojima, T., Takahashi, R., Wang, Y. F., Shen, Y, C., & Lee, C. K. (1993). A cross-national prevalence study of children with emotional and behavioural problems: A WHO collaborative study in the Western Pacific region. *Journal of Child Psychology and Psychiatry, 34,* 307–315.

McKnight, C. C., Crosswhite, F. J., Dossey, J. A., Kifer, E., Swafford, J. O., Travers, K. J., & Cooney, T. J. (1987). *The underachieving curriculum: Assessing U.S. school mathematics from an international perspective.* Champain, IL: Stipes.

Mizuta, I., Zahn-Waxler, C., Cole, P. M., & Hiruma, N. (1996). A cross-cultural study of preschoolers' attachment: Security and sensitivity in Japanese and US dyads. *International Journal of Behavioral Development, 19,* 141–159.

Ni, S. (2000). How should we revise the Marriage Law? *The People's Daily* (Overseas Edition), November 3, p. 5.

Ninio, A. (1990). Early environment and experiences and school achievement in the second grade: An Israeli study. *International Journal of Behavioral Development, 13* (1), 1–22.

Nsamenang, A. B. (1992). *Human development in cultural context: A Third World perspective.* Beverly Hills, CA: Sage.

Nsamenang, A. B., & Lamb, M. E. (1993). The acquisition of socio-cognitive competence by Nso children in the Bamenda Grassfields of Northwest Cameroon. *International Journal of Behavioral Development, 16,* 429–441.

Orlick, T., Zhou, Q. Y., & Partington, J. (1990). Co-operation and conflict within Chinese and Canadian kindergarten settings. *Canadian Journal of Behavioral Science, 22,* 20–25.

Pan, H. W. (1994). Children's play in Taiwan. In J. L. Roopnarine, J. E. Johnson, & F. H. Hooper (Eds.), *Children's play in diverse cultures* (pp. 31–50). Albany: State University of New York Press.

Parke, R. D., & Buriel, R. (1998). Socialization in the family: Ethnic and ecological perspectives. In N. Eisenberg (Ed.), *Handbook of child psychology,* Vol. 3, *Social, emotional, and personality development* (pp. 463–552). New York: Wiley.

Parten, M. B. (1932). Social participation among preschool children. *Journal of Abnormal and Social Psychology, 27,* 342–269.

Prosser, G. V., Hutt, C., Hutt, J., Mahindadasa, K. J., & Goonetilleke, M. D. J. (1986). Children's play in Sri Lanka: A cross-cultural study. *British Journal of Developmental Psychology, 4,* 179–186.

Punamaki, R. (1987). Psychological stress responses of Palestinian mothers and their children in conditions of military occupation and political violence. *Quarterly Newsletter of the Laboratory of Comparative Human Cognition, 9,* 76–84.

———. (1988). Historical-political and individualistic determinants of coping modes and fears among Palestinian children. *International Journal of Psychology, 23,* 721–739.

Ramist, S., & Arbeiter, S. (1984). *Profiles: College-bound seniors, 1983.* New York: College Entrance Examination Board.

Regev, E., Beit-Hallahmi, B., & Sharabany, R. (1980). Affective expression in kibbutz-communal, kibbutz-familial, and city-raised children in Israel. *Child Development, 51,* 232–237.

Rohner, R. P. (1975). *They love me, they love me not: A worldwide study of the effects of parental acceptance and rejection.* New Haven: Human Relations Area Files.

———. (1986). *The warmth dimension: Foundation of parental acceptance-rejection theory.* Newbury Park, CA: Sage.

Rohner, R. P., & Pettengill, S. M. (1985). Perceived parental acceptance-rejection and parental control among Korean adolescents. *Child Development, 56,* 524–528.

Roopnarine, J. L., Johnson, J. E., & Hooper, F. H. (1994). *Children's play in diverse cultures.* Albany: State University of New York Press.

Rosenblatt, R. (1983). *Children of war.* Garden City, NY: Anchor.

Rosenthal, M. (1991). Daily experiences of toddlers in three child care settings in Israel. *Child and Youth Care Forum, 20,* 37–58.

Rosenthal, M., & Zilkha, E. (1987). Mothers and caregivers as partners in socializing the young child. In L. Shamgar-Handelman & R. Palomba (Eds.), *Alternative patterns of family life in modern societies* (pp. 119–131). Rome: IRP–National Institute of Population Research.

Rothbaum, F., Pott, M., Azuma, H., Miyake, K., & Weisz, J. (2000). The development of close relationships in Japan and the United States: Paths of symbiotic harmony and generative tension. *Child Development, 71,* 1121–1142.

Rubin, K. H. (1982). Non-social play in early childhood: Necessarily evil? *Child Development, 53,* 651–657.

———. (1989). *The Play Observation Scale.* Waterloo: University of Waterloo.

Rubin, K. H., Bukowski, W., & Parker, J. G. (1998). Peer interactions, relationships, and groups. In N. Eisenberg (Ed.), *Handbook of child psychology,* Vol. 3, *Social, emotional, and personality development* (pp. 619–700). New York: Wiley.

Rubin, K. H., Chen, X., & Hymel, S. (1993). Socio-emotional characteristics of aggressive and withdrawn children. *Merrill-Palmer Quarterly, 39,* 518–534.

Rubin, K. H., Chen, X., McDougall, P., Bowker, A., & McKinnon, J. (1995). The Waterloo Longitudinal Project: Predicting internalizing and externalizing problems in adolescence. *Development and Psychopathology, 7,* 751–764.

Rubin, K. H., Fein, G., & Vandenburg, B. (1983). Play. In E. M. Hetherington (Ed.), *Handbook of child psychology,* Vol. 4, *Socialization, personality, and social development* (pp. 693–774). New York: Wiley.

Rumboldt, M., Rumboldt, Z., & Pesenti, S. (1994). The impact of war upon the pupils' growth in southern Croatia. *Child: Care, Health and Development, 20,* 189–196.

Rutter, M., Cox, A., Tupling, C., Berger, M., & Yule, W. (1975). Attainment and adjustment in two geographical areas, Part 1: The prevalence of psychiatric disorder. *British Journal of Psychiatry, 126,* 493–509.

Sack, W. H., Clarke, G., Him, C., Dickson, D., Goff, B., Lanham, K., & Kinzie, J. D. (1993). A six-year follow-up study of Cambodian refugee adolescents traumatized as children. *Journal of American Academy of Child and Adolescent Psychiatry, 32* (2), 431–437.

Salter, M. A. (1978). *Play: Anthropological perspectives*. New York: West Point, Leisure Press.

Sears, R. R., Maccoby, E. E., & Levin, H. (1957). *Patterns of child rearing*. New York: Harper & Row.

Shapira, A., & Madsen, M. C. (1974). Between- and within-group cooperation and competition among kibbutz and nonkibbutz children. *Developmental Psychology, 10*, 140–145.

Sigel, I. E., McGillicuddy-DeLisi, A. V., & Goodnow, J. J. (1992). *Parental belief systems: The psychological consequences for children*. Hillsdale, NJ: Erlbaum.

Singer, D. G., & Singer, J. L. (1990). *The house of make-believe*. Cambridge, MA: Harvard University Press.

Smilansky, S. (1968). *The effects of sociodramatic play on disadvantaged preschool children*. New York: Wiley.

Smith, E. M. (1987, April 15). *Chinese trade traditions*. Journal and Courier. Lafayette-West, Lafayette, IN.

Steinberg, L., Dornbusch, S., & Brown, B. B. (1992). Ethnic differences in adolescent achievement: An ecological perspective. *American Psychologist, 47* (6), 723–729.

Stevenson, H. W., Chen, C., & Lee, S. (1993). Mathematics achievement of Chinese, Japanese, and American children: Ten years later. *Science, 259*, 53–58.

Stevenson, H. W., Lee, S., Chen, C., Stigler, J. W., Hsu, C., & Kitamura, S. (1990). Contexts of achievement, *Monographs of the Society for Research in Child Development, 55* (serial no. 221).

Stevenson, H. W., Stigler, J. W., Lee, S., & Lucker, G. W. (1985). Cognitive performance and academic achievement of Japanese, Chinese, and American children. *Child Development, 56*, 718–734.

Stigler, J. W., Lee, S., Lucker, G. W., & Stevenson, H. W. (1982). Curriculum and achievement in mathematics: A study of elementary school children in Japan, Taiwan, and the United States. *Journal of Educational Psychology, 74*, 315–322.

Super, C. M., & Harkness, S. (1986). The developmental niche: A conceptualization at the interface of child and culture. *International Journal of Behavioral Development, 9*, 545–569.

Taharally, L. C. (1991). Fantasy play, language and cognitive ability of four-year-old children in Guyana, South America. *Child Study Journal, 21*, 37–56.

Tamura, T., & Lau, A. (1992). Connectedness versus separateness: Applicability of family therapy to Japanese families. *Family Process, 31*, 319–340.

Thomas, G. (1988). *World education encyclopedia*. New York: Facts on File.

Tieszen, H. R. (1979). Children's social behavior in a Korean preschool. *Journal of Korean Home Economics Association, 17* (3), 71–84.

———. (1982). Density, location, and longitudinal effects on social behavior in two four-year-old groups of Korean preschool children. *Korean Journal of Psychology, 3* (3), 150–158.

Toner, I. J. (1994). Children of "the troubles" in Northern Ireland: Perspectives and intervention. *International Journal of Behavioral Development, 17* (4), 629–647.

Trommsdorff, G. (1985). Some comparative aspects of socialization in Japan and Germany. In I. R. Lagunes & Y. H. Poortinga (Eds.), *From a different perspective: Studies of behavior across cultures* (pp. 231–240). Lisse, Netherlands: Swets & Zeitlinger.

Vygotsky, L. S. (1978). *Mind in society.* Cambridge, MA: Harvard University Press.

Wang, Y. F., Shen, Y. C., Gu, B. M., Jia, M. X., & Zhan, A. I. (1988). A research report on behavior problems of 2,432 school children in an urban area of Beijing [in Chinese]. *Chinese Journal of Mental Health, 2,* 114–115.

Weisz, J. R., Chaiyasit, W., Weiss, B., Eastman, K. L., & Jackson, E. W. (1995). A multimethod study of problem behavior among Thai and American children in school: Teacher reports versus direct observations. *Child Development, 66,* 402–415.

Weisz, J. R., Rothbaum, F., & Blackburn, T. C. (1984). Standing out and standing in. *American Psychologist, 39,* 955–969.

Weisz, J. R., Suwanlert, S., Chaiyasit, W., & Walter, B. R. (1987). Over- and undercontrolled referral problems among Thai and American children and adolescents: The *wat* and *wai* of cultural differences. *Journal of Consulting and Clinical Psychology, 55,* 719–726.

Weisz, J. R., Suwanlert, S., Chaiyasit, W., Weiss, B., Walter, B. R., & Anderson, W. W. (1988). Thai and American perspectives on over- and undercontrolled child behavior problems: Exploring the threshold model among parents, teachers, and psychologists. *Journal of Consulting and Clinical Psychology, 56,* 601–609.

Whiting, B. B., & Edwards, C. P. (1988). *Children of different worlds.* Cambridge, MA: Harvard University Press.

Whiting, B. B., & Whiting, J. W. M. (1975). *Children of six cultures: A psycho-cultural analysis.* Cambridge, MA: Harvard University Press.

Wu, D. Y. H., & Tseng, W. (1985). Introduction: The characteristics of Chinese culture. In W. Tseng & D. Y. H. Wu (Eds.), *Chinese culture and mental health* (pp. 3–13). New York: Academic Press.

Zivcic, I. (1993). Emotional reactions of children to war stress in Croatia. *Journal of American Academy of Child and Adolescent Psychiatry, 32* (4), 709–713.

CHAPTER 3

All the World's Children:
The Impact of Global Demographic Trends and Economic Disparities

Uwe P. Gielen and Oksana Chumachenko

Children are the wealth of a family.

—Nigerian proverb

By 2050, the median age in Europe is expected to rise to 52.3 years.

—Demographer William Frey

Eleven-year-old Fatima has been sitting in front of a carpet-loom for much of the day. Performing a series of well-rehearsed hand movements, she snips away at the short threads emerging from the carpet's knots just a few inches from her face. Like some of the other young girls sitting close by, she has performed this work for several years and, consequently, has grown near-sighted. She can only vaguely make out the green rice shoots glittering in Kashmir's afternoon sun outside the factory.

With puberty approaching, Fatima knows that her carpet-weaving days will soon come to an end. Her family will also need to find a husband for her, a prospect that evokes a mixture of conflicting emotions in Fatima. Her family's fate has recently taken a turn for the worse since two of her older brothers were killed by soldiers "sweeping" her village near the outskirts of Srinargar. Although she has only a vague understanding of the larger world outside her family home, she senses that her future is precarious and that the life looming ahead of her will likely be a difficult one. Because she is barely literate, and given the precarious economic situation of her family, her chances of joining an educated family in marriage are slim.

Many miles to the east of her, Takashi is sitting in front of a computer to gather information for an essay he has been asked to write for one of his school classes.

Living in a small apartment in Hiroshima, Takashi's parents have given him a room so that he can concentrate better on his all-important studies. Like many of his peers, he is visiting a tutorial afterschool program (*juko*) in order to prepare himself for a series of entrance examinations whose outcome will shape his future.

Takashi's room is filled with electronic gadgets, and for years he has been a consumer of *manga* (cartoons) and television programs directed at teenagers like himself. Over the years he has been exposed—through his teachers, parents, and the mass media—to a steady stream of information about the outside world. His ambition is to become a "salaryman," hopefully at the big car company where his uncle works. It is a sensible ambition and Takashi's mind is already filled with some pretty clear notions about the steps he will have to undertake in order to fulfill his dream.

The two fictional youngsters, Fatima and Takashi,[1] live in highly divergent worlds shaped by the different socioeconomic structures of their respective societies, by contrasting demographic structures and trends, religious beliefs and customs, patterns of family life, gender-related ideologies, and the strife that is devastating so many families in the Valley of Kashmir but that finds only a dim echo in Japan's daily news. Whereas Fatima's childhood and emerging adulthood are likely to follow a pattern shared by many other poor girls in Muslim societies, Takashi is pursuing a path that, in its outlines, is shaped by Japan's increasingly global and secular "information society." In this chapter, we are mostly concerned with the economic and demographic trends and forces that help determine the divergent developmental pathways of youths such as Fatima and Takashi.

When we take into account the differences in children's social networks, we can observe two contrasting forms of social life emerge in the postindustrial countries and in the developing countries of Asia, Africa, and Latin America. Many children in the developing world live in traditional but rapidly changing societies that place much emphasis on intricate family relationships, collectivistic patterns of living, early responsibility training for children, traditional gender roles, favoritism toward males, obedience and respect for elders, and the obligation of adolescents and young adults to marry early, be fruitful, and contribute to the common good. Since families tend to be large, children are shaped in the image of comforting and caring siblings as part of a framework of intricate family relationships. The children are expected to learn values, norms, and social roles through task assignment, observation, admonition, and a kind of nonverbal and semiverbal osmosis. Increasingly, however, global influences are undermining the traditional supports of family life and child socialization. Consequently, children's lives in the developing world are now often shaped by hybrid cultural patterns intermingling the old and the new, the local and the imported.

In contrast to traditional societies, many children in the postindustrial countries live in small families or single-parent households, have divorced parents, interact with few or no siblings, occupy their own rooms, are continuously exposed to consumerism and the mass media, are encouraged to pursue a path of self-actualization, and grow up in a world of contested and changing gender roles (Hiner, 1991). Because these youngsters are living in societies placing a premium on innovation and change, they spend many years in school surrounded by peers who strive to create their own teenage culture (Gibbons, this volume).

Traditionally, American and European textbooks on childhood and adolescence have based their theories and findings on the study of mostly Western youths in the postindustrial countries. This holds true even though the great majority of children live in the non-Western and developing countries, a trend that is bound to intensify in the future. In addition, the textbooks pay insufficient attention to the economic and demographic forces that shape the lives of children. In contrast to this scenario, we present here a picture of global childhood as shaped by changing childhood mortality rates, varying fertility patterns, increasing life expectancies, and drastic differences in life chances between the poor, the in-between, and the rich countries. Some of these cross-national differences can be readily observed in the lives of Fatima and Takashi, since in one way or another such differences manifest themselves on a daily basis all around the world.

The recognition of childhood as the basis of all later human development has led to new ways of studying the situation of children on a global scale. Despite some encouraging efforts to increase the access of children and their parents to a stable food supply, safe water, and health and educational services, while simultaneously reducing the spread of preventable diseases and protecting those in danger of exploitation, surviving the first years of life remains a challenge for many of the world's children in the poorer countries. As societies enter the new millennium, accelerated sociocultural change and increasing complexity in an integrated panorama of ecological, demographic, socioeconomic, and technological forces call for a greater investment in the world's next generation.

Drawing on data provided by the United Nations, the World Bank, the Population Reference Bureau, and other sources, this chapter provides an overview of the current state of the world's children by focusing on worldwide economic and demographic disparities and trends. Ten countries representing major regions of the world have been selected on the basis of high population density. Comparing these countries in the context of global statistics, we trace selected trends regarding their economic performance, population increases, fertility and mortality rates, societal age structures, and the prevalence of child labor in many of the poor nations. Delineating these trends sets the stage for a better understanding of children's lives in a broad variety of sociocultural circumstances.

The quality of the data analyzed in this essay varies considerably depending on the studied nations and regions of the world. When comparing various demographic statistics, estimates, and projections, we observed some discrepancies between various sources and dealt with them according to our best judgment.

On the whole, demographic and economic information proves most reliable for the industrialized countries but is sometimes subject to conflicting interpretations and doubt for the poorer countries. This is especially true for information on children's literacy rates and on enrollment figures in educational institutions.

TEN COUNTRIES AND THEIR CHILDREN

Understanding the situation of the children at the beginning of the twenty-first century must begin with a systematic analysis of the global tapestry. The disparities across world regions are evident, with the combined population of the world's rich countries constituting only a quarter of that of the poor countries. According to projections by the United Nations, during the next decade the world is anticipated to witness rapid population growth, such that its projected population will reach 7 billion around the year 2015, and 9–10 billion around the year 2050. Ninety-seven percent of the population increase is expected to take place in the developing countries of Asia, Africa, and Latin America (Davidson, 1994), whose populations are rising by 70 million annually. During the same time period, European nations are expected to experience a sharp population decline.

In 2000 an estimated 2.147–2.175 billion children under the age of eighteen lived in the world. Of these, 604 million could be found in East Asia, 558 million in South Asia, 317 million in sub-Saharan Africa, 195 million in Latin America and the Caribbean, 191 million in industrialized countries, 153 million in the Middle East and North Africa, and 130 million in the post-Soviet countries. (These numbers add up to the lower worldwide estimate quoted above.) Strikingly, at least 86 percent of all children and adolescents are part of the largely non-European, nonwhite majority population in the so-called Third World, and that proportion has been steadily increasing. It is projected that India, China, Pakistan, Indonesia, and Nigeria (and then the United States) will contribute the most to population growth in the coming half century (United Nations Development Programme, 2000). The United States is indeed the only fully industrialized country whose population is projected to grow steadily during the next fifty years, due both to immigration and to a higher fertility rate than is found in the other postmodern societies.

Figure 3.1 depicts child populations for the years 1999–2000 for the following ten countries: Brazil, China, Egypt, Germany, India, Indonesia, Japan, Nigeria, Russia, and the United States. Taken together, these nations not only mirror much of the diversity of humanity but are also the most populous countries in their respective regions. These ten representative countries, ordered from most to least populous with respect to the number of children living in them, are briefly described below, together with some pressing issues faced by each nation.

Figure 3.1

Population Under 18* in Ten Representative Countries (2000)

Source: UNICEF (2000).

*A child who celebrates his or her 18th birthday is considered to be an adult (United Nations Convention on the Rights of the Child, 1989). World's population under 18 in 2000: 2.147–2.175 billion (35% of the world's population).

The world's largest democracy, India, is expected to become the world's most populous nation around the year 2045. Despite India's gradual economic growth since its independence half a century ago, its gross domestic product (GDP) per capita remains among the lowest in the world. The high population growth rate is too fast for the country's expanding infrastructure to accommodate people's needs and ensure adequate living standards: India's total population has increased by 38 percent between 1975 and 2000 (United Nations Development Programme, 2002). Shortages of adequate drinking water breed intestinal ailments and other diseases, which in turn contribute to an increase in infant mortality rates. India's life expectancy is well below the world's average (World Bank, 2001). The ratios for the age groups 0–14, 15–64, and 65+ are 33 percent, 62 percent, and 5 percent of the total population, respectively (Central Intelligence Agency, 2001).

China, the world's third largest country and its most populous nation, is located in East Asia. According to some estimates, it has the world's second largest GDP. (Some other estimates place China third.) Over the past twenty-five years, China's economy has moved from a Soviet-style collectivistic system toward more decentralized economic decision making. And although the more liberal economic policies, which were introduced in the 1980s, have strengthened the nation's economy, its GDP per capita remains fairly low for the region. This trend is characterized in part by the fact that despite the country's rapid industrial expansion and urbanization, the majority of the Chinese population still lives in villages with a rather inadequate food supply for the numerous inhabitants. Marked by an average life expectancy of seventy-one years, China's youth make up one-third of the total population. During 1975–2000, and despite its official one-child-per-family policy, China's total population increased by 27 percent (United Nations Development Programme, 2002). The ratios for the age groups 0–14, 15–64, and 65+ are 25 percent, 68 percent, and 7 percent of the total population, respectively (Central Intelligence Agency, 2001).

Indonesia is by far the largest country lying off the Southeast Asian coast. Eighty-seven percent of its predominantly Muslim population resides in over-populated Java, the most habitable of Indonesia's over 13,600 islands. In response to improved healthcare and living conditions, a moderately high rate of population growth since the 1960s has been affected by an increase in the average life expectancy and a corresponding decline in infant mortality rates (*Encyclopedia Britannica*, 1998). Nonetheless, fertility rates are also declining due to the diffusion of family planning services, birth control, and later marriages. Between 1975 and 2000, Indonesia's total population increased by 37 percent (United Nations Development Programme, 2002). The ratios for the age groups 0–14, 15–64, and 65+ are 30 percent, 65 percent, and 5 percent of the total population, respectively (Central Intelligence Agency, 2001).

Rapid advancement in technology and steady market growth became the symbols of the world's foremost industrial power, the United States, which occupies the middle of the North American continent. Distinguished by the diverse origins of its inhabitants, the population of the United States is considerably larger than that of both Russia, the world's largest country, and Japan, with the world's second (or third) most powerful economy. The country's total population increased by 22 percent between 1975 and 2000 (United Nations Development Programme, 2002). A largely free-enterprise market economy contributes to the country's GDP per capita, which is among the highest in the world. The nation's excellent health services maintain high life expectancy, although they do not necessarily reach every person, especially the urban and rural poor (*Encyclopedia Britannica*, 1998). The ratios for the age groups 0–14, 15–64, and 65+ are 21 percent, 66 percent, and 13 percent of the total population, respectively (Central Intelligence Agency, 2001).

By far the largest country in South America, with a population of approximately 170 million, Brazil occupies a greater landmass than the combined whole of the rest of the continent. The youthfulness of the Brazilian population (half of whom are less than eighteen years of age; see Figure 3.1 and Table 3.1), along with its substantial migration from rural to urban areas, has a direct influence on the nation's high birthrate (*Encyclopedia Britannica*, 1998).

This is particularly true for the cities, where urban people constitute three-fourths of Brazil's total population. There was a 37 percent increase in Brazil's total population between 1975 and 2000 (United Nations Development Programme, 2002). Rapid population growth, however, is affected by relatively high mortality rates due to AIDS, malnutrition, and inadequate healthcare services, which vary according to the income and remoteness of regions. As a consequence, Brazil's life expectancy (67 years) is lower than that of Venezuela (73 years), Colombia (70 years), or Argentina (79 years) (World Bank, 2001). The ratios for the age groups 0–14, 15–64, and 65+ are 29 percent, 66 percent, and 5 percent of the total population, respectively (Central Intelligence Agency, 2001). The country's prospects of dynamic economic advancement are undermined by mounting foreign debts, corruption, tax evasion, enormous economic disparities between the rich and the poor, and widespread poverty (*Encyclopedia Britannica*, 1998). Nevertheless, the nation's developing market economy, based primarily on manufacture, financial services, agriculture, and trade, contributes to one of the highest GDPs per capita among South American countries. Furthermore, Latin American countries such as Brazil and Mexico have in recent years made important advances toward improving children's health and education levels.

Nigeria is the most populous African nation, with one of the world's highest natural population growth rates (5.9 children per woman). The country's demographic trends reflect those of a developing nation. Nigeria's total population mushroomed between 1975 and 2000 by 52 percent (United Nations Development Programme, 2002). The ratios for the age groups 0–14, 15–64, and 65+ are 44 percent, 54 percent, and 2 percent of the total population, respectively (Central Intelligence Agency, 2001). Nigeria's low life expectancy (52 years) is only slightly higher than that of the sub-Saharan region (47 years) (World Bank, 2001), but is much lower than the world's average. One of the fundamental issues in Nigeria concerns the scarcity of adequate health services: significant numbers of people die from preventable diseases such as malaria, tuberculosis, and the like. In addition, there are more than 1.5 million AIDS orphans in the country. The nation's low GDP per capita leaves more than 45 percent of the Nigerians in poverty (Central Intelligence Agency, 2001). Unfortunately, frequent violent altercations over access to water and valuable resources as well as religious tensions contribute to the country's overall socioeconomic and political instability.

Russia is the world's largest country and the sixth most populous nation. A striking demographic feature since the 1940s is the decline in birthrate. Russia's total population increased by only 8 percent between 1975 and 2000 (United Nations Development Programme, 2002). Nonetheless, the country's GDP per capita fails to sustain its population. The ratios for the age groups 0–14, 15–64, and 65+ are 17 percent, 70 percent, and 13 percent of the total population, respectively (Central Intelligence Agency, 2001). The average life expectancy is lower than the world's average (World Bank, 2001). As a result of fundamental political changes, including the conversion of its former centrally planned economic system into a market economy, a highly noticeable deterioration in living standards is experienced by most of the Russian population. As a direct consequence, individuals seek out opportunities for higher salaries and professional advancement elsewhere, thus triggering the exodus of the younger population. Although migration rates have been gradually falling since 1995, there is also the natural population decrease of more than 700,000 annually (Goskomstat Rossii, 2001).

With its Nile-dependent agricultural sector and industrial foundation, Egypt has the largest population in the Arab World and also in northern Africa. Half of the Egyptians reside in rural areas and contribute to the country's high annual population growth. A closer look at the nation's religious structure provides a lucid explanation for a large and rapidly growing nation, which increases by more than 1 million every seven months (World Bank, 2001). It is estimated that more than 90 percent of the population are Muslims (Ahmed, in press). The ratios for the age groups 0–14, 15–64, and 65+ are 35 percent, 62 percent, and 4 percent of the total population, respectively (Central Intelligence Agency, 2001). A 43 percent increase occurred in the country's total population between 1975 and 2000 (United Nations Development Programme, 2002). A 1999 survey indicated that 50 percent of the young people ages 20–25 have never been married (as cited in Ahmed, in press). The educational background of women has been identified as a major determinant in decisions made by these young people (Ahmed, 1991). Overall, life expectancy has been improving since the 1990s and fertility rates have been declining (Ahmed, in press). Egypt's comparatively high (by world standards) infant mortality rate is complemented by a sharp increase in the number of people emigrating in their search for employment elsewhere. Although Egypt has played a leading role in the Arab affairs of the Middle East, the country's GDP per capita remains low in comparison with most non-African countries.

As the world's second most powerful economy, Japan experienced until very recently a dynamic post–World War II economic growth. Characterized by high population density, Japan has one of the world's highest GDPs per capita, very high living standards, and an advanced healthcare system. The country's demographic trends are similar to those of other technologically advanced nations. There was a 12 percent increase in Japan's total population between 1975 and 2000 (United Nations Development Programme, 2002). A dramatic decline in birth and death rates is reflected in the ratios for the age groups 0–14, 15–64, and 65+, which are 15 percent, 68 percent, and 17 percent of the total population, respectively (Central Intelligence Agency, 2001). The decline reflects the effects of the Japanese family's gradual transformation (Naito & Gielen, in press).

Germany has the third most technologically powerful economy after the United States and Japan. As the most populous and one of the richest nations of Western Europe, Germany's GDP per capita is among the world's highest (World Bank, 2001). The country's total population increased by 12 percent between 1975 and 2000 (United Nations Development Programme, 2002). More than 85 percent of all Germans live in urban settings. Germany's population has a long life expectancy, a negative annual population growth, and one of the lowest birthrates when compared to the rest of the world. The ratios for the age groups 0–14, 15–64, and 65+ are 16 percent, 68 percent, and 16 percent of the total population, respectively (Central Intelligence Agency, 2001). At its current rate of growth, one of the many challenges faced by the German society today concerns a disproportionate aging to young population ratio. Specifically, the proportion of the graying population has forced social security expenditures to exceed contributions from the workers (Keller, in press).

As has already been mentioned, almost 99 percent of the world's population growth takes place in the developing nations, whereas Europe is characterized by fewer births than deaths each year. The rich nations are also older, with a much smaller percentage of children under age fifteen as opposed to the poor countries (see Figure 3.2). Such dramatic changes in the composition of the world population place heavy demands on adequate healthcare, social support systems, and public education. Increases in life expectancy have been driven by technological advances in medicine, thus augmenting a palpable gap between the industrialized world and various developing countries such as Nigeria (see Table 3.1). Data provided in Figure 3.3 show that in 2000, the under-five mortality

Table 3.1

Economic and Demographic Indicators in Ten Selected Countries (2000)

	Total Population (in millions)	GDP per capita (PPP US$)[a]	GNI per capita (US$)	Life Expectancy (years)	Fertility Rates (per woman)
USA	283.2	34,142	34,260	77.0	2.0
Japan	127.1	26,755	34,210	81.0	1.3
Germany	82.0	25,108	25,050	77.7	1.3
Russia	145.5	8,377	1,660	66.1	1.2
Brazil	170.4	7,625	3,570	67.7	2.3
China	1,275.0	3,976	840	70.5	1.8
Egypt	67.9	3,635	1,490	67.3	3.4
Indonesia	212.1	3,043	570	66.2	2.6
India	1,008.9	2,358	460	63.3	3.3
Nigeria	113.9	896	260	51.7	5.9

Note: Adapted from the *Human Development Report* (2002) and *2002 World Population Data Sheet*.
[a]PPP (purchasing power parity): A rate of exchange that accounts for price differences across countries, allowing international comparisons of real output and incomes. PPP US$1 has the same purchasing power in the domestic economy as $1 has in the United States.

Figure 3.2
Proportion of Children and Aged in Low-, Middle-, High-Income Countries, and
the World in 2000

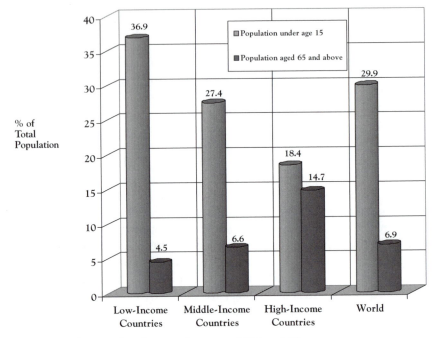

Source: United Nations Development Programme (2002, p. 165).

rates in high-income countries were only 5 percent of those in the low-income
countries. Nevertheless, the death rates of young children have been declining
steadily all around the world between 1970 and 2000, as shown in Figure 3.3.
The decline has been most impressive in the middle-income countries that are
now industrializing at a rapid pace. However, in some of the very poor countries
such as Afghanistan, Sierra Leone, Angola, and Zimbabwe, the ravages of civil
war, spreading HIV epidemics, deteriorating public health systems, and the in-
difference of too many member states of the world community (including the
USA) have kept child mortality rates at very high levels.

SOCIODEMOGRAPHIC FACTORS

Economic Indicators

The demographics of the world are closely related to the countries' overall
economic status (see Table 3.1). Given the dramatic impact of socioeconomic

Figure 3.3
Under-Five Mortality Rates (per 1,000 live births) in 1970 and 2000: Low-, Middle-, High-Income Countries, and the World

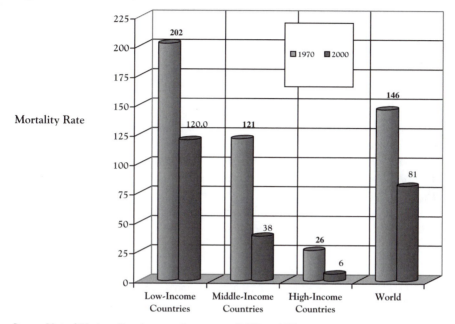

Source: United Nations Development Programme (2002, p. 177).

status on children's welfare, it is important to focus on the economic conditions prevailing in a particular country rather than its geographic location (Population Reference Bureau, 2000a). Although all communities follow certain guidelines for childrearing practices, children's well-being depends to an important degree on their residence in a wealthy or a poor community. The United Nations classifies as "more developed regions" those countries with a gross national product (GNP) per capita of $9,266 or more; "countries in transition" have a GNP per capita of $756–$9,265; and "less developed regions" have GNP per capita of $755 or less (United Nations Development Programme, 2000). However, due to the different exchange rates and the variety of native currencies, it seems preferable to refer to the "gross domestic product per capita" indicator when adjusted for purchasing power (see Table 3.1).

Table 3.1 shows the economic patterns for the ten countries, ranging from the highest GDP per capita (United States: $34,142) to the lowest GDP per capita (Nigeria: $896). With this background, it is possible to contrast different nations against one another for the purpose of shedding light onto some of the main factors affecting children's well-being. For example, by taking Indonesia's and

Japan's GDPs into account, we can predict that Japanese children have concrete chances of survival and productive adulthood, as opposed to Indonesia's many undernourished children, whose number doubled after the recent Asian economic crisis. Thus, allocation of resources and their variations from country to country are fundamental to a newborn's well-being. Essentially, parental investment of time, energy, and resources determines the child's chances for a healthy future.

Fertility Rates

Birthrates and their trends are the most useful indicators for offering insights into the future levels of population (Table 3.1). Fertility rates vary tremendously across world regions (Figure 3.4). Worldwide, the total lifetime number of children born per woman ranges from 1.2 in Eastern Europe to 5.8 in sub-Saharan Africa (Population Reference Bureau, 2000b). Thus, as fertility rates gradually decline in both middle-income and high-income countries, poor countries, particularly in the sub-Saharan region, contribute the most to the world popula-

Figure 3.4
Total Fertility Rates per Woman in 1970–1975 and 1995–2000 in Low-, Middle-, High-Income Countries, and the World

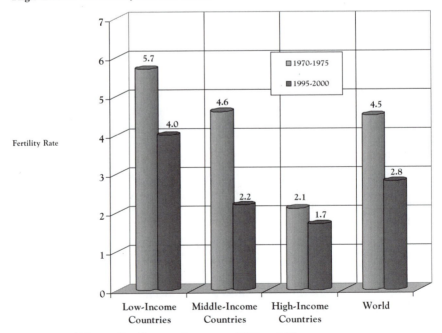

Source: United Nations Development Programme (2002, p. 165).

tion growth, although a rampant AIDS epidemic is beginning to reduce population increases in southern Africa.

The foregoing discussion suggests that children born in industrialized nations, which have much smaller family sizes, are likely to experience different types of threats to their physical health, family influences, developmental changes, and cultural and gender-related pressures when compared to children born in developing countries. Therefore, approaching the topic of female fertility through a multidisciplinary perspective, including considerations derived from evolutionary theory, promotes understanding of the evolved mechanisms of parents' investments into their reproductive patterns that underlie differences in fertility (Blurton-Jones, 1989).

Based on the dramatic decline in Russia's GNP (see Table 3.1), for example, Eberstadt (2001) emphasizes that Russia's death-to-birth ratios are anomalous when compared to the demographic picture of the postwar era. Encouragingly, there has recently been a slight increase in the birthrate (to 1.21 children per woman) since the initial dramatic decline in the mid-1980s (from 2.2 children per woman). In addition, the percentage of the aging population has been increasing, a factor that contributes to the 60 percent increase in the country's death figures.

Various sociocultural forces frequently play an important role in determining the average number of children a woman can bear in an age-specific group (United Nations Development Programme, 2002). Many cultures, for example, hold a traditional view that the number of children (and especially boys) determines the value of a woman—that is, her social status and her contribution to the welfare of the group. Such pronatalist ideologies are especially prevalent in many African and Muslim societies. It is believed that having large numbers of children will increase the likelihood that one's family will succeed in the search for economic and social stability. In contrast, the vast majority of young people in the industrialized countries delay getting married and having children in a time of economic slowdown when unemployment diminishes people's expectations for high salaries and professional advancement. For instance, in Japan, the young generation has been postponing the actual creation of a family in contradiction to long-standing societal norms emphasizing family life. A recent report by the Japanese Ministry of Health, Labor, and Welfare documents an accelerating increase in the median age at first marriage for women (from twenty-five in 1975 to twenty-seven in 2000). Another example in this category is Germany, where the average woman's age when her first child is born is now twenty-eight (Keller, 2000). To counteract such trends, and after the number of births had fallen to a fourteen-year low in 2002, the government of Singapore recently initiated a national campaign to encourage people to fall in love, tie the knot, and have babies. It remains to be seen whether such campaigns will lead to long-lasting changes in fertility rates.

When we consider almost any developing country (excepting China), the picture is reversed. Here, socioeconomic insecurity is translated into both early marriages and the early onset of reproduction. As Table 3.1 indicates, the correlation between poverty and high fertility rates across the world's nations is pronounced. In Nigeria, for instance, the total fertility rate is 5.9 and the gross national income (GNI) per capita is $260. Conversely, Western Europe has a total fertility rate of 1.5 with a GNI per capita of $25,300 (Population Reference Bureau, 2002b).

Various authors have analyzed fertility patterns within the framework of various cultural barriers, such as social customs and taboos. A number of intriguing findings originate in the analysis of birth intervals. Given that the physiological cost of having a boy is greater to the mother than the cost of having a girl, Blanchard and Bogaert (1997) report that birth intervals are longer following a male child rather than a female child. A study by Nath, Leonetti, and Steele (1999) demonstrates that the estimated relative risks of shorter birth intervals are increased for an Indian mother belonging to middle, poor, and very poor income groups, when compared to the upper-income-group mothers. Furthermore, it was also found that higher fertility was associated with compensating effects of having older relatives, especially grandmothers, in the households.

In China, after decades of encouraging reproduction, the government informed its people about the importance of family planning due to an expected population increase to 1.6 billion in the year 2050. The implementation of the "one-child policy" has become a controversial topic despite its major goals of fighting the widespread poverty and ensuring the overall quality of life. According to this plan, each family should have only one child, although in many rural areas, the number of babies born per woman is greater than two. Generally, a second child born without a paid permission does not exist in the legal sense and, therefore, faces numerous obstacles in seeking ways to advance in life. It is illegal for unmarried Chinese women to bear children (Bureau of Democracy, Human Rights, and Labor, 2000). Furthermore, as a direct consequence of the government's promotion of its policy through such incentives as monthly stipends and preferential medical and educational benefits (Bureau of Democracy, Human Rights, and Labor, 2000), Chinese women are reportedly sterilized or forced to abort a pregnancy (United States Committee for Refugees, 2002). Many critics of the one-child policy believe that the long-standing preference for boys has made female infanticide more common. Although the Maternal and Child Health Care Law forbids the use of ultrasound to identify female fetuses and terminate pregnancies, many families, especially in the rural areas, resort to this procedure to meet the demands of labor and specific traditional expectations (Bureau of Democracy, Human Rights, and Labor, 2000). Similar preferences for boys over girls have been reported for various Southeast Asian countries such as Bangladesh, where, as a consequence, a disproportionate number of male babies are allowed to enter this world. In contrast, many female babies are aborted. Other females are omitted from national census figures for a variety of attitudinal and legal reasons.

Mortality Rates

In areas characterized by high infant mortality rates (e.g., Nigeria: 75 infant deaths per 1,000 live births), individuals tend to produce more offspring than individuals in areas with low infant mortality rates (e.g., Germany: 5 infant deaths per 1,000 live births) (United Nations Development Programme, 2002). Despite an impressive record of reduced infant mortality rates throughout the world due to increasingly widespread immunization for preventable diseases, malnutrition, unsanitary conditions, HIV/AIDS and violent conflicts continue to have a detrimental impact on lower-income countries, especially in sub-Saharan Africa (World Bank, 2001). One consequence of the pervasive HIV/AIDS crisis in African countries such as Botswana, Zimbabwe, Swaziland, Lesotho, and Namibia is a steady increase in the number of orphaned children. Most of them will face an exceedingly difficult future. Even now, an estimated 11 million children in sub-Saharan Africa have lost at least one parent due to AIDS, and by 2010 the number will likely increase to about 20 million (Altman, 2002b). Consequently, average life expectancy will soon dip below forty years in many African countries, thereby reversing decades of improvement in health services.

On a more positive note, the world's under-five infant mortality rate (see Figure 3.3) declined more than 10 percent between 1990 and 2000 (from 93 to 83 deaths per 1,000 live births) with corresponding changes occurring in every region of the world (Population Reference Bureau, 2002a). One of the major factors contributing to such an effect appears to be education, especially that of mothers (Ahmed, 1991; Singh & Gielen, 1995). Generally, it is assumed that high rates of low birth weight result from low educational achievement and inadequate nutritional and prenatal care, which usually go hand in hand with various socioeconomic pressures.

Education and Literacy Rates

Current indicators provide conflicting evidence on the number of children enrolled in primary and secondary institutions (see United Nations Development Programme, 2002; World Education Report, 2000; Wagner, this volume). There are, however, indications of a dramatic rise in school enrollment rates as the proportion of young people increases around the world. Overall, literacy rates in industrialized countries such as Japan and Germany are much higher than in developing nations such as Nigeria and India. While the majority of developed countries are close to achieving universal enrollment, many children in the developing nations, especially girls, are still deprived of access to education. The majority of out-of-school youths can be found in Africa, South Asia, and Southeast Asia, regions where gender disparities in schooling are also likely to be most pronounced (Wagner, this volume).

The significant differences in fertility rates that have been found between urban and rural women are primarily a consequence of corresponding differences in levels of female education. Furthermore, children born to women with prenatal care have a greater chance of surviving the first year of life. Unfortunately, too often the social setting dictates whether or not children receive adequate education. In India, for example, many girls internalize the expectations imposed upon them by a patriarchally oriented society, learn to master household tasks, and become child caretakers (Saraswathi, 2000). In this scenario, boys enjoy the privilege of being a male child, with tangible opportunities for academic achievement, as opposed to girls. Similarly, in Mali, West Africa, children are generally cared for by their older siblings, while girls around the age of seven already take on the majority of household chores (Dettwyler, 1994).

According to the Population Reference Bureau (2000a), the birthrate for mothers who have not completed high school is four times higher in the poorest communities than in the wealthiest countries. The 2000 "World Population Data Sheet" (Population Reference Bureau, 2000b) identifies India as the world's second most populous nation, and the country is expected to become a leader in this category by 2045. Although India was a pioneer in implementing a family planning program (1952), the country's annual population growth has reached 15.5 million. Consequently, the Indian government devised the national population policy (2000) to gain control over the country's population growth consistent with its socioeconomic development goals. The policy aims at reaching the replacement-level fertility rate (2.1 children per woman) and achieving universal standards of public health, sanitation, civil and social services, immunization, and education. Since many Indian women do not regulate their reproductive behavior, the policy also captures the importance of educating both women and men about effective family planning. However, recent indications are that fertility rates even among the poorer women have been rapidly declining in some southern states like Kerala and Tamil Nadu. The decline has been less in the already overpopulated and desperately poor northern states such as Uttar Pradesh.

Going to school and becoming fully literate have numerous and mostly positive consequences for children's life chances and their ways of thinking and being. By way of contrast, illiteracy and semiliteracy in today's world condemn a youngster to a life of physical toil, economic hardship, exploitation by others, lower life expectancy, ignorance about family planning, and exclusion from numerous sources of information. Whereas traditional informal education is embedded in family life and the child's round of daily activities, formal education is set apart from the context of his or her everyday life and takes place under the impersonal guidance of experts who are expected to impart superior knowledge and skills (Greenfield & Lave, 1982). Modern formal education makes the child aware of faraway worlds and new ways of thinking, thereby implicitly or explicitly supporting challenges to traditional belief systems, values, and lifeways. Most adolescents know that education is their ticket for a more prosperous, exciting, and satisfying future. It allows them to participate in the creation of a new and increasingly globalized world, however strife-torn it may turn out to be. Child labor, in contrast, enmeshes them in self-perpetuating cycles of poverty.

CHILD LABOR

Overview

Many reports illustrate a clear relationship between low socioeconomic status and school dropout rates, both within and across countries (Population Reference Bureau, 2000a). In societies where people depend on economic subsistence, many children provide an extra set of helpful hands for most of the day, and thus do not enjoy the immediate fruits of primary education, which provides the fundamentals of literacy and other skills for a productive future. If successful integration into the developing economy as well as having an educated citizenry are essential goals of all the nations around the world, then a new workforce must be fully equipped with the applicable reading and writing as well as social and vocational skills.

For instance, following Indonesia's recent economic crisis, it has become very difficult for farming families to survive without children's assistance. According to a 1998 report by the United Nations Children's Fund (2000), multiple threats to basic socioeconomic conditions of this, the world's fourth most populous nation, present a state of dire emergency. Millions of children dropped out of school to earn a living on the streets. The number of teenage prostitutes has also increased in the last four years. Whereas the Eastern Asian crisis seems to be subsiding, the downsides of globalization and modernization have been reflected in the 70 percent loss of Indonesia's currency and the discontinuation of the government. Preceded by a 12.2 percent fall of GDP, the number of Indonesians living in poverty has doubled (World Bank, 2000).

Similar turbulent experiences are evident in Russia's gradual transition from a socialist state to a more democratic form of government. The disintegration of the Soviet Union caused major economic depression and a corresponding deterioration in the nation's social institutions. Corruption continues to be a negative factor in the development of the economy and commercial relations (Human Rights Report, 2000). More than 38 million people fall below the poverty line. Alcoholism, prostitution, drug abuse, and tuberculosis have risen sharply over the last decade and have become catalytic agents of Russia's daily reality, in which too many children are exposed to unhealthy lifestyles. Tragically, the country's living standards are falling and, as a result, Russia is flooded with an orphanage population of adolescents, whose parents can no longer afford to have another mouth to feed in the family. While estimates about the nation-wide number of homeless children are unreliable because they range from 1 to 4 million (Bureau of Democracy, Human Rights, and Labor, 2000), it is clear that their number has increased dramatically since the demise of the Soviet political and economic system.

The Global Picture

The International Labour Organization estimates that more than 250 million children between the ages of five and fourteen are engaged in some form of la-bor. Most children take part in various activities related to intensive manual labor. Knowledge of the selective forces that have been related to child labor can help clarify their catalytic traits within the framework of a particular socio-economic milieu. In agricultural societies, for instance, even young children are expected to contribute to the welfare of the family and the community. The evidence for certain factors leading to child exploitation has been abundantly discussed in the literature (Seabrook, 2001). However, although many thousands of cases have been recorded and analyzed, they represent a highly controversial matter—controversial in terms of the opposing views held by the families, non-governmental organizations, and the child workers themselves.

In its search for socioemotional stability, the young generation often identi-fies itself by the way it contributes to the socioeconomic productivity of its com-munity. Many societies view child labor as a common social obligation and, in some instances, children do not define what they do as work, since their family's poverty does not leave them with much choice. Some children, however, end up in bondage to ruthless employers, in outright slavery, or as teenage prostitutes (Onishi, 2001; see also Aptekar, this volume). HIV infection is a constant threat to prostitutes, and many of them will die young.

It is clear, however, that the little workers of today do not merely suffer from the evil effects of industrialization on their respective societies. Instead, the children's well-being ultimately depends on their society's ability to adequately respond to the immediate effects of a host of global changes and advances, es-pecially in the technological domain. It is possible that at this point in time the social group recognizes the importance of employing its children in order to adapt to many of the new internal and external demands (Seabrook, 2001). In other words, children help their parents mitigate the various strains of living in mod-ernizing societies by utilizing certain techniques they learned from others, such as their peers.

Child labor is a delicate issue, and as such it must be examined within the normative frameworks and economic realities of the respective societies in which it occurs. Scheper-Hughes (1992), for instance, describes a poverty-stricken region of northeastern Brazil, where children are most often raised in single-parent families. Their mothers are low-paid laborers on sugar plantations or serve as maids or as other domestics, but are themselves unable to pay for caretakers. Consequently, older children must assume major responsibilities at an earlier age and learn how to watch their younger siblings or start earning money for the family. A similar situation prevails in many other poor regions of the world.

The fact that most products and services produced by the children in the developing nations are being consumed in the market economies of wealthy nations has important implications. Essentially, living in a competitive environment requires a great deal of physical energy and a quick ability to resist the harsh and callous surroundings. In view of the many children who need to work in hazardous conditions in order to increase their chances of physical and economic survival, it is necessary to understand that although many domestic employers profit more than their vulnerable workers, they themselves are nonetheless governed by the frequently whimsical forces of the global market.

Employers, of course, have always been interested in pursuing wealth that could be acquired in a rapid and cost-effective way. Seabrook (2001) identifies several characteristics of international child employment, including being paid by completed piece, fulfilling the duties of a domestic servant, or serving as an apprentice free of charge. It is implied that in exchange for their labor, children receive priceless practical experience and moral education. However, in reality, children form a major portion of the labor force which is engaged in hazardous activities including handling chemicals and other toxins, and working in factories, glass manufacturing, stone quarries, construction, mines, dumps, and mills (Seabrook, 2001). As children, furthermore, they are least likely to be able to resist exploitation, sexual advances by employers without a conscience, and exposure to toxic environments. In far too many cases, children's working conditions in some of the poorer countries resemble the exploitative conditions described by Charles Dickens and others in nineteenth-century England.

Although much of their time is spent in the deceptively firm and hazardous working environments, the lives of these children are also defined by societal values and family obligations (Arnett, 2002). Those nations that are both poor and embrace collectivistic values are likely to have the largest number of child workers. The Asian Pacific region, for example, has the highest number of working children in the 5–14 age category, 127.3 million in total versus 211 million in the world. In terms of regional incidence, the child-to-work ratio is the highest in sub-Saharan Africa (29 percent). In addition, more than 246 million children are engaged in child labor in the higher age group (15–17 years) (International Labour Organization, 2000).

The failure to promptly educate the youth can only be partially attributed to families' lack of financial resources necessary to compensate for the absence of their school-going children and the additional expenses for the "students." On the other hand, there is another side to the issue in question. The conspicuous remarks of the employers, the families, and the children themselves indicate their mutual reluctance to give up valuable labor time in favor of education. Their argument appears to be even more pertinent in light of a high unemployment rate among recent school graduates all over the world (Seabrook, 2001). In fact, a frequently voiced argument states that when daily work occupies millions of "less fortunate" children, it keeps their minds focused on something "constructive" rather than "deviant." It is common for many tourists, local police, and ordinary citizens, who regularly pass by the clusters of fragile bodies forming the contours of the city's pavements, to view street children as "antisocial" or criminal elements (Aptekar, this volume; Bureau of Democracy, Human Rights, and Labor, 2000).

Furthermore, most families wish to provide their children with certain skills essential to their survival in the immediate environment. Thus, a farmer would teach his children how to cultivate the land, distinguish good seeds from the bad ones, harness the power of domestic animals, and interpret the weather (Seabrook, 2001). An opposed view would be that educational attainment initiates socioeconomic advancement. However, cultural norms dictate specific guidelines for one's contribution to the welfare of the social group and thus monitor the citizens' personal development.

As people become marginalized in their attempts to meet the basics of their everyday existence, educational awareness should ideally be initiated by society through such informal agents as parents and the employers. Although the realization and optimization of basic human rights such as the right to education evolve according to a historical process (Bureau of Democracy, Human Rights, and Labor, 2000), instant "solutions" proposed by outsiders to the problem of child labor often prove ineffective and impractical when compared to gradual improvements in a society's economic performance and the growth of shared cultural understandings about how precious children and their education are. The basic dilemma involved in child labor has been stated as follows: If you stop child labor, you stop the most important human right of all—the right to survive. If, however, you provide decent wages for adults, they will not need to send their children to work (Bhuiyan, as cited in Seabrook, 2001).

ARRIVING AT THE BIG PICTURE

The dramatic demographic and economic changes of the last thirty years have led to divergent physical and social environments for children and adolescents living, respectively, in the poor, the intermediate, and the wealthy nations. Inevitably, these changes are intertwined with dramatic cultural shifts redefining what childhood and parenthood are, can be, and should be. Basic family structures, gender roles, parental ethnotheories and childrearing ideologies, sibling relationships, educational expectations by both parents and children, child labor, consumption patterns, dating practices (if any), adolescents' thoughts about their identities and their possible futures, and youths' exposure to both local and global mass media are all undergoing major culturally structured shifts and redefinitions.

Parenthood: Contrasts Between Traditional and Postindustrial Societies

To illustrate such changes, let us focus for a moment on the most basic question underlying parenthood: Why do parents wish to have children at all, and why do they want either many or only a few children (Kagitçibasi, 1996)? In traditional agricultural and urban settings, parents tend to see children as an insurance that somebody will take care of them in their old age. Given the absence of acceptable social security systems in most of these societies, and given the high mortality rates of both children and adults, being parent to a large number of children is likely to protect one against the possibility of economic destitution and a life of isolation and loneliness. At the same time, children, from early on, can contribute their labor as babysitters for their younger siblings; as water carriers; as workers in the fields, in commercial enterprises, or on the streets; or as maids in other families' homes. In such a situation, to be the parent of many children is truly seen as a blessing. When, for instance, poor Somali Muslim mothers were asked how many children they wished to have, several answered, "As many as possible"—and their actions matched their sentiments (Dybdahl & Hundeide, 1998). Indeed, with seven children per woman, Somalia's birthrate is one of the highest in the world, at a time when Somalia is experiencing a major period of political unrest and economic problems.

Furthermore, parents in many peasant societies prefer boys to girls because when the girls marry, they will join another household and kinship unit. It is the sons—often the oldest—who are expected to take care of their aged parents. As an old Russian saying states: "Feed my parents and I repay a debt, bring up my boys and I make a loan, but provide for a daughter and I throw money out the window." One by-product of such pragmatic, harsh, and economically driven attitudes is the often close bond between mother and oldest son—a situation whose "Freudian implications" have been explored in India by psychoanalyst Sudhir Kakar (1981; see also Sharma, 2003). Emotionally speaking, he finds that many Indian men are in the grip of "maternal enthrallment," a special Indian variant of the Oedipus complex. His example suggests that material interests can lead to special family constellations that, in turn, have profound implications for the long-term emotional development and relationships of children and adults.

In contrast, middle-class parents in postindustrial societies frequently state that they value their children because they provide emotional companionship rather than economic support. Indeed, in the modern world, bringing up children and sending them to school for many years is expensive, and most families can afford only a few children if they wish to protect their own living standards. Given the widespread introduction of pension and old-age insurance systems, and unlike in many of the poor countries, adult children are not usually asked to support their parents financially, although middle-age persons (especially women) are increasingly confronted with the task of taking care of parents suffering from Alzheimer's disease, senility, and other debilitating diseases. In addition, numerous females who have been entering higher educational institutions are postponing the bearing of children. Others remain single or choose not to have any children. We find, consequently, that the higher the percentage of females enrolled in educational institutions and the greater their orientation toward pursuing a career, the lower their birthrate, both within and across countries.

Drastic redefinitions of gender roles, gender role socialization, the treatment of girls and boys inside and outside the family, the desirability of motherhood, and gender-related authority patterns typically accompany the declining birthrates. Feminist ideologies have sprung up among the elite women of the West, are now readily endorsed by otherwise conventional college women, and are slowly spreading to well-educated, Westernized women in the developing world. In contrast, such ideologies have found only a weak echo among the poor and uneducated women in non-Western countries because their life circumstances are so different from those of the highly educated women in the industrialized societies. Once such women are better educated and enjoy better life chances, they, too, will give birth to fewer children and redefine both who they are and who they might and should be.

The Global Transformation of Childhood in Our Times

Based on the foregoing discussion, Table 3.2 compares, in summary form, worldwide differences in children's environments between the poor and the wealthy countries. These differences are presented in ideal-type form—that is, worldwide trends are condensed into a snapshot emphasizing contrasting economic conditions, fertility and mortality patterns, family structures, childrearing goals, gender roles, schooling and labor practices, relationships between the generations, the role of peer groups, and other relevant factors influencing the development of children. It is postulated that economic and demographic forces have a powerful impact on the differences depicted in the table. Without denying the importance of religious, secular, and culture-specific belief systems for the upbringing of children, we may further assume that the belief systems are themselves highly responsive to economic and demographic conditions and changes, although there is often a lag between evolving economic conditions and subsequent cultural transformations.

Table 3.2

Comparison of Children's Environments in Poor and Traditional Countries vs. Wealthy and Postindustrial Countries

	Poor, Traditional Societies	Wealthy, Postindustrial Countries
Economic Basis of Society	Agriculture; subsistence farming; trade; some manufacturing	Information and service industries; involvement in global trade; extensive manufacturing; small agricultural sector
Family Size and Fertility Rates	High fertility rates; large families; pronatalist ideologies	Low fertility rates; small families; motherhood and career concerns frequently in competition
Family Structure and Stability	Low divorce rates; fewer single-parent families; polygamy in African societies	High divorce rates; many single-parent and childless families; increase in variety of family types
Life Expectancy and Mortality Rates	High but declining child mortality rates; low life expectancy	Very low child mortality rates; very high life expectancy
Societal Age Distribution	Children: Elderly ratio very high	Children: Elderly ratio very low and declining further
Impact of HIV/AIDS on Families and Children	Powerful threat especially in southern Africa responsible for numerous orphans; less prevalent in many Muslim societies; female and male victims	Uncommon except among drug users and homosexuals; victims mostly male
Children's Exposure to War	Common Children may be abducted and forced to become soldiers and "war brides"	Rare
Gender Roles	Gender roles sharply distinguished and seen as part of the natural and sacred order; patriarchal and hierarchical conceptions	Contested and less differentiated gender roles; gender roles perceived as changeable and human made; increasing egalitarianism
Schooling, Literacy and Child Labor	Illiteracy and semi-literacy fairly common; many teenagers and some younger children in the labor force; lower school enrollment for females	Universal schooling for both boys and girls; most teenagers enrolled in school; little child labor
Childrearing Goals	Religious piety; conformity; proper manners; loyalty; collectivistic and prosocial attitudes; early responsibility training; child expected to contribute to family welfare	Self-actualization, individuality; independence (especially in the West); success in school; teenagers' ability to navigate in a complex world offering numerous choices and possibilities; secular trends
Parental Reasons for Having Children	It is traditional; economic utility; a spiritual goal; children manifest God's blessing; validation of adult status and social identity	Children provide emotional companionship; having children is an individual preference competing with other preferences; they validate adult status and identity
Length of Adolescence	Brief	Prolonged period
Knowledge and Value Differences Between Generations	Limited but increasing with modernization	Extensive in the knowledge area, less so for basic values
Peer Group Influence	Moderate	Pervasive
Children's Exposure to Mass Media	Limited (especially for girls)	Pervasive
Balance Between Tradition and Innovation	Tradition emphasized but increasing exposure to innovation often introduced from abroad	High rate of economic and cultural change favors innovation over tradition

Given the ideal-type nature of the comparisons, it should not come as a surprise that some societies cannot be placed easily on a linear continuum between the poorest and the wealthiest societies. Saudi Arabia, for instance, is a newly wealthy society whose characteristics fail to match some of the generalizations contained in Table 3.2. Indeed, it may be argued that the religious history of that country can supply better explanations for some of the childrearing conditions (e.g., gender roles) found there than the kind of global analysis presented in this chapter. Nevertheless, a broadly conceived global analysis is the only way to arrive at the "big picture" and to understand, at least in rough outline, what main factors are likely to govern the lives of the world's children over the long run.

The comparisons contained in Table 3.2 can be translated and elaborated into a series of twenty trends that characterize the global transformation of childhood in our times. These trends are certainly not of a linear, uninterrupted, irreversible nature, but they are nevertheless part and parcel of the gradual formation of a dynamic if strife-torn and diversified world community. Driven by technological advances and their pervasive effects, worldwide economic and demographic forces, and global political-economic competition among societies, these broad trends may be summarized as follows: societies, families, parent-child relationships, the role of education in the lives of children, and the nature of adolescence are transformed over time.

Societies

- from agriculture and herding-based subsistence-level societies engaged in limited international trade (if any) to postmodern information societies enmeshed in global economic, political, and cultural systems.
- from societies emphasizing tradition and time-honored sacred archetypes and narratives to those emphasizing innovation and constant change.
- from societies endorsing traditional hierarchically ordered gender roles anchored in patriarchal sacred traditions to societies emphasizing changeable gender roles perceived as human-made and expected to be egalitarian in nature.
- from societies with numerous children to societies with numerous aged persons.

Families

- from families fighting for physical and economic survival to families participating in consumerism.
- from families involved in subsistence activities to families shedding many economic functions.
- from big families to small families.
- from more stable to more unstable families.

- from few to many and diverse family types.
- from families fulfilling numerous economic functions to families emphasizing socioemotional functions. (For more detailed discussions on changing family systems, see Roopnarine & Gielen, in press.)

Parent-Child Relationships

- from parental emphasis on children's obedience, respectfulness, manners, and responsibility toward an emphasis on children's independence, individuality, and self-actualization.
- from authoritarian parents expected to be knowledgeable and in control of their children to more fallible parents ready to learn new (e.g., computer) skills and ideas from their adolescent children.

Educational Institutions and Children's Roles

- from child labor inside and outside the family to children's long-term enrollment in educational institutions.
- from families educating their children informally at home to formal child education outside the family.
- from societies where few girls go to school to societies where females outnumber and outperform males in many educational areas.

Adolescents and Their Future

- from brief adolescence to prolonged adolescence.
- from adolescents' orientation toward authoritative adults to adolescents' involvement in constantly evolving adolescent subcultures.
- from adolescents' desire to learn from the community to adolescents' fascination with a rich variety of mass media produced outside the community.
- from preparing adolescents for known social roles and a known future society to preparing adolescents for unknown social roles making up a society in constant flux.
- from children who as adults will be expected to ensure the long-term economic survival and welfare of their parents to children who are expected to enrich the socioemotional lives of their parents.

As societies transform themselves in these and related ways, they often display a challenging mixture of traditional and modern features. In India, for instance, we may observe all of the following: ancient Hindu rituals and tribal societies pursuing their traditional ways of life, together with modern ways of life emerging, especially among middle-class families in the big cities; modern roads that are built with the help of extensive manual labor and ancient tools; a thriving movie industry depicting ancient gods engaged in futuristic laser-beam warfare;

seemingly traditional villages that are nevertheless deeply affected by the "green revolution" and the national mass media; families that follow both traditional marriage customs and more modern ways of thinking about gender roles; and many other combinations of the old and the new. Not surprisingly, India's childrearing systems increasingly display the same dazzling mixture of ancient and modern features as the other institutions (Sharma, 2003). "Timeless" India, it appears, is finally on the move—and so are many other, formerly traditional societies around the globe.

We may inquire in this context how the lives of Fatima and Takashi, whom we encountered at the beginning of this chapter, fit into the rough picture sketched above. Fatima's work as a carpet weaver, her family surroundings, her marginal literacy, poor economic prospects, exposure to the ravages of civil war, and likely future as a traditional mother with quite a few children—preferably boys, if Allah wills it—mirror, in individual form, many of the characteristics we have attributed to poor and traditional communities and societies. In a corresponding fashion, Takashi's present (and future) existence is mostly shaped by the features of a dynamic, prosperous information society, including small family size, long years of schooling, extensive exposure to peer group and media influence, consumerism, and his prospects for a long and healthy life.

We should not forget, however, that there are many more Fatimas than Takashis in this world, although the contents of most developmental psychology textbooks do not reflect this. Few of these books have much to say about the lives of poor Muslim girls such as Fatima, and as a consequence they tend to remain invisible to the reader.

CONCLUSION

We have sketched a picture of global childhood that emphasizes economic and demographic influences rather than contrasts between collectivistic and individualistic cultural scripts (Greenfield & Cocking, 1994) or the competition between alternative religious, nationalist, and secular ideologies that dominates today's newspaper headlines.

We believe that, in the long run, the transformation of the material basis of societies will prove of central importance in shaping the lives of their children. At the same time, we hope that American life-cycle psychology will continue to grow less ethnocentric in nature and pay more attention to the "big picture" rather than taking as normative the life trajectories of children growing up in postindustrial societies. Even the recent spate of comparisons between American or European children and those residing in East Asian countries (e.g., White, 1993) does not lead to a satisfactory understanding of global childhood, in part because the comparisons leave out too many children in the less technologically advanced countries and sectors.

As educators we need to expand both our own horizons and those of our students by teaching developmental psychology from a truly global perspective, with due consideration for the long-term impact of material factors and for the lives of otherwise invisible children in the poor countries. It is both scientifically desirable and morally appropriate to do so.

NOTE

1. The fictional lives of Fatima and Takashi are based on those of several youngsters whom Uwe P. Gielen has come in contact with in, respectively, Kashmir and Japan.

REFERENCES

Ahmed, R. A. (1991). Women in Egypt and the Sudan. In L. L. Adler (Ed.), *Women in cross-cultural perspective* (pp. 107–133). New York: Praeger.

———. (in press). Egyptian families. In J. L. Roopnarine & U. P. Gielen (Eds.), *Families in global perspective*. Boston: Allyn & Bacon.

Altman, L. K. (2002a). By 2010, AIDS may have 20 million African orphans. *New York Times*, July 11, p. A12.

———. (2002b). Report, reversing estimates, forecasts big increase in AIDS death toll. *New York Times*, July 3, p. A16.

Arnett, J. J. (2002). The psychology of globalization. *American Psychologist, 57*, 774–783.

Blanchard, R., & Bogaert, A. F. (1997). The relation of close birth intervals to the sex of the preceding child and the sexual orientation of the succeeding child. *Journal of Biosocial Science, 29*, 111–118.

Blurton-Jones, N. J. (1989). The cost of children and the adaptive scheduling of births: Toward a sociobiological perspective on demography. In A. Rosa, C. Vogel, & E. Voland (Eds.), *The sociobiology of sexual and reproductive strategies* (pp. 265–282). London: Chapman & Hall.

Bureau of Democracy, Human Rights, and Labor. (2000). *Country reports on human rights*. Available: http://www.state.gov/g/drl/rls/hrrpt/2000/.

Central Intelligence Agency. (2001). *The world factbook 2001*. Available: http://www.bartleby.com/151.

Davidson, A. R. (1994). Problems of rapid population growth. In W. J. Lonner & R. Malpass (Eds.), *Psychology and culture* (pp. 267–272). Needham Heights, MA: Allyn & Bacon.

Dettwyler, K. A. (1994). *Dancing skeletons: Life and death in West Africa*. Prospect Heights, IL: Waveland Press.

Dybdhal, R., & Hundeide, K. (1998). Childhood in the Somali context: Mothers' and children's ideas about childhood and parenthood. *Psychology and Developing Societies, 10* (2), 131–145.

Eberstadt, N. (2001). *The population implosion*. Available: http://www.foreignpolicy.com/issue_marapr_2001/eberstadt.html.

Encyclopedia Britannica. (1998). Chicago: Encyclopedia Britannica.

Goskomstat Rossii [State Committee of the Russian Federation on Statistics]. (2001).

Net migration and natural increase in Russia, 1980–2001. Available: http://www.gks.ru/eng.

Greenfield, P. M., & Cocking, R. R. (Eds.). (1994). *Cross-cultural roots of minority child development.* Hillsdale, NJ: Erlbaum.

Greenfield, P. M., & Lave, J. (1982). Cognitive aspects of informal education. In D. A. Wagner & H. W. Stevenson (Eds.), *Cultural perspectives on child development* (pp. 181–207). San Francisco: W. Freeman.

Hiner, R. (1991). Introduction to J. Hawes & R. Hiner (Eds.), *Children in historical and comparative perspective* (pp. 1–12). New York: Greenwood Press.

International Labour Organization. (2000). *Child labor.* Available: http://www.ilo.org/public/english.

Kagitçibasi, Ç. (1996). *Family and human development across cultures: A view from the other side.* Mahwah, NJ: Erlbaum.

Kakar, S. (1981). *The inner world: A psychoanalytic study of childhood and society in India* (2nd ed.). Delhi, India: Oxford University Press.

Keller, H. (2000). Evolutionary approaches to the life cycle. In A. L. Comunian & U. P. Gielen (Eds.), *International perspectives on human development* (pp. 117–130). Lengerich, Germany: Pabst Science.

———. (in press). The German family: Families in Germany. In J. L. Roopnarine & U. P. Gielen (Eds.), *Families in global perspective.* Boston: Allyn & Bacon.

Naito, T., & Gielen, U. P. (in press). The changing Japanese family: A psychological portrait. In J. L. Roopnarine & U. P. Gielen (Eds.), *Families in global perspective.* Boston: Allyn & Bacon.

Nath, D. C., Leonetti, D. L., & Steele, M. S. (1999). *Analysis of birth intervals in a non-contracepting Indian population: An evolutionary ecology approach.* Seattle, WA: Center for Studies in Demography and Ecology.

Onishi, N. (2001). The bondage of poverty that produces chocolate. *New York Times,* July 29, pp. A1, A6.

Population Reference Bureau. (2000a). *KIDS COUNT international data sheet.* Available: http://www.prb.org or http://www.childtrends.org.

———. (2000b). *2000 World population data sheet.* Available: http:/www.prb.org.

———. (2002a). *Mortality.* Available: http:/www.prb.org.

———. (2002b). *2002 World population data sheet.* Available: http:/www.prb.org.

Roopnarine, J. L., & Gielen, U. P. (Eds.). (in press). *Families in global perspective.* Boston: Allyn & Bacon.

Saraswathi, T. S. (2000). Adult-child continuity in India: Is adolescence a myth or an emerging reality? In A. L. Comunian & U. P. Gielen (Eds.), *International perspectives on human development* (pp. 431–448). Lengerich, Germany: Pabst Science.

Scheper-Hughes, N. (1992). *Death without weeping: The violence of everyday life in Brazil.* Berkeley: University of California Press.

Seabrook, J. (2001). *Children of other worlds.* Sterling, VA: Pluto Press.

Sharma, D. (Ed.). (2003). *Childhood, family, and sociopolitical change in India: Reinterpreting the inner world.* Delhi, India: Sage.

Singh, A., & Gielen, U. P. (1995). Mothers' education, prevalence of contraceptives, and birth attendance by professional health personnel predict under-five mortality rate across 145 countries. Unpublished paper, St. Francis College, New York.

United Nations Children's Fund (UNICEF). (1989). *The convention on the rights of the child*. Available: http://www.unicef.org/crc/convention.htm.

——. (2000). *The state of the world's children*. New York: Oxford University Press.

United Nations Development Programme. (2000). *Human development report*. New York: Oxford University Press.

——. (2002). *Human development report*. New York: Oxford University Press.

United Nations Educational, Scientific, and Cultural Organization (UNESCO). (2000). *World education report 2000*. Available: http://www.unesco.org/education/information/wer.

United States Committee for Refugees (USCR). (2002). *China's one-child policy*. Available: http://www.refugees.org/world/articles/women_rr99_8.htm.

White, M. (1993). *The material child: Coming of age in Japan and America*. New York: Free Press.

World Bank. (2000). *Countries and regions*. Available: http://web.worldbank.org/wbsite/external/countries.

——. (2001). *World Bank atlas*. Washington, DC: International Bank for Reconstruction and Development.

CHAPTER 4

Literacy Development in Global Perspective: A Research and Policy Approach

Daniel A. Wagner

> Literacy represents both a national aspiration and a set of human
> practices anchored in space and time. From this dual existence literacy
> has acquired both a sociopolitical dimension, associated with its role
> within society and the ways in which it is deployed for political, cultural
> and economic ends; and a psychological dimension, associated with
> cognitive and affective properties that lead to greater or lesser individual
> motivation for and competence with writing and print.
> —R. L. Venezky (1991)

CONTEXTS OF LITERACY: PAST AND PRESENT

The history of literacy is long and fascinating, and has been the subject of a considerable number of scholarly studies in recent years (see Wagner, Venezky, & Street, 1999, for a broad overview). While a comprehensive review is beyond the scope of this chapter, it is useful to highlight some areas of relevance, as the reasons for illiteracy over past centuries have much in common with its development and change over time. Historical research indicates that literacy was often transmitted and practiced outside of what we now call formal schooling. For example, as early as the sixteenth century, reading was widespread in Sweden as a function of family and church efforts to teach Bible reading at home (Johansson, 1987). In nineteenth-century Liberia, the Vai people created an indigenous script and have used it ever since for economic and personal written communication (Scribner & Cole, 1981). Likewise, the Native American Cree of northern Canada maintain the use of their syllabic script as a source of cultural identity (Bennett & Berry, 1987).

These illustrative examples outside of formal schooling are representative of only a few of the many interesting cases of literacy development across time and geography. More important, these examples point to a new perspective in literacy research and current literacy efforts. Namely, literacy is a *cultural* phenomenon, and it is practiced in a complex variety of settings and contexts. Literacy, for most children in today's world, is primarily taught in the classroom, but achievement levels are often determined more by the out-of-school determinants than by school factors such as teacher training or textbook quality. Literacy skills as taught in schools all over the globe tell only part of the literacy story, as literacy is practiced in far more varied ways outside of school contexts. It is essential to keep this fact in mind, as literacy development depends on a sensitive understanding of how literacy and culture relate to one another (Wagner, 1991).

The varieties of literacy work—or as is sometimes said, *literacies* (Street, 1999)—in today's world have expanded greatly since the advent of modern public education around the world. More languages are written each year, with scripts, dictionaries, and newspapers to support them. More individuals have increasingly varied skills at using literacy, ranging from information technologies to geographic mapping. Simply said, the world can no longer be characterized as a place where the literate elite dominates the masses of unschooled illiterates. There are relatively few naive illiterates (who know absolutely nothing about scripts or print), but there are many, many individuals with quite limited or restricted literacy skills, such that their own governments might list them as illiterate or functionally illiterate for census purposes. The varieties of literacy, of which school-based literacy tends to be the best understood, mirror the increased social complexity within our rapidly changing societies (Resnick & Resnick, 1989).

In this chapter, I consider literacy in a life-span developmental perspective. While in industrialized countries literacy acquisition begins and is completed largely in childhood and early adolescence, in poor and developing countries, literacy acquisition may take place in later adolescence and adulthood. Thus this analysis takes into account a breadth of research from early childhood through adolescence and into adulthood.

DEFINITIONS OF LITERACY

With the multitude of experts and published works on the topic, one would suppose that there would be a fair amount of agreement on how to define the term *literacy*. On the one hand, most specialists would agree that the term connotes aspects of reading and writing; on the other hand, major debates continue to revolve around such issues as what specific abilities or knowledge count as literacy, and what levels can and should be defined for measurement.

Yet before one can even address the topic of definitions, it is crucial to the separate linguistic dimensions of literacy from formal definitions as used in global literacy statistics. *Literacy* is an English-language term that has its own numerous connotations. Yet other languages have terms for "literacy" and "illiteracy" that carry additional meaning and may have additional, culture-mediated connotations. For example, the Arabic language has no word for "literacy" per se, but only a word for "*illiteracy*" *(umiya)*. Thus, to be literate, in Arabic, is to be nonilliterate, which implies a lower level of literacy than "literacy" in the English language. In French, the term for literacy is usually *alphabetisation*, a word connoting the simple learning of the alphabet—the equivalent of the British primary school phase of "learning one's letters," the most elementary stage of literacy acquisition. Since this term tends to connote negative images for adult learners, it has begun to be replaced by "lettrisme" and "illettrisme" in France today.

Even more troubling than terminology is the surprisingly frequent tendency to append "noncognitive" dimensions of skills and knowledge to the term *literacy*. This happens in many societies and languages, due to the historical pattern of equating the term with education, knowledge, and civilization (Wagner, 1992). Within published works on literacy, one can find a remarkably large compendium of abilities suggested as part of the definition of literacy, such as empowerment, health, democracy, freedom, equality, productivity, technology skill, and so on. Such additions to the meaning of literacy stem from a tendency to commingle the presumed consequences with the term itself. Yet achieving a consensus on the definition of literacy nonetheless remains elusive. Let us consider two of the better known definitions of literacy, the first from early attempts of the United Nations Educational, Scientific, and Cultural Organization (UNESCO) to define literacy; the second from the recent International Adult Literacy Survey sponsored by the Organization of Economic Cooperation and Development (OECD).

> A person is functionally literate when he has acquired the knowledge and skills in reading and writing which enable him to engage effectively in all those activities in which literacy is normally assumed in his culture or group. (Gray, 1956, p. 19)

> The ability to understand and employ printed information in daily activities, at home, at work and in the community—to achieve one's goals, and to develop one's knowledge and potential. (OECD/ Statistics Canada, 2000)

What may we take as an adequate definition of literacy for today's world? Each of the above definitions has been used in major studies of literacy, and each contains some important dimension of literacy that deliberately affected the outcome of its use in data collection. Interestingly, each of these definitions attempts to avoid a traditional dichotomy that once held that literacy was an "all-or-none" entity—that you were *either* a literate *or* an illiterate. Each definition puts the determined level of literacy at a different point, though the most recent definition makes clear that the all-or-none approach is no longer acceptable.

At least part of the controversy over the definition of literacy lies in how people have attempted to study literacy in the first place. The methodologies chosen, which span the social sciences, usually reflect the disciplinary training of the investigator. Thus we find that anthropologists provide in-depth ethnographic accounts of single communities, while trying to understand how literacy is woven into the fabric of community cultural life. Little or no attempt is made at quantifying levels of particular literacy abilities in these studies. By contrast, psychologists and educators have typically chosen to study measurable literacy abilities using tests and questionnaires. While anthropologists primarily use qualitative description to construct a persuasive argument, psychologists tend to use inferential statistics to substantiate claims beyond a numerical level of uncertainty. Both these approaches (as well as those employed in history, linguistics, sociology, and computer science) have value in helping us to understand literacy today. Because literacy is a cultural phenomenon—adequately defined and understood only within each culture, language, and period of time in which it exists—it is not surprising that a single definition of literacy may never be permanently enshrined. For the purposes of this chapter, I will adopt the approach of the aforementioned OECD survey—namely, that some skill levels inevitably must be agreed upon, at least within each cultural group, while leaving open the question of whether a universal definition is plausible or feasible.

POLICIES FOR LITERACY LEARNING IN CHILDREN, YOUTH, AND ADULTS

> [T]he ultimate goal for each country is to meet the basic learning needs of all children, youth, and adults. The focus on providing a necessary level of learning achievement for all is at the core of the meaning of meeting basic learning needs. Access, continued participation, and graduation should therefore be defined only in terms of access to, continued participation in, and graduation from activities that produce the acceptable level of learning achievement. (UNESCO, 1990, p. 43)

The improvement of literacy has not always been a major goal of societies. As has been reviewed elsewhere, literacy in traditional societies has been characterized in part by its "restricted" ownership (such as within the clergy), master-apprenticeship pedagogy for transmitting skills, and the specialized nature of texts (Goody, 1968; Wagner, 1999). Yet with the advent of mass public education in the eighteenth and nineteenth centuries, important changes in the transmission of literacy began to take place. These changes were not, for the most part, preplanned, nor were they without problems. As more countries in the world began to implement mass public education, cultural and national variation has led to considerable diversity in how literacy is transmitted, learned, and retained around the globe. This is not to say that informal patterns of literacy transmission, such as parents reading to children or print media displayed on television, have decreased in importance and frequency—on the contrary. Nonetheless, the locus of change over time has moved to state control through governmental (and intergovernmental) policies that affect literacy instruction of all kinds.

National educational programs are those put into place by governments seeking to extend education on a broad-scale, nationwide basis. All nations currently have formalized educational policies, which tend to be more or less effective depending on such factors as economic development, educational financing, and political stability. The focus of this discussion will be on planned (i.e., formally organized and state-sponsored) literacy development and basic skills instruction in today's societies, which tend to take place principally in four types of contexts: primary education, mass campaigns, adult basic education, and nonformal education.

Primary Education

The core of mass public education, and hence the starting place for literacy for most of the world's population, is primary schooling, beginning with children between the ages of five and seven years. As of 2000, most countries have achieved almost universal primary schooling, though there are a number of countries (principally the "less developed countries") that are still struggling to attain primary education for 60 percent of the school-age population (UNESCO, 2000). It is also apparent that many children in the poorest countries only attend a few grades of school before dropping out (see Figure 4.1), and within most developing countries there is a strong historical disadvantage for girls of school age (see Figure 4.2).

There is, of course, a great deal of variety in the world's primary schools, as there are important differences in language (e.g., national versus local language use), pedagogy (traditional rote learning versus more critical thinking), materials (huge differences in use and availability of textbooks), instructional content (breadth versus depth in particular subjects), and teacher training (the poorest tier of countries have little or no in-service teacher training). Yet there is one curricular topic that is central to all primary school—literacy. The "bottom line" or minimal required cognitive learning for primary school children the world over is to read, write, and calculate by the end of five grades of primary schooling. That some children, within and across nations, achieve greater or lesser success

Figure 4.1
Out-of-School Youth (6–15 years of age) by Region (in millions)

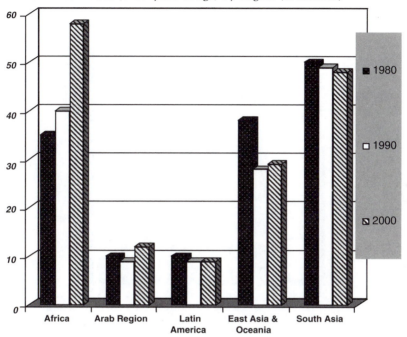

Source: United Nations Development Programme (2002).

in these skills is well known, but there is little disagreement as to the central importance of these three areas of cognitive mastery. It is precisely this consensus among educational policymakers that puts basic literacy skills at the top of the international development agenda, and allows multilateral agencies to play a significant role in educational planning.

It is also this overwhelming interest in primary schooling that gives hope to the notion that illiteracy, someday, will be dramatically reduced. Yet it is also clear that the rates of primary school completion, especially when considering gender and regional disparities (see Figures 4.1 and 4.2), are quite varied, leading to a large number of only partially educated youth, as well as a significant minority who still do not attend any primary school. It is this continuing pool of youth that produces the nearly 1 billion persons (out of an overall world population of 6 billion persons, including children, adolescents, and adults) labeled as "illiterate" today.

While universal primary education is a United Nations goal (UNESCO, 2000), it must be kept in mind that universal access cannot "solve" the problem of illiteracy. "Survival" (or retention) rates within primary schools are still

Figure 4.2
Gender Gap in Adult Literacy Rates by Region, 1980 and 1995
(in percentages)

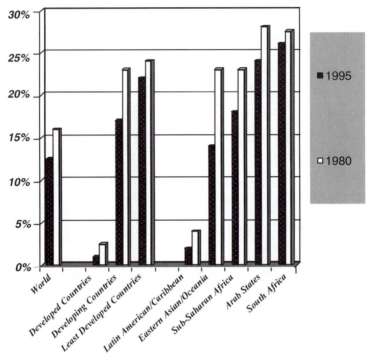

Source: UNESCO (2000).

quite variable, and more than half the children who receive such schooling in the poorest developing countries do not complete five full grades of primary school. Of those who do complete such schooling, as is the case in most industrialized countries, we now know that literacy skills may still be insufficient; and in poor countries, like Bangladesh, we now know that three to four years of poor schooling may leave little or no impact on the basic skills of children and youth (Greaney, Khandker, & Alam, 1999). Finally, with rapid technological change, it is increasingly likely that a person who attended primary school may still lack the particular sets of skills required by an adult a decade or so after completing school. In other words, "technological literacy" is fast becoming part of what country policy makers believe is important to be learned in school, but levels of such technology skills are especially low in developing countries (see Figure 4.3). In sum, in poor countries, it is likely that primary schooling will seldom if ever be sufficient for comprehensive skills training for all citizens. Too many individuals do not complete primary schooling, and those who do may lack the requisite skills for a productive life.

Figure 4.3
Rates of Traditional Illiteracy and Technological Illiteracy Across Regions (in percent)

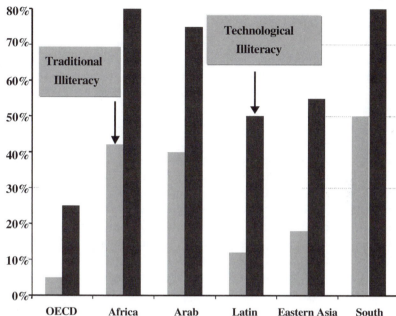

Notes: Literacy data adapted from UNESCO, 2000; technological illiteracy data on OECD adapted from OECD, 2000; while regional data are estimates extrapolated from descriptive accounts, as there is as yet no consensus on a definition of the latter term.

Youth and Adult Literacy Campaigns

In developing countries, where primary school enrollments have only recently begun to cover most of the school-age population, mass campaigns for illiterate youth and adults were, until fairly recently, the preferred "other route" to universal literacy. Literacy campaigns are perhaps the best known of national literacy programs, stemming at least in part from the state-sponsored media campaigns that have usually accompanied these major government efforts. Literacy campaigns, by use of the military "campaign" analogy, have typically tried to enlist large numbers of people and sectors in what is most often a national (rather than local or regional) effort. In the campaign context it is not uncommon to hear language such as the "battle against illiteracy" or to "wipe out" or "eradicate" the "scourge of illiteracy," terminology evocative of the campaign's military origins.

The battlefield analogy may also be seen in media efforts to characterize campaigns as relatively short-lived battles to eliminate illiteracy. This rhetoric is still employed in certain national and multilateral agency proclamations concerning illiteracy. In the view of a number of specialists, this military rhetorical device is ultimately counterproductive to efforts to reduce illiteracy. It implies that the state is in dire peril from illiteracy and illiterates (indeed, the current "threat," evinced in 2002, calls for wiping out "terrorism" through improvements in literacy), and thus puts poor and disadvantaged groups (those who suffer most from illiteracy) in a negative connotation akin to an enemy. Indeed, numerous campaigns, such as those employed following the Russian Revolution (Elkof, 1987), severely penalized (and even punished) those who failed to show up for literacy training. Such penalties—whether explicit or implicit—have had negative consequences in campaigns of the not-too-distant past.

The best-known campaigns stem from those associated with socialist revolutions in such countries as the former Soviet Union, China, Cuba, Ethiopia, and Mozambique. The campaign approach still has adherents, especially in situations of social change. The move away from campaigns is due in part to the fact that countries have found it impossible to maintain a campaign approach for long, whether on literacy, health, or any other worthy activity. It is simply impossible to maintain enthusiasm and media attention for extended periods of time (such as more that two or three years). Furthermore, campaigns are expensive. They typically draw on resources from other sectors of society, such as the national system of schoolteachers or health workers. The extra time spent on literacy is time spent away from tasks for which these professionals have been trained (such as high-quality primary school teaching). In addition, the populations most in need of increased literacy skills are often distinctive or different from the mainstream along such factors as language, ethnicity, and even citizenship (since illiterates may also be migrants from neighboring or previously colonizing states). Given the relatively high expense noted earlier, campaigns typically strive for economies of scale. Consequently, they have tended to treat all illiterates or targets of campaigns as having approximately the same needs, with roughly the same curriculum and so forth. The result is that the campaigns often fail to take into account the key variations in culture and ethnicity that are at the origins of low literacy in the first place.

Nonformal Education

Nonformal and adult basic education typically refers to "first- or second-chance" education programs for youth and adults in both developing and industrialized countries. In developing countries, there are, in addition to campaigns described above, nonformal education (NFE) programs, which became popular in the 1970s with the publication by Coombs and Ahmed (1974) of the World Bank–supported monograph *Attacking Rural Poverty*. Nonformal programs have tended to focus on functional skills, including literacy and numeracy training, to improve development in such sectors as population and health, agriculture, and employment. They also provide second-chance opportunities for children and adolescents who have dropped out of school to get back into school—a major problem in countries with high primary school dropout rates, such as India. Nonformal programs tend to have less rigorous training and lower overall costs than formal schooling, and they can be more accurately targeted to particular development needs. In the past few years, there has been a growth in interest in alternative NFE programs, as exemplified by a recent World Bank report (Lauglo, 2001).

LITERACY ACQUISITION IN CHILDREN, ADOLESCENTS, AND ADULTS

By "literacy acquisition," I refer here to the ways that basic skills (as defined above) are acquired at these different points in the life span and in cultural context. It should be noted that this approach is different from that of standard discussions of reading development, where the "average" child is shown to develop an increasingly sophisticated set of literacy skills that begin before school and continue well beyond secondary school. Here the focus is on beginning skills, which are sometimes acquired at very different points in a person's lifetime.

Literacy Acquisition in Children

The study of literacy acquisition is heavily influenced by research undertaken in the industrialized world. Much of this research might be better termed the study of the acquisition of reading and writing skills, with an emphasis on the relationship between cognitive skills, such as perception, memory, and metalinguistic skills (Snow, Burns, & Griffin, 1998), and reading skills, such as decoding and comprehension. Most of this work has been carried out with school-age children, rather than with adolescents or adults (see Pearson, 1984; Barr, Kamil, Mosenthal, & Pearson, 1991). Relative to industrialized countries, fairly little research on literacy acquisition has been undertaken in the Third World and on non-Western languages (see reviews by region, however, in Wagner et al., 1999). Despite these gaps in the research literature, it is possible to put forward a number of conclusions about how literacy is acquired across different societies. It should be underscored that claims based on the research literature remain relatively weak, given the disparate pieces of evidence available across diverse societies. In reviewing this material, it is helpful to consider children's literacy development within three principal parameters for the collection and interpretation of findings: environmental/cultural, linguistic, and cognitive. Each of these will be considered in turn.

Environmental/cultural. In industrialized countries, it is often assumed that most children grow up in "literate households"—that is, with both parents educated and able to read and write proficiently. While specialists in industrialized countries are now much more likely to discuss the diversity of their respective societies (also useful as explanations for the diversity of literacy achievement in the entire population), the so-called "average child" typically starts to come into contact with written language at about the age of three or four years, beginning with what has been termed the preliterate skills of scribbling and storybook "reading" (Sulzby & Teale, 1991). Subsequently, children are socialized for literacy through many years of attendance in school, reinforced by parents who read and wish their children to read.

Naturally, this normative, schematic, and idyllic portrait of literacy learning in industrialized countries leaves out many children in today's world, both in industrialized countries and in the developing world. With respect to illiteracy or low levels of literacy in former colonies, specialists have stressed the importance of class structure and ethnicity/race as partial explanations of the differential motivation and socialization of young literacy learners. Some claim that many minority and marginalized children in industrialized countries like the United States are alienated and therefore unmotivated to learn to read and write in the cultural structure of the school (e.g., Ogbu, 1980). This approach to understanding social and cultural differences in literacy and school achievement has received increased attention in recent years. A structural approach to children's literacy achievement seems to have only modest attraction to social scientists in developing countries, most of whom see the problem of illiteracy in broader social terms. Rather than focus on those who "fail" in the school system (which is usually the emphasis of Western social scientists), these specialists are mainly concerned with how to provide more literacy to the entire population. Thus, the developing country context is seen as one in which there is simply too little literacy in the environment (e.g., books, newspapers), too few literate parents to teach and add value or "cultural capital" (Bourdieu, 1977) to literacy in the home, and too few children who attend schools for a sufficient number of years to become literate. This perspective largely focuses on the "literate society" (Olson & Torrance, 2001), where parents' literacy abilities and print-in-the-environment (e.g., number of books in the home) often come out as central predictors of children's literacy development (cf. Verhoeven & Snow, 2001).

Overall, when consideration is given to children in low-literate settings in developing or industrialized countries, the environmental/cultural dimension of literacy learning provides a ready explanation for the lack of literacy acquisition among children and youth—whether the basic explanation resides in lack of material resources or the "mismatch" between the culture of the educated (and educators) and those who are "in need" of further education. As societies become more literate (measured in such terms as greater numbers of educated and literate parents), explanations of low literacy begin to become more nuanced, tending toward such issues as language of instruction (the linguistic dimension), and cognitive-psychometric approaches to learning to read and write.

Linguistic. About three decades ago, Downing (1973) published *Comparative Reading*, which surveyed the acquisition of reading skills across different languages and different orthographies. Based on his work and others, we know that mastery of the spoken language is a typical prerequisite for fluent reading comprehension in a given language.

Until fairly recently, it has been taken as "axiomatic" (UNESCO, 1953, p. 11) that learning to read in one's "mother tongue," or first language, is *always* the best educational policy for literacy provision, whether for children or for adults. Based on some frequently cited research studies undertaken in the 1960s and 1970s (e.g., Engle, 1975; see a review in Hakuta, 1986), it has been generally assumed that individuals who have had to learn to read in a second language are at a disadvantage relative to others who learn in their first language. While this generalization probably holds true in many of the world's multilingual societies, more recent research has shown that there may be important exceptions. In one such study, it was found that Berber-speaking children who had to learn to read in standard Arabic in Moroccan schools were able to read in fifth grade just as well as children who were native speakers of Arabic (Wagner, 1993). Adequate research on nonliterate adults who learn to read in a second versus a first language has yet to be undertaken.

We also know that languages that have a relatively close correspondence between the spelling and sounds of written language (such as Spanish) tend to make literacy learning easier than in languages where there exist many exceptions of "sounding out" rules (such as in the English language). Yet it has also been shown, contrary to earlier anecdotal information, that reading problems (and disabilities) exist in all known written languages, even those in which there is no spelling-sound correspondence (such as in Chinese; see Stevenson, Stigler, Lucker, Lee, Hsu, & Kitamura, 1982). Overall, it can be safely said that while important differences exist among written languages, the normal, healthy child, with the proper environment and instruction, ought to be able to learn to read and write. That there remain large individual differences in literacy achievement is usually thought to be explicable by addressing individual-level approaches to literacy learning, as described below.

Cognitive. As noted above, the main body of research on literacy has been conducted in Western industrialized countries, and it has been heavily influenced by the traditions of psychological and cognitive testing developed at the beginning of the twentieth century. This tradition, often called "psychometrics" in the intelligence-testing community, became better known as "cognitive assessment" or "skill assessment" by midcentury. Because studies using psychometric tests (on samples of Western middle-class schoolchildren) demonstrated that reading ability was usually correlated with cognitive skills such as perceptual discrimination, eye movements, and aural (auditory) discrimination, it has been claimed that these skills (the ones that correlate most highly with reading skill) are the basis for effective reading (Barr et al., 1991). This finding, which has been replicated many times, had major ramifications for literacy instruction the world over.

First, it was concluded that these basic cognitive skills (sometimes called "prereading" skills) necessitate direct instruction in the school curriculum. Thus the past several decades have seen a tremendous growth in the use of "basal" textbooks, which stress the learning of cognitive skills and an instructional approach favoring the decomposition of the reading task into simple skill (or subskill) components. One main example is the emphasis on "sounding out" simple pronounceable words or wordlike strings (morphemes).

Second, it was suggested that children who were "slow learners" lacked certain of these basic cognitive skills and therefore required remedial instruction on the component skills (rather than more practice on reading itself). This approach to seeing literacy acquisition as a consequence of the basic cognitive skills or subskills that underlie reading led to a long-term tendency of reading and literacy specialists to emphasize the individual learner as the "cause" of reading deficiencies. Diagnostic terms such as *dyslexia* were often applied to individuals who exhibited such skill deficiencies.

Third, the cognitive approach led to a number of important theories of reading and literacy acquisition. One of the most prominent has been called the "stage theory" of reading (Chall, 1983). In this theory, it was proposed that all children (and, implicitly, adolescents and adults as well) would normally learn to decode the alphabet, learn to read written language, and read to learn from the written language. These are stages that all readers must go through to become proficient in any written language. While this theory has been debated in the United States (cf. Snow et al., 1998), it has yet to be tested widely in other societies.

Finally, since most of the research upon which these conclusions were drawn has been based on Western middle-class children, cultural and linguistic factors have tended to be minimized. It was only with the advent of ethnographic studies, such as those by Street and colleagues (e.g., Street, 2001), that the cognitive perspective came under critical review, particularly with respect to the large-scale literacy problems in Third World countries.

Literacy Acquisition in Adolescents and Adults

Compared to the considerable progress made in understanding the acquisition of literacy in children, far less is known about literacy acquisition in adolescents and adults. Indeed, the research base is so slim that there are few if any major journals that specialize or systematically report on adult literacy research, and there are relatively few university research centers which specialize in research on literacy acquisition in adults. What is known about basic youth and adult literacy acquisition may be conveniently summarized by following the same three approaches used above.

Environmental/cultural. In contrast to the case of young children, adults who do not learn to read and write in industrialized countries are considered to be "failures." Children, while eventually stigmatized in school for failing to read adequately by the end of primary school, are nevertheless given time to develop skills "naturally," through home and school learning. Adult illiterates, on the other hand, are assumed, in most industrialized countries, to already have failed. This distinction is exceedingly important and is one of the key issues in adult literacy work today. Especially in industrialized countries, where the population density of literacy and literacy requirements are relatively high, the illiterate and low-literate individual is often demoralized and rendered helpless by the stigmatization of illiteracy. Consequently, motivation to achieve and to become literate is a critical element in the success of most contemporary literacy programs in industrialized countries.

The situation is not substantially different in developing countries, though the population density of illiteracy is so much higher that the stigmatization factor may be considerably diminished. But this lessening may not have a concomitant effect on the motivational factor mentioned above. Even if literacy in some countries is reserved primarily for the wealthy classes, uneducated and illiterate individuals may, for a variety of sociohistorical reasons, perceive themselves as stigmatized and unable to break the cycle of poverty and illiteracy. Thus, motivation for learning can be just as great a problem for adult literacy programming in developing countries as it is in industrialized ones.

Cultural and environmental explanations for illiteracy and low literacy in industrialized and developing countries are quite similar, and reside typically in an individual's lack of schooling (through nonattendance or premature dropout). As in the case with children, a structural approach to this lack of schooling, and more recently, lack of participation in adult literacy programs and campaigns, may be seen as a sociological and cultural phenomenon. Adult individuals, probably more than young children, are prone to making decisions independently, particularly vis-à-vis their parents, though this can vary significantly across societies. Thus the dual coercive influences of parents and teachers have considerably less impact on the adult learner than on the child learner. As a result, not only are external motivational forces reduced, but, in addition, the incentives for participation in literacy programs may be entirely absent in developing countries.

While statistics on participation in literacy programs are far from adequate, official data on participation are often revealing (and disappointing) for providers of literacy services. It has been estimated, for example, that only one in ten Americans in need of basic skills training is receiving or has received such training as of 1990 (Kirsch & Jungeblut, 1986). In addition, the available evidence suggests that more than half the new adult literacy students in America drop out before completing two weeks of their program (Mickulecky & Drew, 1991). Similarly, it has been frequently reported that low participation rates are an important factor in the inability of many countries with significant adult literacy program investments to make significant progress toward improved adult literacy rates (Lind & Johnston, 1986).

Linguistic. It has been often assumed by national and international development agencies that the language learning characteristics of adults are roughly the same for children. Indeed, I have been unable to find much reference to a child-adult distinction in the policy arena. Generally speaking, UNESCO and literacy policy makers in numerous countries have assumed that, for efficient learning, it is preferable to teach adults (like children) in their native tongue rather than in a second language. The only caveat is that governments, putting learning efficiency aside, may prefer a second (usually metropolitan or European) language for the larger purposes of economic development. The research literature is surprisingly silent on the topic of first- and second-language and literacy learning in adults, even though there has been a heated debate concerning bilingual learning and the education of children.

In second-language learning (oral and aural skills), the available literature seems to be varied in its conclusions. Contrary to popular belief, many specialists believe that adults are faster at second-language learning than are children, particularly with respect to syntax and lexicon; by contrast, children may outdistance adults in learning proper pronunciation of a second language, since their muscular habits are less ingrained (McLaughlin, 1985; Skutnabb-Kangas & Toukomaa, 1976). Thus it is doubtful that adults should be considered "like children" in the domain of second-language learning, as they possess many more lexical items in their native language than do children, and have cognitive and metalinguistic skills that may make second-language learning far easier than it is for children.

The picture of language and literacy learning is even more uncertain with adults. Even if literacy learning in the native tongue is necessarily easier than in a second tongue (and this has yet to be substantiated convincingly in the research literature), it does not follow that adult literacy should always be taught in the native tongue. For example, the presumed cognitive advantage of learning a first literacy in one's native tongue may be small relative to the motivational aspects of learning to read in the second language (especially if the second language has special saliency in a given society). In the few studies that have looked at the preferred language of literacy in adult literacy programs, policy makers have often been surprised to find that many individuals prefer the metropolitan language to the relatively ineffective (for economic purposes) native tongue local language (Lind & Johnston, 1986; Wagner, 1998b).

In sum, linguistic factors in adult literacy acquisition are just beginning to be understood. In many countries—both industrialized and developing—the issue of "which language of literacy" is often bound up in a host of political issues. Often it is difficult to obtain objective information on adult preferences, as lobbyists tend to take opposing positions on the issue of language learning, with governments usually opting for "national" languages, and disadvantaged ethnic groups often opting for the importance of cultural strength, preservation, and resistance through literacy in the native tongue. As many have commented before, it appears to be the case that the scientific findings on the matter of language of literacy will likely be used by one faction or another to support their political agenda.

Cognitive. While there exists a vast literature on the cognitive and psychometric aspects of literacy acquisition in children, the opposite is true in studies of youth and adult literacy acquisition. Work is just beginning on establishing testing equivalencies among the varied standardized tests currently used in countries such as the United States. Since almost no direct assessment of adult skills (i.e., out-of-school literacy and basic skills) has taken place in developing countries, there is little basis upon which to form solid conclusions (see, however, a review in Wagner, 1998a; and a Uganda program evaluation in Okech, Carr-Hill, Kataboire, Kakooza, & Ndidde, 1999). As with language learning, it has usually been assumed (due to lack of relevant data) that adults learn literacy like children do, though perhaps faster or perhaps slower, depending on the research cited. It is often taken for granted, nonetheless, that adults can learn to read in "crash" courses in a matter of weeks or months in literacy campaigns (Arnove & Graff, 1987), even though it is usually assumed that children take years to do so.

POLICY AND LITERACY INSTRUCTION FOR CHILDREN, YOUTH, AND ADULTS

Considerable progress has been made in understanding the acquisition of literacy in children, youth, and adults, though primarily in industrialized societies. Far less is known about literacy acquisition in a truly global perspective and in multilingual societies. Since the bulk of nonliterate people live in these areas of the world, there is much more that needs to be known if we are to improve literacy provision in the coming decades. Similarly, we know almost nothing about the effectiveness of literacy programs in maintaining skills that are taught in the usually short-term programs utilized with adults. This whole area is one in which a greater understanding will be required before major gains will be achieved.

We can also see that there are certain similarities between adult learning and children's learning, such as in the early emphasis on letter learning and pronunciation. But important differences are also apparent. Perhaps most important is the observation that learning to read may have enormously different personal significance to adults than to children, who tend to be socialized by parents and teachers (and even coerced) into literacy. Motivation will depend greatly on these differing perceptions of literacy learning (cf. Verhoeven & Snow, 2001). Moreover, it has been claimed that adults learn through stages more or less like children, from decoding to comprehension (Chall, 1999). Yet there remains substantial disagreement in this area, as in the area of second-language and literacy learning. Until there is a more robust research base on adult literacy learning, credible policy-oriented conclusions will have to wait.

Instruction for Children

Initial reading is taught with remarkable homogeneity the world over, regardless of the language and orthography to be taught. Since the vast majority of world scripts are alphabetic, it is not surprising that the letters of the alphabet are emphasized as the first instructed step toward literacy. The one great exception is that of Chinese, which is a logography of pictorial symbols. Yet it is now standard practice in Chinese schools to first introduce written language in a phonetic form, rather than in pictographs (Taylor, 1999). Of course, the manner in which the alphabet is learned can be quite varied, yet there is a tendency, especially with young children, to emphasize memorization, rhyming, and prosodic recitation as a first way to introduce the script. Instruction of writing also shows similarities across various cultures and writing systems, often with an emphasis on the copying of letters.

Following these initial steps to literacy, there begins what in America is still called a "great debate" about best instructional methods. In fact, there are really various debates, though the most prominent is that described by Chall (1967), which expounds the virtues of the "phonics" or sounding-out methodology as most important to learning to read. Opponents suggest approaches that emphasize "whole language" or a greater focus on comprehension and enjoyment rather than what is seen as too much emphasis on the subskills of reading (such as correct pronunciation). This debate has been raised again more recently by Snow and colleagues (1998). Other debates revolve around such issues as the role of writing and how central it is to reading and literacy in general. Some specialists have suggested that careful writing instruction, building on the natural interests and abilities of children, is the best method to encourage broader literacy skills (Ferreiro & Teberosky, 1982).

Most of our understanding of children's reading instruction, as pointed out above, is heavily weighted toward those countries and languages that have been able to afford basic research on instructional questions, and the large majority of this work has focused on the English language. Clearly, much more needs to be known about best instructional practices in the world's various languages and scripts.

Instruction for Youth and Adults

Pedagogies for youth and adult literacy learners tend to be considerably more varied worldwide than those for children. This seems to be a function of the much more varied purposes of adult literacy and basic education than that of formal schooling (which, as noted earlier, seems to be remarkably similar across today's societies). I turn, therefore, to consider some varied purposes of literacy education. As noted earlier, adult basic education (also known as lifelong learning) typically refers to adults who already completed some formal education, usually primary schooling and some years of secondary schooling. In many countries (particularly in North America and Europe), this type of education focuses on the dropouts from the secondary school system, providing them with part-time coursework to complete a secondary or vocational education diploma. Because of the focus on completion of a formal degree, instruction in adult basic education tends to take the form of standard textbooks, which follow, with some adaptation, the basic subject matters of the (secondary) school curriculum.

There is an increasingly common perception among policy makers that the world is one giant, globalized economy, where the skills of a nation's workers may determine the overall health of national economic development. For this reason, among others, both the industrialized and the industrializing nations seem to have begun a competition to increase the basic skills of their work forces, as evidenced by the publication in the United States of a highly publicized report titled *High Skills or Low Wages: America's Choice* (Tucker, 1990), and in other countries as well (OECD, 2000). A debate in the adult literacy field centers on the transfer of literacy and basic skills. Some specialists have claimed that literacy is so "basic" a skill that it will transfer (and be useful) for a wide range of cognitive tasks, in the workplace, and in everyday life. Others have argued that the evidence to date does not support this assertion, in that skills taught in one type of workplace setting simply are not very useful in other settings (Mickulecky & Drew, 1991).

In developing countries, where research resources have been more scarce, the debate has centered more on which specific skills are most needed for which populations. For example, should breast-feeding mothers be given general courses to teach literacy (which is found to correlate with low infant mortality), or should resources for training be focused on specific pieces of knowledge, such as how to use baby formula if and when necessary? Overall, it is likely that this area of specific skill training in general, and adult literacy more specifically, will receive increased attention in coming years (Wagner, 2000).

CONCLUSION

In Dakar in 2000 the United Nations agencies gathered together to reaffirm their support for a worldwide initiative called "Education for All." Among the many goals set, one that has salience for the present discussion is that of reducing illiteracy by 50 percent in each country of the world by the year 2015. This would seem like a good, reasonable, and certainly laudable goal—if it were not remembered that very similar goals have been stated by the same agencies just about every decade since World War II. While few would debate the importance or urgency of this goal, such targets must confront an important reality—namely, that literacy is a cultural phenomenon; thus to change literacy dramatically is to change our cultures dramatically. On the latter score, there has been a notable resistance among people in many societies. What is needed, in my view, is a set of strategies that incorporate, and appeal to, the developmental, cultural, linguistic, and cognitive domains of individuals in each society—to promote avenues of literacy development that fit with developmental as well as social and cultural dimensions of everyday life. This should not (and will not) be achieved by attempting to confront individuals and social/ethnic groups in the name of a "literacy campaign," but rather through incentives that show individuals and groups the power that literacy can provide them in our ever-changing world.

REFERENCES

Arnove, R. F., & Graff, H. J. (Eds.). (1987). *National literacy campaigns*. New York: Plenum.

Barr, R., Kamil, M. L., Mosenthal, R. B., and Pearson, P. D. (Eds.). (1991). *Handbook of reading research*. Vol. 2. New York: Longman.

Bennett, J. A. H., & Berry, J. (1987). The future of Cree syllabic literacy in Northern Canada. In D. A. Wagner (Ed.), *The future of literacy in a changing world*. New York: Pergamon.

Bourdieu, P. (1977). *Outline of a theory of practice*. Cambridge: Cambridge University Press.

Chall, J. S. (1967). *Learning to read: The great debate*. New York: McGraw-Hill.

———. (1983). *Stages of reading development*. New York: McGraw-Hill.

———. (1999). Literacy learning in children and adults. In D. A. Wagner (Ed.), *The future of literacy in a changing world* (pp. 73–94). New York: Pergamon.

Coombs, P. H., & Ahmed, M. (1974). *Attacking rural poverty*. Baltimore: Johns Hopkins University Press.

Downing, J. (1973). *Comparative reading*. New York: Macmillan.

Elkof, B. (1987). Russian literacy campaigns, 1861–1939. In R. F. Arnove & H. J. Graff (Eds.), *National literacy campaigns* (pp. 123–146). New York: Plenum.

Engle, P. L. (1975). Language medium in early school years for minority language groups. *Review of Educational Research, 45,* 283–325.

Ferreiro, E., & Teberosky, A. (1982). Literacy before schooling. Exeter, N. H.: Heinemann.

Goody, J. (Ed.). (1968). *Literacy in traditional societies.* Cambridge: Cambridge University Press.

Gray, W. S. (1956). *The teaching of reading and writing.* Paris: UNESCO.

Greaney, V., Khandker, S. R., & Alam, M. (1999). *Bangladesh: Assessing basic learning skills.* Washington, DC: World Bank.

Hakuta, K. (1986). *Mirror of language: The debate on bilingualism:* New York: Basic Books.

Johansson, E. (1987). Literacy campaigns in Sweden. In R. J. Arnova & H. Graff (Eds.), *National literacy campaigns: Historical and comparative perspectives.* New York: Plenum.

Kirsch, I., & Jungeblut, A. (1986). *Literacy: Profiles of America's young adults.* Final report of the National Assessment of Educational Progress. Princeton, NJ: Educational Testing Service.

Lauglo, J. (2001). *Engaging with adults.* Washington, DC: World Bank.

Lind, A., & Johnston, A. (1986). *Adult literacy in the Third World: A review of objectives and strategies.* Stockholm: Swedish International Development Agency.

McLaughlin, B. (1985). *Second language learning in childhood* (2nd ed.) Hillsdale, NJ: Erlbaum.

Mickulecky, L., & Drew, R. (1991). Basic literacy skills in the workplace. In R. Barr, M. L. Kamil, R. B. Mosenthal, & P. D. Pearson (Eds.), *Handbook of reading research* (Vol. 2, pp. 669–689). New York: Longman.

OECD/Statistics Canada. (2000). *Literacy in the information age.* Paris: OECD.

Ogbu, J. U. (1980). Literacy in subordinate cultures: The case of Black Americans. Paper presented at the Literacy Conference of the Library of Congress, Washington, DC.

Okech, A., Carr-Hill, R. A., Kataboire, A. R., Kakooza, T., & Ndidde, A. N. (1999). *Evaluation of the functional literacy programme in Uganda 1999.* Kampala: Ministry of Gender, Labour, and Social Development/World Bank.

Olson, D. R., & Torrance, N. (Eds.). (2001). *The making of literate societies.* London: Blackwell.

Pearson, P. D. (Ed.). (1984). *Handbook of reading research.* New York: Longman.

Resnick, D. P., & Resnick, L. B. (1989). Varieties of literacy. In A. E. Barnes & P. N. Stearns (Eds.), *Social history and issues in human consciousness: Some interdisciplinary connections* (pp. 171–196). New York: New York University Press.

Scribner, S., & Cole, M. (1981). *The psychology of literacy.* Cambridge, MA: Harvard University Press.

Skutnabb-Kangas, T., & Toukomaa, P. (1976). *Teaching migrant children's mother tongue and learning the language of the host country in the context of the socio-cultural situation of the migrant family.* Helsinki: Finnish National Commission for UNESCO.

Snow, C. E., Burns, M. S., & Griffin, P. (Eds.). (1998). *Preventing reading difficulties in young children.* Washington, DC: National Research Council.

Stevenson, H. W., Stigler, J. W., Lucker, G. W., Lee, S., Hsu, C. C., & Kitamura, S. (1982). Reading disabilities: The case of Chinese, Japanese, and English. *Child Development, 33,* 1164–1181.

Street, B. V. (1999). The meanings of literacy. In D. A. Wagner, R. L. Venezky, & B. V. Street (Eds.), *Literacy: An international handbook*. Boulder, CO: Westview.

————. (2001). *Literacy and development: Ethnographic perspectives*. London: Routledge.

Sulzby, E., & Teale, W. (1991). Emergent literacy. In R. Barr, M. L. Kamil, R. B. Mosenthal, & P. D. Pearson (Eds.), *Handbook of reading research* (Vol. 2, pp. 727–758). New York: Longman.

Taylor, I. (1999). Literacy in China, Korea and Japan. In D. A. Wagner, R. L. Venezky, & B. V. Street (Eds.), *Literacy: An international handbook* (pp. 423–428). Boulder, CO: Westview.

Tucker, M. (1990). *America's Choice: High Skills or Low Wages*. Washington D. C.: National Center on Education and the Economy.

UNESCO. (1953). The use of vernacular languages in education. *Monograph on fundamental education* (No. 8). Paris: UNESCO.

————. (1990). *World declaration on education for all* (Appendix 1). New York: United Nations.

————. (2000). *Final report of the World Education Forum*. Dakar. Paris: UNESCO.

United Nations Development Programme. (2002). *Human development report*. New York: Oxford University Press.

Venezky, R. L. (1991). The development of literacy in the industrialized nations of the West. In R. Barr, M. L. Kamil, P. B. Mosenthal, & P. D. Pearson (Eds.), *Handbook of reading research* (Vol. 2, pp. 46–67). New York: Longman.

Verhoeven, L., & Snow, C. (2001). *Literacy and motivation: Reading engagement in individuals and groups*. Mahwah, NJ: Erlbaum.

Wagner, D. A. (1991). Literacy as culture: Emic and etic perspectives. In E. M. Jennings & A. C. Purves (Eds.), *Literate systems and individual lives: Perspectives on literacy and schooling* (pp. 11–22). Albany: State University of New York Press.

————. (1992). *Literacy: Developing the future*. UNESCO Yearbook of Education, 1992, Vol. 43. Paris: UNESCO.

————. (1993). *Literacy, culture, and development: Becoming literate in Morocco*. New York: Cambridge University Press.

————. (1998a). *Literacy assessment for out-of-school youth and adults: Concepts, methods, and new directions*. ILI/UNESCO Technical Report. Philadelphia: International Literacy Institute, University of Pennsylvania.

————. (1998b). Putting second language first: Language and literacy learning in Morocco. In A. Durgunoglu & L. Verhoeven (Eds.). *Acquiring literacy in two languages* (pp. 169–184). Mahwah, NJ: Erlbaum.

————. (1999). Indigenous education and literacy learning. In D. A. Wagner, R. L. Venezky, & B. L. Street (Eds.), *Literacy: An international handbook* (pp. 283–287). Boulder, CO: Westview.

————. (2000). "Literacy and Adult Education." Global thematic review prepared for the UN World Education Forum, Dakar, Senegal. Paris: UNESCO. (Reprinted in *Adult Education and Development*, Bonn: IIZ/DVV, in English, French, Spanish.)

Wagner, D. A., Venezky, R. L., & Street, B. V. (Eds.). (1999). *Literacy: An international handbook*. Boulder, CO: Westview.

PART II

Childcare and Parenting

CHAPTER 5

Social Contexts of Weaning: The Importance of Cross-Cultural Studies

Hillary N. Fouts

Cross-cultural studies of child development are important because many Western developmental theories are based solely upon studies of Western children, despite their claims of universal relevance. Studies of small-scale cultures are important in evaluating the relevance of Western theories and also help to illuminate patterns that may be representative of our evolutionary past, because humans have spent approximately 99 percent of their existence living as small-scale hunter-gatherers; only around 10,000 years ago did a transition to other modes and methods of subsistence occur (Phillipson, 1993).

Weaning is an interesting topic because it has implications for several psychological, evolutionary, and anthropological theories (e.g., Ainsworth, 1967; Draper & Harpending, 1987; Hawkes, O'Connell, & Blurton-Jones, 1997; Trivers, 1974). Although many hypotheses about the social and emotional transitions of weaning exist, most researchers have focused their studies on weanling infants' health, counting calories, and calculating the health costs to infants (Clemens, Stanton, Stoll, Shahid, Banu, & Chowdhury, 1986; Gomendio, 1991; Lee, 1987; Lee, Majluf, & Gordon, 1991; Rao & Kanade, 1992).

Weaning has been of popular and academic interest for some time. The timing and health consequences of weaning (Clemens et al., 1986; Cunningham, 1995; Dettwyler, 1995; Habicht, DaVanzo, & Butz, 1986; Harrison, Brush, & Zumrawi, 1992; Lee, 1987; Lee et al., 1991; Martines, Habicht, Ashworth, & Kirkwood, 1994; Nerlove, 1974; Rao & Kanade, 1992) and maternal decision-making (Akin, 1985; Albino & Thompson, 1956; Chowning, 1985; Gray, 1996; Nardi, 1985) have attracted the most attention, whereas the social and emotional components of weaning have rarely been studied systematically despite great theoretical interest (Ainsworth, 1967; Albino & Thompson, 1956; Altmann, 1980; Erikson, 1950; Freud, 1940; Trivers, 1974).

Weaning is more than the physical cessation of breast-feeding; it also marks a social transition. In this chapter I present a discussion of why these social aspects of weaning are important to study cross-culturally. I discuss the importance of viewing weaning cross-culturally by addressing three topics in the "Weaning Compared" section: weaning age, adult- versus child-led weaning, and caregiving contexts of weaning. Within each topic, I discuss several Western scholarly views, differences between these views and the reality of weaning among the Bofi foragers and farmers of Central Africa, and some evolutionary perspectives on various social aspects of weaning.

Throughout this chapter I draw upon quantitative and qualitative data collected during thirteen months of fieldwork among two small-scale populations, Bofi foragers and Bofi farmers. These data were collected for a larger study of weaning, part of which was presented in my dissertation (Fouts, 2002). In this study, I set out to systematically document the social and emotional behavior of weanling children and their caregivers, through observations of twenty-one Bofi farmer children and twenty-two Bofi forager children. Although these samples are small in number, the children were observed using an on-the-mark regimen spanning nine hours of observation (1,080 observational intervals) per child. Taken together, the Bofi farmer children were observed for 189 hours and the Bofi forager children for 194 hours. The behaviors of the farmer and forager children were recorded on a behavioral checklist including categories of child state (e.g., awake, asleep), child-caregiver visual orientation, child attachment behaviors (e.g., reaches for caregiver), child emotional states (e.g., laughing, crying, aggressive), child-caregiver social interactions (e.g., vocalizations, play), child feeding (e.g., nursing, child feeds self), caregiving behaviors (e.g., washing, clothing), caregiver responsiveness (e.g., soothing, scolding), child-caregiver physical positioning (e.g., level of proximity, touching, holding), and maternal work. Parents and other adults were also asked about demographic factors, as well as about such topics as methods and timing of weaning, child reactions to weaning, alloparenting, and birth spacing and fertility. More thorough descriptions of the data collection and analyses are included in my dissertation.

THE BOFI FARMERS AND FORAGERS

The Bofi farmers and foragers provide an interesting case for cross-cultural comparison because they live in the same natural ecology and speak the same language but have very different childcare and cultural practices and are ethnically distinct (Fouts, in press).

Natural Ecology

The Bofi farmers and foragers live in tropical regions of the northern Congo Basin rainforest in the southwest of the Central African Republic. The Bofi foragers subsist primarily through hunting (mostly with large nets) and gathering in the rain forest. A few of the forager families also have small gardens. Similar to other net-hunting foragers (such as the Aka and Mbuti described by Bahuchet [1985] and Hewlett [1996]), Bofi adults and children participate in net-hunting. Bofi forager men, however, also hunt using crossbows, small net traps, and wire traps. Both men and women gather in the forest, though women do the majority of the daily gathering and men solely collect honey. The Bofi foragers collect many species of caterpillars, termites, grubs, snails, wild yams, mushrooms, nuts, and leaves (especially *koko, Gnetum* species), and gain a large portion of their carbohydrates through trade with the Bofi farmers.

The Bofi farmers subsist primarily through "slash and burn" horticulture. Their main crop is manioc, and they also grow coffee, maize, peanuts, tobacco, yams, taro, okra, squash, and a variety of fruits. Farmer men also hunt in the forest using shotguns and snares, and women gather leaves, insects, and mushrooms from time to time; however, the farmers attain most of these forest products through trade with the Bofi foragers. Bofi farmer men usually camp in the forest when they are hunting, and farmer women occasionally stay in forager camps to collect *koko* and caterpillars as well as to trade for them.

Bofi farmer men are responsible for burning fields and for much of the clearing of fields, whereas women perform the majority of the tasks involved in farming, including planting, weeding, harvesting, processing the food grown, as well as clearing some of the fields. Men spend the majority of their time involved in intervillage trading, socializing and politicking within the village, and hunting. Bofi farmer men and women spend most days separately, with women and children mostly in the fields or processing manioc near the fields and men in the village.

Demography

Table 5.1 compares demographic features among the Bofi farmers and foragers. Interestingly, the Bofi farmers and foragers have similar total fertility rates (TFRs) despite their differences in interbirth intervals (IBIs). However, the Bofi farmer TFR has much higher variance (12.38) than the Bofi forager TFR (4.34). In accordance with this finding, Bofi farmer women frequently reported experiencing fertility problems related to sexually transmitted diseases. The Bofi farmer and forager weaning ages (18–24 months and 36–54 months, respectively) coincide with their IBIs, as well as with patterns among other farmers (LeVine, Dixon, LeVine, Richman, Leiderman, Keefer, & Brazelton, 1996) and foragers (Hewlett, 1991). Many anthropologists have proposed that in prehistory, IBIs decreased, along with weaning ages, during demographic transitions from hunting and gathering to food-producing lifeways, due to the availability of easily digestible, calorie-rich foods that could be used to wean children (Ellison, 2001; Hassan, 1979; Larsen, 1995).

Table 5.1
Demographics

	Bofi Farmers *n*=662	Bofi Foragers *n*=318
TFR[a]	5.32	5.54
IBI[b]	2-3 years	3-5 years
Infant Mortality Rate[c]	20.30%	18.80%
Child Mortality Rate[d]	30.60%	40.60%
Monogamous marriages	88.00%	90.38%
Polygynous Marriages	12.00%	9.62%

[a]Total Fertility Rate.
[b]Interbirth Interval.
[c]Birth to 12 months.
[d]Birth to 15 years of age.

Social Organization

The Bofi farmers and foragers have similar infant mortality rates and different child mortality rates (see Table 5.1), perhaps due to the fact that Bofi farmers tend to utilize local pharmacies and hospitals with Western medicine more often than the foragers.

The Bofi farmers and foragers have very similar polygyny rates (see Table 5.1). The Bofi farmers have much lower polygyny rates than other African farming groups (Hewlett, 1991; LeVine & LeVine, 1966), which is perhaps indicative of the low level of wealth accumulation in the villages included in this study. For example, in the two villages studied, the majority of crops were for family consumption and intravillage exchange, and very few individuals sold coffee to national or international companies, which is common in larger nearby villages.

The Bofi farmers and foragers live in close proximity and interact daily in social, economic, and spiritual settings. They are well aware of each others' lifestyles and have access to the same materials and food. Both the Bofi farmers and foragers live patrilocally and are organized into patriclans called *zim*. They are also both exogamous (not marrying within one's own clan).

The Bofi foragers are loosely organized into patriclans, and are patrilocal, though they live patrilocally only after matrilocal bride-service, which usually includes the first two to seven years of marriage. Many couples continue to live matrilocally after bride-service. The Bofi foragers are egalitarian, minimizing any forms of rank including age deference, and thus do not select chiefs. Along with egalitarianism, independence and personal autonomy are highly valued and respected among the Bofi foragers. Because individuals are not given particular rank and power, people also do not sanction the actions of other individuals but respect personal autonomy and independence.

In contrast to the foragers, the Bofi farmers are strictly patrilocal and patri-lineal, and are organized under village and clan chiefs. Respect and deference exist among the farmers and are patterned by an age hierarchy. Accordingly, older individuals punish younger individuals; for example, a seven-year-old may scold her four- or five-year-old sister for misbehaving.

Communalism, putting the interests of one's clan above the interests of indi-viduals, is also a core value among the Bofi farmers. Clans often decide or recommend whom individuals should marry or whether divorce is or is not ap-propriate. Clan chiefs are responsible for settling marriage-related disputes such as disputes over bride-prices and proper marriage patterns (e.g., exogamy).

Childcare

Among Bofi foragers, parent-child relationships in infancy and early child-hood entail high levels of physical contact and holding by both mothers and fathers. Typically, Bofi forager parents hold infants and young children (ages three and under) extensively even when they are working or when the children have fallen asleep. Throughout the day, parents often take turns carrying children in the side-sling.

Starting around two and a half to three years of age, forager children are in-termittently left with adult alloparents (caregivers other than a child's mother or father; e.g., aunts, grandparents) when their parents go to the forest. How-ever, if children protest their parents' leave-taking with intense crying, parents often decide to carry the children with them. Generally, forager children between the ages of three and seven years stay in camp during the day and are left in the care of adult alloparents.

Respect for personal autonomy between forager parents and children is dem-onstrated by the absence of corporal punishment and verbal negations. For ex-ample, children are not punished when they do not comply with parental requests or demands. Occasionally, forager parents speak firmly or raise their voices, but this usually has little effect on children's behavior.

Bofi farmer mothers are the primary caregivers of infants and children under the age of two years. The secondary caregiver is often an older female sibling. In caregiving interviews, the majority of farmer parents stated that mothers and adolescent siblings performed almost all caregiving responsibilities, although many farmer parents also noted that fathers often paid for medicines when the children became ill. Bofi farmer mothers do not hold infants and young chil-dren (under the age of three) as often as forager parents do; farmer mothers of-ten put their infants and young children down on mats and beds while they work or when the children sleep during the day.

Bofi farmer children between the ages of one and a half and six years usually stay in the village during the day. Although fathers may be around the village also, they usually have little contact with their children. The children in the village are frequently involved in multiage, multisex playgroups. These playgroups often roam throughout the village during the day. Two- and three-year-olds frequently have designated alloparents, usually older sisters or female cousins, during the day. Children over the age of three years do not usually have designated alloparents, but older sisters often give them food.

Among the Bofi farmers, children are commonly disciplined, as they are often swatted and spanked for misbehaving. Furthermore, farmer parents frequently use fear to modify their children's behavior; for example, parents and alloparents often purposely evoke fear in children about strangers and places perceived as dangerous, such as the forest.

Weaning Practices

Even before weaning, Bofi farmer children were very reliant on solid food, nursing infrequently. Bofi farmer weaning was initiated by mothers. Starting on a specific morning, mothers usually covered their nipples with red fingernail polish, and/or a bandage to resemble a wound. The mothers then wore their wound simulation for several days in order to make the children afraid to nurse. Bofi farmer mothers reported that this method was very effective and ended breast-feeding quickly. Once weaning was initiated, mothers usually gave children rice or rice gruel (containing rice, sugar, and milk) as a special weaning food. These weaning methods were implemented when children were between eighteen and twenty-four months of age.

As reported by mothers and observed, the majority of Bofi forager children were not weaned by their mothers but instead stopped nursing without overt intervention by their caregivers. Bofi forager mothers all reported that they did not prepare special weaning foods, and that weanling children ate normal adult foods. Bofi forager parents most often reported that their children stopped nursing because their mothers were pregnant, sometimes explaining that pregnancy caused mothers' milk to taste "bad." Bofi forager children typically stopped nursing between the ages of three and four years. Like Bofi farmer children, they were already relying heavily on solid foods, and nursed infrequently prior to the actual cessation of nursing.

WEANING COMPARED

Western images of weaning often contradict weaning patterns in the non-Western world (for a thorough review, see Fouts, 2002; Fouts, Hewlett, & Lamb, 2001). Many of these inconsistencies stem from the fact that weaning in the West differs in many ways from weaning in small-scale cultures. In this section I discuss three topics that often are looked at differently in the Western and non-

Western world: weaning age, who leads weaning (adult or child), and caregiving contexts of weaning.

Weaning Age

American infants are usually weaned before six months of age, even though the American Academy of Pediatrics (1997) recommends at least twelve months of breast-feeding. By contrast, weaning usually occurs in toddlerhood among small-scale groups, with weaning typically occurring among hunter-gatherers between the ages of three and four years, and between one and two years among small-scale food-producers (Ellison, 2001; Konner, 1977). Weaning has different physiological and social implications for infants and toddlers.

Physiological factors. As stated previously, nutrition is one of the most popular topics of weaning studies; most researchers address the nutritional loss to weanling infants and issues involving the contamination of supplementary food (Clemens et al., 1986; Harrison et al., 1992; Martines et al., 1994). Weaning two-, three-, or four-year-olds, however, has different nutritional implications than infant weaning because most toddlers can eat solid food, and often already rely heavily on it prior to weaning. For example, Bofi forager and farmer children were eating the same foods as adults and were no longer nutritionally dependent on nursing, as illustrated by their low preweaning nursing frequencies.

A minority of Bofi farmer mothers reported that they were pregnant when they weaned their last child, whereas the majority of Bofi forager mothers reportedly were pregnant when their child stopped nursing. Furthermore, weaning among the farmers coincides with the cessation of mothers transporting children to the fields. Although no physiological data were collected in this study, these behavioral patterns may suggest that farmer mothers may be increasing their ability to become pregnant by the cessation of both nursing and transporting children. Weaning among the Bofi foragers seems to have less to do with trying to become pregnant, as this usually happens prior to weaning.

Social factors. Clearly, weaning a toddler who is able to verbally express his or her thoughts and feelings is not the same as weaning an infant. Toddlers may react to weaning in different ways than infants; for example, one Bofi farmer mother described how during weaning her son incessantly asked for "everything," including soda, candy, and items of clothing. A Bofi forager mother described how her child stopped nursing because he played with other children frequently and he returned less and less to nurse, eventually "forgetting" about nursing. Despite this Bofi forager mother's depiction, behavioral data showed that overall, Bofi forager children did not spend increasing amounts of time with other juveniles through the weaning process. Instead, nursing, preweaning, and weaned children spent similar amounts of time with juveniles. In contrast, Bofi farmer children spent proportionally more time with juveniles (rather than adults) after weaning than prior to weaning, which is indicative of the caregiving transition that paralleled weaning.

Several theorists have noted that weaning often parallels social transitions. Altmann (1980) explained that weaning often denotes a transition to increasing social independence. Konner (1976a) similarly described how !Kung infants, beginning at the end of the first year, began to show interest in other juveniles, and by the time of weaning (three to four years of age) children had graduated from close relationships with their mothers to close relationships with other juveniles. Konner (1976b) proposed that multiage, multisex playgroups promote children's reproductive fitness, because the younger children can practice sexual and agonistic behaviors while older children practice parental behaviors that are beneficial to their reproductive success. Konner (1976a) described how !Kung children move into closer relationships with other juveniles, beginning after twelve months of age and continuing through the weaning process. Interestingly, only the Bofi farmer pattern was consistent with Konner's descriptions of the !Kung, as Bofi forager weaning did not seem to mark a transition to greater time spent with juveniles.

Adult- versus Child-Led Weaning

Adult-led weaning is the most common type of weaning discussed in the scholarly literature. Furthermore, weaning is typically assumed to be initiated by mothers (Ainsworth, 1967; Albino & Thompson, 1956; Bateson, 1994; Daly & Wilson, 1988; Trivers, 1974). Self-weaning, or child-led weaning, is seldom mentioned in the scholarly literature, although some such examples have been described. For example, Efe forager mothers from Central Africa told Ivey (1993) that children typically decided to cease breast-feeding on their own. Similarly, Conton (1985) indicated that the ideal weaning practice among the Usino of Papua New Guinea involved child-led weaning, although in most cases Usino mothers initiated weaning by putting chili pepper or ginger on their nipples or by leaving their children at home while they traveled.

Weaning practices and the timing of weaning have been documented in many cultures (Ainsworth, 1967; Akin, 1985; Albino & Thompson, 1956; Chowning, 1985; Conton, 1985; Cosminsky, 1985; Gray, 1996; Ivey, 1993; LeVine & LeVine, 1966; Mead, 1935; Millard & Graham, 1985; Minturn & Hitchcock, 1966; Nardi, 1985; Shostak, 1981). Most descriptions of weaning in the literature illustrate how mothers deliberately weaned children by sending weanlings away to relatives' houses temporarily ("weaning doula") or by covering their nipples with unpalatable substances (such as bitter juices and hot peppers) to end breast-feeding within a few days (Ainsworth, 1967; Albino & Thompson, 1956; Gray, 1996; LeVine & LeVine, 1966; Mead, 1935; Raphael & Davis, 1985). Bofi farmer

weaning is therefore quite typical of patterns in other small-scale food produc-
ing groups, where mothers initiated weaning and made their nipples seem unfit
to nurse.

Child-led weaning has different implications than adult-led weaning and
raises interesting questions that have not been previously addressed in the literature. For example, what factors influence a child to stop nursing? Perhaps
the reproductive strategy of the child dictates so, or perhaps external social
pressures are directed at children. Does child-led weaning occur in different
natural and social ecologies than adult-led weaning? For example, in cultures
in which child initiative is valued (e.g., lack of age deference) as among the
Bofi foragers, child-led weaning may be more feasible than in cultures with
strong age deference (e.g., the Bofi farmers). Bofi forager children often take
initiative in other situations (e.g., deciding to help or not help their parents
collect food), whereas Bofi farmer children are often directed by parents and
scolded when they do not comply. The systematic evaluation of these questions is beyond the scope of this chapter, but these questions illustrate how
the typical way Western scholars view weaning (e.g., as adult-led) restricts the
questions that they ask. More cross-cultural studies would enrich and expand
the factors considered in studies of nursing and weaning. The Bofi forager and
farmer weaning patterns suggest that much variability exists in child behavior
(Fouts, 2002), even in similar natural ecologies, suggesting that both cultural
and biological factors may be influential.

Evolutionary perspectives on child-led weaning. What contexts are necessary in order
for self-weaning to coincide with a child's reproductive interests? Altmann's
elaboration (1980) of Trivers's parent-offspring conflict theory (1974) can be applied
to the occurrence of child-led weaning. Trivers's parent-offspring conflict theory was
one of the first to depict children as active agents seeking to secure their own survival,
rather than as passive recipients of parental investment. Trivers argued that children
cannot afford to wait and thus from the moment of conception must contrive to
coerce their parents to invest in them, in order to enhance the offspring's reproductive
interests. Offspring inevitably seek more investment than parents are willing or able
to provide, and thus parent-offspring conflict arises out of disagreement within the
dyad over the optimal level of parental investment. Trivers predicted that conflicts
would occur whenever a parent decreased investment in a child, such as at the time
of weaning; this evidently assumes that mothers initiate weaning. Trivers suggested
that, by weaning, a mother may seek to promote her own reproductive fitness by
conceiving another offspring, whereas the child is still trying to elicit further
investment in order to enhance his or her own fitness.

Konner (1977), like Trivers, describes how weanlings should be expected to
exhibit distress in order to elicit further parental investment in competition with
their younger unborn sibling. Furthermore, he explains how children overcome

this competition and begin to "desire" younger siblings because their siblings possess replicas of their genes and thus promote the weanlings' inclusive fitness. From this point of view, Konner posed a question: "At what age and in what circumstances can children be expected to desire younger siblings, if they have none?" (1977, p. 83). This question is essentially the same question as I have posed in regard to self-weaning: What contexts are necessary in order for self-weaning to coincide with a child's reproductive interests? This is so because, in cases such as the Bofi foragers, mothers are pregnant during weaning and therefore a lack of weaning distress and the presence of self-weaning are likely to promote the reproductive fitness of the unborn offspring. Furthermore, this pattern of child-led weaning allows mothers to easily reallocate energy to the younger offspring. Therefore, child-led weaning may have similar effects as "desiring" younger siblings.

Although Altmann (1980) described marked weanling distress among baboon infants, she cautioned that conflicts of interest between mothers and children do not necessarily lead to conflict characterized by emotional distress and temper tantrums. Instead, Altmann suggested that the resolution to mother-child conflicts depends upon the net cost of the alternative ways of resolving the conflict. For example, do the energetic and social costs of a temper tantrum outweigh the potential benefit of greater parental investment? Altmann showed that a temper tantrum may mean the loss of both feeding and social interaction to baboon infants. Furthermore, Altmann suggested that cooperation and compromise are important elements in the mother-child relationships and are also used to resolve conflicts.

Child-led weaning may well represent a calm resolution of parent-offspring conflict. For example, there may be subtle cues from mothers and other individuals indicating that children should stop nursing, and in certain contexts self-weaning may be the least costly strategy. For example, when the loss of nursing does not have negative health consequences, there may be no great benefit to continued nursing, as a four-year-old's nutritional needs have well surpassed what he or she can gain from nursing alone. Such four-year-olds may gain more benefits by allowing their mothers to reallocate their energy toward younger siblings, thereby increasing their own inclusive fitness. Furthermore, social and reproductive benefits may occur with weaning, as it may provide more opportunities for children to engage in juvenile groups. As reviewed previously, Konner (1976b) suggested that juvenile playgroups enhance the reproductive success of younger and older members of these groups. The Bofi forager weaning pattern was not consistent with Konner's description, however, because weaned children did not spend significantly more time in close proximity to juveniles than did nursing children. Perhaps broader social transitions are not evident among recently weaned four-year-olds but would be evident among older children.

Caregiving Contexts of Weaning

Western images of weaning tend to assume that weaning exclusively involves mothers and children. In the non-Western world, however, fathers and extended kin often play important roles throughout development and are therefore likely to play important roles in weaning as well (Betzig & Turke, 1992; Flinn, 1992; Harkness & Super, 1992; Hawkes et al., 1997; Hewlett, 1991; Lancaster, 1984).

Siblings are the most commonly identified alloparents in the ethnographic literature (Hrdy, 1999; McKenna, 1987; Weisner, 1987). According to McKenna (1987), the various benefits to siblings and other juvenile caregivers include learning to parent and displaying caregiving skills to attract mates. Among the Bofi farmers, siblings and juvenile cousins are indeed the most common alloparents. After weaning, Bofi farmer children were no longer held by mothers and received the majority of their care from other juveniles (for sibling care, see also Maynard, this volume). As Bofi farmer children came to experience less intimate contact with, and physical care from, their mothers and other adults as they were weaned, they spent increasing amounts of time with juveniles. Similar transitions have been observed in other farming groups (LeVine, this volume; LeVine et al., 1996; Weisner, 1987), and among the !Kung (Konner, 1976a). In contrast, among the Bofi foragers, sibling alloparents were uncommon and children continued to receive intimate adult care throughout the weaning process.

Lancaster (1984) proposed that human fathers tend to be uninvolved in infant care and become more involved in offspring care in early childhood around the time of weaning. Bofi farmer fathers were uninvolved in physical childcare through the weaning process. However, many Bofi forager fathers showed high involvement (sometimes equal to maternal care) with children close to weaning and weaned children. Interestingly, Bofi forager fathers appeared less involved with high-frequency nursing children (as depicted by frequencies of holding).

Grandmothers have also been identified as important caregivers. Hawkes and colleagues (1997) proposed in this context that grandmothers (or other related postmenopausal women) may provide considerable resources to weaned children. This hypothesis is based upon the further hypothesis that fathers do not provision their children sufficiently, but instead hunt in order to attract extramarital mates. According to Hawkes and colleagues, this situation makes grandmother provisioning especially important when mothers are nursing and carrying young infants, because mothers are less capable of providing food and care to weaned children at that time. Provisioning by grandmothers is thought to increase a child's chance of survival and allow mothers to decrease interbirth intervals, thereby enhancing both the mothers' and grandmothers' reproductive fitness (Hawkes et al., 1997).

Grandmother help during weaning is described quite commonly in the ethnographic literature. As mentioned above, mothers in some cultures send children to their grandparents' house in order to wean them (Ainsworth, 1967; Raphael & Davis, 1985). Few grandmothers or aunts were involved in childcare among the Bofi farmers, but there were several highly involved grandmothers and aunts among the Bofi foragers. Grandmothers and aunts were especially involved with weaned children whose mothers were pregnant or had a young infant. Despite the widespread awareness of father, grandmother, and sibling care, however, developmental studies continue to emphasize the mother-child dyad, thereby implying that mothers are the only important caregivers throughout the weaning process. The Bofi farmer and forager patterns illustrate how important it is to consider the role of nonmaternal caregivers in the weaning process.

Summary

Weaning age. Weaning has typically been addressed by Western scholars in regard to infants, presumably because of the health risks involved. Toddler-age weaning is much less commonly discussed, yet is most common in non-Western cultures. Weaning in toddlerhood holds different physiological and social implications, especially because children are less reliant on nursing at the time of weaning and because of their ability to express themselves. Juvenile interactions were especially important in the Bofi farmer pattern, whereas among Bofi forager children weaning did not parallel a transition to increased time spent with other juveniles.

Child-led weaning. In the Western scholarly literature, it is typically assumed that mothers initiate weaning, and child-led weaning is rarely addressed. Altmann's elaboration (1980) of parent-offspring theory (Trivers, 1974) provides grounds to discuss why children may not resist weaning and, furthermore, perhaps wean themselves. Several factors may be associated with child-led weaning, including cultural values (such as age egalitarianism) that do not discourage child initiative, negligible nutritional dependence on nursing, and reproductive fitness benefits of weaning.

Caregiving context. Weaning is often assumed to be a mother-child event, as the roles of other caregivers are rarely addressed. The Bofi farmer and forager weanling caregiving contexts both illustrate how nonmaternal care is important throughout the weaning process. Among the Bofi farmers, juvenile care is prevalent after weaning when adult physical care ceases. In contrast, the Bofi forager children receive care from fathers, grandmothers, and aunts, rather than juveniles. These two distinct weanling caregiving patterns illustrate the necessity of considering the overall social context of weaning in order to understand variability in weaning patterns.

NOTE

I offer my thanks to the Bofi farmer and forager families for kindly tolerating my long observations and frequent questions. I am grateful to the government of the Central African Republic and the ECOFAC Ngotto forest project for authorizing this research. I would also like to thank Michael Lamb and Barry Hewlett for comments on earlier drafts of this paper. The research was supported by the National Institute of Child Health and Human Development.

REFERENCES

Ainsworth, M. D. S. (1967). *Infancy in Uganda*. Baltimore: Johns Hopkins University Press.

Akin, K. G. (1985). Women's work and infant feeding: Traditional and transitional practices on Malaita, Solomon Islands. In L. Marshall (Ed.), *Infant care and feeding in the South Pacific* (pp. 207–234). New York: Gordon & Breach.

Albino, R., & Thompson, V. J. (1956). The effects of sudden weaning on Zulu children. *Journal of Medical Psychology, 3–4*, 178–207.

Altmann, J. (1980). *Baboon mothers and infants*. Cambridge, MA: Harvard University Press.

American Academy of Pediatrics. (1997). Breastfeeding and the use of human milk. *Pediatrics, 100* (6), 1035–1039.

Bahuchet, S. (1985). *Pygmées Aka et la forêt centrafricaine: Ethnologie écologique* [Aka Pygmies and the central African forest: An ecological ethnology]. Paris: Selaf.

Bateson, P. (1994). The dynamics of parent-offspring relationships in mammals. *Trends in Evolutionary Ecology, 9* (10), 399–403.

Betzig, L., & Turke, P. (1992). Fatherhood by rank on Ifaluk. In B. S. Hewlett (Ed.), *Father-child relations: Cultural and biosocial contexts* (pp. 111–130). New York: Aldine de Gruyter.

Chowning, A. (1985). Patterns of infant feeding in Kove. In L. Marshall (Ed.), *Infant care and feeding in the South Pacific* (pp. 171–188). New York: Gordon & Breach.

Clemens, J. D., Stanton, B., Stoll, B., Shahid, N. S., Banu, H., & Chowdhury, A. K. (1986). Breast feeding as a determinant of severity in shigellosis. *American Journal of Epidemiology, 123*, 710–720.

Conton, L. (1985). Social, economic, and ecological parameters of infant feeding in Usino, Papua New Guinea. In L. Marshall (Ed.), *Infant care and feeding in the South Pacific* (pp. 97–120). New York: Gordon & Breach.

Cosminsky, S. (1985). Infant feeding practices in rural Kenya. In V. Hull & M. Simposon (Eds.), *Breastfeeding, child health, and child spacing: Cross-cultural perspectives* (pp. 35–54). New Hampshire: Croom Helm.

Cunningham, A. S. (1995). Breast-feeding: Adaptive behavior for child health and longevity. In P. Stuart-Macadam & K. A. Dettwyler (Eds.), *Breast-feeding: Biocultural perspectives* (pp. 243–264). New York: Aldine de Gruyter.

Daly, M., & Wilson, M. (1988). *Homicide*. New York: Aldine de Gruyter.

Dettwyler, K. A. (1995). A time to wean: The hominid blueprint for the natural age of weaning in modern human populations. In P. Stuart-Macadam & K. A. Dettwyler (Eds.), *Breast-feeding: Biocultural perspectives* (pp. 39–73). New York: Aldine de Gruyter.

Draper, P., & Harpending, H. (1987). Parental investment and the child's environment. In J. B. Lancaster, J. Altmann, A. S. Rossi, & L. R. Sherrod (Eds.), *Parenting across the life span: Biosocial dimensions* (pp. 207–236). New York: Aldine de Gruyter.

Ellison, P. T. (2001). *On fertile ground: A natural history of human reproduction.* Cambridge, MA: Harvard University Press.

Erikson, E. H. (1950). *Childhood and society.* London: Norton.

Flinn, M. V. (1992). Paternal care in a Caribbean village. In B. S. Hewlett (Ed.), *Father-child relations: Cultural and biosocial contexts* (pp. 57–84). New York: Aldine de Gruyter.

Fouts, H. N. (2002). The social and emotional contexts of weaning among the Bofi farmers and foragers of Central Africa. Unpublished Ph.D. diss., Washington State University.

———. (in press). Families in Central Africa: A comparison of Bofi farmers and Bofi forager families. In J. L. Roopnarine & U. P. Gielen (Eds.), *Families in global perspective.* Boston: Allyn & Bacon.

Fouts, H. N., Hewlett, B. S., & Lamb, M. E. (2001). Weaning and the nature of early childhood interactions among Bofi foragers in Central Africa. *Human Nature, 12* (1), 27–46.

Freud, S. (1940). An outline of psycho-analysis. *International Journal of Psycho-Analysis, 21,* 27–85.

Gomendio, M. (1991). Parent-offspring conflict and maternal investment in rhesus macaques. *Animal Behaviour, 42,* 993–1005.

Gray, S. J. (1996). Ecology of weaning among nomadic pastoralists of Kenya: Maternal thinking, maternal behavior, and human adaptive strategies. *Human Biology, 68* (3), 437–465.

Habicht, J.-P., DaVanzo, J., & Butz, W. P. (1986). Does breast-feeding really save lives, or are apparent benefits due to biases? *American Journal of Epidemiology, 123* (2), 279–290.

Harkness, S., & Super, C. M. (1992). The cultural foundations of father's roles: Evidence from Kenya and the United States. In B. S. Hewlett (Ed.), *Father-child relations: Cultural and biosocial contexts* (pp. 191–212). New York: Aldine de Gruyter.

Harrison, G. A., Brush, G., & Zumrawi, F. Y. (1992). Interrelations between growth, weaning and disease experience in Khartoum infants. *European Journal of Clinical Nutrition, 46,* 273–278.

Hassan F. A. (1979). Demography and Archaeology. *Annual Review of Anthropology, 9,* 137–160.

Hawkes, K., O'Connell, J. F., & Blurton-Jones, N. G. (1997). Hadza women's time allocation, offspring provisioning, and the evolution of long postmenopausal life spans. *Current Anthropology, 38* (4), 551–577.

Hewlett, B. S. (1991). *Intimate fathers.* Ann Arbor: University of Michigan Press.

———. (1996). Cultural diversity among African Pygmies. In S. Kent (Ed.), *Cultural diversity among twentieth-century foragers* (pp. 215–244). Cambridge: Cambridge University Press.

Hrdy, S. B. (1999). *Mother nature: A history of mothers, infants, and natural selection.* New York: Pantheon Books.

Ivey, P. K. (1993). Life-history theory perspectives on allocaretaking strategies among Efe foragers of the Ituri Forest of Zaire. Unpublished Ph.D. diss., University of New Mexico.

Konner, M. J. (1976a). Maternal care, infant behavior and development among the !Kung. In R. B. Lee & I. DeVore (Eds.), *Kalahari hunter-gatherers* (pp. 218–245). Cambridge, MA: Harvard University Press.

———. (1976b). Relations among infants and juveniles in comparative perspective. *Social Science Information, 4*, 372–402.

———. (1977). Evolutions of human behavior development. In P. H. Leiderman, S. R. Tulkin, & A. Rosenfeld (Eds.), *Culture and infancy* (pp. 69–109). New York: Academic Press.

Lancaster, J. B. (1984). Evolutionary perspectives on sex differences in the higher primates. In A. S. Rossi (Ed.), *Gender and the life course* (pp. 3–27). New York: Aldine.

Larsen, C. S. (1995). Biological changes in human populations with agriculture. *Annual Review of Anthropology, 24*, 185–213.

Lee, P. C. (1987). Nutrition, fertility and maternal investment in primates. *Journal of Zoology London, 213*, 409–422.

Lee, P. C., Majluf, P., & Gordon, I. J. (1991). Growth, weaning, and maternal investment from a comparative perspective. *Journal of Zoology London, 225*, 99–114.

LeVine, R. A., Dixon, S., LeVine, S., Richman, A., Leiderman, P. H., Keefer, C. H., & Brazelton, T. B. (1996). *Child care and culture: Lessons from Africa*. Cambridge: Cambridge University Press.

LeVine, R. A., & LeVine, B. B. (1966). *Six cultures series*. Vol. 2, *Nyansongo: A Gusii community in Kenya*. New York: Wiley.

Martines, J. C., Habicht, J., Ashworth, A., & Kirkwood, B. R. (1994). Weaning in southern Brazil: Is there a "Weanling's Dilemma"? *American Institute of Nutrition*, 1189–1198.

McKenna, J. J. (1987). Parental supplements and surrogates among primates: Cross-species and cross-cultural comparisons. In J. B. Lancaster, J. Altmann, A. S. Rossi, & L. R. Sherrod (Eds.), *Parenting across the life span* (pp. 143–184). New York: Aldine de Gruyter.

Mead, M. (1935). *Sex and temperament in three primitive societies*. New York: William Morrow.

Millard, A. V., & Graham, M. A. (1985). Abrupt weaning reconsidered: Evidence from Central Mexico. *Journal of Tropical Pediatrics, 31*, 229–234.

Minturn, L., & Hitchcock, J. T. (1966). *Six cultures series*. Vol. 3, *The Rajputs of Khalapur India*. New York: Wiley.

Nardi, B. A. (1985). Infant feeding and women's work in western Samoa: A hypothesis, some evidence, and suggestions for future research. In L. Marshall (Ed.), *Infant care and feeding in the South Pacific* (pp. 293–306). New York: Gordon & Breach.

Nerlove, S. B. (1974). Women's workload and infant feeding practices: A relationship with demographic implications. *Ethnology, 13*, 207–214.

Phillipson, D. W. (1993). *African archaeology*. Cambridge: Cambridge University Press.

Rao, S., & Kanade, A. N. (1992). Prolonged breast-feeding and malnutrition among rural Indian children below three years of age. *European Journal of Clinical Nutrition, 46*, 187–195.

Raphael, D., & Davis, F. (1985). *Only mothers know: Patterns of infant feeding in traditional cultures*. Westport, CT: Greenwood Press.

Shostak, M. (1976). A !Kung woman's memories of childhood. In R. B. Lee & I. DeVore (Eds.), *Kalahari hunter-gatherers* (pp. 246–277). Cambridge, MA: Harvard University Press.

———. (1981). *Nisa*. Cambridge, MA: Harvard University Press.

Trivers, R. L. (1974). Parent-offspring conflict. *American Zoology, 14,* 249–264.

Weisner, T. S. (1987). Socialization for parenthood in sibling caretaking societies. In J. B. Lancaster, J. Altmann, A. Rossi, & L. R. Sherrod (Eds.), *Parenting across the life span: Biosocial dimensions* (pp. 237–270). New York: Aldine de Gruyter.

CHAPTER 6

Challenging Expert Knowledge: Findings from an African Study of Infant Care and Development

Robert A. LeVine

In 1973, I met with a pediatrician (T. Berry Brazelton) and a psychiatrist (P. Herbert Leiderman) in an Austrian castle, between the turbulent sessions of a conference on culture and infancy (Leiderman, Tulkin, & Rosenfield, 1977), to discuss a future collaborative study in Africa. The following year my colleagues and I began a two-year field project in southwestern Kenya that included a seventeen-month longitudinal study of twenty-eight infants and their parents. The project produced a detailed portrait of infant care and development in a Gusii community, published as numerous articles and books over the years and finally in our 1994 volume *Child Care and Culture: Lessons from Africa* (LeVine et al., 1994), that brought together our findings on a wide variety of topics. This chapter stems from my dissatisfaction with that book.

In retrospect, I see *Child Care and Culture* as being both too large and too lean—containing a multiplicity of perspectives, data, and insights about African parents, families and infants, but too few definitive conclusions to draw the attention of child development researchers (as implied in Urie Bronfenbrenner's foreword). The book's size and complexity were the product of my desire to integrate perspectives, contexts, and observations in a single monograph. Its restraint was due to my avoidance of interpretations with which my coauthors might disagree. This chapter seeks to remedy those deficiencies by focusing on a few significant points, presented as theoretical challenges for which I take sole responsibility.

Brazelton, Leiderman, and I were brought together by the conviction, based on our previous studies in sub-Saharan Africa, that experienced mothers there had a practical understanding of infant care and development contrasting sharply with expert knowledge in the child development field. We followed Margaret

Mead and John W. M. Whiting in the goal of using data from non-Western cultures to criticize and reframe generalizations about human child development grounded exclusively in our own society. I had myself only a few years earlier attempted to spell out methodological principles for cross-cultural research in a chapter of the third edition of *Carmichael's Manual of Child Psychology* (LeVine, 1970). The newly developed field of infant psychology, with its findings of early infant capacities for processing social experience, seemed ripe for an intensive investigation overseas revealing patterns inaccessible at home that would cause us to think differently about infant experience. (In fact, Charles Super and Sara Harkness, young researchers sponsored by John and Beatrice Whiting and Jerome Kagan, were already beginning their own infant studies in Kenya when we planned our investigation.) We chose southwestern Kenya for the investigation because I had worked there almost twenty years earlier and already had the background knowledge and contacts on which a field study of child development depends. Our data collection program in a Gusii community, as we planned it in the field, covered infant care and early behavioral development, as embedded in the demographic, biomedical, nutritional, and cultural contexts of Gusii parents and children during pregnancy and the first thirty months after birth.

WHAT DO INFANTS NEED?

The child development literature covers a wide spectrum of knowledge claims about the needs of infants, from the certainties delivered by the popular literature of parental advice to the cautiously framed generalizations offered by research investigators in journal articles and handbook chapters. From an anthropological viewpoint, however, even the scientific articles are rarely tentative enough in their conclusions, ignoring as they often do the significance of population-level variation within the human species.

Patterns of reproductive behavior and the care of offspring vary widely across human populations (i.e., geographically bound inbreeding groups at a particular historical period). There are populations in which the prevalent mating system is monogamous and others in which it is polygamous; in some, girls marry at or before puberty and begin bearing children as soon as they can, while in others, the average onset of childbearing is delayed until a woman is in her late twenties. The lifetime fertility of the average woman, calculated as a national rate, currently ranges from 1.2 to 6 or more children. There are populations in which infant mortality during the first twelve months of life is as low as 4 per 1,000 live births and those in which it is over 150. Half a century ago, there were many national populations with infant mortality rates of 200 or more. The infant mortality of the United States was 100 in 1900 but is now 7. In some contemporary populations, breast-feeding is universal, as it was throughout most of human history; in others, like our own, only a minority of infants are breast-fed.

Co-sleeping of mother and child is a widespread practice in much of the world, but not among Europeans and Americans. This evidence of global and historical variation in the parameters of human reproduction and infant care shows that population variability in reproductive outcomes and offspring development is a human species characteristic, part of our biosocial heritage.

There are many other population-level variations that have been found in the symbolic environment of mother and child, from verbal and gestural communication patterns to moral standards, concepts of relationships and developmental goals, and methods of instruction and correction. The social and interpersonal environment of the child also varies greatly at the population level and includes the structure and density of families, sibling and peer groups, the prevalence and types of child labor and schooling, and social boundaries in the local environment of the child. The empirical literature on all of these variations is considerable and has recently been reviewed in several publications (Greenfield & Suzuki, 1998; Harkness & Super, 1995; Shonkoff & Phillips, 2000; Shweder et al., 1998). We need more detailed evidence from more populations than is currently available, but it is abundantly clear that the shape of childhood experience from birth onwards varies in a myriad of ways at the population level, making it impossible to generalize validly about *human* child development on the basis of observations restricted to one population or closely related ones.

Margaret Mead (1930, 1931) and John W. M. Whiting (1954) made this point about the centrality of comparative research to the child development field a long time ago; my formulation only updates some of their arguments. At the present time, there are child development researchers who take the point seriously enough to seek cross-cultural data before launching generalizations about the human species; but there are others who do not. It is fair to say that claims about what human infants need—for their emotional and intellectual development, not just their health and physical growth—are more abundant than the cross-cultural evidence to support them. Many psychologists feel free to draw conclusions unqualified by consideration of population variability, especially when public concerns about mental health and educational achievement are involved.

Psychiatric and educational problems are grounded in a particular population's conceptions of the desirable. Terms like "optimal development," "security of attachment," "developmentally appropriate," and "maternal competence" represent cultural preferences for developmental courses and outcomes, not the findings of empirical research on the human species as a whole.

The problem here is the child development field's dual identity as an ideological advocacy movement for the humane treatment of children and a scientific research endeavor seeking knowledge and understanding of child development. This combination can narrow and distort scientific exploration in the interest of promoting a moral cause. One example is attachment research, with its large claims to scientific knowledge while retaining John Bowlby's vision (1988) of a prescriptive as well as descriptive "developmental psychiatry." Bowlby (1953) was a psychiatrist who launched a successful crusade for the more humane treatment of children in institutional care in the early 1950s, prescribing advice to parents as well in his best-selling book *Child Care and the Growth of Love*. Later, after his concept of "maternal deprivation" was severely criticized by psychologists, he emerged as a biopsychologically oriented developmental theorist (Bowlby, 1958, 1969, 1980), and Mary D. S. Ainsworth organized an empirical research program based in large part on his ideas (Ainsworth et al., 1978). Although her first attachment research was carried out in East Africa in the mid-1950s (Ainsworth, 1967, 1977), Ainsworth and her students never strayed far from the universalistic claims and normative implications of Bowlby's theoretical model. Their resistance to taking seriously cultural differences in findings from the Strange Situation reveals the problem of fusing moral and scientific approaches. By taking the B classification of the Strange Situation as measuring the "optimal" outcome (secure attachment) of "sensitive" mothering, they interpret other outcomes not as indicators of alternative normal developmental pathways but as "suboptimal" responses indicating inadequate mothering, with potentially unhealthy or pathological sequelae in later life. But if suboptimal outcomes are more frequent in populations outside the United States than they are within the United States, then those peoples must be deemed to have a greater frequency of inadequate mothers and psychopathology (or there is something wrong with the method of measuring security of attachment). Having painted themselves into this interpretive corner by adherence to the normative and psychiatric claims of the Bowlby-Ainsworth model, attachment researchers prefer to avoid recognizing the implications of cross-cultural evidence, even when it comes from excellent replications in countries as culturally similar to the United States as Germany (Grossmann et al., 1985; LeVine & Norman, 2001).

Developmentally Appropriate Practice in Early Childhood Programs (Bredekamp & Copple, 1997), published by the National Association for the Education of Young Children, provides another example of the science and ideology problem. In this case, unlike attachment researchers, the authors are not claiming to have produced the developmental framework and research findings themselves. On the contrary, they are attempting to base standards (developmentally appropriate practices, or DAPs) for the care of young children in day care centers, preschools and at home in the United States on scientific knowledge of child development. Given the uneven status of scientific knowledge in child development research, such an effort inevitably exaggerates the definitiveness of the evidence in order to establish an authoritative code for practical work. In the DAPs book there are lists of caregiver behaviors under the headings of "appropriate practices" and "inappropriate practices." The "inappropriate" list seems to me to resemble practices that are culturally preferred among various peoples outside the United States, whereas the "appropriate" list describes the practices preferred by contemporary upper-middle-class Americans, whether or not they are versed in the scientific research literature on child development. In other words, the more one is acquainted with the evidence about cultural variations in the norms for childcare behavior, the more one is likely to see "appropriate" versus "inappropriate" as meaning "ours" versus "theirs" rather than "based on scientific knowledge" versus "based on ignorance of knowledge about child development."

Americans have as much right as anyone else to have culturally preferred practices regarding the care of children. The term *developmental appropriateness*, however, implies that the recommended practices represent more than just one culture's standard of childcare—namely, a universal requirement for healthy behavioral development, much as Vitamin A is necessary for healthy visual development. But what if the DAPs were, as I believe they are, more like peanut butter or nonfat yogurt than like vitamin A—that is, one of many possible (but not universally palatable) packages for promoting the healthy development of children? Like attachment research, though more obviously, the DAPs present an appearance of science-based knowledge in a formula based heavily on cultural ideology. Our findings from the Gusii infant study are relevant to these points.

THE GUSII INFANT STUDY: FACTS TO BE FACED

In this section I shall present four findings from the Gusii infant study that raise questions about parental care and early development, specifically concerning maternal sensitivity, maternal attention, the early development of compliance, and sibling caregiving.

The Gusii are a people of southwestern Kenya who now number well over a million and raise children in environments that differ dramatically from those of the United States. Forty years ago they were an isolated, Bantu-speaking people on the southwestern edge of the Kenya highlands near Lake Victoria who made a living from domestic agriculture and animal husbandry. They had dispersed settlements organized by patrilineal descent, in which each domestic group—consisting of a patriarch, his wives and sons and young children—lived on its own fields and pastures, with a house for each married woman and her children. The men had to marry women from other clans, who moved to their husbands' residence after the payment of bridewealth in cattle. Married women and their children did the routine cultivation and food processing, took care of the domestic animals, and traded in the markets that had been introduced under British colonial rule. Each mother-child household had its own two-room house, but daytime life was spent largely in the front yard. There were initiation ceremonies for boys and girls. Men acted as entrepreneurs and protectors of their families and gained prestige as well as economic benefit from marrying several wives. At the time of my first study, 1955–1957, more than half of all children were raised in polygynous families; each wife lived with her children in a house on her land. Only a few of the children attended school at that time.

By the infant study of 1974–1976, polygyny had sharply declined except among men over age fifty, the average married woman bore nine to ten children (the highest fertility in Kenya and among the highest in the world at that time), and infant mortality was about 80 per 1,000 live births (eight times that of the United States at the time). Our sample mothers breast-fed their infants for an average of sixteen months, sleeping with the babies next to them so as to breast-feed on demand through the night. Each child had siblings available as companions and was expected to attend school and work at home as he or she grew older. Girls played a greater role in infant care and other domestic tasks, including cultivation, although landholdings had diminished and most families lived in part by the fathers' remittances from work in urban areas. The economic context of family life had changed substantially over the previous twenty years, but many cultural values and practices remained the same as during my first period of fieldwork. The hierarchical code of social interaction—the "respect-obedience model" from the child's point of view—remained central to understanding the parental agenda for the child's moral development.

We took a microscopic look at infant care in this context, through three methods of observation on all twenty-eight members of the sample: (1) spot observations of the people and places involved in infant care, rotated over times of day and carried out over the full seventeen months by a young male resident of the community with a high school education; (2) naturalistic observations of caregiver-infant interaction at home, recorded in narrative form for an hour every three months for seventeen months, by a foreign female ethnographer able to speak and understand the Gusii language (Sarah LeVine); and (3) recordings of speech directed to the child at home in periods averaging 105 minutes, recorded in the vernacular by two trained female Gusii high school graduates from outside the community, over an eight-month period. (We also administered Bayley tests and videotaped mother-infant interaction in investigator-structured face-to-face and teaching situations.)

Maternal Sensitivity to Infant Signals

In attachment theory and research, this is the key variable in the infant environment that determines whether a child will become securely or insecurely attached at twelve months of age. We found the Gusii mothers extremely responsive to their infants' distress signals but quite unresponsive to their nondistress vocalizations (i.e., babbling) (Richman, Miller, & LeVine, 1992). At home in the daytime a Gusii mother normally had her infant on her lap or in her arms and responded by jiggling or breast-feeding at the child's first fret before it became a full-blown cry. The Gusii infants at three to four months cried on average less than half as frequently as an American middle-class comparison group (in the Gusii case, some of the crying occurred when the baby was being cared for by a sibling).

When we showed a group of the Gusii mothers a brief videotape of an American mother changing the diaper of her six-week-old infant, they were shocked at the mother's leaving the crying child lying on the changing table momentarily while she turned to pick up a clean diaper. Their visceral reactions and the following conversation left no doubt that they saw the American mother's behavior as blameworthy. For them, the prevention of infant crying through continuous physical contact was not only a device of pragmatic value but also a morally mandated script for maternal behavior.

Maternal speaking in response to infant babbles was not part of that script. The Gusii mothers were observed at home responding verbally to nondistress vocalizations at nine to ten months only 5 percent of the time, while the American mothers in the comparison group responded verbally 20 percent of the time. Gusii mothers did not engage in mock conversations with babies. Some informants said it was senseless to talk to babies, since they cannot comprehend speech; it was better to postpone talking to them until they were two years old, when they could understand what was being said. Furthermore, in the face-to-face videotapes mothers turned away when infants were getting positively excited. Rather than amplifying interactive excitement, as the American mothers did, the Gusii mothers sought to calm their babies in this situation, as in every other situation we observed. A consistent strategy of soothing, keeping infants calm and in physical contact, was pursued throughout the first year as a matter of healthy development that had no place for verbal responsiveness to infant vocalization.

Thus Gusii mothers tended to be highly responsive to infant distress signals and unresponsive to other vocal signals because they were following a normative script that justifies this selective behavior in terms of a folk conception of infant needs. Does this qualify as *maternal sensitivity* in terms of attachment research? The answer could be yes—as Ainsworth (1977, p. 126) found for the Ganda—because Gusii mothers provide comfort rapidly and responsively, protecting their babies from stress as specified in the original formulations of attachment by Bowlby and Ainsworth. But it could be no, because they fail to display other aspects of maternal sensitivity conceptualized in much of the attachment literature as "psychological availability," "positive involvement," and "affectionate" interactions. The first view of maternal sensitivity reduces the mother-infant relationship to a single dimension (comforting distress); the second fleshes out the concept with contemporary American cultural preferences. As originally conceptualized, maternal sensitivity captured a small part of a complex relationship; as used in developmental and clinical studies, it reflects contemporary Anglo-American cultural norms for evaluating maternal care.

Maternal Attention: Gaze and Speech

The mother's visual and verbal engagement with her infant and toddler provides, according to most child development specialists, the stimulation, warmth, and affection required for their normal psychological development. We found that Gusii mothers rarely looked at or spoke to their infants and toddlers, even when they were holding and breast-feeding them. More specifically, only 1 percent of the Gusii mothers' acts toward their infants at nine to ten months (in the coded narrative observations) involved looking, while looking constituted 43 percent of the Boston mothers' behavior (LeVine et al, 1994, p. 197). Furthermore, the Boston mothers looked at their nine- to ten-month-old infants more than three times as frequently as their infants looked at them (28 percent and 8 percent, as a proportion of all the intervals of observation), while the Gusii mothers looked at their infants about the same amount as their infants looked at them (9 percent of all intervals).

Talking was 11 percent of the Gusii mothers' acts toward their nine- to ten-month-old infants, but 29 percent of the Boston mothers' behavior. There were infant-directed utterances from all caregivers combined in only 18.5 percent of the minutes of speech observations of the Gusii infants at ages ranging from three to twenty-seven months. Gusii mothers hardly ever attempted to initiate a conversation with a baby or engaged in prolonged conversational exchange.

The question here is whether the Gusii infants were deprived of the kind of stimulation, affection, and warmth that all children need for normal cognitive and emotional development, or whether infants can develop normally without the kind of maternal attention observable among middle-class Americans.

Compliance: Commands, Threats, and Praise

The Gusii mothers in our sample expected their infants and toddlers to comply with their wishes, and they could be harsh (by American standards) in exerting control over them. They rarely praised their infants or asked them questions but tended to issue commands and threats in communicating with them. Our analysis of infant-directed utterances from all caregivers and at all ages combined showed that 61.4 percent were commands, and after twelve months, negative commands like "Stop!" and "Get away!" became more frequent. Questions, the staple of infant-directed speech in Western middle-class samples, stayed at or under 20 percent during the first twenty-four months, and rose above that level only after two years. Even then, many of the interrogatives were rhetorical questions that have the force of commands or even threats: "Why are you crying?" or "Do you want me to beat you?"

When eighteen of the Gusii mothers and their children ages six to twenty-five months were compared with an equal number of Boston mothers and children of the same ages in a videotaped teaching situation using tasks from the

Bayley test, the American mothers usually praised their children when a task was completed, whereas the Gusii hardly ever did. Yet the Gusii children were more compliant, becoming distressed much less frequently than the Americans and giving no resistance to being pulled and pushed by their mothers, while the American infants resisted in every instance. It would appear that the Gusii mothers succeeded in shaping their infants toward compliance, using speech rarely and in the imperative mode when they did, and avoiding praise even in situations calling for it by American standards.

The Gusii pattern of compliance training contrasts sharply with the normative standards of middle-class Americans. Here are some examples of developmentally *inappropriate* practices for infant or toddler care provided by Bredekamp and Copple (1997):

- Infants are wordlessly and sometimes abruptly moved about at the adult's convenience (p. 72).

- Routines are swiftly accomplished without involving the infant in play or communication. Little or no warm interaction takes place during routines (p. 73).

- Adults are rarely playful with babies (p. 74).

- Adults talk *at* toddlers and do not wait for a response. Adult voices dominate or caregivers do not speak to children because they think they are too young to respond (p. 81).

These could be descriptions of Gusii practices, especially as seen by outsiders. Are these practices developmentally inappropriate or simply inappropriate according to contemporary American cultural standards of interaction, in which compliance to parental wishes is no longer valued as it once was?

Sibling Care

The Gusii mothers frequently delegated daytime care of infants to their other children, including those as young as five or six. This cultural practice would be classified as maternal neglect in the contemporary United States. It is a criminal offense in some states, in accordance with principles often enunciated by experts on childcare and development.

Our observations provided a detailed quantitative picture of the place of siblings in taking care of infants over the first thirty months of life (LeVine et al., 1994, pp. 159–168, 202–210). They showed that mothers are dependent for daytime care on sibling caregivers (mostly girls between six and twelve years of age) during the period when the infant is three to fifteen months old. Although all the infants could walk before age twelve months, they were held by sisters or mother in 42 percent of spot observations at the twelve-to-fifteen-month period

and in 30 percent at fifteen to eighteen months. These elder sisters do not engage the infant in more visual or verbal interaction than the mother, and the
infants cry more when the sister is caring for them than when the mother is doing
so (p. 209, fig. 8.6). By the 1970s, virtually all Gusii girls were going to school,
so mothers had to spread caregiving responsibilities over several daughters if they
could. There were strong correlations between the number of daughters a mother
had and the amount of nonmaternal care the infant received. After the baby
reached fifteen months, there were also significant correlations between the
amount of land the mother was cultivating and the amount of nonmaternal care.
After being weaned at an average age of sixteen months, the children usually
joined the group of older siblings. Although there was a period of more interaction with the mother again when the child was twenty-one to twenty-four
months old and the mother was spending more time at home taking care of the
next baby, the sibling group became the primary context for the child's subsequent socialization.

This pattern raises the question of whether Gusii mothers are neglecting their
infants by putting them in the care of siblings during the first two years and by
confining their exploratory activity during this period, as would be concluded
about an American mother who did so to the same degree.

These four patterns of behavior observed among the Gusii mothers—un-
responsiveness to an infant's positive vocalizations, lack of visual and verbal attention to the infant, strong pressures for compliance, and extensive care of
infants by child siblings, together with lack of praise for the toddler's accomplishments, the virtual absence of mock conversations or extended play dialogues,
and restriction of exploration—are interpretable by the standards of American
child development experts as care that fails to meet the needs of infants. The
practices of Gusii mothers as we observed them would be classified in an American context as developmentally inappropriate, negligent, and possibly abusive.

FACING THE FACTS

The question posed by the Gusii evidence summarized above for "the science
of early childhood development" (as a recent report of the National Academy
of Sciences by Shonkoff and Phillips, 2000, calls it) is: Do Gusii mothers neglect the needs of their infants and toddlers for stimulation, interaction, and
affection, or have these needs been exaggerated by child development specialists
who mistake Anglo-American ideologies of the second half of the twentieth century as the universal requirements of human infants?

Before I attempt to answer this question, I want to emphasize that child development specialists do not speak with a single voice on this question. The
Shonkoff and Phillips report, for example, avoids making claims about what all
infants need, and it takes account, at least in general terms, of cultural variations in alternative developmental pathways. But there are many others, scien-

tists and practitioners in this field, who are certain they know what infants need and identify it with the ideals of childrearing that became prominent in the United States after 1950.

For these child development experts, the child's mental health requires consistently warm and loving care, manifested by a mother lavishing on the infant not only physical caresses but also—and more important—visual engagement and verbal affection in response to vocalization and in extended dialogues involving mutual gaze, questions and answers, and abundant praise. Healthy development also requires maternal avoidance of fear-arousing speech or action and the mother's positive efforts to build competence and self-esteem. In addition, this model posits—perhaps paradoxically—the need to promote independence in the infant through exploratory activity, isolated sleeping arrangements, and early speech development, and it assumes that toddlers will exhibit rebellious behaviors with which mothers will have to deal lovingly yet consistently. Mothers who fail to provide this kind of care are thought to be abusive—due to poverty, family disorganization, or stress—or mentally disturbed, jeopardizing the future mental health of their children.

This is undoubtedly a widespread model for the care of young children in the United States at present, but does it also represent the minimum care for prevention of developmental abnormalities in humans generally or an optimal pattern of maternal care for the human species? Claims that it does represent minimal requirements or optimal standards must pass a test of cross-cultural comparison to be credible. The Gusii mothers clearly raised their infants and toddlers according to a different set of standards; did the development of Gusii children suffer as a result? We do not have the kind of longitudinal data that would provide definitive answers, but we can say that most of the sample children we studied as infants were progressing normally in school and life in their home community at thirteen to fourteen years of age, and those who were not had been hampered by health problems or home conditions that were exceptionally adverse in local terms (LeVine et al., 1994, pp. 267–268). My guess is that the academic skills of the majority were lower than for middle-class American children, but not necessarily than for American children with uneducated parents attending low-quality schools. (The average Gusii mother in our sample had 2.9 years of school, the average father 5.6.) Apart from school skills, most of the sample were said to be average or normal thirteen-year-olds by local standards. We found no evidence to support the prediction that the lack of stimulation, interaction, and affection in infancy and early childhood had led to flagrant abnormalities in later development.

This may seem a weak set of follow-up results on which to base a fundamental critique of widely held assumptions in the child development field, but the critique depends less on our follow-up visit than on the contextual analysis of our data on maternal and nonmaternal care. Working with Gusii mothers convinced us that their perspective on maternal care made sense in practical and moral terms. When viewed in these terms, their practices show not only a greater devotion to their children's welfare than is evident from an American perspective, but also an understanding of possibilities in the development of children that lies beyond the imagination of normal (i.e., Euro-American) child development researchers to date. Each of the four findings from the Gusii infant study can be used to demonstrate this point.

Sensitivity

Are Gusii mothers sensitive or insensitive to infant signals? A global measure of maternal sensitivity, averaging responses to distress and nondistress signals, would equate the Gusii mothers' pattern—extremely responsive to distress and unresponsive to other signals—with that of an American mother who was moderately responsive to both kinds of signals. But they are not equivalent in meaning to the Gusii mothers, who are deliberately responding to one kind of signal and not the other. And if one takes seriously Bretherton's views (1985, 1987) of the infant's "internal working model" of the caregiver, they may not be equivalent to the infant, either. It seems likely that the infant's experience of a mother who is consistently responsive to his distress signals and consistently unresponsive to his positive vocalizations would differ from the infant experience of an American mother who is less consistently responsive to both. The Gusii pattern—particularly if taken together with co-sleeping, breast-feeding on demand, and a high level of physical contact—might foster in Gusii children an internal working model that has not been imagined in attachment research. This conclusion is consistent with Ainsworth's own view (1977, p. 128), based on African data, that breast-feeding (as opposed to responsiveness to signals alone) can become "enmeshed in the organization of the attachment relationship." So can co-sleeping and physical contact, in ways less accessible to observation than overt responses to visible communicative signals.

Discussing her Baltimore study of middle-class Americans, Ainsworth (1977) reported:

> Since we had . . . found that mothers who are responsive to crying signals tend to be responsive to all kinds of infant signals, we concluded that it is this general sensitivity to signals that tends to foster the development of infant communication. (p. 134)

Later she states:

> Since the variables that tend to appear together in one society may appear in different constellations in another, cultural comparisons provide an opportunity to assess the independent influence on development of different infant- and childrearing practices. (p. 143)

The Gusii study gave us the opportunity to observe practices in which types of responsiveness that form a single constellation among middle-class Americans are responded to differentially among the Gusii. While we do not have the data to demonstrate how they influence development, we share Ainsworth's apparent belief that a constellation as different from the American one as the Gusii exhibit might have a distinctive effect that a panhuman concept of maternal sensitivity would have to encompass.

Attention

The lack of Gusii mothers' visual and verbal engagement with their babies may seem from an American perspective like isolation of the child from normal human contact, but this is another domain in which context is important. Gusii babies, like the Kipsigis next door to the Gusii, described by Super and Harkness (1982), are always in the presence of others. They are never put to sleep in a separate room as American infants are, and they are almost always in physical contact with caregivers—mothers or siblings—who are ready to provide comfort. The caregiver does not look at or talk to the baby a great deal, but never excludes the baby from ongoing domestic social interaction. This is not the child-centered interaction of middle-class Americans, and it does not include what Americans consider signs of warmth and affection. But it seems to me likely that Gusii mothers intend, and Gusii babies may feel, a warm and affectionate background experience from all the holding, co-sleeping, and responsive breast-feeding in their normal routines. This could be functionally equivalent to the verbal and visual engagement of Americans in terms of fulfilling basic emotional needs, while building an internal working model of mother-infant relations with distinctive meanings embedded in communicative interaction. We do not know enough about what happens emotionally when the interaction between mother and child deviates from Anglo-American cultural models of emotional expression, but we should be investigating the possibility of alternative forms of engagement rather than assuming that the child's emotional needs are being neglected.

As for cognitive stimulation, it is true that Gusii mothers and other caregivers do not engage in many tutorial interactions or other instructional activities, but the normal environment of Gusii infants and toddlers is more complex interactionally than might be supposed. This environment includes a number of adults and children of various ages engaging in conversation and work activities most of the time the baby is awake. The young child is constantly exposed to social interaction and task performance, first as an observer and then as an "apprentice" (Lave & Wenger, 1991; Rogoff, 1989). Gusii children may not speak at as young an age or with such early verbal fluency as middle-class American children do, but they acquire communicative competence in a grammatically complex language with a great range of implicational nuances. Furthermore, the sibling group, with children who are easier to imitate than parents, seems to provide effective if unintentional scaffolding for the child's rapid acquisition of competence in domestic tasks during the preschool and early school-age years. In the domain of cognitive stimulation as with emotional needs, our own cultural models may blind us to the mental nourishment Gusii children get from their early environment. Gusii mothers, however, presume that each infant and toddler will grow up in an environment rich in speech, social interaction, and activities provided by older children, making it possible for the mother to keep her distance and her authority intact as the supervisor of this scene rather than one of the playmates.

Compliance

Gusii mothers are definitely controlling, unexpressive of positive emotion, and (occasionally) harsh disciplinarians by American standards, but are they abusive to infants and toddlers? The first point to be made here is that they believe their actions that might be coded as "abusive" are in the best interests of the child and the family. They explicitly believe that "children should learn fear" and should be restricted physically even after they can walk, in order to protect them from hazards such as cooking fires, steep hills, and large animals. They want to make sure that young children are respectful and obedient right from the start, not only because it is virtuous but also because it facilitates the domestic work of the household directed by the mother. They think praising children makes them conceited and unwilling to take orders. Their moralization of obedience and hierarchy is not so far from that of nineteenth-century Americans, who held that "children should be seen and not heard" and that parents who "spare the rod spoil the child." Protection is the first priority for Gusii mothers, especially during the dangerous first and second years of life, and then obedience and respect take over as primary goals. It is, once again, important to remember that these children are sleeping with their mothers every night and being held and breast-fed by them every day. Given the context of devoted care, this is a pattern of maternal behavior that would not have been considered abusive a hundred years ago in the United States, although it might be at present.

It may nonetheless seem amazing to contemporary Americans that young children can grow up normally without the kind of enthusiastic and energetic maternal support for their self-esteem, individuality, exploratory tendencies, and personal autonomy that has become standard in the United States and some other Western countries since the mid-twentieth century. In fact, children grew up without that kind of support at earlier times and still do in other parts of the world. Their parents had a different set of moral values to guide and foster their development, not a way of thwarting it. It seems to me more likely that American child development experts have exaggerated the dangers of discipline in early childhood, now conceptualized as "abuse," than that the Gusii mothers we observed were abusive in any sense. Parents of a given culture tend to think their ways are best and that other cultural models of parental practice are morally inferior and dangerous, but this is moral judgment, not science.

Sibling Care

The question of whether siblings who are themselves children should take care of infants and toddlers has also been resolved by insular moral judgment in contemporary American childcare advice and laws. That there are dangers in leaving babies in the care of their five-year-old siblings is reasonable in the context of American housing and family arrangements. It is clear to me, however, as it has been to others who have done fieldwork in Africa and other places where sibling care is customary, that the conditions are very different from those presumed in the American context: there are responsible adults within shouting distance; the children charged with caring seem—and regularly prove themselves to be—capable of assuming the responsibility; the mother is away for a few hours, not the entire day. Research to date has shown no sign of increased risks to child survival or psychological development from sibling care in Africa, and it has pointed to potential advantages in early childhood learning (as pointed out above) and social stimulation (LeVine et al., 1994, pp. 39–42; Sigman et al., 1988). The fact remains, however, that expert opinion in the United States is unanimous in treating this practice as a form of neglect rather than a form of acceptable care, based on a presumption of increased hazards to safety and development.

These considerations lead to my conclusion that evidence from Africa illustrated by the Gusii infant study constitutes a real challenge to knowledge in the child development field as we have received it from those whom we consider experts. All too often culturally valued norms of middle-class America are conflated with conceptions of minimal or optimal standards of maternal care of infants and toddlers in the human species as a whole. Evidence from studies conducted in other cultural settings, like the Gusii infant study, permits us to see that alternative patterns of care based on different moral and practical considerations can constitute normal patterns of development that had not been imagined in developmental theories. The child development field needs to expand its imagination through cross-cultural research in order to generate more valid knowledge of human development and a more critical understanding of our own culture's practices.

REFERENCES

Ainsworth, M. D. S. (1967). *Infancy in Uganda*. Baltimore: Johns Hopkins University Press.

———. (1977). Infant development and mother-infant interaction among Ganda and American Families. In P. H. Leiderman, S. R. Tulkin, & A. Rosenfield (Eds.), *Culture and infancy* (pp. 119–148). New York: Academic Press.

Ainsworth, M. D. S., Blehar, M. C., Waters, E., & Wall, S. (1978). *Patterns of attachment: A psychological study of the Strange Situation*. Hillsdale, NJ: Erlbaum.

Bowlby, J. (1953). *Child care and the growth of love*. London: Penguin.

———. (1958). The nature of the child's tie to his mother. *International Journal of Psychoanalysis*, 39, 350–373.

———. (1969). *Attachment and loss*. Vol. 1, *Attachment*. New York: Basic Books.

———. (1980). *Attachment and loss*. Vol. 3, *Loss*. New York: Basic Books.

———. (1988). *A secure base*. New York: Basic Books.

Bredekamp, S., & Copple, C. (Eds.). (1997). *Developmentally appropriate practice in early childhood programs* (rev. ed.). Washington, DC: National Association for the Education of Young Children.

Bretherton, I. (1985). Attachment theory: Retrospect and prospect. In I. Bretherton & E. Waters (Eds.), *Growing points of attachment theory and research*, Monographs of the Society for Research in Child Development (Vol. 50, Nos. 1–2, pp. 3–35). Chicago: University of Chicago Press.

———. (1987). New perspectives on attachment relations: Security, communication, and working models. In J. D. Osofsky (Ed.), *Handbook of infant development* (2nd ed., pp. 1061–1100). New York: Wiley.

Greenfield, P. M., & Suzuki, L. K. (1998). Culture and human development: Implications for parenting, education, pediatrics, and mental health. In W. Damon (Ed.), *Handbook of child psychology* (5th ed., Vol. 4, pp. 1059–1109). New York: Wiley.

Grossmann, K. A., Grossmann, K. L., Spangler, G., Suess, G., & Unzner, L. (1985). Maternal sensitivity and newborns' orientation responses as related to quality of attachment in northern Germany. In I. Bretherton & E. Waters (Eds.), *Growing points of attachment theory and research*, Monographs of the Society for Research in Child Development (Vol. 50, Nos. 1–2, pp. 233–256). Chicago: University of Chicago Press.

Harkness, S., & Super, C. (1995). Culture and parenting. In M. H. Bornstein (Ed.), *Handbook of parenting* (pp. 211–234). Hillsdale, NJ: Erlbaum.

Lave, J., & Wenger, E. (1991). *Situated learning*. Cambridge: Cambridge University Press.

Leiderman, P. H., Tulkin, S., & Rosenfield, A. (Eds.). (1977). *Culture and infancy: Variations in the human experience*. New York: Academic Press.

LeVine, R. A. (1970). Cross-cultural study in child psychology. In P. Mussen (Ed.), *Carmichael's manual of child psychology* (3rd ed., Vol. 2, pp. 559–612). New York: Wiley.

LeVine, R. A., Dixon, S., LeVine, S., Richman, A., Leiderman, P. H., Keefer, C. H., & Brazelton, T. B. (1994). *Child care and culture: Lessons from Africa*. New York: Cambridge University Press.

LeVine, R. A., & Norman, K. (2001). The infant's acquisition of culture: Early attachment re-examined in anthropological perspective. In C. F. Moore & H. F. Mathews

(Eds.), *The psychology of cultural experience* (pp. 83–104). New York: Cambridge University Press.

Mead, M. (1930). *Growing up in New Guinea: A comparative study of primitive education.* New York: Morrow.

———. (1931). The primitive child. In C. Murchison (Ed.), *A handbook of child psychology* (pp. 669–687). Worcester, MA: Clark University Press.

Richman, A., Miller, P. M., & LeVine, R. A. (1992). Cultural and educational variations in maternal responsiveness. *Developmental Psychology, 28,* 614–621.

Rogoff, B. (1989). *Apprenticeship in thinking.* New York: Oxford University Press.

Shonkoff, J., & Phillips, D. (2000). *From neurons to neighborhoods: The science of early childhood development.* Washington, DC: National Academy Press.

Shweder, R., Goodnow, J., Hatano, G., LeVine, R. A., Markus, H., & Miller, P. (1998). The cultural psychology of development: One mind, many mentalities. In W. Damon (Ed.), *The handbook of child psychology* (5th ed., Vol. 1, pp. 865–937). New York: Wiley.

Sigman, M., Neumann, C., Carter, E., Cattle, D., D'Souza, D., & N. Bwibo. (1988). Home interactions and the development of Embu toddlers in Kenya. *Child Development, 59,* 1251–1261.

Super, C., & Harkness, S. (1982). The infant's niche in rural Kenya and metropolitan America. In L. L. Adler (Ed.), *Cross-cultural research at issue* (pp. 47–55). New York: Academic Press.

Whiting, J. W. M. (1954). The cross-cultural method. In G. Lindzey (Ed.), *The handbook of social psychology* (Vol. 1, pp. 523–531). Cambridge, MA: Addison-Wesley.

CHAPTER 7

Competence and Satisfaction in Parenting Young Children:
An Ecological, Multivariate Comparison of Expressions and Sources of Self-Evaluation in the United States and Argentina

Marc H. Bornstein, O. Maurice Haynes, Liliana Pascual, and Kathleen M. Painter

How parents evaluate their own caregiving is critical to parenting and plays an important role in child development. This chapter reports about sociodemographic, personological, and child developmental sources of two key domains of parenting self-evaluations—namely, competence and satisfaction—and does so in two contrasting cultural contexts, the United States and Argentina.

Parents' evaluations of their own parenting affect parents' sense of self, motivate and shape parenting activities, moderate parenting responses to children, and on these grounds are thought to be significant to long-term child development (see, e.g., Bornstein, 1991, 2002a; Chess & Thomas, 1984; Dix & Grusec, 1985; Goodnow & Collins, 1990; Harkness & Super, 1996; Holloway & Machida, 1992; LeVine, Miller, & West, 1988; Miller, 1988; Palacios & Moreno, 1996; Rubin & Mills, 1992; Sameroff, Seifer, & Elias, 1982; Sigel & McGillicuddy-DeLisi, 2002; Whiting & Whiting, 1975). Feelings of competence and satisfaction relate to parenting behaviors and shape both effort and perseverance in parenting activities. Parents who feel that they are more competent and satisfied (versus parents who feel more negatively about their parenting) can be expected to act with their children in more optimal and effective (warm, sensitive, and responsive) ways (e.g., Baldwin, Cole, & Baldwin, 1982; Bandura, 1977; Johnston & Mash, 1989; Peterson & Seligman, 1984; Ruble, Newman, Rholes, & Altshuler, 1988), and these feelings in turn may inform their perceptions of child behavior (e.g., Panaccione & Wahler, 1986). Parents' self-evaluations of their own parenting also contribute to understanding the full social ecology of child development (see Super & Harkness, 1986).

Competence and satisfaction are intrapsychic constructs and key reflective components of parenting (Hopkins, Marcus, & Campbell, 1984; Patterson,

1980). Each of these specific self-evaluations is associated with favorable maternal mental health and child-related outcomes. Feelings of *competence* at parenting are fundamental and relate directly to the ability of a mother, for example, to organize her parenting and manage interactions with her children. Self-efficacy theory (Bandura, 1986, 1997) asserts that adults who evaluate themselves positively, know what they can do, and understand the likely effects of their actions will be parents who have the potential to act constructively in their children's development. A mother who feels more competent in her role as parent will feel more comfortable engaging her child (Cochran & Niego, 2002). The *satisfaction* that parents derive from childrearing turns on the opportunity they have to find pleasure and interest in relationships with their children and produces direct and indirect influences on their own and their children's behavior and psychological well-being. Greater satisfaction with the maternal role is associated with less depression and prenatal anxiety and with a more favorable adjustment to motherhood (Owen & Cox, 1988). Satisfaction in parenting can lead to different levels of involvement with children, from financial contributions to the family to more immediate nurturance; these feelings, in turn, foster emotional security, mental development, and behavioral adjustment in children.

SOURCES OF COMPETENCE AND SATISFACTION IN PARENTING

Parents' evaluations of their parenting presumably derive from many sources, including personological, situational, sociodemographic, and historical characteristics (see Belsky, 1984; Bornstein, 2002b; Sameroff et al., 1982; Vaughn, Taraldson, Crichton, & Egeland, 1981). The general model that motivated the design of this study followed ecological theory (e.g., Bronfenbrenner, 1989; Bronfenbrenner & Crouter, 1983; see, too, Bornstein, 2002a), and so to evaluate multiple sources of maternal competence and satisfaction in parenting we assessed the contributions of a comprehensive set of factors in context, in mother, and in child. In particular, we focused on culture, but also included socioeconomic status (SES), employment status, social support, education, knowledge of child development, age, personality, and, in recognition of the young child's own potential role in the construction and expression of parenting (Bell, 1968; Bell & Harper, 1977), child gender and language competence.

Context

We were first interested to ascertain what role *culture* might play in mothers' self-evaluations of their parenting. Certainly, culture conditions parents' attitudes and actions in childrearing (see, e.g., Bornstein, 1991; Harkness & Super, 1996; Knight, Cota, & Bernal, 1993). Several considerations guided our selection of two Western Hemisphere countries, the United States and Argentina, as settings in which to compare expressions and assess sources of mothers' self-evaluations of their parenting. On the one hand, the contexts and samples in this study share many structural characteristics related to parenting, including on a national level, a high degree of urbanization and equal preponderance of European heritage populations (approximately 85 percent), and on a social level, a long tradition of educating women, a high level of literacy, a low birthrate, a small family size, and an intact family structure.

However, the United States and Argentina contrast in terms of cultural heritage, economic circumstance, and philosophical orientation pertinent to parenting. The United States is widely recognized as an advanced industrial nation, whereas Argentina is a still-developing country characterized by substantial and continuing economic instabilities with severe consequences for the standard of living. One contemporary perspective on the cultural differences between these two New World nation-states turns on the distinction between individualism and collectivism that describes the relation between the individual and the collectivity that prevails in a given society (e.g., Harwood, Handwerker, Schoelmerich, & Leyendecker, 2001; Kagitçibasi, 1997; Smith & Bond, 1994; Triandis, 1995). Although each culture contains elements of individualism and collectivism, societies vary at the cultural level (Harwood et al., 2001). Individualist cultures tend to emphasize independence, autonomy in choice and action, and social assertiveness; in individualist societies, the ties between individuals are loose. Collectivist cultures tend to emphasize social interdependence, connectedness, and mutual deference or compromise as dominant values; in collectivist societies, people are integrated into stronger, cohesive ingroups, which protect them throughout life in exchange for loyalty. Of fifty countries worldwide studied by Hofstede (1991), the United States ranked first in individualism, whereas Argentina ranked mid-scale, tied for twenty-second, a marked difference. The conceptual status of individualist versus collectivist values differs for groups versus individuals, of course; Hofstede (1980, 1991) himself warned against the "ecological fallacy" of applying culture-level characteristics to individuals. Nonetheless, country scores describe the social systems individuals are likely to have built, and substantial relations obtain between the two levels: persons living in individualistic cultures tend to express idiocentric values and behaviors, and those living in collectivist cultures tend to express allocentric values and behaviors (see Bontempo & Rivero, 1992; Schwartz, 1994). The contrast between the United States and Argentina in individualist-collectivist terms implicates multiple psychological and childrearing differences, including individualist socialization for self-reliance, exploration, and independence versus collectivist socialization for sensitivity, obedience, and duty; independence versus dependence on social support; and reliant focus on self versus others.

Moreover, North and South American cultural styles are thought to contrast in related terms specific to parenting personality and action. Latin South American childrearing values tend to stress authoritarianism, dependency and obedience, reward and punishment (Aguinis, 1988; Durrett, O'Bryant, & Pennebaker, 1975; Eichelbaum de Babini, 1965; Kagan & Ender, 1975; Minturn & Lambert, 1964; Pescatello, 1973). European North American childrearing tends to be of an individualistic nature, where parents rely on their own abilities and resources (Bellah, Madsen, Sullivan, Swindler, & Tipton, 1985; Markus & Kitayama, 1991; Whiting & Child, 1953). Empirically, for example, U.S. mothers report engaging in didactic parenting more than Argentine mothers (Bornstein, Tamis-LeMonda, Pascual, Haynes, Painter, Galperín, & Pêcheux, 1996), and Argentine mothers use direct and controlling statements in speech to children more than U.S. mothers (Bornstein, Tal, Rahn, Galperín, Pêcheux, Lamour, Azuma, Toda, Ogino, & Tamis-LeMonda, 1992). Because the United States and Argentina are alike in so many respects that might be expected to predict maternal self-evaluations of parenting, but still differ in important cultural emphases, we reasoned that an ecological study of sources of maternal self-evaluations could be enriched from a cross-cultural perspective involving these two settings. However, we were also interested in other key sociodemographic and psychosocial factors that might predict competence and satisfaction in parenting and whether and how culture interacts with them.

For example, *socioeconomic status* plays an important part in the expression of diverse aspects of parenting (Hernandez, 1997; Hoff, Laursen, & Tardif, 2002). Not only do socioeconomic circumstances contribute to understanding childrearing techniques (see Bornstein & Bradley, 2002), but parents in a better social position, whose own emotional and physical needs are less at issue, should be able to provide for and respond more positively and effectively to their children. The range of activities and supports available to individuals on account of their different SES circumstances could constitute sources of competence and satisfaction in rearing children (Argyle, 1996). More concretely, mothers' *employment status* has emerged as a significant issue in parenting and developmental research (Crouter & McHale, 1993; Gottfried, Gottfried, & Bathurst, 2002). Career-oriented women generally report less satisfaction in parenting than women in more traditional sex-role orientations (e.g., Power & Parke, 1983). Goldberg and Easterbrooks (1988) found that employed mothers of toddlers were less likely than nonemployed mothers to hold childrearing attitudes that emphasized warmth and firm control.

Social support from significant others (such as spouse, lover, grandparent) constitutes a potentially critical source of parental competence and satisfaction (Belsky, 1984). Mothers appear to develop feelings of competence and satisfaction with their maternal roles through contact with advice givers, role models, and persons who share some of the responsibilities of parenthood within their social network. Even in normative development (all mothers who participated in this study were living in intact families), emotional integration or isolation from potential support networks can enhance or diminish mothers' self-evaluations of their competence and satisfaction in parenting (Cochran & Niego, 2002; Rogosch, Cicchetti, Shields, & Toth, 1995). In considering social support effects on parenting, three aspects are equally critical: the function of social support, the timing of social support, and the sources of social support that are valued culturally. First, social support provides tangible assistance to meet demands and facilitates coping with the effects of stress (Aneshensel, 1986; Heller & Swindle, 1983), and social support influences adult functioning (Cohen & Wills, 1985), including skillful parenting (Cotterell, 1986). Mothers with adequate social support are less harried, feel less overwhelmed, have fewer competing demands on their time, and as a consequence are more available to their babies (e.g., Crockenberg, 1981). Well-supported mothers are less restrictive and punitive with their children than are less well-supported mothers, and contacts with significant others improve the quality of parent-child relationships as well as mothers' sense of their own competence (Crnic, Greenberg, Ragozin, Robinson, & Basham, 1983). Second, the timing of social support is critical and especially valuable when the family is under stress (Quittner, Glueckauf, & Jackson, 1990), as is universally true around the birth of a first or a new baby. Crockenberg (1981) studied social support influences on the security of infant-mother attachment based on interviews conducted at three months: availability of social support facilitated responsive mothering, and social support was the best predictor of secure attachment. Crnic, Greenberg, and Slough (1986) explored relations among early stress, maternal social network supports, and mother-infant functioning during later infancy: stress and support from various ecological sources related to parent and infant outcomes. Burchinal, Follmer, and Bryant (1996) argued that maternal social support during the transition to parenthood might be especially influential in enhancing parenting style. Third, mothers in the United States report that community and friendship supports are beneficial, but support from husbands appears to have the most general positive consequences for maternal competence (Crnic et al., 1983). Mothers (and fathers) who report a weak "parenting alliance" and criticism from a spouse regarding parenting also report lack of self-confidence in parenting (Erel & Burman, 1995; Floyd & Zmich, 1991). However, factors associated with ethnicity or culture, such as differences in collectivism-individualism, could engender variation in parents' use of and responses to social support. For example, social support networks could vary in size, cohesion, or function among European American and Latin American women (Harrison, Wilson, Pine, Chan, & Burie, 1990; Vernon & Roberts, 1985). In spite of such differences, however, it may be that social networks exert similar effects on parenting in Latin American and European American families (MacPhee, Fritz, & Miller-Heyl, 1996). For these reasons, we evaluated and contrasted the reliance of mothers from a more collectivist culture like Argentina and a more individualist one like the United States on sources of social support.

Mother

Other general psychosocial characteristics that might be expected to influence how mothers evaluate competence and satisfaction in their parenting include their own education, knowledge of child development, age, and personality. More *educated* or cognitively aware mothers can be expected to seek out more information about parenting and hence may perceive themselves to be more competent. Kang (1985, cited in Barnard & Martell, 1995) found that mothers' cognitive sophistication was important for explaining parenting competence, and Brunnquell, Crichton, and Egeland (1981) found that mothers who scored higher on intelligence tests were more likely to provide good caregiving. Relatedly, mothers' *knowledge about child development* could also influence their self-evaluations and structure their interactions with their children (McGillicuddy-DeLisi, 1985; Miller, 1988). Knowledge of normative child development positively predicts parenting skills (Stevens, 1984); knowledge of developmental milestones is associated with introducing new experiences (Hess, Kashiwagi, Azuma, Price, & Dickson, 1980); and more knowledgeable mothers rate their children as having easier temperaments and so interact with them more (Sanson & Rothbart, 1995). Understanding the patterns and processes of early development should encourage more realistic expectations of the stages of development and of the skills required of children. Our assumption was that an informed parent acts and responds more positively, skillfully, and effectively than an uninformed parent across childrearing activities and responsibilities. The more knowledgeable parent will therefore be the more competent and satisfied parent.

More proximally still, personological characteristics of the mother can be expected to exert direct effects on self-evaluations of competence and satisfaction in parenting (e.g., Goodnow & Collins, 1990; Miller, 1988; Murphy, 1992; Sigel & McGillicuddy-DeLisi, 2002). If *age* is construed as a marker for maturity, then mothers' age can be expected to relate to parental competence and satisfaction. Younger mothers are known to express less desirable childrearing attitudes and have less realistic expectations for child development than older mothers (see Brooks-Gunn & Chase-Lansdale, 1995); reciprocally, mothers appear to interact with their children in more positively affectionate, stimulating, sensitive, and verbal ways the older they are, and older mothers report being more psychologically ready to assume responsibilities for rearing a child and attain more satisfaction in parenting (e.g., Jones, Green, & Krauss, 1980; Osofsky & Osofsky, 1970; Ragozin, Basham, Crnic, Greenberg, & Robinson, 1982). An individual's *personality* can also function to support or undermine parenting. Presumably, it is the sensitive parent who is able to decenter and to appraise the perspective of the child accurately, to empathize with the child, and to adopt a nurturant orientation. Unfortunately, the literature linking normative personality and parenting is far from extensive (Belsky, 1984; Belsky & Barends, 2002). Nonetheless, greater psychological maturity and integration are expected to predict more competent parenting, whereas higher negative affectivity—expressed as anxiety or depression—and/or severity of mental health impairment would be associated with less competent parenting (Belsky, 1984). More anxious mothers, for example, tend to lose confidence when their usual interactive techniques with children fail (Escalona, 1968). Parenting that is sensitively attuned to children's capabilities and to the developmental tasks children face promotes a variety of valued developmental outcomes, including emotional security, behavioral independence, social competence, and intellectual achievement (Belsky, Lerner, & Spanier, 1985).

Child

Finally, certain characteristics of children doubtless contribute to mothers' self-evaluations of their competence and satisfaction in parenting. Child *gender* could well be one. For example, girls might engender easier parenting than boys, especially in the toddler period studied here (Edwards & Liu, 2002), and so give rise to (the impression of) heightened competence or satisfaction in parenting. Additionally, Goldberg (1977) articulated a model of parent-child interaction that emphasized clarity and consistency of child cues as sources of parental feelings. Toddlers who exhibit more advanced competencies—for example, in their *language* skills—might thereby instill heightened feelings of competence and satisfaction in their mothers. That is, despite similarities in parenting per se, parents of children who present themselves in different ways could reach different conclusions about their competence and satisfaction as parents on account of cognitive or other characteristics of their children (e.g., Sanson & Rothbart, 1995).

OVERVIEW

Understanding self-evaluations of mothers' competence and satisfaction in parenting is integral to understanding variation in parenting, childrearing, parent-child relationships, and possibly child outcomes. Parental adjustment is usually assessed with standardized personality scales; in this cross-cultural, ecological, multivariate study, we assessed mothers' self-evaluations of their competence and satisfaction in parenting using an independent, theoretically based assessment instrument, and we asked how cultural as well as sociodemographic, personological, and child characteristics systematically predicted variation in these effective and affective domains of parenting self-evaluation in U.S. and Argentine mothers.

METHOD

Participants

Altogether, 112 primiparous mothers of twenty-month-old children, including 72 U.S. and 40 Argentine, were interviewed and completed all procedures. Mothers in the Washington, D.C., area were recruited from advertising in newspapers and mailing lists, and mothers in Buenos Aires from hospital birth notifications and patient lists of several medical groups. The samples were selected according to the following inclusive criteria: all women were first-time mothers, mothers were parents by birth, all families were intact with husbands living in the household, and mothers were twenty years of age or older. The samples represented a range from low- to upper-middle-class families as measured by the Hollingshead *Four-Factor Index of Social Status* (Hollingshead, 1975; see also Bornstein, Hahn, Suwalsky, & Haynes, 2002; Gottfried, 1985); the Hollingshead index has been validated as a measure of SES in Argentina (Pascual, Galperín, & Bornstein, 1993). Both parents in the two samples showed a full range of occupational ratings, from semiskilled workers to professionals (measured using the 9-point Hollingshead scale). Approximately 58 percent of U.S. mothers and 50 percent of Argentine mothers were working outside of the home when their child was twenty months of age. To avoid complications of extraneous ethnically based differences among mothers, the U.S. and Argentine samples were restricted to European heritage.

Research on parenting attitudes and activities has concentrated almost exclusively on mothers in recognition of the fact that in most cultures mothers have traditionally assumed primary—if not exclusive—responsibility for early childcare (see Barnard & Solchany, 2002; Hill & Stafford, 1974; Leiderman, Tulkin, & Rosenfeld, 1977; Parke, 2002; Young, 1991). The self-evaluation data on competence and satisfaction in this study were therefore collected directly from mothers. Furthermore, parenting self-evaluations were studied near the end of the child's second year in order to obtain information from mothers whose views of their own parenting had presumably stabilized, who were settled in the maternal role, and who had equivalent experience. All children had been term at birth and healthy since birth, excluding minor illnesses. They were 20.4 months of age on average at the time of observation ($SD = 0.2$). The second-year child is sensitive and responsive to maternal expressions of emotions and feelings, and by the end of the second year children demonstrate the cognitive capacity not only to interpret the physical and psychological states of others but also to share affectively in those states (see Bronson, 1974; Clarke-Stewart & Hevey, 1981; Eisenberg & Valiente, 2002; Zahn-Waxler & Radke-Yarrow, 1990; Zahn-Waxler,

Radke-Yarrow, Wagner & Chapman, 1992). As a consequence, approximately two years postpartum appeared to constitute a formative time from the perspective of children as well as mothers to investigate attitudes about competence and satisfaction in primiparous mothers' parenting. We also investigated potential differences in self-evaluations between mothers of girls and mothers of boys (Leaper, 2002; Maccoby & Jacklin, 1974).

Procedures

All mothers were asked to complete a set of self-report questionnaires in their homes, including sociodemographic information about the family, knowledge of child development, personality, and their children's productive vocabulary. Several steps were taken to promote the validity and cultural appropriateness of the instruments. To assure the equivalence of instruments between cultures, the questionnaires, originally constructed and written in English, were translated into Spanish and then back-translated by bilingual bicultural Argentine natives using standard back-translation techniques (Brislin, 1980, 1986). The translated instruments were then checked for preservation of meaning and cultural appropriateness in each site. Finally, the authors (experienced professionals in psychology and each a native of the countries in the study) also reviewed the instruments for understandableness and cultural appropriateness.

Parenting Competence and Satisfaction

Maternal attitudes toward parenting competence and satisfaction were assessed using the Self-Perceptions of the Parental Role (SPPR) inventory (MacPhee, Benson, & Bullock, 1986). Each item in this inventory has a pair of statements that describe contrasting endpoints of the dimension in question, thereby minimizing socially desirable responses. For example, one competence item states: "Some parents have clear ideas about the right and wrong ways to rear children" but "Other parents have doubts about the way they are bringing up their children"; one satisfaction item states: "Some adults are more content being a parent than they ever thought possible" but "For other adults, being a parent hasn't fulfilled them like they had hoped it would." The respondent chooses the statement that describes her best, and then checks *Sort of true for me* or *Really true for me*. Scores in each scale were the unweighted mean of responses to the items in each category. Possible scores range from 1 = *Low perceived* competence or satisfaction to 5 = *High perceived* competence or satisfaction. There are four response items, weighted 1, 2, 4, and 5 to accord with the absence of a response indicating that the item was equally like and unlike the respondent. (The SPPR has additional items not used here representing scales that assess investment and integration in parenting.) The competence and satisfaction scales have 5 and 6 items, respectively, with high alpha coefficients, 0.78 and 0.80, respectively (MacPhee et al., 1986). SPPR test-retest reliabilities (r) across a twenty-one-day interval for fifty-three mothers of eighteen-month-old infants were 0.86 and 0.88 for competence and satisfaction, respectively (Seybold, Fritz, & MacPhee, 1991). In terms of predictive validity, MacPhee and colleagues (1986) reported that SPPR competence and satisfaction scales correlated with "What I Am Like" scale scores for nurturance and adequacy as a provider.

Sources of Parenting Competence and Satisfaction

Nine predictor measures of maternal competence and satisfaction in parenting included culture, SES, employment status, education, and age. In addition, data on the following maternal predictors were included.

Social support. Social support history was measured on a 6-point scale from 0 = *Not used* to 5 = *Very helpful.* Mothers responded to five categories of role relationships: spouse, mother, mother-in-law, other relatives, and friends and neighbors. This information was collected when children were five months of age because the demands of an infant on a new mother at home are compelling and the mother's early social support is critical to parenting and child outcome (Crockenberg, 1981).

Parenting knowledge. The Knowledge of Infant Development Inventory (KIDI) (MacPhee, 1981) was used to assess mothers' knowledge of childrearing and child development, which forms a knowledge base that may influence parents' self-evaluations of competence and satisfaction. The instrument is composed of seventy-five items covering four general areas: norms and milestones, principles (developmental processes), parenting (strategies), and health and safety (guidelines). The measure used was the proportion of total responses that were correct for each culture.

Maternal personality. Eleven of the sixteen subscales of the Jackson Personality Inventory (JPI) (Jackson, 1976) were self-administered. The JPI is designed to assess a variety of personality traits in adults. Following the factor structure reported for a sample of 215 college students (Jackson, 1976), the principal component of three subscale scores (affectionate interpersonal relations, social participation, and anxiety), accounting for 53.2 percent of their total variance, was used as the single measure of the personality of mothers, specifically anxious sociability.

Social desirability. The Social Desirability Scale (SDS) (Crowne & Marlowe, 1960) uses thirty-three items to assess a respondent's tendency to reply to questions in a socially desirable fashion. This scale was used to estimate the degree to which maternal self-reports may be contaminated in the SPPR and JPI.

Child. Child predictors of maternal competence and satisfaction in parenting included gender and language. Mothers completed the Early Language Inventory (ELI) (Bates, Beeghly, Bretherton, McNew, O'Connell, Reznick, Shore, Snyder, & Volterra, 1984; Bates, Bretherton, & Snyder, 1988) on the basis of their general knowledge of the child. This inventory provides a measure of children's productive vocabulary. Mothers indicated which words in a 643-item checklist they had heard their child spontaneously produce. The total number of words was calculated for each child.

RESULTS

Descriptive Statistics and Country Differences

Parenting competence and satisfaction. Table 7.1 shows the means and standard deviations for competence and satisfaction for each country. Averaged across countries, mothers' reports of their competence ($M = 3.91$, $SD = 0.68$) and satisfaction ($M = 4.60$, $SD = 0.46$) in parenting were comparable to those previously reported by MacPhee and colleagues (1986) for 354 U.S. mothers of twelve- to forty-eight-month-olds. Table 7.1 also presents tests of differences between the two countries on each dependent variable: Mothers in the United States reported greater perceived competence and satisfaction than did mothers in Argentina. In a follow-up test controlling for mothers' SDS, $F(1,106) = 4.47$, $p < 0.04$, partial eta squared (η_p^2) = 0.04, country differences in Competence obtained, $F(1,106) = 17.19$, $p < 0.001$, $\eta_p^2 = 0.14$. In an analogous test controlling for mothers' SDS, $F(1, 106) = 4.17$, $p < 0.05$, $\eta_p^2 = 0.04$, country differences in Satisfaction also obtained, $F(1,106) = 21.52$, $p < 0.001$, $\eta_p^2 = 0.17$. Scores for Competence and Satisfaction shared only 11.9 percent of variance in the United States and 9.7 percent of variance in Argentina; these measures are therefore essentially nonoverlapping and independent, and multiple sources of competence and satisfaction in parenting were therefore investigated separately in a regression framework.

Sources of parenting competence and satisfaction. The means and standard deviations, as well as tests of country differences, of potential predictors of maternal competence and satisfaction are also presented in Table 7.1. Using $\alpha = 0.05$ unadjusted for multiple tests, country differences emerged in six of the eleven predictors. There was no difference in SES between the two groups. In terms of social support, mothers in the United States and Argentina reported finding spouse, mother, and mother-in-law as equally helpful in rearing a new baby, but mothers in the United States reported other relatives and friends and neighbors as more helpful than did mothers in Argentina. The average educational level (measured from the 7-point Hollingshead scale) in the United States was somewhat higher than in Argentina. Mothers in the United States knew more about child development than did mothers in Argentina. U.S. mothers were the same age as Argentine mothers. Mothers' mean standard scores on the personality scales were all close to the U.S. norm ($M = 50$, $SD = 10$) for adult females, and Argentine mothers were more socially anxious than U.S. mothers. The samples

Table 7.1

Maternal Competence and Satisfaction and Potential Predictors by Country

| | United States | | Argentina | | | | |
	Mean	SD	Mean	SD	t	df	$p^a \leq$
Self-evaluation of Maternal Competence	4.09	0.59	3.47	0.82	4.15	59.69	.001
Self-evaluation of Maternal Satisfaction	4.74	0.41	4.31	0.47	4.94	109	.001
Predictors:							
Mother							
Hollingshead SES	48.96	9.34	46.68	12.97	-0.98	110	ns
Social Support from:							
Spouse	4.52	0.89	4.25	1.17	1.37	109	ns
Mother	3.23	1.94	3.12	1.84	.28	108	ns
Mother-in-law	2.01	1.81	1.93	1.93	.24	110	ns
Other relatives	2.61	1.67	1.70	1.77	2.71	110	.008
Friends and neighbors	2.69	1.47	1.12	1.60	5.24	110	.001
Education	5.69	0.87	5.23	1.10	-2.49	110	.01
Knowledge of Child Development	0.81	0.05	0.66	0.10	8.50	49.56	.001
Age	31.48	4.21	29.95	3.66	-1.94	110	ns
Anxious Sociability[b]	-0.15	1.03	0.29	0.88	-2.24	108	.03
Anxiety[c]	49.60	10.24	55.26	5.50			
Affectionate Relations[c]	49.90	7.92	49.82	9.38			
Social Participation[c]	48.72	9.06	53.00	8.79			
Child							
Gender (girls/boys)	40/32		21/19				
Language	124.93	93.97	167.89	90.92	2.26	106	.03

[a]Two-tailed probabilities, unadjusted for multiple tests.
[b]Principal component.
[c]Standard score.

were also balanced with respect to sex of child, χ^2 (1, N = 112) = 0.10, ns. Children's mean language scores were less than 1 SD from the normed average, but larger in Argentina than in the United States. However, using a Bonferroni inequality of 0.0045 to adjust the multiple tests, country differences obtained for only support of friends and neighbors and knowledge of infant development.

Predicting Maternal Competence

Using a relatively liberal criterion (α = 0.15; Bendel & Afifi, 1977), correlations of self-evaluated maternal competence in both countries with each potential source were initially assessed to select the predictors to be used in a multiple regression model. Of the eleven potential sources, three—social support from the spouse, social support from other relatives, and maternal knowledge—met the criterion for inclusion in the regression. Three other predictors were added to the regression model: mothers' education was included because it tended to differ between countries (see "Participants"); mothers' personality was included because its relation with maternal competence was expected to differ by country; and country and terms representing the interactions of each predictor with country were included to test whether relations of predictors with maternal competence differed for the United States and Argentina. Country was represented by a dummy regressor coded 0 for Argentina and 1 for the United States. Prior to their inclusion, predictors were transformed to mean deviation scores to reduce the redundancies between the interaction terms and their components. One Argentine case was missing a score for self-perceived competence, and two Argentine cases were missing SDS scores; the cases were excluded from the final sample. In preliminary regressions of the full model, one case from the United States and two Argentine cases were identified as influential outliers and were also excluded, resulting in a sample size of 106, 71 from the United States and 35 from Argentina.

Eleven pairs of nested regression models—one pair for each of the five predictors, for country, and for the five-country interaction terms—were constructed. Following the notation of Fox (1997), Table 7.2A presents the thirteen regression models used to test the eleven pairs of nested models. The five interaction terms were tested in nested models composed of the full model containing terms for all predictors, the country regressor, and interactions with country (Model 1) and the full model less the specific interaction term (Models 2–6). The five main effects of the predictors—support from other relatives, support from spouse, education, knowledge of child development, and personality—were tested in nested models composed of the full model less the interaction term (Models 2–6) and the full model less the specific interaction term and main term (Models 7–11). The country term was tested in nested models composed of a model with all predictors and the country regressor (Model 12) and a model with predictors only (Model 13). Following Nelder's principle (1977) that main effects are marginal to interaction effects, we do not interpret main effects of predictors that interact.

The multiple regression coefficient for the full model was 0.49, $F(11,94) = 2.71$, $p < 0.005$, explaining 24 percent of the variance in competence. Table 7.2B presents the incremental F-test for each term in the prediction of maternal competence in the two countries. Controlling for relations of other terms in the model with competence, four terms uniquely predicted competence. As we noted in Table 7.1, U.S. mothers reported higher competence than did Argentine mothers, which was borne out by a significantly positive regression

Table 7.2A

Regression Sums of Squares for Models 1–13 Fit to Self-Perceived Competence

Model	Terms	Parameters	Regression Sum of Squares	df
1	E, R, F, P, K, C, ExC, RxC, FxC, PxC, KxC	$\alpha, \beta_1, \beta_2, \beta_3, \beta_4, \beta_5, \gamma, \delta_1, \delta_2, \delta_3, \delta_4, \delta_5$	11.3218	11
2	E, R, F, P, K, C, RxC, FxC, PxC, KxC	$\alpha, \beta_1, \beta_2, \beta_3, \beta_4, \beta_5, \gamma, \delta_2, \delta_3, \delta_4, \delta_5$	10.6269	10
3	E, R, F, P, K, C, ExC, FxC, PxC, KxC	$\alpha, \beta_1, \beta_2, \beta_3, \beta_4, \beta_5, \gamma, \delta_1, \delta_3, \delta_4, \delta_5$	11.3199	10
4	E, R, F, P, K, C, ExC, RxC, PxC, KxC	$\alpha, \beta_1, \beta_2, \beta_3, \beta_4, \beta_5, \gamma, \delta_1, \delta_2, \delta_4, \delta_5$	9.4520	10
5	E, R, F, P, K, C, ExC, RxC, FxC, KxC	$\alpha, \beta_1, \beta_2, \beta_3, \beta_4, \beta_5, \gamma, \delta_1, \delta_2, \delta_3, \delta_5$	11.1936	10
6	E, R, F, P, K, C, ExC, RxC, FxC, PxC	$\alpha, \beta_1, \beta_2, \beta_3, \beta_4, \beta_5, \gamma, \delta_1, \delta_2, \delta_3, \delta_4$	10.6178	10
7	R, F, P, K, C, RxC, FxC, PxC, KxC	$\alpha, \beta_2, \beta_3, \beta_4, \beta_5, \gamma, \delta_2, \delta_3, \delta_4, \delta_5$	9.5006	9
8	E, F, P, K, C, ExC, FxC, PxC, KxC	$\alpha, \beta_1, \beta_3, \beta_4, \beta_5, \gamma, \delta_1, \delta_3, \delta_4, \delta_5$	9.7013	9
9	E, R, P, K, C, ExC, RxC, PxC, KxC	$\alpha, \beta_1, \beta_2, \beta_4, \beta_5, \gamma, \delta_1, \delta_2, \delta_4, \delta_5$	9.4291	9
10	E, R, F, K, C, ExC, RxC, FxC, KxC	$\alpha, \beta_1, \beta_2, \beta_3, \beta_5, \gamma, \delta_1, \delta_2, \delta_3, \delta_5$	9.6248	9
11	E, R, F, P, C, ExC, RxC, FxC, PxC	$\alpha, \beta_1, \beta_2, \beta_3, \beta_4, \gamma, \delta_1, \delta_2, \delta_3, \delta_4$	10.3273	9
12	E, R, F, P, K, C	$\alpha, \beta_1, \beta_2, \beta_3, \beta_4, \beta_5, \gamma$	8.7545	6
13	E, R, F, P, K	$\alpha, \beta_1, \beta_2, \beta_3, \beta_4, \beta_5$	7.2090	5

Terms: E = Education, R = Relatives, F = Father, P = Personality, K = Knowledge, C = Country, XxC = Interaction of X with Country.

coefficient for country. The regression coefficient for social support from other relatives was positive, indicating that greater support from relatives predicted greater perceived competence in parenting. The regression coefficient for mothers' anxious sociability was negative, indicating that anxious sociability predicted lower perceived competence. Finally, the regression coefficient for the interaction of social support from spouse with country was negative, indicating that support from husbands was more predictive of self-perceived competence in Argentina than in the United States. The perception of support from one's spouse may be related to SES in the Argentine culture as it tends to be associated with middle- and upper-middle-class families. The tendency observed in the Argentine society, especially among the new generations of fathers, is that more educated husbands tend to have more active participation in childrearing (e.g., Pascual et al., 1993).

Table 7.2B

Analysis of Variance Table Showing Incremental F-Tests for Terms in Prediction of Maternal Competence

Source	Models Contrasted	β	Sum of Squares	df	F	$p\leq$
Country	12 - 13	.261	1.5454	1	4.065	.05
Social support: Spouse	4 - 9	.006	.0229	1	.060	.81
Social support: Other relatives	3 - 8	.198	1.6186	1	4.258	.04
Education	2 - 7	.173	1.1262	1	2.963	.09
Knowledge of child development	6 - 11	-.117	.2905	1	.764	.38
Personality	5 - 10	-.199	1.5689	1	4.127	.04
Social support: Spouse x Country	1 - 4	-.359	1.8698	1	4.919	.03
Social support: Other relatives x Country	1 - 3	.011	.0019	1	.005	.94
Education x Country	1 - 2	-.214	.6949	1	1.828	.18
Knowledge x Country	1 - 6	.207	.6950	1	1.828	.18
Personality x Country	1 - 5	-.111	.1282	1	.337	.56
Residuals			35.7330	94		
Total			47.0548	106		

Predicting Maternal Satisfaction

Using the same criterion ($\alpha = 0.15$), correlations of self-evaluated maternal satisfaction in parenting in both countries with each potential source were also assessed to select the predictors to be used in a final multiple regression model. Of the eleven potential sources, four—social support from other relatives, social support from friends and neighbors, maternal knowledge of child development, and maternal personality—met the criterion for inclusion in the regression. Two other predictors were added to the regression model: mothers' education was included because it tended to differ between countries, and country and terms representing the interactions of each predictor with country were included to test whether relations of predictors with maternal satisfaction differed for the United States and Argentina. As in the model for competence, country was represented by a dummy regressor coded 0 for Argentina and 1 for the United States, and all predictors were transformed to mean deviation scores. One Argentine case was missing a score for self-perceived satisfaction, and two Argentine cases were missing SDS scores; these cases were excluded from the final sample. In preliminary regressions of the full model, no influential outliers were detected, resulting in a final sample size of 109, 72 from the United States and 37 from Argentina.

Eleven pairs of nested regression models were used to test the prediction of self-perceived satisfaction. Table 7.3A presents the thirteen regression models used to test the eleven pairs of nested models. Except for the inclusion of terms for social support from friends and neighbors and its interaction with country, and the exclusion of terms for social support from spouse and its interaction with country, the pairs of nested models paralleled the models used in the regression of self-perceived competence.

The multiple regression coefficient for the full model was 0.56, $F(11,97) = 3.95$, $p < 0.001$, explaining 31 percent of the variance in satisfaction. Table 7.3B presents the incremental F-test for each term in the prediction of maternal satisfaction in the two countries. Controlling for relations of other terms in the model with satisfaction, two terms uniquely predicted satisfaction. As we noted in Table 7.1, U.S. mothers reported higher satisfaction than did Argentine mothers, which was borne out by a significantly positive regression coefficient for country. The regression coefficient for social support from other relatives was

Table 7.3A
Regression Sums of Squares for Models 1–13 Fit to Self-Perceived Satisfaction

Model	Terms	Parameters	Regression Sum of Squares	df
1	E, R, FN, P, K, C, ExC, RxC, FNxC, PxC, KxC	$\alpha, \beta_1, \beta_2, \beta_3, \beta_4, \beta_5, \gamma, \delta_1, \delta_2, \delta_3, \delta_4, \delta_5$	718622.151	11
2	E, R, FN, P, K, C, RxC, FNxC, PxC, KxC	$\alpha, \beta_1, \beta_2, \beta_3, \beta_4, \beta_5, \gamma, \delta_2, \delta_3, \delta_4, \delta_5$	716406.171	10
3	E, R, FN, P, K, C, ExC, FNxC, PxC, KxC	$\alpha, \beta_1, \beta_2, \beta_3, \beta_4, \beta_5, \gamma, \delta_1, \delta_3, \delta_4, \delta_5$	718204.428	10
4	E, R, FN, P, K, C, ExC, RxC, PxC, KxC	$\alpha, \beta_1, \beta_2, \beta_3, \beta_4, \beta_5, \gamma, \delta_1, \delta_2, \delta_4, \delta_5$	709622.504	10
5	E, R, FN, P, K, C, ExC, RxC, FNxC, KxC	$\alpha, \beta_1, \beta_2, \beta_3, \beta_4, \beta_5, \gamma, \delta_1, \delta_2, \delta_3, \delta_5$	713990.850	10
6	E, R, FN, P, K, C, ExC, RxC, FNxC, PxC	$\alpha, \beta_1, \beta_2, \beta_3, \beta_4, \beta_5, \gamma, \delta_1, \delta_2, \delta_3, \delta_4$	716349.896	10
7	R, FN, P, K, C, RxC, FNxC, PxC, KxC	$\alpha, \beta_2, \beta_3, \beta_4, \beta_5, \gamma, \delta_2, \delta_3, \delta_4, \delta_5$	680613.759	9
8	E, FN, P, K, C, ExC, FNxC, PxC, KxC	$\alpha, \beta_1, \beta_3, \beta_4, \beta_5, \gamma, \delta_1, \delta_3, \delta_4, \delta_5$	620729.136	9
9	E, R, P, K, C, ExC, RxC, PxC, KxC	$\alpha, \beta_1, \beta_2, \beta_4, \beta_5, \gamma, \delta_1, \delta_2, \delta_4, \delta_5$	694829.357	9
10	E, R, FN, K, C, ExC, RxC, FNxC, KxC	$\alpha, \beta_1, \beta_2, \beta_3, \beta_5, \gamma, \delta_1, \delta_2, \delta_3, \delta_5$	686757.064	9
11	E, R, FN, P, C, ExC, RxC, FNxC, PxC	$\alpha, \beta_1, \beta_2, \beta_3, \beta_4, \gamma, \delta_1, \delta_2, \delta_3, \delta_4$	713043.862	9
12	E, R, FN, P, K, C	$\alpha, \beta_1, \beta_2, \beta_3, \beta_4, \beta_5, \gamma$	696096.509	6
13	E, R, FN, P, K	$\alpha, \beta_1, \beta_2, \beta_3, \beta_4, \beta_5$	470676.930	5

Terms: E = Education, R = Relatives, FN = Friends and Neighbors, P = Personality, K = Knowledge, C = Country, XxC = Interaction of X with Country.

Table 7.3B

Analysis of Variance Table Showing Incremental F-Tests for Terms in Prediction of Satisfaction

Source	Models Contrasted	β	Sum of Squares	df	F	$p \leq$
Country	12 - 13	.473	225419.579	1	13.642	.001
Social support: Other relatives	3 - 8	.219	97475.292	1	5.899	.02
Social support: Friend and neighbors	4 - 9	-.093	14793.147	1	.895	.35
Education	2 - 7	.136	35792.412	1	2.166	.14
Knowledge of child development	6 - 11	-.057	3306.034	1	.200	.66
Personality	5 - 10	.122	27233.786	1	1.648	.20
Social support: Other relatives x Country	1 - 3	-.023	417.723	1	.025	.88
Social support: Friends and neighbors x Country	1 - 4	-.108	8999.650	1	.545	.46
Education x Country	1 - 2	-.051	2215.98	1	.134	.72
Knowledge x Country	1 - 6	-.049	2272.255	1	.138	.71
Personality x Country	1 - 5	-.095	4631.301	1	.280	.60
Residuals			1602842.337	97		
Total			2321464.488	108		

positive, indicating that greater support from relatives predicted greater perceived satisfaction in parenting.

DISCUSSION

This study evaluated ecological, psychosocial, and developmental expressions and sources of maternal self-evaluations of competence and satisfaction in parenting in two countries, the United States and Argentina. We sought to investigate mothers' beliefs in these "effective" and "affective" caregiving domains on the grounds that they contribute to understanding parenting more fully and that they have important roles to play in childrearing and child development. We found cultural differences in the levels of maternal self-reported competence and satisfaction in parenting, and we also found that some sources of holding competent and satisfied feelings about one's parenting were the same in these two societies, but others were different.

Before turning to elaborate on these findings, as well as what they have to say about parenting and culture, we note that the criteria data in this study derived from self-reports of mothers about specific sets of parenting beliefs, and the respondents were mothers of children of one specific age from particular populations. These factors limit the generalizability of the findings by parenting domain, population, and setting. Nonetheless, research in parenting is often localized culturally, typically assessed with overgeneralized instruments, and frequently fails to control for confounds in social class and child age, thereby obscuring interpretations of possible cultural differences (see Laosa, 1978; Vega, 1990). By contrast, this cross-cultural, ecological, multivariate study used conceptually targeted criteria instruments with defined populations, and so begins to redress these methodological problems. Furthermore, significant components of parenting entail subjective psychological states that can be assessed indirectly from observed behaviors or others' perceptions (notably the child's), but may be best understood from direct assessments based on self-reports or interviews (Holden & Buck, 2002). Verbal reports of mental activity are common in everyday life, and they constitute critical and valid kinds of data in many areas of cognitive science (Ericson & Simon, 1993). In this study, we also made direct assessments of parenting self-evaluations using theoretically derived instruments. Indeed, from a social cognition viewpoint, such self-evaluations constitute key ways "people make sense of other people and themselves" (Fiske & Taylor, 1984, p. 12). In addition, "accessibility" may constitute a defining characteristic of these particular self-evaluations: those beliefs that are more accessible in the way we measured them could reflect parenting norms or widely held agreements within a culture and relate to, influence, or rationalize parenting behavior quickly or effectively (Bem, 1970; Harkness & Super, 1996; Miller, 1988; Shweder, 1991).

U.S. mothers rated themselves more highly than Argentine mothers in terms of both competence and satisfaction in parenting. It is unlikely that these differences reflect response bias because they obtained even after controlling for social desirability of reporting. In contemporary middle-class Argentine society, parenting is characterized by a degree of insecurity because there are no clear rules about how to behave as a parent: "You never know for sure if you are doing a good job," one mother told us. Argentine middle-class mothers fear making mistakes that could make their children unhappy. They are reflective and hesitant, self-critical and self-questioning. Nor does Argentine society reinforce feelings of security: In its recent history, Argentina has been troubled economically and politically, and social services demeaned or discounted. More specifically, contemporary Argentina lacks a public healthcare system that provides adequate help or advice in childrearing; instead, mothers seek and make do with ad hoc suggestions from relatives or friends. Argentine mothers think they succeed best when parenting tasks are not difficult, and they blame parenting failures on their lack of ability (Bornstein, Haynes, Azuma, Galperín, Maital, Ogino, Painter, Pascual, Pêcheux, Rahn, Toda, Venuti, Vyt, & Wright, 1998). This situation tends to undermine mothers' beliefs in their own part in parenting (Aguinis, 1988; Fillol, 1991; Pascual, 1991; Pascual, Schulthess, Galperín, & Bornstein, 1995). By contrast, U.S. mothers willingly rely on their own abilities;

they are competitive, they want the best for their children, and they feel that the best way to achieve this goal is to prepare themselves to be good parents. U.S. mothers tend to be optimistic and positive when evaluating their parenting: North American culture prizes individual effort, and mothers in the United States see parenting as a kind of personal achievement. Investment in child-rearing is high in U.S. families, and as a consequence mothers tend to feel more confident in themselves (Bellah et al., 1985; Bornstein et al., 1996; Bornstein et al., 1998; Whiting & Child, 1953).

Other between-country differences consisted of finding nonnuclear family relatives and friends and neighbors helpful, and knowledge of child development, both favoring the United States. Mothers in these two samples were equivalent in SES and age; the difference in knowledge of child development held after controlling for maternal education. As to differences in social support, the literature suggests that studies of cultural variation in social networks and childrearing practices should attend to economic confounds. For example, Golding and Baezcondi-Garbanati (1990) found that ethnic differences in social network composition disappeared when income and employment were controlled. We controlled for these factors. Normally, Latin American, relative to North American, groups are believed to have more extensive and more closely knit reciprocal kin relationship networks for social support (e.g., Keefe, Padilla, & Carlos, 1979). Although this may be true, we found that a North American sample reports relatives and friends being more helpful sources of social support.

Among the several potential predictors we measured, the most important contributions to self-evaluations of competence and satisfaction in mothers, beyond culture, were extrinsic aspects of social support and intrinsic aspects of personality. Contributions to self-reported *competence* in parenting in mothers in the two countries consisted of both social support and personological factors. In both cultures, mothers who could appeal for support from relatives other than spouse, mother, and mother-in-law reported higher levels of belief in their parenting competence as did mothers with less social anxiety. The main contributor to self-reported *satisfaction* in mothers in the two countries also consisted of social support from relatives other than spouse, mother, and mother-in-law. Although competence and satisfaction are relatively independent constructs, and mothers in these two societies rated themselves differently on each, a common factor contributing to competence in parenting was personality, and a common factor contributing to both competence and satisfaction in parenting was early social support from extended families. In this connection it is interesting to note that positive personality characteristics support good parenting (Belsky, 1984), just as social support facilitates positive parenting (e.g., Crnic et al., 1983; Crockenberg, 1981; Cutrona & Troutman, 1986): supported mothers are reputedly "warmer" with their young children, for example (Jennings, Stagg, & Connors, 1991). Family social networks can provide parents with regular positive experiences and stable, socially rewarded roles that positively influence self-worth and promote satisfaction. Families also help parents to avoid worries about negative experiences or negative experiences themselves (e.g., economic or legal problems) that otherwise undermine confidence or decrease psychological satisfaction with parenting (Cohen & Wills, 1985).

Amidst the several striking similarities, however, one extrinsic factor functioned differently for competence: Argentine, not U.S., mothers with more social support from their husbands rated themselves as more competent in parenting. In this study, SES, mothers' employment status, education, knowledge of child development, and age as well as child gender and language competence did not help to explain mothers' self-evaluations of their parenting competence or satisfaction. This does not mean that these factors have no role to play, however; the samples from the cultures we studied were matched on most of these variables.

Beyond delimiting predictors of self-evaluations of competence and satisfaction in parenting, data from this study speak to more general issues about parenting, culture, and the interaction of parenting and culture. First, these cross-cultural findings lend support to the notion that parenting ideas are modular (Bornstein, 2002b). Parenting competence and satisfaction were essentially nonoverlapping constructs in mothers in the two societies, and differing sources and cultural conditions exerted differentiating influences on these two self-evaluative domains. Second, culture played a large role. Not only did the two cultures differ in competence and satisfaction, U.S. mothers reported finding relatives and friends and neighbors more helpful to their parenting experiences.

This study also revealed interactions of culture with the domain of parenting assessed. For example, culture interacted with social support differentially to affect parents' self-perceptions of competence. In both the United States and Argentina, social support from relatives exerted a positive effect on mothers' reported competence at parenting, but in addition, in Argentina women with a history of greater spousal social support also reported more competent parenting. Intimate support from husbands is reported to have positive consequences for maternal competence (Crnic et al., 1983), and reciprocally marital conflict, low marital satisfaction, and poor spousal support have been associated with stress in parental competence (Lamb & Elster, 1985). In Latin America, shared parental nurturing appears to be closer to the expected norm, especially among educated middle-class women: Latin Americans relative to European Americans have extensive, close-knit reciprocal relationship networks and reportedly depend on a select few individuals for emotional support (Keefe et al., 1979; see, too, Vega, 1990). In a more collectivist society like Argentina, it is possible that mothers' insecurities about parenting are offset by fathers' more direct involvement in childrearing, and reassured mothers develop confidence in their parenting. Indeed, Argentine mothers report that they want their husbands to take a greater role in childrearing (Bornstein et al., 1996; Pascual et al., 1995). These findings thus comport with predictions from a collectivist-individualist perspective on the role of social support in parenting. For mothers from U.S. and Argentine cultures, parenting competence appears to emerge from wider familial relationships, but for Argentine mothers it tends also to be reinforced by social support within the spousal relationship. East-West contrasts of collectivism-individualism have predominated in the cross-cultural literature; this North-South study compared collectivist and individualist nation-states and identified social support variables thought to involve differences in collectivism and individualism.

Future cross-cultural research in parenting could move to more molar or molecular levels from this starting point. In the one direction, it would be enlightening to uncover what structural forces in society promote or constrain parenting differences and their predictors (Bornstein, 1991). Cochran and his colleagues (Cochran & Niego, 2002; Cochran, Larner, Rile, Gunnarson, & Henderson, 1990) have argued that social capital, group identity, cultural ideology, prejudice, and the like might play telling roles. In the other direction, research could be applied to further differentiate among forms of social support and also to explicate more precisely the processes by which parents utilize self-evaluations about parenting to set social agenda and everyday childrearing choices. With respect to the former, the *type* of social support could matter as much as the source, for example. Kahn and Antonucci (1980) classified support as *affect* (feeling loved and cared for), *aid* (advice, information, or direct intervention in problem solving), and *affirmation* (contributing to the individual's sense that he or she is interpreting events correctly). Examining social supports of different types in different cultural contexts could contribute to deeper insights into differences in the role of social support in parenting. With respect to the latter, self-perceptions reputedly have specific consequences for parenting: In terms of competence, for example, parents who believe that they can exert effects on their children's intelligence or personality tend to adopt more active roles in parenting (McGillicuddy-DeLisi, 1985), and parents who feel efficacious in teaching their children report spending more time actually helping their children (Epstein, 1986). Mothers who receive greater informal support from friends tend to be more emotionally responsive to their children (Crnic et al., 1983) and less punitive (Colletta, 1979; Reis, Barbera-Stein, & Bennett, 1986).

Of course, parents' self-evaluations do not account for the whole of parenting, nor do they monistically shape parents' actions or how their children develop. However, understanding the full scope of parental thinking, including key self-evaluations, can contribute to understanding why and how parents parent the way they do, and helps to provide insight into the full context of child development (Super & Harkness, 1986). Understanding the cultural sources and specialties of parenting competence and satisfaction, such as we have undertaken to do here, opens up new avenues of investigation into the nature of family functioning as well as the possibilities of both predicting and changing parenting beliefs and behaviors in culturally relevant ways.

NOTE

We thank C. Galperín, K. Schulthess, and C. Varron for assistance. Request reprints from Marc H. Bornstein, Child and Family Research, National Institute of Child Health and Human Development, National Institutes of Health, Suite 8030, 6705 Rockledge Drive, Bethesda, MD 20892-7971; tel.: 301-496-6832, fax: 301-480-4039, e-mail: marc_h_bornstein@nih.gov.

REFERENCES

Aguinis, M. (1988). *Un pais de novela* [A fictive country]. Buenos Aires, Argentina: Editorial Planeta.

Aneshensel, C. S. (1986). Marital and employment role strain, social support and depression among adult women. In S. E. Hobfoll (Ed.), *Stress, social support, and women* (pp. 99–114). Washington, DC: Hemisphere.

Argyle, M. (1996). *The psychology of social class*. London: Routledge.

Baldwin, A. L., Cole, R. E., & Baldwin, C. P. (Eds.). (1982). Parental pathology, family interaction, and the competence of the child in school. *Monographs of the Society for Research in Child Development, 47* (serial no. 197).

Bandura, A. (1977). Self-efficacy: Toward a unifying theory of behavioral change. *Psychological Review, 84,* 191–215.

———. (1986). *Social foundations of thought and action*. Englewood Cliffs, NJ: Prentice-Hall.

———. (1997). *Self-efficacy: The exercise of control*. New York: Freeman.

Barnard, K. E., & Martell, L. K. (1995). Mothering. In Marc H. Bornstein (Ed.), *Handbook of parenting: Status and social conditions of parenting*. NJ: Erlbaum.

Barnard, K. E., & Solchany, J. E. (2002). Mothering. In M. H. Bornstein (Ed.), *Handbook of parenting*, Vol. 3, *Status and social conditions of parenting* (2nd ed., pp. 3–25). Mahwah, NJ: Erlbaum.

Bates, E., Beeghly, M., Bretherton, I., McNew, S., O'Connell, B., Reznick, S., Shore, C., Snyder, L., & Volterra, V. (1984). Early language inventory. Unpublished manuscript, Center for Research on Language, University of California, San Diego.

Bates, E., Bretherton, I., & Snyder, L. (1988). *From first words to grammar: Individual differences and dissociable mechanisms*. Cambridge: Cambridge University Press.

Bell, R. Q. (1968). A reinterpretation of the direction of effects in studies of socialization. *Psychological Review, 75,* 81–95.

Bell, R. Q., & Harper, L. (1977). *Child effects on adults*. Hillsdale, NJ: Erlbaum.

Bellah, R. N., Madsen, R., Sullivan, W. M., Swindler, A., & Tipton, S. M. (1985). *Habits of the heart: Individualism and commitment in American life*. New York: Harper & Row.

Belsky, J. (1984). The determinants of parenting: A process model. *Child Development, 55,* 83–96.

Belsky, J., & Barends, N. (2002). Personality and parenting. In M. H. Bornstein (Ed.), *Handbook of parenting*, Vol. 3, *Status and social ecology of parenting* (2nd ed., pp. 415–438). Mahwah, NJ: Erlbaum.

Belsky, J., Lerner, R., & Spanier, G. (1985). *The child in the family.* Reading, MA: Addison-Wesley.

Bem, D. (1970). *Beliefs, behaviors, and human affairs.* Belmont, CA: Brooks/Cole.

Bendel, R. B., & Afifi, A. A. (1977). Comparison of stopping rules in forward regression. *Journal of the American Statistical Association, 72,* 46–53.

Bontempo, R., & Rivero, J. C. (1992, August). Cultural variation in cognition: The role of self-concept in the attitude behavior link. Paper presented at the meeting of the American Academy of Management, Las Vegas, Nevada.

Bornstein, M. H. (1991). Approaches to parenting in culture. In M. H. Bornstein (Ed.), *Cultural approaches to parenting* (pp. 3–19). Hillsdale, NJ: Erlbaum.

———. (Ed.). (2002a). *Handbook of parenting.* Vols. 1–5. Mahwah, NJ: Erlbaum.

———. (2002b). Parenting infants. In M. H. Bornstein (Ed.), *Handbook of parenting* (Vol. 1, pp. 3–39). Mahwah, NJ: Erlbaum.

Bornstein, M. H., & Bradley, R. H. (Eds.). (2002). *Socioeconomic status, parenting, and child development.* Mahwah, NJ: Erlbaum.

Bornstein, M., Hahn, C. S., Suwalsky, J., & Haynes, O. M. (2002). Socioeconomic status, parenting, and child development: The Hollingshead Four-Factor Index of Social Status and the Socioeconomic Index of Occupations. In M. H. Bornstein & R. H. Bradley (Eds.), *Socioeconomic status, parenting, and child development* (pp. 29–82). Mahwah, NJ: Erlbaum.

Bornstein, M. H., Haynes, O. M., Azuma, H., Galperín, C., Maital, S., Ogino, M., Painter, K., Pascual, K., Pêcheux, M. G., Rahn, C., Toda, S., Venuti, P., Vyt, A., & Wright, B. (1998). A cross-national study of self-evaluations and attributions in parenting: Argentina, Belgium, France, Israel, Italy, Japan, and the United States. *Developmental Psychology, 34,* 662–676.

Bornstein, M. H., Tal, J., Rahn, C., Galperín, C. Z., Pêcheux, M. G., Lamour, M., Azuma, H., Toda, S., Ogino, M., & Tamis-LeMonda, C. S. (1992). Functional analysis of the contents of maternal speech to infants of five and thirteen months in four cultures: Argentina, France, Japan, and the United States. *Developmental Psychology, 28,* 593–603.

Bornstein, M. H., Tamis-LeMonda, C. S., Pascual, L., Haynes, O. M., Painter, K., Galperín, C., & Pêcheux, M. G. (1996). Ideas about parenting in Argentina, France, and the United States. *International Journal of Behavioral Development, 19,* 347–367.

Brislin, R. W. (1980). Translation and content analysis of oral and written material. In H. C. Triandis & J. W. Berry (Eds.), *Handbook of cross-cultural psychology* (Vol. 1, pp. 389–444). Boston: Allyn & Bacon.

———. (1986). The wording and translation of research instruments. In W. J. Lonner & J. W. Berry (Eds.), *Field methods in cross-cultural research* (pp. 137–164). Newbury Park, CA: Sage.

Bronfenbrenner, U. (1989). Ecological systems theory. In R. Vasta (Ed.), *Annals of child development* (Vol. 6, pp. 187–249). Greenwich, CT: JAI Press.

Bronfenbrenner, U., & Crouter, A. C. (1983). The evolution of environmental models in developmental research. In W. Kessen (Ed.), P. H. Mussen (Series Ed.), *Hand-*

book of child psychology, Vol. 1, History, theory, and methods (pp. 357–414). New York: Wiley.

Bronson, W. C. (1974). Mother-toddler interaction: A perspective on studying the development of competence. Merrill-Palmer Quarterly, 20, 275–301.

Brooks-Gunn, J., & Chase-Lansdale, P. L. (1995). Adolescent parenthood. In M. H. Bornstein (Ed.), Handbook of parenting (Vol. 3, pp. 113–149). Mahwah, NJ: Erlbaum.

Brunnquell, D., Crichton, L., & Egeland, B. (1981). Maternal personality and attitude in disturbances of child rearing. American Journal of Orthopsychiatry, 51, 680–691.

Burchinal, M. R., Follmer, A., & Bryant, D. M. (1996). The relations of maternal social support and family structure with maternal responsiveness and child outcomes among African American families. Developmental Psychology, 32, 1073–1083.

Chess, S., & Thomas, A. (1984). Origins and evolution of behavior disorders from infancy to early adult life. New York: Brunner/Mazel.

Clarke-Stewart, K. A., & Hevey, C. M. (1981). Longitudinal relations in repeated observations of mother-child interaction from 1 to 2½ years. Developmental Psychology, 17, 127–145.

Cochran, M., Larner, M., Rile, D., Gunnarson, L., & Henderson, C. R. (1990). Extending families: The social networks of parents and their children. Cambridge: Cambridge University Press.

Cochran, M., & Niego, S. (2002). Parenting and social networks. In M. H. Bornstein (Ed.), Handbook of parenting, Vol. 4, Applied parenting (2nd ed., pp. 123–148). Mahwah, NJ: Erlbaum.

Cohen, S., & Wills, T. A. (1985). Stress, social support, and the buffering hypothesis. Psychological Bulletin, 98, 310–357.

Colletta, N. (1979). Support systems after divorce: Incidence and impact. Journal of Marriage and the Family, 41, 837–846.

Cotterell, J. L. (1986). Work and community influences on the quality of child rearing. Child Development, 57, 362–374.

Crnic, K. A., Greenberg, M. T., Ragozin, A., Robinson, N., & Basham, R. (1983). Effects of stress and social support on mothers and premature and full-term infants. Child Development, 54, 209–217.

Crnic, K. A., Greenberg, M. T., & Slough, N. M. (1986). Early stress and social support influences on mothers' and high-risk infants' functioning in late infancy. Special issue: Social support, family functioning, and infant development, Infant Mental Health Journal, 7, 19–33.

Crockenberg, S. B. (1981). Infant irritability, mother responsiveness, and social support influences on the security of infant-mother attachment. Child Development, 52, 857–865.

Crouter, A. C., & McHale, S. M. (1993). The long arm of the job: Influences of parental work on childrearing. In T. Luster & L. Okagaki (Eds.), Parenting: An ecological perspective (pp. 179–202). Hillsdale, NJ: Erlbaum.

Crowne, D. P., & Marlowe, D. (1960). A new scale of social desirability independent of psychopathology. Journal of Consulting Psychology, 24, 349–354.

Cutrona, C. E., & Troutman, B. R. (1986). Social support, infant temperament, and parenting self-efficacy: A mediating model of postpartum depression. Child Development, 57, 1507–1518.

Dix, T. H., & Grusec, J. E. (1985). Parent attribution processes in the socialization of children. In I. E. Sigel (Ed.), *Parental belief systems* (pp. 201–234). Hillsdale, NJ: Erlbaum.

Durett, M. E., O'Bryant, S., & Pennebaker, J. W. (1975). Child-rearing reports of White, Black, and Mexican-American families. *Developmental Psychology, 11,* 871.

Edwards, C. P., & Liu, W. (2002). Parenting toddlers. In M. H. Bornstein (Ed.), *Handbook of parenting,* Vol. 2, *Children and parenting* (2nd ed., pp. 45–71). Mahwah, NJ: Erlbaum.

Eichelbaum de Babini, A. M. (1965). *Educacion familiar y status socioeconomico* [Socialization within the family and socioeconomic status]. Buenos Aires: Instituto de Sociologia.

Eisenberg, N., & Valiente, C. (2002). Parenting and children's prosocial and moral development. In M. H. Bornstein (Ed.), *Handbook of parenting,* Vol. 5, *Practical parenting* (2nd ed., pp. 111–142). Mahwah, NJ: Erlbaum.

Epstein, J. L. (1986). Parents' reactions to teacher practices of parent involvement. *Elementary School Journal, 86,* 277–294.

Erel, O., & Burman, B. (1995). Interrelatedness of marital relations and parent-child relations: A meta-analytic review. *Psychological Bulletin, 118,* 108–132.

Ericson, K. A., & Simon, H. A. (1993). *Protocol analysis: Verbal reports as data.* Cambridge: MIT Press.

Escalona, S. K. (1968). *The roots of individuality: Normal patterns of development in infancy.* Chicago: Aldine.

Fillol, T. R. (1991). *Social factors in economic development: The Argentine case.* Westport, CT: Greenwood Press.

Fiske, S. T., & Taylor, S. E. (1984). *Social cognition.* New York: Random House.

Floyd, F. J., & Zmich, D. E. (1991). Marriage and the parenting partnership: Perceptions and interactions of parents with mentally retarded and typically developing children. *Child Development, 62,* 1434–1448.

Fox, J. (1997). *Applied regression analysis, linear models, and related methods.* Thousand Oaks, CA: Sage.

Goldberg, S. (1977). Social competence in infancy: A model of parent-infant interaction. *Merrill Palmer Quarterly, 23,* 163–177.

Goldberg, W. A., & Easterbrooks, M. A. (1988). Maternal employment when children are toddlers and kindergartners. In A. E. Gottfried & A. W. Gottfried (Eds.), *Maternal employment and children's development: Longitudinal research* (pp. 121–154). New York: Plenum.

Golding, J. M., & Baezconde-Garbanati, L. A. (1990). Ethnicity, culture, and social resources. *American Journal of Community Psychology, 18,* 465–486.

Goodnow, J. J., & Collins, W. A. (1990). *Development according to parents. The nature, sources, and consequences of parents' ideas.* London: Erlbaum.

Gottfried, A. E., Gottfried, A. W., & Bathurst, K. (2002). Maternal and dual-earner employment status and parenting. In M. H. Bornstein (Ed.), *Handbook of parenting,* Vol. 2, *Biology and ecology of parenting* (2nd ed., pp. 207–229). Mahwah, NJ: Erlbaum.

Gottfried, A. W. (1985). Measures of socioeconomic status in child development research: Data and recommendations. *Merrill-Palmer Quarterly, 31,* 85–92.

Harkness, S., & Super, C. M. (Eds.). (1996). *Parents' cultural belief systems: Their origins, expressions, and consequences*. New York: Guilford Press.

Harrison, A. O., Wilson, M. N., Pine, C. J., Chan, S. Q., & Burie, R. (1990). Family ecologies of ethnic minority children. *Child Development, 61*, 347–362.

Harwood, R. L., Handwerker, W. P., Schoelmerich, A., & Leyendecker, B. (2001). Ethnic category labels, parental beliefs, and the contextualized individual: An exploration of the individualism/sociocentrism debate. *Parenting: Science and Practice, 1*, 217–236.

Heller, K., & Swindle, R. W. (1983). Social networks, perceived social support, and coping with stress. In R. D. Felner, L. A. Jason, J. N. Moritsugu, & S. S. Farber (Eds.), *Preventive psychology: Theory, research, and practice* (pp. 87–103). New York: Pergamon.

Hernandez, D. J. (1997). Child development and the social demography of childhood. *Child Development, 68*, 149–169.

Hess, R. D., Kashiwagi, K., Azuma, H., Price, G. C., & Dickson, W. P. (1980). Maternal expectations for mastery of developmental tasks in Japan and the United States. *International Journal of Psychology, 15*, 259–271.

Hill, C. R., & Stafford, F. P. (1974). Allocation of time to preschool children and educational opportunity. *Journal of Human Resources, 9*, 323–341.

Hoff, E., Laursen, B., & Tardif, T. (2002). Socioeconomic status and parenting. In M. H. Bornstein (Ed.), *Handbook of parenting*, Vol. 2, *Biology and ecology of parenting* (2nd ed., pp. 231–252). Mahwah, NJ: Erlbaum.

Hofstede, G. (1980). *Culture's consequences: International differences in work-related values*. London: Sage.

———. (1991). *Cultures and organizations: Software of the mind*. London: McGraw-Hill.

Holden, G. W., & Buck, M. J. (2002). Parental attitudes toward childrearing. In M. H. Bornstein (Ed.), *Handbook of parenting*, Vol. 3, *Status and social conditions of parenting* (2nd ed., pp. 537–562). Mahwah, NJ: Erlbaum.

Hollingshead, A. B. (1975). The four factor index of social status. Unpublished manuscript, Yale University.

Holloway, S. D., & Machida, S. (1992). Maternal child-rearing beliefs and coping strategies: Consequences for divorced mothers and their children. In I. E. Sigel, A. V. McGillicuddy-DeLisi, & J. J. Goodnow (Eds.), *Parental belief systems: The psychological consequences for children* (pp. 249–265). Hillsdale, NJ: Erlbaum.

Hopkins, J., Marcus, M., & Campbell, S. B. (1984). Postpartum depression: A critical review. *Psychological Bulletin, 95*, 498–515.

Jackson, D. N. (1976). *Jackson personality inventory manual*. Goshen, NY: Research Psychologists Press.

Jennings, K. D., Stagg, V., & Connors, R. E. (1991). Social networks and mothers' interactions with their preschool children. *Child Development, 62*, 966–978.

Johnston, C., & Mash, E. (1989). A measure of parenting satisfaction and efficacy. *Journal of Clinical Child Psychology, 18*, 167–175.

Jones, F. A., Green, V., & Krauss, D. R. (1980). Maternal responsiveness of primiparous mothers during the postpartum period: Age differences. *Pediatrics, 65*, 579–583.

Kagan, S., & Ender, P. B. (1975). Maternal response to success and failure of Anglo-American, Mexican-American, and Mexican children. *Child Development, 46*, 452–458.

Kagitçibasi, Ç. (1997). Individualism and collectivism. In J. W. Berry, M. H. Segall, & Ç. Kagitçibasi (Eds.), *Handbook of cross-cultural psychology* (2nd ed., Vol. 3, pp. 1–49). Boston: Allyn & Bacon.

Kahn, R. I., & Antonucci, T. C. (1980). Convoys of social support: A life-course approach. In P. B. Baltes & O. G. Brim (Eds.), *Life-span development and behavior* (Vol. 3, pp. 253–286). New York: Academic Press.

Keefe, S. E., Padilla, A. M., & Carlos, M. L. (1979). The Mexican-American extended family as an emotional support system. *Human Organization, 38,* 144–152.

Knight, G. P., Cota, M. K., & Bernal, M. E. (1993). The socialization of cooperative, competitive, and individualistic preferences among Mexican American children: The mediating role of ethnic identity. *Hispanic Journal of Behavioral Sciences, 15,* 291–309.

Lamb, M. E., & Elster, A. B. (1985). Adolescent mother-infant-father relationships. *Developmental Psychology, 21,* 768–773.

Laosa, C. M. (1978). Maternal teaching strategies in Chicano families of varied educational and socioeconomic levels. *Child Development, 49,* 1129–1135.

Leaper, C. (2002). Parenting girls and boys. In M. H. Bornstein (Ed.), *Handbook of parenting, Vol. 1, Children and parenting* (2nd ed., pp. 189–225). Mahwah, NJ: Erlbaum.

Leiderman, P. H., Tulkin, S. R., & Rosenfeld, A. (Eds.). (1977). *Culture and infancy: Variations in the human experience.* New York: Academic Press.

LeVine, R. A., Miller, P. M., & West, M. M. (Eds.). (1988). *Parental behavior in diverse societies. New directions for child development.* San Francisco: Jossey-Bass.

Maccoby, E. E., & Jacklin, C. N. (1974). *The psychology of sex differences.* Stanford, CA: Stanford University Press.

MacPhee, D. (1981). Manual for the Knowledge of Infant Development Inventory. Unpublished manuscript, University of North Carolina.

MacPhee, D., Benson, J. B., & Bullock, D. (1986). Influences on maternal self-perceptions. Paper presented at the Fifth Biennial International Conference on Infant Studies, Los Angeles, April.

MacPhee, D., Fritz, J., & Miller-Heyl, J. (1996). Ethnic variations in personal social networks and parenting. *Child Development, 67,* 3278–3295.

Markus, H. R., & Kitayama, S. (1991). Culture and the self: Implications for cognition, emotion, and motivation. *Psychological Review, 98,* 224–253.

McGillicuddy-DeLisi, A. V. (1985). The relationship between parental beliefs and children's cognitive level. In I. E. Sigel (Ed.), *Parental belief systems: The psychological consequences for children* (pp. 7–24). Hillsdale, NJ: Erlbaum.

Miller, S. (1988). Parents' beliefs about children's cognitive development. *Child Development, 59,* 259–285.

Minturn, L., & Lambert, W. W. (1964). *Mothers of six cultures: Antecedents of childrearing.* New York: Wiley.

Murphy, D. A. (1992). Constructing the child: Relations between parents' beliefs and child outcomes. *Developmental Review, 12,* 199–232.

Nelder, J. A. (1977). A reformulation of linear models. *Journal of Royal Statistical Society, A. 140,* Part 1, 48–77.

Osofsky, H. J., & Osofsky, J. D. (1970). Adolescents as mothers: Results of a program for low-income pregnant teen-agers with some emphasis upon infants' development. *American Journal of Orthopsychiatry, 40,* 825–834.

Owen, M. T., & Cox, M. J. (1988). Maternal employment and the transition to parenthood. In A. E. Gottfried & A. W. Gottfried (Eds.), *Maternal employment and children's development: Longitudinal research* (pp. 85–119). New York: Plenum.

Palacios, J., & Moreno, M. C. (1996). Parents' and adolescents' ideas on children: Origins and transmission of intracultural diversity. In S. Harkness & C. M. Super (Eds.), *Parents cultural belief systems: Their origins, expressions, and consequences* (pp. 215–253). New York: Guildford Press.

Panaccione, V. F., & Wahler, R. G. (1986). Child behavior, maternal depression, and social coercion as factors in the quality of child care. *Journal of Abnormal Psychology, 14,* 263–278.

Parke, R. D. (2002). Fathers and families. In M. H. Bornstein (Ed.), *Handbook of parenting,* Vol. 3, *Status and social conditions of parenting* (2nd ed., pp. 27–73). Mahwah, NJ: Erlbaum.

Pascual, L. (1991). Democracy and educational reforms in Argentina: Possibilities and limitations. Paper presented at the annual conference of the Comparative and International Education Society, Pittsburgh, PA.

Pascual, L., Galperín, C., & Bornstein, M. H. (1993). La medición del nivel socioeconómico y la psicología evolutiva: El caso Argentino [Measurement of socioeconomic status and developmental psychology: The Argentine case]. *Revista Interamericana de Psicologia/Interamerican Journal of Psychology, 27,* 59–74.

Pascual, L., Schulthess, L., Galperín, C., & Bornstein, M. (1995). Las ideas de las madres sobre la crianza de los hijos en Argentina [Mothers' ideas about childrearing in Argentina]. *Interamerican Journal Psychology, 29,* 23–38.

Patterson, G. (1980). Mothers: The unacknowledged victims. *Monographs of the Society for Research in Child Development* (serial no. 186).

Pescatello, A. (Ed.). (1973). *Female and male in Latin America: Essays.* Pittsburgh: University of Pittsburgh Press.

Peterson, C., & Seligman, M. E. P. (1984). Causal explanations as a risk factor for depression: Theory and evidence. *Psychological Review, 91,* 347–374.

Power, T. G., & Parke, R. D. (1983). Patterns of mother and father play with their 8-month-old infant: A multiple analyses approach. *Infant Behavior and Development, 6,* 453–459.

Quittner, A. L., Glueckauf, R. L., & Jackson, D. N. (1990). Chronic parenting stress: Moderating versus mediating effects of social support. *Journal of Personality and Social Psychology, 59,* 1266–1278.

Ragozin, A. S., Basham, R. B., Crnic, K. A., Greenberg, M. T., & Robinson, N. M. (1982). Effects of maternal age on parenting role. *Developmental Psychology, 18,* 627–634.

Reis, J., Barbera-Stein, L., & Bennett, S. (1986). Ecological determinants of parenting. *Family Relations, 35,* 547–554.

Rogosch, F. A., Cicchetti, D., Shields, A., & Toth, S. L. (1995). Parenting dysfunction in child maltreatment. In M. H. Bornstein (Ed.), *Handbook of parenting* (Vol. 4, pp. 127–159). Mahwah, NJ: Erlbaum.

Rubin, K. H., & Mills, R. S. L. (1992). Parents' thoughts about children's socially adaptive and maladaptive behaviors: Stability, change, and individual differences. In I. Sigel, J. Goodnow, & A. V. McGillicuddy-DeLisi (Eds.), *Parental belief systems* (pp. 41–68). Hillsdale, NJ: Erlbaum.

Ruble, D., Newman, L. S., Rholes, W. S., & Altshuler, J. (1988). Children's "naive psychology": The use of behavioral and situational information for the prediction of behavior. *Cognitive Development, 3,* 89–112.

Sameroff, A., Seifer, R., & Elias, P. (1982). Sociocultural variability in infant temperament ratings. *Child Development, 53,* 164–173.

Sanson, A., & Rothbart, M. K. (1995). Child temperament and parenting. In M. H. Bornstein (Ed.), *Handbook of parenting* (Vol. 4, pp. 299–321). Mahwah, NJ: Erlbaum.

Schwartz, S. H. (1994). Beyond individualism and collectivism: New cultural dimensions of values. In U. Kim, H. C. Triandis, Ç. Kagitçibasi, C. Choi, & G. Yoon (Eds.), *Individualism and collectivism: Theory, method, and applications* (pp. 85–122). Newbury Park, CA: Sage.

Seybold, J., Fritz, J., & MacPhee, D. (1991). Relation of social support to the self-perceptions of mothers with delayed children. *Journal of Community Psychology, 19,* 29–36.

Shweder, R. A. (1991). *Thinking through cultures: Expeditions in cultural psychology.* Cambridge, MA: Harvard University Press.

Sigel, I. E., & McGillicuddy-DeLisi, A. V. (2002). Parental beliefs and cognitions: The dynamic belief systems model. In M. H. Bornstein (Ed.), *Handbook of parenting,* Vol. 3, *Status and social conditions of parenting* (2nd ed., pp. 485–508). Mahwah, NJ: Erlbaum.

Smith, P. B., & Bond, M. H. (1994). *Social psychology across cultures.* Boston: Allyn & Bacon.

Stevens, J. H. (1984). Child development knowledge and parenting skills. *Family Relations, 33,* 237–244.

Super, C. M., & Harkness, S. (1986). The developmental niche: A conceptualization of the interface of child and culture. *International Journal of Behavioral Development, 9,* 546–569.

Triandis, H. C. (1995). *Individualism and collectivism.* Boulder, CO: Westview.

Vaughn, B., Taraldson, B., Crichton, L., & Egeland, B. (1981). The assessment of infant temperament: A critique of the Carey Infant Temperament Questionnaire. *Infant Behavior and Development, 4,* 1–17.

Vega, W. A. (1990). Hispanic families from the 1980s: A decade of research. *Journal of Marriage and the Family, 52,* 1015–1024.

Vernon, S. W., & Roberts, R. E. (1985). A comparison of Anglos and Mexican Americans on selected measures of social support. *Hispanic Journal of Behavioral Sciences, 7,* 381–399.

Whiting, B., & Whiting, J. (1975). *Children of six cultures.* Cambridge, MA: Harvard University Press.

Whiting, J. W. M., & Child, I. L. (1953). *Child training and personality: A cross-cultural study.* New Haven: Yale University Press.

Young, K. T. (1991). What parents and experts think about infants. In F. S. Kessel, M. H. Bornstein, & A. J. Sameroff (Eds.), *Contemporary constructions of the child* (pp. 79–90). Hillsdale, NJ: Erlbaum.

Zahn-Waxler, C., & Radke-Yarrow, M. (1990). The origins of empathic concern. *Motivation and Emotion, 14,* 107–130.

Zahn-Waxler, C., Radke-Yarrow, M., Wagner, E., & Chapman, M. (1992). Development of concern for others. *Developmental Psychology, 28,* 1038–1047.

PART III

Two Themes in Children's Lives:
Gender Roles and Siblings

CHAPTER 8

Gender Roles in Childhood and Adolescence

Deborah L. Best

As psychologists interested in development and culture, why should gender also be of interest to us? Perhaps because it is one of the most salient of physical features distinguishing between human beings. As proof of its salience, what is the first question that is asked following the announcement of the birth of a healthy child? "Is it a boy or a girl?" This gender label affects almost every aspect of that child's subsequent life.

As infants, girls and boys are so similar that they are often difficult to distinguish from one another. However, throughout early childhood and into adolescence, boys and girls develop distinct differences in appearance, mannerisms, ways of talking, styles of dress, interests and games, and preferred playmates. Children learn the gender role for their sex—the behaviors and social roles that are expected of males and females in their particular society.

Munroe and Munroe noted in *Cross-Cultural Human Development* (1975/1994) that in all known human societies, there are modal sex differences in physical characteristics (e.g., primary and secondary sex characteristics), behavior, and at the adult level a division of labor. For children, sex differences are reported in child behavior (e.g., in forty-five countries, nurturance, responsibility, obedience, self-reliance, achievement, independence; Barry, Bacon, & Child, 1967), and in child training (thirty-four of thirty-five countries with full ratings). Sexual dimorphism appears very early in life (e.g., higher basal metabolism, more muscle development, higher pain threshold of male neonates; Rosenberg & Sutton-Smith, 1972) and continues, resulting in the well-known adult physical differences (e.g., for males, greater height, more massive skeleton, higher muscle-to-fat ratio, higher blood oxygen capacity, more body hair, primary and secondary sex characteristics) (d'Andrade, 1966; Tanner, 1961). Both physical and behavioral differences have been well documented across cultural groups (Munroe & Munroe, 1975/1994), suggesting that sex and gender have a pervasive influence on almost every aspect of individual and communal life.

DEFINITIONS OF GENDER

Gender researchers (Deaux, 1985; Deaux & LaFrance, 1998; Ruble & Martin, 1998) often differentiate between the words "sex" and "gender," with the former referring to biological aspects of masculinity and femininity that presumably reflect the effects of nature, and the latter referring to the psychosociocultural aspects, which are constructed by culture. Using separate terms for gender and sex sets up an arbitrary, unnecessary dichotomy between biological and environmental influences (Fausto-Sterling, 2000; Hoyenga & Hoyenga, 1993). Human beings are products of both biology and environment, past and present, simultaneously and inseparably.

BIOLOGICAL ASPECTS OF GENDER

Even though gender and sex are often treated as categorical variables, biologists point out that in measuring any of a number of biological differences between males and females, many attributes are on a continuum rather than falling into a clean dichotomy or typology. For example, people differ in levels of testosterone; some are at the higher end of the continuum, as with most males, others at the lower end, as with most females, and still others range across the middle at levels that are below the typical male but above the typical female. Interestingly, anthropologists have noted a third gender category, the berdache, distinct from homosexuals or transsexuals, in some nineteenth-century Native American cultures, in which an individual performed some prescribed role behaviors inconsistent with the originally assigned gender role (Kessler & McKenna, 1978). Moreover, in most biological definitions of gender, chromosomes, hormones, gonads, and external anatomy are the determinative factors.

Biological Determinism

When similarities in gender differences in behavior are found across cultures, this is often used as support for the role of genes and hormones, which implies complete genetic or biological determinism. Biological determinism assumes that any biological influence or bias always leads to an irreversible sex difference, making biology both the necessary and sufficient cause of sex differences. Biology is neither. The long-standing nature-nurture controversy within developmental psychology has shown that biology does not cause behavior and that such a notion is quite naive.

Sex chromosomes or sex hormones are neither necessary nor sufficient to cause behaviors; they simply change the probability of occurrence of certain behaviors (Hoyenga & Hoyenga, 1993; Stewart, 1988). The gene-behavior pathway is bidirectional (Gottlieb, 1983), and somewhat like people inherit genes, they may "inherit" environments by living close to parents and family.

Probabilistic Epigenesis

Genes and environment sometimes act similarly on growth and development, and at all times, the developmental process reflects the impact of both. As a result, a particular phenotype may come from a gene or from a given developmental environment or both (Cairns, Gariépy, & Hood, 1990; Gottlieb, 1997). Genes and environments tend to influence the same developmental processes with equivalent outcomes that work through different mechanisms. As a result, life history strategies (evolutionary patterns of adaptation that differ by developmental stage) can be altered by both genes and developmental environments (Hoyenga & Hoyenga, 1993). Both genes and environment affect brain anatomy—affecting the child's intellectual abilities and traits—and both can lead to stability and change. Indeed, in the sexually dimorphic process, gender is the added factor that may affect the form of the interaction between genes and environmental context.

PSYCHOSOCIOCULTURAL ASPECTS OF GENDER

Psychological aspects of gender refer to behavioral differences between males and females, how they interact with people and things in their environments. The gender of rearing usually determines gender identity, gender roles, gender stereotypes, gender-role ideology, and other cultural-environmental aspects of gender, and these are the focus of the present chapter.

Multidimensional View of Sex-Typing

Sex-typing, the development of gender-related differences in children, changes continuously with age and is considered to be a multidimensional process (Huston, 1983). Huston has proposed a taxonomic view of gender, distinguishing between constructs and content areas. Ruble and Martin (1998) modified Huston's matrix, which represents sex-typing across six areas (biological gender, activities and interests, personal-social attributes, gender-based social relationships, stylistic and symbolic content, and gender-related values) and includes four content aspects (beliefs, self-perception, preferences or attitudes, and behavioral tendencies). Gender-related differences are found in all areas, but few studies have addressed the interrelationships among the areas, and even fewer of these relationships have been examined cross-culturally (e.g., one exception is Cheung

Mui-ching's examination [1986] of gender stereotypes and self- and ideal-self descriptions of adolescents).

Cultural Influences on Gender Development

Even though biological factors may impose predispositions and restrictions on development, sociocultural factors are important determinants of development (Best & Williams, 1993; Munroe & Munroe, 1975/1994; Rogoff, Gauvain, & Ellis, 1984). Culture has profound effects on behavior, prescribing how babies are delivered, how children are socialized, how they are dressed, what is considered intelligent behavior, what tasks children are taught, and what roles adult men and women will adopt. Children's behaviors, even behaviors that are considered biologically determined, are governed by culture. Cultural universals in gender differences are often explained by similarities in socialization practices, while cultural differences are attributed to differences in socialization.

Children grow up within other people's scripts, which guide their actions long before the children themselves can understand or carry out the culturally appropriate actions. For developmental researchers, one of the crucial tasks is to identify the mechanism responsible for the changes seen across time. This means that researchers must unpackage broadly defined cultural variables to identify what aspects or processes are responsible for the development of particular behavioral outcomes. Gender should be examined not only in relation to culture (e.g., social systems, practices, myths, beliefs, rituals), but also in the context of the history and economics of the society (Mukhopadhyay & Higgins, 1998). Identification of the mechanisms within a culture that are responsible for age-related developmental change must also account for variation among individuals within the cultural group as well as variation between cultures.

Not only is the subject of study, the child or parent, changing across time, this change takes place in a cultural system that is itself changing. Thus, developmental change is the emerging synthesis of several major factors interacting over time, what Cole (1999) refers to as a bio-social-behavioral shift—changes in the relations between a child's biological makeup, the social world in which he or she lives, and the resulting behaviors that occur. Several illustrative examples of this interplay are (1) a mother's influence on her child's prenatal development through the foods and other substances that she ingests (biological) or (2) the songs she sings (social, cultural) during the last weeks of pregnancy, which can be heard in utero and become preferred (DeCasper & Fifer, 1980); (3) the cultural practices that surround the birth of a child in various societies; and, relevant to the discussion of gender, (4) the parent's interpretation (e.g., "Is it a boy or is it a girl?") of the child's biological sex characteristics following birth.

Even when particular behaviors are assumed to be heavily biologically determined, cultural practices can play an important role in shaping them. For example, lengths of sleeping bouts are modified by culturally determined demands on mothers' time, and the course of sitting and walking are influenced by childcare practices (Super & Harkness, 1982). Cultural practices shape children to fit different life circumstances.

SOCIALIZATION OF BOYS AND GIRLS

"Baby X" studies (i.e., studies in which the sex of the infant is not known to participants) in the United States have shown that parents and young adults treat infants differently depending on whether they think they are interacting with a girl or a boy (Rubin, Provezano, & Luria, 1974; Seavey, Katz, & Zalk, 1975; Sidorowicz & Lunney, 1980). Boys are described as big and strong and are bounced and handled more physically than girls, who are described as pretty and sweet and are handled more gently. Even before birth, after finding out their child's sex via ultrasound, parents described girls as "finer" and "quieter" than boys, who were described as "more coordinated" than girls (Sweeney & Bradbard, 1989). Parental presumptions such as these reflect the impact of culture on parents' memory of their own past and their assumptions about their child's future. However, culture is a dynamic influence that changes across time. In the United States, parents of the 1950s would never have assumed their daughters would grow up to be soccer players in college, but many parents today would certainly have this expectation.

Such parental expectations are not peculiar to the United States. Greenfield and her colleagues (Greenfield, Brazelton, & Childs, 1989) report that shortly after birth, Zinacanteco babies in Mexico are given objects that are gender appropriate. A father reported giving his son "three green chilies to hold so that it would know to buy chili when it grew up." According to the Zinacanteco saying, "In the newborn baby is the future of our world." Parents assume that things in the future will be as they have been in the past, an assumption of continuity.

Behavioral differences between girls and boys are often attributed to differences in socialization. Barry, Bacon, and Child (1957) examined socialization practices in over 100 societies and found that generally boys are reared to achieve and to be self-reliant and independent while girls are reared to be nurturant, responsible, and obedient. However, when Hendrix and Johnson (1985) reanalyzed these data, they found no evidence of a general sex differentiation in socialization, and instead of being polar opposites, the instrumental-expressive components were orthogonal, unrelated dimensions with similar emphases in the training of girls and boys. For both male and female socialization factors, self-reliance and independence had strong positive loadings, and nurturance loaded negatively.

In a meta-analysis, Lytton and Romney (1991) examined 158 North American studies of socialization and found the only significant effect was for the encouragement of sex-typed behaviors. In seventeen additional studies from other

Western countries, there was a significant sex difference for physical punishment, with boys receiving a greater amount than girls. Differential treatment of boys and girls decreased with age, particularly for disciplinary strictness and encouragement of sex-typed activities.

Overall, socialization studies suggest that there may be subtle differences in how parents treat boys and girls. These differences are only occasionally significant, perhaps due to the ways the behaviors are measured or which parent is being observed. Fathers play an especially important role in signaling the types of behaviors they consider appropriate, particularly for their sons, who have fewer accessible male role models and for whom deviations are considered more undesirable (Jacklin, DiPietro, & Maccoby, 1984; Langlois & Downs, 1980). Even if parents do not differentiate between daughters and sons, the same parental treatment may affect girls and boys differently. Research in the United States suggests that gender lessons are finely focused on specific behaviors and that learning often occurs during transitional periods in development when new abilities first emerge, particularly during the toddler period and during adolescence (Beal, 1994).

Parents' behaviors communicate the importance of gender via their reactions to their children's behavior and by the organization of activities within the family. Parent behaviors, as well as those of peers, teachers, and other socialization agents, help shape sex-appropriate behaviors, toy choices, playmates, and other activities. Peers, task assignment, caretaking, and the educational environment are among the cultural influences that help to socialize children's gender-role behaviors.

Peers

Throughout childhood and adolescence, peers play an important role in socialization. In some cultures, boys and girls are separated by the end of infancy (Whiting & Edwards, 1988), and in others, children play freely within mixed age and gender groups (Rogoff, 1990). Peer influence increases as children grow older, helping to structure the transition between childhood and adulthood (Edwards, 1992). Maccoby (1998) suggests that peers may play as important a role as parents, if not more so, in the socialization of gender roles.

Maccoby (1988, 1998) has identified three major gender-linked phenomena in children's social development: gender segregation, differentiation of interaction styles, and group asymmetry. Both with American children and cross-culturally (Whiting & Edwards, 1988), as early as age three, there is a powerful tendency for children to seek out playmates of their own sex and to avoid children of the other sex, and this tendency strengthens throughout grade school. These segregated playgroups differ in their interaction styles and activities. Boys strive for dominance, play rough, take risks, "grandstand," and are reluctant to reveal weaknesses to each other. In contrast, girls self-disclose more, try to maintain positive social relationships, and avoid open conflict. Same-sex playgroups provide children with useful socialization experiences and the venue for construction of social norms, but there is an asymmetry in these groups. Compared with girls' groups, boys' groups are more cohesive, more exclusionary, and more separate from adult culture.

Maccoby (1998) has found that behavioral compatibility, avoidance of aggression or rough-and-tumble play, and matching activity levels cannot by themselves account for gender segregation of playgroups. She proposes an interplay between biology (differences in metabolic rate, activity level, arousability, maturation rates of language and inhibitory mechanisms, prenatal hormones), socialization (role of fathers, more emotion talk with girls, role of peer group, cultural practices), and cognition (self-identity, cultural stereotypes, scripts). Segregation of play groups leads to different activities and toy choices, which in turn may lead to differences in intellectual and emotional development (Block, 1983).

Examination of peer interactions of two- to ten-year-olds from the Six Culture Study and from six additional samples (Edwards, 1992; Edwards & Whiting, 1993) showed a robust, cross-culturally universal same-gender preference that emerges after age two. By middle childhood, gender segregation is found frequently, perhaps in part motivated by a desire for self-discovery (Edwards, 1992). Age-mates who resemble the child in abilities and activity preferences also provide the greatest opportunity for competition and conflict.

Gender segregation also results from culturally prescribed adolescent initiation rites, which are found in many cultures. Initiation rites are designed to separate initiates from their families, to socialize them to culturally appropriate sexuality, dominance, and aggression, to create peer-group loyalty, and to solidify political ties. Collective rituals, more common for boys than girls, are found more frequently in warrior societies that emphasize gender differences in adult activities (Edwards, 1992). Western education has begun to change initiation rites, but vestiges remain in many cultures.

Task Assignment

Examining children's learning environments in various cultures shows how cultural differences in socialization processes affect the development of gender roles. Learning environments were investigated in the Six Culture Study (Edwards & Whiting, 1974; Minturn & Lambert, 1964; Whiting & Edwards, 1973), which examined aggression, nurturance, responsibility, and help- and attention-seeking behaviors of children ages three to eleven in Okinawa (Japan), the Mixtecans in Mexico, the Philippines, India, the Gusii in Kenya, and the United States. Fewer gender differences were found in the three groups (the United States, the Philippines, Kenya) where both boys and girls cared for younger siblings and performed household chores. In contrast, more differences were found in the samples (India, Mexico, Okinawa) where boys and girls were treated dissimilarly, with girls assuming more responsibility for siblings and household tasks. Indeed, the fewest gender differences were found between American girls and boys, who were assigned few childcare or household tasks.

Bradley (1993) examined children's labor in ninety-one Standard Cross-Cultural Sample cultures (Murdock & White, 1969) and found that children younger than age six perform little work, whereas children older than ten perform work similar to that of same-gender adults. Both boys and girls do women's work (e.g., fetching water) more frequently than men's (e.g., hunting), and children tend to do chores that adults consider demeaning or unskilled. Women monitor children's work while simultaneously socializing with their daughters. These joint tasks provide help for the mother, which she also needs. Parents report that along with providing care in parents' old age, an important benefit of having children is children's labor.

Caretaking

Analyzing data from 186 societies, Weisner and Gallimore (1977) found that in most cases, mothers, female adult relatives, and female children are the primary caretakers of infants. However, when those infants reach early childhood, both-sex peers share caretaking responsibilities. Sibling caretakers play an important socialization role in societies where two- to four-year-olds spend more than 70 percent of every day with their child nurses. Because mothers in such societies spend much of their time in productive activities, they are not devoted exclusively to mothering (Greenfield, 1981; Minturn & Lambert, 1964), even though children in all cultures see mothers as responsible for children (see also Maynard, this volume).

Moreover, in 20 percent of eighty cultures surveyed (Katz & Konner, 1981), fathers were rarely or never near their infants. Father-infant relationships were close in only 4 percent of the cultures, but even when close, fathers spent only 14 percent of their time with their infants and only gave 6 percent of the actual caregiving. In most societies, paternal interactions with children are characterized by play (Munroe & Munroe, 1975/1994).

Father absence has been associated with both effeminate and violent or hypermasculine behaviors (Katz & Konner, 1981; Segall, 1988; Whiting, 1965). When fathers are absent for extended periods of time due to war (Stolz, 1954) or lengthy sea voyages (Gronseth, 1957; Lynn & Sawrey, 1959), their sons display effeminate overt behaviors, high levels of dependence, excessive fantasy aggression, as well as some overly masculine behaviors. Compared with father-present children, father-absent children are more aggressive (Amato & Keith, 1991; Stevenson & Black, 1988).

Fathers pay less attention to female offspring than to males and promote sex-typed activities more than mothers (Lytton & Romney, 1991). Mothers are equally involved in the caretaking of sons and daughters, but fathers tended to be more involved as caretakers of sons (Rohner & Rohner, 1982). Mackey (Mackey, 1981, 1985; Mackey & Day, 1979) observed parents and children in public places in ten different cultures and found that girls were more often in groups with no adult males, while boys were frequently found in all-male groups, and these differences increased with age.

Education

Educational settings also greatly influence the development of children's gender roles. Observations of Japanese and American fifth graders indicate that teachers in both countries paid more attention to boys, particularly negative attention, and the greater attention was not due to off-task or bad behavior (Hamilton, Blumenfeld, Akoh, & Miura, 1991).

Parents' beliefs about academic performance can also have a profound impact upon children's achievements. Serpell (1993) found that education was considered to be more important for Zambian boys than girls, and fathers made schooling arrangements even though mothers were primarily responsible for childcare. In China, Japan, and the United States, mothers expect boys to be better at mathematics and girls to be better at reading (Lummis & Stevenson, 1990), even though they perform equally well in some aspects of both disciplines.

CULTURAL PRACTICES THAT INFLUENCE BEHAVIORS OF MALES AND FEMALES

The previous section examined specific aspects of socialization, but there are broader cultural influences on gender that provide an important context for gender-role learning. Among these practices are the status of women, gender division of labor, religious beliefs and values, economic factors, and political participation.

Status of Women

Ethnographic evidence suggests that women's "status" is multidimensional and includes economic indicators, power, autonomy, prestige, and ideological dimensions (Mukhopadhyay & Higgins, 1988; Quinn, 1977). Asymmetry in status between men and women may be due to women's reproductive roles and physical differences as well as the complexity of the society (Berry, 1976; Ember, 1981).

What is considered masculine and feminine may differ across cultures, but the literature suggests two possible cultural universals. At least to some degree, every society assigns traits and tasks according to gender (Munroe & Munroe, 1975/ 1994); and in no society is the status of women superior to that of men, while the reverse is common (Hoyenga & Hoyenga, 1993; Population Crisis Committee, 1988; Whyte, 1978).

Gender Division of Labor

Analysis of ethnographic records of jobs and tasks in 244 different societies found that men were involved with hunting, metalwork, weapon making, and travel farther from home, while women were responsible for cooking and food preparation, carrying water, caring for clothing, and making things used in the home (d'Andrade, 1966). Women's participation in subsistence activities was consistent with childrearing activities (Brown, 1970; Segal, 1983), and men had major childrearing responsibilities in only 10 percent of the eighty cultures examined (Katz & Konner, 1981).

Recent decreases in infant mortality and advances in technology have made it possible for women to participate more extensively in the labor force outside the home (Huber, 1986). However, compared with men, women remain economically disadvantaged and are paid less than their male counterparts (Ottaway & Bhatnagar, 1988). Even in societies where women are active in the labor force, there has not been a commensurate reduction in their household duties (Population Crisis Committee, 1988). In the United States, Switzerland, Sweden, Canada, Italy, Poland, and Romania, the overwhelming majority of household work is performed by women, regardless of the extent of their occupational demands (Calasanti & Bailey, 1991; Charles & Höpflinger, 1992; Vianello, Siemienska, Damian, Lupri, Coppi, d'Arcangeloo, & Bolasco, 1990; Wright, Shire, Hwang, Dolan, & Baxter, 1992).

The difficulty in eliminating gender divisions in labor is illustrated by the Israeli kibbutz, established in the 1920s, where there was a deliberate attempt to develop egalitarian societies (Rosner, 1967; Snarey & Son, 1986; Spiro, 1956, 1995). Initially there was no sexual division of labor. Both women and men worked in the fields, drove tractors, worked in the kitchen and in the laundry. However, with time and increases in the birthrate, women found they could not undertake many of the physical tasks that men were capable of doing. Women soon found themselves in the roles they had tried to escape—cooking, cleaning, laundering, teaching, caring for children. Somewhat surprisingly, the kibbutz attempts at equitable division of labor had little effect on the children. Kibbutz-raised children and Swedish children showed no differences in how they conceptualized typical female and male sex-role behaviors nor in their sex-typed self-attributions (Carlsson & Barnes, 1986).

Religious Beliefs and Values

Religious and cultural views of gender roles and family honor influence perceptions of women and their working outside the home (Rapoport, Lomski-Feder, & Masalha, 1989), as well as the role models children see. For instance, ideals of personal and family honor in Latin America and the Middle East link the manliness of men (*machismo, muruwwa*) with the sexual purity of women (*vergüenza, 'ird*), and these influence the division of labor within the family (Youssef, 1974). Some religious communities prescribe proper roles and behavior for males and females, and children are brought up consistent with these views.

Economic Factors

Economic factors appear to influence gender-related cultural practices. Brideprice, compensation for the loss of a daughter's economic contributions to her family (Heath, 1958), is found more frequently where her contributions are substantial. Dowry accompanies the bride when her economic contributions to her family are relatively small. Cronk (1993) theorized that relative to females, the reproductive success of males is affected more by socioeconomic factors, particularly in societies where men may have more than one wife and where they must pay bridewealth for their wives. Consequently, when parents have high socioeconomic status so that sons can pay for wives, males are favored, but when parents have low status, females are favored because they can be married off to wealthier, higher-status neighbors.

Sex-biased parental investment in children may be affected by socioeconomic conditions. Among the Mukogodo of central Kenya, who are at the bottom of the regional hierarchy of regional wealth and prestige, the male-female birth ratio is about equal, but the 1986 census recorded ninety-eight girls and sixty-six boys under four years of age. Although there is no evidence of male infanticide, it is likely that boys' higher death rate is due to favoritism toward girls. Compared with sons, daughters are breast-fed longer, are generally well-fed, and visit the doctor more often. Because men in the Mukogodo area can have as many wives as they can afford, women are in short supply and as a result they all find husbands.

In sharp contrast, in most other traditional parts of the world (e.g., India, China, Turkey, Korea), cultural practices favor boys, who are highly valued by their families and whose birth leads to great rejoicing (Kagitçibasi, 1982). Brideburning (Ghadially & Kumar, 1988), wife beating (Flavia, 1988), and female infanticide (Krishnaswamy, 1988) are cultural practices that demonstrate the lack of concern for women in some traditional Indian cultures. In the United States (Oakley, 1979; Pooler, 1991) and in non-Western countries (Arnold, Bulatao, Buripakdi, Chung, Fawcett, Iritani, Lee, & Wu, 1975), preference for boys continues to be strong even though many of the religious traditions and economic circumstances that created the preference for sons no longer apply in contemporary society.

Female Political Participation

Across cultures, men are more involved in political activities and possess greater power than women (Ember, 1981; Masters, 1989; Ross, 1985, 1986). The long-standing stereotyped dichotomy of public/male versus private/female suggests that men are in the public eye, active in business, politics, and culture, while women stay at home, caring for home and family (Peterson & Runyan, 1993). However, this dichotomy is not supported by cross-cultural studies showing women actively working and in public life outside the home and men being more involved with their families (Vianello et al., 1990).

Moreover, Gibbons, Stiles, and their colleagues (Gibbons, Lynn, Stiles, Berducido, Richter, Walker, & Wiley, 1993; Gibbons, Stiles, & Shkodriani, 1991) have shown that adolescents in a variety of cultures conceptualize the female gender role to encompass both homemaking and employment outside the home. Adolescents' images of women reflect the change in conditions and attitudes toward women around the world.

THEORIES OF SEX-ROLE DEVELOPMENT

Even though there is theoretical disagreement about the sources of influence and the course of sex-role development, most theories recognize the role of gender information readily available in the child's culture. While maturational theories have gone out of vogue, many of the assumptions about the role of biological influences remain important and have been incorporated into other, more current theories of sex-role development, such as evolutionary theory and social role theory.

Evolutionary Theories

Evolutionary psychology has grown out of early-nineteenth-century evolutionary thinking (e.g., Spencer, Haeckel, Lamarck; see Dixon & Lerner, 1999), which is represented by Darwin's (1872) observations of human and animal emotional expression. The forces of natural selection shape the morphological features of the organism, which in turn shape behavioral and psychological tendencies (Kenrick & Luce, 2000). Humans and animals inherit brains, bodies, and specific behavioral mechanisms that are equipped to adapt to their environments and to solve the recurrent problems confronted during their ancestral past. Evolutionary success is measured not by survival but ultimately by reproductive success. Sexual selection (e.g., attracting a mate; Geary, 1998) and differential parental investment (e.g., nutritional cost of carrying a fetus, provision of food, protection from predators; Trivers, 1985) may account for many of the sex differences found throughout the animal kingdom.

Sex differences in physical development and reproductive life history are linked to sex differences in social behaviors, such as mate preferences (Buss, 1989; Kenrick & Keefe, 1992), aggression (Daly & Wilson, 1988), sexuality (Daly & Wilson, 1988), and childcare (Geary, 1998). Several evolutionary theorists assume that some cultural variation in behavior results from a flexible genetic program unfolding in variable environments (Kenrick & Luce, 2000). For example, Öhman (1986) describes an open genetic program in which a cultural pool of information helps structure learning episodes for members of the social group.

In an effort to strengthen their views, evolutionary theorists dealing with gender have borrowed experimental psychology's concept of preparedness, which grew out of research with animal taste aversion and with the development of human phobias (Rozin & Kalat, 1971; Seligman, 1971). They propose that males and females enter the world biologically prepared to experience their environments differently and that these experiences shape sex-appropriate behaviors. While this is an interesting application, there presently are no data to support the extension of the preparedness mechanism from the learning of food avoidance (poison) and fear responses (e.g., from the predatory defense system—fear of snakes, spiders; from dominance/submissiveness system—social fears) to gender-related social behavior.

Many current researchers find the broad outline of evolutionary theory to be correct, but criticisms of the theory point to the difficulty in testing the propositions and assumptions. Perhaps the most serious weakness of evolutionary approaches is that they do not account for the precise developmental mechanisms by which gender-differentiated values and norms are transmitted to individuals within a cultural group (see also Fouts, this volume).

Social Role Theory

According to social role theory, the differences between male and female behaviors are a result of the different social roles that they play, which in turn are based on the sexual division of labor. The division of labor and the gender hierarchy of power and status are a function of the differences in reproductive activities and the physical size and strength of women and men (Wood & Eagly, 1999), with differences typically favoring men (Eagly, Wood, & Diekman, 2000). The contrasting social positions of men and women result in different gender roles, which include both beliefs (descriptive norms) and expectations (injunctive norms; Cialdini & Trost, 1998) about what men and women do. Dispositional assumptions about the sexes have grown into cultural stereotypes (Ross, 1977) that reflect the differential distribution of the sexes into social roles. Because women are more frequently associated with the domestic role, the characteristics thought to exemplify homemakers are ascribed to women in general.

Likewise, characteristics thought to typify providers are ascribed to men in general (Eagly et al., 2000). Cultural expectations promote conformity to gender roles and influence how people think about themselves and their perceptions of masculinity and femininity. Indeed, gender stereotypes often become the rationalizations that justify differential sex-role distributions (Hoffman & Hurst, 1990; Williams & Best, 1982/1990).

One of the most serious criticisms of social role theory is that physical sex differences are not the entire story, and they themselves need to be accounted for. Social role theory stops short of explaining why the two social structures of sexual division of labor and gender hierarchy are common to almost all cultural groups. Furthermore, social role theory does not identify the mechanisms by which social structures exert their influence on individuals and groups within various cultural settings.

Social role theory could be strengthened by considering Van Leeuwen's formulation (1978) of an ecological model to account for sex differences in behavior. Briefly, she proposes that in sedentary, high-food-accumulating societies, training for males and females will differ greatly and females will receive more training to be nurturant and compliant. In contrast, in low-food-accumulating societies (e.g., hunting societies), there will be little division of labor by sex, with both men and women contributing to subsistence, so there will be no need to train either females or males to be nurturant and compliant. Cross-cultural variations in gender-related variables are most likely a product of socialization practices that vary in their degrees of compliance training.

Social Learning Theory

In the 1960s, Sears and his colleagues (Sears, Maccoby, & Levin, 1957; Sears, Rau, & Alpert, 1965) revised Freud's notions of sex-role development to be consistent with learning theory's principles of reinforcement and modeling. The socialization of sex-typed behaviors was said to result from differential parenting behaviors, warmth and emotional support from mothers and control and discipline from fathers. Bandura (Bandura, 1969; Bussey & Bandura, 1984) and Mischel (1970) expanded the cognitive aspects of social learning theory by emphasizing the role of modeling and expectations in the differential treatment of boys and girls.

Because observational learning is a powerful process, modeling is important in the development of sex-typing. Gender stereotypes can be passed from parent to child, from one generation to the next, and from one child to another (Hoyenga & Hoyenga, 1993). Girls are systematically exposed to fewer same-sex models with power and prestige than are boys, a process that must affect the development of stereotypes.

While there is substantial cross-cultural evidence that social learning plays an important role in gender-role learning, it is clear that by itself, social learning is not a sufficient explanation. The cross-cultural patterns of differential treatment of boys and girls demonstrate wide variation and are not consistently tied to differential behavior (Bronstein, 1984; Lamb, Frodi, Hwand, Frodi, & Steinberg, 1982; Russell & Russell, 1987; Sagi, Lamb, Shoham, Dvir, & Lewkowicz, 1985). Task assignment and models available in the larger cultural context provide differential learning opportunities for boys and girls and encourage distinct behaviors. Indeed, childhood culture differs from that of adult culture, and peer group socialization may be a more important carrier of social change than are parents.

Cognitive Stage Theories

Even though Piaget made use of biological concepts, such as reflexes and tendencies of assimilation, accommodation, and organization, he was not a maturationist. He did not believe that the invariant stages of cognitive development that he described were wired into the genetic code. Children themselves constructed them as they interacted with their environments, and they represented increasingly more sophisticated ways of thinking. For Piaget, development was an active construction process in which children developed schemes, or action structures, to deal with their environments (Ginsberg & Opper, 1969). For Piaget, environmental effects on development could be partitioned into physical experience (manipulations of objects) and social interactions, but the two were not independent (Ginsberg & Opper, 1969).

Building on Piaget's ideas, Kohlberg (1966) developed a cognitively oriented theory of gender development. Children seek out information and experiences that are appropriate for their own sex, and their understanding of gender develops through a series of stages from gender identity or labeling (achieved by two and a half years), through gender stability (by three and a half years), and finally gender consistency or constancy (by four and a half to five years). The impact of external forces and experiences on children's developing gender-role orientation is governed by the child's emerging cognitive structure.

The Munroes (Munroe, Shimmin, & Munroe, 1984) tested cognitive development theory in a cross-cultural study with children in American Samoa, Belize, Kenya, and Nepal. They expected to find that gender classification would be more salient for children in the cultures that emphasized sex distinctions in their socialization practices (e.g., Kenya, Nepal). Because the latter stages of gender understanding are dependent on cognitive structural factors, they were expected to be less influenced by culture and to appear at approximately the same time for all groups. They found that children's stages of gender understanding conformed to those found in the United States, but contrary to expectations, the culture-specific predictions were not supported. These data provide some support for the propositions of cognitive development theory in a cross-cultural context.

While current gender development research recognizes the importance of cognitive factors, it has been difficult to demonstrate an antecedent relationship between the stages of gender identity and sex-typed behaviors (Bussey, 1983). Children appear to learn sex-appropriate behaviors before they can translate these behaviors into words. Furthermore, there appears to be a two-process model for boys (acceptance of masculine behavior, rejection of feminine behavior) and a one-process model for girls (acceptance of same-sex behavior only). It would be interesting to see whether these same gender-identity acquisition processes are found across different cultural groups.

Gender Schema Theories

Schema theorists assume that individuals develop notions about gender, and these ideas organize and bias their behavior, thinking, and attention to information in their environments. Gender development is a transactional process in which environmental information about what it means to be male or female stimulates the creation of gender schemas or theories, which in turn facilitate gender-related processing of newly incoming information (Martin, 2000). Cumulative experience within social contexts that activate gender schemas leads to a more automatic use of gender-related knowledge. As a result, children come to see themselves and others in terms of gender distinctions: boys-girls, females-males, masculinity-femininity, women-men. The cognitive construction of gender concepts is both descriptive and prescriptive, and gender stereotypes are used to evaluate the appropriateness of behaviors.

The cognitive development approach to gender proposes a multidimensional model (Huston, 1983; Ruble & Martin, 1998) of gender-related constructs from gender identity, gender stereotypes, gender scripts, self-perceptions of masculinity and femininity, and expectations about others' gender-appropriate behaviors. Interrelationships among these constructs have been hypothesized, but only a few have been tested developmentally or cross-culturally, and even fewer have been related to gendered behaviors (e.g., interaction styles, segregation of play groups; Maccoby, 1998).

DIFFERENCES IN MALE AND FEMALE GENDER-ROLE BEHAVIORS

Research across cultures has shown consistent patterns of differences in the behaviors of males and females in four areas: nurturance, aggression, proximity to adults, and self-esteem.

Nurturance

Edwards and Whiting (1980) found in the Six Culture Study that between ages five and twelve, gender differences in nurturance were most consistent in behavior directed toward infants and toddlers rather than in behavior directed toward mothers and older children. Because infants elicit more nurturant behavior than do older children, girls, who spent more time with infants, displayed more nurturance than boys, who did not engage in as much interaction with infants.

These findings are consistent with Barry, Bacon, and Child's finding (1957) that compared with boys, girls were socialized to be more nurturant (82 percent of cultures), obedient (35 percent of cultures), and responsible (61 percent of cultures). Boys, on the other hand, were socialized to be more achieving (87 percent of cultures) and self-reliant (85 percent of cultures) than girls. In 108 cultures, Welch, Page, and Martin (1981) found more pressure for boys to conform to their roles than for girls, who also had greater role variability.

Aggression

Cross-culturally, prepubertal boys have consistently shown higher levels of aggression, competitiveness, dominance-seeking, and rough-and-tumble play than girls (Ember, 1981; Freedman & DeBoer, 1979; Strube, 1981). When examining data from the Six Cultures project and additional African samples, Whiting and Edwards (1988) found sex differences in aggression and dominance, but contrary to their earlier findings, aggression showed no decrease with age and was more physical among the oldest boys. In playground observations in Ethiopia, Switzerland, and the United States (Omark, Omark, & Edelman, 1975), boys were more aggressive than girls, and similar patterns were found in four !Kung bushmen villages of Africa's Kalahari and in London (Jones & Konner, 1973). Observations in four nonindustrial cultures found more frequent aggression in boys than girls (Munroe, Hulefeld, Rodgers, Tomeo, & Yamazaki, 2000). While both girls and boys are segregated by sex, aggregation-by-sex was associated most strongly with episodes of aggression by boys.

Mothers in the Six Culture Study generally react similarly to boys' and girls' aggression, but there was some differential aggression training in Okinawa and the United States that suggested the importance of the father's role in socializing boys' aggression (Minturn & Lambert, 1964). In Western European countries, acceptance of aggression is similar for males and females, but there are gender differences in the forms of aggression. Initially, males are more restrained, but when they act, they are more violent (Ramirez, 1993) than females, who are more emotional and use shouting and verbal attacks (Burbank, 1987).

At the other end of the spectrum, Boehnke and colleagues (Boehnke, Silbereisen, Eisenberg, Reykowski, & Palmonari, 1989) examined the development of prosocial motivation in schoolchildren from West Germany, Poland, Italy, and the United States. By age twelve, but not before, girls exhibited more mature motives in their responses to hypothetical situations that provided opportunity for prosocial action.

Proximity to Adults and Activity

Observing five- to seven-year-olds at play in eight cultures (Australian Aboriginal, Balinese, Ceylonese, Japanese, Kikuyu, Navajo, Punjabi, Taiwanese), Freedman (1976) determined that boys ran in larger groups, covered more physical space, and engaged in more physical and unpredictable activities than girls, who were involved in more conversations and games with repeated activities. Usually, girls are found closer to home (Draper, 1975; Munroe & Munroe, 1971; Whiting & Edwards, 1973). Boys interact more with other boys, and girls interact more with adults (Jones & Konner, 1973; Omark et al., 1975; Whiting & Edwards, 1973). Both task assignment (Whiting & Edwards, 1973) and behavioral preferences may contribute to these gender differences (Draper, 1975). Children's drawings in nine cultures, which may reflect differences in preferences, showed that boys draw more vehicles, monsters, and violence-related themes than do girls, who draw more flowers (Freedman, 1976).

Self-Esteem

Even though gender-role attributions are similar, girls seem less satisfied with being girls than boys are with being boys (Burns & Homel, 1986), and boys perceive themselves to be more competent than girls (Dongen-Melman, Koot, & Verhulst, 1993). However, girls' dissatisfaction is not consistently manifested in lower self-esteem (Calhoun & Sethi, 1987). Adolescent girls in Nepal, the Philippines, and Australia had lower opinions of their physical and mathematical abilities than did boys, but girls in Australia and Nigeria felt more competent in reading (Watkins & Akande, 1992; Watkins, Lam, & Regmi, 1991). Nigerian boys believed they were more intelligent than did girls (Olowu, 1985).

In summary, differences between girls and boys in nurturance, aggression, and mobility are robust and consistently found across cultures (Ember, 1981), but self-esteem differences are less consistent. Culture shapes the social behaviors of children by determining the company they keep and the activities that engage their time. Such experiences can minimize, maximize, or even eliminate gender differences in social behaviors.

GENDER ROLES AND STEREOTYPES

Gender roles and behaviors develop within the context of cultural stereotypes about male-female differences. In the United States, children as young as two years of age stereotype objects as masculine or feminine (Thompson, 1975; Weinraub, Clemens, Sockloff, Etheridge, Gracely, & Myers, 1984), and by age three to four, children use stereotypic labels accurately with toys, activities, and occupations (Edelbrock & Sugawara, 1978; Guttentag & Longfellow, 1977).

In Africa, similar gender stereotyping of toys is found where girls play with dolls and boys construct vehicles and weapons (Bloch & Adler, 1994). By age four to five, Sri Lankan village children exhibit gender differences in play, similar to those found with British children (Prosser, Hutt, Hutt, Mahindadasa, & Goonetilleke, 1986). Boys display more negative behaviors and more fantasy object play while girls show more fantasy person play. Although cultural factors may determine the content of children's play, only a few behaviors show culturally specific forms.

Development of Sex-Trait Stereotypes

Children in the United States acquire knowledge of sex-trait stereotypes somewhat later than stereotypic knowledge of toys and occupations (Best, Williams, Cloud, Davis, Robertson, Edwards, Giles, & Fowles, 1977; Reis & Wright, 1982; Williams & Best, 1982/1990). Using the Sex Stereotype Measure (SSM) to assess children's knowledge of adult-defined stereotypes, research with European American children revealed a consistent pattern of increasing knowledge from kindergarten through high school, similar to a typical learning curve. Stereotype knowledge increases dramatically in the early elementary school years, and scores plateau in the junior high years. African American children's scores also increased with age but were lower than those of the European American children, reflecting subcultural variation in stereotype knowledge.

Stereotypes are more differentiated in the early years and become more flexible as children grow older (Biernat, 1991; Trautner, Helbing, Sahm, & Lohaus, 1988). Children show a growing recognition of the similarities between the sexes, which may lead to the incorporation of gender-incongruent information into their gender stereotypes and self-construals (Hanover, 2000).

Cross-Cultural Findings

Williams and Best and their colleagues (1982/1990) administered the SSM II to five-, eight-, and eleven-year-olds in twenty-five countries. Across all countries, the percentage of stereotyped responses rose from around 60 percent at age five to around 70 percent at age eight. Strong, aggressive, cruel, coarse, and adventurous were traits consistently associated with men at both age levels, and weak, appreciative, soft-hearted, gentle, and meek were traits consistently associated with women.

Male and female stereotype scores were unusually high in Pakistan and relatively high in New Zealand and England. Scores were atypically low in Brazil, Taiwan, Germany, and France. Although between countries there was variation in the rate of learning, there was a general developmental pattern in which stereotype acquisition begins prior to age five, accelerates during the early school years, and is completed during the adolescent years.

Girls and boys learned the stereotypes at the same rate, but there was a tendency for male-stereotype traits to be learned somewhat earlier than female traits. In seventeen of the twenty-four countries studied, male stereotype items were better known than female items. Germany was the only country where there was a clear tendency for the female stereotype to be better known than the male. In contrast, female stereotype items were learned earlier than male items in Latin/ Catholic cultures (Brazil, Chile, Portugal, Venezuela), where the adult-defined female stereotype is more positive than the male (Neto, Williams, & Widner, 1991; Tarrier & Gomes, 1981).

In predominantly Muslim countries, five-year-olds associate traits with the two sexes in a more highly differentiated manner, and they learn the stereotypes, particularly the male items, at an earlier age than children in non-Muslim countries. Initially, children in predominantly Christian countries are slower in learning the stereotypes, perhaps reflecting the less-differentiated nature of the adult stereotypes, particularly in Catholic countries.

Using a combined measure of traits and roles, Albert and Porter (1986) examined the gender stereotypes of four- to six-year-olds in the United States and South Africa and found stereotyping increased with age. South African children stereotyped the male role more than did U.S. children, but there were no country differences for the female role. South African children from liberal Christian and Jewish backgrounds stereotyped less than children from more conservative religious groups. In the United States, religious background was not a factor.

Looking at older children, eleven to eighteen years of age, Intons-Peterson (1988) found that, compared with American children, Swedish children attributed more instrumental qualities to women. Gender stereotypes were more similar in Sweden than in the United States, perhaps reflecting the egalitarian Swedish cultural philosophy. Surprisingly, in Sweden ideal occupational choices differed by gender, with young Swedish women reporting interests in service occupations, such as flight attendant, hospital worker, and nanny, and young Swedish men reporting interests in business occupations. In contrast, ideal occupations for the sexes overlapped in the United States, with both groups listing doctor/dentist/attorney and business executive as their top choices. Given the similarities found across diverse countries with the different measures used, sex stereotypes appeared to be universal, with culture modifying rate of learning and minor aspects of content.

CONCLUSIONS AND FUTURE CHALLENGES

Gender differences have fascinated social scientists for decades, and with the growing interest in culture, questions regarding the joint effects of these variables should continue to intrigue researchers for years to come. It is remarkable to see that pancultural similarities in sex and gender greatly outweigh the cultural differences that are found. Indeed, the ways in which male-female relationships are organized are remarkably similar across social groups. With the many technological advances that have shrunk the world, longitudinal studies within societies undergoing rapid socioeconomic development should address concomitant changes in gender roles and behaviors.

In spite of the fact that males and females are biologically more similar than different, persons in traditional or in modern industrialized societies can expect to live qualitatively different lives based upon their gender. The relatively minor biological differences between the sexes can be expanded or reduced by cultural practices and socialization, resulting in gender differences in roles and behaviors that are generally modest but in some cases culturally important. Furthermore, few researchers have studied the relationship between cultural practices, such as initiation rites—a typical anthropological topic—and the development of the individual—a topic usually confined to the psychological domain.

The range of variation and diversity in familial and peer relationships seen across cultural groups provides a exceptional opportunity for examining gender-related social development. Future studies of gender roles across cultural groups should address how social relationships and behaviors change with age to identify the mechanisms that contribute to the development of gendered behaviors. Cross-cultural researchers have only begun to explore these social and behavioral issues with children in other societies.

REFERENCES

Albert, A. A., & Porter, J. R. (1986). Children's gender role stereotypes: A comparison of the United States and South Africa. *Journal of Cross-Cultural Psychology, 17,* 45–65.

Amato, P. R., & Keith, B. (1991). Parental divorce and the well-being of children: A meta-analysis. *Psychological Bulletin, 110,* 26–46.

Arnold, F., Bulatao, R., Buripakdi, C., Chung, B. J., Fawcett, J. T., Iritani, T., Lee, S. J., & Wu, T. S. (1975). *The value of children: Introduction and comparative analysis* (Vol. 1). Honolulu: East-West Center Population Institute.

Bandura, A. (1969). Social learning theory of identificatory process. In D. A. Goslin (Ed.), *Handbook of socialization theory and research* (pp. 213–262). Chicago: Rand McNally.

Barry, H., III, Bacon, M. K., & Child, I. L. (1957). A cross-cultural survey of some sex differences in socialization. *Journal of Abnormal and Social Psychology, 55,* 327–332.

————. (1967). Definitions, ratings and bibliographic sources of child-training practices of 110 cultures. In C. S. Ford (Ed.), *Cross-cultural approaches* (pp. 293–331). New Haven: HRAF Press.

Beal, C. R. (1994). *Boys and girls: The development of gender roles*. New York: McGraw-Hill.

Berry, J. W. (1976). Sex differences in behavior and cultural complexity. *Indian Journal of Psychology, 51*, 89–97.

Best, D. L., & Williams, J. E. (1993). Cross-cultural viewpoint. In A. E. Beall & R. J. Sternberg (Eds.), *Perspectives on the psychology of gender* (pp. 215–248). New York: Guilford.

Best, D. L., Williams, J. E., Cloud, J. M., Davis, S. W., Robertson, L. S., Edwards, J. R., Giles, H., & Fowles, J. (1977). Development of sex-trait stereotypes among young children in the United States, England, and Ireland. *Child Development, 48*, 1375–1384.

Biernat, M. (1991). Gender stereotypes and the relationship between masculinity and femininity: A developmental analysis. *Journal of Personality and Social Psychology, 61*, 351–365.

Bloch, M. N., & Adler, S. M. (1994). African children's play and the emergence of the sexual division of labor. In J. L. Roopnarine, J. E. Johnson, & F. H. Hooper (Eds.), *Children's play in diverse cultures* (pp. 148–178). Albany: State University of New York Press.

Block, J. H. (1983). Differential premises arising from differential socialization of the sexes: Some conjectures. *Child Development, 54*, 1335–1354.

Blurton-Jones, N. G., & Konner, M. (1973). Sex differences in behavior of London and Bushman children. In R. P. Michael & J. H. Crook (Eds.), *Comparative ecology and behavior of primates* (pp. 690–749). London: Academic.

Boehnke, K., Silbereisen, R. K., Eisenberg, N., Reykowski, J., & Palmonari, A. (1989). Developmental pattern of prosocial motivation: A cross-national study. *Journal of Cross-Cultural Psychology, 20*, 219–243.

Bradley, C. (1993). Women's power, children's labor. *Cross-Cultural Research, 27*, 70–96.

Bronstein, P. (1984). Differences in mothers' and fathers' behaviors toward children: A cross-cultural comparison. *Developmental Psychology, 20*, 995–1003.

Brown, J. K. (1970). A note on the division of labor by sex. *American Anthropologist, 72*, 1073–1078.

Burbank, V. K. (1987). Female aggression in cross-cultural perspective. *Behavior Science Research, 21* (1–4), 70–100.

Burns, A., & Homel, R. (1986). Sex role satisfaction among Australian children: Some sex, age, and cultural group comparisons. *Psychology of Women Quarterly, 10*, 285–296.

Buss, D. M. (1989). Sex differences in human mate preferences: Evolutionary hypotheses tested in thirty-seven cultures. *Behavioral and Brain Sciences, 12*, 1–49.

Bussey, K. (1983). A social-cognitive appraisal of sex-role development. *Australian Journal of Psychology, 35*, 135–143.

Bussey, K., & Bandura, A. (1984). Influence of gender constancy and social power on sex-linked modeling. *Journal of Personality and Social Psychology, 47*, 1292–1302.

Cairns, R. B., Gariépy, J. L., & Hood, K. E. (1990). Development, microevolution, and social behavior. *Psychological Review, 97,* 49–65.

Calasanti, T. M., & Bailey, C. A. (1991). Gender inequality and the division of household labor in the United States and Sweden: A socialist-feminist approach. *Social Problems, 38,* 34–53.

Calhoun G., Jr., & Sethi, R. (1987). The self-esteem of pupils from India, the United States, and the Philippines. *Journal of Psychology, 121,* 199–202.

Carlsson, M., & Barnes, M. (1986). Conception and self-attribution of sex-role behavior: A cross-cultural comparison between Swedish and kibbutz-raised Israeli children. *Scandinavian Journal of Psychology, 27,* 258–265.

Charles, M., & Höpflinger, F. (1992). Gender, culture, and the division of household labor: A replication of U.S. studies for the case of Switzerland. *Journal of Comparative Family Studies, 23,* 375–387.

Cheung Mui-ching, F. (1986). Development of gender stereotypes. *Educational Research Journal, 1,* 68–73.

Cialdini, R. B., & Trost, M. R. (1998). Social influence: Social norms, conformity, and compliance. In D. T. Gilbert, S. T. Fiske, & G. Lindzey (Eds.), *The handbook of social psychology* (4th ed., Vol. 2, pp. 152–192). Boston: McGraw-Hill.

Cole, M. (1999). Culture in development. In M. H. Bornstein & M. E. Lamb (Eds.), *Developmental psychology: An advanced textbook* (4th ed., pp. 73–123). Mahwah, NJ: Erlbaum.

Cronk, L. (1993). Parental favoritism toward daughters. *American Scientist, 81,* 272–279.

Daly, M., & Wilson, E. O. (1988). *Sex, evolution, and behavior* (2nd ed.). Belmont, CA: Wadsworth.

d'Andrade, R. (1966). Cultural meaning systems. In R. A. Shweder & R. A. LeVine (Eds.), *Culture theory: Essays on mind, self, and emotion* (pp. 88–122). New York: Cambridge University Press.

Darwin, C. (1872). *The expression of emotions in man and animals.* London: Murray.

Deaux, K. (1985). Sex and gender. *Annual Review of Psychology, 36,* 49–81.

Deaux, K., & LaFrance, M. (1998). Gender. In D. T. Gilbert, S. T. Fiske, & G. Lindzey (Eds.), *The handbook of social psychology* (4th ed., Vol. 1, pp. 788–827). Boston: McGraw-Hill.

DeCasper, A. J., & Fifer, W. P. (1980). Of human bonding: Newborns prefer their mothers' voices. *Science, 208,* 1174–1176.

Dixon, R. A., & Lerner, R. M. (1999). History and systems in developmental psychology. In M. H. Bornstein & M. E. Lamb (Eds.), *Developmental psychology: An advanced textbook* (pp. 3–45). Mahwah, NJ: Erlbaum.

Dongen-Melman, J. E. W. M. van, Koot, H. M., & Verhulst, F. C. (1993). Cross-cultural validation of Harter's self-perception profile for children in a Dutch sample. *Educational and Psychological Measurement, 53,* 739–753.

Draper, P. (1975). Cultural pressure on sex differences. *American Ethnologist, 2* (4), 602–616.

Eagly, A. H., Wood, W., & Diekman, A. B. (2000). Social role theory of sex differences and similarities: A current appraisal. In T. Eckes & H. M. Trautner (Eds.), *The developmental social psychology of gender* (pp. 123–174). Mahwah, NJ: Erlbaum.

Edelbrock, C., & Sugawara, A. I. (1978). Acquisition of sex-typed preferences in pre-school-aged children. *Developmental Psychology, 14*, 614–623.

Edwards, C. P. (1992). Cross-cultural perspectives on family-peer relations. In R. D. Parke & G. W. Ladd (Eds.), *Family-peer relationships: Modes of linkages* (pp. 285–315). Mahwah, NJ: Erlbaum.

Edwards, C. P., & Whiting, B. B. (1974). Women and dependency. *Politics and Society, 4*, 343–355.

———. (1980). Differential socialization of girls and boys in light of cross-cultural research. *New Directions for Child Development, 8*, 45–57.

———. (1993). "Mother, older sibling, and me": The overlapping roles of caretakers and companions in the social world of 2–3 year olds in Ngeca, Kenya. In K. MacDonald (Ed.), *Parent-child play: Descriptions and implications* (pp. 305–329). Albany: State University of New York Press.

Ember, C. R. (1981). A cross-cultural perspective on sex differences. In R. H. Munroe, R. L. Munroe, & B. B. Whiting (Eds.), *Handbook of cross-cultural human development* (pp. 531–580). New York: Garland.

Fausto-Sterling, A. (2000). *Sexing the body: Gender politics and the construction of sexuality.* New York: Basic Books.

Flavia. (1988). Violence in the family: Wife beating. In R. Ghadially (Ed.), *Women in Indian society: A reader* (pp. 151–166). New Delhi, India: Sage.

Freedman, D. G. (1976). Infancy, biology, and culture. In L. P. Lipsitt (Ed.), *Developmental psychobiology: The significance of infancy* (pp. 35–54). Hillsdale, NJ: Erlbaum.

Freedman, D. G., & DeBoer, M. M. (1979). Biological and cultural differences in early child development. *Annual Review of Anthropology, 8*, 579–600.

Geary, D. C. (1998). *Male, female: The evolution of human sex differences.* Washington, DC: American Psychological Association.

Ghadially, R., & Kumar, P. (1988). Stress, strain, and coping styles of female professionals. *Indian Journal of Applied Psychology, 26* (1), 1–8.

Gibbons, J. L., Lynn, M., Stiles, D. A., de Berducido, E. J., Richter, R., Walker, K., & Wiley, D. (1993). Guatemalan, Filipino, and U.S. adolescents' images of women as office workers and homemakers. *Psychology of Women Quarterly, 17*, 373–388.

Gibbons, J. L., Stiles, D. A., & Shkodriani, G. M. (1991). Adolescents' attitudes toward family and gender roles: An international comparison. *Sex Roles, 25*, 625–643.

Ginsberg, H., & Opper, S. (1969). *Piaget's theory of intellectual development: An introduction.* Englewood Cliffs, NJ: Prentice-Hall.

Gottlieb, G. (1976). Conceptions of prenatal development: Behavioral embryology. *Psychological Review, 83*, 215–234.

———. (1983). The psychobiological approach to development. In P. H. Mussen (Series Ed.) and M. M. Haith & J. J. Campos (Vol. Eds.), *Handbook of child psychology,* Vol. 2, *Infancy and developmental psychobiology* (pp. 1–26). New York: Wiley.

———. (1997). *Synthesizing nature-nurture: Prenatal roots of instinctive behavior.* Mahwah, NJ: Erlbaum.

Greenfield, P. M. (1981). Child care in cross-cultural perspectives: Implications for the future organization of child care in the United States. *Psychology of Women Quarterly, 6*, 41–54.

Greenfield, P. M., Brazelton, T. B., & Childs, C. P. (1989). From birth to maturity in Zinacantan: Ontogenesis in cultural context. In V. Bricker & G. Gosen (Eds.),

Ethnographic encounters in southern Mesoamerica: Celebratory essays in honor of Evon Z. Vogt (pp. 177–216). Albany: Institute of Mesoamerican Studies, State University of New York.

Gronseth, E. (1957). The impact of father absence in sailor families upon the personality structure and social adjustment of adult sailor sons (Part 1). In N. Anderson (Ed.), *Studies of the family* (Vol. 2, pp. 97–114). Göttingen: Vandenhoeck and Ruprecht.

Guttentag, M., & Longfellow, C. (1977). Children's social attributions: Development and change. In C. B. Keasey (Ed.), *Nebraska Symposium on Motivation* (pp. 305–341). Lincoln: University of Nebraska Press.

Hamilton, V. L., Blumenfeld, P. C., Akoh, H., & Miura, K. (1991). Group and gender in Japanese and American elementary classrooms. *Journal of Cross-Cultural Psychology, 22,* 317–346.

Hanover, B. (2000). Development of the self in gendered contexts. In T. Eckes & H. M. Trautner (Eds.), *The developmental social psychology of gender* (pp. 177–206). Mahwah, NJ: Erlbaum.

Heath, D. B. (1958). Sexual division of labor and cross-cultural research. *Social Forces, 37,* 77–79.

Hendrix, L., & Johnson, G. D. (1985). Instrumental and expressive socialization: A false dichotomy. *Sex Roles, 13,* 581–595.

Hoffman, C., & Hurst, N. (1990). Gender stereotypes: Perceptions or rationalization? *Journal of Personality and Social Psychology, 58,* 197–208.

Hoyenga, K. B., & Hoyenga, K. T. (1993). *Gender-related differences: Origins and outcomes.* Boston: Allyn & Bacon.

Huber, J. (1986). Trends in gender stratification, 1970–1985. *Sociological Forum, 1,* 476–495.

Huston, A. C. (1983). Sex-typing. In P. H. Mussen (Ed.), *Handbook of child psychology* (4th ed., Vol. 4, pp. 387–467). New York: Wiley.

Intons-Peterson, M. J. (1988). *Gender concepts of Swedish and American youth.* Hillsdale, NJ: Erlbaum.

Jacklin, C. N., DiPietro, J. A., & Maccoby, E. E. (1984). Sex typing behavior and sex typing pressure in child/parent interaction. *Archives of Sexual Behavior, 13,* 413–425.

Kagitçibasi, Ç. (1982). Old-age security value of children: Cross-national socioeconomic evidence. *Journal of Cross-Cultural Psychology, 13,* 29–42.

Katz, M. M., & Konner, M. J. (1981). The role of the father: An anthropological perspective. In M. E. Lamb (Ed.), *The role of the father in child development* (2nd ed.; pp. 155–185). New York: Wiley.

Kenrick, D. T., & Keefe, R. C. (1992). Age preferences in mates reflect sex differences in human reproductive strategies. *Behavioral and Brain Sciences, 15,* 75–91.

Kenrick, D. T., & Luce, C. L. (2000). An evolutionary life-history model of gender differences and similarities. In T. Eckes & H. M. Trautner (Eds.), *The developmental social psychology of gender* (pp. 35–63). Mahwah, NJ: Erlbaum.

Kessler, S. J., & McKenna, W. (1978). *Gender: An ethnomethodological approach.* New York: Wiley.

Kohlberg, L. (1966). A cognitive-developmental analysis of children's sex-role concepts and attitudes. In E. E. Maccoby (Ed.), *The development of sex differences* (pp. 82–173). Palo Alto, CA: Stanford University Press.

Krishnaswamy, S. (1988). Female infanticide in contemporary India: A case study of Kallars of Tamilnadu. In R. Ghadially (Ed.), *Women in Indian society: A reader* (pp. 186–195). New Delhi, India: Sage.

Lamb, M. E., Frodi, A. M., Hwand, C. P., Frodi, M., & Steinberg, J. (1982). Mother- and father-infant interaction involving play and holding in traditional and non-traditional Swedish families. *Developmental Psychology, 18,* 215–221.

Langlois, J. H., & Downs, C. (1980). Mothers, fathers, and peers as socialization agents of sex-typed play behavior in young children. *Child Development, 51,* 1217–1247.

Lummis, M., & Stevenson, H. W. (1990). Gender differences in beliefs and achievement: A cross-cultural study. *Developmental Psychology, 26,* 254–263.

Lynn, D. B., & Sawrey, W. L. (1959). The effects of father-absence on Norwegian boys and girls. *Journal of Abnormal Social Psychology, 59,* 258–262.

Lytton, H., & Romney, D. M. (1991). Parents' differential socialization of boys and girls: A meta-analysis. *Psychological Bulletin, 109,* 267–296.

Maccoby, E. E. (1988). Gender as a social category. *Developmental Psychology, 24,* 755–765.

———. (1998). *The two sexes: Growing up apart, coming together.* Cambridge, MA: Belknap Press.

Mackey, W. C. (1981). A cross-cultural analysis of adult-child proxemics in relation to the Plowman-Protector Complex: A preliminary study. *Behavior Science Research, 3–4,* 187–223.

———. (1985). *Fathering behaviors: The dynamics of the man-child bond.* New York: Plenum.

Mackey, W. C., & Day, R. (1979). Some indicators of fathering behaviors in the United States: A cross-cultural examination of adult male-child interaction. *Journal of Marriage and the Family, 41,* 287–299.

Martin, C. L. (2000). Cognitive theories of gender development. In T. Eckes & H. M. Trautner (Eds.), *The developmental social psychology of gender* (pp. 91–121). Mahwah, NJ: Erlbaum.

Masters, R. D. (1989). Gender and political cognition: Integrating evolutionary biology and political science. *Political and Life Sciences, 8,* 3–39.

Minturn, L., & Lambert, W. W. (1964). *Mothers of six cultures: Antecedents of child rearing.* New York: Wiley.

Mischel, W. (1970). Sex-typing and socialization. In P. H. Mussen (Ed.), *Carmichael's manual of child psychology* (Vol. 2, pp. 3–72). New York: Wiley.

Mukhopadhyay, C. C., & Higgins, P. J. (1998). Anthropological studies of women's status revisited: 1977–1987. *Annual Review of Anthropology, 17,* 461–495.

Munroe, R. L., Hulefeld, R., Rodgers, J. M., Tomeo, D. L., & Yamazaki, S. K. (2000). Aggression among children in four cultures. *Cross-Cultural Research, 34,* 3–25.

Munroe, R. L., & Munroe, R. H. (1971). Effect of environmental experiences on spatial ability in an East African society. *Journal of Social Psychology, 83,* 3–10.

————. (1975/1994). *Cross-cultural human development*. Prospect Heights, IL: Waveland Press.

Munroe, R. H., Shimmin, H. S., & Munroe, R. L. (1984). Gender understanding and sex role preference in four cultures. *Developmental Psychology, 20*, 673–682.

Murdock, G. P., & White, D. R. (1969). Standard cross-cultural sample. *Ethnology, 8*, 329–369.

Neto, F., Williams, J. E., & Widner, S. C. (1991). Portuguese children's knowledge of sex stereotypes: Effects of age, gender, and socioeconomic status. *Journal of Cross-Cultural Psychology, 22*, 376–388.

Oakley, A. (1979). *Becoming a mother*. Oxford: Martin Robertson.

Öhman, A. (1986). Face the beast and fear the face: Animal and social fears as prototypes for evolutionary analysis of emotion. *Psychophysiology, 23*, 123–145.

Olowu, A. A. (1985). Gender as a determinant of some Nigerian adolescents' self-concepts. *Journal of Adolescence, 8*, 347–355.

Omark, D. R., Omark, M., & Edelman, M. (1975). Formation of dominance hierarchies in young children: Action and perspective. In T. Williams (Ed.), *Psychological anthropology* (pp. 289–315). The Hague: Mouton.

Ottaway, R. N., & Bhatnagar, D. (1988). Personality and biographical differences between male and female managers in the United States and India. *Applied Psychology: An International Review, 37*, 201–212.

Peterson, V. S., & Runyan, A. S. (1993). *Global gender issues*. Boulder, CO: Westview.

Pooler, W. S. (1991). Sex of child preferences among college students. *Sex Roles, 25*, 569–576.

Population Crisis Committee. (1988, June). *Country rankings of the status of women: Poor, powerless, and pregnant*. Issue brief no. 20. Washington, DC: Author.

Prossner, G. V., Hutt, C., Hutt, S. J., Mahindadasa, K. J., & Goonetilleke, M. D. J. (1986). Children's play in Sri Lanka: A cross-cultural study. *British Journal of Developmental Psychology, 4*, 179–186.

Quinn, N. (1977). Anthropology studies of women's status. *Annual Review of Anthropology, 6*, 181–225.

Ramirez, J. M. (1993). Acceptability of aggression in four Spanish regions and a comparison with other European countries. *Aggressive Behavior, 19*, 185–197.

Rapoport, T., Lomski-Feder, E., & Masalha, M. (1989). Female subordination in the Arab-Israeli community: The adolescent perspective of "social veil." *Sex Roles, 20*, 255–269.

Reis, H. T., & Wright, S. (1982). Knowledge of sex-role stereotypes in children aged three to five. *Sex Roles, 8*, 1049–1056.

Rogoff, B. (1990). *Apprenticeship in thinking: Cognitive development in social context*. New York: Oxford University Press.

Rogoff, B., Gauvain, M., & Ellis, S. (1984). Development viewed in its cultural context. In M. H. Bornstein & M. E. Lamb (Eds.), *Developmental psychology: An advanced textbook* (pp. 533–571). Hillsdale, NJ: Erlbaum.

Rohner, R. P., & Rohner, E. C. (1982). Enculturative continuity and the importance of caretakers: Cross-cultural codes. *Behavior Science Research, 17*, 91–114.

Rosenberg, B. G., & Sutton-Smith, B. (1972). *Sex and identity*. New York: Holt, Rinehart, & Winston.

Rosner, M. (1967). Women in the kibbutz: Changing status and concepts. *Asian and African Studies, 3,* 35–68.

Ross, L. (1977). The intuitive psychologist and his shortcomings: Distortions in the attribution process. In L. Berkowitz (Ed.), *Advances in experimental social psychology* (Vol. 10, pp. 173–220). New York: Academic Press.

Ross, M. H. (1985). Female political participation: A cross-cultural explanation. *American Anthropologist, 88,* 843–858.

———. (1986). The limits to social structure: Social structural and psychocultural explanations for political conflict and violence. *Anthropological Quarterly, 59,* 171–176.

Rozin, P., & Kalat, J. W. (1971). Specific hungers and poison avoidance as adaptive specializations of learning. *Psychological Review, 78,* 459–486.

Rubin, J. Z., Provezano, F. J., & Luria, Z. (1974). The eye of the beholder: Parents' views on sex of newborns. *American Journal of Orthopsychiatry, 44,* 512–519.

Ruble, D. N., & Martin, C. L. (1998). Gender development. In W. Damon (Series Ed.) and N. Eisenberg (Vol. Ed.), *Handbook of child psychology,* Vol. 3, *Social, emotional, and personality development* (5th ed., pp. 933–1016). New York: Wiley.

Russell, G., & Russell, A. (1987). Mother-child and father-child relationships in middle childhood. *Child Development, 58,* 1573–1585.

Sagi, A., Lamb, M. E., Shoham, R., Dvir, R., & Lewkowicz, K. (1985). Parent-infant interaction in families on Israeli kibbutzim. *International Journal of Behavioral Development, 8,* 273–284.

Sears, R. R., Maccoby, E. E., & Levin, H. (1957). *Patterns of child rearing.* Palo Alto, CA: Stanford University Press.

Sears, R. R., Rau, L., & Alpert, R. (1965). *Identification and child rearing.* Palo Alto, CA: Stanford University Press.

Seavey, C. A., Katz, P. A., & Zalk, S. R. (1975). Baby X: The effect of gender labels on adult responses to infants. *Sex Roles, 1,* 103–110.

Segal, E. S. (1983). The structure of division of labor: A tentative formulation. *Behavior Science Research, 18,* 3–25.

Segall, M. (1988). Psycho-cultural antecedents of male aggression: Some implications involving gender, parenting, and adolescence. In N. Sartorious, P. Dasen, & J. W. Berry (Eds.), *Psychological implications for healthy human development* (pp. 71–92). Beverly Hills, CA: Sage.

Seligman, M. E. P. (1971). Phobias and preparedness. *Behavior Therapy, 2,* 307–320.

Serpell, R. (1993). *The significance of schooling: Life-journeys in an African society.* New York: Cambridge University Press.

Sidorowicz, L. S., & Lunney, G. S. (1980). Baby X revisited. *Sex Roles, 6,* 67–73.

Snarey, J., & Son, L. (1986). Sex-identity development among kibbutz-born males: A test of the Whiting hypothesis. *Ethos, 14,* 99–119.

Spiro, M. E. (1956). *Kibbutz: Venture in utopia.* New York: Schocken Books.

———. (1995). *Gender and culture: Kibbutz women revisited.* New Brunswick, NJ: Transaction.

Stevenson, M. R., & Black, K. N. (1988). Paternal absence and sex role development: A meta-analysis. *Child Development, 59,* 793–814.

Stewart, J. (1988). Current themes, theoretical issues, and preoccupations in the study of sexual differentiation and gender-related behaviors. *Psychobiology, 16*, 315–320.

Stolz, L. M. (1954). *Father relations of war-born children.* Palo Alto, CA: Stanford University Press.

Strube, M. J. (1981). Meta-analysis and cross-cultural comparison. *Journal of Cross-Cultural Psychology, 12*, 3–20.

Super, C. M., & Harkness, S. (1982). The infants' niche in rural Kenya and metropolitan America. In L. L. Adler (Ed.), *Cross-cultural research at issue* (pp. 47–55). New York: Academic Press.

Sweeney, J., & Bradbard, M. R. (1989). Mothers' and fathers' changing perceptions of their male and female infants over the course of pregnancy. *Journal of Genetic Psychology, 149*, 393–404.

Tanner, J. M. (1961). *Education and physical growth.* New York: International Universities Press.

Tarrier, N., & Gomes, L. F. (1981). Knowledge of sex-trait stereotypes: Effects of age, sex, and social class on Brazilian children. *Journal of Cross-Cultural Psychology, 12*, 81–93.

Thompson, S. K. (1975). Gender labels and early sex role development. *Child Development, 46*, 339–347.

Trautner, H. M., Helbing, N., Sahm, W., & Lohaus, A. (1988). Unkenntnis–Rigidität–Flexibilität: Ein Entwicklungsmodell der Geschlechtsrollen-Stereotypisierung [Unawareness–rigidity–flexibility: A developmental model of gender-role stereotyping]. *Zeitschrift für Entwicklungspsychologie und Pädagogische Psychologie, 19*,105–120.

Trivers, R. L. (1985). *Social evolution.* Menlo Park, CA: Benjamin/Cummings.

Van Leeuwen, M. S. (1978). A cross-cultural examination of psychological differentiation in males and females. *International Journal of Psychology, 13*, 87–122.

Vianello, M., Siemienska, R., Damian, N., Lupri, E., Coppi, R., d'Arcangelo, E., & Bolasco, S. (1990). *Gender inequality: A comparative study of discrimination and participation.* Newbury Park, CA: Sage.

Watkins, D., & Akande, A. (1992). The internal structure of the self description questionnaire: A Nigerian investigation. *British Journal of Educational Psychology, 62*, 120–125.

Watkins, D., Lam, M. K., & Regmi, M. (1991). Cross-cultural assessment of self-esteem: A Nepalese investigation. *Psychologia, 34*, 98–108.

Weinraub, M., Clemens, L. P., Sockloff, A., Etheridge, R., Gracely, E., & Myers, B. (1984). The development of sex role stereotypes in the third year: Relationships to gender labeling, gender identity, sex-typed toy preferences, and family characteristics. *Child Development, 55*, 1493–1503.

Weisner, T. S., & Gallimore, R. (1977). My brother's keeper: Child and sibling caretaking. *Current Anthropology, 18*, 169–190.

Welch, M. R., Page, B. M., & Martin, L. L. (1981). Sex differences in the ease of socialization: An analysis of the efficiency of child training processes in preindustrial societies. *Journal of Social Psychology, 113*, 3–12.

Whiting, B. B. (1965). Sex identity conflict and physical violence: A comparative study. Special issue, *American Anthropologist, 67*, 123–140.

Whiting, B. B., & Edwards, C. P. (1973). A cross-cultural analysis of sex differences in the behavior of children aged three to eleven. *Journal of Social Psychology, 91*, 171–188.

———. (1988). *Children of different worlds: The formation of social behavior.* Cambridge, MA: Harvard University Press.

Whyte, M. K. (1978). *The status of women in preindustrial societies.* Princeton: Princeton University Press.

Williams, J. E., & Best, D. L. (1982/1990). *Measuring sex stereotypes: A multination study* (rev. ed., 1990). Newbury Park, CA: Sage.

Wood, W., & Eagly, A. H. (1999). The origins of the division of labor and gender hierarchy: Implications for sex differences in social behavior. Unpublished manuscript.

Wright, E. O., Shire, K., Hwang, S. L., Dolan, M., & Baxter, J. (1992). The non-effects of class on the gender division of labor in the home: A comparative study of Sweden and the United States. *Gender and Society, 6*, 252–282.

Youssef, N. H. (1974). *Women and work in developing societies.* Berkeley, CA: Institute of International Studies.

CHAPTER 9

Sibling Interactions

Ashley E. Maynard

There is a notion in the developmental literature that the child's internal model of relationships uses the parent-child dyad (usually the mother-child dyad) as a prototype (Azuma, 1994; Dunn, 1992; Lebra, 1994). Indeed, the role of parents as guides of development has received much attention in psychology (see Bornstein, 1991, 1995, for reviews). Parents are said to arrange activities and experiences for their children that foster their optimal development (Gallimore, Goldenberg, & Weisner, 1993). Much research has documented the ways that parents serve as cultural transmitters for children by exposing them to various activities, belief systems, and artifacts according to their goals for them (e.g., Bearison, 1991; Whiting & Edwards, 1988). But parents, of course, are not the only source of guidance in children's development. Siblings also are effective socializers of each other (Rogoff, 1991; Stewart, 1983; Tobin, Wu, & Davidson, 1989; Zukow, 1989a). Interactions with siblings serve important functions in development because they allow children to practice roles and to observe more skilled partners (Rogoff, 1990).

The role of siblings in early childhood socialization has received much attention in recent years (e.g., Abramovitch, Corter, & Lando, 1979; Kendrick & Dunn, 1980; Nuckolls, 1993b; Weisner, 1987; Zukow, 1989a; Zukow-Goldring, 1995, 2002). Research in Western cultures has focused on the effects of a new sibling on the mother's relationship with the firstborn (e.g., Kendrick & Dunn, 1980), on the role of siblings in children's cognitive development (e.g., Teti, Bond, & Gibbs, 1988; Zukow, 1989b), and on the role of siblings in children's social and emotional development (e.g., Dunn, 1989; Dunn & Munn, 1986; Howe & Ross, 1990; Teti & Ablard, 1989; Whiting & Edwards, 1988). The study of sibling relationships in non-Western cultures has added to our understanding of the role that siblings may play in development (Marshall, 1983; Nuckolls, 1993a; Whiting & Edwards, 1988; Whiting & Whiting, 1975). Extensive studies of sibling caretaking in many agrarian societies highlight the role of siblings as guides for one another in cultural practices (Maynard, 2002b; Weisner & Gallimore, 1977; Zukow-Goldring, 1995, 2002).

In many of the world's cultures the sibling relationship is an ideal relationship, forming the prototype for other social relationships outside the family (Marshall, 1983; Maynard, 1999b; Nuckolls, 1993a; Weisner, 1993b). In such cultures, siblings maintain lifelong bonds and obligations to one another. For example, in the Zinacantec Maya culture of Chiapas, Mexico, the older brother–younger brother relationship serves as a prototype for relationships outside the family. People know how to behave in terms of status, a concept which stems from the older brother–younger brother paradigm (Vogt, 1969).

In this chapter, I explore the roles that siblings play in each other's lives around the world, emphasizing cultural influences on sibling interactions. Sibling interactions are conceived as part of an overall ecocultural project engaged in by families. The ecocultural approach is consistent with an evolutionary approach, and both are considered throughout the chapter. The studies reported here demonstrate the significant impact of siblings on each other's development. In the first section I consider the cultural context that surrounds sibling relationships, with a focus on sibling caretaking practices as a form of social support used in many cultures. I then examine the impact that siblings have on each other's development in several domains: social and emotional development, cognitive development, language socialization, and play.

THE ROLE OF CULTURE IN SIBLING INTERACTIONS

In the words of Weisner (1989a, p. 14, his emphasis), "Siblings always *matter*." Siblings are in a different age cohort than their parents and may share perspectives foreign, or at least unfamiliar, to the parents (Bryant, 1992; Dunn, 1983). Because they are biologically related and close in age, siblings may be especially effective at helping each other understand the cultural practices they are exposed to in development. An evolutionary view supports this idea of altruism expressed to those who share one's genes. Siblings exhibit altruism as they provide each other with examples of behavior and initiate each other into cultural practices (Martini, 1994; Maynard, 2002b; Zukow, 1989b; Zukow-Goldring, 1995, 2002).

Wherever children develop in the world, sibling relationships are important, though the degree of importance varies from culture to culture and throughout the life span. Siblings may play different roles in each other's lives depending on the local ecocultural goals for development. Different cultures define how siblings should interact with each other and with other relatives and neighbors; what resources, including both material and personnel, they should have individually; what should be shared among them; and how they should work and sleep (Weisner, 1989a; Whiting & Edwards, 1988). All of these aspects of interaction are influenced by people's cultural values. It is important to take the entire package of culture, including cultural values, into account when considering sibling interactions and their impact on development. Ecocultural theory provides a framework for understanding the important impact that siblings have on one another.

Ecocultural Theory

In ecocultural theory, development is an ecocultural project (Weisner, 1984) influenced by the interaction between the surrounding ecology and cultural practices for the care and raising of children (LCHC, 1986; Super & Harkness, 1986; Weisner, 1989b; Whiting & Edwards, 1988). The cultural place is centrally located in research questions and methods using ecocultural theory. The major premise is that the entire package of culture influences the developing child: for example, each family member's role in the family subsistence activities, how much time the siblings spend together, and whether or not older siblings are responsible for the care of the younger ones—all affect sibling relationships and a child's ultimate development. There are various ecocultural influences on sibling interactions, including availability of personnel to care for children, cultural beliefs about sex roles and goals for child development, and whether or not a sibling group shares lifelong obligations to each other, such as economic reciprocity and arrangement of marriages (Weisner, 1987).

The role of siblings is an important part of the ecocultural project, and conversely, the cultural place is primary in the study of sibling relationships (Weisner, 1993b). Taken-for-granted cultural values may affect sibling interactions and the role that siblings have in each other's lives. In those cultures where independence is a primary goal for child development, such as the United States (Greenfield, 1994), siblings will find themselves more independent of one another. On the other hand, in cultures where interdependence is a primary goal for development, siblings may be more dependent on one another for their social, cognitive, and biological needs (Kim & Choi, 1994; Zukow-Goldring, 1995, 2002). Raising the issue of the cultural place brings forth many more questions about sibling relationships. First, who is a sibling? What is the form that the sibling relationship should take? How should siblings relate to one another during childhood and adulthood? Once culture is seen as a set of practices adapted to local conditions it becomes clear that the sibling relationship is part of a complex system of cultural practices that are adapted to a cultural place. Adaptation to a cultural niche has a place within an evolutionary framework as parents and caretakers socialize children to adapt to their local environments and practices.

The Sibling Relationship: Who Is a Sibling?

Biological and evolutionary theory tell us that siblings are those individuals who share parents and therefore 50 percent of their genes. Linguistics and ecocultural theory have a varied answer to the question of who is considered a sibling: it depends on the cultural place. In the United States, Europe, and other Western cultures, siblings are defined as those people who share parents, and therefore, on average, 50 percent of their genetic material. The English language goes so far as to denote a special term for a "stepsibling," who is the child of a spouse of one's parent, conceived from another union. In this case no genes are shared. In the American system of genealogy, cousins share even less genetic material than siblings, and they are often even less involved in each other's lives.

This is not the case in many cultures of the world, where aunts, uncles, cousins, and siblings-by-baptism may be considered as important as genetic siblings. These siblings are sometimes called "classificatory siblings" by Western researchers, to indicate a kinship category (Nuckolls, 1993a; Watson-Gegeo & Gegeo, 1989). In some cultures, such as in the Solomon Islands and some parts of India, people who are not genetic siblings, and therefore share a smaller percentage (or none) of their genes, may be referred to as siblings and have the same obligations as genetic siblings (Watson-Gegeo & Gegeo, 1989; Zukow-Goldring, 2002). In Pukapuka Atoll in Oceania, there is a sibling term (*taina*) that is applied in modern times not only to those with blood relations but also to other members of the village, members of the same church, and "created kin" (Hecht, 1981, p. 61). In Pukapuka, *taini* are expected to share resources. In the Marquesas Islands, cousins may be considered to be a part of the sibling group or they may be considered part of separate groups (Kirkpatrick, 1981). Marquesan siblings are expected to share resources and workload, and to engage each other in an informal way. Thus, who is classified as a sibling, and what the relationship should therefore entail, is relative to the cultural place.

It is likely that parents socialize children according to their developmental goals for the siblings' future relationships, whether they are related by blood or not. This finding fits within an evolutionary framework if it is interpreted as a way to increase possible resources in one's ecocultural niche. Non–genetically related siblings who have obligations to one another may ensure each other's success and survival. It is important for researchers interested in doing sibling research to find out who among a group are considered siblings, what their relationship entails, what their future obligations might be to one another, and how these behaviors are socialized by parents and other caretakers.

Influences on Sibling Interactions

In American culture, the parent-child relationship is more primary than the sibling relationship (Weisner, 1993b). Parents often look for ways to reduce sibling rivalry and foster positive sibling relationships (Mendelson, 1990; Stoneman & Brody, 1993). Parents manage the sibling relationship, rather than siblings managing their own relationship. The sibling relationship is part of the constellation of family relationships, led by the parents. Stoneman and Brody (1993) propose a family systems model of sibling relations within the family context. In their study of American families, they find several variables important in fostering positive sibling relationships: direct parental behavior, which children imitate; parental discipline; intrafamily differences in parenting as experienced by the siblings; and consistency of parenting strategies with all siblings. The focus here is on the parents trying to influence siblings to get along, in an environment of fairness. Individual needs and goals are considered primary in children's development.

In Western cultures, sibling interactions are affected by parents' presence, and having a sibling changes the way an earlier-born child interacts with the parents. In American homes, mothers' presence has been found to reduce the quantity of time siblings spend interacting (Corter, Abramovitch, & Pepler, 1983). Kendrick and Dunn (1980) found that, for children growing up in England, the arrival of a second child affects the first child's interactions with the mother. When the mother was interacting with the new baby, there was an increase in confrontation and nurturance with the first child. When mothers were not busy with the new baby, there was a decrease in attention to the first child compared to before the birth. Howe and Ross (1990) found that American sibling interactions were more negative when the mother paid attention to one child at the expense of the other. Attachment style may influence the effects of a new sibling on an earlier-born child's distress. Securely attached infants were found to be less distressed by their mothers' attentiveness to a younger sibling than less securely attached infants (Teti & Ablard, 1989).

In non-Western cultures the sibling relationship is often more primary than the parent-child relationship, and parents worry less about fostering positive sibling relationships, usually because the siblings work out their own relations rather well, without intervention from adults (Martini, 1994; Whiting & Edwards, 1988; Zukow-Goldring, 1995, 2002). Abaluyia children of Kenya, for example, automatically seek out siblings or other peers for support as much or more than the mother (Bryant, 1992; Weisner, 1987). This may be because mothers are working and children are accustomed to relying on each other for social support more than their American counterparts are. Abaluyia children are sibling caretakers: older children help take care of their younger siblings. Older children are assigned roles to ensure the safety and well-being of younger children. Sibling caretaking is a widely used practice in which children rely on each other for social support. The practice of sibling caretaking has important influences on the ways that siblings relate to one another.

SIBLING CARETAKING

Sibling caretaking is a primary form of childcare in many agrarian societies (Weisner & Gallimore, 1977; Whiting & Edwards, 1988; Zukow-Goldring, 1995, 2002). In the practice of sibling caretaking, older siblings are responsible for the care of their younger siblings. This care may range from keeping the child happy and entertained while an adult is within earshot to feeding, bathing, and taking full responsibility for the child's complete safety and well-being while the adult is away. Care by older siblings frees adult caretakers to perform subsistence tasks such as cooking or working in a field. Sibling caretakers do more than just provide basic biological needs of their charges; they are effective socializers of each other (Maynard, 2002b; Rogoff, 1991; Stewart, 1983; Zukow-Goldring, 1995, 2002).

Siblings may provide special care because they are related to the child genetically and they are in the same relative age cohort compared to the parents. Children seem to benefit, both cognitively and socially, from interacting with caregivers other than their parents (Hill, 1991). In cultures with sibling caretaking, both the caregiver and the sibling being cared for benefit from such care. Sibling caregiving promotes interdependence and prosocial behavior in children (Weisner & Gallimore, 1977; Whiting & Edwards, 1988).

Adults' Roles in Guiding Sibling Caretaking

Adults in societies in which there is child caretaking do not consider that they are shirking their duties as caregivers (Whiting & Edwards, 1988; Whittemore & Beverly, 1989). Parents closely supervise sibling caretaking and typically give children increasingly complex tasks, initiating them into the role of child caretaker (Whiting & Edwards, 1988; Weisner, 1989a; Zukow-Goldring, 1995). For instance, in the Maya community of Nabenchauk in Chiapas, Mexico, a child of three years might get a clean cloth for the mother to diaper the infant or fetch a bar of soap as the mother bathes the younger infant sibling. An older child might actually bathe the infant herself (Maynard, unpublished field notes, 1995).

The responsibilities that parents give to children reflect the children's developing abilities and their interest in new babies. Children start to take more interest in younger children around the age of four (Weisner, 1982), and most sibling caretakers range in age from five to ten years (Zukow-Goldring, 1995, 2002). This appears to be an affordance of evolution, given that natural birth spacing in nonindustrialized, hunter-gatherer societies is three to four years. As the older sibling is maturing, she (and sometimes he) will become quite interested in the infant, wanting to be more involved in its care. As the child matures cognitively and emotionally, he or she becomes ready to take care of younger siblings (Weisner, 1993a). Sibling caretakers exhibit many of the same behaviors as parents, showing that they have internalized cultural models for caretaking behaviors (Zukow, 1989b). While it appears that children who take the role of caretaker for a younger sibling are being prepared for adult roles (Essman, 1977; Weisner, 1987), adults do not always describe the delegation of caretaking and instruction in caretaking as training the child caretaker for a future parenting role (Whittemore & Beverly, 1989).

In many cultures parents hold good caretaking skills in high regard. Among the Kwara'ae of Melanesia, for example, children are rewarded for being good sibling caretakers (Watson-Gegeo & Gegeo, 1989). Thus, both children and adults take sibling caretaking very seriously, since children who are good at caretaking gain higher status. In Kwara'ae society, child caretakers play a bigger role than parents in introducing their younger siblings to cousins and other children with whom they will have relationships throughout their lives. As a whole, the Kwara'ae village is a much richer environment for children and families because there are distributed resources that are not found in each individual household. This probably promotes a sense of reliance on shared resources and a long-term connection among age-mates, who will grow together as a community throughout their lives.

The Study of Sibling Care in Europe and the United States

Sibling caretaking relationships have also been studied in Europe and the United States, with a predominantly different set of methods. As opposed to the ethnographic approaches employed in more agrarian cultures, most studies in Europe and the United States have relied on questionnaire and behavioral inventory studies to ask questions about sibling caretaking. In a questionnaire and inventory study of both parent and sibling caretaking behaviors, Bryant (1989) related sibling care to children's social and emotional development and placed sibling caretaking practices in the web of family caretaking practices. She asked how the sibling interactions relate to the parents' caretaking interactions. She found seven factors in caretaking practices: paternal support, sibling nurturance, sibling challenge, paternal and sibling punishment, maternal and sibling concern, paternal protectiveness, and paternal indulgence. Her quantitative results suggest a stronger effect of sibling interactions over parent-child interactions in social and emotional development.

There have been few ethnographic studies of sibling caretaking in the United States and Europe. Notable examples are the study of siblings in "Orchard Town," a pseudonym for a community studied by Beatrice and John Whiting in their Six Cultures Study (Whiting & Whiting, 1975), and a study of children in South Carolina (Heath, 1983). Further study of sibling interactions in activities in the United States and Europe, through a more ethnographic approach, would help to elucidate this important relationship.

Summary

Sibling caretaking practices are adapted to an ecocultural place. An evolutionary view helps explain the use of the help of older children to take care of younger ones: attentional and physical resources (for labor) are used where they are more likely to ensure the survival of offspring. In agrarian societies, adults, capable of doing hard labor, use their energy and strength for the work of supporting the family as they socialize siblings to care for their younger charges. The socioeconomic situation interacts with the cultural goals for children's development.

THE IMPACT OF SIBLING INTERACTIONS ON SOCIAL AND COGNITIVE DEVELOPMENT

Siblings have been found to affect each other's social development as well as their cognitive development. There is an ongoing question in the literature about the relationship between family size and cognitive success. In this section the effects of siblings on social and cognitive development will be considered, along with issues raised by evolutionary theory such as the effect of number of siblings and sibling conflict.

Social Development

Sibling interactions are a major arena for children to learn about social support and the social world more generally. Children need to figure out how other family members, and still others in the world outside of the home, will behave and respond in various situations. They also need to understand others' feelings in order to behave appropriately. The sibling relationship is one in which young children exhibit relatively mature skills of cooperation, sharing and comforting, conciliation and teasing (Dunn, 1992; Martini, 1994; Maynard, 2002b; Watson-Gegeo & Gegeo, 1989; Weisner & Gallimore, 1977; Zukow-Goldring, 1995, 2002). Sibling interactions are associated with aspects of prosocial behavior in both the family and school contexts in the preschool period (Dunn, 1992). These capabilities may be importantly fostered in sibling interactions (Dunn & Munn, 1986).

There are social benefits for both older and younger siblings. Older siblings may learn the skills of caretaking, including providing nurturance and guidance. Younger siblings receive this care and benefit from it. The older sibling has a role as a model for the younger sibling. Younger siblings pay a lot of attention to older siblings as they look for appropriate ways to behave and as they look for ways to participate in activities (Dunn & Kendrick, 1982a; Martini & Kirkpatrick, 1992; Zukow, 1989b). Younger siblings imitate older siblings more than they are imitated (Pepler, Abramovitch, & Corter, 1981), and they receive guidance from older brothers or sisters (Maynard, 2002b; Zukow, 1989b), rather than the other way around. When urban American children had positive images of their older siblings, the sibling relationship served as a buffer for adjustment in such areas as delinquency, academic success, and mental health (Widmer & Weiss, 2000).

Parents in various cultures around the world believe it is important for children to be competent in giving and receiving social support, and they may train children in various social practices (Lebra, 1994; Watson-Gegeo & Gegeo, 1989; Weisner, 1989a; Zukow, 1989a; Zukow-Goldring, 1995, 2002). Two areas in which children receive such training are sharing and cooperation. In American society, sharing is often considered a source of conflict among siblings (Mendelson, 1990). In many agrarian societies, children learn to share from a very early age, and sharing is not a source of conflict in the sibling group. For example, Solomon Islanders train infants to share as early as six months of age (Watson-Gegeo & Gegeo, 1989). Watson-Gegeo and Gegeo describe the development of children's sharing in the Solomon Islands: children share on request by eighteen months of age, share without any prompting by three years, and by the age of six give food willingly to a younger sibling if there is not enough food for everyone. Martini and Kirkpatrick (1992) also describe early sharing among children in the Marquesas Islands: by the age of three years Marquesan siblings share with each other freely.

In addition to sharing, cooperation between siblings has been found to promote prosocial behaviors. Cooperation may take different forms in different cultures. In societies valuing independence and personal choice, such as the United States, cooperation may be based on an ethic of compromise or on taking turns at getting one's wishes: "I get what I want this time and you'll get what you want next time." In agrarian societies, cooperation may be based more on a social hierarchy. Older siblings have higher status and get more respect from younger siblings. For this respect they provide care and nurturance to the younger siblings. Younger siblings, on the other hand, become accustomed to listening to and following the will of an older child (Maynard, unpublished field notes, 1997; Ochs, 1988; Zukow-Goldring, 1995, 2002). Overall, it appears that cooperation with siblings leads to cooperation in other types of interactions. For example, Dunn and Munn (1986) found that British children who grew up with a sibling who cooperated with them in a high proportion of their interactions became more cooperative than children whose siblings did not cooperate as much with them.

Cognitive Development

Interacting with siblings also has influences on a child's cognitive development. As with social development, most cognitive benefits of interacting with siblings are not unidirectional. Interacting with siblings increases cognitive functioning for both parties involved (Cicirelli, 1975). Children may display cognitive capacities earlier with their siblings than with other peers or adults or when they are alone (Azmitia & Hesser, 1993; Weisner, 1989a). For example, Weisner (1989a) found that children sometimes display cognitive and social capacities earlier in interaction with their siblings than with an experimenter in a laboratory situation. This could be because children relate more to siblings than to experimenters. Or this could be because sibling caretakers break down activities into their component parts and provide models of appropriate conduct to children (Zukow, 1989b). Both siblings and adult caretakers in Zukow's Mexican and American samples used scaffolding in their interactions with young children, but sibling caretakers accommodated to children more than adults. These findings suggest an important role of siblings in cognitive development.

There are two major domains where siblings have been found to play a role in each other's cognitive development: perspective taking and providing guidance or teaching.

Perspective taking. Perspective taking involves understanding the point of view of another person. Children may be asked to indicate what someone else can see (Piaget, 1951) or how someone else would feel in a given situation (Eisenberg & Mussen, 1989). Sibling nurturance has been found to predict American children's later social perspective taking (Bryant, 1987) and to affect children's school behaviors and adjustment (Gallimore, Tharp, & Speidel, 1978; Weisner, Gallimore, & Jordan, 1988).

Positive sibling relations are related to perspective-taking skills of the older child (Howe & Ross, 1990). If the older child can appropriately assess the younger child's point of view or desires, sibling relations may be more positive. However, perspective taking may not be necessary for children to respond appropriately to a child's needs. Although on the surface it seems necessary to take the perspective of a sibling in distress in order to respond appropriately, Howe and Ross (1990) found that sibling response to distress was related to the intensity of the younger sibling's upset, and not to perspective-taking abilities. It may be that early attention to distress leads to the development of perspective-taking abilities at a cognitive level as children try to meet the needs of their younger siblings more efficiently and sensitively.

Interacting with siblings enhances children's perspective taking (Lewis et al., 1996; Perner, Ruffman, & Leekam, 1994; Ruffman, Perner, Naito, Parkin, & Clements, 1998). Lewis and colleagues (1996) found that children who interacted with an extended kin network, including multiple siblings, were precocious in their acquisition of false belief compared with children who interacted with a more limited kin group. In their studies in Japan and England, Perner and his colleagues found that the more siblings a child has, the more likely he is to understand the classic false-belief task. That is, children with more siblings have a better understanding that others may hold beliefs that are actually false relative to the true state of the world, and that beliefs may change according to changes in the world. Having a *younger* sibling does not appear to influence children's performance on the false-belief task (Perner et al., 1994).

Sibling teaching. Siblings can be especially effective teachers of their younger siblings because they are related, they are emotionally close, and they are close in age. Older siblings often serve as guides or models for their younger siblings (Maynard, 2002b; Zukow-Goldring, 1995, 2002). Older siblings may accrue advantages in cognitive functioning from teaching their younger siblings (Meisner & Fisher, 1980), and younger siblings receive the benefits of guidance. In the peer-tutoring literature, it has been shown that peer tutoring can benefit both the tutor and the tutee (Lepper, Aspinwall, Mumme, & Chabay, 1990; Weisner et al., 1988). Sibling teaching has similar effects.

The scope of past research on sibling teaching is limited. Dunn and Kendrick (1979) mention that they have noticed older siblings teaching and caring for their younger siblings, but they do not describe these interactions. Most studies have focused at one age, usually a sibling teacher age six and a target child age eighteen months to four years. One recent study of young children's semantic development compared six-year-old siblings' approach to teaching with that of mothers in a picture categorization task (Perez-Granados & Callanan, 1997). Mothers labeled categories and objects more than siblings. The target children, age four, labeled more objects and categories themselves when they were working with their mothers than they did when they were working with their siblings.

Most studies of sibling teaching have been conducted in laboratory settings (e.g., Cicirelli, 1972, 1973; Stewart, 1983), with protocols designed for experimental control but perhaps lacking in ecological validity. Some researchers have studied sibling interaction in children's home environments (e.g., Lamb, 1978; Pepler, Abramovitch, & Corter, 1981), but they have not considered what develops in the process of teaching younger siblings.

Ethnographic studies of sibling interactions indicate that siblings do teach each other to do everyday things. Sibling caretakers introduce younger siblings to new languages, language routines, and appropriate ways to behave (Ochs, 1988; Watson-Gegeo & Gegeo, 1989; Zukow-Goldring, 1995, 2002). In this way, they teach their younger siblings to become competent members of their cultures. In a study in Central Mexico, Zukow (1989a) described examples of older siblings engaging their younger charges in more advanced play than what the younger ones had been previously engaged in on their own. In the Marquesas, Martini (1994) found that sibling caretakers socialize each other to become competent at managing stratified social roles, respecting the complex social hierarchy of Marquesan culture. Maynard (2002b) used ethnographic video data to

examine the development of sibling teaching in the context of caretaking interactions. Older siblings ages three to eleven years were observed as they engaged their younger, two-year-old siblings in everyday activities. They provided
verbal and nonverbal guidance to incorporate the two-year-olds into the sibling
group activity. The oldest sibling caretakers, ages eight to eleven, were able to
structure tasks, provide necessary materials, simplify tasks into doable parts, guide
the bodies of learners, and provide both verbal and nonverbal feedback to help
their youngest siblings do a task. The six- and seven-year-olds also could set up
materials, but their teaching involved many directives without much task sim-
plification, explanations, or feedback. The three- to five-year-old children mainly
served as observational models, engaging in side-by-side activities with learners. The growing body of ethnographic work elucidates the ways that siblings
engage each other in everyday teaching activities.

Questions Raised by Evolutionary Theory Concerning Cognitive and Social Development in the Sibling Group

An evolutionary theory of siblings suggests that a person is more likely to help
a sibling, who shares half of his genes, than an unrelated person. Evolutionary
theory raises the question of how siblings will behave as they compete with each
other for resources while protecting them as carriers of half of each other's genes.
From a classic evolutionary perspective, the number of siblings one has should
increase conflict because of diminishing resources. Taken another way, however,
the number of siblings may also have a positive impact on children's social and
cognitive development: a greater number of siblings could be either an impediment to controlling resources or a resource itself.

Number of siblings. In the United States, a debate has gone on for many years
regarding the issue of family size and children's educational performance. Several
researchers concluded that having more siblings led parents to overdivide their
material and attentional resources among siblings, resulting in a pattern of firstborns
outperforming later-borns on scholastic aptitude tests and other measures of cognitive
ability (Downey, 1995; Zajonc, 1986). Zajonc (1986) concluded that, in terms of
cognitive development, it was better for a child to come from a smaller family rather
than a larger one. Research in recent years, however, in both agrarian cultures and
in the United States, has shown that there are positive effects, in both social and
cognitive development, of having more than one sibling.

Much recent research shows that having more than one sibling can enhance
children's social and cognitive development. For example, Tambashe and Shapiro
(1996) found that women in Zaire who grew up with more siblings had easier
social transitions into marriage in adulthood. Children with more siblings were
found to achieve success on false-belief tasks earlier than children with fewer

siblings (Lewis, Freeman, Kyriakidou, Maridaki-Kassotaki, & Berridge, 1996). Children who had multiple siblings who were both older than and younger than they were showed advanced theory-of-mind abilities (Peterson, 2001). Maynard (2002a) found that children with a greater number of older siblings were the beneficiaries of more opportunities for complex, scaffolded instruction than those children who had a smaller number of older siblings. In her Zinacantec Maya sample, Maynard found that siblings in multiage playgroups each served as teachers for young two-year-olds in ways that exhibited their developmental capabilities: three- to five-year-olds served as observational models; six- to seven-year-olds served to bring necessary items and provide some verbal instruction; and eight- to eleven-year-olds provided appropriate verbal and nonverbal help, including sensitive scaffolding of tasks. Thus, the two-year-old siblings with more than one older sibling were able to take advantage of more of these available teaching characteristics than children with only one older sibling. The scaffolding of the two-year-olds' learning is distributed among all the older siblings of a particular group.

Having more than one sibling available for care of the younger ones is also beneficial for parents who go away from home to work, as in many cultures in Africa (e.g., the Abaluyia of Kenya). Children in these cases are left in the complete care of siblings while parents work (Weisner & Gallimore, 1977). The sibling relationship becomes central to children's daily routines, and maintaining positive sibling relationships, therefore, becomes critical. Siblings must learn to manage conflict when it arises.

Sibling conflict. Sibling relationships are not always smooth and easy. The more siblings, the more potential for conflict among them. Siblings may find themselves dominated by others or in conflict with others over material goods. The ways that sibling conflict is characterized vary across cultures. In agrarian societies, sibling groups are usually stratified in a hierarchy where older siblings have authority over the younger ones (Zukow-Goldring, 2002). Older children assume responsibility for the happiness and well-being of the younger siblings. That responsibility often entails the wielding of power: older siblings can tell younger siblings what to do to avoid harm, to stay out of the way of adult work, and to behave well (Weisner & Gallimore, 1977; Whiting & Edwards, 1988). Younger children learn to accept that authority and follow the lead of the older siblings. The sibling group maintains homeostasis through this accepted authority system, rarely requiring intervention from adults.

In Great Britain and the United States, sibling conflict is characterized as a struggle based on sibling rivalry (Mendelson, 1990). Conflict is thought of as something that helps an individual to develop particular socioemotional skills and to internalize rules for social conduct (Zukow-Goldring, 2002). The sibling relationship is typically managed by the parents, who intervene to help resolve sibling conflicts. Thus the parents maintain homeostasis as the children gradually internalize social rules.

Summary

Across the world, siblings must learn to get along with each other and with others they meet in contexts outside the home. Siblings learn social and cognitive skills as they interact. Just as having more than one sibling may be beneficial in guiding the youngest sibling's learning, having more than one sibling may give children more opportunities to deal with greater conflict, to observe a wider range of emotional profiles, and to therefore develop greater agility with social skills. Having more than one sibling may be a resource or an impediment, depending on the particular ecocultural context. The relationship between number of siblings, birth spacing, and the distribution of resources needs to be investigated in both within- and between-culture studies to separate cultural values from economic issues.

THE IMPACT OF SIBLING INTERACTIONS ON LANGUAGE DEVELOPMENT

Language is a powerful tool in the socialization of children. Through linguistic interactions in social contexts children acquire their culture's values, rules, and roles (Blake, 1994; Ochs, 1986; Schieffelin, 1990). Researchers who study language socialization carefully link patterns of child language behavior with the social organization of a cultural place, and with members' values and beliefs (Ochs, 1982). Different cultural models are expressed in cultures' linguistic norms (d'Andrade, 1992; Ochs, 1982; Quinn & Holland, 1987). Parents and other socializing agents, such as sibling caretakers, express to children this linguistic cultural knowledge to indicate the appropriate behavior expected of children as they gain involvement in cultural practices (Ochs, 1982).

Language Socialization of Caretaking Skills

Caretaking behaviors are encouraged in many different kinds of linguistic interactions with children. Sibling caretakers engage in dialogues with their charges to teach them culturally appropriate means of speaking and behaving, including empathic response (Watson-Gegeo & Gegeo, 1989; Zukow-Goldring, 1995, 2002). Harkness (1977) found that mothers and child caretakers in East African Kipsigis society explain concepts and situations and repeat utterances to young children. The Kaluli, a people in Papua New Guinea, use a term to elicit empathy in their children; adults also appeal to children to elicit feelings of compassion in them (Schieffelin, 1990). Give-and-take and sharing are very important in Kaluli society, and children are socialized from a very early age, with verbal and nonverbal instruction in these behaviors. Girls and boys are socialized differently in Kaluli society; mothers are more accommodating with boys and "abrupt" with daughters. Infant girls are urged to attend to what is happening outside the mother-child dyad, to attend to the surrounding social environment. This is training for girls' future roles as mothers and reflects a concern for others. Boys and, more so, girls are faced outward to see what the mother is seeing, to see things from her perspective. Sibling caregivers learn to educe sharing and empathy and to face children outward in the same manner as adults. This is in contrast to the face-to-face interactions found so frequently in American mother-child dyads.

Caregivers' Socialization of Language

Caregivers also socialize children to use language in culturally appropriate ways. In her many studies of language socialization, Zukow has outlined the form and function of linguistic interactions in early child development (Zukow, 1989b, 1990; Zukow-Goldring & Ferko, 1994; Zukow-Goldring, 1996). Among populations in the United States and Central Mexico, Zukow finds that Euro-American and Latino caregivers use rich linguistic interactions to socialize children's language. They revise their own miscomprehended speech utterances in order to engage infants in the events of the moment. Both adult and sibling caregivers are adept at coordinating verbal and nonverbal discourse in order to help children understand what is happening. These interactions lead to close involvement in activities. For example, Zukow (1989b) describes the ways in which Mexican adult and child caretakers facilitate comprehension of young children; in an instance where the child appears to misunderstand a situation, caretakers provide both verbal and nonverbal information to help make things clear for the child. This is an important message from the caregiver to the child: "I see that you do not understand. I want you to understand so that we can relate to each other. This is what is going on."

African culture stresses social relations and the social impact of behaviors. Rabain-Jamin (1994) found that African immigrant mothers guided their children's activity with more visual and verbal input, and stressed the importance of social bonds and interactions with people, as opposed to the French mothers' focus on interaction with objects. One interesting feature of mother-child interaction was mothers' relating the babies' emotional states to an absent third party. In these interactions, the mother describes for the baby the situation ("Who made fun of my baby? Who hit Kajja?" [Rabain-Jamin, 1994, p. 161]), giving an explanation for the baby's apparent distress. This kind of interaction lets the child know that the mother is concerned about how he or she is feeling and helps in managing the child's mood. Indeed, Rabain-Jamin points out that one reason the mothers referred to a third party was that "discomfort should leave the body and enter into a social relationship" (p. 161).

In Africa, Melanesia, and Samoa, triadic conversations may also involve a present third part, where the mother, older sibling, and infant participate together in language socialization practices (Ochs, 1988; Rabain-Jamin, 1998; Schieffelin, 1990; Watson-Gegeo & Gegeo, 1989). In these interactions, mothers engage younger and older siblings to help the two understand others' perspectives emotionally and cognitively. Children also learn to take each other's perspective in the course of these triadic interactions. Controlled studies could help determine whether this kind of training leads to earlier perspective-taking and empathy skills in these children.

In the United States, older siblings have been found to adjust their speech to younger infants (Dunn & Kendrick, 1982b; Shatz & Gelman, 1973), using "motherese" when speaking with babies. Zukow-Goldring (1997) explains that the higher pitch, exaggerated speech contours, slower tempo, and simplified utterances of this speech enhance sibling and adult caregivers' socialization of attention.

SIBLINGS AT PLAY

Play serves important social and cognitive functions in children's development (Corsaro & Schwarz, 1991; Lancy, 1996; Scales, Almy, Nicolopoulou, & Ervin-Tripp, 1991). Play permits children to explore their environment, to learn about objects, and to solve problems (Garvey, 1990). In play, children learn to understand others and to practice roles they will assume as they mature (Chen & Kaspar, this volume; Corsaro, 1985; Haight & Miller, 1993; Vygotsky, 1978).

Play, as with other domains of development, is also affected by ecocultural models and values. For example, whether or not parents support play and how much parents participate affect the role of play in siblings' lives. In agrarian societies, play occurs predominantly outside the realm of adult activities (Farver, 1999; Gaskins, 1999; Martini, 1994; Maynard, 2002b; Watson-Gegeo & Gegeo, 1989; Zukow, 1989b). Children may play while adults work. As long as children do not interfere with adult work, play is usually tolerated and sometimes encouraged. A notable exception is the Yucatec Maya described by Gaskins (1996, 1999). Gaskins finds that Yucatec Maya families do not support play. For example, Yucatec parents do not provide toys or otherwise encourage play.

Play can be a very powerful engine for sibling interactions. In a Vygotskian view, play is a way for the child to deal with real-life situations and to exhibit behaviors slightly ahead of behaviors exhibited in other domains. Interacting with siblings and peers in play helps children take on roles and participate in cultural practices (Vygotsky, 1978; Zukow-Goldring, 1995, 2002). Indeed, even though much of children's play is imaginary, we observe that much of children's play is based on real-life events. Play often reproduces the adult world within the context of peer culture. It is with play that children "come to grasp, refine and extend features of the adult world in the creation of their own peer world" (Corsaro, 1985, p. 62). Children express their understandings of their worlds in their play activities. They also develop new ways of being in the culture.

Children develop cultural knowledge through role-play (Vygotsky, 1978). Role-play indicates their conception and use of social information like status, roles, and norms (Corsaro, 1985; Martini, 1994; Maynard, 1999a, 1999b; Vygotsky, 1978; Zukow-Goldring, 1995, 2002). Play provides an arena for children to practice what they know, to teach, to learn, and to try on future roles. In the case of the Yucatec Maya, for whom play is not a predominant form of role practice, future roles are practiced by the early assumption of chores and participation in household work (Gaskins, 1996, 1999).

Older siblings often structure younger children's play (Gaskins, 1999; Martini, 1994; Maynard, 2002b; Watson-Gegeo & Gegeo, 1989; Zukow-Goldring, 1995, 2002). Zukow (1986) used ethnographic data to demonstrate that play with siblings was significantly more advanced than play with adult caregivers. Older siblings were adept at engaging toddler siblings in elaborate role-playing scenes from everyday life. In the Zinacantec Maya community studied by Maynard (1999a, 1999b, 2002b), siblings structure play activities for their younger charges to keep them out of the way of adults and to keep then entertained and happy. The long-term cognitive and social effects of sibling play are being studied longitudinally (Maynard, unpublished field data, 2000).

CONCLUSION

No matter where they are developing in the world, siblings have an impact on each other's lives. Sibling caretaking provides a special glimpse into the potential for children to guide and teach each other, as they become competent members of their cultures. Sibling interactions influence many areas of children's development: socially, cognitively, linguistically, and in play. It is important to consider sibling relationships in the study of human development. We must understand how the sibling relationship relates with other relationships in the larger family and societal contexts.

The study of sibling interactions can add greatly to our understanding of human development. For example, a recent study by Whaley and her colleagues (Whaley, Sigman, Beckwith, Cohen, & Espinosa, 2000) contradicts the prevailing view that African children in Kenya participate in less *en face* interaction with their caregivers than their American counterparts. By taking into account siblings and caregivers other than the mother, Whaley and her colleagues showed that Kenyan and American children actually receive roughly the same amount of *en face* communication. Previous studies of infant-caregiver interactions had apparently focused solely on mother-infant interaction, without taking into account the role of sibling caretakers in Kenyan society. Because they understood the role of siblings and other caregivers in their Kenyan subjects' lives, Whaley and her colleagues were able to show that Kenyan siblings provide some types of care that their mothers do not provide. The focus for research thus shifts from a Kenyan "interaction deficit" to a deeper question about the pervasive role of interactions with infants, the ways that such interactions support development, and the ways that care is distributed among people in a society. Future studies of sibling interactions in their cultural contexts will help us to understand human development as a set of adaptations to particular ecocultural niches.

REFERENCES

Abramovitch, R., Corter, C., & Lando, B. (1979). Sibling interaction in the home. *Child Development, 51*, 1268–1271.

Azmitia, M., & Hesser, J. (1993). Why siblings are important agents of cognitive development: A comparison of siblings and peers. *Child Development, 64*, 430–444.

Azuma, H. (1994). Two modes of cognitive socialization in Japan and the United States. In P. Greenfield & R. Cocking (Eds.), *Cross-cultural roots of minority child development* (pp. 275–284). Hillsdale, NJ: Erlbaum.

Bearison, D. J. (1991). Instructional contexts of cognitive development: Piagetian approaches to sociogenesis. In L. T. Landsmann (Ed.), *Culture, schooling, and psychological development* (pp. 56–70). Norwood, NJ: Ablex.

Blake, I. K. (1994). Language development and socialization in young African-American children. In P. Greenfield & R. Cocking (Eds.), *Cross-cultural roots of minority child development* (pp. 167–195). Hillsdale, NJ: Erlbaum.

Bornstein, M. H. (1991). *Cultural approaches to parenting*. Hillsdale, NJ: Erlbaum.

———. (1995). *Handbook of parenting*, Vol. 3, *Status and social conditions of parenting*. Hillsdale, NJ: Erlbaum.

Bryant, B. K. (1987). Mental health, temperament, family, and friends: Perspectives on children's empathy and social perspective taking. In N. Eisenberg & J. Strayer (Eds.), *Empathy and its development* (pp. 245–270). New York: Cambridge University Press.

———. (1989). The child's perspective of sibling caretaking and its relevance to understanding social-emotional functioning and development. In P. G. Zukow (Ed.), *Sibling interaction across cultures: Theoretical and methodological issues* (pp. 143–164). New York: Springer-Verlag.

———. (1992). Sibling caretaking: Providing emotional support during middle childhood. In F. Boer & J. Dunn (Eds.), *Children's sibling relationships: Developmental and clinical issues* (pp. 55–69). Hillsdale, NJ: Erlbaum.

Cicirelli, V. G. (1972). The effect of sibling relationship of concept learning of young children taught by child-teachers. *Child Development, 43*, 282–287.

———. (1973). Effects of sibling structure and interaction on children's categorization style. *Developmental Psychology, 9*, 132–139.

———. (1975). Effects of mother and older sibling on the problem-solving behavior of the younger child. *Developmental Psychology, 11* (6), 749–756.

Corsaro, W. A. (1985). *Friendship and peer culture in the early years.* Norwood, NJ: Ablex.

Corsaro, W. A., & Schwarz, K. (1991). Peer play and socialization in two cultures: Implications for research and practice. In B. Scales, M. Almy, A. Nicolopoulou, & S. Ervin-Tripp (Eds.), *Play and the social context of development in early care and education* (pp. 234–254). New York: Teachers College Press.

Corter, C., Abramovitch, R., & Pepler, D. J. (1983). The role of the mother in sibling interaction. *Child Development, 54* (6), 1599–1605.

d'Andrade, R. G. (1992). Schemas and motivation. In R. G. d'Andrade & C. Strauss (Eds.), *Human motives and cultural models* (pp. 23–44). Cambridge: Cambridge University Press.

Downey, D. B. (1995). When bigger is not better: Family size, parental resources, and children's educational performance. *American Sociological Review, 60* (5), 746–761.

Dunn, J. (1983). Sibling relationships in early childhood. *Child Development, 54,* 787–811.

———. (1989). Siblings and the development of social understanding in early childhood. In P. G. Zukow (Ed.), *Sibling interaction across cultures: Theoretical and methodological issues* (pp. 106–116). New York: Springer-Verlag.

———. (1992). Sisters and brothers: Current issues in developmental research. In F. Boer & J. Dunn (Eds.), *Children's sibling relationships: Developmental and clinical issues* (pp. 1–17). Hillsdale, NJ: Erlbaum.

Dunn, J., & Kendrick, C. (1979). Interaction between young siblings in the context of family relationships. In M. Lewis & L. A. Rosenblum (Eds.), *The child and its family* (pp. 143–168). New York: Plenum.

———. (1982a). *Siblings: Love, envy, and understanding.* Cambridge, MA: Harvard University Press.

———. (1982b). The speech of two- and three-year olds to infant siblings: "Baby Talk" and the context of communication. *Journal of Child Language, 9,* 579–597.

Dunn, J., & Munn, P. (1986). Siblings and the development of prosocial behavior. *International Journal of Behavioral Development, 9,* 265–284.

Eisenberg, N., & Mussen, P. (1989). *The roots of prosocial behavior in children.* Cambridge: Cambridge University Press.

Essman, C. S. (1977). Sibling relations as socialization for parenthood. *Family Coordinator, 26* (3), 259–262.

Farver, J. (1999). Activity setting analysis: A model for examining the role of culture in development. In A. Göncü (Ed.), *Children's engagement in the world: Sociocultural perspectives* (pp. 99–127). New York: Cambridge University Press.

Gallimore, R., Goldenberg, C., & Weisner, T. S. (1993). The social construction and subjective reality of activity settings: Implications for community psychology. *American Journal of Community Psychology, 21* (4), 537–559.

Gallimore, R., Tharp, R. G., & Speidel, G. E. (1978). The relationship of sibling caretaking and attentiveness to a peer tutor. *American Educational Research Journal, 15* (2), 267–273.

Garvey, C. (1990). *Play.* Cambridge, MA: Harvard University Press.

Gaskins, S. (1996). How Mayan parental theories come into play. In S. Harkness & C. Super (Eds.), *Parents' cultural belief systems* (pp. 345–363). New York: Guilford.

———. (1999). Children's daily lives in a Mayan village: A case study of culturally constructed roles and activities. In A. Göncü (Ed.), *Children's engagement in the world: Sociocultural perspectives* (pp. 25–61). New York: Cambridge University Press.

Greenfield, P. M. (1994). Independence and interdependence as developmental scripts: Implications for theory, research, and practice. In P. M. Greenfield & R. R. Cocking (Eds.), *Cross-cultural roots of minority child development* (pp. 1–39). Hillsdale, NJ: Erlbaum.

Haight, W., & Miller, P. (1993). *The ecology and development of pretend play*. Albany: State University of New York Press.

Harkness, S. (1977). Aspects of social environment and first language acquisition in rural Africa. In C. E. Snow & C. E. Ferguson (Eds.), *Talking to children: Language input and acquisition* (pp. 309–316). Cambridge: Cambridge University Press.

Heath, S. B. (1983). *Way with words: Language, life, and work in communities and classrooms*. Cambridge: Cambridge University Press.

Hecht, J. A. (1981). The cultural contexts of siblingship in Pukapuka. In M. Marshall (Ed.), *Siblingship in Oceania: Studies in the meaning of kin relations* (pp. 53–77). Ann Arbor: University of Michigan Press.

Hill, M. (1991). The role of social networks in the care of young children. In M. Woodhead, P. Light, & R. Carr (Eds.), *Growing up in a changing society* (pp. 97–114). London: Routledge.

Howe, N., & Ross, H. S. (1990). Socialization, perspective-taking, and the sibling relationship. *Developmental Psychology, 26* (1), 160–165.

Kendrick, C., & Dunn, J. (1980). Caring for second baby: Effects on interaction between mother and firstborn. *Developmental Psychology, 16* (4), 303–311.

Kim, U., & Choi, S. (1994). Individualism, collectivism, and child development: A Korean perspective. In P. Greenfield & R. Cocking (Eds.), *Cross-cultural roots of minority child development* (pp. 227–257). Hillsdale, NJ: Erlbaum.

Kirkpatrick, J. (1981). Meanings of siblingship in Marquesan society. In M. Marshall (Ed.), *Siblingship in Oceania: Studies in the meaning of kin relations* (pp. 17–51). Ann Arbor: University of Michigan Press.

Lamb, M. E. (1978). Interactions between eighteen-month-olds and their preschool-aged siblings. *Child Development, 49* (1), 51–59.

Lancy, D. (1996). *Playing on the mother ground: Cultural routines for children's development*. New York: Guilford Press.

LCHC (Laboratory of Comparative Human Cognition). (1986). Contribution of cross-cultural esearch to educational practices. *American Psychologist, 41*, 1049–1058.

Lebra, T. S. (1994). Mother and child in Japanese socialization: A Japan-U.S. comparison. In P. M. Greenfield & R. R. Cocking (Eds.), *Cross-cultural roots of minority child development* (pp. 259–274). Hillsdale, NJ: Erlbaum.

Lepper, M. R., Aspinwall, L. G., Mumme, D. L., & Chabay, R. W. (1990). Self-perception and social-perception processes in tutoring: Subtle social control strategies of expert tutors. In J. M. Olson & M. P. Zanna (Eds.), *Self-inference processes: The Ontario symposium*, Vol. 6, *Ontario symposium on personality and social psychology* (pp. 217–237). Hillsdale, NJ: Erlbaum.

Lewis, C., Freeman, N. H., Kyriakidou, C., Maridaki-Kassotaki, K., & Berridge, D. M. (1996). Social influences on false belief access: Specific sibling influences or general apprenticeship? *Child Development, 67,* 2930–2947.

Marshall, L. B. (1983). *Siblingship in Oceania: Studies in the meaning of kin relations.* Lanham, MD: University Press of America.

Martini, M. (1994). Peer interactions in Polynesia: A view from the Marquesas. In J. P. Roopnarine, J. E. Johnson, & F. H. Hooper (Eds.), *Children's play in diverse cultures* (pp. 73–103). Albany: State University of New York Press.

Martini, M., & Kirkpatrick, J. (1992). Parenting in Polynesia: A view from the Marquesas. In J. L. Roopnarine & D. B. Carter (Eds.), *Parent-child socialization in diverse cultures* (pp. 199–223). Norwood, NJ: Ablex.

Maynard, A. E. (1999a). Cultural teaching: The social organization and development of teaching in Zinacantec Maya sibling interactions. Unpublished Ph.D. diss., University of California, Los Angeles.

———. (1999b). The social organization and development of teaching in Zinacantec Maya sibling play. In P. Greenfield (Chair), *Cultural context and developmental theory: Evidence from the Maya of Mexico.* Symposium conducted at the meeting of the American Anthropological Association, Chicago.

———. (2002a). The social organization of development. Unpublished manuscript, University of Hawaii at Manoa.

———. (2002b). Cultural teaching: The development of teaching skills in Maya sibling interactions. *Child Development, 73* (3), 969–982.

Meisner, J. S., & Fisher, V. L. (1980). Cognitive shifts of young children as a function of peer interaction and sibling status. *Journal of Genetic Psychology, 136,* 247–253.

Mendelson, M. J. (1990). *Becoming a brother: A child learns about life, family, and self.* Cambridge: MIT Press.

Nuckolls, C. W. (1993a). An introduction to the cross-cultural study of sibling relations. In C. W. Nuckolls (Ed.), *Siblings in South Asia: Brothers and sisters in cultural context* (pp. 19–41). New York: Guilford Press.

———. (1993b). *Siblings in South Asia: Brothers and sisters in cultural context.* New York: Guilford Press.

Ochs, E. (1982). Talking to children in Western Samoa. *Language in Society, 11,* 77–104.

———. (1986). From feelings to grammar: A Samoan case study. In B. B. Schieffelin & E. Ochs (Eds.), *Language socialization across cultures* (pp. 251–272). Cambridge: Cambridge University Press.

———. (1988). *Culture and language development: Language acquisition and socialization in a Samoan village.* Cambridge: Cambridge University Press.

Pepler, D. J., Abramovitch, R., & Corter, C. (1981). Sibling interactions in the home: A longitudinal study. *Child Development, 52* (4), 1344–1347.

Perez-Granados, D. R., & Callanan, M. A. (1997). Conversations with mothers and siblings: Young children's semantic and conceptual development. *Developmental Psychology, 33* (1), 120–134.

Perner, J., Ruffman, T., & Leekam, S. R. (1994). Theory of mind is contagious: You catch it from your sibs. *Child Development, 65,* 1225–1238.

Peterson, C. C. (2001). Influence of siblings' perspectives on theory of mind. *Cognitive Development, 15* (4), 435–455.

Piaget, J. (1951). *The origins of intelligence in children*. New York: International Universities Press.

Quinn, N., & Holland, D. (1987). Culture and cognition. In D. Holland & N. Quinn (Eds.), *Cultural models in language and thought* (pp. 3–40). Cambridge: Cambridge University Press.

Rabain-Jamin, J. (1994). Language and socialization of the child in African families living in France. In P. M. Greenfield & R. Cocking (Eds.), *Cross-cultural roots of minority child development* (pp. 147–166). Hillsdale, NJ: Erlbaum.

———. (1998). Polyadic language socialization strategy: The case of toddlers in Senegal. *Discourse Processes, 26,* 43–65.

Rogoff, B. (1990). *Apprenticeship in thinking*. New York: Oxford University Press.

———. (1991). The joint socialization of development by young children and adults. In M. Lewis & S. Feinman (Eds.), *Social influences and socialization in infancy* (pp. 253–280). New York: Plenum.

Ruffman, T., Perner, J., Naito, M., Parkin, L., & Clements, W. A. (1998). Older (but not younger) siblings facilitate false belief understanding. *Developmental Psychology, 34* (1), 161–174.

Scales, B., Almy, M., Nicolopoulou, A., & Ervin-Tripp, S. (1991). *Play and the social context of development in early care and education*. New York: Teachers College Press.

Schieffelin, B. B. (1990). *The give and take of everyday life: Language socialization of Kaluli children*. Cambridge: Cambridge University Press.

Shatz, M., & Gelman, R. (1973). *The development of communication skills: Modifications in the speech of young children as a function of listener*. Monographs of the Society for Research in Child Development. Chicago: University of Chicago Press.

Stewart, R. B. (1983). Sibling interaction: The role of the older child as teacher for the younger. *Merrill-Palmer Quarterly, 29* (1), 47–68.

Stoneman, Z., & Brody, G. H. (1993). Sibling relations in the family context. In Z. Stoneman & P. Waldman Berman (Eds.), *The effects of mental retardation, disability, and illness on sibling relationships: Research issues and challenges* (pp. 3–30). Baltimore, MD: Brookes.

Super, C. M., & Harkness, S. (1986). The developmental niche: A conceptualization at the interface of child and culture. *International Journal of Behavioral Development, 9,* 1–25.

Tambashe, B. O., & Shapiro, D. (1996). Family background and early life course transitions in Kinshasa. *Journal of Marriage and the Family, 58* (4), 1029–1037.

Teti, D. M., & Ablard, K. E. (1989). Security of attachment and infant-sibling relationships: A laboratory study. *Child Development, 60* (6), 1519–1528.

Teti, D. M., Bond, L. A., & Gibbs, E. D. (1988). Mothers, fathers, and siblings: A comparison of play styles and their influence upon infant cognitive level. *International Journal of Behavioral Development, 11* (4), 415–432.

Tobin, J. J., Wu, D. Y. H., & Davidson, D. H. (1989). *Preschool in three cultures: Japan, China, and the United States*. New Haven: Yale University Press.

Vogt, E. Z. (1969). *Zinacantán: A Maya community in the highlands of Chiapas*. Cambridge, MA: Harvard University Press.

Vygotsky, L. S. (1978). *Mind in society*. New York: Cambridge University Press.

Watson-Gegeo, K. A., & Gegeo, D. W. (1989). The role of sibling interaction in child socialization. In P. G. Zukow (Ed.), *Sibling interaction across cultures: Theoretical and methodological issues* (pp. 54–76). New York: Springer-Verlag.

Weisner, T. S. (1982). Sibling interdependence and child caretaking: A cross-cultural view. In M. E. Lamb & B. Sutton-Smith (Eds.), *Sibling relationships: Their nature and significance across the lifespan* (pp. 305–327). Hillsdale, NJ: Erlbaum.

———. (1984). Ecocultural niches of middle childhood: A cross-cultural perspective. In W. A. Collins (Ed.), *Development during middle childhood: The years from six to twelve* (pp. 334–369).Washington, DC: National Academy Press.

———. (1987). Socialization for parenthood in sibling caretaking societies. In J. B. Lancaster, J. Altmann, A. S. Rossi, & L. R. Sherrod (Eds.), *Parenting across the life span: Biosocial dimensions* (pp. 237–270). Hawthorne, NY: Aldine.

———. (1989a). Comparing sibling relationships across cultures. In P. G. Zukow (Ed.), *Sibling interaction across cultures: Theoretical and methodological issues* (pp. 11–25). New York: Springer-Verlag.

———. (1989b). Cultural and universal aspects of social support for children: Evidence from the Abaluyia of Kenya. In D. Belle (Ed.), *Children's social networks and social supports* (pp. 70–90). New York: Wiley.

———. (1993a). Ethnographic and ecocultural perspectives on sibling relationships. In Z. Stoneman & P. W. Berman (Eds.), *The effects of mental retardation, disability, and illness on sibling relationships: Research issues and challenges* (pp. 51–83). Baltimore, MD: Brookes.

———. (1993b). Overview: Sibling similarity and difference in different cultures. In C. W. Nuckolls (Ed.), *Siblings in south Asia: Brothers and sisters in cultural context* (pp. 1–17). New York: Guilford Press.

———. (1996). Why ethnography should be the most important method in the study of human development. In R. Jessor, A. Colby, & R. A. Shweder (Eds.), *Ethnography and human development: Context and meaning in social inquiry* (pp. 305–326). Chicago: University of Chicago Press.

Weisner, T. S., & Gallimore, R. (1977). My brother's keeper: Child and sibling caretaking. *Current Anthropology, 18* (2), 169–190.

———. (1985, December). The convergence of ecocultural and activity theory. Paper presented at the annual meeting of the American Anthropological Association, Washington, DC.

Weisner, T. S., Gallimore, R., & Jordan, C. (1988). Unpackaging cultural effects on classroom learning: Native Hawaiian peer assistance and child-generated activity. *Anthropology and Education Quarterly, 19* (4), 327–353.

Whaley, S. E., Sigman, M., Beckwith, L., Cohen, S., & Espinosa, M. P. (2000). Cultural differences in caregiving in Kenya and the United States: The importance of multiple caregivers and adequate comparison groups. Unpublished manuscript, University of California, Los Angeles.

Whiting, B. B., & Edwards, C. P. (1988). *Children of different worlds: The formation of social behavior.* Cambridge, MA: Harvard University Press.

Whiting, B. B., & Whiting, J. M. (1975). *Children of six cultures: A psycho-cultural analysis.* Cambridge, MA: Harvard University Press.

Whittemore, R. D., & Beverly, E. (1989). Trust in the Mandinka way: The cultural context of sibling care. In P. G. Zukow (Ed.), *Sibling interactions across cultures: Theoretical and methodological issues* (pp. 26–53). New York: Springer-Verlag.

Widmer, E. D., & Weiss, C. C. (2000). Do older siblings make a difference? The effects of older sibling support and older sibling adjustment on the adjustment of socially disadvantaged adolescents. *Journal of Research on Adolescence, 10* (1), 1–27.

Youngblade, L. M., & Dunn, J. (1995). Social pretend with mother and sibling: Individual differences and social understanding. In A. D. Pellegrini (Ed.), *The future of play theory: A multidisciplinary inquiry into the contributions of Brian Sutton-Smith* (pp. 221–240). New York: State University of New York Press.

Zajonc, R. B. (1986). The decline and rise of scholastic aptitude scores: A prediction derived from the confluence model. *American Psychologist, 41* (8), 862–867.

Zukow, P. G. (1986). The relationship between interaction with the caregiver and the emergence of play activities during the one-word period. *British Journal of Developmental Psychology, 4,* 223–234.

Zukow, P. G. (1989a.) *Sibling interaction across cultures. Theoretical and methodological issues.* New York: Springer-Verlag.

———. (1989b). Siblings as effective socializing agents: Evidence from central Mexico. In P. G. Zukow (Ed.), *Sibling interaction across cultures: Theoretical and methodological issues* (pp. 79–105). New York: Springer-Verlag.

———. (1990). Socio-perceptual bases for the emergence of language: An alternative to innatist approaches. In C. Dent & P. G. Zukow (Eds.), The idea of innateness: Effects on language and communication research. Special issue, *Developmental Psychobiology, 23,* 679–704.

Zukow-Goldring, P. G. (1995). Sibling caregiving. In M. H. Bornstein (Ed.), *Handbook of parenting,* Vol. 3, *Status and social conditions of parenting* (pp. 177–208). Hillsdale, NJ: Erlbaum.

———. (1996). Sensitive caregivers foster the comprehension of speech: When gestures speak louder than words. *Early Development and Parenting, 5* (4), 195–211.

———. (1997). A social ecological realist approach to the emergence of the lexicon: Educating attention to amodal invariants in gesture and speech. In C. Dent-Read & P. G. Zukow-Goldring (Eds.), *Evolving explanations of development: Ecological approaches to organism-environment systems* (pp. 199–250). Washington, DC: American Psychological Association.

———. (2002). Sibling caregiving. In M. Bornstein (Ed.), *Handbook of Parenting,* Vol. 3, *Status and social conditions of parenting* (2nd ed.). Mahwah, NJ: Erlbaum.

Zukow-Goldring, P. G., & Ferko, K. R. (1994). An ecological approach to the emergence of the lexicon: Socializing attention. In V. John-Steiner, C. P. Panofsky, & L. W. Smith (Eds.), *Sociocultural approaches to language and literacy: An interactionist perspective* (pp. 170–190). Cambridge: Cambridge University Press.

PART IV

Adolescents in the Global Village

CHAPTER 10

Adolescents in the Developing World

Judith L. Gibbons

Most information about adolescents' daily activities, social interactions, and well-being originates in the industrialized Western world. But the large majority of the world's adolescents live in developing countries. At the present time, 86 percent of ten- to twenty-four-year olds live in developing nations, and the percentage continues to rise (Boyd, Ashford, Haub, & Cornelius, 2000). Add to this number the adolescents who live in traditional, nonindustrial societies within developed nations (e.g., the Inuit in the Canadian arctic, Aborigines in traditional communities in Australia), and the majority of the world's teenagers might well be called "the forgotten 90 percent."

In a recent review of adolescent development (Steinberg & Morris, 2000), the international diversity of the adolescent experience was overlooked; a short section on diversity was limited to ethnic minority and poor youth within the United States. One reason for the paucity of studies from developing countries is a lack of resources with which to conduct and publish research (Adair, Pandey, Begum, Puhan, & Vohra, 1995). Perhaps a more important reason is that psychologists in developing countries have often, fittingly, turned their attention to addressing pressing social problems rather than building or testing theories. The ensuing applied research can often illuminate an aspect of the lives of adolescents. For example, in a study of adolescent pregnancy in Nicaragua (Berglund, Lifjestrand, De Maria Marín, Salgado, & Zelaya, 1997), it was found that girls who had close friends were less likely to become pregnant as teenagers. So a protective function of adolescent friendship was elucidated.

DEVELOPING COUNTRIES, MODERNIZATION, AND INDUSTRIALIZATION

The very notion of developing countries implies change, such that many of the influences on adolescents in developing countries stem from the social changes in their society. Among the social changes are modernization, industrialization, and urbanization. Although there are a number of theories that predict that rapid social change leads to stressful lives for adolescents, the empirical evidence for this effect is limited. Moreover, adolescents' successful adaptation to stress may be engendered by protective factors such as strong family and community ties (Dasen, 2000).

Some of the consequences for adolescents of rapid social change have been well-described in ethnographies from the Harvard Adolescence Project (Burbank, 1988; Condon, 1988; Davis & Davis, 1989; Hollos & Leis, 1989). For example, there were profound changes in Holman, a remote community in the Canadian arctic, in the twenty-two years prior to Condon's 1982 research trip (Condon, 1988). In 1960, housing units were first provided by the Canadian government and within ten years all of the Inuit community had settled in houses. A school and a medical clinic were introduced. There was enhanced communication with the outside world as a result of the new air strip, the introduction of television, and school trips to Toronto. Snowmobiles, running water, and electricity changed the daily lives of the Holman inhabitants. Adolescents enrolled in formal education, engaged in competitive sports, and developed a more worldly outlook (Condon, 1988).

One of the few longitudinal studies to look at social change during development is a study from the Sudan (Cederblad & Rahim, 1986). Demographic and mental health data on 197 children (ages three to fifteen) living in three small villages outside Khartoum, Sudan, were first collected during 1964 and 1965. Almost twenty years later, more than half of the participants were located and surveyed a second time. During the intervening years, the city of Khartoum had expanded and the villages had been absorbed into the urban spread. Rather than subsisting on agriculture and animal husbandry, residents had taken jobs in manufacturing and service industries. There were increased services providing for education, health, communication, and transportation. Family structure had changed from predominantly polygyny to predominantly monogamy and the average family size had decreased. Most of the study's participants had come of age during the period of most rapid social change. The changes were broad, including not only urbanization but also modernization and Westernization. Under conditions of rapid social change, the most important childhood predictor of mental health as an adult was the type of occupation of the father. Children who had fathers with more modern jobs (manufacturing or clerical) fared better than those whose fathers held more traditional jobs (e.g., farmer or bricklayer). There are many possible mediators of this relationship, including parental beliefs and socialization for success and more educational opportunities in families in which fathers held modern jobs. The congruity between the fathers' experiences and the opportunities available to the developing adolescents is likely to be an important factor.

Global, as opposed to local, social changes may also be altering the lives of adolescents. Schlegel (2000) has described the spread of global culture, evident in music preferences and fashion, its impact on adolescents, and the unique meaning that adolescents may bring to the use of the international symbols. She provides two examples of practices adopted by adolescents far from the original source—the celebration of St. Valentine's Day among Polish adolescents and the popularity of reggae music among Moroccan adolescents. Like Dasen (2000), Schlegel also notes that community factors may influence adolescents' responses to the social changes. Two communities in Nigeria—one that had held to traditional ways and another that was rapidly modernizing—were contrasted by Hollos and Leis (1989). It was found that there was more conflict between adolescents and their parents in the traditional village and more intergenerational cooperation in the modernizing village. Perhaps, in communities facing social change, adolescent well-being may be fostered by a "modern" perspective shared by adolescents and their parents (Cederblad & Rahim, 1986; Hollos & Leis, 1989).

The spread of Western popular music to remote corners of the globe may have far-reaching effects on adolescents' lives (Arnett, 2001). For example, young people growing up in Kathmandu enjoy rock, heavy metal, and rap (Liechty, 1995; cited in Arnett, 2001). Among the Chambri of Papua New Guinea, many adolescents are fans of Pepsi Fizz, a television show of popular music videos that feature international musicians as well as local Papua New Guinea performers (Gewertz & Errington, 1996).

DIVERSITY OF ADOLESCENTS' CONDITIONS

A second truism is that adolescents in developing countries live in diverse circumstances. The contexts of adolescents' lives vary by socioeconomic condition, gender, urban or rural residence, educational opportunity, and access to media and material goods.

From the Indian perspective, Saraswathi (1999) has pointed out that the adolescent life stage is defined differently for youth of different socioeconomic groups and differently for boys and girls. She explains that, in India, continuity between childhood and adulthood is the norm for some adolescents, especially girls from the lower and middle socioeconomic groups. Through early responsibilities for household chores and childcare, girls learn to be mothers and wives. For boys from the lower socioeconomic conditions, the necessity to earn money preempts advanced schooling, leading to premature entry into an adult lifestyle. Among the middle socioeconomic groups, boys may be encouraged to focus on educational attainment, and peer groups may assume greater importance. Among wealthy young persons in India, increased access to vehicles and cash may allow a certain amount of independence and may also promote consumerism.

Saraswathi's observations about the importance of material products in defining trends in adolescent development may not be limited to India (Saraswathi, 1999). For adolescents in developing nations, as well as for adolescents in the Western world, material possessions may become symbols of group membership, status, and identity. A comparison of the lifestyles of Japanese and U.S. teenagers was titled *The Material Child* (White, 1993). The tastes shared by teenagers from the two countries included fashions, music, and electronic equipment. A study of adolescent identity development in postapartheid South Africa described "Coca-Cola kids," youth who had embraced Western values of individualism, competition, and materialism (Stevens & Lockhat, 1997). In rural north China, intergenerational squabbles have emerged over the young peoples' embrace of materialistic values, their display of new clothes, leather shoes, expensive cigarettes, and cassettes (Yan, 1999).

Another major way in which adolescents differ from each other is in urban versus rural residence. Because urban centers offer a greater variety of occupational pursuits, increased opportunities for education, better healthcare, and increased access to media, cities may afford platforms for positive development. On the other hand, urban residence can also increase the risk of exploitation, prostitution, drug use, and diseases such as AIDS (Arnett, 2001).

Of the urban-rural differences, attendance at school may have the most pervasive effects on adolescents' lives, not just because of education per se, but because schooling allows adolescents to spend large amounts of time with their peers. In a review of the life stage of adolescence in several parts of the developing world, Caldwell and his colleagues (Caldwell, Caldwell, Caldwell, & Pieris, 1998) have pointed out the increased opportunities for social interaction, especially between boys and girls, that often accompany formal education. Among the Yoruba of Nigeria in sub-Saharan Africa, schooling

> removed children from the house or farm and from the control of their elders. It transferred their obedience to a nonrelative, frequently brought boys and girls together, induced and even taught them to play, and often left mixed groups to go to school and return home unsupervised, presenting the opportunity for sexual and other mischief. (p. 139)

Even among adolescents who do not attend school, urban settings may provide enhanced opportunities to be part of a group of peers. Several researchers have noted the close friendships of Latin American street children, relationships that provide companionship, support, and protection (Aptekar, 1988; Aptekar, this volume; Campos et al., 1994).

However, the extraordinary diversity among children and adolescents of developing countries does not permit easy categorization into urban and rural (Liddell, 1998). Liddell has pointed out that children are affected differently by rural to urban migration depending on whether they migrate with their mothers or their fathers to urban centers, by whether the resettlement community supports traditional values, and by the strength of ties to the rural community. The complexity of family and household structure may not be captured by the rural/urban distinction. A study of families in Guatemala, for example, found differences in household structure among six types of families—three rural (traditional indigenous, modified indigenous, rural Latino) and three urban (low socioeconomic urban, middle socioeconomic urban, and high socioeconomic urban) (Méndez-Domínguez, 1983).

This review focuses on the daily activities of adolescents in the developing world, their social relationships with peers, siblings, and friends, and their well-being. The diversity of adolescents' experience, related to their gender, socioeconomic situation, educational opportunities, and the rural-urban context will be considered.

DAILY ACTIVITIES

The daily activities of adolescents provide the social and physical contexts for development. "Where adolescents spend time, doing what, and with whom provides a first approximation of what their lives are like" (Csikszentmihalyi & Larson, 1984, p. 84). In addition, what they are doing in the present constrains, focuses, and creates opportunities for their futures.

A major consideration for adolescents who live in developing nations is that they are less likely than adolescents in developed nations to attend secondary school. While virtually all adolescents in more developed countries have some secondary schooling, current estimates are that 57 percent of boys and 48 percent of girls living in developing countries attend secondary school (Boyd et al., 2000). These rates of schooling vary greatly by country, even within a region. While fewer than 25 percent of adolescents in the Sudan attend school, more than 90 percent of teenagers in Libya do so. While many nations of sub-Saharan Africa, such as Burundi, Ethiopia, Rwanda, Niger, and Senegal, have attendance rates below one-fourth, over 90 percent of adolescents in South Africa attend secondary schools. Within Latin America, only about one-fourth of Guatemalan adolescents attend secondary school, whereas over three-fourths of teenagers in Chile and Argentina do so (Boyd et al., 2000). School attendance creates opportunities for occupational success in the industrialized world, as well as increasing opportunities for peer interaction as described above.

There are a number of ways of studying daily activities, including observation, retrospective surveys, and contemporaneous methods. Contemporaneous records of time use by adolescents can be sampled using the innovative "experience sampling method" (ESM), the so-called beeper procedure in which a beeper signals respondents to record their activities and their feelings at random points throughout the day (Csikszentmihalyi & Larson, 1987).

Although most ESM studies and other formal time-use studies have been done within the United States and Europe (e.g., Alsaker & Flammer, 1999), a study of Indian adolescents (Larson, Verma, & Dworkin, 2002) revealed daily activities and associated moods that differed from the typical Western pattern. In that study, urban middle-class eighth-graders in India spent about one-third of their waking hours in school classrooms (approximately the same percentage as a comparable group in the United States). They spent approximately one-fifth of their waking hours alone, slightly less than the time spent by U.S. adolescents. However, the biggest differences emerged in time spent with family and time spent with friends. Indian adolescents spent about 40 percent of their time with family (more than the U.S. students) and less than 10 percent of their time with friends (less than half of that spent by U.S. students). Most time with families was spent watching television, doing homework, or eating, with few differences between girls and boys. Although adolescents in both countries spent more time with their mothers and siblings than with their fathers, Indian adolescents had more contact with and more conversations with their fathers than did U.S. adolescents. Also, Indian adolescents experienced more positive emotions when with their families than did U.S. adolescents (Larson et al., 2002). In sum, consistent with the notion that India is a collectivistic culture with a high value placed on family relationships, adolescents' daily activities and emotions reflected both physical proximity to and positive feelings about family members. Moreover, this study shows that even when school attendance is similar, there are cultural differences in the way adolescents spend their time.

In ethnographic studies such as those in the Harvard Adolescence Project, typical daily activities of adolescents have been reported. The lives of adolescents living in Morocco, in Nigeria, in the remote Canadian arctic, and in communities of Australian Aborigines have been described (Burbank, 1988; Condon, 1988; Davis & Davis, 1989; Hollos & Leis, 1989).

Although they live in an industrialized country, the adolescents of Hohman Island in the Canadian arctic have much in common with adolescents in developing nations (Condon, 1988). In that remote environment, adolescent boys spend the long days of the arctic summer playing hockey. They might also go snowmobiling or hunting, visit with friends, or watch television. Time-use diaries showed that girls more often spent time playing with younger siblings, washing dishes, shopping, and visiting with friends.

Ijo adolescents in rural Nigeria spent about half the day in school (Hollos & Leis, 1989). After school, girls tended younger siblings and helped their mothers in shops and with food preparation. Boys would sometimes run errands, but in general had more free time to "stroll around," look for girls, goof off, play records, and go to the movies. Spot observations revealed that girls spent about three times as much time working and half as much time playing as did boys.

About half of Moroccan adolescents in Zawiya attend school (Davis & Davis, 1989). After washing up and combing her hair, a typical adolescent girl attends school for about three hours, then goes home for chores such as fetching water, washing laundry, taking care of younger siblings, household cleaning, and cooking. Leisure time is scarce, but younger girls play active games like hopscotch or jump rope, and older girls just talk. The typical boy was occupied with school classes, prayer, homework, hanging out with friends, playing soccer, and watching television. Boys and girls who are not in school work at paid jobs or in the household.

Among the Aborigines of Australia, typical days were described only for adolescent girls (Burbank, 1988). Depending on their status (as mothers or employees), they spent time working, in childcare, or in helping their own mothers. The plentiful leisure time was spent conversing, socializing, playing cards, walking around, visiting friends, and listening to music.

As the above examples illustrate, girls in developing countries are often responsible for a great deal of childcare. Among the Nso of Cameroon, by the time they reach adolescence most girls have raised younger siblings (Nsamenang & Lamb, 1994). This is distinctly different from the pattern of time use among adolescents in the developed world, and also different from the activities of urban middle-class adolescents in India (Larson et al., 2002). Werner (1979) has pointed out that child caretaking by other children, particularly girls, is the most common worldwide pattern. The development of socially responsible and nurturing behavior might be a consequence of children's care of infants (Whiting & Whiting, 1975). One might advance the hypothesis, then, that adolescents living in developing countries, particularly girls, would be likely to develop an ethic of care and helpfulness to a greater extent than adolescents living in the developed world (see also Maynard, this volume).

One cross-cultural study that compared urban middle- and high-income adolescent girls in Sri Lanka and the United States only partially supported the hypothesis (Stiles, Gibbons, & de Silva, 1996). Girls from both countries endorsed individualistic values, with greater attention to relationships higher among older adolescents. However, Sri Lankan girls were more likely than U.S. girls to define themselves in terms of group identities.

A more direct test of this hypothesis was conducted among individual adolescents living in the industrialized world, in Sydney, Australia. Grusec and her colleagues studied the consequences of assigning different household tasks to adolescents (Grusec, Goodnow, & Cohen, 1996). They found that adolescents who performed family-care tasks (e.g., "setting or clearing a table, helping prepare a meal, working in the garden, fetching things for others, cleaning up a space that is shared with others, feeding pets") developed a greater concern for others than did adolescents who were assigned self-care tasks, such as cleaning one's own room. The greater concern for others was noted in specific behaviors of spontaneous helpfulness and also in mothers' ratings of the adolescents' concern for others.

In summary, reports of daily activities suggest that adolescents in the developing world are less likely to attend school than are adolescents in the developed world. Even among middle-class urban adolescents who attend school, adolescents in the developing world may spend less time with peers and more time with their families. Especially in rural or preindustrial societies, adolescents are likely to be engaged in productive tasks. For girls, this often involves caretaking of younger children, an activity that might promote the development of prosocial nurturant values.

SOCIAL RELATIONSHIPS

Peers

Without discounting the overwhelming importance of the family in adolescent development, a central feature of the adolescent stage is the greater time spent with peers than previously (Schlegel & Barry, 1991; Seltzer, 1989). In developed countries much of the time with peers occurs in classrooms, but a great deal of a teenager's "free time" is also spent with peers (Alsaker & Flammer, 1999). A comparison of time use among urban middle-class adolescents from the United States and India revealed that Indian adolescents spend less time with their friends; although they report positive feelings about being with their friends, they are less positive than are U.S. adolescents (Larson et al., 2002). A study of Chilean adolescents showed that spending time with friends was among the top choices for preferred free-time activities for both boys and girls (Avendaño, Valenzuela, Correa, Almonte, & Sepúlveda, 1988). In a few preindustrial societies, peers may be the primary agents of socialization (Schlegel & Barry, 1991).

Results obtained from a study in a highland Guatemala town (Rogoff, 1981) illustrate a typical time course of the pattern of association between children and their peers as they reach adolescence. Both boys' and girls' time spent with adult women dropped linearly with age, so that by early adolescence they spent only about 40 percent of their time with adult women. Boys' time in the presence of men, very limited during early childhood, took an upturn at about age ten, attributed to boys' increasing ability to help out with men's work. Older children and young adolescents spent more time than did younger children in the presence of other children, especially during activities such as play, running an errand, childcare, and feeding animals.

Peer Groups

In their cross-cultural study of 178 preindustrial societies represented in the "Human Relations Area Files," Schlegel and Barry (1991) determined that peer groups during adolescence are mostly same-gender. Boys' peer groups are larger than those of girls, often having fourteen or more members. The groups tend to share activities (Schlegel & Barry, 1991) such as practicing adult behaviors, engaging in productive labor, or enforcing community standards. The most frequent group activity was engaging in leisure.

A quote from an ethnographic study of the Maya of Zinacantan in Chiapas, Mexico, illustrates the activities of boys' groups:

> By the age of twelve to fourteen, boys are believed to be "formed." They may walk to and from the Lowlands alone, and are able to take down loads of toasted tortillas for the farming groups and return with loads of maize. When they are at home, they often wander around together with groups of related boys, who watch for the approach of strangers and go out in groups to visit with them. They sometimes go to San Cristóbal together to buy and sell in the market. (Vogt, 1970, p. 67)

Among the various types of activities engaged in by boys' groups, two activities were associated with antisocial behavior by adolescent boys. At the societal level, both military activities and religious activities were significantly correlated with antisocial behavior (Schlegel & Barry, 1991). The association between groups of teenage boys engaged in military activities and antisocial behavior is reasonable; perhaps the training for aggressiveness "spills over" into other activities. The association between religious groups and antisocial behavior is less clear, but causation may point in the other direction. In a contemporary study of the popularity of a Christian youth group in Papua New Guinea, there was a simultaneous claim from community elders and social workers that young people were falling into antisocial ways, including marijuana use and crime (Gewertz & Errington, 1996). One might see the formation of religious groups as efforts to perceived delinquency among youth.

Schlegel and Barry (1991) also provide a number of examples of groups of adolescent boys making positive contributions to the community. For example, boys' groups actively participated in organizing celebrations and enforcing community standards. A contemporary example of community participation by adolescents is the formation of political parties and activist groups among adolescents in Latin America (Aptekar, 1988).

Among the Inuit, congregation of peers into same-sex groups occurred about the same time as puberty. Boys' groups were larger and often centered around competitive sports activities. Girls more often gathered in small groups in private rather than public settings (Condon, 1988). Girls spent less time with their peers, in part, because of their greater household responsibilities.

For boys' groups, peer bonding is stronger and amount of time spent with peers is greater in societies in which adolescents experience some separation from their parents (Schlegel & Barry, 1991). In general, boys' groups are more competitive than girls' groups (Schlegel & Barry, 1991). There were no differences, however, in the average amount of cooperation shown in boys' and girls' groups.

That peers have greater influence on boys than on girls is a major conclusion of Schlegel and Barry's study (1991) of preindustrial societies. Boys spend more time with their peers, while girls spend the majority of their time in groups of women of various ages. Schlegel and Barry contend that the differences in predominant social settings between girls and boys have powerful implications for development. Specifically, they argue that boys are more likely to find a voice in the relatively egalitarian peer group and to learn to participate through competition and cooperation in the give-and-take of public life. Girls learn the skills needed to function within smaller, more hierarchical groups.

This hypothesis is at odds with the dominant explanation of gender differences that emerges from studies of children's play groups in developed nations. Maccoby (1998) reviews evidence that from an early age children prefer same-gender playmates and form separate boys' and girls' play groups. She argues that boys' groups are both more hierarchical and more competitive than girls' groups, thus training boys for competitive and hierarchical stances in the workplace, romantic relationships, and parental roles.

The hypotheses converge on the greater competitiveness of boys' versus girls' peer groups. However, they diverge on the primary socializing influence that differentiates girls and boys. Do girls learn a more cooperative style through their less competitive play groups or a more hierarchical style through their participation with older and younger women in household chores?

Adolescents' peers not only serve a socializing function but may also serve as referents in drawing comparisons with the self. In one of the few contemporary cross-national studies of adolescents and their peers, Seltzer and Waterman (1996) studied eleven- to eighteen-year-olds' perceived congruence with their peers. The theory that framed the study, labeled "dynamic functional interaction" (Seltzer, 1982), proposes that adolescents are drawn to each other during early adolescence because of perceived similarities, and they use their peers to confirm their similarity. Adolescents of four countries—the United States, Scotland, Costa Rica, and the Philippines—were asked to state their own opinion and the opinion of their peers on a variety of topics. With increasing age, the adolescents from the United States and Scotland showed increasing divergence between their self-ratings and their perceptions of peer ratings, suggesting an increasing independence of thought. Adolescents in Costa Rica failed to show an age-related trend, and adolescents in the Philippines showed the opposite trend. Filipino adolescents, particularly girls, perceived greater similarity with their peers with increasing age. This study confirms that the typical developmental course differs for adolescents of different nationalities, and suggests the hypothesis that adolescents of developing countries see themselves as becoming more like their peers as they grow older.

A recent review of self-concept and person perception in adolescents revealed a similar phenomenon, that for many adolescents in the developing world the Western model of increasing autonomy and independence failed to apply (Gibbons, 2000). In two studies from India, adolescents showed an age-related increase in defining the self in relation to others (Kuebli, Reddy, & Gibbons, 1998), and boys from a lower socioeconomic status showed an age-related increase in group identification (Reddy & Gibbons, 1999). In sum, there is a suggestion that adolescents living in developing countries show age-related increases in perceiving important others as similar to, connected to, or even part of the self. This developmental phenomenon may reflect the collectivist culture of many developing countries (Hofstede, 1983; Markus & Kitayama, 1991).

Friendship

Research from industrialized Western countries has shown that friendships are important to adolescents. More than younger children, adolescents stress the importance of intimacy in their friendships. They value trustworthiness and loyalty in their friends.

One study of adolescents in contemporary nations included adolescents from two developing countries (Bangladesh and Turkey) as well as adolescents from eight developed countries (Australia, Germany, Italy, Israel, Hungary, Japan, Taiwan, and the United States) (Offer, Ostrov, Howard, & Atkinson, 1988). Most adolescents of both genders, older and younger, in all ten countries denied that they had a difficult time making friends. They disagreed with the statement that they would rather be alone than with others their age, and they said that they would like to help their friends. That is, there was virtually universal endorsement of the importance of and ease of establishing friendship, and no differences between adolescents living in more developed or less developed nations.

In their ethnography of contemporary Moroccan adolescents, Davis and Davis (1989) devoted an entire chapter to friendship, perhaps reflecting the importance of the topic to their subjects. Most adolescents in Zawiya reported a single same-sex friend. The two most important qualities in a friend were trustworthiness and reciprocity. Problems arose if the friend proved to be untrustworthy or failed to reciprocate. For example, sixteen-year-old Sa'id argued with a friend who had borrowed many books but refused to lend a book in return. An added concern, more important for girls, was the preservation of one's reputation. Eighteen-year-old Aisha emphasized that she would not go around with girls with bad reputations because her own reputation would suffer (Davis & Davis, 1989).

Hollos and Leis (1989) have described adolescent friendships among the Ijo of Nigeria. For example, both fourteen-year-old Timinepere and fourteen-year-old Omiebi had same-sex, same-age best friends with whom they walked to school. However, the boys had additional time to be together in the evening, while the girls' evenings were spent at home doing household chores. Girls more often mentioned the role of friends as confidants, whereas boys saw friends as those with whom they goofed off. Friendships during adolescence were described as emotionally close, but often short-lived (Hollos & Leis, 1989).

Friends were considered very important among the Inuit of Holman, with most adolescents listing only same-sex friends in response to an inquiry (Condon, 1988). Having a good sense of humor was the most important quality of a friend, and especially among older teenagers, a friend was someone to confide in and to give you advice (Condon, 1988). Johnny Apiuk described the development of psychological closeness: "I have the same group of friends as before, but I can talk with them better" (Condon, 1988, p. 120).

In sum, the evidence from the Harvard Adolescence Project suggests that friendships are important to adolescents in both the developed and the developing world and that intimacy and trustworthiness in friends are universally highly valued. Nonetheless, there is some evidence for differences in the roles of friends in the lives of adolescents from developing and developed countries. As described above, U.S. adolescents experienced more positive affect when in the company of friends than did Indian adolescents (Larson et al., 2002). Another recent study comparing the relationships of adolescents in Indonesia and the United States revealed some differences in friendship (French, Rianasari, Pidada, Nelwan, & Burmester, 2001). Intimacy with a same-sex friend was rated equally high in the two samples, but U.S. students rated their friendships higher in companionship, conflict, and satisfaction than did Indonesian students.

Siblings

Studies of the role of siblings in adolescent development suggest that siblings may play a variety of roles, including caregiver, buddy, critic, rival, and casual relative (Stewart, Beilfuss, & Verbrugge, 1995; cited in Arnett, 2001). Much of the literature from developed countries has explored conflict in sibling relationships, and studies suggest that conflict may serve developmental functions (Raffaelli, 1992). In cross-national studies, relationships with siblings have been largely neglected. However, a recent comparison of Indonesian and U.S. adolescents revealed that intimacy with siblings was equally high in the two samples, but that Indonesian adolescents rated their sibling relationships as higher in companionship and lower in conflict. Among boys, relationships with siblings were also more satisfying than in the United States (French et al., 2001).

The ethnologies of the Harvard Adolescent Project suggest that siblings may play important roles in adolescents' development, particularly in the developing world. Relative age and gender of the sibling are most likely important factors as well (see also Maynard, this volume).

One of the clearest examples of the importance of siblings is found among the Ijo (Hollos & Leis, 1989, p. 90): "The most important long-term relationship for youth in Amakiri and Ebiama is the one between siblings." Brothers and sisters provide lifelong help for each other, including older siblings helping the younger with education. The closest ties are between youth who share both a mother and a father. In their daily lives, adolescent girls, such as Timinepere, are responsible for much of the care of their younger siblings. Adolescent boys do not have so much responsibility for direct care, but may let younger brothers tag along with them. There are specific differences among the various relationships of brother-sister, sister-sister, and brother-brother as well. Informants among the adolescents of Nigeria repeatedly emphasized the differences between friends and siblings, in that "siblings are forever" (Hollos & Leis, 1989, p. 106).

Sibling bonds are similarly close and lifelong among the Inuit (Condon, 1988). Even following marriage and establishment of a separate household, older siblings often help out their younger brothers and sisters by giving them things and helping with their education. Because of the high rates of adoption, many adolescents have half siblings and adoptive siblings as well as full siblings; these relationships are supportive, too.

Age differences that are important in Moroccan culture are also evident in sibling relationships (Davis & Davis, 1989, p. 80): "Older siblings are to be obeyed," especially older brothers. In return, older brothers protect their sisters from boys' attentions, serve as role models for their younger brothers, and sometimes help them in material ways. Sisters often reported very close ties with each other, although they were rarely best friends.

In explaining the importance of social context in children's development, Rogoff (1990) has pointed out the role of older siblings in increasing children's cognitive skills. Rogoff explains that when she gave novel baby toys to Mayan mothers in Guatemala, the mothers summoned older siblings and showed them how to use the toy in playing with the baby (see Maynard, this volume).

In their study of preindustrial societies, Schlegel and Barry (1991) found that in most societies adolescents had close relationships with older siblings and were often subordinate to them. There was more contact between siblings of the same gender than between those of opposite gender.

Overall, this research suggests that siblings are important in the lives of adolescents in the developing world, especially since they tend to have several of them. Sibling relationships may be closer, with less conflict, than in the developed world. Many adolescents in developing nations may have been cared for by an older sibling, and in turn, be responsible for the caretaking of younger brothers and sisters. (These generalizations are less true for China because of its one-child policy.)

ADOLESCENT WELL-BEING IN INTERNATIONAL PERSPECTIVE

Macrosocial factors, such as national wealth, high life expectancy, availability of education, and gender equality, have been consistently related to adolescent well-being and happiness. Within developing countries, social conditions vary widely, and well-being may be linked to socioeconomic status and gender.

The examination of well-being stems from the numerous cross-national studies that have linked indicators of well-being, including life satisfaction and happiness, to socioeconomic indicators (Diener, Diener, & Diener, 1995; Veenhoven, Ehrhardt, Ho, & de Vries, 1993). A question that will be addressed is whether there is evidence that the adolescents experience lesser well-being in developing countries.

Cross-national studies of adolescents allow the study of the national demographic and cultural correlates of well-being in adolescents. Offer and his colleagues (1988) studied the self-image of younger adolescents (ages thirteen through fifteen) and older adolescents (ages sixteen through nineteen) of ten countries. According to the United Nations, two of those countries (Turkey and Bangladesh) are categorized as developing nations, and seven (Australia, Germany, Italy, Israel, Hungary, Japan, and the United States) as developed (United Nations Development Programme, 2001). There are no national statistics from Taiwan. The World Bank divides developing countries into three income categories; Bangladesh is in the lowest of those categories, and Turkey is in the middle-income category (Salem Press, 1999). Turkey and Bangladesh are characterized by a relatively low average income, less than universal secondary education, a high proportion of adolescents in the population, and rapid urbanization (United Nations Development Programme, 1998, 2001).

Offer and colleagues (1988) found that adolescents were happier in wealthier countries, as indicated by their country's gross national product. A positive body image in adolescents was correlated with individual wealth (per capita income of the country) (Offer et al., 1988). Good peer relationships were associated with higher educational expenditure per capita and with a quality of life index that included literacy, life expectancy, and infant mortality.

One of the best predictors of adolescent well-being was the percentage of fourteen- to eighteen-year-olds in the population. In countries with high proportions of young people, adolescents reported more negative affect, poorer social relationships, and more signs of anxiety or loneliness (Offer et al., 1988). Developing countries are characterized by higher percentages of young people. In the year 2000, 20 percent of the population in more developed countries was age ten to twenty-four and 29 percent of the population in developing countries was in that age range (Boyd et al., 2000). The proportions for Turkey and Bangladesh were 29 percent and 36 percent respectively (Boyd et al., 2000). Thus, a macrosocial factor that characterizes developing countries has also been linked to lesser well-being in adolescents.

One may also look at well-being in adolescents by examining its opposite—depression. In general, depression is negatively correlated with happiness among adolescents (del Barrio, Moreno-Rosset, López-Martinez, & Olmedo, 1997). In a later report, Offer and his colleagues calculated the percentage of adolescents from each of the ten countries who endorsed a subset of depressive items indicating sadness, loneliness, emotional emptiness, hopelessness, and thoughts of death (Offer, Ostrov, Howard, & Atkinson, 1992). They reported the data separately for younger males, younger females, older males, and older females for each sample.

In order to test the relationship of rates of adolescent depression in different countries with cultural and demographic indicators, the depression scores from Offer's study were reanalyzed for the present chapter. Depression scores were correlated with the scores for individualism-collectivism, power-distance, uncertainty-avoidance, and masculinity-femininity for each nation as reported by Hofstede (1983). Because the well-being of adolescents has also been linked to demographic indicators such as the gross national product, the depression rates of Offer's study were also correlated with the per capita gross national product, the Human Development Index (HDI) of the United Nations, the Gender Development Index (GDI) of the United Nations, and indicators of population growth and urbanization in those nations from 1970 to 1995 (United Nations Development Programme, 1998). The HDI is based on indicators of well-being such as life expectancy, literacy rate, enrollment in education, and gross domestic product per capita. The GDI tabulates the same variables in terms of gender disparities. Adolescent depression rates in nine of the ten samples (there were no United Nations indicators for Taiwan) were negatively correlated with the HDI and the GDI for those countries. The correlation with the GDI was $r(9) = -0.62$, $p < 0.05$ and with the HDI, $r(9) = -0.62$, $p < 0.05$ (one-tailed tests). See Figure 10.1 for a graph of the relation between the Composite Depression Score and the Human Development Index, and Figure 10.2 for a graph of the relation between Composite Depression Score and the Gender Development Index. When separate analyses were done for younger girls, younger boys, older girls, and older boys, the depression scores for all groups except older boys correlated negatively with HDI and GDI. The significant correlations ranged from -0.68 to -0.80. Depression among adolescents was not correlated with rates of population growth, urbanization, or with any of the cultural dimensions as defined by Hofstede (1983).

These findings suggest that adolescents who live in nations where there is general well-being—including high life expectancy, availability of education, economic prosperity, and gender equality—are less likely to suffer from depression. Although individualism is correlated with human development and gen-

Figure 10.1
Adolescents' Depressive Mood (Offer et al., 1992) and Human
Development Index

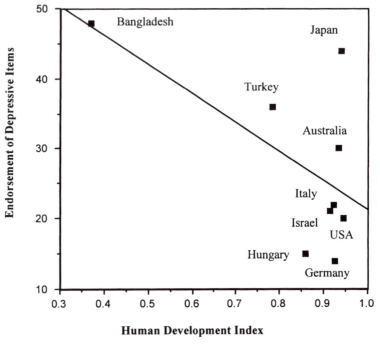

Human Development Index

der development, the correlation of depression with individualism (based on eight countries for which data were available) was not significant, $p = 0.1$ (one-tailed test).

Factors such as national prosperity and gender disparities in education are distal from the lives of most adolescents. Remaining to be discovered are the factors that mediate society's effects on adolescent depression. For example, what are the effects of economic privation on the families, schools, and social environments of adolescents? What specific proximal factors impact the well-being of adolescents? For example, in a study of the effects of poverty on adolescents' school performance it was found that the effects of poverty were completely mediated by stressful life events, parenting, and feelings of "not fitting in" at school (Felner, Brand, DuBois, Adan, Mulhall, & Evans, 1995). Poor economic conditions at a national level may impact adolescent well-being if adolescents believe that few jobs are available to them. The question of how national economic factors and gender stratification impact the lives of adolescents remains to be addressed.

Figure 10.2
Adolescents' Depressive Mood (Offer et al., 1992) and Gender
Development Index

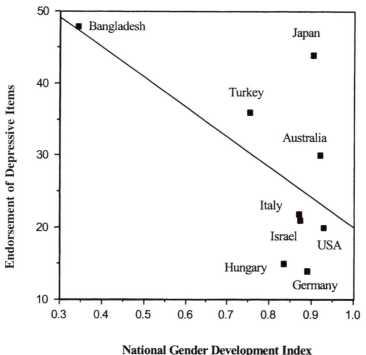

National Gender Development Index

Although ethnographic studies do not provide the large numbers of cases necessary for statistical comparison, there is some evidence that adolescents in Morocco, Nigeria, Hohman Island, Canada, and Aboriginal Australia (Burbank, 1988; Condon, 1988; Davis & Davis, 1989; Hollos & Leis, 1989) might have been experiencing stress. Condon noted that alcohol use was on the rise in Hohman Island, along with an "alarming increase in suicide rate among teenagers" (Condon, 1988, p. 184). Davis and Davis (1989) observed an increasing use of drugs by Moroccan adolescents, including smoking kif (a form of cannabis), drinking alcohol, and sniffing inhalants. Because the sample of adolescents in the large-scale studies were "middle-class" and urban (Offer et al., 1988), the findings cannot be generalized to adolescents in traditional societies. It is likely that traditional societies provide sources of support that lessen the negative effects of living in a developing country (Condon, 1988; Dasen, 2000). The general finding that adolescents living in developing countries experience lesser well-being may be limited to urban settings.

CONCLUSION

Although there is great diversity among adolescents living in developing countries, all are affected to some extent by the demographics of their nation—rapid urbanization, modernization, less access to education, and a higher percentage of adolescents in the population. Cross-national studies of middle-class and urban adolescents suggest that in developing countries adolescents are likely to experience lesser well-being, higher rates of depression, and greater gender disparities than adolescents living in more developed countries.

In the developing world, especially in rural settings, adolescents may be more likely to spend their time in productive activities, and girls are especially likely to take care of younger siblings. Peer groups assume greater importance at adolescence, and boys, especially, may be strongly socialized through their participation in groups with other boys. The gender differences may be greater in the developing world than in urban Western settings. Close relationships with friends appear to be universally valued among adolescents, but some adolescents in developing countries may spend less time with their friends and have less emotional engagement than adolescents in the developed world. On the other hand, siblings may be more important to adolescents in the developing world.

Exposure to international media is spreading to remote corners of the globe, including rural China, Papua New Guinea, and Kathmandu. However, adolescents appear to use the media in different ways, adapting their use to unique cultural and developmental purposes.

In sum, the large numbers of adolescents who are growing up in the developing world pose a challenge for developmental theorists. The dominant standpoint of developmental psychology, that adolescence is a period of increasing independence and autonomy in thought and action, is challenged by research on adolescents in developing countries. The developmental trajectories for self-concept, perceived similarity to peers, and group identity appear to follow a different course among some adolescents in developing countries.

NOTE

I would like to thank Natalie Humphrey for collecting references, the Beaumont Faculty Development Fund of Saint Louis University for providing financial support during the preparation of this manuscript, and Jeffrey Arnett for providing critical comments on an earlier version of the manuscript.

REFERENCES

Adair, J. G., Pandey, J., Begum, H. A., Puhan, B., & Vohra, N. (1995). Indigenization and development of the discipline: Perceptions and opinions of Indian and Bangladeshi psychologists. *Journal of Cross-Cultural Psychology, 26,* 392–407.

Alsaker, F. D., & Flammer, A. (1999). *The adolescent experience: European and American adolescents in the 1990s.* Mahwah, NJ: Erlbaum.

Aptekar, L. (1988). *Street children of Cali.* Durham, NC: Duke University Press.

Arnett, J. J. (2001). *Adolescence and emerging adulthood: A cultural approach.* Upper Saddle River, NJ: Prentice-Hall.

Avendaño, A., Valenzuela, C., Correa, F., Almonte, C., & Sepúlveda, G. (1988). Cracterísticas del desarrollo psicosocial en adolescentes de 16 a 19 años en seguimiento longitudinal. III Futuro laboral: Aspectos religiosos y recreación. [Labor expectancies, religious activities, and use of free time in Chilean adolescents]. *Revista Chilena de Pediatría, 59,* 96–101.

Berglund, S., Lifjestrand, J., De Maria Marín, F., Salgado, N., & Zelaya, E. (1997). The background of adolescent pregnancies in Nicaragua: A qualitative approach. *Social Science & Medicine, 44,* 1–12.

Boyd, A., Ashford, L., Haub, C., & Cornelius, D. (2000). *The world's youth 2000.* Washington, DC: Population Reference Bureau.

Burbank, V. K. (1988). *Aboriginal adolescence: Maidenhood in an Australian community.* New Brunswick, NJ: Rutgers University Press.

Caldwell, J. C., Caldwell, P., Caldwell, B. K., & Pieris, I. (1998). The construction of adolescence in a changing world: Implications for sexuality, reproduction, and marriage. *Studies in Family Planning, 29,* 137–153.

Campos, R., Antunes, C. M., Raffaelli, M., Halsey, N., Ude, W., Greco, M., Greco, D., Ruff, A., Rolf, J., & Street Youth Study Group (1994). Social networks and daily activities of street youth in Belo Horizonte, Brazil. *Child Development, 65,* 319–330.

Cederblad, M., & Rahim, S. I. (1986). Effects of rapid urbanization on child behaviour and health in a part of Khartoum, Sudan, Part 1: Socio-economic changes 1965–1980. *Social Science & Medicine, 22,* 713–721.

Condon, R. G. (1988). *Inuit youth: Growth and change in the Canadian arctic.* New Brunswick, NJ: Rutgers University Press.

Csikszentmihalyi, M., & Larson, R. (1984). *Being adolescent: Conflict and growth in the teenage years.* New York: Basic Books.

———. (1987). Validity and reliability of the Experience-Sampling Method. *Journal of Nervous Mental Disorders, 175,* 526–536.

Dasen, P. R. (2000). Rapid social change and the turmoil of adolescence: A cross-cultural perspective. *International Journal of Group Tensions, 29,* 17–50.

Davis, S. S., & Davis, D. A. (1989). *Adolescence in a Moroccan town.* New Brunswick, NJ: Rutgers University Press.

del Barrio, V., Moreno-Rosset, C., Lopez-Martinez, R., & Olmedo, M. (1997). Anxiety, depression and personality structure. *Personality & Individual Differences, 23,* 327–335.

Diener, E., Diener, M., & Diener, C. (1995). Factors predicting the subjective well-being of nations. *Journal of Personality and Social Psychology, 69,* 851–864.

Felner, R. D., Brand, S., DuBois, D. L., Adan, A. M., Mulhall, P. F., & Evans, E. G. (1995). Socioeconomic disadvantage, proximal environmental experiences, and socioemotional and academic adjustment in early adolescence: Investigation of a mediated effects model. *Child Development, 66,* 774–792.

French, D. C., Rianasari, M., Pidada, S., Nelwan, P., & Burmester, D. (2001). Social support of Indonesian and U.S. children and adolescents by family members and friends. *Merrill-Palmer Quarterly, 47,* 377–394.

Gewertz, D., & Errington, F. (1996). On PepsiCo and piety in a Papua New Guinea "modernity." *American Ethnologist, 23,* 476–493.

Gibbons, J. L. (2000). Personal and social development of adolescents: Integrating findings from preindustrial and modern industrialized countries. In A. L. Communian & U. P. Gielen (Eds.), *International perspectives on human development* (pp. 403–429). Lengerich, Germany: Pabst Science.

Grusec, J. E., Goodnow, J. J., & Cohen, L. (1996). Household work and the development of concern for others. *Developmental Psychology, 32,* 999–1007.

Hofstede, G. (1983). Dimensions of national cultures in fifty countries and three regions. In J. B. Deregowski, S. Dziurawiec, & R. C. Annis (Eds.), *Expiscations in cross-cultural psychology* (pp. 335–355). Lisse, Netherlands: Swets & Zeitlinger.

Hollos, M., & Leis, P. E. (1989). *Becoming Nigerian in Ijo Society.* New Brunswick, NJ: Rutgers University Press.

Kuebli, J. E., Reddy, R., & Gibbons, J. L. (1998). Perceptions of others in self-descriptions of children and adolescents in India. *Cross-Cultural Research, 32,* 217–240.

Larson, R., Verma, S., & Dworkin, J. (2002). Adolescents' family relationships in India. In J. J. Arnett (Ed.), *Readings on adolescence and emerging adulthood* (pp. 133–141). Upper Saddle River, NJ: Prentice-Hall.

Liddell, C. (1998). Conceptualising "childhood" in developing countries. *Psychology and Developing Societies, 10,* 35–53.

Liechty, M. (1995). Media, markets, and modernization: Youth identities and the experience of modernity in Kathmandu, Nepal. In V. Amit-Talai & H. Wulff (Eds.), *Youth cultures: A cross-cultural perspective* (pp. 166–201). New York: Routledge.

Maccoby, E. E. (1998). *The two sexes: Growing up apart, coming together.* Cambridge, MA: Harvard University Press.

Markus, H. R., & Kitayama, S. (1991). Culture and the self: Implications for cognition, emotion, and motivation. *Psychological Review, 98,* 224–253.

Méndez-Domínguez, A. (1983). Family and household structures in Guatemalan society. *Journal of Comparative Family Studies, 14,* 229–255.

Nsamenang, A. B., & Lamb, M. E. (1994). Socialization of Nso children in the Bamenda grassfields of northwest Cameroon. In P. M. Greenfield & R. R. Cocking (Eds.), *Cross-cultural roots of minority child development* (pp. 133–146). Hillsdale, NJ: Erlbaum.

Offer, D., Ostrov, E., Howard, K. I., & Atkinson, R. (1988). *The teenage world: Adolescents' self-image in ten countries.* New York: Plenum Medical.

———. (1992). A study of quietly disturbed and normal adolescents in ten countries. *International Annals of Adolescent Psychiatry, 2,* 285–299.

Raffaelli, M. (1992). Sibling conflict in early adolescence. *Journal of Marriage and the Family, 54,* 652–663.

Reddy, R., & Gibbons, J. L. (1999). School socio-economic contexts and adolescent self-descriptions in India. *Journal of Youth and Adolescence, 28,* 619–631.

Rogoff, B. (1981). Adults and peers as agents of socialization: A highland Guatemalan profile. *Ethos*, 9, 18–36.

———. (1990). *Apprenticeship in thinking: Cognitive development in social context.* New York: Oxford University Press.

Salem Press (Eds.). (1999). *Economics basics*, Vol. 2, *Labor economics, world economies.* Pasadena, CA: Author.

Saraswathi, T. S. (1999). Adult-child continuity in India: Is adolescence a myth or an emerging reality? In T. S. Saraswathi (Ed.), *Culture, socialization, and human development: Theory, research, and applications in India* (pp. 213–232). New Delhi: Sage.

Schlegel, A. (2000). The global spread of adolescent culture. In L. J. Crockett & R. K. Silbereisen (Eds.), *Negotiating adolescence in times of social change* (pp. 71–88). Cambridge: Cambridge University Press.

Schlegel, A., & Barry, H., III. (1991). *Adolescence: An anthropological inquiry.* New York: Free Press.

Seltzer, V. C. (1982). *Adolescent social development: Dynamic functional interaction.* Lexington, MA: Lexington Books.

———. (1989). *The psychosocial worlds of the adolescent: Public and private.* New York: Wiley.

Seltzer, V. C., & Waterman, R. P. (1996). A cross-national study of adolescent peer concordance on issues of the future. *Journal of Adolescent Research*, 11, 461–482.

Steinberg, L., & Morris, A. S. (2000). Adolescent development. *Annual Review of Psychology*, 52, 83–110.

Stevens, G., & Lockhat, R. (1997). "Coca-cola kids": Reflections on black adolescent identity development in post-apartheid South Africa. *South African Journal of Psychology*, 27, 250–255.

Stewart, R. B., Beilfuss, M. L., & Verbrugge, K. M. (1995, March). That was then, this is now: An empirical typology of adult sibling relationships. Paper presented at the biennial meeting of the Society for Research on Child Development, Indianapolis.

Stiles, D. A., Gibbons, J. L., & de Silva, S. S. (1996). Girls' relational self in Sri Lanka and the United States. *Journal of Genetic Psychology*, 157, 191–203.

United Nations Development Programme (1998). *Human development report 1998.* New York: Oxford University Press.

———. (2001). *Human development report 2001: Making new technologies work for human development.* New York: Oxford University Press.

Veenhoven, R., Ehrhardt, J., Ho, M. S. D., & de Vries, A. (1993). *Happiness in nations: Subjective appreciation of life in fifty-six nations, 1946–1992.* Rotterdam, Netherlands: Erasmus University.

Vogt, E. Z. (1970). *The Zinacantecos of Mexico: A modern Maya way of life.* New York: Holt, Rinehart, & Winston.

Werner, E. E. (1979). *Cross-cultural child development: A view from Planet Earth.* Monterey, CA: Brooks/Cole.

White, M. (1993). *The material child: Coming of age in Japan and America.* New York: Free Press.

Whiting, B., & Whiting, J. W. (1975). *Children of six cultures*. Cambridge, MA: Harvard University Press.

Yan, Y. (1999). Rural youth and youth culture in north China. *Culture, Medicine, and Psychiatry, 23*, 75–97.

CHAPTER 11

Adolescence in the Twenty-First Century: A Worldwide Survey

Jeffrey Jensen Arnett

When we look back at the twentieth century, we can see that it was a time of astounding change for adolescents all over the world. In the West, typical fifteen-year-olds in 1900 who lived in Europe and North America had long before completed any schooling they would receive, and spent most of their days working alongside adults on farms and in factories (Kett, 1977). Their leisure, too, was often spent with family or at least under the watchful eyes of parents or other adults (Bailey, 1989). In the early twenty-first century, typical fifteen-year-olds in these countries are in school among their peers for the better part of each day (Flammer & Alsaker, 1999). After school as well, a substantial amount of their time is spent among peers and friends—playing sports, hanging around, and working in part-time service jobs (Flammer, Alsaker, & Noack, 1999; Steinberg & Cauffman, 1995). Much of their leisure includes electronic media, on an average day about two hours of television and three or more hours of music (Flammer et al., 1999; Roberts, Foehr, Rideout, & Brodie, 1999).

The degree of change in the twentieth century was also dramatic for adolescents in non-Western countries. Most non-Western countries had not industrialized nearly as much as the West in 1900, but by 2000, countries such as Japan and South Korea had developed highly industrialized, information-based economies much like the West, and countries in many other parts of the world are headed in the same direction. Young people in non-Western countries were also deeply affected in the twentieth century by historical events specific to their countries—for example, the rise of communism in China and the independence movement in India.

What can we say about adolescents' prospects for the twenty-first century in countries around the world? Predicting the future is always a risky enterprise.

Who would have predicted, in 1900, that the young people of 2000 would typically remain in school into their early twenties, or that they would typically become sexually active about ten years before they marry; or that they would spend a considerable amount of their leisure time listening to recorded music, watching images flicker on a television, or surfing the Internet?

Nevertheless, speculating about the future can be a useful way of assessing the present. In this chapter I will examine the prospects for adolescents in the twenty-first century in six regions of the world: sub-Saharan Africa, northern Africa and the Middle East, India, East Asia, Latin America, and the West. Rather than attempt an exhaustive survey in the limited space of this chapter, for each region I identify several key issues facing the young people of the twenty-first century. Then I discuss three issues that will be important for young people across the world: globalization, equality of wealth and opportunity, and the increasing divergence between urban and rural areas.

As background, Table 11.1 presents demographic information for the different regions of the world. The table demonstrates that the experiences of young people in the twenty-first century will be vastly different depending on where they are born.

Table 11.1
Demographic Characteristics of Young People in Different World Regions

Region	% enrolled in secondary school males females		Average age at first marriage (females)	% females giving birth by age 20
Sub-Saharan Africa	29	23	19	52
North Africa	63	57	21	24
India	59	39	20	49
East Asia	77	70	23	8
Latin America	n.a.	n.a.	21	35
North America	99	98	25	19
Europe	97	100	24	n.a.

Source: Population Reference Bureau (2000).

SUB-SAHARAN AFRICA

In 1900, most African countries were not countries at all but colonies dominated by European countries such as Great Britain, France, and Germany. Gradually, in the course of the twentieth century, all of Africa gained political independence. However, for most African countries independence was not the end of their troubles but just the beginning. Sub-Saharan Africa has especially struggled during the twentieth century, and as the twenty-first century begins it is plagued by numerous serious problems. Three of the most important problems facing Africa's young people are chronic poverty, war, and an epidemic of HIV/AIDS.

Africa has been described as "a rich continent whose people are poor" (Nsamenang, 1998). The countries of Africa are extremely rich in natural resources such as oil, gold, and diamonds. Unfortunately, due to exploitation by the West followed by corruption, waste, and war in the postcolonial period, this natural wealth has not translated to economic prosperity for the people of Africa. On the contrary, living standards in Africa have actually declined in the past fifty years, and an increasing number of young Africans live in poverty (Nsamenang, 1998). Furthermore, sub-Saharan Africa has the worst performance of any region of the world on virtually any measure of living standards, including per capita income, access to clean water, life expectancy, infant mortality, and prevalence of disease (Nsamenang, 2002).

War was also a frequent part of life for Africans in the twentieth century. Following the wars of independence, there were many wars between African countries. There were many civil wars as well; the country boundaries drawn by European powers often ignored traditional tribal boundaries and antagonisms, and after independence tribal rivalries often revived and resulted in civil wars. Young people have been and continue to be at the heart of these wars, as soldiers. Those who are not soldiers also find their lives disrupted when their parents are involved in the fighting, or when the war comes to their own village, or when they are forced to become refugees.

As if poverty and war were not enough to daunt the prospects of young people in Africa, there is an even bigger threat to their future on the threshold of the twenty-first century: an epidemic of HIV/AIDS. Of the deaths that took place from AIDS worldwide in 1999, 85 percent were in Africa (Bartholet, 2000). In some African countries, more than one-fourth of adults are currently infected with HIV. Already there are 10 million African children under age fifteen who have lost their mother or both parents to AIDS—90 percent of the world's total of AIDS orphans.

The AIDS epidemic will affect young Africans mainly in three ways (Bartholet, 2000; Nsamenang, 2002). First, many of them will be required to assume the leadership of their families due to their parents' deaths. Second, many of them will be forced into even deeper poverty by their parents' deaths and may end up joining the millions of AIDS orphans who have already become street children in African cities, where they are vulnerable to illness, malnutrition, and sexual exploitation. Third, many young Africans will become AIDS victims themselves in the twenty-first century if vast changes are not made soon in the prevalence of safe sex practices.

For adolescents growing up in sub-Saharan Africa today, these conditions present a grim prospect. Growing up in poverty means that adolescents often will be struggling simply to survive rather than being able to develop their abilities and enjoy their youth. War brings disruption to their lives and death to many of them. HIV/AIDS has the potential to devastate the continent and is already in the process of doing so. However, it may be that young people will be the ones to reverse these grim trends and set Africa onto a better path toward the future.

NORTHERN AFRICA AND THE MIDDLE EAST

Northern Africa and the Middle East have in common that they are regions where the Muslim religion is the predominant influence on all aspects of cultural life. For the young people of this region in the twenty-first century, three key issues are the continued strength of Islam, patriarchal family relationships, and the subordination of women.

Currently, the strength of Islam in the region varies, from countries in which all government policies are based on Islamic principles and texts (e.g., Kuwait and Saudi Arabia), to countries that have a semblance of democracy and diversity of opinion but where the influence of Islam is nevertheless strong (e.g., Jordan and Morocco). During the twentieth century the course of history in the West was generally toward secularism, as the influence of the Christian religion faded in the cultural life of most Western countries. Will North Africa and the Middle East follow a similar path in the twenty-first century, toward secularism and away from a foundation in Islam? The young people of these countries may be the ones to determine the answer. Right now there is evidence that many of them have been influenced by globalization and are highly attracted to the popular culture and information technologies of the West (e.g., Booth, 2002; Davis & Davis, 1989; Malik, 2000). Nevertheless, Islam currently remains strong, even among the young.

Patriarchal authority in the family has a long tradition in Arab societies and is supported by Islam (Booth, 2002; Malik, 2000). This means that the father's authority in the family is to be obeyed unquestioningly. There is to be no "authoritative" discussion of family rules in Muslim families. Even to suggest such a thing would be considered an unacceptable affront to the authority of the parents, especially the father. Will this view of the father's authority survive the twenty-first century? Again, a look at the West would suggest that it would not, because in the West there was also a tradition of patriarchal authority in the family that no longer exists. The tensions arising from globalization, with its promotion of a worldwide youth culture, would also seem to undermine patriarchal authority. Still, it may be that the tradition of Islam will remain strong enough to support the father's paramount authority.

The third issue of importance with regard to young people in North Africa and the Middle East in the twenty-first century is the position of women. Islamic societies have a long tradition of subordinating women by keeping tight control over their appearance and behavior (Booth, 2002). In the most restrictive Islamic societies girls and women are required to wear a garment that covers them from head to toe (e.g., a chador or a burqa) anytime they leave their household. In these societies, Muslim women are not allowed to go out of the house unaccompanied by a male (Malik, 2000). In all Islamic societies, virginity before marriage is highly prized, and violation of this taboo can result in the most severe punishments, even death. Girls are less likely than boys to receive an education past primary school, especially in rural areas (Booth, 2002). Women are generally discouraged from working outside the home, although the percentage of working women varies from a high of 24 percent in Egypt to a low of 4 percent in Saudi Arabia (Makhlouf & Abdelkader, 1997). The controversial and terribly painful practice of female circumcision continues to be prevalent in most northern African and Middle Eastern countries (Hatfield & Rapson, 1996).

Will these practices continue through the twenty-first century? Or will young women in this region gain a wider scope of autonomy and equal rights as the century progresses? It is impossible to say right now. So far, the practices described here have remained remarkably resistant to the influence of globalization and to criticisms within these countries as well.

INDIA

India is a complex society, with numerous religions, dozens of languages, and a population of over 1 billion people. In the twentieth century, India gained its independence from Great Britain through peaceful means, following the strategy of nonviolent resistance devised by Mohandas K. Gandhi. India has maintained a democracy since obtaining independence in 1947—a remarkable feat, given the diversity of its people and the high rate of illiteracy. In the twenty-first century, the main issues facing young people in India will be school versus work, the tradition of early arranged marriages, the caste system, and the rights of women.

Currently, India is one of the few countries in the world that does not have compulsory education for children (Verma & Saraswathi, 2002). Consequently, about one-third of fifteen- to nineteen-year-olds are illiterate. Illiteracy is especially high among adolescent girls, nearly 50 percent (PROBE, 1999). Many parents, especially in rural areas, do not believe that girls should be educated beyond a minimal ability to write letters and keep household accounts. Access to education is much higher in urban areas, for girls as well as boys, and despite high illiteracy India also has a large number of highly educated young people, especially in fields such as medicine and information technologies. Nevertheless, many rural areas in India have few schools, and the available schools tend to be poorly funded and staffed by teachers who are poorly trained.

Also contributing to high illiteracy in India is widespread child and adolescent labor. India is one of the countries where child and adolescent labor is most common, in a wide range of jobs such as carpet weaving, mining, cigarette manufacturing, and gem polishing, often in extremely unsafe and unhealthy conditions (Burra, 1997). Parents often would prefer to have their children and adolescents working, and thus contributing to the family income, rather than attending school. Consequently, the government has taken few steps to restrict child and adolescent labor (see also Gielen & Chumachenko, this volume).

The state of child and adolescent labor in India is very similar to the situation in Western countries 100 years ago. It is possible that in the course of the twenty-first century primary and secondary education in India will become compulsory, and children and adolescents will focus on developing knowledge and skills for adult work rather than entering the workplace at an early age. However, this will happen only if an organized movement develops to abolish child and adolescent labor, as happened in the West.

With regard to marriage, India has a long tradition of young marriages. In the past, children were often married even before reaching puberty, and even now about half of India's young people marry in their teens (Verma & Saraswathi, 2002). Early marriages are especially common in rural areas. Furthermore, most marriages in India are arranged by the parents. Young people often contribute to the decision and may reject a person their parents recommend, but for the most part they rely on their parents to choose a marriage partner for them. Even urban, highly educated Indians prefer to have an arranged marriage (Pathak, 1994).

The endurance of the tradition of arranged marriage is a reflection of the collectivist beliefs of Indian society and the trust and closeness that often exist between Indian young people and their parents. But will this practice survive the twenty-first century? The continued practice of arranged marriages even among highly educated, urban young people suggests that it may.

Another issue facing young Indians in the twenty-first century is the status of the caste system. According to this tradition, people are born into a particular caste based on their moral and spiritual conduct in their previous life (reincarnation is central to the Hindu beliefs held by most Indians). A person's caste then determines his or her status in Indian society. Only persons of elite castes are considered to be eligible for positions of wealth and power. Persons of lower castes are considered worthy only of the lowest-paying, dirtiest, lowest-status jobs. Also, marrying outside one's caste is strongly discouraged.

Attempts have been made in India throughout the twentieth century to abolish the caste system, especially since independence, and the attempts have been partially successful. The Indian government has affirmative action–type programs that give preference to persons from lower castes for certain government jobs and educational opportunities. However, the caste system is deeply embedded in Indian tradition, and it remains strong. Young people from lower castes continue to be less likely to attend school than young people from higher castes, which restricts the jobs available to them (Verma & Saraswathi, 2002). Although the lower castes are becoming increasingly well-organized and effective as a political force in India, it is difficult to believe the caste system will be abolished entirely by the end of the twenty-first century.

Finally, rights for women are likely to be an important issue affecting the lives of young people in India during the twenty-first century. Like many societies, India has a long tradition of holding women to be of inferior status from birth onward. As noted, girls are less likely than boys to receive even enough education to become literate. Even for girls who are fortunate to obtain a good education, often there is little opportunity for them to develop a career, because of the belief that the role of women should be restricted to that of wife and mother. Prostitution of adolescent girls has also become a major problem in India. Increasingly, brothel owners seek out young adolescent girls as prostitutes. Because of their youth, they are regarded as less likely to have HIV/AIDS, and so men are willing to pay more to have sex with them (Thapar, 1998).

Will the opportunities for young women in India improve over the twenty-first century? One hopeful sign is that girls who do get the opportunity to attend school generally outperform boys academically (Verma & Saraswathi, 2002). Also, in middle-class urban families many young women are now pursuing professional careers. This may indicate that opportunities for young women will continue to expand.

EAST ASIA

East Asia comprises a vast and diverse area, ranging from countries that are highly industrialized (e.g., Japan) to countries that have recently industrialized (e.g., South Korea) to countries that are rapidly industrializing (e.g., China). Nevertheless, these countries share certain common characteristics and certain common challenges in the twenty-first century. Some of the major issues affecting young people are likely to be the tradition of filial piety, arranged marriages and dating, intense pressure at the secondary school level, and the rights of women.

The cultures of East Asia have been profoundly influenced by Confucianism, which is a set of beliefs and precepts attributed to the philosopher Confucius, who lived from about 550 to 480 B.C.E. One of the central tenets of Confucianism is filial piety, which means that children are expected to respect, obey, and revere their parents, especially the father. This principle applies not just in childhood but in adolescence and adulthood as well, as long as their parents live. In fact, it even applies beyond death; ancestor worship is common in Asian cultures. Part of filial piety is the expectation that the children, in particular the oldest son, have the responsibility for caring for their parents when the parents become elderly. Often this includes having the parents live in the children's household.

East Asian cultures are becoming more individualistic under the influence of globalization (Naito & Gielen, in press; Stevenson & Zusho, 2002). Can filial piety survive this trend? There is evidence that adolescents' relationships with their parents are changing. Some studies indicate that parents are much less likely to demand obedience from their adolescents now than in the past (Park & Cho, 1995). However, in general, East Asian adolescents still expect that they will take care of their parents as their parents grow older (e.g., Cho & Shin, 1996; Feldman et al., 1992). Thus it may be that the tradition of filial piety will endure in the twenty-first century, but in a modified, less traditional form. Because all East Asian countries have a low birthrate (less than two children per woman), in many families there may be no son to take care of the elderly parents, and this duty may fall instead on a daughter.

One aspect of the authority of parents in East Asian cultures is the tradition of arranged marriages, in which parents choose a mate for their child. This tradition remains strong in East Asian cultures, even in cultures that have become highly industrialized (Cho & Shin, 1996). However, like filial piety, the tradition of arranged marriage has become modified in response to increased individualism. Today, in Asian cultures, the "semi-arranged marriage" is the most common practice (Lee, 1998). This means that parents influence the mate selection of their children but do not simply decide it without the children's consent. Parents may introduce a potential mate to their child. If the child has a favorable impression of the potential mate, they date a few times. If they agree that they are compatible, they marry. Another variation of semi-arranged marriage is that young people meet a potential mate, but seek their parents' approval before proceeding to date the person.

It is difficult to say if semi-arranged marriage will be an enduring form, or if it is a transitional stage on the way to the end of the tradition of arranged marriage. Although semi-arranged marriages are now common, it is also increasingly common for young people to choose their own marriage partner. Recreational dating remains rare in Asian cultures, but it is more common than in the past, and it seems likely to grow in the future.

The Confucian tradition places a strong emphasis on education, which is one of the reasons for the intense focus on education in the lives of young people in Asian cultures today. High school tends to be highly pressured for young people in Asian societies, because performance on college entrance exams determines to a large extent their path through adult life. In South Korea, for example, many high school students spend more than seventy hours a week in class or studying (Migliazzo, 1993)!

There is increasing criticism of this system within Asian societies, by those who argue that young people should not be subjected to such pressure at a young age and should be allowed more time for fun. Also, as Asian economies are becoming more flexible in response to global economic pressures, attending a certain college is no longer an absolute guarantee of a secure, well-paying job for life. However, the tradition of intense focus on secondary school education continues to be strong and seems likely to endure well into the twenty-first century.

In Asian societies as in so much of the world, females have fewer rights and opportunities than males. With regard to education, boys receive more support from parents than girls for pursuing higher education. In Japan, for example, girls are discouraged from applying to the elite universities and are expected instead to enter junior colleges and pursue traditionally female occupations such as early childhood education (Naito & Gielen, in press; Stevenson & Zusho, 2002). Parents are reluctant to make the same sacrifices for higher education for girls as they do for boys, in part because it is sons and not daughters who are expected to support the parents in their old age. In the workplace, similar discrimination exists, with women being the first to be fired when cutbacks are made, because of the view that they are less likely to need the money to support a family (Stevenson & Zusho, 2002). Given the pervasiveness of sexism in human societies throughout history, it is difficult to be optimistic that it will be totally eliminated in the twenty-first century, in Asia or anywhere else.

LATIN AMERICA

Like Asia, Latin America comprises a vast land area of diverse cultures. And, as in Asia, in Latin America there are certain common characteristics that unite these cultures. Latin American countries share a common history of colonization by southern European powers, particularly Spain, and a common allegiance to the Catholic religion. For young people in Latin America, two of the key issues for the twenty-first century are political stability and economic growth.

The twentieth century was one of great political instability in most of Latin America. Most Latin American countries became independent (mostly from Spain) in the nineteenth century or early in the twentieth century. However, in the course of the twentieth century, most of them suffered continued instability. Sources of this instability included military coups followed by military dictatorships, communist revolutions, and civil wars between communist and anticommunist forces.

As the twentieth century begins, prospects look much brighter for adolescents in Latin America. Although political instability continues in countries such as

Colombia and Peru, for the most part Latin American countries have now established stable democracies (Welti, 2002). This means that young Latin Americans of the twenty-first century are much less likely than in the twentieth century to have to fight in a war, and much more likely to be able to express their ideas and beliefs freely.

The political instability of the twentieth century led to considerable economic instability (Welti, 2002). Despite having great natural resources, the countries of Latin America have not prospered economically. Even now, with mostly stable democracies, Latin American countries continue to experience economic difficulties, due to governmental corruption and mismanagement as well as to large international debt burdens accumulated from previous economic crises. The period from 1980 to 1990 is known in Latin America as the "lost decade," because the economies of the continent fared so poorly, and the 1990s were not much better.

For the young people of Latin America, this means that their economic prospects are grim as they enter the twenty-first century. Unemployment among adults is high throughout Latin America, and unemployment among young people is even higher, in most countries at least double the rate for adults, as high as 50 percent (Welti, 2002). However, prospects for young people are likely to improve during the twenty-first century. With more enduring political stability, economic growth in Latin America is likely to improve. Young people in Latin America are obtaining increased education, which should help prepare them for the increasingly information-based global economy (Welti, 2002). Also, the birthrate has declined sharply in Latin America in the past two decades, and consequently the children who are now growing up should face less competition in the job market as they enter adolescence and emerging adulthood.

THE WEST

For young people in the West, in many ways the twenty-first century holds bright prospects. Western societies have well-established, stable democracies, and economies that are generally healthier than in the rest of the world. Young people in the West generally have access to opportunities for secondary and higher education, and in terms of work they have a wide range of occupations from which to choose. Because Western societies are highly affluent, most young people have a wide range of leisure opportunities, such as sports and music. However, the West has its problems as well. For young people, the principle issues of the twenty-first century involve education, unemployment, immigrants, and health-risk behavior.

Young people in Western countries are obtaining increased education, with many of them remaining in school through their early twenties. However, educational opportunities are not evenly distributed in most Western countries.

Young people in minority groups often attend college at rates considerably lower than among young people in the majority culture. Furthermore, some critics have argued that Western countries produce far more college graduates than the economy really needs, so that many of them end up underemployed, in jobs with skills that do not require a college education (Cote & Allahar, 1996). Still, it seems likely that in the twenty-first century, with the economy headed rapidly toward an increased focus on information technologies, the jobs available requiring higher education will continue to expand, and the proportion of young people attending college will continue to expand accordingly.

Unemployment is another problem faced by young people in the West as we enter the twenty-first century. Despite the impressive efforts that European countries make to promote a smooth entry into the workplace for young people, unemployment among the young is a serious problem in most European countries. This is especially true for the countries of southern Europe, where youth unemployment (ages fifteen to twenty-four) has remained stubbornly over 20 percent for many years (Lagree, 1995). Unemployment among adults (age twenty-five and older) is also high in southern Europe relative to the north, but youth unemployment is especially high. Consistently across Europe, in the north as well as the south, and the east as well as the west, the youth unemployment rate is about twice as high as the unemployment rate for adults (Arnett, 2002).

In the United States, unemployment is also higher among young people than among adults, and it is especially high among young Latinos and African Americans living in urban areas (Wilson, 1996). Similar disparities are reported in Europe between immigrant youth and the majority population (e.g., Bois-Reymond & van der Zande, 1994; Sansone, 1995). Throughout Western countries, young minorities are disadvantaged in the workplace in part because of lower levels of education and training and in part because of prejudice and discrimination from the majority (Kracke et al., 1998; Liebkind & Kosonen, 1998). Although opportunities for minorities improved in most Western countries during the twentieth century, it is an open question whether or not minorities in the West will reach true equality of opportunity with the majority populations in the course of the twenty-first century.

European societies tend to be much more homogeneous than the United States, but most European countries have allowed substantial immigration in recent decades, from Eastern Europe and from a variety of developing countries. Most Europeans have been tolerant and accepting of immigration, and young people tend to be more favorable toward immigration than older people (Kracke et al., 1998; Westin, 1998). However, when anti-immigrant acts do occur, they tend to be committed by peer groups of young working-class men in their late teens and early twenties (Westin, 1998), especially young men who are members of the "skinhead" youth subculture. These acts include verbal harassment, attacks on refugee centers, and even random murders of immigrants. Immigration will be an important issue in Europe in the next century, as European countries make a decision about how much immigration to allow and how to address the problem of the small proportion of young people who are disposed to commit violent acts against immigrants.

Finally, young people in the West are more likely to engage in behavior that holds risks for their health than are young people in the rest of the world. In many ways, Western young people at the dawn of the twenty-first century are the healthiest generation in history (Arnett, 2002). Unlike the Western young people of 1900, and unlike young people in developing countries today, very few Western young people of the twenty-first century will die of infectious diseases before they reach maturity. Unlike the Western young people of 1900, and unlike young people in developing countries today, very few Western young people of the early twenty-first century are subject to extremely unsafe and unhealthy working conditions in mines and factories (Kett, 1977).

Nevertheless, young people in the West face health problems and challenges of their own in the twenty-first century. For Western adolescents and emerging adults today, the primary threats to their health arise from their behavior. The most serious threats are automobile fatalities and homicides, both of which are far more prevalent in the United States than in other Western countries (National Highway Traffic Safety Administration, 2001; Rockett, 1998). Graduated licensing shows promise in reducing automobile fatalities among young people in the United States (Preusser, Zador, & Williams, 1993), but rates of fatalities are likely to remain high as long as young people in American society rely heavily on automobiles for transportation and leisure—far into the twenty-first century, in other words.

With regard to homicide, the prevalence of unregulated firearms in American society—200 million, by recent estimates—makes it difficult to be hopeful that homicides among young people will be reduced anytime soon. Regulation of gun ownership is a controversial issue in American society, and the United States has been reluctant to adopt the kind of gun control laws that have long been typical of other Western countries. Even if such laws were passed in the twenty-first century, one can only speculate how long it would take to achieve any kind of legal control over 200 million firearms.

Cigarette smoking among young people is another health-risk behavior worth noting, because it is—in the long run—the source of more illness and mortality than automobile fatalities and homicides combined, and because the majority of persons who smoke begin as adolescents, in their middle teens (U.S. Department of Health and Human Services, 1994). Smoking has decreased among young people in most Western countries since the 1960s (e.g., Buzzi & Cavalli, 1994; Galambos & Kolaric, 1994). However, rates of smoking among young people have changed little (or even increased) in recent years and remain strikingly high, so that is difficult to predict whether or not smoking will remain a common form of health-risk behavior for young people through the twenty-first century.

COMMON ISSUES

Although young people in various parts of the world face challenges distinctive to their region and their society, some issues will be common to young people all over the world in the twenty-first century. Three of these issues are globalization, equality of wealth and opportunity, and the urban-rural split.

The Future of Globalization

Globalization is affecting cultures around the world, as increased economic integration brings cultures and countries into more frequent contact with each other and as media spread common information and entertainment to every part of the globe. For the most part the direction of influence has been from the West outward, as Western political forms, economic practices, and media content are adopted by cultures in other parts of the world (Schlegel, 2000a). Western influences have often been embraced first and most enthusiastically by young people in non-Western cultures (Dasen, 2000; Schlegel, 2000a).

Globalization is certain to continue into the twenty-first century, but two questions concerning globalization concern how far it will extend and whether its effects will be positive or negative for young people. The first of these questions is difficult to answer. Globalization took place at a rapid pace in the second half of the twentieth century, but this does not mean it will continue to occur at the same pace. There is some evidence that many cultures are devising new forms of dress, media, and economic practices that combine Western influences with indigenous forms. Will these hybrid forms continue to occur? Or is this a middle stage on the way to total Westernization and the creation of a more or less homogeneous global culture? The answer will probably become clear in the course of the twenty-first century.

Is globalization good or bad for young people? There is probably not a clean either/or answer to this question. Globalization may be good if it provides young people with greater opportunities than they have had in the past. As their economies develop and become more connected to the rest of the world, young people in developing countries may have a wider range of educational and occupational possibilities from which to choose. Girls, in particular, may see their opportunities increased as globalization proceeds. Also, as more countries develop stable democratic institutions, ethnic and religious hatreds may diminish, and young people may become less likely to die in ethnic and religious conflicts.

On the other hand, globalization holds a variety of perils for young people as well. Currently many young people in developing countries are being exploited, often by international companies that regard them as a source of plentiful, desperate, and easily exploitable labor. Also, young people may become alienated from the ways of their own culture as a consequence of globalization, and conflict with parents often increases as young people in changing societies develop interests and beliefs that differ sharply from those of their parents (e.g., Burbank, 1988; Liechty, 1995). Young people in developing countries may develop aspirations and expectations for their lives, based on what they have seen or read about the West, that are unattainable in the cultures where they live. The result may be increased disenchantment and alienation among the young.

Equality of Wealth and Opportunity

Currently, resources of wealth and opportunity available to young people are distributed extremely unevenly around the world. Young people in the middle class and above in the majority cultures of industrialized countries have many advantages. They have access to high-quality healthcare from the womb onward. They are provided with a good education throughout childhood, and most of them are able to obtain higher education if they wish. They have access to a variety of leisure opportunities, including a vast range of media and often the opportunity to travel to various parts of their own country and the world.

At the other extreme are young people around the world who are growing up in desperate conditions. Even now, at the beginning of the twenty-first century, many children grow up without even the most basic healthcare, such as childhood vaccinations, so that they reach adolescence in poor health if they reach it at all. Hundreds of millions of young people—in fact, the majority of the world's young people—grow up with almost nothing in the way of material resources and spend their youth as well as their adult lives working strenuously to survive from one day to the next. There are tens of millions of street children in the world, who live without families and who are subject daily to threats to their health and their lives (Raffaeli & Larson, 1999). Their prospects in adolescence and beyond are bleak. In the West, too, particularly in the United States, many young people grow up with few resources, with little to inspire hope for their futures.

Will these conditions change in the course of the twenty-first century? Will the world move toward greater equality of opportunity for all young people, regardless of the conditions they have been born into through no choice of their own? It is difficult to say, but currently there is little question that the world is moving in the opposite direction—toward greater inequality of wealth and opportunity, as the rich get richer in industrialized countries, and the poor get poorer and more numerous around the world.

The Urban-Rural Split

Although I have been discussing young people in this chapter according to region and country, it is important to recognize that each region and country is diverse. In particular, it is notable that in developing countries, young people in urban areas face conditions much different than young people in rural areas (Booth, 2002; Nsamenang, 2002; Welti, 2002). In urban areas, young people typically have greater access to education and healthcare. On the other hand, they are also more likely to be subject to exploitation by adults, in prostitution or industrial labor. In rural areas, young people are less likely to attend school and often spend their days working in agriculture or other work with adults. On the other hand, they are more likely to have the support and care of a stable extended family.

Globalization is affecting urban areas in developing countries far more than rural areas, so far. Consequently, young people in urban areas are growing up in increasingly different ways from those of than young people in rural areas. Will this disparity become more extreme in the course of the twenty-first century? Or will young people in rural areas become increasingly swept up in globalization, as their urban counterparts are? Currently, in many developing countries, young people are leaving their rural villages when they reach adolescence or emerging adulthood and heading for what they believe to be the promise of greater wealth and opportunity in the big cities. However, many of them are finding that when they reach the cities, opportunities are not what they expected, and there are threats of exploitation that they had not anticipated (Nsamenang, 2002). It is difficult to predict what will happen with regard to the urban-rural split in the twenty-first century, but it is important to keep it in mind when considering the prospects for young people in developing countries.

CONCLUSION

In this chapter we have looked ahead to what adolescence may be like during the century to come. We have seen that the young people of the world face futures of remarkable diversity, from the challenges of disease, exploitation, and illiteracy in developing countries to the challenges of unemployment, relations between minority and majority cultures, and health-risk behavior in industrialized countries. In some respects, the future of adolescents worldwide is bleak. AIDS remains an incurable and deadly disease and is devastating Africa. Adolescent girls receive less opportunity for education than boys do everywhere in the world except the West. Youth unemployment is an intractable problem worldwide.

Still, who would trade the future of adolescents in the twenty-first century for the future of young people at any time in the past? In 1900, the problems faced by young people were different but were in many ways more daunting than the problems of young people today: high rates of childhood mortality due to lack of effective vaccinations and medical interventions, rampant exploitation in the workplace, few opportunities for education beyond elementary school, and (for boys) a high likelihood of being a combatant in a future military conflict. Although these problems still exist in some parts of the world, in many other parts of the world they have been overcome. This allows us to hold out the hope that many of the problems described here will be a thing of the past by the end of the twenty-first century.

REFERENCES

Arnett, J. J. (2002). Adolescents in Western countries in the twenty-first century: Vast opportunities—for all? In B. B. Brown, R. Larson, & T. S. Saraswathi (Eds.), *The world's youth: Adolescence in eight regions of the globe* (pp. 307–343). New York: Cambridge University Press.

Bailey, B. L. (1989). *From front porch to back seat: Courtship in twentieth-century America.* Baltimore: Johns Hopkins University Press.

Bartholet, J. (2000). The plague years. *Newsweek,* January 17, pp. 32–37.

Bois-Reymond, M., & van der Zande, I. (1994). The Netherlands. In K. Hurrelmann (Ed.), *International handbook of adolescence* (pp. 270–286). Westport, CT: Greenwood Press.

Booth, M. (2002). Arab adolescents facing the future: Enduring ideals and pressures for change. In B. B. Brown, R. Larson, & T. S. Saraswathi (Eds.), *The world's youth: Adolescence in eight regions of the globe* (pp. 207–242). New York: Cambridge University Press.

Burbank, V. (1988). *Aboriginal adolescence.* New Brunswick, NJ: Rutgers University Press.

Burra, N. B. (1997). *Born to work: Child labor in India.* New Delhi: Oxford University Press.

Buzzi, C., & Cavalli, A. (1994). Italy. In K. Hurrelmann (Ed.), *International handbook of adolescence* (pp. 224–233). Westport, CT: Greenwood Press.

Cho, B. E., & Shin, H. Y. (1996). State of family research and theory in Korea. In M. B. Sussman & R. S. Hanks (Eds.), *Intercultural variation in family research and theory: Implications for cross-national studies* (pp. 101–135). New York: Haworth Press.

Cote, J. E., & Allahar, A. L. (1996). *Generation on hold: Coming of age in the late twentieth century.* New York: New York University Press.

Dasen, P. (2000). Rapid social change and the turmoil of adolescence: A cross-cultural perspective. *International Journal of Group Tensions, 29,* 17–49.

Davis, S. S., & Davis, D. A. (1989). *Adolescence in a Moroccan town.* New Brunswick, NJ: Rutgers.

Flammer, A., & Alsaker, F. D. (1999). Time use by adolescents in international perspective: The case of necessary activities. In F. D. Alsaker & A. Flammer (Eds.), *The adolescent experience: European and American adolescents in the 1990s* (pp. 61–84). Mahwah, NJ: Erlbaum.

Flammer, A., Alsaker, F. D., & Noack, P. (1999). Time use by adolescents in international perspective: The case of leisure activities. In F. D. Alsaker & A. Flammer

(Eds.), *The adolescent experience: European and American adolescents in the 1990s* (pp. 33–60). Mahwah, NJ: Erlbaum.

Fletcher, M. A. (2000). California minority youth treated more harshly, study says. *Washington Post*, February 3, p. A-16.

Galambos, N., & Kolaric, G. C. (1994). Canada. In K. Hurrelmann (Ed.), *International handbook of adolescence* (pp. 92–107). Westport, CT: Greenwood Press.

Hatfield, E., & Rapson, R. L. (1996). *Love and sex: Cross-cultural perspectives*. Boston: Allyn & Bacon.

Kett, J. (1977). *Rites of passage: Adolescence in America, 1790 to the present*. New York: Basic Books.

Kracke, B., Oepke, M., Wild, E., & Noack, P. (1998). Adolescents, families, and German unification: The impact of social change on anti-foreigner and antidemocratic attitudes. In J. Nurmi (Ed.), *Adolescents, cultures, and conflicts* (pp. 149–170). New York: Garland.

Lagree, J. C. (1995). Young people and employment in the European community: Convergence or divergence? In L. Chisholm, P. Buchner, H. H. Kruger, & M. du Bois-Reymond (Eds.), *Growing up in Europe: Contemporary horizons in childhood and youth studies* (pp. 61–72). New York: Walter de Gruyter.

Lee, B. (1998). The changes of Korean adolescents' lives. Unpublished manuscript, Department of Human Development and Family Studies, University of Missouri.

Liebkind, K., & Kosonen, L. (1998). Acculturation and adaptation: A case of Vietnamese children and youths in Finland. In J. Nurmi (Ed.), *Adolescents, cultures, and conflicts* (pp. 199–224). New York: Garland.

Liechty, M. (1995). Media, markets, and modernization: Youth identities and the experience of modernity in Kathmandu, Nepal. In V. Amit-Talai & H. Wulff (Eds.), *Youth cultures: A cross-cultural perspective* (pp. 166–201). New York: Routledge.

Makhlouf, H., & Abdelkader, M. (1997). *The current status of research and training in population and health in the Arab region and the future needs*. Cairo: Cairo Demographic Center.

Malik, S. (2000, February). Arab adolescents facing the third millenium. Paper presented at the meeting of the Study Group on Adolescence in the Twenty-First Century, Washington, DC.

Migliazzo, A. C. (1993). Korean leadership in the twenty-first century: A profile of the coming generation. *Korea Journal* (Winter), 60–67.

Naito, T., & Gielen, U. P. (in press). The changing Japanese family: A psychological portrait. In J. L. Roopnarine & U. P. Gielen (Eds.), *Families in global perspective* (pp. 63–84). Boston: Allyn & Bacon.

National Highway Traffic Safety Administration (NHTSA) (2001). *Traffic safety facts, 2000*. Washington, DC: Author.

Nsamenang, A. B. (1998). Work organization and economic management in sub-Saharan Africa: From a Eurocentric orientation toward an Afrocentric perspective. *Psychology and Developing Societies, 10*, 75–97.

———. (2002). Adolescence in sub-Saharan Africa: An image constructed from Africa's triple inheritance. In B. B. Brown, R. Larson, & T. S. Saraswathi (Eds.), *The world's youth: Adolescence in eight regions of the globe* (pp. 61-104). New York: Cambridge University Press.

Park, I. H., & Cho, L. J. (1995). Confucianism and the Korean family. *Journal of Comparative Family Studies, 26,* 1134–1170.

Pathak, R. (1994). The new generation. *India Today,* January 31, pp. 72–87.

Population Reference Bureau (2000). *The world's youth 2000.* Washington, DC: Author.

Preusser, D. F., Zador, P. L., & Williams, A. F. (1993). City curfew ordinances and teenage motor vehicle fatalities. *Accident Analysis and Prevention, 25,* 641–645.

PROBE (1999). *Peoples' report on basic education.* New Delhi: Oxford University Press.

Raffaelli, M., & Larson, R. W. (Eds.). (1999). *Homeless and working adolescents around the world: Exploring developmental issues.* New Directions in Child and Adolescent Development no. 85. San Francisco: Jossey-Bass.

Roberts, D. F., Foehr, U. G., Rideout, V. J., & Brodie, M. (1999). *Kids & media @ the millenium: A comprehensive national analysis of children's media use.* New York: Henry J. Kaiser.

Rockett, I. R. H. (1998). Injury and violence: A public health perspective. *Population Bulletin, 53* (4), 1–40.

Sansone, L. (1995). The making of a black youth culture: Lower-class young men of Surinamese origin in Amsterdam. In V. Amit-Talai & H. Wulff (Eds.), *Youth cultures: A cross-cultural perspective* (pp. 114–143). New York: Routledge.

Schlegel, A. (2000a). The global spread of adolescent culture. In L. Crockett & R. K. Silbereisen (Eds.), *Negotiating adolescence in times of social change* (pp. 71–88). Cambridge: Cambridge University Press.

———. (2000b, April). The global spread of adolescent culture. Paper presented at the biennial meeting of the Society for Research on Adolescence, Chicago.

Steinberg, L., & Cauffman, E. (1995). The impact of employment on adolescent development. In R. Vasta (Ed.), *Annals of child development, 11,* 131–166. London: Jessica Kingsley.

Stevenson, H. W., & Zusho, A. (2002). Adolescence in China and Japan: Adapting to a changing environment. In B. B. Brown, R. Larson, & T. S. Saraswathi (Eds.), *The world's youth: Adolescence in eight regions of the globe* (pp. 141–170). New York: Cambridge University Press.

Thapar, V. (1998, November). Family life education in India: Emerging challenges. Background paper for the National Convention on Family Life Education, New Delhi, India.

U.S. Department of Health and Human Services (1994). Preventing tobacco use among young people: A report of the Surgeon General. Atlanta, GA: Author.

Verma, S., & Saraswathi, T. S. (2002). Adolescents in India: Street urchins or Silicon Valley millionaires? In B. B. Brown, R. Larson, & T. S. Saraswathi (Eds.), *The world's youth: Adolescence in eight regions of the globe* (pp. 105–140). New York: Cambridge University Press.

Welti, C. (2002). Adolescents in Latin America: Facing the future with skepticism. In B. B. Brown, R. Larson, & T. S. Saraswathi (Eds.), *The world's youth: Adolescence in eight regions of the globe* (pp. 276–306). New York: Cambridge University Press.

Westin, C. (1998). Immigration, xenophobia, and youthful opinion. In J. Nurmi (Ed.), *Adolescents, cultures, and conflicts* (pp. 225–241). New York: Garland.

Wilson, W. J. (1996). *When work disappears: The world of the new urban poor.* New York: Knopf.

PART V

The Adaptation of Immigrant Children in the United States

CHAPTER 12

The Adaptation and Acculturation of Children from Immigrant Families

Andrew J. Fuligni

Children have figured prominently in the dramatic rise in international migration that has occurred in the past few decades. In the United States, the number of children with immigrant parents reached 13.8 million in 1997, representing almost one-fifth of the population of American children (Rumbaut, 1998). These trends are perhaps nowhere more apparent than among groups from Latin America and Asia, who account for the majority of the foreign-born population in the United States (U.S. Bureau of the Census, 1997). It has been estimated that more than half of all Latin American children and approximately 90 percent of those from Asian families have at least one foreign-born parent (Landale & Oropesa, 1995, as cited in Rumbaut, 1995). The United States is not alone in experiencing these demographic changes. Canada, Australia, Germany, and other European countries have also taken in large numbers of immigrant families and their children in recent years (United Nations Commission on Population and Development, 1997).

Social scientists, policy makers, and practitioners alike have expressed concern as to how such a large and diverse group of children will adapt in their new societies. How will they perform in school, given the dramatic variations in their cultural and linguistic backgrounds? Will the transition to a new and different society have a negative impact upon their psychological and behavioral adjustment? What is the process by which these children acculturate to their new societies? In this chapter, the adaptation of children from immigrant families in the United States will be used as a focal point in order to attempt to answer these questions. Research has only recently caught up with the rapid increase in immigration in the United States, but a number of studies have begun to paint a surprising portrait of the children from immigrant families. Rather than asking whether these unique children will adjust to American society, the question now seems to be: How can they be doing so well?

PATTERNS OF ADJUSTMENT

In systematic studies of nonclinical populations, the children from immigrant families in the United States demonstrate a remarkable level of general adjustment. In fact, they often appear to be better off than their peers from American-born families. Students with immigrant parents, including children who themselves are foreign-born, tend to receive grades in school that are equal to or even higher than those of students whose parents were born in the United States (Kao & Tienda, 1995). The students' success is evident across many different subjects, including English. Similarly surprising results have been found regarding the age at which foreign-born children enter the United States. The secondary school performance of relatively recent arrivals tends to equal or even surpass the achievement of foreign-born students who entered this country at younger ages (Fuligni, 1997; Rumbaut, 1997a).

Fewer studies have been conducted on the broader behavioral and psychological adjustment of immigrant children. Yet findings are beginning to emerge that are consistent with those from the research on academic achievement. In recent analyses of data from the National Longitudinal Study of Adolescent Health ("Add Health"), a nationally representative study of over 20,000 adolescents, youths from immigrant families exhibit healthier adjustment than their peers from American-born families across a variety of outcomes (Harris, 1998). First-generation adolescents (foreign-born) and second-generation adolescents (American-born with immigrant parents) are less likely to engage in delinquent and violent acts, to use drugs and alcohol, and to have had sex. In addition, teens from immigrant families are less likely to be in poor health, to be obese, to have asthma, and to have missed school due to a health or emotional problem. Among immigrant families themselves, first-generation youths tend to be healthier and less likely to engage in risky behavior than their second-generation counterparts. Similar to academic achievement, foreign-born adolescents who immigrated to the United States at later ages evidence fewer problem behaviors and better physical health.

The findings regarding the psychological health of children from immigrant families tend to be more complex, but there is little evidence that this group suffers the great distress commonly expected of them. Despite feeling that they have less control over their lives and that they are less popular, youths from immigrant families report a level of self-esteem equal to that of their peers from native-born families (Kao, 1998). In the Add Health study, there are no overall differences in depressive feelings and positive well-being according to the adolescents' generation (Harris, 1998). Other studies have observed that immigrant adolescents actually tend to have fewer psycho-somatic problems and less psychological distress than those from latter generations (Steinberg, 1996).

Children from immigrant families tend to exhibit positive adjustment even when they are compared to American-born children of the same ethnic back-grounds. For example, immigrant Mexican youths are less likely to have engaged in delinquent or violent acts, to have used drugs or alcohol, and to have asthma than their Mexican peers from later generations (Harris, 1998). The same is true for adolescents from other Latin American and Asian backgrounds. In addition, the similar or even higher psychological well-being among youths from immigrant families as compared to those from native-born families holds up within different ethnic groups (Harris, 1998; Steinberg, 1996). The findings regarding academic achievement, however, tend to be somewhat mixed. Some studies have observed consistent generational differences among all ethnic groups (Steinberg, 1996), but others have reported that the success of immigrant students relative to their peers from the same ethnic group tends to be most evident among Asian youths and less apparent among Latin American adolescents (Fuligni, 1997; Kao & Tienda, 1995). In addition, the rate at which immigrant Latin American students drop out of U.S. schools is slightly higher (24 percent) than the rate for American-born Latin American youths (18 percent) (McMillen, 1997).[1]

Despite the overall success of the children from immigrant families, important variations in adjustment exist within the population itself. Children from Asian countries receive higher grades than those from Europe, who in turn have more academic success than those from Latin American countries (Fuligni; 1997; Kao & Tienda, 1995). Similarly, immigrant Chinese children tend to exhibit lower rates of risk behavior and better physical health outcomes than immigrant children from Latin America (Harris, 1998). Differences also exist among Asian and Latin American children themselves. Immigrant Filipino youths engage in more risky behavior than Chinese adolescents, with rates comparable to those among Latin American immigrants (Harris, 1998). In addition, immigrant Mexican students do worse on standardized tests than other Latin American students, such as those from Cuba and Colombia (Rumbaut, 1997a).

These variations, while significant, do not change the picture of generally positive adjustment among children from immigrant families. When compared to American-born children of similar ethnic backgrounds, those from immigrant families exhibit better physical health, less involvement in risky behavior, and similar or even greater academic achievement and psychological well-being. The only exception to this trend seems to be that immigrant Latin American students have more difficulty completing high school in the United States than their later-generation peers.

Socioeconomic Factors

Given the many challenges of adjusting to a new and different society, how do the children from immigrant families present such a consistent picture of successful development? One possible explanation could be that these children come from more advantaged family backgrounds. Indeed, some immigrant parents received advanced education in their home countries and have come to the United States seeking greater professional opportunities. Over 40 percent of foreign-born Filipinos have received bachelor's degrees, as compared to only 20 percent of the general American-born population (U.S. Bureau of the Census, 1993). But many other immigrant parents, such as those from Latin America and Southeast Asia, tend to come from much lower educational backgrounds. For example, only 4 percent of immigrant Mexican adults have graduated from college. Variations in educational attainment produce major differences in family income, with the immigrant Filipinos and Mexicans earning approximately $48,000 and $22,000, respectively (U.S. Bureau of the Census, 1993).

Socioeconomic factors alone do not explain the differences in adjustment between children from immigrant and American-born families. Generational differences in academic achievement, behavioral adjustment, and psychological well-being remain after controlling for parental education and income (Fuligni, 1997; Harris, 1998; Kao & Tienda, 1995; Steinberg, 1996). In fact, generational differences often become greater after such controls, reflecting the fact that many immigrant children do better than would be expected based on their backgrounds. For example, when compared to youths with parents of similar levels of education and income, children from immigrant Latin American families evidence slightly higher educational outcomes than students from native-born Latin American families (Kao, 1998). In the Add Health study, youths from immigrant families actually report significantly less emotional distress and more positive well-being than their peers from American-born families after their families' socioeconomic status is taken into account (Harris, 1998).

Rather than explaining generational differences in adjustment, socioeconomic factors seem to be more important for the ethnic variations within the population of children from immigrant families itself. Immigrant groups differ dramatically in their economic backgrounds, with those from Asia tending to be more educated and to work in higher-paying occupations than those from Latin America (U.S. Bureau of the Census, 1993). Families from Laos, Cambodia, Mexico, and El Salvador find themselves in worse economic conditions than other Asian and Latin American groups. These variations, along with differences in the manner in which the families are treated and afforded opportunities in this country, are likely to be important sources of the generally poorer outcomes for children from Latin America and certain countries in Southeast Asia (Portes & Rumbaut, 1996).

Psychosocial Factors

To explain the success of immigrant children relative to their native-born peers, one must turn to a collection of psychosocial factors that seem to motivate the children to seek success in school while protecting them from psychological and behavioral difficulties.

Value of education. Immigrant families see education as the best way that their children can succeed in American society. Regardless of their ethnic or socioeconomic backgrounds, foreign-born parents tend to place a great importance on school achievement (Caplan, Choy, & Whitmore, 1991; Gibson & Bhachu, 1991; Suárez-Orozco & Suárez-Orozco, 1995). Families from countries as different as India, Mexico, China, and Cuba all emphasize academic success and aspire for their children to attend college. Acutely aware of the challenges that their children face, immigrant parents try to minimize these difficulties by comparing them to the relative lack of educational opportunities in their native countries (Matute-Bianchi, 1991; Ogbu, 1991). Some parents will also encourage their children to view education as a way to avoid the often menial jobs in which the parents find themselves.

The children from immigrant families quickly internalize their parents' emphasis on educational achievement. In a study of adolescents from Latin American and Asian backgrounds, students from immigrant families endorsed every attitude and value regarding education more strongly than their peers with American-born parents (Fuligni, 1997). First- and second-generation students placed more importance upon learning mathematics and English, aspired to higher levels of educational attainment, valued academic success more, and spent more time studying and doing homework than those from native-born families. These attitudes and behaviors, in turn, statistically accounted for the higher grades of immigrant students. Similarly high levels of academic motivation have been observed in numerous ethnographies of specific immigrant populations (e.g., Gibson & Bhachu, 1991; Suárez-Orozco & Suárez-Orozco, 1995).

The educational emphasis of immigrant families likely enhances more than just their children's academic achievement. In general, students who value educational success and put effort into their studies tend to have better psychological well-being and less frequent involvement in risky behaviors such as substance use and delinquency (Steinberg, 1996). Focusing on education, therefore, probably prevents the children from immigrant families from getting involved in activities that may threaten their psychological and behavioral adjustment. Instead of creating undue pressure, the motivation to achieve may actually provide immigrant students with a clear direction that helps them to navigate a new and different society.

Family obligation. Many immigrant families, such as those from Asia and Latin America, come from collectivistic traditions that emphasize family members' responsibilities and obligations to one another (Chilman, 1993; Shon & Ja, 1982). With immigration, these traditions take on immediate and practical importance because foreign-born parents often know very little about American society. Children, who assimilate more quickly, help their families with negotiating the official tasks and more informal demands of the new country (Zhou, 1997). The children from immigrant families feel a profound sense of duty and obligation to their families, both in the present and in the future. They are more likely than those from American-born families to believe that they should help their parents financially and have their parents live with them when the children become adults (Fuligni, Tseng, & Lam, 1999).

Children from immigrant families view school success as one of the most important ways that they can assist their families. Parents often emigrate to the United States in order to provide their children with better opportunities, including the chance to pursue education through and even beyond secondary school. Some students say that they would feel guilty about not trying hard in school, given the many personal and professional sacrifices their parents made to come to this country (Caplan et al., 1991; Suárez-Orozco & Suárez-Orozco, 1995). Other children believe that their educational attainment will help them to secure employment and support the family in the future. Students from immigrant families will often cite such indebtedness and responsibility as their primary motivations to do well in school (Zhou & Bankston, 1998).

While not yet empirically documented, the sense of responsibility to the family likely keeps immigrant children from engaging in the relatively more risky activities of American-born children and adolescents. At a basic level, children and youths who assist and spend time with their families have fewer opportunities to become involved in delinquency or substance use. In addition, the obligations associated with immigrant families provide children with integral roles within the family. These roles delineate a set of expectations, such as supporting the family's reputation and well-being, that may keep immigrant children from engaging in activities that would disappoint or embarrass the family in the larger immigrant community (Zhou & Bankston, 1998).

Nevertheless, there is some recent evidence that very high levels of family obligations may not be so advantageous for children. Fuligni, Tseng, and Lam (1999) found that while a moderate sense of responsibility was associated with higher academic achievement, those adolescents who indicated the strongest endorsement of their obligations tended to receive school grades just as low as or even lower than those with the weakest endorsement. This curvilinear association is exemplified by the poor Latin American immigrants, studied by Suárez-Orozco and Suárez-Orozco (1995), who feel the need to cut back on their studies when their families face economic distress. The students value education, but the more immediate need to help their families at home or on the job can interfere with the students' progress at school. It is currently unknown how such a high level of responsibility to the family may affect the students' broader psychological and behavioral adjustment as well as their long-term economic adjustment.

Cultural identity. Despite the pressure to conform to Americanized ethnic and racial categories, immigrant families and their children tend to avoid such labels and instead retain their original cultural identities. Adolescents from immigrant families relate more to nationalistic identities, such as Mexican or Chinese, than to pan-ethnic or hyphenated labels such as Latino or Asian American (Rumbaut, 1994). It is not surprising that immigrant families would claim identities tied to their cultures of origin. But immigrant parents sometimes employ such identifications as a way to keep their children from adopting undesirable "American" attitudes and behaviors, such as laziness, materialism, and selfishness (Gibson & Bhachu, 1991; Sung, 1987). Certain immigrant groups also feel the need to distance themselves from the negative stereotypes associated with American ethnic categories. For example, some West Indian adolescents with African backgrounds prefer not to be identified with American blacks because of the low expectations that American society has for such youths (Waters, 1994). Similarly, immigrant Mexican youths will sometimes resist labels such as Mexican American, Latino, or Chicano (Matute-Bianchi, 1991).

Studies have recently suggested that such cultural identifications have important implications for children's adjustment. West Indian and Mexican youths who identify with their parents' cultural origins tend to be more attached to school and attain greater academic success than their peers who assume the more Americanized ethnic identities (Matute-Bianchi, 1991; Waters, 1994). It is unclear, however, what produces an association between identity and adjustment. Distancing themselves from American ethnic labels may enable immigrant children to avoid the negative stereotypes that act to depress the achievement of minority students (Steele, 1997). Cultural labels chosen by immigrant children and adolescents can also be confounded with social class, and such identifications can be just as much reactions to as producers of their experiences in American society. For example, Waters (1994) observed that the West Indian youths who did not identify with their parents' cultural origin tended to be from lower socioeconomic backgrounds and were more likely to report that they had experienced discrimination in the United States. The dynamics of cultural identification among children from immigrant families present a particular challenge to researchers. The process appears to be of great significance for the children's adjustment, but it is currently not well understood.

Summary

Despite the concerns of many observers, the children from immigrant families display a truly remarkable degree of adjustment across a variety of domains.

These children do well with the help of a collection of values and traditions that provide the children with a clear direction, a responsible role, and a strong cultural identity. Latin American children tend to have more difficulties than their counterparts from Asia, but even those from Latin America appear to be adjusting more successfully than their American-born peers of similar socioeconomic and ethnic backgrounds.

The question remains as to whether the children from immigrant families will maintain their successful adjustment through adolescence and into adulthood. Up to this point, research on this population has almost exclusively relied upon cross-sectional designs that compare different children according to their birthplace or age of immigration. Despite the implication from these studies that more time spent in the United States diminishes children's overall adjustment, we currently do not know whether exposure to American society brings about changes in the attitudes and behaviors of individual children. On the one hand, children's value of education and identifications with their families and cultures may remain constant through their lives, enabling them to overcome challenges to their attainments as adults. On the other hand, the children's cumulative experiences in this country may lead them to acculturate to the seemingly less advantageous values and activities of their American-born peers.

A LONGITUDINAL APPROACH TO ACCULTURATION

In order to understand how exposure to a new society affects children and adolescents, many observers have turned to the concept of acculturation (e.g., Buriel & De Ment, 1997; García-Coll & Magnusson, 1997; Matute-Bianchi, 1991; Park & Buriel, 1998; Szapocznik & Kurtines, 1993). Various definitions and models of acculturation have been offered, but the concept generally refers to the changes that take place among newcomers as they come in contact with a new society (Berry & Sam, 1997). Debates occur over issues such as whether acculturation involves a unidirectional shift from native to host culture or a more multidimensional negotiation of old and new traditions (e.g., Buriel & De Ment, 1997). Some observers question whether acculturation is indeed inevitable or even desirable (Berry & Sam, 1997; Rumbaut, 1997a; Steinberg, 1996). Yet there seems to be a general agreement that the concept of acculturation involves some type of adjustment or change within individuals as a result of their exposure to the host culture.

Unfortunately, acculturation has rarely been studied as a process of individual change over time. Instead, acculturation is often inferred from cross-sectional studies that have examined individual and group differences in adjustment according to factors such as birthplace, age of immigration, language proficiency, and the ethnic composition of social networks (e.g., Feldman, Mont-Reynaud, & Rosenthal, 1992; Fuligni, 1997; Kao & Tienda, 1995; Knight, Bernal, Garza,

Cota, & Ocampo, 1993; Suárez-Orozco & Suárez-Orozco, 1995). These studies provide needed information about within-group variation, but they reveal very little about the changes that result from children's experiences in a new society. Cross-sectional studies often possess confounding factors that prevent strong conclusions about the process of acculturation. For example, children who differ in terms of their language ability also vary greatly in terms of their families' socioeconomic backgrounds (Bradby, 1992). It is unclear, therefore, whether an increase in a student's language proficiency will improve academic performance if the family's economic conditions do not change. Investigators can attempt to control for some of these confounds in their analyses, but the fundamental drawback of cross-sectional designs can never be rectified statistically. These models simply do not assess individual change over time.

Given the limitations of cross-sectional designs, there is a great need for studies that track the same children as they encounter and negotiate the potential differences between their cultural traditions and those of the host society. In this section, an approach for studying acculturation is described in which children from different generations and societies are simultaneously followed across time and development. This comparative longitudinal approach allows investigators to isolate acculturative change from shifts that would have occurred through the course of development had immigration not occurred. The design also offers the potential of examining acculturation in terms of both the level and the developmental progression of different aspects of adjustment. Finally, this approach allows investigators to explore variations in change with important implications for how the sources of acculturation are assessed. The intent is not to present a comprehensive and definitive theory of acculturation. Rather, the purpose is to describe a general framework that can be used to examine acculturative change regardless of a study's specific topic, method, or theoretical orientation.

A Comparative Approach

One possible effect of acculturation on immigrant children will be used to present this approach. Many of the recent immigrants to the United States come from societies that place a strong importance on the role of education in children's development. Chinese immigrants, for example, have often been raised in cultures that see academic pursuits as the main focus of children's lives (Ho, 1981; Stevenson, Chen, & Lee, 1992; see also Chen & Kaspar, this volume). American society, in contrast, places relatively less emphasis upon education. Children in the United States spend much less time in school each year than their counterparts in East Asian countries (Stevenson & Stigler, 1992). American students consistently place less value on education and spend less time studying than their counterparts in Taiwan, Hong Kong, and mainland China (e.g., Fuligni & Stevenson, 1995). What happens, then, to the children of Chinese immigrant families when they enter the United States? Does the children's value of education decline as they gain more exposure to American society, its students, and its schools?

Cross-sectional studies that have compared East Asian children living in East Asian societies with East Asian children living in the United States offer the hint that such a disconcerting effect of acculturation may indeed occur. Chen and Stevenson (1995) have observed that Asian American children place less importance on education than their counterparts in Asia. Fuligni (1997) has further noted that the academic values of Chinese children within the United States decline with each successive generation: American-born students have lower educational aspirations, place less value on doing well in school, and study less often than their immigrant peers.

Yet it is unclear whether these group differences are due to acculturation. Chinese families who decide to leave their home countries for the United States may possess a preexisting inclination toward American norms and values. Immigrant Chinese students often emphasize education more than their native-born peers because they believe it be their primary route to success as newcomers to American society (Sue & Okazaki, 1990; Sung, 1987). Other factors, ranging from economic to historical, can also contribute to the group differences. The variations between Chinese children of different societies and generations, therefore, do not necessarily mean that the educational values of individual immigrants will decline as they spend more time in the United States. To explore whether acculturation erodes the academic emphasis of children from Chinese immigrant families, one must observe the same children and their exposure to American society over time.

The difficulty with studying acculturation longitudinally is that time spent in a new society is going to be confounded with common developmental changes during childhood and adolescence. For example, one may observe that the value of education among immigrant children declines as they progress through secondary school and conclude that these students are assimilating to the deemphasis on academics among American adolescents. The problem with this conclusion is that a decline in academic motivation during secondary school is a well-documented developmental trend in the United States (Eccles, Midgely, Wigfield, Buchanan, Reuman, Flanagan, & Mac Iver, 1993). Immigrant and native-born students may both show declines in their value of education while still remaining far apart in terms of their overall level of academic motivation.

To avoid confounding acculturative and developmental changes, investigators should simultaneously study both immigrant and native-born children over time. Comparing the longitudinal trends in both groups would then indicate whether any changes observed among immigrant children can be attributed to acculturation. For example, Figure 12.1A presents a hypothetical graph in which a decline in academic motivation has been observed among both immigrant and native-born adolescents. The parallel lines indicate that while both groups ex-

Figure 12.1A
Changes in the Value of Education Among Immigrant and Native-Born Children
That Indicate a Lack of Acculturation

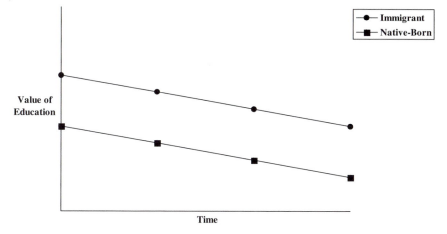

Figure 12.1B
Changes in the Value of Education Among Immigrant and Native-Born Children That
Indicate an Effect of Acculturation on the Level of the Immigrant Children's Value

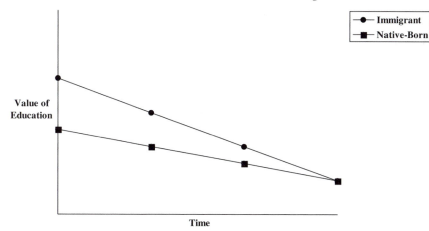

perience changes in their motivation, the values of the immigrant students have
not come any closer to those of the native-born adolescents. In this case, it can
be argued that acculturative change has not occurred. In contrast, Figure 12.1B
shows trends in which the values of the immigrant students have changed faster,
so that they gradually approximate those of native-born students. Such evidence
for a convergence in the academic motivation of the adolescents from the different groups would seem to indicate an effect of acculturation.

Ideally, investigators would begin studying immigrant children before they emigrated or soon after they have entered the host country. Otherwise, one may miss an acculturative effect that occurred before the study began. For example, the parallel trends observed in Figure 12.1A may have been preceded by a narrowing of the difference between the two groups of children. Given the difficulty of sampling families prior to their departure from their countries of origin or immediately after their immigration, this may be a problem that many investigators cannot avoid. If so, any conclusions regarding a lack of acculturation must be limited to the period being studied. Yet even such bounded findings will be revealing, as they will offer insights into the existence of acculturative change during specific developmental periods. For example, the acculturation of academic values may be more likely to occur during a time of other educational changes—such as the transition to secondary school—than during periods of relative stability. Such findings would help determine whether and why children are more susceptible to acculturative change during some periods of development as compared to others.

Investigators can compare several groups of children in order to provide a richer portrait of the acculturation process. For example, native-born children with immigrant parents often appear similar to immigrant children in terms of their attitudes and behaviors regarding education (Fuligni, 1997; Kao & Tienda, 1995). The native-born group in Figures 12.1A and 12.1B, therefore, can be split according to the nativity of their parents in order to determine whether native-born children with immigrant parents also go through a process of acculturation.

Portes and Rumbaut (1996) argue that the question about acculturation is not whether children will adapt to the United States, but to which aspects of American society will they acculturate. Given the diversity of norms and values in American society, investigators should considering including several different native-born comparison groups. One can compare immigrant Chinese children with native-born children from both Chinese American and European American families. More refined subgroups of native-born children may also be selected. For example, immigrant Chinese adolescents will encounter many different peer crowds—ranging from gang members to academic stars—when they settle in existing ethnic communities (Sung, 1987). Additional ethnic and cultural groups within the immigrants' areas of settlement could also have an important influence on the children's development. Such can be the case in urban areas, such as Los Angeles and New York City, where several immigrant and ethnic groups often live in close proximity to one another (Fix & Passel, 1994).

The comparisons shown in Figures 12.1A and 12.1B are useful in determining the effect of acculturation on the level of the immigrant students' values, but one cannot tell whether the developmental change itself is the result of acculturation. It is possible that while the difference between immigrant and native-born students remains constant over time, a developmental decline in the motivation of immigrant students is a direct result of their exposure to native-born students. In this case, it is useful to undertake the task of estimating the developmental trends of children remaining in the immigrants' countries of origin. Figures 12.2A and 12.2B include hypothetical changes that incorporate such trends. In Figure 12.2A, the children from the country of origin exhibit

Figure 12.2A
Changes in the Value of Education among Immigrant and Native-Born Children, and Children from the Immigrants' Country of Origin, That Indicate a Lack of Acculturation

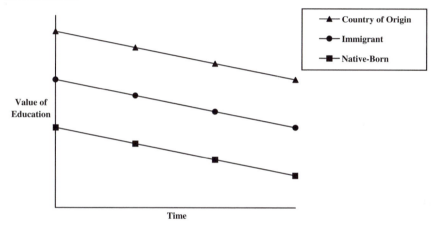

Figure 12.2B
Changes in the Value of Education Among Immigrant and Native-Born Children That Indicate an Effect of Acculturation on the Developmental Trends of the Immigrant Children's Value

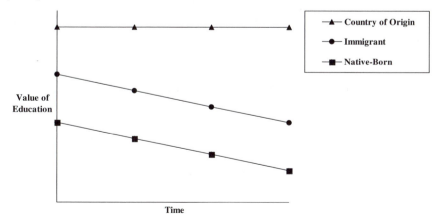

developmental changes similar to those of the children in the other two groups. There appears to be no acculturation of either the level or the developmental trend of the educational values of the immigrant children. Figure 12.2B, however, shows a result that would indicate an effect of acculturation on the developmental change among the immigrant children. The immigrant students do not share the values of the children from native-born families, but they do follow the norm of a declining value of education while the children in the country of origin do not exhibit such a drop.

Comparing immigrant children with those from their countries of origin can be problematic because of the inherent selection factors involved in emigration (Portes & Rumbaut, 1996). Investigators should attempt to match the two groups in terms of factors such as region in the country of origin, socioeconomic status, and even intent to emigrate, if possible. Yet there will always be a bias in terms of which families and children eventually do immigrate to the United States. This bias may be due to the motivation and ability of some families to leave their countries of origin and enter a new society, the selective nature of the host country's system of determining which petitioners may enter the country, or both. For this reason, comparing the average value of education among immigrants with that of children in the immigrants' countries of origin cannot be considered a good test of acculturation. It is less obvious how selection factors may influence the developmental trends of the immigrant students' values, but selection may still play an unspecified role. Differences in the developmental trends between these two groups should therefore be interpreted with caution, but such variations may still be suggestive of a subtle yet interesting effect of acculturation.

Variations Within and Between Immigrant Children

A unique benefit of a longitudinal approach is the ability to examine variation in acculturative change within individual children and adolescents. As with developmental change, acculturation is unlikely to occur in only the simple linear fashion represented in Figures 12.1 and 12.2. Immigrant children probably alternate between periods of relative stability and times of rapid change in their attitudes and behaviors, depending upon events in their lives or the specific period of their development (García-Coll & Magnusson, 1997). For example, as shown in Figure 12.3, immigrant Chinese students may maintain a strong value of education for many years in early and middle childhood. During adolescence, when the students enter secondary school and gain more exposure to native-born students from different ethnic groups, the students' educational orientation could change dramatically within a short period of time. Additional patterns of change are possible, but one cannot explore these interesting acculturative trends without a longitudinal design. Longer time spans and additional repeated measure-

Figure 12.3
Variation in the Changes in the Value of Education Within Immigrant Children According to Developmental Period

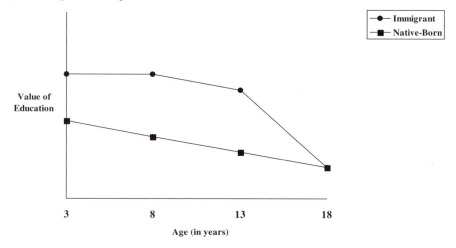

ments increase the ability to plot complex patterns of change over time in studies of immigrant children (Collins & Horn, 1991).

Variations in acculturative change will also occur between different immigrant children. Immigrants vary in their desire to assimilate to the host country, and factors such as children's socioeconomic status, ethnicity, and gender will be associated with differential exposure to aspects of the new society (Berry & Sam, 1997; García-Coll & Magnusson, 1997). For example, boys within American society tend to place less value on education, receive lower grades in school, and are more likely to engage in delinquent behaviors than girls (Henderson & Dweck, 1990; McCord, 1990). Given the gender segregation of children's peer groups, boys from immigrant Chinese families may be more likely than girls to encounter native-born students who place a lower value on education. As a result, as shown in Figure 12.4, a decreased emphasis on academics might occur more quickly with immigrant Chinese boys than with Chinese girls. One can easily imagine similar variations according to factors such as children's economic background. Poor immigrant children, who are more likely to attend impoverished and underachieving schools, may lose their interest in education more quickly than their wealthier counterparts in more successful schools. Investigators should carefully consider theoretically meaningful sources of variation such as these, and attempt to use these factors to predict differences in acculturative change between immigrant children.

Documenting individual differences in change within children over time has value beyond establishing the possible range of variation in acculturation.

Figure 12.4
Variation in the Changes in the Value of Education Between Immigrant Children
According to Gender

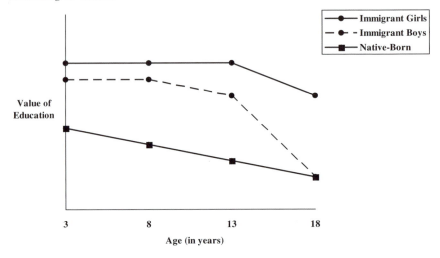

Combining the two levels of analyses provides perhaps the best way to discover
the possible sources of acculturative change. Up to this point, investigators have
relied upon cross-sectional studies that have examined the relations between
various outcomes and indices such as language proficiency, interactions with
nonimmigrants, and involvement with popular culture and leisure activities such
as music and entertainment (e.g., Buriel, 1993; Knight, Bernal, Garza, Cota, &
Ocampo, 1993; Marin, 1993; Saldana, 1995; Szapocznik, Scopetta, Kurtines, &
Aranalde, 1978). These factors may indeed be sources of acculturative change,
but one cannot make that conclusion from cross-sectional studies because it is
unclear whether observed correlations are due to preexisting individual differences. An association between having native-born friends and a lower value of
education could simply reflect a Chinese immigrant child who disliked school
prior to entering the United States. In order to infer that a particular factor may
be a source of acculturative change, one must observe that the factor is associated with actual changes in the attitudes or behaviors of individual children.

Investigators should therefore simultaneously measure possible sources and
developmental outcomes longitudinally in order to determine whether particular factors produce acculturative change *within* immigrant children over time.
At the same time, investigators can assess variations *between* immigrant children
in terms of both the sources and the amount of change. For example, one may
observe that encountering native-born peers does reduce the educational values
of Chinese immigrants who previously placed great importance upon their
schooling. One may also find that the educational emphasis of immigrant boys

drops more precipitously when they encounter native-born peers because the boys' friends tend to place a lower value on schooling more than do the friends of immigrant girls. Such a combination of within- and between-person analyses has been increasingly called for in the study of psychological and developmental change (Kenny, Kashy, & Bolger, 1998; Bryk & Raudenbusch, 1992). The combination would likewise provide a more sophisticated understanding of the sources of acculturative change than cross-sectional studies, and it represents perhaps the greatest benefit of a comparative longitudinal design.

Finally, investigators should examine variation in acculturative change across many different developmental outcomes. Recent observers have questioned the traditional view that acculturation involves a unidirectional shift from traditional to host cultures (Portes & Zhou, 1993; Rumbaut, 1997a). Some have offered alternative two-dimensional models in which individuals may be high or low on dimensions of both the traditional and host cultures. For example, Buriel and De Ment (1997) suggested the immigrants could be either (1) simultaneously oriented to both the traditional and host cultures, (2) oriented to only the traditional or the host culture, or (3) alienated from both cultures. Yet even these two-dimensional frameworks may overgeneralize the process. Immigrant children and their families most likely select some aspects of the host society and not others, such as rapidly learning English and U.S. popular culture but rejecting the emphasis on independence from parents and dating during high school (Gibson & Bhachu, 1991; Zhou & Bankston, 1998). By simultaneously studying changes across a variety of domains, one can better capture the complex negotiations that lie at that heart of the acculturation process among children and adolescents.

CONCLUSION

Research on acculturation needs to move from cross-sectional to longitudinal designs in order to study actual change over time. By following several groups of children longitudinally, investigators can address many important features of the acculturation process. One can disentangle acculturative change from developmental shifts, examine the effects of acculturation on both the level and the developmental progression of children's adjustment, determine the particular aspects of the host society to which immigrant children may be acculturating, and explore possible sources of acculturation by analyzing variations in change.

The approach described in this chapter is intended to be general and flexible. Investigators can examine different aspects of children's adjustment using a variety of methods, including ethnographies, surveys, and experiments. One need not be limited to thinking about quantitative changes in specific outcomes, as there may be qualitative changes in children's acculturation that cannot be accurately represented in terms of increases or decreases. The only requirement of this approach is the comparative study of change over time among different groups of children. Through such comparative longitudinal studies, investigators may even gain insights that reach beyond the topic of acculturation. A child's move from one society to another is a valuable natural experiment that scholars should mine. A better grasp of the effects of such a dramatic transition could enhance our understanding of the more general ways that cultural traditions and social settings shape the development of all children.

NOTES

Support for the preparation of this chapter was provided by a Faculty Scholars Award from the William T. Grant Foundation and a FIRST Award from the National Institute of Child Health and Human Development. Sections of this chapter previously appeared as: Fuligni, A. J. (1998). The adjustment of children from immigrant families. *Current Directions in Psychological Science, 7*, 99–103. Copyright © 1998 American Psychological Society; and Fuligni, A. J. (2001). A comparative longitudinal approach to acculturation among children from immigrant families. *Harvard Educational Review, 71* (3), 556–578. Copyright © 2001 The President and Fellows of Harvard College.

1. The percentage of *all* foreign-born Latin American youths ages sixteen to twenty-four years who were either not enrolled in school or did not receive a high school degree (the traditional criteria used to determine dropout rates) is actually 46 percent. Yet this high figure is misleading because almost half (43 percent) of the Latin American immigrants in this age range never enrolled in U.S. schools because they entered the United States after the age of eighteen and/or because they came in search of employment rather than education. Therefore, the dropout rate among those immigrant youths who actually enrolled in a U.S. school (24 percent) is a better indicator of their adjustment to U.S. schools and a fairer comparison to the dropout rate among American-born youths (McMillen, 1997).

REFERENCES

Berry, J. W., & Sam, D. L. (1997). Acculturation and adaptation. In J. W. Berry, M. H. Segall, & Ç. Kagitçibasi (Eds.), *Handbook of cross-cultural psychology*, Vol. 3, *Social behavior and applications* (pp. 291–326). Needham, MA: Allyn & Bacon.

Bradby, D. (1992). *Language characteristics and academic achievement: A look at Asian and Hispanic eighth graders in NELS:88*. Washington, DC: U.S. Government Printing Office.

Bryk, A. S., & Raudenbusch, S. W. (1992). *Hierarchical linear models: Applications and data analysis methods*. Newbury Park, CA: Sage.

Buriel, R. (1993). Acculturation, respect for cultural differences, and biculturalism among three generations of Mexican American and Euro American school children. *Journal of Genetic Psychology, 154*, 531–543.

Buriel, R., & De Ment, T. (1997). Immigration and sociocultural change in Mexican, Chinese, and Vietnamese American families. In A. Booth, A. C. Crouter, & N.

S. Landale (Eds.), *Immigration and the family: Research and policy on U.S. immigrants* (pp. 165–200). Hillsdale, NJ: Erlbaum.

Caplan, N., Choy, M. H., & Whitmore, J. K. (1991). *Children of the boat people: A study of educational success.* Ann Arbor: University of Michigan Press.

Chen, C., & Stevenson, H. W. (1995). Motivation and mathematics achievement: A comparative study of Asian-American, Caucasian-American, and East Asian high school students. *Child Development, 66,* 1215–1234.

Chilman, C. S. (1993). Hispanic families in the United States: Research perspectives. In H. P. McAdoo (Ed.), *Family ethnicity: Strength in diversity* (pp. 141–163). Newbury Park, CA: Sage.

Collins, L. M., & Horn, J. L. (1991). *Best methods for the analysis of change.* Washington, DC: American Psychological Association.

Eccles, J. S., Midgely, C., Wigfield, A., Buchanan, C. M., Reuman, D., Flanagan, C., & Mac Iver, D. (1993). Development during adolescence: The impact of stage-environment fit on young adolescents' experiences in schools and in families. *American Psychologist, 48,* 90–101.

Feldman, S. S., Mont-Reynaud, R., & Rosenthal, D. A. (1992). When East moves West: The acculturation of values of Chinese adolescents in the U.S. and Australia. *Journal of Research on Adolescence, 2* (2), 147–173.

Fix, M., & Passel, J. S. (1994). *Immigration and immigrants: Setting the record straight.* Washington, DC: Urban Institute.

Fuligni, A. J. (1997). The academic achievement of adolescents from immigrant families: The roles of family background, attitudes, and behavior. *Child Development, 68,* 261–273.

Fuligni, A. J., & Stevenson, H. W. (1995). Time-use and mathematics achievement among Chinese, Japanese, and American high school students. *Child Development, 66,* 830–842.

Fuligni, A. J., Tseng, V., & Lam, M. (1999). Attitudes toward family obligations among American adolescents from Asian, Latin American, and European backgrounds. *Child Development, 70,* 1030–1044.

García-Coll, C., & Magnusson, K. (1997). The psychological experience of immigration: A developmental perspective. In A. Booth, A. C. Crouter, & N. Landale (Eds.), *Immigration and the family: Research and policy on U.S. immigrants* (pp. 91–132). Mahwah, NJ: Erlbaum.

Gibson, M. A., & Bhachu, P. K. (1991). The dynamics of educational decision making: A comparative study of Sikhs in Britain and the United States. In M. A. Gibson & J. U. Ogbu (Eds.), *Minority status and schooling: A comparative study of immigrant and involuntary minorities* (pp. 63–96). New York: Garland.

Harris, K. M. (1998). The health status and risk behavior of adolescents in immigrant families. In D. J. Hernandez (Ed.), *Children of immigrants: Health, adjustment, and public assistance* (pp. 286–347). Washington, DC: National Academy Press.

Henderson, V. L., & Dweck, C. S. (1990). Motivation and achievement. In S. S. Feldman & G. R. Elliot (Eds.), *At the threshold: The developing adolescent* (pp. 308–329). Cambridge, MA: Harvard University Press.

Ho, D. Y. F. (1981). Traditional patterns of socialization in Chinese society. *Acta Psychologica Taiwanica, 23,* 81–95.

Kao, G. (1998). Psychological well-being and educational achievement among immigrant youth. In D. J. Hernandez (Ed.), *Children of immigrants: Health, adjustment, and public assistance* (pp. 410–477). Washington, DC: National Academy Press.

Kao, G., & Tienda, M. (1995). Optimism and achievement: The educational performance of immigrant youth. *Social Science Quarterly, 76,* 1–19.

Kenny, D. A., Kashy, D. A., & Bolger, N. (1998). Data analysis in social psychology. In D. Gilbert, S. Fiske, & G. Lindzey (Eds.), *Handbook of social psychology* (pp. 233–265). New York: McGraw-Hill.

Knight, G. P., Bernal, M. E., Garza, C. A., Cota, M. K., & Ocampo, K. A. (1993). Family socialization and the ethnic identity of Mexican-American children. *Journal of Cross-Cultural Psychology, 24,* 99–114.

Landale, N. S., & Oropesa, R. S. (1995). *Immigrant children and the children of immigrants: Inter- and intra-ethnic group differences in the United States.* Population research Group (PRG) Research Paper no. 95-2. East Lansing: Institute for Public Policy and Social Research, Michigan State University.

Marin, G. (1993). Influence of acculturation on familism and self-identification among Hispanics. In M. E. Bernal & G. P. Knight (Eds.), *Ethnic identity: Formation and transmission among Hispanics and other minorities* (pp. 181–196). Albany: State University of New York Press.

Matute-Bianchi, M. E. (1991). Situational ethnicity and patterns of school performance among immigrant and non-immigrant Mexican-descent students. In M. A. Gibson & J. U. Ogbu (Eds.), *Minority status and schooling: A comparative study of immigrant and involuntary minorities* (pp. 205–248). New York: Garland.

McCord, J. (1990). Problem behaviors. In S. S. Feldman & G. R. Elliot (Eds.), *At the threshold: The developing adolescent* (pp. 414–430). Cambridge, MA: Harvard University Press.

McMillen, M. (1997). *Dropout rates in the United States: 1995.* Washington, DC: U.S. Government Printing Office.

Ogbu, J. U. (1991). Immigrant and involuntary minorities in comparative perspective. In M. A. Gibson & J. U. Ogbu (Eds.), *Minority status and schooling: A comparative study of immigrant and involuntary minorities* (pp. 3–36). New York: Garland.

Parke, R. D., & Buriel, R. (1998). Socialization in the family: Ethnic and ecological perspectives. In W. Damon & N. Eisenberg (Eds.), *Handbook of child psychology* (5th ed.), Vol. 2, *Social, emotional, and personality development* (pp. 463–552). New York: Wiley.

Portes, A., & Rumbaut, R. G. (1996). *Immigrant America: A portrait* (2nd ed.). Berkeley: University of California Press.

Portes, A., & Zhou, M. (1993). The new second generation: Segmented assimilation and its variants. *The Annals of the American Academy of Political and Social Science, 530,* 74–96.

Rumbaut, R. G. (1994). The crucible within: Ethnic identity, self-esteem and segmented assimilation among children of immigrants. *International Migration Review, 28,* 748–794.

———. (1995). The new Californians: Comparative research findings on the educational progress of immigrant children. In R. G. Rumbaut & W. A. Cornelius (Eds.),

California's immigrant children: Theory, research, and implications for educational policy (pp. 17–70). San Diego: Center for U.S.-Mexican Studies, University of California.

———. (1997a). Paradoxes (and orthodoxies) of assimilation. *Sociological Perspectives, 40* (3), 483–511.

———. (1997b). Ties that bind: Immigration and immigrant families in the United States. In A. Booth, A. C. Crouter, & N. Landale (Eds.), *Immigration and the family: Research and policy on U.S. Immigrants* (pp. 3–46). Mahwah, NJ: Erlbuam.

———. (1998, March). Transformations: The post-immigrant generation in an age of diversity. Paper presented at the annual meeting of the Eastern Sociological Society, Philadelphia.

Saldana, D. H. (1995). Acculturative stress: Minority status and distress. In A. M. Padilla (Ed.), *Hispanic psychology: Critical issues in theory and research* (pp. 43–56). Thousand Oaks, CA: Sage.

Shon, S. P., & Ja, D. Y. (1982). Asian families. In M. McGoldrick, J. K. Pearce, & J. Giordano (Eds.), *Ethnicity and family therapy* (pp. 208–228). New York: Guilford Press.

Steele, C. M. (1997). A threat in the air: How stereotypes shape intellectual identity and performance. *American Psychologist, 52,* 613–629.

Steinberg, L. (1996). *Beyond the classroom: Why school reform has failed and what parents need to do.* New York: Simon & Schuster.

Stevenson, H. W., Chen, C., & Lee, S. Y. (1992). Chinese families. In I. E. Sigel (Series Ed.) and J. L. Roopnarine & B. Carter (Vol. Eds.), *Annual advances in applied developmental psychology,* Vol. 5, *Parent-child socialization in diverse cultures* (pp. 17–33). Norwood, NJ: Ablex.

Stevenson, H. W., & Stigler, J. W. (1992). *The learning gap.* New York: Simon & Schuster.

Suárez-Orozco, C., & Suárez-Orozco, M. M. (1995). *Transformations: Immigration, family life, and achievement motivation among Latino adolescents.* Stanford, CA: Stanford University Press.

Sue, S., & Okazaki, S. (1990). Asian-American educational achievement: A phenomenon in search of an explanation. *American Psychologist, 45,* 913–920.

Sung, B. L. (1987). *The adjustment experience of Chinese immigrant children in New York City.* New York: Center for Migration Studies.

Szapocznik, J., & Kurtines, W. M. (1993). Family psychology and cultural diversity: Opportunities for theory, research, and application. *American Psychologist, 48,* 400–407.

Szapocznik, J., Scopetta, M. A., Kurtines, W., & Aranalde, M. A. (1978). Theory and measurement of acculturation. *Interamerican Journal of Psychology, 12,* 113–130.

United Nations Commission on Population and Development (1997). *International migration and development: The concise report.* New York: United Nations.

U.S. Bureau of the Census (1993). *We the American: Foreign born.* Washington, DC: U.S. Government Printing Office.

———. (1997). *Current population reports: The foreign-born population: 1996.* Washington, DC: U.S. Government Printing Office.

Waters, M. C. (1994). Ethnic and racial identities of second-generation black immigrants in New York City. *International Migration Review, 28*, 795–820.

Zhou, M. (1997). Growing up American: The challenge confronting immigrant children and children of immigrants. *Annual Review of Sociology, 23*, 63–95.

Zhou, M., & Bankston, C. L. (1998). *Growing up American: How Vietnamese children adapt to life in the United States.* New York: Russell Sage.

CHAPTER 13

Factors Tied to the Schooling of Children of English-Speaking Caribbean Immigrants in the United States

Jaipaul Roopnarine, Pauline F. Bynoe, and Ronald Singh

Among the diverse ethnic and linguistic groups that constitute the large numbers of new immigrants in the United States are people from the Caribbean. Population movement from the Caribbean to the United States is not a new phenomenon. It dates back to the nineteenth century (Foner, 2001a; Marshall, 1982; Vickerman, 2001). But it was not until after World War II that widespread migration from the Caribbean to the United States began in earnest. The decades subsequent to World War II witnessed sizable influxes of immigrants from the Spanish-, English-, and French-speaking countries of the Caribbean to the United States (see Foner, 2001a; Grosfougel, 1997; Roopnarine & Shin, 2003). By 1990, an estimated 2.7 million people had migrated from the Caribbean to the United States, and this number grew to over 3.5 million in 1998 (U.S. Department of Justice, Immigration and Naturalization Service [INS], 1998). These figures do not include undocumented people. The growth in population movement has been so sharp that some 50 percent of Dominicans have relatives in the United States (Rumbaut, 1997), and in some cases this may be true of immigrants from the English-speaking Caribbean in North America and Europe as well. Table 13.1 presents a breakdown of immigrants from different Caribbean countries to the United States between 1988 and 1998.

A popular destination for Caribbean immigrants to the United States is the New York City area (e.g., Brooklyn, Queens, Bronx, Jersey City, and Newark). More than 50 percent of non-Hispanic African Caribbeans reside in New York City (Kalmijin, 1996; Rong & Brown, 2001), among them 40 percent of all Jamaicans who migrated between 1990 and 1994 (Vickerman, 2001). Table 13.2 displays the residential patterns of newly arriving Caribbean immigrants in the five boroughs of New York City (New York City Department of Planning, 1999).

Table 13.1
Caribbean Immigrants to the United States: 1988–1998

Country	1988-1992	1993-1998
Barbados	7,367	5,413
Belize	10,978	4,397
Dominican Republic	179,481	222,165
Dominica	4,113	3,607
Grenada	5,009	4,202
Guyana	51,628	44,117
Haiti	127,317	84,340
Jamaica	113,245	100,063
Montserrat	647	517
St. Kitts and Nevis	3,807	2,413
St. Lucia	3,568	3,108
St. Vincent and Grenadines	3,994	3,131
Trinidad and Tobago	31,496	36,898

With the surge of immigrants from the Caribbean are concomitant increases in the school-age population of children born to immigrant parents and those who migrated with their parents. It is estimated that currently about one in five children in the United States lives in an immigrant household (Suárez-Orozco & Todorova, 2001). There are about 14 million children in the United States whose parents are immigrants (Portes & Rumbaut, 1990). The nation's largest school districts are saturated with children from immigrant families. For example, about 48 percent of the children in the New York City public schools are from immigrant households (Suárez-Orozco, 2001), with a significant number from the Caribbean. There is a troubling tendency for some groups of children of immigrants (e.g., those of color) to be concentrated in substandard schools in inner urban centers (Suárez-Orozco, 2001). The responsibility for providing appropriate, high-quality educational experiences for children of immigrants and

Table 13.2

Recent Immigrants from the Selected Countries of the Caribbean in the Different Boroughs of New York City (1990–1996)

| Country | | | Boroughs | | | |
	Bronx	Brooklyn	Manhattan	Queens	Staten Island	Total
Barbados	273	2,903	183	561	25	3,945
Grenada	112	3,042	91	199	17	3,461
Guyana	6,137	17,335	785	17,497	150	41,909
Haiti	316	14,673	1,045	4,959	60	21,053
Jamaica	13,221	19,427	1,421	10,602	148	44,819
St. Vincent	106	2,236	61	226	13	2,624
Trinidad and Tobago	1,592	13,132	968	5,478	255	21,425

Source: Newest New Yorkers: 1995–1996, New York City Department of Planning, September, 1999.

immigrant children can be taxing to most large metropolitan areas that are currently in the throes of financial problems and massive teacher shortages.

As with social scientists, mental health and medical professionals, policy makers, and educators (Berry, 1998; Gopal-McNicol, 1993; Munroe-Blum, Boyle, Offord, & Kates, 1989; Gibson & Ogbu, 1991; Pawliuk, Grizenko, Chan-Yip, Gantous, Matthew, & Nguyen, 1996; Suárez-Orozco, 2001), our general concerns have their roots in the psychosocial adjustment and educational experiences of children of immigrants and immigrant children and their families. In this chapter, the focus is on factors within the family and the family-school interface that, we believe, are pivotal to providing quality educational services to children of families who immigrated from the English-speaking countries of the Caribbean (e.g., Barbados, Belize, Grenada, Guyana, Jamaica, Trinidad and Tobago, and the other smaller islands of the eastern Caribbean) to the United States. There is increased interest in the education of immigrant children of color in general (e.g., disproportionate special education placements, school failure, gender disparity in achievement), the differential school success rates among children of immigrants (Fuligni, 2001; Fuligni, this volume; Rong & Brown, 2001; White-Davis, 1996), selective assimilation patterns of Caribbean immigrant families, the conditions of the schools that immigrant children and the children of immigrants of color attend, and the parental knowledge base about the "cultural and educational scripts" regarding schooling in the United States (Lopez, 2001).

Accordingly, we thought that shedding further light on beliefs, goals, and educational processes within the family and in schools that bear on the education of young children (up to eight years of age) of English-speaking Caribbean immigrants might be useful in informing and sharpening practices within the broad educational community. Furthermore, by focusing on the initial encounters of children with formal schooling, we are poised to identify factors that place children of immigrants on good footing for a successful school career, and to arrest those that may stand in the way. Altogether, we direct attention to the processes of adjusting to a new society, parent-child relationships and the implications for children's schooling, parental beliefs about schooling, parent-teacher relationships, culturally appropriate practices and the early childhood curriculum, and factors that affect children's performance in school.

THE DYNAMIC PROCESSES OF ACCULTURATION

How do immigrant families structure/restructure their lives in a new cultural community, and what implications might this have for understanding school outcomes in the United States? Do teachers and other school personnel recognize the varied backgrounds, entry points, and patterns of adjustment associated with immigrant families and their children? An often-misguided assumption is that immigrants and their children have little or no prior knowledge of the United States and its cultural underpinnings. That is, all "immigrants start at some point near American cultural ground zero and then proceed only post arrival to 'become American' in word, deed, and ultimately thought" (Rumbaut, 1997, p. 948). This could not be further from the truth. Immigrants from different parts of the world enter the United States with diverse backgrounds and skills: from highly educated professionals with good English skills, who may have traveled to the United States prior to migration, or at the very least have some working knowledge of the culture through the mass media (e.g., immigrants from Asia), to those who are less skilled and may have limited knowledge about life in the United States (e.g., immigrants from Latin America) (Foner, 2001a). Diversity is also mirrored in the socioeconomic lives and accomplishments of new immigrants. As Rumbaut (1997) states, "Different immigrant nationalities account at once for the highest and lowest rates of education, self-employment, homeownership, poverty, welfare dependency, and fertility, as well as the lowest rates of divorce and female-headed single-parent families, and the highest proportions of children under age 18 residing with both parents" (p. 947). In view of the various levels of professional skills and English language competence, familiarity with life in the United States, and socioeconomic starting points, the adjustment process for new immigrant groups is likely to follow divergent pathways.

In framing our discussion on Caribbean immigrant families and schooling in the United States, we move away from the linear "assimilationist" perspective on immigrant adjustment (for good discussions, see DeWind & Kasinitz, 1997;

and Rumbaut, 1997), but adhere to the notion that movement from one society to another for an extended stay would require some level of acculturation or integration, the complexity of which varies and evolves over time (Rumbaut, 1997) and is likely bidirectional (Foner, 1997). Just as the adjustment process does not begin upon entry to a new country, it does not end with the acquisition of employment, housing, and schooling for children. In terms of the latter, as families adjust to their new society, there is the possibility that they are changing the very institutions they interact with and shaping the delivery of educational and social services they seek (Foner, 1997, 2001a).

The assimilationist framework has dominated much of the discourse on and analysis of immigrant adjustment to a new society (DeWind & Kasinitz, 1997). A major tenet of this view is that over time people move away from natal-culture values, behavioral practices, and beliefs toward the incorporation of those in their new society. The process is set in motion by cultural assimilation or acculturation, which may be a prelude to structural, identificational, attitude-receptional, behavioral-receptional, and civic assimilation (Gordon, 1964; Zhou, 1997). It is argued that the degree to which different immigrant groups successfully meld with dominant culture views and life in American society depends on ethnicity, social class, intermarriage, length of residence, level of education, intensity of contact with the dominant culture, and English-language competence (Warner & Srole, 1945; Zhou, 1997). Although it continues to be hailed as having good explanatory power in defining current waves of immigrant incorporation into American society (Alba & Nee, 1997; DeWind & Kasinitz, 1997), the assimilationist perspective has been criticized on several grounds: for not considering the role of immigrants as architects in shaping their own lives and opportunities in the new society; for being wed to the notion of a unified set of values, beliefs, and behaviors that all immigrant groups aspire to; and for seeing other cultural beliefs and practices as less desirable and ineffectual for life in the United States (Zhou, 1997).

Noting the shortcomings of the assimilationist perspective, segmented assimilation theory considers the socioeconomic structure of American society and the different starting points of immigrants in telescoping their eventual destinies (Zhou, 1997). This theory proposes that due to the social and economic stratification of American society, the children of new immigrants experience different patterns of adaptation that may result in various social and economic outcomes: acculturation and integration into middle-class American life; retrenchment and membership in the underclass; and economic integration into the middle class, with the process of acculturation occurring at a slower pace and with more calculated attempts to maintain seminal natal-culture beliefs and practices. Not unlike the assimilationist framework, in Zhou's theory (1997), ethnicity (its advantages and disadvantages), network relationships and support (social capital), education and social class, and other sociodemographic factors (e.g., length of residence, gender) are all seen as influencing the acculturation process.

In the New York City area, English-speaking Caribbean immigrants constitute ethnic enclaves in Brooklyn (e.g., Crown Heights and Flatbush areas), Queens (e.g., Richmond Hill), North Bronx (Crowder, 1999), Jersey City, Newark, and East Orange, New Jersey. They often settle in neighborhoods once occupied by European immigrants or adjacent to African Americans or other ethnic groups from the Caribbean. For them, the process of acculturation appears paradoxical. The presumed advantages that many Caribbean immigrant families accrue through their English-language skills (see Folkes, 1996, for a discussion of Creole, Creolese)—greater exposure to American culture through trade, music, tourism, the media, and social ties between relatives in the Caribbean and United States—may be offset by ethnic membership. That is, being people of color, English-speaking Caribbean immigrants must confront issues in housing, education, and occupational discrimination that still plague American society. Not accustomed to being designated a "minority group" in the Caribbean, these immigrants quickly become aware of the inequities in American society that are attributed to skin color and class (Vickerman, 2001; Waters, 1999; Zhou, 1997). It is well documented that these two factors affect upward economic mobility, school spending and the quality of neighborhood schools, and the general quality of family life (Oropesa & Landale, 1997; Waters, 1999; Wilson, 1996). So what patterns of adjustment do English-speaking immigrant families and their children assume in setting up life in America?

Similar to other immigrant groups, English-speaking Caribbean immigrants are far from being homogeneous. Quite a few are in unskilled jobs, but others have joined the civil service and teaching professions in the New York City area en masse (Grasmuck & Grosfoguel, 1997; Roopnarine, 1999), and levels of educational achievement and home ownership have risen over the last two decades (e.g., 30.3 percent of Jamaicans owned homes and 14.7 percent were college graduates in 1990—U.S. Bureau of the Census, 1993); in the sample of a recent study, 28 percent of men and 22 percent of women were college graduates (Roopnarine, 1999; Vickerman, 2001). We agree with Zhou (1997) that, generally, immigrant incorporation in the United States assumes different paths that result in different economic, social, political, and educational accomplishments. However, we believe that for certain immigrant groups, social, educational, and economic mobility is sabotaged by ethnic membership, a point made repeatedly by Zhou and others (Alba & Nee, 1997; Vickerman, 2001); groups with darker skin may experience delayed acculturation in terms of economic, social, and educational gains (Gans, 1992). For Caribbean immigrants, it is suggested that skin color weighs heavily in interacting with neighborhood factors (access to quality housing, schools, and businesses; ethnic density), ethnic identity, class (education and income), gender, and social networks in determining how successfully families and children negotiate their way through daily life in America (Foner, 1997; Rumbaut, 1997). Through their parents' experiences and in their own encounters with social and educational institutions, children of Caribbean immigrants come to inherit the burden of skin color.

As might be surmised from what has been discussed so far, more contemporary conceptual frameworks on immigrant adjustment shy away from a unidimensional and linear treatises on the topic (Zhou, 1997). Such is the case for considerations of the educational achievement of children of immigrants. In this regard, a trimodal pattern of adaptation to schooling has been proposed: some children exceed their nonimmigrant peers in general attitudes toward education and academic performance; there are those whose academic performances are on par with a vast majority of children in the United States; and then there are children of immigrants who perform rather poorly in school (Suárez-Orozco, 2001). One of the major problems with research on immigrants is that the adaptation of children and their parents is rarely viewed longitudinally (Fuligni, this volume) or in concert. It is conceivable that the adjustment experiences of parents and children converge at some points but diverge at others.

Taking into account what has already been said about skin color and class, Caribbean immigrant parents' adjustment patterns, parental psychology about their child's schooling, their degree of involvement in their child's schooling in the United States, and the quality and quantity of their own schooling would combine to produce differential educational outcomes in their children during the early childhood years. Obviously, other factors such as family structure, economic and social resources, gender of child, age of entry into the United States, "ideologies of optimism," and other social and psychological factors may also have a hand in the adjustment process and school performance of young children of Caribbean immigrants (see Suárez-Orozco, 2001; Rumbaut, 1997; Zhou, 1997). Building on prior research and models of acculturation (e.g., Berry, 1998; Foner, 1997; Gibson, 1988; Zhou, 1997), we offer a handful of untested permutations of adjustment scenarios in Caribbean immigrant families that should be interpreted along a continuum. By no means are they meant to be exhaustive or deny the confluence of forces at play in the immigrant adjustment process.

Beginning with a *synchronous parent-child adjustment pattern*, Caribbean immigrant parents consciously weave natal-culture values and beliefs about childrearing and schooling with those present in the United States. In these situations parent-child relationships are more sanguine and children have unbridled support for intellectual and social pursuits from parents. This posture is primed to optimize psychological and educational outcomes in children (Berry, 1998).

By contrast, in a *asynchronous parent-child adjustment pattern*, parents push natal-culture scripts about childrearing and schooling at all cost while ignoring the cultural and educational metamorphosis in their children—claiming to understand life in America, when in reality these parents may not. They mostly refuse to change their stand on various matters, proclaiming that the beliefs and practices they were brought up with in the Caribbean can serve children well in the United States (e.g., a good spanking now and then is not so bad; children should listen to their parents no matter what). There is strong support for these beliefs in what have been termed multilocal binational families (Foner, 1997; Caribbean immigrants literally ship their children to the home country to be "straightened out"). In some domains, young children show a better level of understanding of, and an inclination toward, the practices and beliefs about life and the milieu of schooling inherent in the United States. At times, they become "family experts" on these issues and outpace their parents in the adjustment process. As these children unleash the cultural and educational acumen acquired in the United States, they are likely to challenge the rhythms of cultural life and expectations in the immigrant household. Alienation between parents and children and diminished school outcomes, due to parent-child tensions, are not unexpected.

But not all parents who hold on to natal-culture beliefs and practices about childrearing and education are undermining their children's adjustment and schooling. There are families who gradually relinquish natal-culture beliefs and practices in a *staggered pattern* (see Gibson, 1988; Zhou, 1997). They see a good immersion in Caribbean beliefs and practices initially (e.g., a strong hand in parenting) as laying the groundwork for coping with life in a new society. These parents show a propensity to grow along with their children, relinquishing and modifying old patterns of behaviors, en route to embracing those in their new society that are more functional. It is declared that children raised in these households eventually adjust to and perform well in school.

Finally, there are those situations in which both parents and children experience *extreme adjustment and cultural difficulties*. When this scenario is coupled with socioeconomic woes, families and children experience severe hardship. Parents may experience prolonged psychological and social dysfunction and eventually become disenfranchised from mainstream life. For most children, their mental health and schooling can be severely compromised. Within these clinically and economically distressed families, there is the likelihood that a small number of children are able to insulate themselves, because of personality factors and coping styles, from the hardships of their parents. This small cohort may continue to be plagued by adjustment problems but performs reasonably well in school.

PARENT-CHILD RELATIONSHIPS

The nature and quality of parent-child relationships among diverse groups of immigrant families and their relevance for schooling have been the focus of systematic investigations (Chao, 1994; Roopnarine, 1999; Suárez-Orozco &

Todorova, 2001). Both psychological and sociological studies (e.g., Arnold, 1997; Millette, 1998) have pointed to the stresses and strains in parent-child and couple relationships post-immigration, and to the role of the family in providing a haven for devising strategies to cope with the challenges of facing life in a new society (Foner, 1997). Educational studies have investigated different aspects of the immigrant home environment for supporting academic achievement (e.g., strong emphasis on education, heavy investment in homework, family work ethic) (Lopez, 2001; Rumbaut, 1997). Yet others (Berry, 1998) have articulated the prudence of blending natal-culture childrearing practices with those of the new society in determining healthy child development outcomes (Berry, 1998). The aim in this segment is to attend to issues tied to parent-child relationships in Caribbean immigrant families that may have "crossover effects" on young children's schooling.

A basic premise has been that parents are children's first teachers and the home-school partnership is vital in charting a course for good yields from schooling (Comer, 1988; Sigel, 1985). An underlying difficulty may be that immigrant families are unfamiliar with the processes and demands of schools in the United States. Bridging knowledge and expectations about childrearing (e.g., behavior management) and educational practices between the home and school environments can facilitate educational planning. In keeping with theoretical frameworks (e.g., developmental niche; Super & Harkness, 1997) and research evidence (Darling & Steinberg, 1993) that emphasize the role of parental beliefs, practices, goals, and styles in shaping childrearing and education, we offer a glimpse as to how parenting style, parental discipline techniques (as reflective of one aspect of parental management), sources of parent-child conflict, and resilience bound to community support are intertwined with the schooling of children of Caribbean immigrants. The hope is that teachers and other school personnel who are "in tune" with immigrant families' childrearing practices and beliefs and expectations about schooling will be at a distinct advantage in their efforts to meet the educational needs of the children they teach and to solicit high levels of parental involvement in school-related activities.

Parenting Style

Based on over forty years of research (for a good review, see Darling & Steinberg, 1993), parenting style and its influence on children's academic performance and social competence has occupied center stage in the parenting literature. After studying largely European American families, proponents (e.g., Baumrind, 1967) of the importance of this construct suggest that an authoritative style that is more democratic, as opposed to authoritarian or permissive, in its approach is desirable for raising children who are self-reliant and self-assured. The relative importance attributed to parenting styles as they pertain to families from diverse cultural backgrounds has raised a bit of controvery. There are parents who govern their children's lives (Chao, 1994), make decisions for them throughout childhood (Shin, 2001), and mix high control with loving displays and acceptance during social and cognitive transactions with them. Stated differently, there are parents who engage in an active process of child training that is quite measured. Additionally, in other families, such as the Aka in central Africa, parents are seemingly permissive yet raise children who acquire the skills necessary to survive in their immediate environment (Hewlett, 1992). A case can be made that Baumrind's classic parenting typologies and their presumed outcomes are less clear when applied to non–European American groups (Chao, 1994, 2001; see also LeVine, this volume). Nevertheless, the authoritative style is widely accepted in academic and clinical circles as optimal for childrearing.

The parenting styles of adults in the Caribbean are characterized as a mixture of authoritarian punitive control, and indulgence (Leo-Rhynie, 1997; see also Gopaul-McNicol, 1993; Payne & Furnham, 1992) and permissiveness, depending on the ethnic group (Roopnarine, Bynoe, Singh, & Romel, in press). If we use the findings of the North American studies on parenting styles as a gauge, the childrearing formulas employed by Caribbean parents might spell trouble for children's positive development. Of the two studies we could find that examined the parenting styles of Caribbean immigrant parents, one provided evidence of the existence of an authoritarian style among families residing in Newark, New Jersey (DeYoung & Zigler, 1994), whereas the other reported that parents had the highest scores on the authoritative dimension of the Buri Parental Authority Questionnaire in families in the New York metropolitan area (Roopnarine, 1999). Our intuition is that newly arriving Caribbean immigrant parents in the United States basically hold on to internal working models about childrearing that are firmly planted in the expectations of respect for parents and teachers and the display of manners and obedience. However, there is uncertainty about their utility in the United States. To this end, some (e.g., Foner, 1997) have hinted that qualitative changes in approaches to parenting are inevitable as Caribbean families begin to confront practices in their own lives and those in their new communities.

At this juncture, research findings on the effects of parenting styles and levels of parental involvement on schooling in different family configurations in Caribbean immigrant families are nonexistent. Preliminary research on Caribbean immigrant families has failed to draw significant associations between parenting styles and kindergarten or prekindergarten children's early academic skills (Roopnarine, 1999). A key question remains as to whether other factors such as parental beliefs, goals and expectations for children, gender, family structure and multiple sources of support for education, regular monitoring of school progress, and parent-teacher relationships exercise more influence on the early schooling of children of Caribbean immigrants than parental style per se. These potential associations remain largely unexplored.

Discipline and Punishment

Perhaps more a part of the nomenclature of authoritarian than other parenting styles, much has been written about the harsh discipline techniques employed by Caribbean parents (Payne, 1989) and, to a lesser extent, Caribbean immigrant parents in the United States (Gopaul-McNicol, 1993; Trasher & Anderson, 1988). The essential connections we want to make embody the potentially harmful effects of severe punishment on children's psychosocial adjustment and the transfer of parental expectations about discipline from the home to the classroom environment. Emboldened by the desire to keep children "in line," Caribbean immigrant parents often complain that American society is "too lax" when it comes to disciplining children (Roopnarine, 1999). The overall desire is to have swifter enforcement of strong discipline at home and in schools when behavioral transgressions occur. Anecdotally, teachers working with children of Caribbean immigrants in the New York City area suggest that parents often make such requests of them (Bynoe, 1997).

In the face of empirical evidence on the impact of harsh discipline on childhood development (Rohner, Bourque, & Elordi, 1996; Turner & Finkelhor, 1996), Caribbean immigrant parents who use assertive and physically punishing management strategies could create psychological distress in young children, which in turn might conspire against school adjustment and academic performance (Arnold, 1997). Furthermore, cultural discrepancies in modes of discipline between the home and school contexts can be perplexing to young children and strain parent-teacher relationships. As children become more firmly entrenched in schooling, they are likely to make mental note of methods of discipline valued by the school community.

Sources of Parent-Child Difficulties

Not surprisingly, a chief source of difficulty for Caribbean immigrant parents stems from attempts to discipline and exercise authority over their children. In this vein, they view American society as infringing on their freedom to be effective parents. Simultaneously, children become aware of "their rights" as individuals in American society, and some openly question extreme parental authority by rebelling or being disobedient (as one Caribbean immigrant parent remarked, "You cannot hit these children, they are ready to call 911") (Arnold, 1997; see also Foner, 1997). The challenges marshaled by their children were quite distressing to some Caribbean immigrant parents, who manifested signs of despair and depression (Arnold, 1997). Equally disquieting were concerns about being charged with possible abuse when harsh punishment was employed at home (parents report to us that they keep their children at home if they have bruises rather than run the risk of being suspected of abuse).

Difficulties may also originate from prolonged separation and reunification with parents due to serial migration. In a longitudinal study of immigrant student adaptation in the United States (Suárez-Orozco & Todorova, 2001), 85 percent of sample youths were separated from one or both parents during the migration process (only in 11 percent of Dominican, 4 percent of Central American, 4 percent of Haitian, and 15 percent of Mexican families did all members come together as immigrants), and the length of separation from mothers and/ or fathers was of extended duration. Twenty-five percent of Dominican and 34 percent of Haitian children were separated from their mothers for more than 5.2 years. On average, West Indians in England were separated from their children for 5.2 years due to migration (Arnold, 1997).

These separations can be very painful to children as they are forced to renounce their primary attachment figures and forge relationships with new caregivers. With limited resources for counseling agencies or personnel in developing countries, children are often left to mourn the loss of contacts with attachment figures privately (Roopnarine & Shin, 2003). Relatedly, parents reported extreme sadness in leaving very young children behind (Suárez-Orozco & Todorova, 2001). With the euphoria surrounding parent-child reunions behind them, relationships in immigrant families can be difficult for both parents and children. Upon reunification, children who were separated from parents were more likely to express depressive symptoms than those who immigrated with their parents, and there were feelings of disorientation as children had to reestablish relationships with parental figures who had also changed or were in new relationships (Suárez-Orozco & Todorova, 2001). Data on Caribbean children in England indicated that they were distraught, withdrawn, and resentful, and that their parents had difficulty communicating with them (Arnold, 1997; Cheetham, 1972; Sewell-Coker, Hamilton-Collins, & Fein, 1985).

Resilience and Broad Support for Education

As noted previously, Caribbean immigrant families in the New York City area live in densely populated ethnic enclaves, establish multilocal and binational families with ties to their countries of origin and other communities in North America (e.g., Toronto, Miami, Los Angeles). They set up businesses (restaurants, real estate, beauty salons) and informal childcare and child-minding alliances, build churches and assemblies, and find employment and housing for relatives and friends upon their arrival in the United States (Vickerman, 2001). In the immigrant neighborhoods, the businesses serve as emblems of economic success and the interpersonal networks provide social capital that reinforce cultural values that may inoculate some children against school and social failure. Parental involvement in children's schooling may not always be reflected in direct contacts with teachers or investment in designing school curricula (Lopez,

2001). Instead, Caribbean immigrant parents stress the inherent value of education for upward mobility and as a "tonic" for discrimination (Rong & Brown, 2001). They offer anecdotes from their own lives to motivate their children to learn. In short, the social resources within the family and community can buffer some of the noxious effects of poor schools and economic hardship.

Taken together, the areas of parenting considered provide a window for comprehending continuities and discontinuities between the home experiences of Caribbean immigrant children and those in their schools and society at large. Clearly, some of the practices (e.g., discipline) of Caribbean immigrant parents are at odds with those advanced by schools in the United States and may cause anxiety in young children who are introduced to situations where they must learn to cope with methods of behavior management that are sometimes conflicting. Teachers are also in a precarious position since they must be sensitive to the different child training methods in their students' home environment and culture, while ardently advocating for the respectful treatment of children. Turning to styles of parenting, it is not yet known whether the admixture of parenting styles displayed by Caribbean immigrant parents have deleterious effects on children's academic and social competence. There is reason to believe that more autocratic forms of parental behaviors among Caribbean immigrants are disconcerting to young children and could be a source of distress for them (Arnold, 1997; Roopnarine, 1999). Adjustment problems linked to separation and reunification with parents are likely to be manifested in school (Suárez-Orozco, 2001). Amid the wide range of issues they confront during the adjustment process, Caribbean immigrant parents tap into an elaborate network of kinship and nonkinship members for support for childrearing and the education of young children.

BELIEFS ABOUT SCHOOLING

Research findings spelled out in several volumes on childhood development (Goodnow & Collins, 1991; Harkness & Super, 1996; Siegel, 1985) confirm the importance of parental belief systems in childrearing and education. Parental cultural beliefs or ethnotheories about caring for and educating children are important not only in articulating parental goals and desires for children but also in the structuring of cognitive and social experiences at home and school. For example, based on their beliefs about education, parents may demand specific experiences for children in and out of school (e.g., strict discipline, school uniforms, homework). The direct and indirect influences of parental belief systems have been delineated in several papers (e.g., Sigel & McGillicuddy-DeLisi, 2002). Our primary focus is on the interplay between immigrant parents' beliefs about early educational training and those that guide practices in their children's schools.

To get a better handle on Caribbean immigrant parents' beliefs about different dimensions of schooling and children's school experiences, it is first necessary to outline briefly the current system of education that exists in the Caribbean. Patterned after what was in place in England at the time of colonial occupation, most English-speaking Caribbean countries implemented principles of educational training that were narrowly focused on rote memory (Holder, 1998; Scott-MacDonald, 1997), strict obedience to authority figures, harsh discipline and punishment techniques (e.g., flogging children, making them stand by the blackboard with hands outstretched; see Anderson & Payne, 1994), academic tracking and elitism, narrowly defined subject areas often void of emphasis in the arts, and highly structured and formal methods of instruction (Evans, 1997). In the process of changing, elements of these practices persist today as Caribbean educators strive to implement an educational system that is more culturally and academically relevant to Caribbean students.

Taking into account the recent of arrival of sizable numbers of English-speaking Caribbean immigrants (Foner, 2001a), it is proposed that, as was the situation with parenting behaviors, the fundamental ingredients of the above mentioned ideas about schooling (internal working models) migrate with Caribbean parents to the United States, but they may become reorganized due to exposure to concepts about schooling and parenting that are more democratically oriented (Foner, 1997). Put differently, over time parents are likely to revise some of their educational and childrearing goals for their children after considering institutional practices and demands placed on them in their new communities. Bearing this in mind, we examine English-speaking Caribbean immigrant parents' ethnotheories about two components of early childhood education that have ties to their country of origin: a rigorous academic curriculum and extensive homework for young children.

Beliefs About the Early Childhood Curriculum

What constitutes appropriate early childhood education has been an ongoing debate for decades. Views on the structure and content of experiences within early childhood settings span practices that are based on constructivist principles to those driven by behavioral psychology (Roopnarine & Johnson, 2000). All of this is further complicated by the fact that different cultures have their own sets of beliefs about the meaning and value of early childhood education (Holloway, 1999; Tobin, Wu, & Davidson, 1989). In the United States, the National Association for the Education of Young Children (NAEYC) (Bredekamp & Copple, 1997) has recommended goals and practices for developmentally appropriate education for young children, and other august organizations (e.g., Committee on Early Childhood Pedagogy, National Academy of Sciences and National Research Council, 1999) have convened to discuss early childhood educational goals in global perspective. Typically, what is espoused has a constructivist base emerging out of the thinking of Jean Piaget and other cognitive developmentalists (e.g., Bruner, 1999; Sigel, 1991, 2000). With sensitive and appropriate adult guidance, the child is permitted unlimited elbow room to explore and discover the object environment and to formulate its own understanding of the world. This philosophical orientation acknowledges the child's cognitive and social developmental levels in educational planning and the preparation of the classroom environment. A play-based curriculum is encouraged, and rigorous academic activities are frowned upon, as they are seen as causing undue anxiety for children early in their lives (Elkind, 1981, 1987). Considerations of the child's socioemotional and cognitive needs are paramount in the creation of educational goals (Bredekamp & Copple, 1997).

Advocated as the "ideal" way of educating young children, the developmentally appropriate practices philosophy does not appeal to everyone in the educational establishment or to some groups of parents from diverse ethnic backgrounds. As a result, there are heated debates about the merits of constructivist early childhood education as opposed to more formal-instructional approaches (see Rescorla, Hyson, & Hirsh-Pasek, 1991; Roopnarine & Johnson, 2000). And in several cultural/ethnic groups, parents place a good deal of stock in more rigorous academic training for young children. For example, Indo-Canadian parents (Ghuman, 1994), Chinese parents (Hong & Lee, 1999; Tobin, Wu, & Davidson, 1989), Korean American parents (Farver, Kim, & Lee, 1995), Korean immigrants in New Zealand (Renwick, 1997), and others insist on school curricula that are interlaced liberally with academic content. On the whole, English-speaking Caribbean immigrants' beliefs about the early childhood curriculum closely mesh with those of the aforementioned groups. What, then, do Caribbean immigrant parents believe children should learn during the early childhood years in preschool and kindergarten?

A Strong Focus on Academics

For a majority of Caribbean immigrant parents, there seems to be an internal debate between a "child-centered" approach to education that is more relaxed and tailored to the child's developmental level and the educational customs and practices they were brought up with in the Caribbean. Despite this inner turmoil, few would venture to explore it publicly. From parents' own remarks, there remains an affinity for full-scale academic training starting in the preschool years. When asked what they thought their prekindergarten or kindergarten child should learn in school, Caribbean immigrant parents in the New York City area overwhelmingly mentioned academic skills: ABCs, mathematics, reading, and spelling (Roopnarine, 1999). Even more striking were their responses as to why this was important for young children. Invariably, mothers and fathers see the preschool period as watershed years during which it is easier for children to learn basic academic concepts that will give them a "good start" or "head start" when formal schooling becomes more intense. Thus, they cast the early childhood years as a critical time when children's minds are more "absorbent" to learning the fundamental academic skills that are crucial to later schooling (Roopnarine, 1999).

To elucidate the potency of Caribbean immigrant parents' ethnotheories about early education, let us consider their ideas about rigorous academic training in the context of those of other cultural/ethnic groups. When opinions were solicited about "the most important thing children should learn in preschool," 40 percent of Caribbean immigrant mothers and 55 percent of Caribbean immigrant fathers (sixty mothers and fifty-eight fathers) placed academics as most important to the early childhood curriculum (Roopnarine, 1999). By comparison, 2 percent of Japanese, 22 percent of American, and 37 percent of Chinese parents were inclined to do so (Tobin, Wu, & Davidson, 1989). Endorsements that are parallel to those reported by Caribbean immigrant parents regarding academic rigor early in the child's life have been recorded among Latina mothers in Boston (Holloway, Rambaud, Fuller, & Eggers-Pierola, 1995), Asian mothers in the northeastern United States (Parmar, Harkness, Super, & Johnson, 2001), and Korean American mothers in the Los Angeles area (Farver, Kim, & Lee, 1995). Regardless of whether such beliefs are a product of cultural emphasis, they pose a serious challenge to the universalistic guidelines purported by NAEYC, a point we will return to later.

Homework and More Academics at Home

The costs and benefits of homework for very young children are far from clear. Some detest the practice of homework for young children so much that they recommend its abolishment (Kralovec & Buell, 2000); others provide guidelines for its appropriate use (Hong & Milgram, 2000). Cross-national data indicate that there is a greater emphasis on homework in other cultures and among immigrant groups than among children of nonimmigrant groups in the United States. First-grade children in Taiwan (8.2 hours) and Japan (3.9 hours) spend more time on homework each week than similar-age children in the United States (1.2 hours). This trend is also evident among fifth graders (for children in Taiwan, 12.9 hours; for children in Japan, 6.0 hours, for children in the United States, 4.2 hours). Similarly, children in Taiwan and Japan had more favorable attitudes toward homework than children in the United States (mean ratings for first graders: Taiwan 3.8, Japan 3.2, and United States 2.5; mean ratings for fifth graders: Taiwan 3.6, Japan 2.8, and United States 2.2) (Stevenson & Lee, 1991). Older children of immigrants and those who immigrated to the United States before age twelve (1.5 generation) (Mexican, Vietnamese, Laotian,

Hmong, and Filipino), enrolled in schools in the San Diego region, spent over 2 hours per day doing homework compared to less than an hour for students of nonimmigrant parents. Hmong children spent the most time (2.9 hours a day) on homework initially. In the San Diego study, hours spent in homework was strongly associated with grade-point averages, while the reverse was the case for watching television (Rumbaut, 1997).

For Caribbean immigrant parents, ample homework assignments go hand in hand with an early academic regimen. These parents fully accept the view that a lot of homework is quite appropriate for prekindergarten- and kindergarten-age children. In his Caribbean immigrant families and schooling study, Roopnarine (1999) found that 83 percent of Caribbean immigrant mothers and 78 percent of Caribbean immigrant fathers thought that homework was quite appropriate for their prekindergarten or kindergarten children. On average, mothers (N = 60) estimated that their child spent 5.9 hours per week on homework (fathers estimated 4.5 hours). Homework as a potential burden to children during the preschool, kindergarten, and early grade school years was rarely, if ever, considered by Caribbean immigrant parents. To them, more academic work at home can only buttress what is learned in school (Roopnarine, 1999).

From the preceding findings, it appears that these beliefs about academic training for young children among Caribbean immigrant families may collide with those of the much touted scientific child-development knowledge-derived practices suggested by NAEYC. It is not simply that early childhood teachers and administrators trained in the tradition of developmentally appropriate practices would at once abhor these beliefs; these parents would be seen as having unreasonable demands and expectations of young children that might jeopardize their psychological and educational functioning later on. As LeVine (this volume) argues so persuasively, our child-development knowledge base in the West is biased, and experts have been quick to treat childrearing and educational practices that are different from white middle-class norms as maladaptive and, hence, inappropriate for raising psychologically healthy and educationally competent children. Are we at such a comfortable spot in our scientific knowledge about childhood development across different cultural groups to introduce and back educational practices for *all* children with such certainty? A perusal of the child-development literature reveals an increase in research information on diverse groups of children over the last two decades, but this research is far from complete.

Dichotomizing practices into developmentally "appropriate" and "inappropriate" categories is worrisome (LeVine, this volume). It has a supercilious tone because it rejects outright practices in other cultural groups (not vocalizing to children all the time, use of negation, direct correction of errors, not praising children openly, shaming) that are central to the socialization of children; they are rendered "insensitive" and ultimately inappropriate by NAEYC standards.

Given concerns about school failure among children of color in the United States, why not be more receptive to experimenting with educational practices that include some of the beliefs of immigrant parents? At the very least, why not entertain these views in national dialogues about educational reform before dismissing them without a coherent grasp of their adaptive significance within particular cultural groups? We address the issue further in the section below on culturally appropriate practices and the school curriculum.

PARENT-TEACHER RELATIONSHIPS: UNEASY ALLIANCES

Under the current status of schooling policies and practices at the national and local levels, the drive to provide high-quality education for Caribbean immigrant children is of extreme importance because of the overrepresentation of these children in low-performing schools, where overcrowding and diminished teacher quality prevail. In urban schools, children of immigrants are caught in the high-stakes game of national academic standards and accountability (Suárez-Orozco, 2001). With the different waves of school reforms in the United States, the responsibility ascribed to improving academic standards and school outcomes sits squarely with the major players: teachers, administrators, parents and students. Immigrant parents are implicitly expected and judged on their ability to understand, negotiate, and navigate the public school system and to explicitly partner with school personnel in schooling practices. In staying close to the overall focus of this chapter, we examine the sometimes tenuous relationships between teachers and Caribbean immigrant parents.

Because of the different acculturation processes among Caribbean immigrants and their children, parent-teacher relationships are expected to vary correspondingly. Table 13.3 maps out parent-teacher relationships and educational potential in Caribbean immigrant children relative to the four adjustment patterns laid out earlier. Predictably, in families in which parents and children operate from an integrative cultural framework, there is likely to be greater support for children's educational experiences at home and in school than in family configurations in which there are major discrepancies in beliefs about schooling and childrearing between the home environment and those that predominate in the new society. Again, we recognize the complex set of interrelated variables that contribute to positive school outcomes in immigrant children, but we feel that the joint partnership between immigrant parents and schools in fashioning education for young children of immigrants, at a time when the family is in transition, can attenuate some of the difficulties associated with early schooling. Two aspects of this relationship are considered next.

Public school policies often require the engagement of parent representatives in school governance bodies as a requisite for funding. This policy to practice initiative is exemplified in the Elementary and Secondary Education Act (ESEA)

Table 13.3

Continuum of Acculturation Potential for Schooling

	Parents/Caregivers	Teachers	Students
Synchronous	-Consciously blending natal and adopted beliefs -Unbridled support for intellectual and social pursuits -Sanguine relationship with child -Progressive ability to navigate and negotiate schooling process -Articulation of expectations	-Clarity of parents' intent and effort -Consistent and overt accountability for the teaching-learning dynamic -Clear protocols for viable communication -Acknowledge and consider the parents' role	-Joint effort with parent to identify and adopt most useful guidance techniques -Sanguine relationship with parent -Compounding ability to advocate on own behalf - Aware of expectations -Psychosocial and educational potential optimized
Asynchronous	Dogmatic application of natal beliefs and practices. -Claim to understand notions of American life but refuse to consider them -Believe that natal values must be transferred	-Idiosyncratic understanding of parents' intent and effort -Tacit and covert accountability for the teaching-learning process	-May possess a pragmatic understanding of home culture milieu -Dissonance between family and social milieus -(May) become the family expert -Become alienated over time -Diminished learning outcomes
Staggered	-Entrenched in natal beliefs and practices -Co-dependent relinquishment and modification of old behaviors -Expectations evolve	-Delayed understanding of parents' intent and effort -Tacit accountability for the teaching-learning process becomes defined and overt -Expectations evolve -May require guidance to affirm best practices	-Progressive adjustment over time that is reflective of duality with parents -Expectations evolve -Appropriate learner outcomes over time
Disoriented/ Disorganized	-Extreme adjustment and cultural difficulties -Prolonged psycho-social dysfunction -Eventual disenfranchisement from mainstream society	-Convoluted understanding of parents' intent and effort -Ambivalent about ability to identify and address needs -Referrals to support services	-Compromised mental health -Dysfunction in school milieu - Negated learning outcomes

and the Individuals with Disabilities Education Act (IDEA). In Caribbean immigrant communities, Title I budget allocation represents a primary source of school spending and a legislated means to promote and protect parental involvement by stipulating 10 percent of the budget for this purpose. Schools are required to establish and execute plans that support effective involvement of parents in their children's education irrespective of socioeconomic status or individual differences (Bynoe, 1997). The difficulty is that for Caribbean immigrant parents, the construct of "parent as schooling partner and advocate" (Harry, 1995) is rather new. There is an absolute shift from passive or nonexistent access to school policy and practice in the natal culture to open requests for parental involvement by schools in the United States. A regular complaint from teachers of children of Caribbean immigrants is a lack of parental involvement in school-related activities (no contacts with parents, little familiarity with school structure) (Clay, 1995).

Teachers also seem ill equipped to successfully reach out to parents in this important home-school partnership. They appear to lack basic knowledge about childrearing beliefs and practices in these families, their natal-culture beliefs about schooling, and the linguistic competencies of children and their parents (e.g., Jamaican and Guyanese Creolese, Trinidadian Bhojpuri) (Irish, 1995). Given that we discussed discrepancies in beliefs and practices about discipline and schooling between Caribbean immigrant parents and the school system earlier, our focus shifts to the language of communication. Within the educational establishment, nonstandard English use is suspect, considered negatively (Cummins, 1996; Folkes, 1996), and is rarely incorporated into social commerce with parents or children. It is not beyond teachers to lace conversations with the use of educational terminology and acronyms. Caribbean parents refer to these encounters as "alphabet soup meetings." In conducting workshops for parents in the New York City area, the second author frequently finds that she has to explain the underlying meaning of educational terminologies and acronyms to parents (e.g., "MIS 1" did not mean that a child was "missing something" but rather that he or she had been enrolled in the Modified Instructional Program for children with learning disabilities). Teachers seem blatantly unaware that parents miss their intended messages or lack a full understanding of the language of schools. The problem is compounded by the fact that educational guidelines for students from non-English-speaking nations are more clearly defined than for students from the Creolese-speaking countries of the Caribbean. School districts' protocols for students from Anglophone-Caribbean immigrant families remain nonspecific (Irish, 1995). The conundrum is clear; in combination, the low levels of parental involvement and inadequate understanding of school practices and ignorance of the child's home culture and language can undermine parent-teacher communication and affect levels of participation in children's schooling (Marshall, 2001).

Ostensibly, viable parent-teacher relationships can be achieved if both constituents join forces to consciously examine and clarify their intent, and make an effort to improve pedagogical practices. In part, effective parent-teacher-child relationships depend on the teacher's effort to practice culturally relevant pedagogy. That is, teachers must seek congruence between children's learning experiences at home and at school (Ladson-Billings, 1995, 2000) while demonstrating behaviors that show a determination to eliminate intentional and unintentional biases about Caribbean families (Gopaul-McNicol, 1993). Concurrently, the establishment of community-based support entities (e.g., Caribbean Women's Health Center) that inform and empower Caribbean immigrants about the language and routines of schooling during the acculturation process would assist parents to acquire the knowledge and develop the skills necessary to engage their children in the schooling process more successfully.

CULTURALLY APPROPRIATE PRACTICES AND THE EARLY CHILDHOOD CURRICULUM

The designations of "minority status" and "culturally diverse" are not monolithic terms. Rather, there is heterogeneity within ethnic groups that must be considered in the discussion of what is culturally appropriate and for whom (Artiles & Trent, 1997; Bynoe, 1998). The present mosaic of peoples, languages, and inter- and intracultural variability in Caribbean immigrant communities beg such considerations. The notion of unilateral majority or minority suggests that if not the former, then the latter occurs by default (Ladson-Billings, 2000; Ogbu, 1987). A sufficiently documented phenomenon is that the performance of minority groups within schools in the United States, has historically been measured with reference to educational practices and assessment tools that are aligned with the majority culture (Hillard, 1997). This is so whether it pertains to the issue of school readiness criteria or K–12 curricula (see Marshall, 2001).

A good deal has been written on culturally relevant practices (Hyun & Marshall, 1997; Ladson-Billings, 2000; Derman-Sparks & Ramsey, 2000), and developmentally appropriate practices (Bredekamp & Copple, 1997). Irrespective of cultural beliefs about the ontogeny of development in diverse cultural groups, school readiness criteria for young children are embedded in hierarchically arranged skills and competencies that children are expected to acquire in the domains of cognition, speech and language, gross and fine motor skills, social and emotional development, and so on. These chronologically ordered skills and competencies are the barometers by which different aspects of typical and atypical development are discerned. Developmentally appropriate practices depend on these skills to orchestrate the scope and sequence of curriculum for young children and the accreditation of early childhood programs across the country (Bredekamp, 1987; Bredekamp & Copple, 1997).

It is perhaps not extraordinary to assert that the determination of appropriate versus inappropriate development is largely affected by the constituents involved in the discourse and, as has been stated, the scientific data behind childhood development. On a common sense level, the core aspects of appropriateness and inappropriateness are rendered suspect without the incorporation of cultural competence among the teacher/evaluator, the student, and the family. Cultural competence refers to the ability to function effectively in one's culture of origin through communication and successfully within group relationships (Ladson-Billings, 2000). Teachers must recognize biases and perceptions in their own cultural frames as a prerequisite to developing instructional strategies and assessment tools for working with children of Caribbean immigrants. These requisites permit the teaching-learning process to be influenced by the experiences of the students and their learning styles. For instance, the inductive, auditory, lecture-format instructional approaches (teacher-centered) used by teachers in the Caribbean (Clay, 1995; Gopaul-McNicol, 1993) can be intermingled with other techniques to influence the acquisition of early academic skills in current classrooms. This teacher-centered approach differs fundamentally from the ubiquitous child-centered constructivist approach (Fosnot, 1989; Waite-Stupiansky, 1997) in that students are encouraged to construct meaning by bridging cultural referents with curriculum frames or in conjunction with standard curriculum (Ladson-Billings, 2000). These considerations for the teaching-learning process move the emphasis away from NAEYC designations of appropriate and inappropriate development specifically and encourage accommodation of the student's individualistic needs based on culture and learning styles, while providing opportunities to optimize learning. It is unlikely that standard methods of pedagogy or educational practices alone will be in the best educational interest of children of Caribbean immigrants.

FACTORS THAT AFFECT CHILDREN'S SCHOOL PERFORMANCE

There is scientific agreement that demonstrates parents' involvement in children's academic pursuits at home and at school, the pervasive emphasis on the importance of education by parents and other family members, parents' monitoring of school progress, frequent parent-teacher contacts, and parental involvement in school management and governance as well as input in school curricula all contribute to successful schooling (Comer, 1988; Roopnarine, 1999; Stevenson, Chen, & Uttal, 1990). We also know that factors such as race, class, and gender, the quality of schools (teacher qualifications, school resources, etc.), and parents' educational attainment significantly influence school outcomes (Ford, 1995; Harry, 1995). However, for Caribbean immigrant families there are other considerations that may figure into the equation on successful school achievement:

- While parental involvement in school-related activities and management are symbolic of the new push to utilize parental support for school success, the meaning and manifestations of the construct itself require careful attention. Parental involvement may occur outside of school (examples from life, daily emphasis on education, community networks; see Lopez, 2001); the demands of work and familial responsibilities as well as the family's legal status in the United States are bound to determine the level of interface with schools (Marshall, 2001). The parent as partner in the schooling process and as an advocate for the child intrinsically and extrinsically is not endemic to certain immigrant groups (Harry, 1995). It is clear that for immigrant families, parental involvement in schooling has many faces and may be impeded by a constellation of family-functioning variables.

- The ability to comparatively transpose the language used in the country of origin or home environment (Creolese or Creole) to that used in the educational system (Gopaul-McNicol, 1993) and the ability to decipher and acquire the discrete properties of the language of the school as an institution are likely to have beneficial effects on the child's well-being and subsequently on academic performance (Ovando & Collier, 1998).

- Recent educational reforms in the United States have coincided with active periods of immigration from the Caribbean. In the past, this has created a combustible situation where schools in metropolitan areas were scrambling to accommodate children they did not understand, while establishing new educational standards and accountability. As the focus on standards and accountability tightened, there was a perceived inability of teachers and students to meet prescribed educational standards. Unwittingly, children were blamed for low academic performance. This quagmire forced young children of Caribbean immigrants to rely on parents, who shouldered the responsibility of assisting them to stave off the tide of negative portrayals and diminished academic performance. To wit: these families are no strangers to rigorous academic standards (Ziegler & Folkes, 1995).

CONCLUSION

In this chapter, we have examined some factors within the home and school environment that have implications for the education of children of English-speaking Caribbean immigrants of color. These may also apply to the large numbers of children whose families immigrated from other parts of the Caribbean and Latin America to the United States. The research and theorizing on the educational achievement of children of Caribbean immigrants is rather meager (Irish, 1995; Rong & Brown, 2001), despite the increased presence of these children in major urban school districts (e.g., New York). By focusing on the diverse adjustment patterns of Caribbean immigrant families—including parent-child relationships, parental ethnotheories about early education, parent-teacher relationships, factors that influence schooling, and the curriculum—we have attempted to draw attention to the complex and interrelated issues that are at play in the schooling of children of immigrants of color in the United States. We hope that this chapter will stimulate additional dialogue and research on the topic.

REFERENCES

Alba, R. D., & Nee, V. (1997). Rethinking assimilation theory for a new era of immigration. *International Migration Review, 31*, 826–874.

Anderson, S., & Payne, M. (1994). Corporal punishment in elementary education: Views of Barbadian school children. *Child Abuse and Neglect, 18*, 377–386.

Arnold, E. (1997). Issues in re-unification of migrant West Indian children in the United Kingdom. In J. L. Roopnarine & J. Brown (Eds.), *Caribbean families: Diversity among ethnic groups* (pp. 243–258). Norwood, NJ: Ablex.

Artiles, A., & Trent, S. (1997). Forging a research program on multicultural preservice teacher education in special education: A proposed analytic scheme. In J. Lloyd, E. Kameenui, & D. Chard (Eds.), *Issues in educating students with disabilities* (pp. 275–304). Mahwah, NJ: Erlbaum.

Baptiste, D. A. (1990). The treatment of adolescent immigrants and their families in cultural transition: Issues and recommendations. *Contemporary Family Therapy, 12*, 3–22.

Baptiste, D. A., Hardy, K. V., & Lewis, L. (1997). Clinical practice with Caribbean immigrant families in the United States: The intersection of emigration, immigration, culture, and race. In J. L. Roopnarine & J. Brown (Eds.), *Caribbean families: Diversity among ethnic groups* (pp. 275–303). Norwood, NJ: Ablex.

Baumrind, D. (1967). Child care practices anteceding three patterns of preschool behavior. *Genetic Psychology Monographs, 75*, 43–88.

———. (1996). The discipline controversy revisited. *Family Relations, 45*, 405–414.

Berry, J. W. (1998). Acculturation and health: Theory and research. In S. S. Kazarian & D. R. Evans (Eds.), *Cultural clinical psychology: Theory, research, and practice* (pp. 39–57). New York: Oxford University Press.

Bredekamp, S. (1987). *Developmentally appropriate practice in early childhood programs serving children from birth through age eight.* Washington, DC: National Association for the Education of Young Children.

Bredekamp, S., & Copple, C. (Eds.). (1997). *Developmentally appropriate practice in early childhood programs* (Rev. ed.). Washington, DC: National Association for the Education of Young Children.

Bruner, J. (1999). Global perspectives on early childhood education. Keynote address for the Committee on Early Childhood Pedagogy, National Academy of Sciences, National Research Council, Washington, DC.

Bynoe, P. (1997, November). What have you taught my child? A protocol for viable parent-teacher communication. Paper presented at the Council for Exceptional Children Annual Conference, New York.

———. (1998). Rethinking and retooling teacher preparation to prevent perpetual failure by our children. *Journal of Special Education, 32*, 37–40.

Bynoe, P., & Trent, S. (1995, April). Policy and legislation: Implications for African-American exceptional learners. Paper presented at the annual meeting of the Council for Exceptional Children, Indianapolis.

Chao, R. (1994). Beyond parental control and authoritarian parenting style: Understanding Chinese parenting through the cultural notion of training. *Child Development*, 65, 1111–1119.

———. (2001). Extending research on the consequences of parenting style for Chinese Americans and European Americans. *Child Development*, 72, 1832–1843.

Cheetham, J. (1972). *Social work with immigrants.* London: Routledge & Kegan Paul.

Clay, C. (1995). Perspectives on the teaching and learning needs of Caribbean students: A survey of teachers and administrative staff of a Brooklyn elementary public school. In G. Irish (Ed.), *Caribbean students in New York*, Occasional Paper no. 1 (pp. 91–101). New York: Caribbean Diaspora Press.

Comer, J. P. (1988). Educating poor minority children. *Scientific American*, 259 (5), 42–48.

Committee on Early Childhood Pedagogy, National Academy of Sciences and National Research Council. (1999). *Global perspectives on early childhood education.* Washington, DC.

Crowder, K. (1999). Residential segregation of West Indians in the New York/New Jersey metropolitan area: The roles of race and ethnicity. *International Migration Review*, 33, 79–113.

Cummins, J. (1996). *Negotiating identities: Education for empowerment in a diverse society.* Los Angeles: California Association for Bilingual Education.

daCosta, E. (1985). *Reunion after long-term disruption of the parent-child bond in older children: Clinical features and psychodynamic issues.* Toronto: Clark Institute of Psychiatry.

Darling, N., & Steinberg, L. (1993). Parenting style as context: An integrative model. *Psychological Bulletin, 113,* 487–496.

Derman-Sparks, L. & Ramsey, P. (2000). A framework for culturally relevant, multicultural, and antibias education in the twenty-first century. In J. L. Roopnarine & J. E. Johnson (Eds.), *Approaches to early childhood education.* (pp. 379–404). Columbus, OH: Merrill/Prentice-Hall.

DeWind, J., & Kasinitz, P. (1997). Everything old is new again? Processes and theories of immigrant incorporation. *International Migration Review, 31,* 1096–1111.

DeYoung, Y., & Zigler, E. F. (1994). Machismo in two cultures: Relation to punitive child-rearing practices. *American Journal of Orthopsychiatry, 64,* 386–395.

Diaz-Rico, L., & Weed, K. (2002). *The cross-cultural, language, and academic development handbook* (2nd ed.). Boston: Allyn & Bacon.

Elkind, D. (1981). *The hurried child.* Reading, MA: Addison-Wesley.

———. (1987). *Miseducation: Preschoolers at risk.* New York: Knopf.

Evans, H. (1991). *Teachers' and students' perceptions of teaching, learning and schooling in the all-age school.* Final report to the Ministry of Education, Kingston, Jamaica.

Farver, J. A. M., Kim, Y. K., & Lee, Y. (1995). Cultural differences in Korean- and Anglo-American preschoolers' social interaction and play behaviors. *Child Development*, 66, 1088–1099.

Farver, J. A. M., & Shin, Y. L. (1997). Social pretend play in Korean- and Anglo-American preschoolers. *Child Development, 68,* 544–556.

Folkes, K. (1995). Issues of assessment and identification of Anglo-Caribbean students in a migratory environment. In G. Irish (Ed.), *Caribbean students in New York*, Occasional Paper no. 1. (pp. 27–38). New York: Caribbean Diaspora Press.

Foner, N. (1978). *Jamaican farewell: Jamaican migrants in London*. Berkeley: University of California Press.

———. (1994). *Ideology and social practice in the Jamaican diaspora*. Working Paper no. 65. New York: Russell Sage.

———. (1997). The immigrant family: Cultural legacies and cultural changes. *International Migration Review, 31*, 961–974.

———. (2001a). Introduction: New migrants in New York. In N. Foner (Ed.), *New immigrants in New York* (pp. 1–31). New York: Columbia University Press.

———. (Ed.). (2001b). *Islands in the city: West Indian migration to New York*. Berkeley: University of California Press.

Ford, B. (1995). African American community involvement processes and special education: Essential networks for effective education. In B. Ford, F. Obiakor, & J. Patton (Eds.), *Effective education of African American exceptional learners* (pp. 235–273). Austin, TX: Pro-Ed.

Fosnot, C. (1989). *Enquiring teachers, enquiring learning: A constructivist approach for teaching*. New York: Teachers College Press.

Fuligni, A. (2001). A comparative longitudinal approach to acculturation among children from immigrant families. *Harvard Educational Review, 71*, 566–578.

Gans, H. J. (1992). Second-generation decline: Scenarios for the economic and ethnic futures of the post-1965 American immigrants. *Ethnic and Racial Studies, 14*, 173–192.

Ghuman, P. A. S. (1994). Indo-Canadian parentsí perceptions of Canadian schooling. *Multicultural Education Journal, 12*, 21–31.

Gibson, M. (1988). *Accommodation without assimilation: Sikh immigrants in an American High School*. Ithaca: Cornell University Press.

Gibson, M., & Ogbu, J. (Eds.). (1991). *Minority status and schooling: A comparative study of immigrant and involuntary minorities*. New York: Garland.

Goodnow, J. J., & Collins, W. A. (1991). *Development according to parents: The nature, sources, and consequences of parents' ideas*. Hillsdale, NJ: Erlbaum.

Gopaul-McNicol, S. (1993). *Working with West Indian families*. New York: Guilford Press.

Gordon, M. M. (1964). *Assimilation in American life: The role of race, religion, and national origin*. New York: Oxford University Press.

Grasmuck, S., & Grosfoguel, R. (1997). Geopolitics, economic niches, and gendered social capital among recent Caribbean immigrants in New York City. *Sociological Perspectives, 40*, 339–363.

Grosfoguel, R. (1997). Colonial Caribbean migrations to France, the Netherlands, Great Britain, and the United States. *Ethnic and Racial Studies, 20*, 594–612.

Harkness, S., & Super, S. (Eds.). (1996). *Parental cultural belief systems: Their origins, expressions, and consequences*. New York: Guilford Press.

Harry, B. (1995). African-American families. In B. Ford, F. Obiakor, & J. Patton (Eds.), *Effective education of African-American Exceptional learners: New perspectives* (pp. 211–234). Austin, TX: Pro-Ed.

Hewlett, B. (1992). The parent-infant relationship and socio-emotional development among Aka Pygmies. In J. L. Roopnarine & D. B. Carter (Eds.), *Parent-child socialization across cultures* (pp. 153–176). Norwood, NJ: Ablex.

Hilliard, A. G., III. (1997). The structure of valid staff development. *Journal of Staff Development*, 18, 28–33.

Holder, C. (1998, Winter–Spring). Making ends meet: West Indian economic adjustment in New York City 1900–1952. *Wadabagei: A Journal of the Caribbean and Its Diaspora*, 1 (1), 31–84.

Holloway, S. (1999). Beyond the "average native": Cultural models of early childhood education in Japan. Address to the Committee on Early Childhood Pedagogy, National Academy of Sciences, National Research Council, Washington, DC.

Holloway, S. D., Rambaud, M. F., Fuller, B., & Eggers-Pierola, C. (1995). What is "appropriate practice" at home and in child care? Low-income mothers' view on preparing their children for school. *Early Childhood Research Quarterly*, 10, 451–473.

Hong, E., & Lee, K. (1999). *Chinese parents' awareness of their children's homework style and homework behavior and its effects on achievement.* Las Vegas: University of Nevada Press.

Hong, E., & Milgram, R. M. (2000). *Homework: Motivation and learning preference.* Westport, CT: Greenwood Press.

Hyun, E., & Marshall, J. D. (1997). Theory of multiple/multiethnic perspective-taking ability for teachers' developmentally and culturally appropriate practice (DCAP). *Journal of Research in Childhood Education*, 11, 188–199.

Irish, G. (Ed.). (1995). *Caribbean students in New York.* Occasional Paper no. 1. New York: Caribbean Diaspora Press.

Johnson, J. (2001). Taiwanese teacher educators', teachers', and parents' views on play. Paper presented at the Association for the Study of Play meetings, San Diego.

Kalmijin, M. (1996). The socioeconomic assimilation of Caribbean American blacks. *Social Forces*, 74, 911–930.

Kralovec, E., & Buell, J. (2000). *The end of homework: How homework disrupts families, overburdens children, and limits learning.* New York: Beacon Press.

Ladson-Billings, G. (1995). Multicultural teacher education: Research, practice, and policy. In J. Banks & C. Banks (Eds.), *Handbook of research on multicultural education* (pp. 747–749). New York: Macmillan.

———. (2000). Fighting for our lives: Preparing teachers to teach African American children. *Journal of Teacher Education*, 51 (3), 206–214.

Leo-Rhynie, E. (1997). Class, race, and gender issues in child rearing in the Caribbean. In J. L. Roopnarine & J. Brown (Eds.), *Caribbean families: Diversity among ethnic groups* (pp. 25–55). Norwood, NJ: Ablex.

Lopez, G. R. (2001). The value of hard work: Lessons on parental involvement from an (im)migrant household. *Harvard Educational Review*, 70, 417–437.

Marshall, D. I. (1982). Migration as an agent of change in the Caribbean Island ecosystem. *International Social Science Journal*, 34, 451–467.

Marshall, J. A. (2001). *Minority learning disabled students in segregated and integrated classes.* University Microfilm no. 99-92356. Dissertation Abstracts International, Tempe, AZ.

Maxime, J. (1986). Some psychological models of black concept. In S. Ahmed, J. Cheetham, & J. Small (Eds.), *Social work with black children and their families* (pp. 100–116). London: Batsford Press.

McGillicuddy-DeLisi, A. V. (1982). Parental beliefs about developmental processes. *Human Development*, 25, 192–200.

Millette, R. (1998). West Indian families in the United States. In R. Taylor (Ed.), *Minority families in the United States: A multicultural perspective* (2nd ed., pp. 46–59). Upper Saddle River, NJ: Prentice-Hall.

Munroe-Blum, H., Boyle, M. H., Offord, D., R., & Kates, N. (1989). Immigrant children: Psychiatric disorder, school performance, and service utilization. *American Journal of Orthopsychiatry, 59,* 510–519.

New York City Department of Planning. (1999). *Newest New Yorkers: 1995–1996.* September.

Ogbu, J. (1987). Variability in minority school performance. A problem in search of an explanation. *Anthropology and Education Quarterly, 18,* 312–334.

Oropesa, R. S., & Landale, N. S. (1997). In search of the new second generation: Alternative strategies for identifying second generation children and understanding their acquisition of English. *Sociological Perspectives, 40,* 427–455.

Ovando, C., & Collier, V. (1998). *Bilingual and ESL classrooms: Teaching in multicultural contexts.* Boston: McGraw-Hill.

Parmar, P., Harkness, S., Super, C. M., & Johnson, J. E. (2001). Cross-cultural study of parents' ethnotheories of play and learning: Effects on home routines and children's behavior in preschool. Paper presented at the meeting of the Society for Cross-Cultural Research, San Diego.

Pawliuk, N., Grizenko, N., Chan-Yip, A., Gantous, P., Matthew, J., & Nguyen, D. (1996). Acculturation style and psychological functioning in children of immigrants. *American Journal of Orthopsychiatry, 66,* 111–121.

Payne, M. (1989). Use and abuse of corporal punishment: A Caribbean view. *Child Abuse and Neglect, 13,* 389–401.

Payne, M., & Furnham, A. (1992). Parental self-reports of childrearing practices in the Caribbean. *Journal of Black Psychology, 18,* 19–36.

Phinney, J., Lochner, B., & Murphy, R. (1990). Ethnic identity development and psychological adjustment in adolescence. In A. Stiffman & L. Davis (Eds.), *Ethnic issues in adolescent mental health* (pp. 53–72). Newbury Park, CA: Sage.

Portes, A., & Rumbaut, R., G. (1990). *Immigrant America: A portrait.* Berkeley: University of California Press.

Pressar, P. R., & Graham, P. M. (2001). Dominicans: Transnational identities and local politics. In N. Foner (Ed.), *New immigrants in New York* (pp. 251–273). New York: Columbia University Press.

Renwick, M. (1997). *Your children: Our schools. A guide to Korean parents in New Zealand early childhood educational services and primary schools.* New Zealand: New Zealand Council for Educational Research.

Rescorla, M. L., Hyson, M. C., & K. Hirsh-Pasek, K. (Eds.). (1991). Instruction in early childhood: Challenge or pressure. *New Directions for Child Development, 53.* San Francisco: Jossey-Bass.

Rohner, R., Bourque, S., & Elordi, C. (1996). Children's perceptions of corporal punishment, caretaker acceptance, and psychological adjustment in a poor, biracial community. *Journal of Marriage and the Family, 58,* 842–852.

Rong, X. L., & Brown, F. (2001). The effects of immigrant generation and ethnicity on educational attainment among young African and Caribbean blacks in the United States. *Harvard Educational Review, 70,* 537–565.

Roopnarine, J. L. (1999). Parental involvement, ethnotheories about development, parenting styles, and early academic achievement in Caribbean-American children. Paper presented in the Department of Applied Psychology, New York University.

Roopnarine, J. L., Bynoe, P. F., Singh, R., & Romel, S. (in press). Caribbean families in English-speaking countries: A rather complex mosaic. In J. L. Roopnarine & U. P. Gielen (Eds.), *Families in global perspective*. Boston: Allyn & Bacon.

Roopnarine, J. L., & Johnson, J. E. (Eds.). (2000). *Approaches to early childhood education* (3rd ed.). Upper Saddle River, NJ: Merrill, Prentice Hall.

Roopnarine, J. L., & Shin, M. (2003). Caribbean immigrants from English-speaking countries: Sociohistorical forces, migratory patterns, and psychological issues in family functioning. In L. L. Adler & U. P. Gielen (Eds.), *Migration: Immigration and emigration in international perspective* (pp. 123–142). Westport, CT: Greenwood.

Roopnarine, J. L., Shin, M., Jung, K., & Hossain, Z. (2003). Play and early development and education: The instantiation of parental belief systems. In O. Saracho & B. Spodek (Eds.), *Contemporary issues in early childhood education*. Greenwich, CT: Information Age.

Rumbaut, R. G. (1997). Assimilation and its discontents: Between rhetoric and reality. *International Migration Review, 31*, 923–960.

Rutter, M. (1972). *Maternal deprivation reassessed*. Hammondsworth, UK: Penguin.

Rutter, M., Yule, W., Berger, M., Morton, J., & Bagley, C. (1974). Children of West Indian immigrants, Part 1: Rates of behavioral deviance and psychiatric disorder. *Journal of Child Psychiatry, 15*, 241–262.

Salem, D., Zimmerman, M., & Notaro, P. (1998). Effects of family structure, family process, and father involvement on psychosocial outcomes among African American adolescents. *Family Relations, 47*, 331–341.

Scott-Macdonald, K. (1997). The status of child care supports for Jamaican families. In J. L. Roopnarine & Brown, J. (Eds.), *Caribbean families: Diversity among ethnic groups* (pp. 147–176). Norwood, NJ: Ablex.

Sewell-Coker, B., Hamilton-Collins, J., & Fein, E. (1985). West Indian immigrants. *Social Casework, 60*, 563–568.

Shin, M. (2001). Beyond independent children and authoritative parenting: Korean mothers' perspective. Unpublished Ph.D. diss., Syracuse University.

Sluzki, C. E. (1979). Migration and family conflict. *Family Process, 18*, 379–390.

Sigel, I. (1985). A conceptual analysis of beliefs. In I. Sigel, A. McGillicuddy-DeLisi, & J. Goodnow (Eds.), *Parental belief systems: The psychological consequences for children* (2nd ed., pp. 345–371). Hillsdale, NJ: Erlbaum.

———. (1991). Preschool education: For whom and why? In L. Rescorla, M. C. Hyson, & K. Hirsh-Pasek (Eds.), Instruction in early childhood: Challenge or pressure. *New Directions for Child Development, 53*, 83–91.

———. (2000). Educating the young thinker model, from research to practice: A case study of program development, or the place of theory and research in the development of educational programs. In J. L. Roopnarine & J. E. Johnson (Eds.), *Approaches to early childhood education* (pp. 315–340). Columbus, OH: Merrill/ Prentice-Hall.

Sigel, I., & McGillicuddy-DeLisi, A. (2002). Parental beliefs are cognitions: The Dynamic Belief Systems model. In M. H. Bornstein (Ed.), *Handbook of parenting* (2nd ed., Vol. 3, pp. 485–508). Mahwah, NJ: Erlbaum.

Stevenson, H. W., Chen, C., & Uttal, D. H. (1990). Beliefs and achievement: A study of black, white, and Hispanic children. *Child Development, 61,* 518–523.

Stevenson, H. W., & Lee, S. Y. (1991). Contexts of achievement: A study of American, Chinese, and Japanese children. *Monographs of the Society for Research in Child Development, 55* (1–2) (serial no. 221).

Suárez-Orozco, C., & Todorova, I. (2001). The transnationalization of families: Immigrant separations and reunifications. Paper presented to the American Family Therapy Academy, Miami, FL.

Suárez-Orozco, M. (2001). Globalization, immigration, and education: The research agenda. *Harvard Educational Review, 71,* 345–365.

Super, C., & Harkness, S. (1997). The cultural structuring of child development. In J. Berry, P. Dasen, & T. Saraswathi (Eds.), *Handbook of cross-cultural psychology: Basic processes and human development* (pp. 1–39). Needham, MA: Allyn & Bacon.

Szapocznik, J., & Kurtines, W. (1993). Family psychology and cultural diversity: Opportunities for theory, research, and application. *American Psychologist, 48,* 400–407.

Thompson, P., & Bauer, E. (2000). Jamaican transnational families: Points of pain and sources of resilience. *Wadabagei, 2,* 1–36.

Tobin, J., Wu, D. Y. H., & Davidson, D. H. (1989). *Preschool in three cultures: Japan, China, and the United States.* New Haven: Yale University Press.

Trasher, S., & Anderson, G. (1988). The West Indian family: Treatment challenges. *Social Casework: The Journal of Contemporary Social Work* (March), 171–176.

Turner, H. A., & Finkelhor, D. (1996). Corporal punishment as a stressor among youth. *Journal of Marriage and the Family, 58,* 155–156.

U.S. Bureau of the Census. (1993). *1990 Census of Population and Housing.* Washington, DC: U.S. Government Printing Office.

U.S. Department of Justice, Immigration and Naturalization Service (INS) (1998). *Statistical Yearbook of the Immigration and Naturalization Service.* Washington, DC: U.S. Government Printing Office.

Vickerman, M. (2001). Jamaicans: Balancing race and ethnicity. In N. Foner (Ed.), *New immigrants in New York* (pp. 201–228). New York: Columbia University Press.

Voltz, D. (1995). Learning and cultural diversities in general and special education classes: Frameworks for success. In B. Ford (Ed.), *Multiple voices for ethnically diverse exceptional learners* (pp. 1–11). Reston, VA: Council for Exceptional Children.

Waite-Stupiansky, (1997). Building understanding together: A *constructivist approach to early childhood.* Boston: Delmar.

Warner, W. L., & Srole, L. (1945). *The social system of American ethnic groups.* New Haven: Yale University Press.

Waters, M. (1999). *Black identities: West Indian immigrant dreams and American realities.* Cambridge, MA: Harvard University Press.

White-Davis, G. (1995). Recommendations for enhancing the education of English-speaking Caribbean students in the New York public schools. In G. Irish (Ed.), *Caribbean students in New York.* Occasional Paper no. 1. (pp. 133–143). New York: Caribbean Diaspora Press.

Wilson, W. J. (1996). *When work disappears: The world of the new urban poor.* New York: Knopf.

Zhou, M. (1997). Segmented assimilation: Issues, controversies, and recent research on the new second generation. *International Migration Review, 31,* 975–1008.

Ziegler, P., & Folkes, K. (1995). Language enrichment initiatives for creole-speaking immigrant students from Caribbean cultures. In G. Irish (Ed.), *Caribbean students in New York* (pp. 103–110). New York: Caribbean Diaspora Press.

CHAPTER 14

The Acquisition of English and Maintenance of First Language by Immigrant Children and Adolescents in North America

Gisela Jia

For immigrant children and adolescents in North America, learning English as a second language is an important part of their adaptation to the new world. Meanwhile, gaining English proficiency also has different consequences for their first or native language proficiency. Understanding the processes by which they acquire English and maintain their first language has both practical and theoretical significance. In this chapter, I review the traditional psychological research in the area of learning English as a second language by immigrants, present the major empirical advances that have recently occurred in this field, and discuss their theoretical and practical implications. This review focuses on immigrants in North America, as most recent studies have been conducted with this population.

TRADITIONAL FOCUS ON AGE DIFFERENCES IN SECOND-LANGUAGE ACQUISITION

From the late 1960s to the late 1980s, many psychological studies on the acquisition of English by immigrants focused on examining the Critical Period Hypothesis (CPH). First developed by Lenneberg (1967), the CPH proposes that brain maturation causes the human language-learning mechanism[1] to decline after a certain age. This decline is assumed to result from genetically preprogrammed interactions of various aspects of brain maturation (e.g., lateralization, neuronal interconnections, chemical changes, and brain weight changes), and is functionally independent of other aspects of behavioral development (e.g., cognitive and social development). This hypothesis has aroused substantial interest in psychology and related fields because of its potential to shed light on the nature of the human language-learning mechanism. The possible existence of a critical period for second-language acquisition also implies an optimal age for the initiation of foreign- and second-language education.

To empirically examine the CPH, researchers have turned to second-language (L2) acquisition, because in contrast to what normally occurs with first-language (L1) acquisition, people can be exposed to L2 at different ages. Hence, L2 acquisition has been used as a case study for the CPH. The most popular approach involves comparing L2 proficiency of immigrants who learned English as L2 at various ages (usually indexed by arrival age in the United States or Canada) and have stayed in the L2-speaking countries for a number of years (e.g., Asher & Garcia, 1969; Johnson, 1992; Johnson & Newport, 1989; Oyama, 1976, 1978; Patkowski, 1982). Studies adopting this approach are generally referred to as long-term attainment studies. Researchers have studied a variety of language groups and various aspects of L2 proficiency, and all have demonstrated a decline of L2 proficiency with increasing arrival age, a phenomenon known as long-term L2 attainment decline.

Asher and Garcia (1969) asked seventy-one Cuban child and adult immigrants in California with arrival age between one and nineteen years to read four English sentences. With increasing arrival age, these immigrants spoke English with a stronger Cuban accent. Oyama (1976, 1978) found the same trend with Italian immigrants in the United States. To assess morphology and syntax, Patkowski (1982) used ratings of grammatical accuracy in taped conversations and found that with increasing arrival age, participants made more grammatical production errors. Johnson and Newport (1989) had forty-six native Chinese and Korean speakers with at least five years of U.S. residence and arrival age between three and thirty-nine judge the grammaticality of 270 English sentences auditorily presented to them. Again, a younger arrival age was associated with a better performance on the task. Using a reading version of the same grammaticality judgment task, Johnson (1992) also found a similar but weaker trend with twenty-seven native Chinese and Korean speakers.

These findings of decreasing L2 proficiency with increasing arrival age have been largely referred to as the long-term L2 attainment decline because it indicates L2 attainment after supposedly sufficient L2 input has occurred. The causes of the long-term L2 attainment decline have been a topic of much debate (for reviews, see Birdsong, 1998; Harley & Wang, 1997; and Marinova-Todd, Marshall, & Snow, 2000). While some hold long-term L2 decline as evidence of a neurobiologically based and domain-specific Critical Period for L2 acquisition (e.g., Johnson, 1992; Johnson & Newport, 1989; Patkowski, 1990), others propose cognitive, social, and environmental factors as major causes of this phenomenon (e.g., Bialystok & Hakuta, 1994, 1998; Snow, 1983; Snow & Hoefnagel-Höhle, 1987).

During the past decade, this long-standing debate has prompted several empirical advances that have increased the scope and depth of the investigation of English acquisition by immigrants. Findings from these recent studies indicate that L2 acquisition is shaped by multiple factors, with age being only one of them. More specifically, cognitive, social, and cultural factors all make contributions to L2 acquisition. These advances have transformed the field from one that merely focuses on a single psychological theory (namely, the CPH) to one that views L2 acquisition as part of the dynamic adaptation process of immigrants. The following is a review of the major studies that have come along with four major empirical advances.

ARRIVAL AGE IS NOT THE WHOLE STORY: MULTIPLE PREDICTORS OF L2 PROFICIENCY

Consistent with long-existing traditional theories of environmental, social, and attitudinal influences on L2 acquisition (e.g., Gardner & Lambert, 1959; Lambert, 1967), researchers have started to examine multiple predictive factors of long-term L2 attainment by immigrants (Flege, Yeni-Komshian, & Liu, 1999; Jia & Aaronson, 2002; Jia, Aaronson, & Wu, 2002).

Flege and colleagues (1999) studied 240 native Korean speakers living in the Washington, D.C., area. Their English grammatical proficiency was measured with a 144-sentence grammaticality judgment task, and their English pronunciation accuracy was measured by having judges rate the degree of foreign accent in twenty-one imitated English sentences. Additionally, a thirty-nine-item questionnaire elicited comprehensive information on these immigrants' language learning experiences. Similar to the standard finding from previous research (e.g., Johnson & Newport, 1989), arrival age was the best predictor of L2 proficiency, accounting for 68 percent of the variance in pronunciation accuracy and 49 percent of the variance in grammatical proficiency. A younger arrival age was associated with both higher grammatical and pronunciation proficiency. However, several other factors also uniquely predicted a significant amount of L2 proficiency variance. More media input in L2 (e.g., movies, videos, television, and radio), as well as stronger integrative motivation (e.g., to have American friends) and instrumental motivation (e.g., to have a good job), were all uniquely associated with significantly higher L2 proficiency. Consistent with these findings, Birdsong and Molis (2001) found that more L2 use predicted higher English grammatical proficiency in a study with sixty-one native Spanish speakers.

The strong predictive power of arrival age can be an overestimation of its role because it is significantly related to other potentially relevant factors. For example, younger arrivals tend to have stayed longer in the United States and to have received more education in the United States. To separate the predictive effects of arrival age and education in the United States, a matched-group analysis was conducted (Flege et al., 1999). Two groups of participants were randomly selected. They differed in the number of years of education received in the United States (15.1 versus 8.9 years), but their arrival ages were matched (mean = 12.3 years). The results indicated that the two groups did not differ in the accuracy of English pronunciation, but the group with more U.S. education did significantly better than the other group on the sentences testing rule-based grammatical knowledge (e.g., the use of *cooked* rather than *cooks* in a context in which past tense is required). These findings suggest that proficiency in the rule-based grammatical structures was better predicted by an environmental variable, education in the United States, rather than arrival age.

Jia and colleagues (in press) studied 112 adult nonnative English speakers who immigrated to the United States between ages one and thirty-eight. Their English grammatical proficiency was measured with one listening and one reading grammaticality judgment task. In a questionnaire, participants also rated their family members' (e.g., father, mother, and siblings) English proficiency in speaking, reading, and writing on 4-point scales. After a set of multiple regression analyses, both arrival age and mother's English proficiency remained significant predictors of performance on the two tasks: younger arrival age and higher English proficiency of the mothers were associated with higher English proficiency of the participants. For the listening task, mothers' English proficiency uniquely explained the same amount of L2 performance variance (21 percent) as arrival age (22 percent). For the reading task, mother's L2 proficiency explained more performance variance than arrival age did (15 percent versus 7 percent). Although these data are correlational, supplementary interviews with the participants revealed that, for the most part, language environment influenced language proficiency, rather than vice versa. For example, many bilinguals reported that when interacting with their parents, they chose how much English to use based on their parents' English proficiency.

Taken together, environmental and attitudinal variables other than arrival age, including the amount of English use, family members' English proficiency, and motivation can all predict immigrants' long-term English attainment.

FIRST LANGUAGE MATTERS: COMPARISONS OF MULTIPLE LANGUAGE GROUPS

Another group of recent studies has demonstrated that bilinguals with different first languages have different levels of L2 proficiency. When education and language-learning backgrounds are matched, European-language speakers tend to have higher English proficiency and weaker arrival-age effects in comparison to Asian-language speakers.

Bialystok and Miller (1999) tested the English grammatical proficiency of thirty-three native Chinese speakers and twenty-eight native Spanish speakers in Canada using both listening and reading grammaticality judgment tasks. The native Spanish speakers, as a group, demonstrated higher English proficiency and weaker arrival-age effects in comparison to the native Chinese speakers. Interestingly, the native Chinese speakers had more problems with English structures that are absent in Chinese, including plurals, articles, and different collocation restrictions.[2]

Birdsong and Molis (2001) studied sixty-one native Spanish speakers whose language-learning backgrounds matched those of the forty-six native Chinese speakers studied by Johnson and Newport (1989). Participants in both samples were undergraduates, graduates, faculty, and staff in first-rank universities. Both studies used exactly the same listening grammaticality judgment task with the same procedures. Consistent with findings of Bialystok and Miller (1999), as a group the Chinese speakers scored significantly lower than the Spanish speakers (87.9 percent versus 93.1 percent). Then each language group was separated into four subgroups according to arrival age: ages 3–7, 8–10, 11–16, and 17–44 years. Native Spanish and Chinese speakers did not differ in their L2 performance if they arrived in the United States younger than age ten. The total group differences were mainly due to the fact that the Spanish speakers in the two older groups scored significantly higher than their Chinese counterparts (see Figure 14.1).

However, possibly depending on the difficulty level of the proficiency task used, language-group differences can also occur among younger arrivals. McDonald (2000) compared a group of fourteen native Spanish speakers with a group of fourteen native Vietnamese speakers who all started to learn English when younger than age five. On an English grammaticality judgment task, the native Spanish speakers scored 92.8 percent, not significantly different from monolingual English speakers. The Vietnamese speakers scored 87.2 percent, significantly lower than the Spanish speakers and the monolinguals. Significantly, the Vietnamese speakers particularly had trouble with English structures that are absent in Vietnamese, such as plurals, articles, and third-person subject-verb agreement. Given the fact that all of the Vietnamese speakers had attended English-speaking schools ever since age five, learning L2 at a young age (e.g., within the supposedly Critical Period) seems not to be able to guarantee a native-level L2 attainment.

Jia and colleagues (Jia & Aaronson, 2002; Jia et al., 2002) compared the English proficiency of a group of European-language speakers and a group of Asian-language speakers in the New York City area. The European group consisted of thirty-two native speakers of Russian, Spanish, Polish, German, Italian, or Haitian Creole. The Asian group included seventy-two native speakers of Chinese (Mandarin and Cantonese) or Korean. The two groups were matched in arrival age, age of English instruction, length of U.S. residence, and number of years of U.S. education. L2 proficiency was measured with one listening and one reading grammaticality judgment task. The Asian group scored significantly lower than the European group on the listening task (85 percent versus 92 per-

Figure 14.1

Accuracy (% Correct) in an English Grammaticality Judgment Task by Native Chinese Speakers (Johnson & Newport, 1989) and by Native Spanish Speakers (Birdson & Molis, 2001)

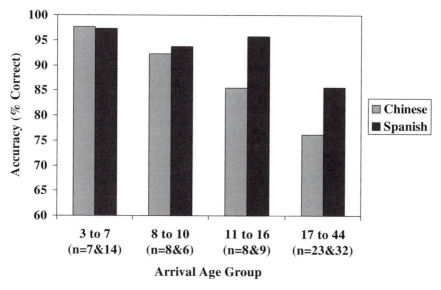

cent) as well as on the reading task (88 percent versus 91 percent). This tendency occurred for all of the eleven grammatical structures for the listening task and six of the eleven structures for the reading task. For the Asian group, a younger arrival age predicted significantly higher total accuracy scores on the listening task ($r = -0.76, p < 0.01$) and higher accuracy scores on all eleven grammatical structures; arrival age also predicted higher total accuracy scores on the reading task ($r = -0.53, p < 0.01$) and higher accuracy scores on eight of the eleven grammatical structures. For the European group, no arrival-age effect was found with overall performance on either task, except for the performance on one rule type for the listening task (articles) and another rule type for the reading task (predicate structure).

In light of these findings, one may ask, why does long-term L2 attainment vary among different language groups? The language groups are associated with different L1 linguistic attributes as well as different social and cultural behaviors. Regarding linguistic attributes, European languages usually are linguistically closer to English whereas Asian languages are linguistically further from English. As a nonlinguistic but approximate indicator of linguistic distance, Odlin (1997) used the different lengths of language courses at the Foreign Service Institute of the U.S. State Department designed to help L1 English speakers with similar language-learning aptitudes to reach comparable levels of proficiency in different foreign languages. The average length of Asian-language classes was substantially longer than the length of European-language classes. Consistent with this phenomenon, the Vietnamese speakers (McDonald, 2000) and Chinese speakers (Bialystok & Miller, 1999) had particular trouble with English structures that are absent in their native languages, such as plurals, articles, third-person singular present, and subject-verb agreement.

Socially and culturally, in comparison to Asian-language speakers, European-language speakers tended to use English more frequently (Birdsong & Molis, 2001; McDonald, 2000). In the study reported by Jia and colleagues (in press), in comparison to the Asian mothers, European mothers were reported to speak better English. In addition, European-language speakers reported stronger motivation to learn English because of the beauty of the language, did less preparation of grammar before speaking English, and had a stronger identity with American culture.

Taken together, when major learning variables are equal, immigrant groups speaking different first languages have different levels of long-term L2 attainment and different degrees of arrival-age effects. Across the several studies reviewed, speakers of the European languages showed a higher proficiency and smaller arrival-age effect than speakers of the Asian languages. These findings suggest that factors associated with different bilingual groups, such as L1-L2 linguistic distance, as well as social and cultural behaviors related to language learning and use, can all be independent predictors of L2 proficiency. However, reasons for these social and cultural differences among various L1 groups and their causal links to language proficiency are not fully understood and merit further research.

A BILINGUALISM PERSPECTIVE: SIMULTANEOUS EXAMINATION OF L1 AND L2 PROFICIENCY

Another advance has come as the result of studies that have examined immigrants' proficiency in not only English but also their first language. Bilinguals' two languages can closely interact with each other at different levels (Grosjean, 1989; Heredia & Altarriba, 2001). A better understanding of how L1 is maintained among immigrants can shed light on the processes of L2 acquisition as well as identify factors related to heritage-language maintenance. Studies that have simultaneously examined L1 and L2 proficiency have consistently found that, with increasing arrival age, L1 proficiency increases and L2 proficiency decreases. Such trends have been found with the accuracy of pronunciation of Korean-English bilinguals (Yeni-Komshian, Flege, & Liu, 2000) and Italian-English bilinguals (Flege, Munro, & MacKay, 1995), with the speed and accuracy of lexical retrieval of Russian-English bilinguals (McElree, Jia, & Litvak, 2000) and of Spanish-English bilinguals (Kohnert, Bates, & Hernandez 1999), and with grammatical proficiency of Chinese-English bilinguals (Jia & Aaronson, 1999; Jia et al., 2002).

Flege and colleagues (1995) studied 240 native Italian speakers who began to learn English in Canada between the ages of two and twenty-three, and who had lived in Canada for an average of thirty-two years. Although the focus of the study was on arrival-age effects on L2, the researchers observed that as arrival age increased, the self-evaluated pronunciation accuracy in English decreased, but accuracy in Italian increased.

Yeni-Komshian and colleagues (2000) reported the first empirical demonstration in the realm of pronunciation, of the negative correlation between L1 and L2 in relation to arrival ages. These researchers studied 240 native Korean speakers who immigrated to the United States between the ages of one and twenty-three and had lived in the country for more than ten years. Participants were divided into ten groups based on their arrival ages in the United States. Participants imitated twenty-four English sentences and fourteen Korean sentences. Ten monolingual judges of each language rated the pronunciation proficiency along a 9-point scale, with 1 for "very poor pronunciation" (Korean) or "very strong accent" (English) and 9 for "very good pronunciation" (Korean) or "no accent" (English). These numbers were then converted to z-scores so that proficiency in L1 and L2 were directly comparable (see Figure 14.2). As arrival age increased, accuracy in L2 pronunciation decreased, but accuracy in L1 increased. Those who immigrated to the United States younger than age

Figure 14.2

Average Pronunciation Proficiency (z-scores) in English (L2) and Korean (L1) by 10 Korean Bilingual (KB) Groups with Different Ages of Arrival (AOA) in the United States

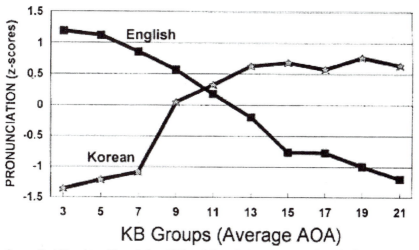

Source: Yeni-Komshian, Flege, & Liu, 2000, p. 140, with the permission of Cambridge University Press.

eleven pronounced English more accurately than Korean, whereas those who arrived in the United States older than age eleven pronounced Korean more accurately than English. Significantly, for the whole group of participants, more accurate pronunciation in one language predicted less accurate pronunciation in the other, $r = -0.65$, $p < 0.001$.

Using a speed-accuracy trade-off paradigm, McElree and colleagues (2000) compared the speed and accuracy with which twenty-six native Russian speakers retrieved conceptual information in L1 and L2. Participants made categorical judgment of 216 pairs of English words and 216 pairs of Russian words. Younger arrivals (mean U.S. arrival age = 8.6 years) recognized L2 words faster and more accurately than L1 words, while the older arrivals (mean U.S. arrival age = 16.8 years) had the opposite pattern. Medium-age arrivals (mean U.S. arrival age = 12.3 years) showed similar speed and accuracy in L1 and L2 word recognition.

Kohnert and colleagues (1999) focused only on native Spanish speakers who were exposed to English at around age five. Participants were divided into five groups according to their ages at the time of the study, ages 5–7, 8–10, 11–13, 14–16 years, and young adults, with twenty participants in each age group. They named pictures in either Spanish or English in 100 trials. The 5–7 age group was more accurate in naming pictures in Spanish (51 percent accuracy) than in English (32 percent accuracy). The gap narrowed after age seven, and the 8–10 and 11–13 groups obtained the same levels of accuracy in both languages. The trend reversed after age thirteen, with the 14–16 age group being more accurate in English (86 percent accuracy) than in Spanish (70 percent accuracy), and the young adult group also being more accurate in English (94 percent accuracy) than in Spanish (85 percent accuracy). The speed of picture naming also showed the same patterns as accuracy.

Jia and colleagues (Jia & Aaronson, 1999; Jia et al., 2002) studied forty-four native Mandarin Chinese speakers in New York City with at least five years of U.S. residence and arrival ages between three and thirty-eight years. Their grammatical proficiency was measured with one listening grammaticality judgment task in Mandarin and one in English. A younger arrival age predicted lower accuracy on the L1 task, $r = 0.55$, $p < 0.001$, but higher accuracy on the L2 task, $r = -0.69$, $p < 0.001$. Accuracy in the L1 and L2 tasks also had a significant negative correlation, $r = -0.33$, $p < 0.05$, indicating that higher proficiency in one language predicted lower proficiency in the other.

These results are consistent with findings from large-scale survey studies. With a longitudinal survey study of 3,063 U.S. high school immigrant students of thirty-five nationalities and a wide range of socioeconomic levels, Rumbaut (1998) found that younger arrivals reported an increasing preference for and proficiency in L2 (English) and a decreasing preference for and proficiency in

L1 over a three-year period. Krashen (1996) reviewed a group of survey studies showing the same trend in the Spanish-speaking populations in the United States.

Considering that upon U.S. arrival, immigrants of all ages usually have L1 as their only or dominant language, these recent findings indicate that younger arrivals generally switch their dominant language from L1 to L2, whereas older arrivals generally maintain L1 as their dominant language. The dominant-language switch and maintenance processes are different from the additive and subtractive learning processes proposed by Lambert (1978) in certain ways. When both L1 and L2 have social value and respect in a learning setting, additive L2 learning occurs: learners add a second, socially relevant language to their repertoire of language skills. When L1 does not enjoy sufficient respect in a learning setting, subtractive learning occurs: L2 slowly replaces L1. However, I suggest that the dominant-language switch or maintenance processes are preferable ways to describe the dynamic changes of immigrants' L1 and L2 proficiency because these terms emphasize the relative proficiency of the two languages, whereas additive and subtractive learning do not. For example, dominant-language maintenance clearly indicates that an individual's L1 remains stronger than his or her L2, whereas additive learning can occur even though L2 grows stronger than L1. Hence, dominant-language maintenance and additive learning are overlapping but not identical concepts.

The dominant language switch and maintenance processes are group trends that do not exclude the possibility that some individuals maintain comparably high levels of proficiency in more than one language due to their exceptional language-learning abilities or unique environmental demands. Examples of such environmental demands are bilingual programs in which both L1 and L2 proficiency are targets of academic achievement. Studies have found that L1 and L2 proficiency are usually positively correlated with each other in such programs (for a comprehensive review of these studies, see Cummins, 1991). The reason may be that the bilingual programs provide learners with both motivation and structured learning opportunities to master two languages. However, participants in the reviewed studies mostly went through immersion programs, and L1 had never been a target of their academic achievement.

The theme of dominant-language switch or maintenance emerging from recent research raises both theoretical and applied questions, the answers to which can deepen our understanding not only of arrival age effect on long-term L2 attainment, but also of the context in which immigrants of different ages become bilinguals. What are the ongoing processes of dominant-language switch or maintenance? Why do younger arrivals in general switch to L2 as their dominant language, and older arrivals in general maintain their L1 dominance? Would going through the different processes expose younger and older arrivals to different learning conditions, and if so, what are the differences?

TRACKING LANGUAGE PROFICIENCY AND ENVIRONMENT OVER TIME: LONGITUDINAL RESEARCH

Evidently, the long-term attainment approach has its limits in answering these questions because it only captures a snapshot of bilinguals' language proficiency, and information on the learning context can only be obtained through retrospective self-report. A more suitable approach to addressing these questions would involve a longitudinal design with multiple research methods, including language tasks to measure proficiency changes, as well as interviews and observations to assess the learning context.

Two decades ago, longitudinal studies were initiated to explore the processes of L2 acquisition (e.g., Cancino, Rosansky, & Schumann, 1978; Hakuta, 1978). Most of these were single case studies lasting between three and ten months, and age differences in L2 acquisition were rarely examined. Snow and Hoefnagel-Höhle (1977, 1978) conducted the most extensive longitudinal study on age differences in L2 acquisition by following forty-seven English speakers from ages three to sixty years who were learning Dutch in Holland for a year. Interestingly, the older learners (age of arrival in Holland = adult or 12–15) initially were better than the younger ones (age of arrival in Holland = 8–10, 6–7, or 3–5) in L2 pronunciation, morphology, and syntax, a phenomenon that disappeared after four to five months. Possibly due to the large sample size, information about language environment was not obtained. Nevertheless, these studies have helped to lay the groundwork for more recent research.

Jia and Aaronson (2001, 2002) reported a three-year longitudinal study to assess the changes in both language environment and language proficiency. Participating in the study were ten Chinese children and adolescents, five girls and five boys, ages five to sixteen when they immigrated to the New York City area. These ten children and adolescents were Anna (f5), Betty (f6), Carl (m7), Dianna (f8), Eric (m9), Frank (m9), Gary (m12), Hua-lei (f12), Jing-lan (f15), and Kang-da (m16). Participants' pseudonyms are specified with their gender and arrival age in the parentheses. Data collection started from the beginning of their English immersion and continued until relatively stable English proficiency was achieved three years after immigration. Various aspects of participants' language environments and changes in L1 and L2 proficiency were measured with controlled language tasks, detailed structured interviews with participants and their parents, and observations of participants' language use in various situations. The following is a review of some findings from the study.

Specific Processes of Dominant Language Switch or Maintenance

The study documented the specific dominant-language switch or maintenance processes ongoing at three related levels: language preference, language use, and language proficiency. Based on participants' self-report and observations, all of them started L2 immersion with preference for L1, but within a year, younger arrivals (with arrival age of nine or younger) had switched their language preference from Chinese to English, while older arrivals (with arrival age of 12 or older) maintained their preference for Chinese across all three years of study. Consistent with this language-preference switch or maintenance pattern, younger arrivals used L2 more often and older arrivals used L1 more often in leisure activities and peer interactions.

In contrast to the immediate language preference and use switches from L1 to L2 among younger arrivals, their performance on some language tasks indicated that they only started to surpass older arrivals in L2 grammatical abilities during the third year of the study. This marked the beginning of the long-term L2 attainment decline documented in the long-term attainment studies. This does not contradict the findings that older learners had higher L2 proficiency than younger learners during the first year of L2 immersion (Snow & Hoefnagel-Höhle, 1977, 1978), because the earliest L2 proficiency data analyzed to date were obtained at the end of the first year of L2 immersion. Taken together, the long-term L2 attainment decline seems to be primarily a long-term effect that starts to appear after a delay.

Although all participants had Chinese as their dominant language in the beginning of English immersion, older arrivals had higher L1 proficiency as shown by parental reports. Across the three years, the older arrivals maintained their L1 proficiency at a native level and suffered little L1 attrition. L1 proficiency of the younger arrivals underwent three types of changes: development, no change, and loss. Listening and speaking abilities grew among some of them or remained unchanged. The limited reading and writing abilities were almost completely lost. Therefore, in comparison to older arrivals, the younger ones had lower L1 proficiency to start with, and the development stop and attrition of L1 overwhelmed the limited development that occurred. These processes jointly contributed to the long-term L1 attainment increase with increasing arrival age documented in long-term attainment studies (e.g., Jia et al., 2002; Yeni-Komshian et al., 2000).

Age Differences in Language Environment

Younger arrivals were exposed to a richer L2 environment and poorer L1 environment in comparison to the older arrivals throughout the three years of study. The following are discussions of several aspects of language environment examined.

Speaking with family members. Consistent with the language preference transition patterns, younger arrivals used more English in conversations with their parents, whereas the older ones exclusively used L1. While all participants predominantly spoke L1 at home during Year 1 and Year 2, during Year 3 all of the younger arrivals began to talk to their parents in English although their parents generally used Chinese. This language-code mismatch occurred in 10 to 35 percent of the conversations between the younger arrivals and their parents. In contrast, this situation did not occur at all for any of the older arrivals. Consequently, parents of the younger and older arrivals had different reactions to their children's language use at home. Most of the parents of the younger arrivals insisted on using L1 at home in response to their children's increasing loss of L1 and reluctance to use L1. In contrast, the parents of the older arrivals pushed their children to speak English at home so that the parents could practice. However, their children generally refused to do so.

Speaking with friends. Across all three years, the younger arrivals made more predominantly L2-speaking friends whereas the older ones made more predominantly L1-speaking friends (see Figure 14.3). Most of the younger arrivals increased the number of L2-speaking friends and decreased the number of L1-speaking friends throughout the three years. The average percentage of their L2-speaking friends increased from 65 percent in Year 1 to 90 percent in Year 2 and 93 percent in Year 3. In contrast, the older arrivals only increased the percentage of L2-speaking friends from 10 percent in Year 1 to 17 percent in Year 2 and 29 percent in Year 3. In comparison to older arrivals, the younger ones not only spoke and listened to L2 more, they also had a greater ratio of L2 speech output to input. Although older arrivals received substantial L2 input during school instruction, they produced L2 output in only limited situations. Many studies have demonstrated that natural conversations in L2 can facilitate L2 acquisition (e.g., Chesterfield, Barrows-Chesterfield, Hayes-Latimer, & Chávez, 1983; Johnson, 1983). In addition, the demand for L2 speech output increases attention to syntactic structures (e.g., Donato, 1994; Swain, 1995) and the ways in which meanings are expressed (e.g., Pica, Holliday, Lewis, & Morgenthaler, 1989). This subsequently helps learners modify their own speech to achieve their communication goals.

Watching television. Younger arrivals in the study watched English television more often and watched a greater variety of programs than the older ones did. Past research on the influence of watching television on L1 acquisition has shown that the cartoons and commercials watched by younger children contain linguistic redundancy and repetition of specific linguistic structures in a colloquial style with simple syntax (Sharma, 1995). From watching television, monolingual children learn object names and relationships, attributes, action words, and body parts. Verbal routines seen on television are later used in children's play activities (Rice & Woodsmall, 1988). These results may well generalize to bilingual children.

Reading. Participants read books and newspapers in addition to their required school reading. The language used in reading differed for the younger and older arrivals. The younger group read more in L2 than in L1, and vice versa for the older group.

Figure 14.3
The Percentage of Predominantly English-Speaking Friends Participants Had
During the First Three Years of Residence in the United States

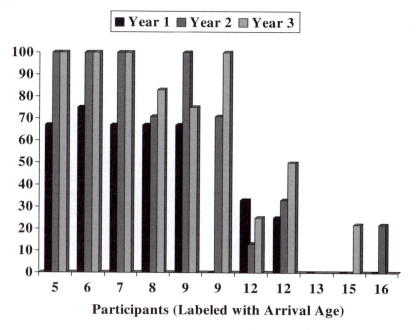

Participants (Labeled with Arrival Age)

For the younger group, 76 percent of their book reading was in L2 during Year 1, and the proportion increased to 99 percent in Year 2 and 97.9 percent in Year 3. For the older group, 17 percent of their book reading was in L2 during Year 1, and the proportion increased to only 33 percent in Year 2 and 31 percent in Year 3. Research on both L1 and L2 acquisition has shown that increased reading leads to higher reading proficiency and general language proficiency (see Krashen, 1993, for a review). In the L1 literature, increased reading has been found to be an independent contributor to the development of verbal abilities (e.g., Cunningham & Stanovich, 1991), the acquisition of a receptive vocabulary (Leseman & de Jong, 1998), and productive vocabulary (McKeown & Curtis, 1987). Similar gains have also been found for L2 acquisition in bilingual reading research (Elley, 1991; Elley & Mangubhai, 1983).

Notably, age differences in the language preference and use transitions over time seemed to occur independently of language proficiency. Despite comparable ability to communicate in L2 in many situations, younger arrivals chose to use L2 more than the older ones. Interestingly, other investigators have also noted the discrepancy between language proficiency and willingness to communicate in L2 among adult L2 learners. L2 learners' motivation to communicate with other L2 speakers, rather than their L2 proficiency, has been found to be an important causal factor of the willingness to use L2 (see MacIntyre, Clement, Dornyei, & Noels, 1998, for a review). The discrepancy between language proficiency and willingness to use L2 can partially explain the transition from the advantage of older learners (e.g., Snow & Hoefnagel-Höhle, 1977, 1978) to the long-term L2 attainment declines (e.g., Flege et al., 1999) that have been separately documented in the literature. That is, across time, the environmental differences accumulate and lead to proficiency differences. A substantial amount of qualitative data from the longitudinal study further shows that cognitive, social, and psychological factors interactively led to the environmental differences.

Factors Contributing to Environmental Differences

Developing L1 proficiency. A large body of research literature in L1 acquisition has documented continuing L1 development throughout childhood and adolescence (e.g., Braine, Brooks, Cowan, Samuels, & Tamis-LeMonda, 1993; Gaddes & Crockett, 1975; Heath, 1999). Findings from the longitudinal study indicate that developing L1 proficiency is an important cognitive factor in L2 acquisition. As a function of age and previous education, L2 learners of different ages start L2 immersion with different levels of L1 proficiency.

For example, when asked if, and why, she preferred speaking English over Chinese, Betty (f6) replied, based on her knowledge that single English words often require more than one Chinese character, "Yeah, because it (English) go [sic] faster. Yeah, you don't have to say two word [sic] in, in one. . . . Like 'friend,' you don't have to say Peng2-You3. Two word [sic] in only one word. That's easier." When asked if, and why, he found Chinese more difficult than English, Frank (m9) complained about the substantially greater number of homophones in Chinese than in English.

The younger arrivals, with limited L1 reading abilities in the beginning of L2 immersion, almost started their literacy in L2. In contrast, the older participants arrived in the United States as fluent Chinese readers, with the knowledge of between 2,000 and 5,000 Chinese characters. Consequently, soon after exposure to English reading and writing instructions and demands, the younger arrivals started to report a lack of interest in further developing their Chinese reading and writing skills. For example, Frank (m9) felt that the Chinese logographic writing system was harder than the English alphabetic system: "Chinese is like harder to write," he said. "English is easier to write . . . because you just have to know ABCDEFG, the 26 letters. But in Chinese, you have to draw a lot of stuff to get it."

These and related points were voiced by most of the younger arrivals during the interviews, soon after their exposure to English reading and writing instruction. In contrast, the older arrivals all felt that Chinese was easier than English due to their superior L1 skills, and subsequently continued to prefer and use Chinese.

At a more specific linguistic level, L1 proficiency impacts L2 lexical acquisition. A series of studies has shown that for beginning adult L2 learners, word forms in L2 indirectly access concepts via word forms in L1, but advanced L2 learners have direct access to concepts for word forms in both languages (e.g., Kroll & Stewart, 1994). These skill-related differences in L2 lexical acquisition have analogies in age-related differences found in the current longitudinal study. Younger children had acquired fewer L1 words upon their arrival in the United States and then learned new L2 words for new concepts. For example, Anna started to play piano after she came to the United States at age five, and learned to say "hit the key" in English. Both "hit" and "key" were the first lexical labels she learned for the related concepts because she had never learned the Chinese (L1) equivalents "tan2" for "hit" and "qin2-jian4" for "key." Therefore she learned "hit" and "key" by directly mapping L2 words to concepts. These English words became her L1 words learned through similar processes for L1 acquisition (direct mapping of word forms and concepts) and allow younger learners to acquire L2 lexical items efficiently. Significantly, findings like these indicate that younger children's greater proficiency in L2 is partially a consequence of a normal experience that is more readily available to them due to their less developed L1 proficiency.

Peer preference and social abilities. Interactions among peer preferences, social abilities, and age-related pragmatics also fostered a relatively richer L2 environment for younger arrivals and richer L1 environment for older arrivals. According to the child and parental interviews, as well as direct observations, participants of various ages showed different peer preferences. Children younger than nine had friends with diverse cultural and language backgrounds, including European, Hispanic, and Asian. Their friends were from readily available sources, such as the same class and neighborhood. They predominantly spoke English with each other. Participants in the middle age range (twelve to thirteen years) made mostly Chinese- and Korean-speaking friends and spoke Chinese with the former and English with the latter. Their friends were from both the same and different classes. The two oldest participants, Jing-lan (f15) and Kang-da (m16), were the most selective, with almost exclusively L1-speaking friends, who came from the same region of China as they did, during the first two years of L2 immersion. These findings are consistent with age differences in peer preferences that have been extensively documented in nonimmigrant populations. Younger children develop friendships based on concrete activities and thus choose playmates who are close at hand. In contrast, older children view friendship in terms of intangible factors such as similar interests and cultural identities, as well as mutual consideration and understanding. Therefore they choose friends based on similarities in race, ethnicity, sex, and social class (Hartup, 1996; Kupersmidt, De Rosier, & Patterson, 1995).

These different peer choices subsequently influenced their language use. For example, among the younger participants, the motivation to be similar to their peers made them feel "irregular" if they could not speak L2 fluently, but not so when their L1 had stopped developing or had been lost. When asked how she felt about speaking English but not Chinese with her peers, Betty (f6) replied, "I feel regular. . . . I'm not embarrassed or something. I feel regular." Significantly, younger children's strong motivation to use L2 was not completely caused by language proficiency. For example, when asked about her language preference, Dianna (f8), who explicitly acknowledged that her Chinese was better, replied, "I like to speak English a little tiny bit more because I want to. Usually I was talking in English with my friends. . . . I don't like to talk with Cathy, because she doesn't know how to speak a lot of English."

Age-related differences in social abilities also contributed to different peer interactions. The highly developed social abilities of the adolescents enabled them to find L1-speaking friends from various social settings and somewhat distant geographic areas. In contrast, the younger children's limited social abilities and parental restrictions on mobility meant that they made friends with others who happened to be physically close, such as children in the same class or those living on the same block. Differences in social abilities also affected how much L2 proficiency is essential to satisfy their daily pragmatic needs. For example, Anna (f5) wet her pants in kindergarten at the beginning of the study because she did not know how to ask for the bathroom in English. Also, on some days she did not receive the school breakfast because she could not tell her teacher in English that she had not eaten at home. These pragmatic needs provided strong motivation for a young child to master the new language as quickly as possible. In contrast, older arrivals' greater cognitive and social abilities enabled them to handle the daily problems with limited English skills.

Different levels of social and cognitive abilities also led to different understandings of language choice during peer interactions. Younger children felt socially obligated, as if by "majority rule," to speak only English in school, whereas older ones felt that they had control over that aspect of their environment. When asked whether she spoke Chinese with peers in school, Anna (f5) stated, "Oh, there is [sic] a lot of Chinese people [in school], but . . . they don't speak Chinese. . . . They can't speak Chinese in school . . . because nobody speaks Chinese in school. It's an English school." In contrast, Hua-lei (f12) reported that she preferred to speak Chinese with peers in school because "there's [sic] so many Chinese in the school."

Cultural preferences. Based on child and parental interviews and interviewer observations, older participants' preference for their native culture and younger participants' preference for American culture also shaped their language use for peer interactions, television watching, and leisure reading. Although the older participants were linguistically capable of dealing with L2 speakers, they preferred to interact with peers from the same culture. By doing so, they were able to talk about familiar

Chinese movies and songs, to exchange CDs and information related to their favorite Chinese movie stars and singers, and to go to Chinese restaurants. In contrast, younger children, who had fewer native cultural experiences to share with others from the same background, were more curious about the broader popular American peer culture, such as baseball games and television shows. For example, Eric (m9) reported that he watched television a lot just to learn about popular television shows and baseball games so that he could join his classmates in relevant conversations. All of the younger children watched cartoons, movies, and television shows that were popular among typical American children of their age, such as *Batman*, Disney cartoons, *Fox 5 Kids* (New York City only), *Hercules*, *Power Rangers*, *Xena*, *Titanic*, and *Pokemon*. Cultural preference also influenced participants' reading activities. Younger children's English reading included book series such as Disney stories, Babysitters Club, and Goosebumps. Older participants' Chinese reading included Chinese classics, as well as news about China and Chinese movie and popular singers. Although little psychological research has focused on age differences in the speed and degree of acculturation by immigrants, the current findings are consistent with those of an anthropological study on this topic. Minoura (1992) studied a group of seventy-three Japanese children who immigrated to the United States at different ages and an additional group of children who returned to Japan after residing in the United States. It was found that a younger arrival age was associated with faster and more thorough acculturation, and the years between ages nine and fourteen seemed to be a sensitive period for the incorporation of the meaning system of the host culture.

SUMMARY, IMPLICATIONS, AND FUTURE RESEARCH DIRECTIONS

The findings reviewed indicate that English attainment and native-language maintenance by immigrant children and adolescents in North America are predicted and influenced by multiple variables. Traditional psychological research has repeatedly shown that arrival age in the host country is a robust predictor of long-term English attainment: a younger arrival age predicts higher English proficiency after several years of English immersion. As the first recent advance in the field, a number of environmental and attitudinal variables have also been found to uniquely predict English proficiency independently of arrival age. Higher English proficiency is associated with more English use (Birdsong & Molis, 2001; Flege et al., 1999), more years of education in the host country (Flege et al., 1999), family members' higher English proficiency (Jia & Aaronson, 2002; Jia et al., 2002), and stronger motivation in learning English (Flege et al., 1999). Due to the inherent limitations of the long-term attainment type of research design, we cannot go beyond correlational interpretations to reach causal conclusions. Hence, one challenge for future researchers is to explore the causal mechanisms linking these environmental and attitudinal variables to language attainment. Equally important, many other major environmental variables remain to be explored, including the socioeconomic status of the immigrant families, and the type of bilingual programs that immigrant children and adolescents receive.

As the second advance in the field, researchers have started to compare multiple immigrant groups with different first languages (Bialystok & Miller, 1999; Birdsong & Molis, 2001; Jia & Aaronson, 2002; Jia et al., 2002; McDonald, 2000). The results consistently indicate that when major learning variables are controlled, speakers of European languages (e.g., Spanish and Russian) tend to achieve higher English proficiency and show less strong arrival-age effects than do speakers of Asian languages (e.g., Chinese, Korean, and Vietnamese). The results also suggest that what seems to be responsible for European-language speakers' advantages are the closer linguistic distance between L1 and L2, mothers (or parents) with higher L2 proficiency, a stronger motivation to learn L2, and a stronger identity with the host culture. These findings, from a different angle, have strengthened the view that English learning is sensitive to environmental and attitudinal variables, as well as previously learned L1 linguistic structures. The findings also suggest that methods of teaching English as a second language should be sensitive to learners' linguistic and cultural backgrounds.

As the third advance in the field, researchers have started to examine not only English proficiency but also how much L1 immigrants of different ages maintain. The findings indicate that a younger arrival age predicts higher proficiency in L2 but lower proficiency in L1 (Flege et al., 1995; Jia & Aaronson, 1999, 2002; Kohnert et al., 1999; McElree et al., 2000; Yeni-Komshian et al., 2000). The relative levels of L1 and L2 proficiency have opposite patterns among younger and older arrivals, and as a group, younger immigrants tend to switch their dominant language from L1 to L2, whereas older immigrants tend to maintain L1 as their dominant language.

As the fourth advance, larger-scale and longer-term longitudinal design has just begun to be used in this research area. The longitudinal study reviewed in this chapter (Jia & Aaronson, 2001, 2002) offered us detailed information about immigrants' L2 acquisition that is hard to obtain through long-term attainment studies. Younger arrivals, within the first year of immersion, switched their language preference from L1 to L2, while older arrivals maintained their preference for L1 the three years of the second study. Consistently, younger arrivals were exposed to significantly richer L2 environments and poorer L1 environments, but the reverse was found for older arrivals. These age differences in language environment were related to developmental differences in L1 proficiency and in peer as well as cultural preferences. These findings indicate that cognitive, social, and cultural factors jointly shape the course of L2 acquisition and L1 maintenance or loss by immigrant children and adolescents.

Contradictory to the assumption that immigrants in general are reluctant to give up their heritage languages, the rapid L1 attainment among younger immigrants has also been documented by a rich set of survey studies in the field of bilingual education (see Krashen, 1996, for a review). Significantly, immigrants who have lost their heritage language have been shown to unwillingly suffer from impaired communications with their family members and their heritage culture communities (Cho & Krashen, 1998; Kouritzin, 1999; Wong-Fillmore, 1991). If we agree that bilingualism or multilingualism can improve the well-being of individuals and our nation (see Krashen, 1998, for a review of studies supporting this point), we should find ways to better preserve immigrants' heritage languages, which are a natural source of bilingualism and multilingualism.

The long-standing debate on whether the long-term L2 attainment decline along increasing arrival age can support the CPH has inspired all of these empirical advances and transformed the field into one that is more comprehensive and in-depth. Regarding answers to the debate, the findings reviewed in this chapter have failed to provide sufficient evidence for the CPH. Although a younger arrival age is robustly and uniquely associated with higher English proficiency, arrival age covaries with other variables that play causal roles in L2 acquisition, such as learning environment and attitudes that are influenced by cognitive, social, and cultural factors. Actually, due to inherent methodological constraints, behavioral studies are not likely to yield sufficient evidence for the CPH. In the future, a real breakthrough in our understanding of the contribution of neurological factors to age differences in L2 acquisition should come from research that simultaneously tracks changes in brain functioning, L1 and L2 proficiency, language environment, and the interactions of all these variables.

Although going beyond the limited focus on age differences marks a breakthrough in psychological research in L2 acquisition by immigrants, other fields can benefit from explicitly taking age differences into account. For example, one such field is the research on the efficiency of bilingual programs. If immigrants of different ages learn English differently due to their different levels of cognitive, social, and cultural resources, the optimal timing and methods of teaching English to immigrants of different ages may vary.

Basic research in L2 acquisition also has the potential to provide valuable information for the ongoing research and practice in the area of bilingual speech and language disorders, and efforts are much needed to bridge these two areas of science and practice. A major problem in diagnosing and treating speech and language disorders of immigrants with limited English proficiency is the lack of norms in both L1 and L2 proficiency that have ages of learning English and L1 backgrounds factored in. Developing such norms requires reliable information about the changes of L1 and L2 proficiency of immigrants of different ages over an extended age span. Future research design in basic L2 acquisition should strive to take these needs into account.

NOTES

1. Although there may be a variety of learning mechanisms and strategies responsible for language learning, the conventional term *language-learning mechanism* in the language development literature will be used to refer to the entire set.

2. An example of an ungrammatical sentence in this category is "My parents arrived the airport yesterday." English requires the collocation of the intransitive verb *arrive* and the preposition *at*, whereas Chinese only requires the transitive verb *dao4-da2*.

REFERENCES

Asher, J., & Garcia, R. (1969).The optimal age to learn a foreign language. *Modern Language Journal, 53*, 334–341.

Bialystok, E., & Hakuta, K. (1994). *In other words*. New York: Basic Books.

———. (1998). Confounded age: Linguistic and cognitive factors in age differences for second language acquisition. In D. Birdsong (Ed.), *Second language acquisition and the Critical Period Hypothesis* (pp. 161–181). Mahwah, NJ: Erlbaum.

Bialystok, E., & Miller, B. (1999). The problem of age in second-language acquisition: Influences from language, structure, and task. *Bilingualism: Language and Cognition, 2*, 127–145.

Birdsong, D. (Ed.). (1998). *Second language acquisition and the Critical Period Hypothesis*. Mahwah, NJ: Erlbaum.

Birdsong, D., & Molis, M. (2001). On the evidence for maturational constraints on second language acquisition. *Journal of Memory and Language, 44*, 235–249.

Braine, M. D. S., Brooks, P. J., Cowan, N., Samuels, M., & Tamis-LeMonda, C. (1993). The development of categories at the semantics/syntax interface. *Cognitive Development, 8*, 465–494.

Cancino, H., Rosansky, E. J., & Schumann, J. H. (1978). The acquisition of English negatives and interrogatives by native Spanish speakers. In E. M. Hatch (Ed.), *Second language acquisition* (pp. 207–230). Rowley, MA: Newbury House.

Chesterfield, R., Barrows-Chesterfield, K. B., Hayes-Latimer, K., & Chávez, R. (1983). The influence of teachers and peers on second language acquisition in bilingual preschool programs. *TESOL Quarterly, 17* (3), 401–419.

Cho, G., & Krashen, S. (1998). The negative consequences of heritage language loss and why we should care. In S. D. Krashen, L. Tse, & J. McQuillan (Eds.), *Heritage language development* (pp. 31–39). Culver City, CA: Language Education Associates.

Cummins, J. (1991). Interdependence of first- and second-language proficiency in bilingual children. In E. Bialystok (Ed.), *Language processing in bilingual children* (pp. 70–89). New York: Cambridge University Press.

Cunningham, A. E., & Stanovich, K. E. (1991). Tracking the unique effects of print exposure in children: Associations with vocabulary, general knowledge, and spelling. *Journal of Educational Psychology, 83*, 264–274.

Donato, R. (1994). Collective scaffolding in second language learning. In J. P. Lantolf & G. Appel (Eds.), *Vygotskian approaches to second language research* (pp. 33–56). Norwood, NJ: Ablex.

Elley, W. B. (1991). Acquiring literacy in a second language: The effect of book-based programs. *Language Learning, 41*, 375–411.

Elley, W. B., & Mangubhai, F. (1983). The impact of reading on second language learning. *Reading Research Quarterly, 19*, 53–67.

Flege, J. E., Munro, M. J., & MacKay, I. R. A. (1995). Factors affecting strength of perceived foreign accent in a second language. *Journal of the Acoustical Society of America, 97*, 3125–3134.

Flege, J. E., Yeni-Komshian, G. H., & Liu, S. (1999). Age constraints on second-language acquisition. *Journal of Memory and Language, 41*, 78–104.

Gaddes, W. H., & Crockett (1975). The Spreen-Benton aphasia tests, normative data as a measure of normal language development. *Brain and Language, 2*, 257–280.

Gardner, R. C., & Lambert, W. E. (1959). Motivational variables in second language acquisition. *Canadian Journal of Psychology, 13*, 266–272.

Grosjean, F. (1989). Neurolinguists, beware! The bilingual is not two monolinguals in one person. *Brain and Language, 36*, 3–15.

Hakuta, K. (1978). A report on the development of grammatical morphemes in a Japanese girl learning English as a second language. In E. M. Hatch (Ed.), *Second language acquisition* (pp. 132–147). Rowley, MA: Newbury House.

Harley, B., & Wang, W. (1997). The Critical Period Hypothesis: Where are we now? In A. M. B. de Groot & J. F. Kroll (Eds.), *Tutorials in bilingualism: Psycholinguistic perspectives* (pp. 19–51). Hillsdale, NJ: Erlbaum.

Hartup, W. W. (1996). The company they keep: Friendships and their developmental significance. *Child Development, 67*, 1–13.

Heath, S. B. (1999). Dimensions of language development: Lessons from older children. In A. S. Masten (Ed.), *Minnesota symposia on child psychology*, Vol. 29, *Cultural processes in child development* (pp. 59–75). Mahwah, NJ: Erlbaum.

Heredia, R. R., & Altarriba, J. (2001). Bilingual language mixing: Why do bilinguals code-switch? *Current Directions in Psychological Science, 10*, 164–168.

Jia, G., & Aaronson, D. (1999). Age differences in second language acquisition: The Dominant Language Switch and Maintenance Hypothesis. In A. Greenhill, H. Littlefield, & C. Tano (Eds.), *Proceedings of the twenty-third Boston University Conference on Language Development* (pp. 301–312). Somerville, MA: Cascadilla Press.

———. (2002). Learning English as a second language by U.S. immigrants: What accounts for their ultimate attainment in the new language? In Y. Shirai, H. Kobayashi, S. Miyata, K. Nakamura, T. Ogura, & H. Sirai (Eds.), *Studies in language sciences* (Vol. 2, pp. 259–270). Japan: Kurosio.

———. (2003). A longitudinal study of Chinese children and adolescents learning English in the U.S. *Applid Psycholinguistics, 24*, (1), 131–161.

Jia, G., Aaronson, D., & Wu, Y. H. (2002). Long-term language attainment of bilingual immigrants: Predictive factors and language group differences. *Applied Psycholinguistics, 23* (4), 599–621.

Johnson, D. M. (1983). Natural language learning by design: A classroom experiment in social interaction and second language acquisition. *TESOL Quarterly, 17*, 55–68.

Johnson, J. (1992). Critical Period effects in second language acquisition: The effect of written versus auditory materials on the assessment of grammatical competence. *Language Learning, 42*, 217–248.

Johnson, J., & Newport, E. (1989). Critical Period effect in second language learning: The influence of maturational state on the acquisition of English as a second language. *Cognitive Psychology, 21*, 60–69.

Kohnert, K. J., Bates, E., & Hernandez, A. E. (1999). Balancing bilinguals: Lexical-semantic production and cognitive processing in children learning Spanish and English. *Journal of Speech, Language, and Hearing Research, 42*, 1400–1413.

Kouritzin, S. G. (1999). *Face(t)s of first language loss*. Mahwah, NJ: Erlbaum.

Krashen, S. (1993). *The power of reading*. Englewood, CO: Libraries Unlimited.

———. (1996). *Under attack: The case against bilingual education*. Culver City, CA: Language Education Associates.

———. (1998). Heritage language development: Some practical arguments. In S. D. Krashen, L. Tse, & J. McQuillan (Eds.), *Heritage language development* (pp. 3–13). Culver City, CA: Language Education Associates.

Kroll, J. F., & Stewart, E. (1994). Category interference in translation and picture naming: Evidence for asymmetric connections between bilingual memory representations. *Journal of Memory and Language, 33*, 149–174.

Kupersmidt, J. B., De Rosier, M. E., & Patterson, C. P. (1995). Similarity as the basis for children's friendships: The roles of sociometric status, aggressive and withdrawn behavior, academic achievement, and demographic characteristics. *Journal of Social & Personal Relationships, 12*, 439–452.

Lambert, W. E. (1967). The social psychology of bilingualism. *Journal of Social Issues, 23*, 91–109.

———. (1978). Cognitive and socio-cultural consequences of bilingualism. *Canadian Modern Language Review, 34*, 537–547.

Lenneberg, E. (1967). *Biological foundations of language*. New York: Wiley.

Leseman, P. P. M., & de Jong, P. F. (1998). Home literacy: Opportunity, instruction, co-operation, and social-emotional quality predicting early reading achievement. *Reading Research Quarterly, 33*, 294–318.

MacIntyre, P. D., Clement, R., Dornyei, Z., & Noels, K. A. (1998). Conceptualizing willingness to communicate in a L2: A situational model of L2 confidence and affiliation. *Modern Language Journal, 82*, 545–562.

Marinova-Todd, S. H., Marshall, D. B., & Snow, C. E. (2000). Three misconceptions about age and L2 learning. *TESOL Quarterly, 34*, 9–34.

McDonald, J. L. (2000). Grammaticality judgments in a second language: Influences of age of acquisition and native language. *Applied Psycholinguistics, 21*, 395–423.

McElree, B., Jia, G., & Litvak, A. (2000). The time course of conceptual processing in three bilingual populations. *Journal of Memory and Language, 42*, 229–254.

McKeown, M. G., & Curtis, M. E. (Eds.). (1987). *The nature of vocabulary acquisition*. Hillsdale, NJ: Erlbaum.

Minoura, Y. (1992). A sensitive period for the incorporation of a cultural meaning system: A study of Japanese children growing up in the United States. *Ethos, 20*, 304–339.

Odlin, T. (1997). *Language transfer: Cross-linguistic influence in language learning*. New York: Cambridge University Press.

Oyama, S. (1976). A sensitive period for the acquisition of a nonnative phonological system. *Journal of Psycholinguistic Research, 5,* 261–283.

———. (1978). The sensitive period and comprehension of speech. *Working Papers on Bilingualism, 16,* 1–17.

Patkowski, M. S. (1982). The sensitive period for the acquisition of syntax in a second language. In S. D. Krashen, R. C. Scarcella, & M. H. Long (Eds.), *Child-adult differences in second language acquisition* (pp. 52–63). Rowley, MA: Newbury House.

———. (1990). Age and accent in a second language: A reply to James Emil Flege. *Applied Linguistics, 11,* 73–89.

Pica, T., Holliday, L., Lewis, N., & Morgenthaler, L. (1989). Comprehensible output as an outcome of linguistic demands on the learner. *Studies in Second Language Acquisition, 11,* 63–90.

Rice, M. L., Woodsmall, L. (1988). Lessons from television: Children's word learning when viewing. *Child Development, 59,* 420–429.

Rumbaut, R. G. (1998). Passages to adulthood: The adaptation of children of immigrants in Southern California. In D. J. Hernandez (Ed.), *Children of immigrants: Health, adjustment, and public assistance* (pp. 478–545). Washington, DC: National Academy Press.

Sharma, V. (1995). On children's mass media communication. *Psycho-Lingua, 25,* 85–96.

Snow, C. E. (1983). Age differences in second language acquisition: Research findings and folk psychology. In K. M. Bailey, M. H. Long, & S. Peck (Eds.), *Second language acquisition studies* (pp. 141–150). Rowley, MA: Newbury House.

Snow, C. E., & Hoefnagel-Höhle, M. (1977). Age differences and the pronunciation of foreign sounds. *Language and Speech, 20,* 357–365.

———. (1978). Age differences in second language acquisition. In E. M. Hatch (Ed.), *Second language acquisition* (pp. 333–344). Rowley, MA: Newbury House.

———. (1987). The critical period for language acquisition: Evidence from second language learning. *Child Development, 49,* 1115–1128.

Swain, M. (1995). Three functions of output in second language learning. In G. Cook & B. Seidlhofer (Eds.), *Principle and practice in applied linguistics* (pp. 125–144). Oxford: Oxford University Press.

Wong-Fillmore, L. W. (1991). When learning a second language means losing the first. *Early Childhood Research Quarterly, 6,* 323–346.

Yeni-Komshian, G., Flege, J. E., & Liu, S. (2000). Pronunciation proficiency in the first and second languages of Korean-English bilinguals. *Bilingualism: Language and Cognition, 3,* 131–149.

PART VI

Difficult Adjustments

The Changing Developmental Dynamics of Children in Particularly Difficult Circumstances: Examples of Street and War-Traumatized Children

Lewis Aptekar

DEVELOPMENTAL DIFFERENCES AMONG STREET CHILDREN

The children that the United Nations Childen's Fund (UNICEF, 1986) refers to as "in particularly difficult circumstances" are those whose suffering entails the highest risk to mental health. They include children traumatized by war, or natural and technological disasters, and those living and working without parents (street children). Other children also face especially difficult circumstances, either from extreme poverty, severe malnutrition, forced prostitution, labor exploitation, or excessive family violence. Each of these latter groups faces its own trials and tribulations, so much so that they are beyond the scope of this chapter. The two categories that are the focus here, adolescents traumatized by war and street children, face their own developmental difficulties.

Fifteen years ago, UNICEF estimated that there were about 300 million street children worldwide (1987). At that time, street children were defined according to two dimensions, the time spent in the street and the absence of contact with responsible adults. What the definition did was characterize street children as prematurely living and working without parents, a bit like premature adults. They are, in essence, living in two worlds, one characterized by childhood dependence and the other by adult independence.

There were several problems with this definition; some were simply factual, while others ignored how the children perceived their experiences and the cultural context of childhood (Aptekar, 1994). By understanding street children within a cultural context (and with regard to gender distinctions), we can re-examine the Western view that presents street children as victims of abuse or neglect, or as delinquents ready for reeducation. Instead, we can see how they have learned strategies for coping in economically (and sometimes emotionally) challenging circumstances.

In fact, the view that it is abusive parents who are at the root of the problem of street children is a bit ethnocentric. Whereas in the West abusive parents are seen as having mental disorders, and they abuse in ways which deliberately hurt the child, in non-Western cultures abuse comes less often from parents than from society. Take, for example, the numerous instances of how political contexts invoking the "superior interests of the state" have led to the most painful forms of child abuse. During the "Dirty War" in Argentina, children were tortured in front of their parents in order to motivate the parents to offer information to the state. Children in Iran were given the status of martyrs after serving as human shields in the war against Iraq. In these cases, abuse comes under state authority.

The importance of the state as an agent of child abuse is also evident in the case of China's one-child policy. Children born to families that already have a child are "out of plan" and amount to nearly 40 percent of the annual births. Yet by virtue of the state's policy, they do not officially exist. Hidden by parents who fear sanctions for having an excess birth, an unknown number remain unregistered and therefore deprived of social services. As a result of the one-child policy, the gender distribution has been modified by the increase in the numbers of female infanticides and differential abortions. Thus, while Chinese parents positively desire a child's birth, the birth is simultaneously defined by the state in stigmatizing terms. These examples illustrate that worldwide child abuse is not solely, or even mainly, the result of the wrongdoing of a few psychopathological parents; it is more likely to be a result of state policy.

The original definition of "street children" claimed that these children came from poor families, almost always headed by women living in urban areas of the developing world. They either neglected them, which led to their going to the streets, or the children were actively thrown out of the house, often because a series of stepfathers treated them badly. Not only did this beg the question of why only a small percentage of poor and neglected or abused children went to the streets while the vast majority didn't, but it also ignored the fact that as many as 90 percent of street children in developing cultures maintained contact with their families, and most of them contributed a portion of what they earned to them. Over the years, research showed that rather than being abandoned, street children almost always left home in a measured manner, initially staying away for a night or two, then adding to the time spent away from their homes (Aptekar, 1988, 1989, 1994). Gradually, the amount of time they spent with other children increased until they were matriculated into the street culture.

Other studies questioned the generally accepted characteristics about street children. The general view was that they were either pitiful and in need of help, or delinquent and in need of incarceration, but research found that as a group, many street children were better off than their counterparts living at home. A study in Guatemala and Colombia that compared the degree of malnutrition between street children and their poor counterparts who lived at home found that street children had living conditions on the street that were often better than those at home (Connolly, 1990). A study in Honduras found similar results (Wright, Kaminsky, & Wittig, 1993). In South Africa, street children ate more nutritiously while escaping the daily abuse they might have faced at home (Donald & Swartz-Kruger, 1994). In Brazil, street children were both more intelligent and less likely to abuse drugs than their poor, stay-at-home counterparts (Baizerman, 1988).

So it is possible, at least when considering the context of developing countries, that instead of succumbing to abuse or neglect, becoming a street child might also be a positive coping strategy (even if filled with difficulty). In a developmental context, street children can be seen as a case in which adolescence begins earlier and ends sooner than what would be considered ideal in the West (Aptekar, 1992; Aptekar & Stocklin, 1996).

Gender Differences

However, to make any claims about the aggregate, without first considering the gender differences, means repeating perhaps the most fundamental mistake of the original view of street children—namely, that the category referred to all street children, instead of street boys and street girls. Thus the differences between the genders were minimized. When one considers the statistics, it is clear that there is a predominance of street boys in the developing world, 90 percent in many African countries, over 80 percent in Jamaica and other Caribbean countries, and more than 75 percent worldwide (Aptekar, 1994; Aptekar & Ciano, 1999). This striking gender difference is important for another reason. Since in most cultures girls are more likely to be abandoned and abused than boys, if being a street child is mainly the result of neglect or abuse, then one would have expected a much higher proportion of girls.

The gender bias was not the only overgeneralized statement about street children. Another bias described the families from which the street children allegedly came. Three hypotheses pointed to family dysfunction as the major reason for the origins of street children: (1) that urban poverty led to a breakdown of family and moral values, (2) that their aberrant families abandoned, abused, or neglected their children, and (3) that street children were an almost inevitable adverse side effect of modernization.

In a study conducted in Nairobi, Kenya (Aptekar & Ciano, 1999; Aptekar et al., 1995), the authors visited a mother of four boys and two girls who lived with four of her six children in one room no bigger than a small bedroom in an American middle-class home. Two blankets, hung up by clothespins, divided the room. Behind one blanket was the mother's loft, behind the other, three levels of shelves, each of which was used for a bed.

In one corner was a small one-burner propane stove that was surrounded by two pots and a stool. The only source of light in the house was from the front door. Open sewage ran from the front door through the walkway and down to the front of the house, where it met the drainage from other homes.

The woman was nearly able to support herself and her children by selling illegal beer. She never attended school, had no job skills, and was illiterate. Her two oldest boys, half brothers well into their teens, both lived and made a living on the streets. They came home periodically, usually with a gift, and were very welcome. Their mother had taught them that the time they could stay at home without making a contribution ended shortly before puberty. The male children accepted this. They preferred the streets to their home, particularly since they could come home when they needed to do so.

One cultural interpretation of this mother's situation would describe her as irresponsible and immoral. However, she can also be seen as coping adequately. She taught her two oldest boys to make their own way, she found a means to feed the other four children at home, and she fulfilled her hopes of educating as many of her children as possible by using the sale of illegal brew to pay the children's school fees. In short, the children's period of dependence ended early and their adolescent independence was accelerated. The authors showed that the cultural notion that single poor mothers were, by virtue of being single and poor, irresponsible and incapable of raising moral and productive children represented a culturally ethnocentric point of view.

To pejoratively label these families, in large part because the mothers have developed their own cultural criteria for the supervision and protection of their children (different from those espoused by the middle and upper social classes), acts to compound rather than solve the problem. Not only does the pejorative attitude condemn the hard effort of mothers, it also dismisses the fact that unmarried mothers can raise children without a husband. Indeed, it even discounts the judgment of street children who leave unhealthy homes, such as girls who have been physically or sexually abused.

It is by looking more closely at street boys and street girls, rather than street children, that erroneous notions of family deviance become much easier to understand. Research has found that most (but not all) street boys are taught by their mothers to cope with the necessity of having to live in a very limited economic environment by becoming independent at a far earlier age than the dominant society deems appropriate (Aptekar, 1992, 1994). Thus, when compared to other poor boys and to the other boys in the family, street boys are the more resilient, since the less resilient boys are unable to leave home.

The opposite situation exists for street girls. Mothers teach their daughters how to cope with the vagaries of poverty by staying at home and out of the streets. Thus, street girls (for the most part) are often more psychopathological than their sisters who stay at home. These girls begin street life much later than boys, usually not before they are ten years of age. Even though they may appear to be alone, they are most often being supervised by an older sibling. As girls become pubescent, they are perceived (and evaluated) in sexual terms. By the time they are young women, they follow in their mother's footsteps by having children, usually many and by different men, who as a rule do not view them as legitimate wives and thus do not see them as worthy of continued financial support.

Because boys are expected to bring income into the house by living on the streets, while girls are expected to stay at home and help with the household chores, the street boys and street girls relate to their families of origin differently. They also probably come from different types of families. It is quite common for street boys to remain connected to their mothers; indeed, they often contribute part of their incomes to them. On the other hand, because girls are taught that they are supposed to remain at home, street girls often have distant and more difficult relationships with their families of origin (for more information, see Aptekar & Ciano, 1999; and Aptekar et al., 1995).

Taken together, all of the above information suggests that street boys commonly are on the streets because they have been brought up to be independent, while street girls are on the streets because they are fleeing a very difficult situation. Their mental health is therefore considerably worse than that of the boys. Considering that all over the developing world as many 90 percent of street children are male, we can say that contrary to popular opinion, the vast majority of street children are not psychopathological or otherwise delinquent and drug-abusing. Many have developed adequate coping strategies, which allow them to function at least as well as their poor counterparts who spend less time in public view. These coping strategies include finding a niche in the economic market, which gives them sufficient income to eat and clothe themselves. They are also able to find and take advantage of programs that serve them, and are sufficiently informed about their physical health to stay reasonably healthy. They form close friendships with their peers, finding themselves in many cases belonging to strong communities. At the same time, they consistently maintain some form of connection to their family of origin.

Who, then, are we talking about when we use the term "street children"? Essentially, they are young people—too young, from their society's perspective— who are living without parental or adult supervision in the cities of the developing world. There are important gender differences that must be considered. The reasons for them being on the streets cannot be explained by poverty, although it appears that poverty in most cases, though not all, is a necessary condition for them in the developing world, but not in the developed world, as we shall see. The results of the philosophy of the state and of wars fought by ethnic or political groups also contribute to the prevalence of street children. In the past fifteen years, perhaps the most important reason for children going to the streets in the developing world is because they have been orphaned due to war or HIV/AIDS.

Differences Between the Developing and the Developed World

The second major problem with the original statements about street children is that they ignored the differences between street children in the developing and the developed world. In the developed world, one quickly notes that there are as many, if not more, female compared to male street children, and when one looks into the background of these children, one discovers that many do not come from poor, one-parent families. Instead, their origins are often middle class and their family structure is what might be considered the ideal nuclear family, with two parents and a couple of siblings.

In the developed world, street children are pushed out of their families because of abuse that comes from one or more of their psychopathological parents or guardians. (The interested reader can see Smollar, 1999, for more information about poverty and abuse. Sometimes both were given as the major reasons children took to the streets in the United States.) An additional factor, and one that seems to account for a good deal of the male street children in the developed world, is homosexuality. Adolescent males were simply either afraid to "come out" to their parents and fled, or if they did "come out" they were forced out of their homes. They have the highest risk of self-destructive acts, including suicide (Kruks, 1991; Kurtz, Kurtz, & Jarvis, 1991).

In the developed world, there are also far fewer street children. This has less to do with mental health or poverty of families (in fact, the mental health of the families of origin of the street children might be better in the developing world than in the developed world) than it has to do with the power of the civil community. In the developed world, the state is wealthy enough to police the streets and supports enough facilities to confine children who will not conform to the rules and regulations of what is considered appropriate child or adolescent development.

In the developed world, street boys are not raised for early independence as they are in many developing countries, and they do not have the skills or experience to help them cope on the streets. Their mental health is considerably more precarious than that of their male counterparts in the developing world. There are no mental health differences between girls on the streets in the developed world and girls on the streets in the developing world. Both suffer.

There are also a couple of other important parallels between street children in the developed and the developing world. Adolescents all over the world are living more and more under an international culture that comes from the West, mostly from movies, music, and the multinational corporations. No matter where one goes (even the most remote places on Earth), no matter how poor the people there are, one always seems to find some evidence of this. Recently I was taken to a small rural Indian village, a day north of Bombay, and discovered that not only was there extreme poverty, the village had a communal satellite dish. This gave street children the opportunity to idealize what they saw. It is clear that one of the easiest ways to make conversation with a street child in the developing world is to talk about Nike shoes or the latest rock group in London or New York. No matter how poor they may be, they find a way to get the goods they see on television, or, more likely, to adjust what they have to look like them.

Another parallel between street children in the developed world and street children in the developing world is that as difficult as life is for street children, the worst problem they face is public animosity (Aptekar, 1994; Aptekar & Abebe, 1997). In the case of girls, this often takes the form of sexual abuse, while in the case of boys, it often takes the form of public hostility. In many places in the world, street and working children have been assassinated for no more than petty crimes and haughty behavior. In fact, the number of street children killed in Brazil supersedes the total casualties in the civil war in Lebanon.

I reported on a boy in Nairobi, Simon, a fifteen-year-old adolescent, who was murdered by a police reservist (Aptekar & Ciano, 1999). So many poor, unkempt children had already been mistreated that his demise would not have aroused much concern, except that he was shot five times at point-blank range, kicked into the gutter, and then spat upon. Evidently, Simon had stolen a signal lens from a parked car. How was it that Simon's relatively minor crime aroused such anger in the police officer?

Ironically, the connection between Simon and the larger group of street children was not as clear as it might have seemed to the reservist. Simon was a street child, but he also had loving parents who were full of grief and were present at his funeral. In their mourning, they talked about his good character, his sensitivity to others, and particularly his contributions to his family and younger siblings.

Like the majority of the public in many parts of the world, it appears that the reservist construed a scenario about street children that did not include loving parents or good character. The connection between adequate "parenting" and lack of character is the main point that the dominant culture makes about the origins of street children. In fact, street children, in nearly all cultures in the world, have become symbols of moral judgment because they violate the norms that most cultures give to children. They do this by not being under the same roof as their parents, by working instead of going to school, and by assuming the right to enjoy the fruits of their work as they choose (such as consuming alcohol). What makes the climate so volatile is that the phenomenon of children taking on the roles of adults is peaking at a time when many societies are moving away from traditional codes of conduct. These codes originated by birthrights and long-accepted roles of authority. Now conduct is based on rational values, democratic choices, and a worldwide adolescent culture based on the Western entertainment media.

Like the alleged murderer of Simon, who seemingly quickly (and falsely) made a connection between large-scale societal problems and the petty problems of minor delinquency caused by some street children, other murderers of street children justify their actions in self-righteous moral terms, seeing themselves as heroes in cultures rapidly approaching moral decay.

Street children have become cultural scapegoats, portrayed as carriers of all the large-scale social problems, including inequality of income, changing family values with concomitant alterations in the roles of men and women, and the reduction in personal security in the context of an overly romanticized past.

Finally, the press in many countries must share the blame for contributing to public outrage. They dramatize the "bad boy" image of street children and intimidate the public. The image emphasizes worst-case scenarios, such as the youngest children on the streets, the severely intoxicated, and the most delinquent. While this approach sells newspapers (and raises money), it does not contribute to an accurate assessment of the situation. It has become widespread in many African countries to hear that street children are carrying syringes filled with contaminated HIV-positive blood and are threatening anyone who refuses to give them money with lethal injections. Not one case of this alleged behavior has actually ever been authenticated, yet the public's perception is that it is a common occurrence.

In short, what we learn from street children is that the period of adolescence is determined more by the dominant society's definition of appropriate behavior for people under the age of majority. We learn that adolescence is a period of status related less to the well-being or the capabilities of teenagers than to extraneous cultural factors that come from other societal factors.

DEVELOPMENTAL DIFFERENCES AMONG ADOLESCENTS TRAUMATIZED BY WAR

In the past fifteen years, the frequency of wars has increased, and there have been more and more civilians casualties. Nearly 90 percent of the war-related deaths during this time occurred to noncombatants, and of them more than half were children (UNICEF, 1986). In the past dozen years, more than 2 million children have been killed in wars, and nearly 5 million more have been disabled. Add to this another 12 million children who were made homeless and another 1 million orphaned or living without their parents (UNICEF, 1997). Furthermore, the horrors of these wars—where rape and decapitation of children and women were documented as a purposeful policy—have increased. Far from being senseless or irrational, war has become more rational; at whatever human costs, it is designed to win. These costs include targeting health workers to prevent healthcare, destroying schools to prevent education, and ruining places of religion to prevent a spiritual life.

Yet the emotional reaction to these events has been surprisingly difficult to ascertain. The classical symptoms of posttraumatic stress disorder (PTSD) are recurrent distressing mental imagery (expressed through sleep disturbance, intrusive daytime thoughts, and/or phobic responses). In addition, there is also an overaroused startle response. (See the *Diagnostic Statistical Manual [IV-TR]* of the American Psychiatric Association [2000] or the *International Classification of Diseases and Related Health Problems* of the World Health Organization [1992] for further information.)

There are problems with trying to find these classical symptoms. One is that some highly traumatized adolescents do not show these signs. This might be because symptoms are different in different cultures and therefore go unnoticed, which has been the case with some war-traumatized adolescents coming from the developing world to the West as refugees. Several studies of highly traumatized Cambodian children and adolescents living as refugees in the United States did not reveal the classical symptoms (Kinzie et al., 1986). The participants of these studies were severely traumatized, having experienced the death of family members. They witnessed the killings of relatives, they were beaten, and they were starved. The authors explained that the relative absence of the Western symptoms of PTSD was related to the participants' past cultural reactions to education and teachers. The American schoolteachers helped these youngsters find part-time jobs. They promoted Cambodian culture in their schools and provided ample opportunities to help them learn about American culture. Under their cultural framework, it would have been impolite not to adjust to school, since their teachers were doing so much to help them. In fact, the authors contrasted this resilient approach with what has been found in the West, where adolescents are more likely to respond to trauma by acting out in delinquency and drug abuse. Wisely, the authors realized that although their responses were not in line with the traditional Western definition of PTSD, these children were still under a great deal of posttraumatic stress. In addition, depressive symptoms and drug and alcohol abuse were also commonly experienced.

Another reason for the lack of diagnosis of PTSD might be that Westerners working in the developing world do not notice different symptoms that may be subtle and rarely found in the West, yet are still debilitating. These include elective mutism, hysterical blindness, and other dissociative disorders like shaking or falling down. Sometimes the psychosocial manifestations of trauma also include a pathological difficulty in facing new challenges and various problems associated with engaging unnecessarily in self-destructive relationships with people (Aptekar, Paardekooper, & Kuebli, 2000; Aptekar & Giel, 2002). While these symptoms may not constitute PTSD, they certainly override the process of coming to terms with the larger issues of grief and recovery that these adolescents have to face.

In fact, it can be difficult to know whether adolescents in some cultures actually have mental disorders as we understand them in the West, or whether they are possessed by spirits, which is how they are described in their own cultures. Perhaps it can be difficult to know if there are differences between the two.

Another question concerns the effects of living where the horrendous is common. In Cambodia (1970), a large percentage of the population was killed, and in Rwanda (1994), 14 percent of the population was slaughtered in three months. In Mozambique (1975–1992), 48 percent of the healthcare facilities and 45 percent of the schools were destroyed. Do the adolescents in these places become accustomed to suffering, or do they suffer as much as we might expect someone from the West (where these tragedies have not been experienced recently) would?

It seems likely that, as Rutter (1990) points out, resilience (and by inference, mental disorders such as PTSD) is not merely a fixed reaction to particular traumatic events—that is, the amount and severity of trauma cannot be added and then used to predict behavior. Instead, reactions to trauma are mitigated or exaggerated by the person's perception of events. For example, among adolescents exposed to war in Ireland (Conroy, 1987; Hosin & Cairns, 1984), Palestine (Baker, 1990; Punamaki, 1988, 1989), and South Africa (Straker, 1991), there were considerable psychological differences in response to war trauma. Those who believed that the cause was just and that fighting for it was appropriate exhibited much less psychopathology than the adolescents in the same traumatic circumstances who did not have political convictions.

I and my colleagues have described a group of war-traumatized displaced Ethiopian adolescents in a refugee camp called Kaliti (Aptekar, Paardekooper, & Kuebli, 2000). In this study, seven of ten suffered from lack of water, and six of ten from lack of food; a third of them had witnessed the death of a family member, nearly a third felt that they were near death themselves, and a quarter viewed their experience as torture. Given their terrible ordeal, a case could have been made to expect a good deal of psychopathology. Instead, we found a relative lack of psychopathology, which we attributed to several factors. One was the importance and value the community members received from their spiritual beliefs. They were actively religious. Even after they came to grips with the loss of their loved ones and the demise of their material lives, with faith and philosophy they were able to cope.

Another mitigating factor was the adolescents' ability to take some solace in comparing their adolescence to that of their parents'. By comparison, they felt they had much for which to be thankful. They recalled that their parents were routinely prevented from playing with the opposite sex and even from playing with those of their own gender. Their fathers were made to work under the direct guidance of their grandfathers. If they were allowed to play with other boys, they were considered to be straying from their chores. Their mothers were confined to their homes.

In contrast, these adolescents had the benefits of living in close contact with other adolescents. Their parents granted them more personal choices of lifestyle and, most important, the parents of these adolescents allowed them to interact with one another across gender lines. This was in line with what was found among Eritrean orphans traumatized by war and famine (Wolff et al., 1995). What accounted for their well-being was not individual counseling but the child-centered group care they received. This care was characterized by changing traditional roles that allowed for an earlier end to adolescence.

The parents of these adolescents gave them authority to respond to their circumstances. Traditionally, taking care of those who were in need was a role assigned to elders, but in Kaliti this role was taken over by adolescents. One reason for this was that many of the elders were no longer alive. By helping others, these adolescents were not only taking over adult roles far earlier than tradition dictated, they were able to help themselves. This is also consistent with the literature. For instance, Folkman (1997) reported that the act of providing care to terminally ill patients was not just a depressing and difficult psychological process but also brought with it positive mental health. Adolescent caregivers, in caring for and coming to terms with the grim reality of their loved ones, actually found they were also maturing and finding their own meaning in life. These adolescent caregivers were engaged in fulfilling the culturally meaningful goal of helping their loved ones die in dignity. As Frankl (1963) pointed out among Holocaust survivors, adequate mental health (even in relative terms) came to those who were able to create some redeeming value from the losses that were so omnipresent. More recently, Miller (1996) found a lack of PTSD among Guatemalan adolescent refugees in Chiapas, Mexico. He suggested that the reason for this was the personal meanings they found in their circumstances.

The importance of the community in aiding the mental health of war-traumatized adolescents has been found among Rwandan genocide survivors (Geltman & Stover, 1997). These authors reported that how the participants of their study would ultimately come to terms with their experience would depend less on traditional mental health services based on trying to help individuals cope with what they had been through than on the community's ability to change its social values.

Gender Differences

While there were reasons for mitigating mental health problems, it was clear that many young people in Kaliti were far from carefree. Almost every day, the older boys could be seen in large numbers, often twenty or more, playing a card game called "conqueror" with the older men for ten-cent coins. They sat together, hour upon hour, sharing the few cigarettes between them, while dropping the card or pairs of cards to the bamboo table with exaggerated yet routine bodily movements, almost like a nervous tic. The only interruption was the shuffling of the double deck for the next game.

With no work to be had and no secure future to contemplate, they could not help but be influenced by their elders, whose lack of hope (either because of their own trauma or because there was no work) spread a listless disappointment over every moment. These adolescent boys did not come to grips with the grim reality of having little opportunity outside of government whim, nor did they move to find a way past their impasse. They did not talk about their dead parents or the sights and smells of their shared traumatic memories, nor did they acknowledge what lay in their refugee community. The latrines remained clogged, the small children unschooled, the elderly hungry and lonely. The boys were languishing in a kind of developmental no-man's land, hanging around with the men but not quite growing into adulthood.

The behavior of these young men was most conspicuous in what they did not do. They did not commence working on these problems. They did not begin an association for a common buying power in basic foods or medicines. They did nothing about the loan sharks who charged usurious rates to widows with children. In contrast, the behavior of the older girls was conspicuous. The girls found some employment in a food-for-work program, either for themselves, if they had children, or by substituting in the program for their mothers. They also eased the family burden by doing household chores and caring for relatives.

Researchers (Aptekar, Paardekooper, & Kuebli, 2000) believe that the girls were less troubled in part because they were less traumatized, but also because of developmental differences. Girls of this developmental time are less stressed by family disruptions and less needy of a peer community than the boys (see Schlegel & Berry, 1991, for cross-cultural gender differences on this developmental point). They also had more options for finding some type of work and found an easier niche in the refugee camp, continuing their traditional roles as family caregivers.

This is not to say that the girls were without burdens; far from it. They had only their mothers to rely upon at home and had to take on a larger amount of family work. The difficulty was also increased for the girls who had aspirations beyond those of the traditional female. For example, female adolescents who wanted to attend school were a financial burden to their families, who had to pay school fees, supply extra clothes, and incur the indirect cost associated with the lack of possible income. As with young females in other cultures, their hopes of bettering themselves increased their immediate problems, often in quite a painful way.

This was certainly the case for Eskedar, a withdrawn young woman of seventeen who preferred spending most of her time doing her schoolwork. But she also had considerable family responsibilities. She lived with her brother of eight years of age and her mother, who was dying of tuberculosis and most probably AIDS. For the most part, her mother was so sick that she was unable to get out of bed. Eskedar knew that for her to continue school, she would be consuming the minimal resources of her family, already taxed due to her mother's need of medicines. She dealt with this by going to school hungry, coming home hungry, and remaining hungry while she ministered to her mother at night. Although her mother encouraged her to go to school, Eskedar obviously knew that the more she was at school, the more her mother was left without care and food. While Eskedar was studying, her mother's coughing rang through the tent, doing nothing to reduce the difficult and contradictory thoughts that sped through her mind. After several months of this tension, Eskedar began to go to a friend's house after school because she could not bear to see her mother so sick at home, nor could she give up on her dream of getting schooling. Other female adolescents shared her burden.

There were other aspects of adolescent development in times of war trauma that we learned from our work in Kaliti. There was a conspicuous absence of delinquency, child abuse, and neglect. We believe this might be due to something the Rohners (1980) claim—that child abuse will be high in places with certain characteristics, such as where there are many unwanted children, where the only caretakers are the children's parents, where fathers are not involved in childrearing, and where families are not connected to their communities. The absence of these factors in the refugee camp (with the possible exception of the latter) was pronounced. What we learned from this was that Westerners might well overrate the effects of poverty on mental disorders, while ignoring many moderating variables such as the ones the Rohners have listed.

The conspicuous absence of delinquency, child abuse, and neglect in Kaliti also led us to believe that Westerners might place too much emphasis on particular forms of family interactions that we assume to be abusive. There is probably not a child in Ethiopia who has been raised without physical discipline. Such discipline could easily be claimed to be abusive, at least in the Western context. Permissiveness, exploration of possible alternatives, and giving voice to children's inquiries and demands are simply not part of the Ethiopian point of view regarding appropriate childrearing. Yet being together through thick and thin is an important aspect of cultural strength.

In Kaliti, conflicts between parents and adolescents were minor. Family members continued to be united, and the community insisted on family ties, so much so that adult status depended upon it, even if it meant being considerably more flexible in defining the criteria. The new criteria not only increased the value of secular education for both genders and allowed women secular opportunities, they also offered a far more lenient approach to accepting young men and women in all their activities.

PROBLEMS IN COLLECTING RESEARCH DATA WHEN WORKING WITH STREET CHILDREN AND WAR-TRAUMATIZED ADOLESCENTS

When conducting research with both of these populations, it is particularly important to collect both quantitative and qualitative data and use what has been referred to as a triangulation of methods. This means selecting three or more methods, each of which is chosen to offset some of the inherent problems of the others (Segall, 1983).

While it is common to follow the appropriate cross-cultural methodology in many areas, sometimes the practical realities that can lead to invalid data are ignored. For example, I observed a recent research protocol that included translating testing materials developed in the West, establishing local norms, training local data gatherers, and otherwise working on the issues of taking tests in one culture and using them in another.

However, when the data collectors finally went to gather data, they proceeded in groups of four, carrying with them the papers they needed to administer the protocol. The children knew when they were coming and that they would be paid to take the tests. The data collectors were chosen from among the brightest and most competent university students in the local culture. They came from privileged backgrounds, and were not familiar with the living conditions of the adolescents in the refugee camp (in other cases street children). Because of this and other social-class differences, the researchers tended to stay by themselves, to the extent that they all sat together in one tent to collect the data, ate lunch together, and left together at the end of the day. In fact, the very training they undertook to prepare themselves for this work solidified them as a social group themselves, which increased their lack of intermingling with the traumatized adolescents. One of the many problems that this caused was a decrease in the many types of information that could have been gathered; after all, who wants to talk about personal things when one's peers are in earshot?

Because the research participants were paid to finish the protocol, which took several hours, and because they were so poor, they vied for the option to participate. Because the test takers did not know the children, they were not aware that some of them bought the names of others.

In addition, the sample was drawn from a list made by organizations whose continued funding depended on the size of the population, which led to numbers being inflated. Thus there were many names of children who were never found. This helped children take the tests more than once, which meant getting paid more than once. Unfortunately, it also meant that the data taken from one person were being compared to other people with significantly different demographics.

Once the children sat for the testing, there was no check on how accurately they were responding. Many research participants rushed through their tests so as to complete them and get paid. They were much more interested in getting the money than telling some person they never knew the accurate details of their awful experiences. In some cases they just lied, making up complete stories about themselves, including past traumas, because they thought that their fictitious circumstances would bring them more aid. Because the data collectors were being paid piecemeal, they too had their reasons to complete the protocols quickly, at the expense of accuracy.

Many of these research problems could have been avoided had the data collectors and the people in charge of the study worked more closely together, but the above example is a paradigm that is too common in this field. Someone plans the research with children in particularly difficult circumstances in a far-off location, and such planners have their own agendas in collecting data. Rarely is the information validated. Needless to say, it is also important to be clear about whether or not the child is being paid to give answers, or being forced to give answers in return for placement in a program or to obtain services.

Another source of research bias comes from where the data are collected, since whether the data are collected on the streets, in a refugee camp, in the child's home, or with or without parents being present can influence the results. Time also distorts information. The flow of symptoms of PTSD, for example, routinely fluctuates, and often does not even manifest itself until a considerable time has passed after the person has been traumatized. By asking the same questions more than once and in more than one place, it is possible to check for variation in answers, thus increasing reliability.

By increasing the amount of data that are performance-related or of a projective nature, many of the problems resulting from the children's distortion of information can be dealt with. Photos can be taken from magazines and used as projective techniques. One can use the photos to elicit the respondents' thoughts about the relationships between the adolescents that the respondents are seeing in the photos, or the wishes that the adolescents in the photos might have for their future. Adolescents, even if they are not literate (which is common in this field), can build their own life story by cutting out photos from magazines. While this procedure does not provide standardized data, it may help the researcher gain a sense of how reliable the standardized, but not culturally normed, data are. It should also be pointed out that in addition to a low level of literacy, there is the problem of ascertaining the children's true age, and of course all standardized tests are normed on age.

Performance-related tests, including projective techniques like sociograms of social networks, as well as drawings of their families or of the important people in their lives, or of their daily life routines, are valuable in judging how accurately the respondents are reporting information. Some homemade projective techniques such as incomplete sentences and the Three Wishes Test are also helpful in this way. In addition, researchers may make use of the Q-sort procedure by asking the children to arrange cards in such a way that they reflect their preferences or their fears in ordinal amounts.

It is also valuable to obtain quantitative data, such as how many children participate in a certain program, or how many pass a certain place in a given period of time. Using random time samplings in collecting ethnographic data—that is, collecting data both during the day and during the night, during the week as well as during the weekends, and in all kinds of weather—helps to reduce the bias of time-skewed data. Random medical examinations of the children can be used to determine their nutritional level as well as their abuse of drugs. All of this information can be quantified.

A much overlooked and extremely important method of getting accurate psychological data from these adolescents is the mental status exam (MSE). Essentially, the mental status exam is the psychological equivalent of a physician's physical exam. The MSE includes an assessment of the child's appearance, memory, thought processes, language abilities, motor behavior, intelligence, and judgment. It also provides information about the child's attitudes toward strangers.

While it is true that understanding and interpreting an MSE does takes some training, it is certainly not beyond a researcher's grasp to do so. As soon as the researcher makes contact with a street child, the MSE should begin. The researcher can observe the child's appearance. Is the child clean or dirty? Are there any wounds, and if so, are they cared for or untreated? Does the child have any tremors? Are there any unusual facial distortions or movements, or any stereotypical or repetitive movements or mannerisms? Does the child's pace exhibit other signs of agitation? Or are the child' s movements too slow and labored? Is the amount of eye contact appropriate? What is the child's attitude toward strangers and toward people whom he or she knows?

What is the child's speech like? Is the tone appropriate, is the flow of speech slow or pressured, is the tone quality unusual, is the volume appropriate? What is the level of vocabulary? Does the child have a problem finding words and the names of well-known objects? Is he or she misusing words?

There are other things to observe, such as the children's mood and, over time, their range of moods. One can ask about their goals and evaluate how realistically they perceive themselves as well as their insight into their problems, and what kinds of judgments they are making about their lives. Certain games can be played with them that will help ascertain their level of simple arithmetic or their memory.

It is impossible to arrive at an accurate understanding of these adolescents without obtaining various sources of data. In the aggregate, it is particularly important to understand society's attitude toward the adolescents and to understand the historical context of the children being studied. Information can also be gleaned from archival data such as press reports and written documents from governments and nongovernmental organizations, and from civil and criminal laws. It is valuable to see how the children are presented by the media.

Focus groups composed of parents, of persons who worked with the children, and of those who do not know them at all can yield important information. We used this method to help us define street children from several perspectives, and found that different people's knowledge and attitudes about street children contributed to their estimates of their numbers, which ranged from 1,000 to 100,000 in Nairobi, and from 5,000 to 1.5 million in Kenya (Aptekar & Ciano, 1999). The themes for the focus groups can be chosen by the participants, by the issues brought up by the children, or by research questions. The adolescents can be present or absent.

Two additional problems are particularly important and unfortunately too widespread in this field. Authors routinely overgeneralize their findings by moving from a small and often nonrandom sample to a statement that suggests a much larger population. For example, a nonrandom sample of forty street boys may lead to a statement like "Nearly all street children in Uganda are HIV positive or addicted to drugs."

Second, there are problems with verifying numbers. No matter how much the author discounts the validity of his or her numbers by saying that they were obtained from invalid standardized tests, the reader still tends to believe in them, if for no other reason than to use them in his or her own literature reviews. Then the next person down the line uses them more easily, and so forth.

Research Problems Associated with Street Children

Some problems are particular to conducting research with street children. One of these is a obtaining a sample, which depends upon knowing the dimensions of the population, which of course relates to a clear definition of who is being studied. For instance, there has been confusion between street children and working children who at a young age are on the streets during the day but return to their families at night. While it is probably not accurate to see street children and working children as two distinct groups, because they fall on a continuum that often changes with such circumstances as family dynamics, economic circumstances, and other factors (Aptekar, 1994), there are considerable differences between them. As stated at the outset, the focus of this chapter is not on the end of the continuum of working children, who while living at home are exploited in the workplace because they are too young to be working or because their working conditions are unsafe or exploitative. India and several other Asian countries have often received the brunt of public exposure about this. (I am thinking of the children forced to make carpets, for example, and who as a result lose their health and childhood [Gielen & Chumachenko, this volume].)

Another problem is the bias toward inflating the numbers of street children (which can also be true of war-traumatized adolescents). There are several reasons for this. The higher the number, the larger the problem, and the larger the problem, the more likely donors are to contribute funds. Once funds are flowing there will be more programs, and each of these employs several people, who are apt to inflate the numbers. Finally, the press is biased toward increasing the numbers, which it often does by reporting worst-case scenarios—the youngest child on the street, the most drug-dependent, the severest delinquent acts, and so on. This is what sells newspapers. There is a field of research here, one that falls under the rubric of the sociology of information or the sociology of knowledge.

In our work in Kenya (Aptekar & Ciano, 1999), we began a process that helped to establish a valid procedure for choosing a sample of street children. We started with a map of Nairobi. By using former street children and others who were working with street children, we were able to identify the areas in the city that had high concentrations of street children. We laid this over the map of the city. We made and numbered grids on this new map.

We then asked local people who were known by the street children to walk these areas each night for two weeks. We used these sleeping places (which in Kenya are called *choums*) to define the households. Households are the central concept in a census and were lacking in former estimates of street children in a particular space. We then placed the *choums* on the map of the city. This gave us areas of the city with high and low concentrations of street children. This map was divided into equal grids, which were then labeled with high or low concentrations of households. We then selected a stratified random sample of the high and low areas of households for collecting census data.

The census takers collected data on the numbers of street children in each *choum* in the randomly selected areas for three successive nights and then at weekly intervals for three weeks. Each data collection team had the same structured interview format. All of this helped us ascertain a rough estimate of the numbers of street children, the degree to which they moved from household to household, and the gender ratio.

Each census team was composed of two people, because we knew that street children are not good reporters of demographic information, such as age and family circumstances; thus while one member of the team asked the child's age, the other made an independent estimate of the child's age. Similar procedures were used for comparing the children's stated tribal affiliation with physical characteristics and language skills. The degree of discrepancy gave us some idea about the validity of information the child was supplying, and by using this procedure three times, we had some notion of the reliability. The census data were then ready to be used for an estimation of the population, which in turn was used to determine how large the samples had to be in order to arrive at useful statistical comparisons.

Having an estimate of the numbers of street children in the population helps to ascertain several important pieces of information; for example, we could estimate how many of them were using the programs that were being offered. We used the program records to check which children living in which *choums* were visiting which programs, and how consistently they visited them. In this case, a surprising fact emerged: there were more than enough programs for the children, because originally the number of programs had grown from the available but inflated estimates of how many children there were. The problem was the lack of organized services. There were too many feeding programs, so that word went out among the children about which one to go to on a particular day.

We used this procedure to answer some important hypotheses. We chose a stratified random sample of street children with different degrees of street experience, from those who had just arrived to the streets to those who had been around a while. When we coupled this with various measures of mental health, we were able to get an idea if the length of time on the streets diminished their mental health.

We were also able to draw a sample of siblings who stayed at home, because we were trying to figure out why some poor children became street children but most did not, and why within a single family only some of the children became street children. The siblings at home were to provide a kind of control group. While we found it was quite easy to choose an adequate-size sample of street boys, it was nearly impossible to get a large enough random sample of street girls, so we had to choose them nonrandomly. Solving these research problems would make for a good study.

In the case of street children, we found that either in ethnographic conversations or from paper-and-pencil tests, they were not reliable reporters. Like other nomadic entertainers (Berland, 1982) they make their living by manipulating their audiences, either by begging or by devising schemes to get work. The data collector is rarely exempt from their skills. It has been our experience that much too much emphasis is placed on giving questionnaires, which are particularly insensitive to this problem. Hutz and Koller (1999) discuss these and other methodological issues in doing research with street children.

It is common to stress the importance of creating trust and a relationship with street children (and, for that matter, with war-traumatized children) before doing research with them. Yet in my experience, almost no one who collects data has such a unique relationship to street children that it will reduce the distortion of facts that the children are likely to produce. In some cases, the relationship of trust or friendship is just as likely to lead to increased distortion as it is to reduce it, because the more the children are familiar with you, the more adept they are at manipulating information to get what they want. Some data collectors overromanticize the children, which tends to create a bias toward resilience, while others overdramatize the children, making the children seem worse off than they are.

To help with this distortion, we have used more than one person to collect data. I suggest that researchers routinely match the children's answers between different data collectors. In one case, we used a group of data collectors from different academic disciplines, ethnic groups, genders, social status, ages, and so forth, and charted how street children responded differently to different people given the same question. In fact, in the Kenya study, some correlations were stronger between data collectors than they were between information gleaned from different children (Aptekar & Ciano, 1999).

Finally, here are my Ten Commandments for prospective researchers in the field of street children:

1. Think about how your ethnocentrism defines the nature of childhood.
2. Judge how the children of poor families cope in the context of their culture.
3. Avoid pitying the children or stretching their resilience.
4. Be clear about how the sample was drawn and who the children are.
5. Don't forget gender differences.
6. Use both narrative and numbers, but understand the shortcomings of each.
7. Don't accept what the children say to you as factual.
8. Use projective methods, performance-based tests, and observe their mental status.
9. Collect data about how the children are seen in their society.
10. Don't overgeneralize your results.

PROBLEMS IN SUPPLYING MENTAL HEALTH SERVICES

For several years I was collegial with an elderly priest who had been working with street children for nearly four decades (Aptekar et al., 1995). Each Monday night, he conducted work on the streets of a large African city with several young men and women who were interested in learning how to work with street children. It was my pleasure to accompany him. One rainy evening, we stopped to talk to a group of about a dozen boys who were living at the back of a dead-end alley. After talking with them about getting help, we bought each of them a bag of chips and we were off to the next group of children, who received the same treatment. As was the custom at the end of each evening, we sat down to discuss the evening's work over chicken and chips. Later, on our way home, we encountered a group of seven girls about thirteen to fifteen years old. They came into the street, stopped our car, and pointed to one girl who had stayed behind in the shadows. This girl clearly had a high fever and was delusional. She was suffering from malaria, an overdose of drugs, or even syphilis. Whatever the reason for the girl's illness, the girls implored the priest to take their sick companion to the hospital. He refused and told them he would check on her in the morning. As we drove back to where I was staying, I asked him why he left the girl in such a crisis. He said that it was past ten o'clock at night, and if he took her to the hospital, he would not get home until past one in the morning. He had mass to say at six and a full day of street work already planned to do afterward. "I have to draw the line somewhere."

When I saw him leave this sick young girl alone in the rainy night, I felt betrayed. He wasn't living up to the moral standards of his calling. I found myself evaluating forty years of good work by a single late night's decision. Only later did I come to realize a painful fact: when one is working with this population of adolescents, there are always more troubled children than there are resources to help them. At some point everyone has to turn his or her back, if for no other reason than to move forward to the next day.

The priest's refusal to administer to the sick child, a decision learned from decades of experience, was based on the greater good. I had mistaken my own cultural view about the righteous life and made a judgment about what was appropriate and inappropriate to helping street children. I did this in spite of the fact that each time I visited a program for street children, no matter what continent or hemisphere, people spoke disparagingly about another program across town. They also spoke badly about people helping in a different style than their own. I have seen the religious assail the secular, tough disciplinarians complain about the easygoing, those in favor of offering shelter but not family fight against those that favor fostering, and so on.

My own quick judgments were inappropriate for several reasons. There is little correlation between a program's official policy and the way the child experiences the program. Street children are also very different from each other, and their needs change over time. There is, in short, plenty of room for nearly all philosophies and nearly every style of help. What keeps diversity, experimentation, and variety from flourishing in the work with street children can often be traced to ethnocentric values emphasizing that only perfect programs, based on Western approaches, are valuable.

In fact, the question is larger. Whether or not to give help, what kind of help, and how to deliver it, are major problems for the humanitarian aid worker. In fact, it is far more difficult to help than one might expect (Aptekar & Giel, 2002). At one point, I had been given some $200 from an American friend who had seen a videotape that I had made of the refugee camp outside of Addis Ababa, Ethiopia, and who wanted to help. I gave some of it to particular groups in need, one of which was a collection of about 120 adolescent orphans. I held a meeting with them to do this, but even before it started, there was jockeying for favor. One young man claimed to be an orphan but was not on the list we had made of eligible orphans. He kept demanding that I give him something. There were two members of our camp's sports team who had fractured their legs while playing in a game. They stayed in the tent and kept asking for money. They claimed that because they were on our sports team, they deserved compensation. One young woman who was partially paralyzed, probably due to a stroke, waited outside in the rain to ask for transport money to go to the doctor.

When I made my way out of the meeting with the orphans, I went into a private tent with four of my assistants to give the remainder away. Before we started, I told the four that I had a fixed amount of money to spend and asked them to help make the decisions about how to give it away. First to enter was Asnake, a twenty-one-year-old war-orphaned boy who was working as a waiter earning 100 birr per month (about 7 birr per U.S. dollar). A week earlier, he had missed a meeting I'd had with the orphans because of work, so he was not on the list and therefore did not receive the 50 birr I gave to the other orphans. He was offered only 20 birr.

Next came a young man in his early twenties wearing a red University of Indiana sweatshirt. He came in with a prescription for an antibiotic. He looked healthy. He was not given any money. Next was an indigent young mother, who was given five birr for food. Then a woman breast-feeding a baby came in; she was also given five birr for food.

About this time, a young man with mental health problems showed up. He stood in the doorway, blocking the way for others to enter and refusing to leave unless we gave him money. He said he needed money for school and for transport, then showed us his clavicle, which was protruding, and said it was dislocated. He demanded money to go to the doctor. He was reminded that the day before he was given money to visit the psychiatric hospital, but he didn't go. He refused to leave. Finally, one helper gave him a birr, but this was not enough. He still refused to budge. The standoff lasted several minutes before he was offered another birr. Finally he left, but only for a short time. He returned twice, causing us to spend less time with the others.

Abush, a young man who lost a leg when he stepped on a mine, came in next, looking for money for transport to a job prospect. He was refused. Then there was a woman who wanted money for transport to visit her children, who were being fostered in Addis Ababa. She was turned down. We continued seeing people and making judgments about their claims for a couple of hours, but as word got out that we were giving out money, the crowd grew rather than diminished. Each person had a case, but eventually we ran out of money, leaving many people still queuing.

As we left the tent, many people said that we had previously promised to see them (and in fact this was true for some of them). They all felt that they deserved help, and certainly felt that they needed it. The criteria we used to determine who actually got the money were not pretty to examine. Furthermore, I had to consider that the most needy were not even able to get out of bed to ask.

It was just logistically impossible (and this still begs the question of one's professional and moral responsibilities) to give each of them what they wanted. As a result, there were questions that needed to be answered. Should I give to only some people and face the challenge of favoritism, or should I give to the camp committee, expecting that at least some of the money would be siphoned off for "administrative fees"? In either case, and not unimportant, how would I stop giving after I started?

The bottom line was that these people would have to accept that we were helpless, no matter how well meaning, to meet all of their demands. We had to accept that the only way we could help any of them was to have them accept that not everyone was going to be helped. What one needs in this work is a heavy coat of armor, however it might be formed or made to fit. At one point, I learned that Sister Mary from the Italian Comboni Order, the order that specialized in working with "outcasts," had been providing a feeding program for the indigent in a neighborhood where I was working. The first time I met her, the Sister—in a rather long-winded account of her work—told me that it was difficult to work in this field (whether with street children or with war refugees), because at a fundamental level, one could never finish the job. Usually, when people said that it was difficult to work in this field, they would either mean that it was difficult to work with the government or that it was difficult because the people never stopped asking for help. No matter what they were given, they were never satisfied. At first I thought that this was what the Sister was saying, but later I learned that what she really wanted to say was that God's work was never done.

I remember leaving Sister Mary's compound one day. There was a young woman with a ten-month-old girl waiting to see her. The little girl had been completely burned all over her face. A soiled white piece of cotton cloth was wrapped around her head as if she had a toothache, but it was still possible to see a gag-inducing red pimple protruding from the cornea of one eye. As the woman reached out to say hello to Sister Mary, I could see that the fingers of her hands were burned to the stubs. Sister Mary welcomed her in her arms and complained to the girl's mother that the child had a runny nose.

Sister Mary developed a way of helping, probably as subconsciously as consciously, to keep her going. She had continued by finding a way to ignore the incurably obvious and embrace the barest of possibilities. The most important thing, and in many cases the most difficult, is to find a way to stay in the field. Without being able to do more, and because this work can be so overwhelming, only the least sensitive remain.

THE NEED TO MAKE DIFFICULT CULTURAL CHOICES

Apart from the logistical problems of trying to help, other problems exist because of cultural differences. Perhaps the first place to start is with the United Nations Convention on the Rights of the Child, which offers a promising opportunity for helping street and war-traumatized children but also poses problems that similar laws across cultural barriers carry. On the one hand, by bringing in all that is diverse among cultural variations of children's lives, the convention can contribute to defining what is universal about children's rights. It can clarify when certain behaviors are abusive regardless of the cultural beliefs that promote them. On the other hand, because it is international law, the convention must accept enough exceptions to Western practices of appropriate child development to avoid ethnocentricity.

One place to start figuring out how to help today's street children is with the definition of childhood and adolescence. Many people in the West have a concept of child development based on an ideal child who is seen as innocent and in need of constant attention. Although this child might commonly be found in certain cultures, to incorporate this concept of children across cultures poses problems.

In the developing world, there are many instances of what to a Westerner must seem to be unusually harsh forms of training for early independence. Many ten-year-old children, for example, are expected to earn a living, take care of their own basic needs, and contribute to the general welfare of their family, yet they are not (and perhaps should not be) given the privileges and responsibilities of adults. Is their society out of compliance with the United Nations convention, and have they therefore been abused?

When people of material comfort work with street children, many preconceived ideas about children, which are often ethnocentric and moralistic, can be challenged. For example, it is far too easy for a person from the West to use Western morality and assume that street children are deprived. I describe here a fairly typical workday for two Colombian children that explains how this affects poor children in the streets (Aptekar, 1988). Every morning in Cali, Colombia, Roberto and Antonio, two eleven-year-old street children, went to the El Paradiso restaurant, where they washed the front sidewalk with a hose in exchange for leftover food, *sobres*. On one particular day, Antonio put the plastic bag of *sobres* over his shoulder, and the two of them went to a quiet side street, sat down in the shade, and emptied the food, which was lumped together in a mass about the size of a small pillow. They ate some of it and took the rest to a blind man, with whom they traded for a few pesos and a couple of cigarettes.

Getting on the bus that was going to the cemetery, they asked the driver to let them ride for free so that they might ask for food, since, they said, they were starving. On the bus, Roberto put on a pitiful expression and began to sing soulfully about the difficulties of having a sick mother whom he was trying to support. The song concluded with "Could you give my mother a few pesos so she could go to the doctor?" He got a few pesos, enough to pay for their ride to the cemetery. Meanwhile, Antonio lodged himself in the exit well, standing in the way of exiting passengers, offering them his hand so they might climb down more easily. Most of the passengers ignored him, some were indignant and made comments to the bus driver, a few found his performance amusing and gave him a coin.

Once at the cemetery, the two boys met a few older friends and exchanged some of the bus money with them for a ladder, which they carried over to an area where relatives were visiting a loved one's grave. As it was nearly impossible to place wreaths on the higher gravesites, Roberto and Antonio rented out the use of the ladder.

In the evening, they went to the *sexta* (Sixth Avenue, an avenue of shops and restaurants on the fashionable side of town), where, because of their disordered and disheveled appearance, the boys were perceived as a menace. After receiving some malignant looks and rude comments from people, they stopped on a side street, where a young and rather affluent couple was dining. When the boys asked them for food, the couple tried to ignore them. The two boys, sensing that they were intruding on a special occasion, were insistent, thinking that they were likely to be paid to leave the diners alone. Finally, the man who was dining told them in a loud voice to leave. This only indicated to the boys that they were winning the battle of nerves. The diner called the waiter for help, who halfheartedly told the boys to go. They were back in a few moments. Roberto approached the table from one side, asking once more for something to eat, while Antonio came from the other side and grabbed a piece of meat off the woman's plate. Running and laughing, they receded into the darkened street (Aptekar, 1988).

These two boys have a peripatetic way of life; they stalk different places to find something that can be sold dearer in another place. They rotate between routines and places known for their lucrative possibilities. They live in a group in which they have emotional ties only among themselves, and they travel among the sedentary. One study of the Qalander (Berland, 1982), a peripatetic group of entertainers in Pakistan who traveled from village to village having animals act and performing magic tricks for their audiences, illustrates what happens in this situation. Like the two Colombian boys, the Qalander children developed routines while roaming through several sedentary communities, and both groups of children were treated very pejoratively during these encounters.

The Qalander children were trained from an early age to study the reactions of their potential audiences. As they traveled through different areas, they practiced the appropriate regional accents and adjusted their clothes and methods of presentation to take advantage of each subculture's expectations. By the time the children were the age of Roberto and Antonio, they had learned to dance in front of potential patrons, to control their performing bears and monkeys in order to arouse the public's interest, to juggle and do magical tricks, and to do sexually suggestive impersonations.

Each time the nomadic Qalander came to a local village, community members discussed, often with great alarm and anger, what could be done to keep them from performing. These citizens tried to keep them out of public view, where their theatrical way of life, they feared, would create too much curiosity and interest among their children.

As Roberto and Antonio roamed through the streets of Cali, performing various acts of bold, orchestrated performances, they, like the Qalander children peripatetic entertainers (indeed, there are many other peripatetic entertainers, including the "Gypsies"), found a way to live off the sedentary groups they "entertained" by their varied antics.

The very term "street children," a name given by the sedentary middle class, hides its own paradox. Streets are a public environment whose degree of safety depends upon the control of the civic politic, but children belong to the family, a private environment considered off-bounds to public scrutiny. The term "street children" is thus an oxymoronic moniker that reveals the origins of this form of exaggerated hostility toward them. What endangers street children, more than their poverty or the lack of adult supervision, is the degree to which they are treated with hostility, and this can only be understood in the context of the unique environment in which they need to make a living.

Again, the United Nations Convention on the Rights of the Child can serve poor children by leading in the difficult task of deciding which behaviors toward children are universally reprehensible and where to draw the line between cultural relativism and child neglect or abuse, but it also can lead toward cultural hegemony. In this case, although the convention states that all children should have the benefit of their childhood and not be forced into premature adult responsibilities, the question remains, at what point can a child be considered an adult?

What the escapades of Roberto and Antonio suggest is that many street children, rather than being passive recipients of abuse or neglect, are more like young adults who use their knowledge of human behavior to survive. Instead of perceiving the children as the pathological result of abuse or neglect, they can also be seen as well adapted by their ability to turn impoverished conditions into economic opportunities.

By assuming the right to live as they choose (either attending or not attending school, entering public restaurants for something to drink or eat, becoming intoxicated when and where they desire, and working to support themselves), poor children have taken on many of the qualities associated with adulthood. They have done this in full public view. As a result, they have received sanctions, in many cases of immense proportion.

Although the convention has incorporated into international law what has been described as the child's right to childhood (i.e., certain inalienable rights), in the case of poor children this will be difficult to apply unless we educate the public about young children assuming adulthood earlier than certain cultural expectations allow. If we can do this, we might be able to negotiate a peace in the troubled space where the children assume adult roles and where the public views and responds to them with such fear and anger.

Many poor working children put to test the question of cultural relativism in childrearing. While some studies have shown how miserable their childrearing is, others point to the children's resilience in the face of adversity. Perhaps the truth lies somewhere in between and brings up the question, are the lives of poor working and street children abusive, or do they live in an appropriate but culturally different set of circumstances? Coming to terms with the apparent dichotomy between cultural relativism and universalism, which is at the heart of helping street children, is one central problem and the main task of the Convention.

One task in working with street children ought to be redirecting public concern, but unfortunately all but a handful of the tens of thousands of people devoted to helping street children work directly with poor children to change their behavior. This leaves the important work of changing society's attitudes toward poor children almost completely neglected. Whether this is because direct care is easier to administer and evaluate than community development is not clear, but whatever the reason for ignoring public health, the difficulty of changing the public's perception is not easy.

Sometimes cultural hegemony is easy to accept, but it is rarely unanimously accepted, even in the case of genital alteration of female adolescents. In other cases, particularly in the field of mental health, cultural hegemony is subtler but so thick that to bridge cultural differences is professionally taxing and morally ambiguous. Every couple of months, the Christian Relief and Development Association (CRDA), a self-styled mega–nongovernmental organization composed of all the groups working with refugees in Ethiopia, has held a meeting to coordinate programs, thus avoiding duplication while serving as a focal organization for donors and the government. They had written a report that called for giving priority assistance to women and children. While their rationale was based on Western gender relations that would be helpful in getting funding from Western donors, the approach made less sense in the local cultural context.

In local terms, a case could have been made in the opposite direction, that the men should have received the priority. The women were already working in a food-for-work project (a public project funded by donor countries) and were involved with their traditional roles in childrearing and heading the household. They were too busy, but better off than the men, who sat and played cards, chewed *chat*, and were unable to find work, though desperate for it.

Although it was possible to view the behavior of these young men as culturally appropriate to their cultural gender roles, it was also possible to see them as emasculated from their culture's gender-specific roles and clinically depressed.

As young men they moved from their rural homes into the cities and competed successfully to gain access to the minuscule salaried economy, some in the military and many in what might be referred to as the military-industrial economy. They had worked on tasks that were far greater even in imagination than they had ever dreamed of. They learned to be mechanics for tanks and transport vehicles, and some worked on airplanes and naval ships. In the civilian sector, they refined oil, learning and assuming command of the technology that it required. They earned enough to buy homes, electrify them, and have refrigerators. Their children were fed and clothed and attended school. The family had medical care. They were a part of the small Ethiopian middle class.

Now they had lost the power to support their families. They were no longer warriors or providers, nor part of a team of men working together to reach a challenging goal. They were war victims, not physically wounded but certainly injured (they were behaving like patients in a hospital daycare recovery room) and deserving of attention. Giving priority to children and women would make the men even more withdrawn and less involved. This would place yet more stress on the women in their families. Even the families who were able to make it intact through this ordeal would find themselves in more stress and disharmony than they were already experiencing.

When the assumption of female and child priorities was challenged, many in the CRDA meeting countered by saying that if money was given to men, the men would use it for drink, while the women would use it appropriately. Ethiopian men (and also, by implication, men of the Third World) were treated pejoratively. If this accusation were true, would this not be even more reason that they should be targeted for help?

In other cases, cultural factors impeded our understanding and treatment of mental health problems. It was estimated that 2.6 million Ethiopian adults and about 3 million children suffered from psychiatric disorders (Araya & Aboud, 1993). There were long-standing descriptors for mental illness in Ethiopia, which included people who wandered naked on the streets and talked to themselves (*ibd, kewes*). *Wofefe* referred to people whose mood fluctuated suddenly. *Bisichit* described people who were greatly irritable, intensely gloomy or severely anxious. *Abshiu* referred to people who were aggressive because of being intoxicated. (See Araya and Aboud, 1993, and Kortman, 1987, for additional terms.)

Therefore, it was not that there were differences in the symptoms of mental disorders, it was the cultural reason given for these behaviors that made treating them a problem. In the West, mental disorders are assumed to come from childhood experiences, ongoing mental stressors, and physiological dispositions, while in Ethiopia mental illness is believed to be caused by evil spirits (the main ones being the *buda* and the *zar* [Vecchiato, 1993a, 1993b]). As a result, very few Ethiopians with mental disorders would be served in secular offices. Almost all the mental health services were provided in churches or in areas designated for spiritual value.

Ethiopian healers, the cultural equivalent of Western clinicians, went through training by passing through rites of passage within a religious context. This is different from attending graduate school. While the healer's training called for accepting the unknown, the Westerner is trained to find rational truth. In short, the Ethiopian healer was more likely to receive insight into the clinical process from prayer than from academic conferences.

As a result of these cultural differences, clients had different expectations. In the West, a client would form an alliance with a "professional" healer and expect that this help would be based on secular natural science theories and principles. When an Ethiopian client had (what in the West would be called) a mental health problem, he or she would go to a healer. The client would be likely to supplicate him- or herself to God (or to other forms of the supernatural).

Ethiopian clients would acknowledge their own weakness and give themselves to the all-powerful healer, while in the West the client would look forward to reasoned dialogue between counselor and client. The Western client expects that therapy will include occasional emotional arousal, but mostly he or she expects to have controlled verbal recollections of past and current events. In contrast, Ethiopians clients expect to be taken over by spiritual possession. In the West, clients expect to learn to react to social situations differently, to control their behavior, or to make cognitive changes, while Ethiopian clients expect to be told what to do, which is often done in an elaborate ceremony that would be considered irrational in the West.

In short, the philosophy behind mental health services in the West is secular humanism and the therapy democratic, while in Ethiopia the philosophy is religious and the practice authoritarian (see Kleinman, 1988, for more information on how to compare the causes of mental health problems and therapies across cultures). To work in this context often means denying what one knows to be right, while accepting what one knows to be incorrect.

If you are one of the many mental health workers who deal with individual street children or with adolescents traumatized by war, you may wish to adopt the following rules:

1. Examine your culturally bound beliefs about child development.

2. Embrace alternative family structures as legitimate.

3. Do not confuse poverty with psychopathology.

4. Accept young people in adult roles.

5. Work with these adolescents without forcing them to accept your moral point of view.

6. Refrain from quick judgment against others who work with these groups but operate from different cultural points of view.

7. Give psychotherapy only to those who need it, and give the rest of the children practical help.

8. Focus on the child, not the drug.

9. Do your best to increase income generation and self-efficacy.

10. Educate the public, the most difficult and potentially the most reward-ing task you can undertake.

CONCLUSION

This chapter has stressed the importance of understanding trauma in refer-ence to the adolescent's phenomenological interpretation of it. Phenomeno-logical factors mitigated against antecedent traumas and severity of current situational difficulties to produce less than the expected amount of psycho-pathology. This seemed to be particularly true for the adolescents in the refu-gee camp and for street children. This helps to explain why many antecedent traumatic factors have been mentioned as ameliorating and exaggerating psychopathology in adolescent development. (See Losel & Bliesener, 1990, and Aptekar & Stocklin, 1996, for reviews of this literature.)

There are, however, two variables that have been found to be mitigating fac-tors in several different cultures. One of these is a stable psychological rela-tionship with at least one parent, or at least having a parent or an adult caretaker present and calm in the midst of trauma (Ajudukovic & Ajudukovic, 1993; Gabarino, Kostelny, & Dubrow, 1991a, 1991b; McCallin & Fozzard, 1990; McFarlane, 1990; Zeidner, Klingman, & Itzkovitz, 1993). This seems to hold particularly true for children and preadolescents, the clear effects waning with age (see Terr, 1990, 1991, for the contrary point of view). What this chapter has shown is that community and peers are also vitally important.

The second mitigating factor found in the literature is that positive inter-personal relations with people, when combined with an active approach to problem solving, are particularly helpful in reducing psychopathology (Garbarino, Kostelny, & Dubrow, 1991a, 1991b; Hobfoll et al., 1991; Ressler, Boothby, & Steinbeck, 1988; Saylor, 1993; Wertleib et al., 1990). It appears that in the two groups discussed in this chapter, this is particularly important. Certainly, street children find solace with other young adults, living what in the West might be called a premature adulthood. The same can be said of the adolescents in the refugee camp. By being able to freely associate with each other (in sharp contrast to the past), they were able to greatly improve their capacity to cope.

Although this chapter, after exploring some of the developmental distinc-tions of these two groups, has examined research and intervention problems and then offered some suggestions for clinical work, the reader ultimately should not lose sight of the fact that working in this field addresses some essential research questions for the social scientist. To the researcher, the question of applicability hits in its fullest form. What value, if any, is there in doing research on these children? What might constrain or facilitate the transfer of research into policy and practice? For the practitioner, the assumption and responsibility of privilege are put to the test. How do counselors balance professionalism and social responsibility? Fortunately, the field also offers many opportunities to help us understand better not only the diversity of adolescent behavior but also the cross-cultural diversity of attitudes toward adolescence.

REFERENCES

American Psychiatric Association. (1994). *The diagnostic and statistical manual of mental disorders* (4th ed.). Washington: American Psychiatric Press.

———. (2000). *The diagnostic and statistical manual of mental disorders* (IV-TR). Washington: American Psychiatric Press.

Ajudukovic, M., & Ajudukovic, D. (1993). Psychological well-being of refugee children. *Child Abuse and Neglect, 17,* 843–854.

Aptekar, L. (1988). *Street children of Cali.* Durham, NC: Duke University Press.

———. (1989). Characteristics of the street children of Colombia. *Child Abuse and Neglect: The International Journal, 13* (3), 427–439.

———. (1992). Are Colombian street children neglected? The contributions of ethnographic and ethnohistorical approaches to the study of children. *Anthropology and Education Quarterly, 22* (4), 326–349.

———. (1994). Street children in the developing world: A review of their condition, *Cross-Cultural Research, 28* (3), 195–224.

Aptekar, L., & Abebe, B. (1997). Conflict in the neighborhood: Street children and the public space. *Childhood, 4* (4), 477–490.

Aptekar, L., Cathey, P. J., Ciano, L., & Giardino, G. (1995). Street children in Nairobi, Kenya. *African Urban Quarterly, 10,* 1–26.

Aptekar, L., & Ciano, L. (1999). Street children in Nairobi, Kenya: Gender differences and mental health. In M. Rafaelli & R. Larson (Eds.), *Developmental issues among homeless and working street youth: New directions in childhood development* (pp. 35–46). San Francisco: Jossey-Bass.

Aptekar, L., & Giel, R. (2002). Walks in Kaliti, life in a shelter. In J. De Jong (Ed.), *War and violence: Public mental health in the sociocultural context* (pp. 337–366). New York: Plenum-Kluwer.

Aptekar, L., Paardekooper, B., & Kuebli, J. (2000). Adolescence and youth among displaced Ethiopians: A case study in Kaliti camp. *International Journal of Group Tensions, 29* (1–2), 101–135.

Aptekar, L., & Stocklin, D. (1996). Growing up in particularly difficult circumstances: A cross-cultural perspective. In J. Berry, P. R. Dasen, & T. S. Saraswathi (Eds.), *Handbook of cross-cultural psychology,* Vol. 2, *Basic processes and development psychology* (2nd ed., pp. 377–412). Boston: Allyn & Bacon.

Araya, M., & Aboud, F. (1993). Mental illness. In H. Kloos & A. Zein (Eds.), *The ecology of health and disease in Ethiopia* (pp. 493–506). Boulder, CO: Westview.

Baizerman, M. (1988). Street kids: Notes for designing a program for youth of and on the streets. *Child Care Worker, 6* (11), 13–15.

Baker, A. M. (1990). The psychological impact of the intifadah on Palestinian children in the occupied West Bank and Gaza. *American Journal of Orthopsychiatry, 60* (4), 496–505.

Berland, J. (1982). *No five fingers are alike.* Cambridge, MA: Harvard University Press.

Connolly, M. (1990). Adrift in the city: A comparative study of street children in Bogota, Colombia, and Guatemala City. In N. Boxhill (Ed.), *Homeless children: The watchers and the waiters* (pp. 129–149). New York: Haworth Press.

Conroy, J. (1987). *Belfast diary.* Boston: Beacon Press.

Donald, D., & Swartz-Kruger, J. (1994). The South African street child: Developmental implications. *South African Journal of Psychology, 24* (4), 169–174.

Folkman, S. (1997). Positive psychological states and coping with severe stress. *Social Science Medicine, 45,* 1207–1221.

Frankl, V. (1963). *Man's search for meaning.* New York: Washington Square Press.

Gabarino, J., Kostelny, K., & Dubrow, N. (1991a). *No place to be a child: Growing up in a war zone.* Lexington, MA: Lexington Books.

———. (1991b). What children can tell us about living in danger. *American Psychologist, 46,* 376–383.

Geltman, P., & Stover, E. (1997). Genocide and the plight of children in Rwanda. *Journal of the American Medical Association, 277* (4), 289–294.

Hobfoll, S., Spielberger, C., Breznitz., S., Figley, C., Folkman, S., Leper-Green, B., Meichenbaum, D., Milgram, N., Sandler, I., Sarason, I., & van der Kolk, B. (1991). War related stress: Addressing the stress of war and other traumatic events. *American Psychologist, 46,* 848–855.

Hosin, A., & Cairns, E. (1984). The impact of conflict on children's ideas about their country. *Journal of Psychology, 118,* 161–168.

Hutz, C., & Koller, S. (1999). Methodological and ethical issues in research with street children. In M. Raffaelli & R. Larson (Eds.), *Homeless and working youth around the world: Exploring developmental issues* (pp. 59–70). San Francisco: Jossey-Bass.

Kinzie, J., Sack, W., Angell, R., Manson, S., & Rath, B. (1986). The psychiatric effects of massive trauma on Cambodian children, Part 1: The children. *Journal of American Academy of Child Psychiatry, 25,* 370–376.

Kleinman, A. (1988). *Rethinking psychiatry.* New York: Free Press.

Kortman, F. (1987). Popular, traditional, and professional mental health care in Ethiopia. *Transcultural Psychiatric Research Review, 24,* 255–274.

Kruks, G. (1991). Gay and lesbian homeless/street youth: Special issues and concerns. *Journal of Adolescent Health, 12,* 515–518.

Kurtz, P., Kurtz, G., & Jarvis, S. (1991). Problems of maltreated runaway youth. *Adolescence, 26,* 543–552.

Losel, F., & Bliesener, T. (1990). Resilience in adolescence: A study of the generalizabilty of protective factors. In K. Hurrelemann & F. Losel (Eds.), *Health hazards in adolescence* (pp. 299–320). New York: Walter de Gruyter.

McCallin, M., & Fozzard, S. (1990). *The impact of traumatic events on the psychological well-being of Mozambican women and children.* Geneva: International Catholic Child Bureau.

McFarlane, A. C. (1990). An Australian disaster: The 1983 bush fires. *International Journal of Mental Health, 19*, 36–47.

Miller, K. (1996). The effects of state terrorism and exile on indigenous Guatemalan refugee children: A mental health assessment and an analysis of children's narratives. *Child Development, 67* (1), 89–106.

Punamaki, R. (1988). Historical-political and individualistic determinants of coping modes and fears among Palestinian children. *International Journal of Psychology, 23*, 721–739.

———. (1989). Factors affecting the mental health of Palestinian children exposed to political violence. *International Journal of Mental Health, 18*, 63–79.

Ressler, E., Boothby, N., & Steinbock, D. (1988). *Unaccompanied children: Care and protection in wars, natural disasters, and refugee movements.* New York: Oxford University Press.

Rohner, R., & Rohner, E. (1980). Antecedents and consequences of parental rejection: A theory of emotional abuse. *Child Abuse and Neglect, 4*, 189–198.

Rutter, M. (1990). Pychosocial resilience and protective mechanisms. In J. Rolf, A. Masten, D. Cicchetti, K. Neuchterlein, & S. Weintraum (Eds.), *Risk and protective factors in the development of pscyhopathology* (pp. 181–214). Cambridge: Cambridge University Press.

Saylor, C. (Ed.). (1993). *Children and disaster.* New York: Plenum Press.

Schlegel, A., & Berry, H. (1991). *Adolescence: An anthropological inquiry.* New York: Free Press.

Segall, M. (1983). On the search for the independent variable in cross-cultural psychology. In S. H. Irvine & J. Berry (Eds.), *Human assessment and cultural factors* (pp. 122–137). New York: Plenum.

Smollar, J. (1999). Homeless youth in the United States: Description and development issues. In M. Raffaelli & R. Larson (Eds.), *Homeless and working youth around the world: Exploring developmental issues* (pp. 47–58). San Francisco: Jossey-Bass.

Straker, G. (1991). *Faces in the revolution: The psychological effects of violence on township youth in South Africa.* Cape Town, South Africa: David Phillip.

Terr, L. (1990). *Too scared to cry.* New York: Harper and Row.

———. (1991). Childhood traumas: An outline and overview. *American Journal of Psychiatry, 148*, 10–20.

UNICEF. (1986). *Children in situations of armed conflict.* New York: Author.

———. (1987). *The state of the world's children: 1987.* Oxford: Oxford University Press.

———. (1997). *The state of the world's children: 1997.* Oxford: Oxford University Press.

Vecchiato, N. (1993a). Illness, therapy, and change in Ethiopian possession cults. *Journal of International African Institute, 63* (2), 176–195.

———. (1993b). Traditional medicine. In H. Kloos & Z. Zien (Eds.), *The ecology of health and disease in Ethiopia* (pp. 157–178). Boulder, CO: Westview.

Wertleib, D., Weigel, C., Springer, T., & Feldstein, M. (1990). Temperament as a moderator of children's stressful experiences. *American Journal of Orthopsychiatry, 57*, 234–245.

Wolff, P., Tesfai, B., Egasso, H., & Aradom, T. (1995). The orphans of Eritrea: A comparison study. *Journal of Child Psychology and Child Psychiatry and Allied Disciplines*, 36 (4), 633–644.

World Health Organization. (1992). *International classification of diseases and related health problems* (10th ed.). Geneva: World Health Organization.

Wright, J. D., Kaminsky, D., & Wittig, M. (1993). Health and social conditions of street children in Honduras. *American Journal of Diseases of Children, 147*, 279–283.

Zeidner, M., Klingman, A., & Itzkovitz, R. (1993), Anxiety, control, social support and coping under threat of missile attack: A semi-projectile assessment. *Journal of Personality Assessment, 60*, 435–457.

CHAPTER 16

Cross-Cultural Perspectives on Developmental Psychopathology

Thomas M. Achenbach

Systematic research on child psychopathology has a relatively short history. Cross-cultural comparisons of child psychopathology have a still shorter history. However, such comparisons are now proliferating rapidly. One reason for the proliferation of cross-cultural comparisons is a growing awareness of the need to deal more effectively with children's behavioral and emotional problems. Mental health workers in many cultures are recognizing the value of standardized assessment for meeting needs such as epidemiology, training, evaluating treatment outcomes, and helping immigrant and refugee children. Because of a lack of indigenous instruments, those who seek to improve assessment of children's problems often look for well-standardized instruments that have been developed elsewhere. An important step in applying instruments developed in one culture to children of another culture is to compare findings from the two cultures.

This chapter presents an approach that has generated assessment instruments that have been translated into sixty-nine languages and have been used in some 5,000 published studies from sixty cultures (Bérubé & Achenbach, 2004). Table 16.1 lists languages into which the instruments have been translated.

THE EMPIRICALLY BASED PARADIGM

Our approach is called the empirically based paradigm for assessment and taxonomy of psychopathology. It is summarized in Table 16.2. This paradigm has spawned standardized rating forms for assessing problems and competencies according to reports by parents, teachers, caregivers, direct observers, psychometrists, clinical interviewers, and the subjects themselves.

Table 16.1

Translations of Empirically Based Assessment Instruments[a]

Afrikaans	Czech	Japanese	Sepedi (South
Albanian	Danish	Kannada	Africa)
American Sign	Dutch	Kiembu (Kenya)	Serbo-Croatian
Language	Estonian	Korean	Sinhala
Amharic (Ethiopia)	Finnish	Latvian	Slovenian
Arabic	Flemish	Lithuanian	Sotho (South
Armenian	French (Canadian	Maltese	Africa)
Australian Sign	& Parisian)	Marathi	Spanish (Castilian
Language	Ga (Ghana)	Norwegian	& Latin
Bahasa-Indonesia	German	Papiamento-Aruba	American)
Bahasa-Malaysia	Greek	Papiamento-	Swahili
Bengali	Gujerati (India)	Curacao	Swedish
Bosnian	Haitian Creole	Polish	Tagalog
British Sign	Hebrew	Portuguese	(Philippines)
Language	Hindi	Portuguese Creole	Thai
Bulgarian	Hungarian	Romanian	Tibetan
Cambodian	Icelandic	Russian	Turkish
Catalan (Spain)	Iranian (Farsi,	Samoan	Ukrainian
Chinese	Persian)	Saami (Norwegian	Vietnamese
Croatian	Italian	Laplanders)	Zulu

[a]Language into which at least one instrument has been translated.

As an example of the rating forms, Figure 16.1 shows the first page of the Child Behavior Checklist (CBCL), which is designed to be filled out by parents of children between the ages of 1.5 and 5 years. The CBCL comprises descriptions of behavioral and emotional problems that can be rated with a minimum of inference. Parents are asked to circle 0 if the item is *not true* of their child, *1* if it is *somewhat or sometimes true*, and *2* if it is *very true or often true*. If parents cannot read, an interviewer can read the form aloud and record the answers.

Table 16.2

Components of the Empirically Based Paradigm

Standardized procedures are used to assess problems reported for large samples of subjects.

1. Assessment data are analyzed quantitatively to detect associations among problems.

2. Syndromes are derived from identified associations among problems.

3. Scales for scoring individuals are constructed from items forming the syndromes.

4. Each scale is normed from data on large samples of subjects.

5. New cases can be evaluated via the same assessment procedures that were used to derive the syndromes.

6. Taxonomic constructs are formed from syndromes that are robust across samples and assessment procedures.

7. The taxonomic constructs are operationally defined in terms of scales scored from each source of data.

Figure 16.1
Child Behavior Checklist for Ages 1.5 to 5 Years

Please print. Be sure to answer all items.

CHILD BEHAVIOR CHECKLIST FOR AGES 1½ - 5

For office use only
ID #

CHILD'S FULL NAME	First Mary	Middle Sue	Last Lin

PARENTS' USUAL TYPE OF WORK, even if not working now. Please be specifio—for example, auto mechanic, high school teacher, homemaker, laborer, lathe operator, shoe salesman, army sergeant.

CHILD'S GENDER	CHILD'S AGE	CHILD'S ETHNIC GROUP OR RACE
☐ Boy ☒ Girl	3	Chinese

FATHER'S TYPE OF WORK: _Engineer_

MOTHER'S TYPE OF WORK: _Teacher_

TODAY'S DATE

Mo. _3_ Date _3_ Yr. _01_

CHILD'S BIRTHDATE

Mo. _1_ Date _1_ Yr. _98_

THIS FORM FILLED OUT BY: (print your full name)

Lee Lin

Please fill out this form to reflect *your* view of the child's behavior even if other people might not agree. Feel free to write additional comments beside each item and in the space provided on page 2. *Be sure to answer all items.*

Your relationship to child:

☒ Mother ☐ Father ☐ Other (specify):

Below is a list of items that describe children. For each item that describes the child *now or within the past 2 months*, please circle the *2* if the item is *very true* or *often true* of the child. Circle the *1* if the item is *somewhat or sometimes true* of the child. If the item is *not true* of the child, circle the *0*. Please answer all items as well as you can, even if some do not seem to apply to the child.

0 = Not True (as far as you know)   1 = Somewhat or Sometimes True   2 = Very True or Often True

0 (1) 2 1. Aches or pains (without medical cause; *do not* include stomach or headaches)
0 (1) 2 2. Acts too young for age
(0) 1 2 3. Afraid to try new things
(0) 1 2 4. Avoids looking others in the eye
(0) 1 2 5. Can't concentrate, can't pay attention for long
(0) 1 2 6. Can't sit still, restless, or hyperactive
(0) 1 2 7. Can't stand having things out of place
(0) 1 2 8. Can't stand waiting; wants everything now
(0) 1 2 9. Chews on things that aren't edible
0 (1) 2 10. Clings to adults or too dependent
(0) 1 2 11. Constantly seeks help
(0) 1 2 12. Constipated, doesn't move bowels (when not sick)
0 1 (2) 13. Cries a lot
(0) 1 2 14. Cruel to animals
(0) 1 2 15. Defiant
(0) 1 2 16. Demands must be met immediately
(0) 1 2 17. Destroys his/her own things
(0) 1 2 18. Destroys things belonging to his/her family or other children
(0) 1 2 19. Diarrhea or loose bowels (when not sick)
(0) 1 2 20. Disobedient
0 (1) 2 21. Disturbed by any change in routine
0 (1) 2 22. Doesn't want to sleep alone
0 (1) 2 23. Doesn't answer when people talk to him/her
(0) 1 2 24. Doesn't eat well (describe): _____
_____
(0) 1 2 25. Doesn't get along with other children
0 (1) 2 26. Doesn't know how to have fun; acts like a little adult
(0) 1 2 27. Doesn't seem to feel guilty after misbehaving
0 (1) 2 28. Doesn't want to go out of home
0 (1) 2 29. Easily frustrated

(0) 1 2 30. Easily jealous
(0) 1 2 31. Eats or drinks things that are not food—*don't* include sweets (describe): _____
_____
0 (1) 2 32. Fears certain animals, situations, or places (describe): _Big dogs_
_____
0 (1) 2 33. Feelings are easily hurt
(0) 1 2 34. Gets hurt a lot, accident-prone
(0) 1 2 35. Gets in many fights
(0) 1 2 36. Gets into everything
0 (1) 2 37. Gets too upset when separated from parents
0 (1) 2 38. Has trouble getting to sleep
(0) 1 2 39. Headaches (without medical cause)
(0) 1 2 40. Hits others
(0) 1 2 41. Holds his/her breath
(0) 1 2 42. Hurts animals or people without meaning to
0 (1) 2 43. Looks unhappy without good reason
(0) 1 2 44. Angry moods
0 (1) 2 45. Nausea, feels sick (without medical cause)
(0) 1 2 46. Nervous movements or twitching (describe): _____
_____
(0) 1 2 47. Nervous, highstrung, or tense
(0) 1 2 48. Nightmares
(0) 1 2 49. Overeating
(0) 1 2 50. Overtired
(0) 1 2 51. Shows panic for no good reason
(0) 1 2 52. Painful bowel movements (without medical cause)
(0) 1 2 53. Physically attacks people
(0) 1 2 54. Picks nose, skin, or other parts of body (describe): _____

Be sure you have answered all items. Then see other side.

Derivation of Syndromes

Syndromes of co-occurring problems have been identified by factor-analyzing problems reported for clinical samples. The syndromes are scored on profiles that display scale scores in relation to norms based on large samples of peers. Figure 16.2 shows a profile scored for thirteen-year-old Richard from the CBCL for ages six to eighteen completed by his mother (Achenbach & Rescorla, 2001). The profile displays eight syndromes that were derived by factor-analyzing the 0-1-2 scores of problems on CBCLs completed for large samples of clinically referred children by their parents. The syndromes have been given the following descriptive titles to summarize the problems that constitute them: "Anxious/Depressed," "Withdrawn/Depressed," "Somatic Complaints," "Social Problems," "Thought Problems," "Attention Problems," "Rule-Breaking Behavior," and "Aggressive Behavior." Beneath the title of each syndrome are the abbreviated versions of the problem items that compose the syndrome. To the left of each item is the parent's 0, 1, or 2 rating of the item, plus the number that the item bears on the CBCL.

Between each syndrome's title and the items that compose the syndrome are the total score (sum of 1 and 2 scores on the items of the syndrome), the T score (a standard score based on a national normative sample), and the percentile (the percentile-equivalent of the syndrome score in the national normative sample).

Above the syndrome scales is a graphic display of a profile that shows how the child's scores on each syndrome compare with scores obtained by children in the national normative sample in terms of the T scores listed to the left of the graphic display. The two broken lines printed across the graphic display demarcate a borderline clinical range. Scores above the top broken line are in the clinical range (above the 97th percentile of the national normative sample). Scores below the bottom broken line are in the normal range (below the 93rd percentile of the national normative sample). And scores between the broken lines are considered to be in the borderline range, because they are high enough to be of concern but are not so deviant as to be clearly in the clinical range.

Internalizing and Externalizing Groupings of Problems

On the left side above the graphic display of Figure 16.2, the title "Internalizing" designates the leftmost trio of syndromes, which were found to group together in a second-order factor analysis. On the right side above the graphic display, the title "Externalizing" designates the rightmost pair of syndromes, which were found to group together in the second-order factor analysis. To view children's problems in terms of these broad groupings, we add the scores of the internalizing and externalizing syndromes, respectively. The Internalizing and Externalizing scores, plus the Total Problems score (sum of all problem-item scores), are displayed in another graph in relation to national norms.

Figure 16.2

Profile of Syndromes Scored for Thirteen-Year-Old Richard from the Child Behavior Checklist for Ages Six to Eighteen Completed by His Mother

ID: 111189-101
Name: Richard Jennings
Clinician: Peters

CBCL/6-18 - Syndrome Scale Scores for Boys 12-18
Gender: Male
Age: 13
Date Filled: 06/06/2001
Birth Date: 11/11/1987
Agency: CMHC
Verified: Yes

Informant: Catherine Jennings
Relationship: Biological Mother

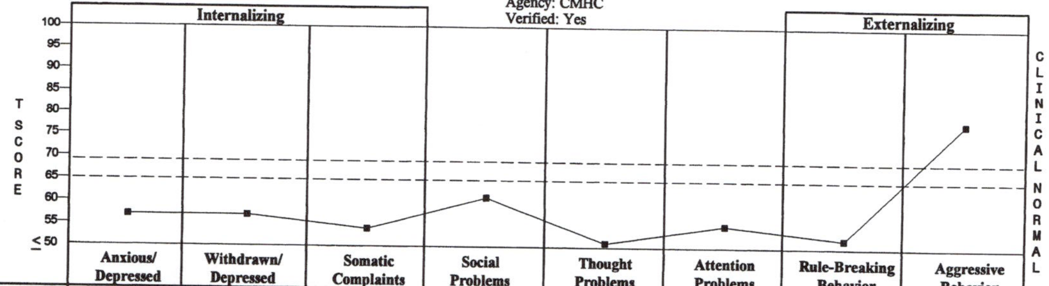

Internalizing | Externalizing

	Anxious/ Depressed	Withdrawn/ Depressed	Somatic Complaints	Social Problems	Thought Problems	Attention Problems	Rule-Breaking Behavior	Aggressive Behavior
Total Score	4	3	1	4	1	5	2	22
T Score	57	57	54	61	51	55	52	78-C
Percentile	76	76	65	87	54	69	58	>97

Anxious/Depressed
1 14.Cries
0 29.Fears
0 30.FearSchool
0 31.FearDoBad
0 32.Perfect
1 33.Unloved
1 35.Worthless
0 45.Nervous
0 50.Fearful
0 52.Guilty
0 71.SelfConsc
0 91.TalkSuicide
1 112.Worries

Withdrawn/Depressed
0 5.EnjoysLittle
0 42.PreferAlone
1 65.WontTalk
0 69.Secretive
0 75.Shy
0 102.LacksEnergy
1 103.Sad
1 111.Withdrawn

Somatic Complaints
0 47.Nightmares
0 49.Constipate
0 51.Dizzy
0 54.Tired
0 56a.Aches
0 56b.Headaches
0 56c.Nausea
0 56d.EyeProb
0 56e.SkinProb
0 56f.Stomach
0 56g.Vomit

Social Problems
0 11.Dependent
1 12.Lonely
0 25.NotGetAlong
0 27.Jealous
0 34.OutToGet
0 36.Accidents
1 38.Teased
0 48.NotLiked
1 62.Clumsy
0 64.PreferYoung
0 79.SpeechProb

Thought Problems
0 9.MindOff
1 18.HarmSelf
0 40.HearsThings
0 46.Twitch
0 58.PicksSkin
0 59.SexPartsP
0 60.SexPartsM
0 66.RepeatsActs
0 70.SeesThings
0 76.SleepLess
0 83.StoresUp
0 84.StrangeBehv
0 85.StrangeIdeas
0 92.SleepWalk
0 100.SleepProblem

Attention Problems
2 1.ActsYoung
1 4.FailsToFinish
1 8.Concentrate
1 10.SitStill
0 13.Confused
0 17.Daydream
0 41.Impulsive
1 61.PoorSchool
0 78.Inattentive
0 80.Stares

Rule-Breaking Behavior
0 2.Alcohol
0 26.NoGuilt
0 28.BreaksRules
0 39.BadFriends
0 43.LieCheat
0 63.PreferOlder
0 67.RunAway
0 72.SetsFires
0 73.SexProbs
0 81.StealsHome
0 82.StealsOut
0 90.Swears
0 96.ThinksSex
0 99.Tobacco
0 101.Truant
0 105.UsesDrugs
0 106.Vandalism

Aggressive Behavior
2 3.Argues
2 16.Mean
2 19.DemAtten
2 20.DestroyOwn
1 21.DestroyOther
1 22.DisbHome
1 23.DisbSchool
1 37.Fights
0 57.Attacks
2 68.Screams
2 86.Stubborn
2 87.MoodChang
0 88.Sulks
0 89.Suspicious
0 94.Teases
1 95.Temper
1 97.Threaten
1 104.Loud

B = Borderline clinical range; C = Clinical range

Broken lines = Borderline clinical range

It is important to note that the Internalizing and Externalizing groupings of problems do not constitute mutually exclusive categories to which individuals are assigned. Instead, like the syndrome scales, Internalizing and Externalizing are quantified in terms of sums of scores on the relevant items. Although individuals may be classified as being relatively high on Internalizing versus Externalizing, individuals can obtain scores that are low on both groupings, high on both groupings, or that show any other pattern on the two groupings.

Multi-Informant Assessment

Because manifestations of behavioral and emotional problems may vary with the context and interaction partner, the authors of the instruments have sought to identify syndromes that have counterparts in assessment data obtained from informants who see the subjects under different conditions. Figure 16.3 shows different levels of scale scores at which behavioral and emotional problems can be analyzed in ratings obtained from parents, teachers, and youths.

The eight syndromes under the headings "Internalizing," "Mixed," and "Externalizing" in Figure 16.3 are called *cross-informant syndromes*, because they were derived from a combination of parent, teacher, and self-ratings. The computer software for scoring individuals can compare data from multiple informants in order to identify similarities and differences in what they report about the subject. Cross-informant and cross-cultural comparisons can be made between item scores and between scale scores. Figure 16.4 illustrates bar graph comparisons of syndrome scores obtained by thirteen-year-old Richard from ratings by his mother, father, two teachers, and himself.

The bar graphs in Figure 16.4 show that ratings by all informants placed Richard in the borderline or clinical range on the Aggressive Behavior syndrome, indicating high consistency in reports of aggression across informants and contexts. On the Attention Problems syndrome, both teachers scored Richard in the clinical range, but ratings by his mother, father, and himself were in the normal range. This suggests that Richard's attention problems were specific to the classroom context, as perceived by his teachers. On the Anxious/Depressed syndrome, Richard's self-ratings were in the clinical range, but ratings by the four adults were in the normal range. This suggests that Richard was experiencing affective distress that was not evident to his parents and teachers.

DSM-Oriented Scales

In addition to empirically based syndromes, the rating forms can be scored in terms of scales that are oriented toward categories of the fourth edition of the American Psychiatric Association's *Diagnostic and Statistical Manual of Mental Disorders* (DSM) (1994). The DSM-oriented scales comprise problem items that

Figure 16.3
Different Levels of Scale Scores at Which Behavioral and Emotional Problems Can Be Analyzed in Ratings by Different Informants

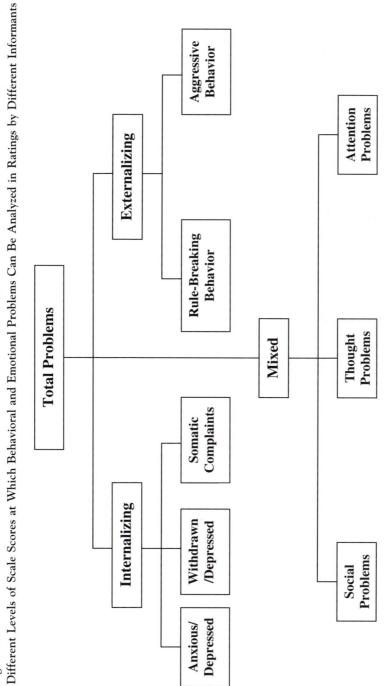

Figure 16.4

Side-by-Side Comparisons of Syndrome Scale Scores Obtained by Thirteen-Year-Old Richard from Ratings by His Mother, Father, Two Teachers, and Himself

Cross-Informant Comparison - Syndrome Scale T Scores CBCL/TRF/YSR (2001 Version)

ID: 111189 Name: Richard Jennings Gender: Male Birth Date: 11/11/1987 Comparison date: 07/07/2001

Form	Eval ID	Age	Informant Name	Relationship	Date	Form	Eval ID	Age	Informant Name	Relationship	Date
CBC1	101	13	Catherine Jennings	Biological Mother	06/06/2001	YSR5	103	13	Self	Self	06/06/2001
CBC2	102	13	Carl Jennings	Biological Father	06/06/2001						
TRF3	104	13	Bernard Chavez	Classroom Teacher {M}	06/06/2001						
TRF4	105	13	Marie Caruso	Classroom Teacher {F}	06/06/2001						

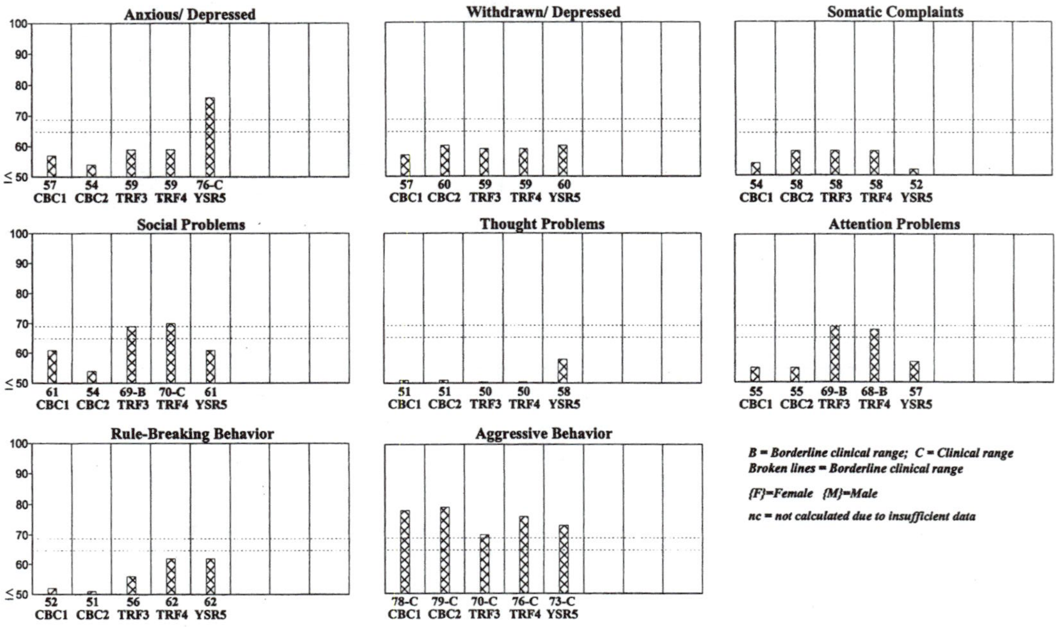

mental health experts from sixteen cultures around the world rated as being very consistent with particular DSM diagnostic categories. Like the empirically based syndromes, the DSM-oriented scales are displayed on profiles that show each child's scores in relation to scores for normative samples of children of the child's gender and age rated by parents, teachers, or the children themselves.

CROSS-CULTURAL APPLICATIONS OF THE EMPIRICALLY BASED APPROACH

The empirically based approach is especially compatible with cross-cultural applications, because the assessment instruments provide concrete descriptions of problems that can be easily scored by a variety of informants without specialized training. This makes it possible to obtain data on large epidemiological and clinical samples at minimal cost, without the need for highly trained professionals.

In numerous countries, a starting point for the application of the empirically based instruments has been to obtain data on general population and clinical samples in order to compare local scores with scores obtained in other countries and to provide baseline scores for clinical assessment and research (e.g., Lambert, Knight, Taylor, & Achenbach, 1994; MacDonald, Tsiantis, Achenbach, Motto-Stefanidi, & Richardson, 1995; Verhulst, Akkerhuis, & Althaus, 1985; Weisz et al., 1987). Many of these efforts have used sampling and assessment procedures similar enough to permit statistical comparisons of problems scored on the items and scales of the profile that was shown in Figure 16.2.

Cross-Cultural Findings

To illustrate the comparisons across multiple cultures, Figure 16.5 shows the mean Total Problems score on the CBCL completed by general population samples of parents in twelve cultures (Crijnen, Achenbach, & Verhulst, 1997). Cultures were included only if at least 80 percent of the selected parents completed the CBCL. The total N in this study was 13,697 children.

Figure 16.5 shows a line indicating the mean Total Problems score for all the cultures that provided data. This is called the *omnicultural mean score* (Ellis & Kimmel, 1992). Twelve cultures provided data for ages six through eleven. Averaged across both genders at these ages, the omnicultural mean Total Problems score was 22.4. Sweden's mean of 13.3 was the lowest, while Puerto Rico's mean of 35.2 was the highest. Sampling and socioeconomic status (SES) differences could have contributed to the difference between the Swedish and Puerto Rican scores, because the Puerto Rican sample was a probability sample of the entire island, with a 96 percent completion rate, the highest of any culture. By contrast, the Swedish sample was drawn from randomly selected schools in the

Figure 16.5
Mean CBCL Total Problems Scores Obtained by General Population Samples of Six- to Eleven-Year-Olds in Twelve Cultures

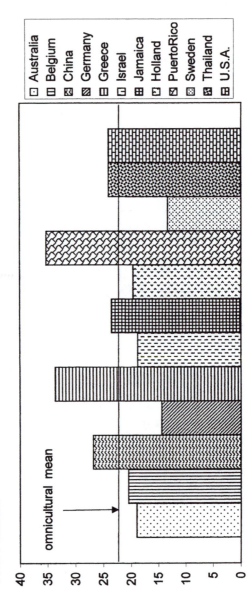

Culture

Uppsala and Stockholm areas, where SES is high even for Sweden, and where the completion rate was 84 percent. The higher SES and lower completion rate in Sweden could have reduced mean problem scores below what would be found with more fully representative samples, such as the Puerto Rican sample.

Moving away from the extremes of Puerto Rico and Sweden, Greece was relatively high, with a mean score of 33.6, while Germany was relatively low, with a mean score of 14.4. All the rest were within 4 points of the omnicultural mean, including such different cultures as Australia, Belgium, China, Israel, Jamaica, the Netherlands, Thailand, and the United States. Across all the cultures, girls obtained significantly higher Internalizing scores, whereas boys obtained higher Externalizing scores. There were no significant interactions between gender and culture for Total Problems, Externalizing, or Internalizing, indicating that the gender differences in rates of different kinds of problems were similar in all the cultures.

Cross-cultural comparisons of scores on the eight syndromes showed that the United States and Puerto Rico obtained significantly higher scores than other cultures on several syndromes, especially Aggressive Behavior, as shown in Figure 16.6 (Crijnen, Achenbach, & Verhulst, 1999). Systematic cross-cultural comparisons of children's aggressive behavior assessed with other standardized measures have evidently not been done. However, the finding of relatively high Greek scores on the Anxious/Depressed syndrome have been borne out in other studies (see MacDonald et al., 1995). Like the more global Total Problems, Externalizing, and Internalizing scales, scores for the eight syndromes showed negligible interactions between gender and culture. Thus, even though one gender obtained higher mean scores than the other on certain syndromes, these gender differences tended to be quite consistent across cultures.

Cross-Cultural Comparisons of Syndrome Structure

In addition to cross-cultural comparisons of scale scores, there have been some cross-cultural comparisons of the structure of the syndromes derived from principal components analyses. The strongest test of the cross-cultural comparability of syndromes was done on CBCLs scored for 4,674 Dutch children who were referred for mental health services (de Groot, Koot, & Verhulst, 1994). An exploratory factor analysis was done on half the Dutch sample. Data for the other half of the Dutch sample were then subjected to confirmatory factor analyses that separately tested the factor model derived from the Dutch exploratory analyses and the American cross-informant syndrome model.

Based on three goodness-of-fit indices, the confirmatory factor analyses of the Dutch validation sample showed identical levels of fit with the factors obtained from the Dutch exploratory analysis and with the American cross-informant syndromes. Dutch scores on the CBCL thus yielded the same syndrome structure

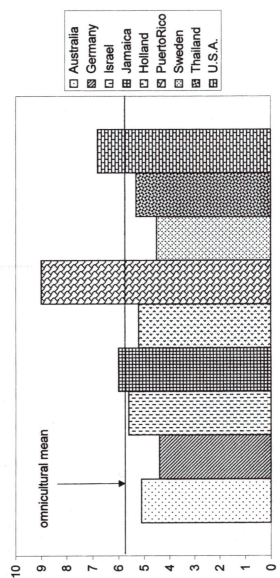

Figure 16.6
Mean CBCL Aggressive Behavior Syndrome Scores Obtained by Children in Nine Cultures

as did the combination of American scores on the CBCL, Teacher's Report Form, and Youth Self-Report on which the cross-informant syndrome constructs were based. Dutch longitudinal studies have also produced results similar to U.S. longitudinal studies with respect to the long-term stability of syndrome scores and their ability to predict signs of disturbance such as suicidal behavior and substance abuse (Achenbach, Howell, McConaughy, & Stanger, 1998; Verhulst, Koot, & van der Ende, 1994).

Another Dutch study has shown that CBCL scores obtained at ages two and three significantly predicted psychiatric diagnoses at ages ten and eleven (Mesman & Koot, 2001). Studies in non-Western cultures, such as China and Taiwan, have also demonstrated many significant correlates of the scale scores (e.g., Liu, Sun, Uchiyama, & Okawa, 2000; Yang, Soong, Chiang, & Chen, 2000).

Although many significant correlates of the scale scores have been found in many cultures, this does not mean that there are no cross-cultural differences. As reported earlier, significant cross-cultural differences have been found in Total Problems scores and in some syndrome scores (Crijnen et al., 1997, 1999). The degree to which particular patterns are adaptive or maladaptive may also vary from one culture to another. For example, Chen and Kaspar (this volume) have suggested that certain Internalizing problems may be accompanied by good adjustment in China. Nevertheless, it is possible for children in most cultures to manifest many combinations of problem behaviors. Studies in China and Taiwan, for example, have shown high levels of Internalizing problems that may be associated with other problems such as enuresis and academic pressure (Liu et al., 2000; Yang et al., 2000).

Secular Trends

So far, I have been describing concurrent comparisons between different cultures. However, cultures may not be static with respect to psychopathology. To find out whether rates of psychopathology are changing within particular cultures, it is necessary to assess representative samples of people via the same standardized assessment procedures across relatively long intervals. Using the Child Behavior Checklist, we have compared general population samples across a thirteen-year period in the United States (Achenbach & Howell, 1993). Using the Teacher's Report Form (TRF) to obtain teachers' ratings, we have also compared general population samples across an eight-year period. Figure 16.7 shows the mean Total Problems scores for a general population sample assessed with the CBCL in 1976 and a demographically similar sample assessed in 1989, plus demographically similar samples assessed with the TRF in 1981–1982 and 1989.

Figure 16.7 shows that there were parallel increases in problem scores according to both parent and teacher ratings. Analyses of demographic variables showed no significant interactions between these secular changes and gender, SES, age,

Figure 16.7
Mean CBCL and TRF Total Problems Scores Obtained by American
Children in Different Years

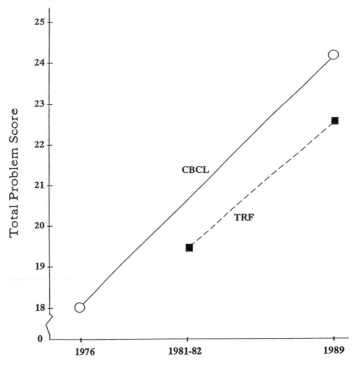

or African American versus white ethnicity. The increases in problems were thus consistent across these demographic variations. Moreover, analyses of syndrome scores and scores on specific problem items showed that the increases spanned a broad spectrum of problems. Although the increases were small in terms of Cohen's criteria (1988) for effect sizes, accounting for 4 percent of the variance in CBCL Total Problems scores, the increases were significant on many items and all syndromes. This suggests that certain cultural factors (e.g., decline of intact families, increased exposure to violence) may have been detrimental to many children's development, although individual children may have reacted differently. Some children, for example, may have become more aggressive or delinquent than they would otherwise have been. By contrast, other children may have become more depressed or withdrawn than they would otherwise have been. The author and colleagues have now finished another national survey that enables us to compare problems reported on the CBCL for a new sample of children assessed in 1999 with the samples that we assessed in 1989 and 1976. Analyses reveal significant declines in CBCL Total Problems scores from the

1989 levels (Achenbach, Dumenci, & Rescorla, 2001). The research team has also obtained teacher and self-reports for comparison with those obtained earlier.

In a similar comparison of Dutch children assessed with the CBCL in 1983 and 1993, Verhulst, van der Ende, and Rietbergen (1997) found smaller changes in problem scores. The few significant changes in scale scores reflected increases in the Somatic Complaints, Thought Problems, and Delinquent Behavior (now called Rule-Breaking Behavior) syndromes. The Dutch researchers are conducting another large survey that will enable them to test secular changes over twenty years.

Cross-Cultural Comparisons of Competencies

The instrument that has been most often used for cross-cultural comparisons of children's problems, the Child Behavior Checklist, also assesses competencies in terms of children's involvement in sports, other activities, organizations, jobs and chores, relationships with significant others, and school functioning. The cross-cultural differences on the competence items and scales have generally been larger than on the measures of problems. There may be at least three reasons for finding larger cross-cultural differences in competencies than in problems. First, there are cultural differences in the number of activities that are available to children and in parents' preferences for keeping their children at home (Achenbach et al., 1990; MacDonald et al., 1995).

Second, there may be cultural differences in what parents regard as positive kinds of adaptive functioning. For example, even though American and Dutch children obtain very similar scores in ratings of problems, some competence items show considerably larger differences than the problem items. One such item asks parents to indicate how many close friends their child has. This item was scored much lower by Dutch parents than American parents, because in the Netherlands people are expected to have only one really close or "genuine" friend (echt vriend), whereas the term "close friends" has a broader meaning for Americans (Achenbach, Verhulst, Baron, & Akkerhuis, 1987).

A third possible reason for larger differences in competence scores is cultural differences in response sets. As an example, on competence items where parents rate their children as below average, average, or above average, the mean scores for normative samples of American children are between the average and the above-average points. This indicates a positive response bias whereby American parents tend to rate their children above average, as so aptly captured by Garrison Keillor in Lake Wobegon, where all the children are above average. In French normative samples, by contrast, the mean scores are between below-average and average (Stanger, Fombonne, & Achenbach, 1994). This suggests that French parents have a negative response bias whereby they tend to make more critical comparisons of their children with what they perceive to be average.

Although competence items may add to the validity of assessment procedures within each culture, cross-cultural differences appear to be greater in responses to these kinds of items than in response to the behavior problem items, which parents rate with considerable similarity across a wide range of cultures. The greater cross-cultural similarity in problem scores suggests that the 0-1-2 ratings may be less susceptible to cultural differences in response sets than are the scoring systems for competence items.

Future Directions

Work is presently under way to compare self-ratings by adolescents in diverse cultures (Verhulst et al., 2003). We are also extending the empirically based paradigm to adulthood and old age, which will facilitate cross-cultural comparisons of psychopathology and competencies across the life span (Achenbach, Newhouse, & Rescorla, 2004; Achenbach & Rescorla, 2003). To further test the cross-cultural robustness of syndrome structures, we are performing confirmatory factor analyses of samples from multiple cultures to determine which syndromes are most robust across cultures and which ones are more variable. If cultural variations in syndrome structure are not too great, syndrome constructs will be derived on the basis of multicultural data in order to capture cross-culturally robust patterns of problems that may underlie specific phenotypic variations. The identification of such patterns would be especially useful for cross-cultural behavior genetic research. To date, some of the empirically based syndromes, especially the Aggressive Behavior syndrome, have shown high heritability in samples from several countries (Edelbrock, Rende, Plomin, & Thompson, 1995; Ghodsian-Carpey & Baker, 1987; Gjone, Stevenson, & Sundet, 1996; van den Oord, Verhulst, & Boomsma, 1996). Further cross-cultural research on syndrome structure may make it possible to more precisely separate genetic from environmental influences on particular patterns of problems.

SUMMARY AND CONCLUSION

Practical needs for improving the assessment of behavioral and emotional problems have prompted applications of empirically based assessment across a wide range of cultures. Published reports from sixty cultures indicate that this methodology can be successfully used under diverse conditions. Problems reported by parents have shown considerable similarity across numerous cultures, including similar gender differences. The strongest test to date of cross-cultural similarity in syndrome structure has shown very similar syndromes among American and Dutch children referred for mental health services. Tests of secular trends have revealed significant increases and then decreases in problems reported for American children, but smaller changes for Dutch children. Cross-cultural comparisons of parent-reported competencies have shown larger differences than for problems, probably owing to larger differences in value judgments and in opportunities related to particular forms of competence. Current extensions of the empirically based paradigm include using a new U.S. national sample to update norms and to extend analyses of secular trends to twenty-three years; extension of the empirically based approach across the life-span in the United States and other cultures; multicultural comparisons of data from additional informants; and derivation of syndrome constructs from multicultural data.

REFERENCES

Achenbach, T. M., Bird, H. R., Canino, G. J., Phares, V., Gould, M., & Rubio-Stipec, M. (1990). Epidemiological comparisons of Puerto Rican and U.S. mainland children: Parent, teacher, and self reports. *Journal of the American Academy of Child and Adolescent Psychiatry, 29,* 84–93.

Achenbach, T. M., Dumenci, L. & Rescorla, L. A. (2001). Are American children's problems still getting worse? A twenty-three-year comparison. *Journal of Abnormal Child Psychology, 31,* 1–11.

Achenbach, T. M., & Howell, C. T. (1993). Are American children's problems getting worse? A thirteen-year comparison. *Journal of the American Academy of Child and Adolescent Psychiatry, 32,* 1145–1154.

Achenbach, T. M., Howell, C. T., McConaughy, S. H., & Stanger, C. (1998). Six-year predictors of problems in a national sample, Part 4: Young adult signs of disturbance. *Journal of the American Academy of Child and Adolescent Psychiatry, 37,* 718–727.

Achenbach, T. M., Newhouse, P. A., & Rescorla, L. A. (2004). *Manual for the ASEBA Older Adult Forms and Profiles.* Burlington: University of Vermont Research Center for Children, Youth, and Families.

Achenbach, T. M., & Rescorla, L. A. (2001). *Manual for the ASEBA School-Age Forms and Profiles.* Burlington: University of Vermont Research Center for Children, Youth, and Families.

Achenbach, T. M., & Rescorla, L. A. (2003). *Manual for the ASEBA Adult Forms and Profiles.* Burlington: University of Vermont Research Center for Children, Youth, and Families.

Achenbach, T. M., Verhulst, F. C., Baron, G. D., & Akkerhuis, G. W. (1987). Epidemiological comparisons of American and Dutch children, Part 1: Behavioral/emotional problems and competencies reported by parents for ages four to sixteen. *Journal of the American Academy of Child and Adolescent Psychiatry, 26,* 317–325.

American Psychiatric Association. (1994). *Diagnostic and statistical manual of mental disorders (DSM-IV).* Washington, DC: Author.

Bérubé, R. L., & Achenbach, T. M. (2004). *Bibliography of published studies using ASEBA instruments: 2004 edition.* Burlington: University of Vermont, Department of Psychiatry.

Cohen, J. (1988). *Statistical power analysis for the behavioral sciences* (2nd ed.). New York: Academic Press.

Crijnen, A. A. M., Achenbach, T. M., & Verhulst, F. C. (1997). Comparisons of problems reported by parents of children in twelve cultures: Total Problems, Externalizing, and Internalizing. *Journal of the American Academy of Child and Adolescent
Psychiatry, 36*, 1269–1277.

———. (1999). Comparisons of problems reported by parents of children in twelve cultures: The CBCL/4–18 syndrome constructs. *American Journal of Psychiatry, 156*,
569–574.

de Groot, A., Koot, H. M., & Verhulst, F. C. (1994). Cross-cultural generalizability of
the CBCL cross-informant syndromes. *Psychological Assessment, 6*, 225–230.

Edelbrock, C., Rende, R., Plomin, R., & Thompson, L. A. (1995). A twin study of competence and problem behavior in childhood and early adolescence. *Journal of Child
Psychology and Psychiatry, 36*, 775–785.

Ellis, B. B., & Kimmel, H. D. (1992). Identification of unique cultural response patterns
by means of item response theory. *Journal of Applied Psychology, 77*, 177–184.

Ghodsian-Carpey, J., & Baker, L. A. (1987). Genetic and environmental influences on
aggression in four- to seven-year-old twins. *Aggressive Behavior, 13*, 173–186.

Gjone, H., Stevenson, J., & Sundet, J. M. (1996). Genetic influence on parent-reported
attention-related problems in a Norwegian general population twin sample.
Journal of the American Academy of Child and Adolescent Psychiatry, 35, 588–596.

Lambert, M. C., Knight, F., Taylor, R., & Achenbach, T. M. (1994). Epidemiology of
behavioral and emotional problems among children of Jamaica and the United
States: Parent reports for ages six to eleven. *Journal of Abnormal Child Psychology, 22*, 113–128.

Liu, X., Sun, Z., Uchiyama, M., Li, Y., & Okawa, M. (2000). Attaining nocturnal urinary
control, nocturnal enuresis, and behavioral problems in Chinese children aged
six through sixteen years. *Journal of the American Academy of Child and Adolescent Psychiatry, 39*, 1557–1564.

MacDonald, V., Tsiantis, J., Achenbach, T. M., Motto-Stefanidi, F., & Richardson, S. C.
(1995). Competencies and problems reported by parents of American and Greek
six- to eleven-year-old children. *European Child and Adolescent Psychiatry, 4*, 1–13.

Mesman, J., & Koot, H. M. (2001). Early preschool predictors of preadolescent internalizing and externalizing DSM-IV diagnoses. *Journal of the American Academy
of Child and Adolescent Psychiatry, 40*, 1029–1036.

Stanger, C., Fombonne, E., & Achenbach, T. M. (1994). Epidemiological comparisons
of American and French children: Parent reports of problems and competencies
for ages six to eleven. *European Child and Adolescent Psychiatry, 3*, 16–29.

van den Oord, E. J. C. G., Verhulst, F. C., & Boomsma, D. I. (1996). A genetic study of
maternal and paternal ratings of problem behaviors in three-year-old twins. *Journal
of Abnormal Psychology, 105*, 349–357.

Verhulst, F. C., Achenbach, T. M., van der Ende, J., Evol, N., Lambert, M. C., Leung, P.
W. L., Silva, M. A., Zilber, N., & Zubrick, S. R. (2003). Comparisons of problems reported by youths from seven countries. *American Journal of Psychiatry, 160*,
1479–1485.

Verhulst, F. C., Akkerhuis, G. W., & Althaus, M. (1985). Mental health in Dutch children, Part 1: A cross-cultural comparison. *Acta Psychiatrica Scandinavica, 72*
(Suppl. 323).

Verhulst, F. C., van der Ende, J., & Rietbergen, A. (1997). Ten-year time trends of psycho-pathology in Dutch children and adolescents: No evidence for strong trends. *Acta Psychiatrica Scandinavica*, 96, 7–13.

Verhulst, F. C., Koot, H. M., & van der Ende, J. (1994). Differential predictive value of parents' and teachers' reports of children's problem behaviors: A longitudinal study. *Journal of Abnormal Child Psychology*, 22, 531–546.

Weisz, J. R., Suwanlert, S., Chaiyasit, W., Weiss, B., Achenbach, T. M., & Walter, B. R. (1987). Epidemiology of behavioral and emotional problems among Thai and American children: Parent reports for ages six to eleven . *Journal of the American Academy of Child and Adolescent Psychiatry*, 26, 890–897.

Yang, H-J., Soong, W-T., Chiang, C-N., & Chen, W. J. (2000). Competence and behav-ioral/emotional problems among Taiwanese adolescents as reported by parents and teachers. *Journal of the American Academy of Child and Adolescent Psychiatry*, 39, 232–239.

Epilogue

CHAPTER 17

Cross-Cultural Human Development: Following the Yellow Brick Road in Search of New Approaches for the Twenty-First Century

Harry W. Gardiner

If I were to describe the current standing of cross-cultural human development and the direction it might take in the early years of the new millennium in only one word, that word would be one that has appeared before in this book: *contextualization*. It refers to the view that behavior cannot be meaningfully studied or fully understood independent of its ecocultural context.

As many readers may recognize, this is not an entirely new approach. It is firmly rooted in George Herbert Mead's *symbolic interactionism* (1934), Kurt Lewin's *field theory* (1951), as well as Urie Bronfenbrenner's original *ecological systems approach* (1975, 1979, 1989) and his more recently evolving *bioecological model* (1999), to mention just a few ancestors of the approach. What *is* noteworthy is the frequency with which research linking contextualization and development is appearing in contemporary literature. In the pages that follow, I shall briefly comment on the origins of research on cross-cultural development, consider its relationship to other social sciences, evaluate where it is today, and speculate about its future.

This program represents a significant challenge, but I find myself in agreement with my longtime colleague John Berry, who, in his autobiography in Michael Bond's book *Working at the Interface of Cultures*, said: "My view is that the ecological perspective is a continuing and evolving theme in thinking about the origins and functions of human diversity, and that a periodic attempt to synthesize and organize such thoughts into frameworks is a useful exercise" (Berry, 1997, pp. 139–140).

Organizing and synthesizing some recent thoughts on cross-cultural human development is the goal of this chapter as well as a large part of what appears in a recent book on the topic (Gardiner & Kosmitzki, 2004). For the purpose of this chapter, I define *cross-cultural human development* as "cultural similarities and differences in developmental processes and their outcomes as expressed by behavior in individuals and groups" (Gardiner & Kosmitzki, 2002, p. 4).

CULTURE AND DEVELOPMENT

In the early days of this discipline, it was accurately (and frequently) pointed out that developmental psychology was neither cross-cultural nor interdisciplinary in its approach, while cross-cultural psychology failed to be developmental in its approach. For example, in 1981, Theodore Schwartz wrote that "anthropologists had ignored children in culture while developmental psychologists had ignored culture in children" (p. 4). However, in the past two decades, and particularly during the last five years, progress has been dramatic and we may be approaching what I like to call *the age of development*.

Four years ago, Super and Harkness (1997), discussing cultural structuring in child development, pointed out, "An enduring theme in studies of child development across cultures has been the idea of the environment as a communicative medium. In this metaphorical contextualization, two systems—the individual and the contextual—interact, each sending 'messages' that are assimilated into the other's respective internal organizations. Historically, cultural researchers, like early developmentalists, focused their attention on messages from the environment to the child; only more recently have cultural theorists, following trends in developmental psychology, recognized the agency of the individual and the bidirectionality of influence" (p. 8). Over the years, students have heard me make a similar point when I have said, "Not only do parents raise children, children raise parents." I believe this is an area we have neglected for too long and look forward to seeing additional research done in the future.

RELATIONSHIP TO OTHER SOCIAL SCIENCES

In an article published two years before the turn of this new century, titled "Cross-Cultural Psychology as a Scholarly Discipline," Segall, Lonner, and Berry (1998) posed a question: "Can it still be necessary, as we approach the millennium (as measured on the Western, Christian calendar), to advocate that all social scientists, psychologists especially, take culture seriously into account when attempting to understand human behavior?" (p. 1101). Although substantial advances have taken place, the answer, unfortunately, is yes! Yet circumstances have vastly improved and continue to get even better.

While cross-cultural psychology and cross-cultural human development both have long historical ties with general psychology, there are also connections to other social sciences, most notably sociology and anthropology. Although they often focus on kindred topics and frequently make use of similar concepts, approaches, and methodologies, the interface between the two disciplines has not always been a smooth one. For example, some twenty years ago, Super (1981) recognized that "[f]or the past few decades they [anthropology and psychology] seem to have withdrawn from the interface, especially with regard to infancy, to tend to their own theories. Success in this direction requires both sound ethnographic knowledge of the culture as well as a quantitative baseline of information about infants' daily lives" (p. 247). More recently, Weisner (1997) declared that ethnography is especially well adapted for understanding human development and culture, particularly where families and the societies in which they exist are attempting to pursue their objectives in "their cultural world."

Finally, while examining the relationship between anthropology and psychology, Gustav Jahoda (1982), an exceptional scholar with close ties to both disciplines and a sincere appreciation and understanding of each, made the point that "[a]nthropologists have always been concerned with psychology, even if unwittingly. However, this interest has not been reciprocated by psychologists and psychology has, in many respects, remained narrowly culture-bound, largely ignoring the wider perspectives provided by anthropology" (back cover). Fortunately, in more recent years, proponents of these two disciplines have begun to show greater appreciation for each other's points of view, although some are not yet ready to work closely with each other.

I believe our goal in the future should be to search for threads of common interest between psychology and its sister disciplines and nurture them where they exist. Cooperative research efforts can only help to refine and sharpen our understanding of human behavior and the vital role culture plays in determining similarities and differences. Not to do so is like trying to clap with one hand!

THEORETICAL VIEWS AND PARADIGMS

One of the current debates highlighting efforts aimed at linking psychology and culture, including development, focuses on theorists and researchers employing two divergent approaches: those of *cross-cultural psychology* and those of *cultural psychology*. It is impossible, within the scope of this chapter, to attempt to unravel even a few of the threads that weave their way through this debate. There is no question that it will continue to be an important issue and one would do well to know as much as possible about it. In this regard, interested readers are directed to writings by Cole (1998), Gardiner (2001), Jahoda and Krewer (1997), Jessor, Colby, and Shweder (1996), Shweder and Sullivan, 1993), and a proposed synthesis offered by Triandis (2000).

Perhaps these divergent views will one day merge or, at the very least, find a way to coexist. Valsiner and Lawrence (1997) recognize this possibility in their comment that "[t]he two disciplines converge in their interests in the contextualization of the person's life course. Each carries with it the potential for treating person-cultural contextual interactions as central units of analysis for understanding how lives change" (p. 83). A similar view is expressed by Kagitçibasi (1996), who remarks, "I work from a cultural and cross-cultural perspective. A cultural approach is presupposed by contextualism, and a cross-cultural approach is required for the unambiguous interpretation of the observed cultural differences" (p. 2). Again, it is my desire and expectation that ways can be found to resolve our differences and work toward some common goals.

EVOLVING TRENDS

Although there is an expanding literature on cross-cultural human development, it remains a relatively new area and not yet fully organized. An effort aimed at integrating existing research is found in Gardiner and Kosmitzki's recent book *Lives Across Cultures: Cross-Cultural Human Development* (2004). Let us briefly focus on two of the evolving trends mentioned there.

Contextual Influences

In a commentary on parenting in diverse cultures, Stevenson-Hinde (1998), expanding on research carried out by Marc Bornstein and his colleagues (1998), proposes a model that allows more accurate measurement and greater understanding of parenting *practices* and *styles* within cultural contexts. Researchers planning studies of cultural similarities and differences in parenting can benefit from consideration of this model. Along similar lines is earlier integrative work by Darling and Steinberg (1993) based on traditional socialization approaches (Baumrind, 1967, 1971; Maccoby & Martin, 1983) and principles of global parent practices.

Finally, there is the approach utilized by Zevalkink (1997) that focuses on how a specific aspect of parenting relates to a particular child behavior (e.g., maternal support and attachment security), cautious selection of assessment methods, evaluation of cultural contexts by means of multiple methods (e.g., ethnographic interviews and participant observation), and use of multiple samples within a single culture to search for socioeconomic differences. This last point helps to mitigate the common assumption that groups chosen by researchers are "typical" of a particular culture—a point made in several of the earlier chapters in this volume.

Applications to Social Policy Issues

As part of his 1969 presidential address to members of the American Psychological Association, George Miller encouraged his listeners to "give psychology away." Now, following more than 100 years of developmental research and several decades of gathering information on cultural similarities and differences, I believe the time has come to "give cross-cultural (and cultural) psychology (as well as cultural anthropology) away" by devoting increased attention to successfully applying our theoretical findings to practical social policy issues.

More than thirty years ago, while teaching and doing research in Thailand, I wrote an article in which I suggested a two-year moratorium on conducting any more psychological research so we could sit back, read what had been done, try to make sense of it, and begin to make practical use of it. I did not think anyone would actually do this and, of course, no one did. Three decades later, I remain convinced that it is a good idea.

A good beginning, aimed at more closely linking theory and practice (as well as "giving" research away), is the work of Çigdem Kagitçibasi and her "Turkish Early Enrichment Project" for mothers and children (1996). Focusing on early childhood care and education, and using principles established during her twenty years of research in developmental and cross-cultural psychology, Kagitçibasi has transformed her country in ways that will be felt long into the new century. Her work has clearly demonstrated that cross-cultural developmental findings can be used to establish intervention strategies and policy positions relevant to children and families within a variety of cultural contexts.

Expressing her own opinion that contextual theory should be more closely connected to practical application, Kagitçibasi (1996) states that "[t]he weight of the evidence points to a contextual approach in early intervention, particularly in adverse socioeconomic conditions where there is less-than-adequate support for human development" (p. 184). Her success with Turkish mothers serves as a model for others interested in blending contextualization in human development with the application of cross-cultural findings to important social policy issues.

Another example is the work of Mishra, Sinha, and Berry (1996) examining the psychological adaptation of tribal groups in India. Three groups (the Oraon, Birhar, and Asur), differing in settlement and occupation patterns, were compared in terms of cultural lifestyles, patterns of child socialization, cognitive behavior, and acculturation attitudes and experiences. Similar to Kagitçibasi's research, the focus was on the application of findings, this time to problems of acculturative stress. The authors successfully introduced strategies for reducing such stress and providing better psychological adaptation. A similar approach could be applied to issues of immigration and problems of refugee resettlement seen almost daily throughout the world.

One part of the world where the application of psychological principles to societal problems *has* been made a priority is Africa (see also Aptekar, this volume). Mike Durojaiye (1987, 1993), a pioneer in African cross-cultural psychology (and once an officemate of mine during our doctoral studies at Manchester University in England), has stated, "There is a serious effort to make psychology an indigenous discipline useful to national development" (1987, p. 25). Other important work is Mundy-Castle's analysis (1993) of rapid modernization and its psychological effects on peoples living in African communities and Nsamenang's studies and proposals (1992) for improving African family life and childrearing practices through the practical use of indigenous findings.

WHERE DO WE GO FROM HERE?

As we look to the future, several important and challenging questions present themselves. What kinds of cross-cultural human development studies need to be carried out in the future? How similar or different should this research be to that currently being conducted? In what ways will these new studies contribute to our understanding of human development and the ever-changing and increasingly complex world in which people live? What implications will future findings have for the design and construction of new developmental theories, and how will these new theories affect even newer studies?

While the questions are easy to ask, finding appropriate answers is not. In this context, let me suggest a few possibilities. For example, researchers conducting future developmental studies should seriously consider making greater use of the triangulation design in which multiple concepts and methods are used to study a single phenomenon. A good illustration is a cross-cultural investigation by Dreher and Hayes (1993) consisting of an ethnographic study of marijuana use among rural Jamaican women along with standardized clinical evaluations of the development and health status of their children. In the words of the authors, "The methodological combination of ethnography and standardized instruments is not just a matter of coming at the same question from qualitative and quantitative perspectives. Rather, it is an essential feature of cross-cultural research. Ethnography tells us what questions to ask and how to ask them. The open-ended inquiries commonly associated with ethnography, however, may sacrifice comparability when answers fall into different domains. Standardized instruments, administered in as consistent a manner as possible, enhance comparability but are useful only when preliminary determination of the appropriate range and categories of responses are accompanied by ethnographic observations and interviews" (p. 227).

If you finish reading this chapter and go away with only one piece of information, this is what I would like you to take with you: I look forward to future cross-cultural research efforts focusing on developmental comparisons within cultural contexts that attempt to combine, in part, the ethnographic approaches of the anthropologist, the psychological theories and methodologies of the psychologist, and the social policy concerns of the sociologist.

In addition to highly creative and pioneering studies aimed at breaking new ground, I would like to see more attention given to clarifying, modifying, and extending exiting knowledge and theories through careful (and well designed) replication of previous findings deserves more attention. This is a frequently ignored (and often unappreciated) undertaking in which many findings may or may not be confirmed when viewed within sociocultural settings other than the ones in which they were originally conducted.

Recently, Super and Harkness (1999) published an extremely important chapter titled "The Environment as Culture in Developmental Research" (in a volume edited by Friedman & Wachs, *Measuring Environment Across the Life Span: Emerging Methods and Concepts*), which lays the foundation for answering many of the questions raised in this chapter. Specifically, they outline several methods of data collection that permit measurement of the three subsystems in their developmental niche framework.

LESSONS LEARNED AND WINDOWS OPENED TO THE FUTURE

At the beginning of this chapter, I stated that if I were to choose one word to describe the direction that the study of cross-cultural human development would take in the years ahead, it would be *contextualization*, or viewing behavior within the ecocultural context in which it takes place. It is clear from the preceding chapters that many authors in this volume share this view. In fact, the importance of studying the developmental context in order to better understand behavior is stressed so often that can it be viewed as a common theme connecting many of the contributions.

Another point made earlier in this chapter was the importance of bringing psychology and its sister disciplines closer together by developing interdisciplinary cooperative research efforts involving participants from a variety of cultural backgrounds along with a greater sensitivity to each other's theories, methodologies, unique research difficulties, and central social issues. It is encouraging to see that a number of authors in this volume have done, and are continuing to do, exactly this in their cross-cultural research on children and adolescents. Again, this becomes a general theme and, as such, bodes well for the future of the field: it provides models, as well as rich examples, for others to follow.

The chapters in this book, written by a variety of researchers—psychologists and anthropologists as well as seasoned leaders and younger scholars—represent the best in historical overviews and literature reviews of topics on the cutting edge of the field. The number and variety of cultural settings presented in these investigations is truly astounding, thereby providing a global perspective on a range of critically important issues not found anywhere else. Although the chapters were written independently and focus on a diversity of topics, approaches, and findings, several additional themes emerge and weave their way throughout the pages of this book. For example, a significant number of authors comment on the lack of well-designed studies from developing countries, the need to look more closely at the daily lives and activities of children, such as greater attention to sibling relationships and parental belief systems, and the importance of viewing behavior in other than Western perspectives.

Several authors (Achenbach; Wagner; Aptekar; Gielen & Chumachenko; Fuligni; and Roopnarine, Bynoe, & Singh) join with Gardiner in stressing the need to place greater emphasis on applications to social policy issues such as immigration, acculturation, literacy and illiteracy, poverty, war, and education. The importance of parenting styles and methods of childcare play a central role in the work of Roopnarine, Bynoe, and Singh, while demonstrations of the resiliency of children and adolescents are emphasized in the studies by Aptekar, Fuligni, and Roopnarine, Bynoe, and Singh. And my plea for more longitudinal studies is echoed (and in many cases clearly demonstrated) in studies by Achenbach, Fuligni, and Jia.

Finally, as researchers begin to design their present and future cross-cultural studies of children and adolescents, they would do well to first consider Gielen and Chumachenko's discussion of twenty worldwide trends in childrearing environments and Aptekar's "Ten Commandments" for conducting research with street children, which has application to other topics as well.

Perhaps an appropriate way to end this chapter is to quote the closing lines I wrote for *Lives Across Cultures* (Gardiner & Kosmitzki, 2002): "Ahead of us lie tremendous challenges and opportunities. Speculating about where our cross-cultural journey will take us next is difficult. Wherever we go, it is certain to be an interesting and exciting adventure. Perhaps some of you will be the pioneer theorists and researchers who take us to the next point on this journey" (p. 274). I eagerly look forward to that day.

Like Dorothy and her three friends (the scarecrow, tin man, and lion), all of whom landed in the magical kingdom of Oz and had many fascinating and wonderful new cultural adventures (as well as misadventures), we need to have the brains, the heart, the courage, and the sense of adventure to follow our own yellow brick road in search of new approaches that will help us understand human development in the early years of the twenty-first century and beyond.

REFERENCES

Baumrind, D. (1967). Child care practices anteceding three patterns of preschool behavior. *Genetic Psychology Monographs, 75,* 43–88.

———. (1971). Current patterns of parental authority. *Developmental Psychology Monographs, Part 2, 4* (1), 1–103.

Berry, J. (1997). Cruising the world: A nomad in Academe. In M. H. Bond (Ed.), *Working at the interface of cultures: Eighteen lives in social science* (pp. 138–153). London: Routledge.

Bornstein, M. H., Haynes, O. M., Azuma, H., Galperin, C., Maital, S., Ogino, M., Painter, K., Pascual, L., Pecheux, M. G., Rahn, C., Toda, S., Venuti, P., Vyt, A., & Wright,

B. (1998). A cross-national study of self-evaluations and attributions in parenting: Argentina, Belgium, France, Israel, Italy, Japan, and the United States. *Developmental Psychology, 34,* 662–676.

Bronfenbrenner, U. (1975). Reality and research in the ecology of human development. *Proceedings of the American Philosophical Society, 119,* 439–469.

———. (1979). *The ecology of human development: Experiments by nature and design.* Cambridge, MA: Harvard University Press.

———. (1989). Ecological systems theory. In R. Vasta (Ed.), *Six theories of child development* (Vol. 6, pp. 187–250). Greenwich, CT: JAI Press.

———. (1999). Environments in developmental perspective: Theoretical and operational models. In S. L., Friedman & T. D. Wachs (Eds.), *Measuring environment across the life span* (pp. 3–28). Washington, DC: American Psychological Association.

Cole, M. (1998). *Cultural psychology: A once and future discipline.* Cambridge, MA: Belknap Press.

Darling, N., & Steinberg, L. (1993). Parenting style as context: An integrative model. *Psychological Bulletin, 113,* 487–496.

Dreher, M. C., & Hayes, J. S. (1993). Triangulation in cross-cultural research in child development in Jamaica. *Western Journal of Nursing Research, 15* (2), 216–229.

Durojaiye, M. O. (1987). Black Africa. In A. R. Gilgen & C. K. Gilgen (Eds.), *International handbook of psychology* (pp. 24–36). New York: Greenwood Press.

———. (1993). Indigenous psychology in Africa: The search for meaning. In U. Kim & J. W. Berry (Eds.), *Indigenous psychologies: Research and experience in cultural context* (pp. 211–220). Newbury Park, CA: Sage.

Gardiner, H. W. (2001). Culture, context, and development. In D. Matsumoto (Ed.), *Handbook of culture and psychology* (pp. 101–117). New York: Oxford University Press.

Gardiner, H. W., & Kosmitzki, C. (2002). *Lives across cultures: Cross-cultural human development* (2nd ed.). Boston: Allyn & Bacon.

———. (2004). *Lives across cultures: Cross-cultural human development* (3rd ed.). Boston: Allyn & Bacon.

Jahoda, G. (1982). *Psychology and anthropology: A psychological perspective.* London: Academic Press.

Jahoda, G., & Krewer, B. (1997). History of cross-cultural and cultural psychology. In J. W. Berry, Y. H. Poortinga, & J. Pandey (Eds.), *Handbook of cross-cultural psychology: Theory and method* (Vol. 1, pp. 1–42). Boston: Allyn & Bacon.

Jessor, R., Colby, A., & Shweder, R. A. (1996). *Ethnography and human development: Context and meaning in social inquiry.* Chicago: University of Chicago Press.

Kagitçibasi, Ç. (1996). *Family and human development across cultures.* Mahwah, NJ: Erlbaum.

Lewin, K. (1951). *Field theory in social science.* New York: Harper.

Maccoby, E. E., & Martin, J. A. (1983). Socialization in the context of the family: Parent-child interaction. In P. H. Mussen (Series Ed.) & E. M. Hetherington (Vol. Ed.), *Handbook of child psychology,* Vol. 4, *Socialization, personality, and social development* (4th ed., pp. 1–101). New York: Wiley.

Matsumoto, D. (Ed.). (2001). *Handbook of culture and psychology.* New York: Oxford University Press.

Mead, G. H. (1934). *Mind, self, and society.* Chicago: University of Chicago Press.

Miller, G. A. (1969). Psychology as a means of promoting human welfare. *American Psychologist, 24,* 1063–1075.

Mishra, R. C., Sinha, D., & Berry, J. W. (1996). *Ecology, acculturation, and psychological adaptation.* Thousand Oaks, CA: Sage.

Mundy-Castle, A. C. (1993). Human behaviour and national development: Conceptual and theoretical perspectives. *Ife Psychologia, 1,* 1–16.

Nsamenang, A. B. (1992). *Human development in cultural context: A Third World perspective.* Newbury Park, CA: Sage.

Schwartz, T. (1981). The acquisition of culture. *Ethos, 9,* 4–17.

Segall, M. H., Lonner, W. J., & Berry, J. W. (1998). Cross-cultural psychology as a scholarly discipline: On the flowering of culture in behavioral research. *American Psychologist, 53,* 1101–1110.

Shweder, R. A, & Sullivan, M. A. (1993). Cultural psychology: Who needs it? *Annual Review of Psychology, 44,* 497–523.

Stevenson-Hinde, J. (1998). Parenting in different cultures: Time to focus. *Developmental Psychology, 34,* 698–700.

Super, C. M. (1981). Cross-cultural research on infancy. In H. C. Triandis & A. Heron (Eds.), *Handbook of cross-cultural Psychology,* Vol. 4, *Developmental psychology* (pp. 17–54). Boston: Allyn & Bacon.

Super, C. M., & Harkness, S. (1997). The cultural structuring of child development. In J. W. Berry, P. R. Dasen, & T. S. Saraswathi (Eds.), *Handbook of cross-cultural psychology* (2nd ed., Vol. 2, pp. 1–39). Boston: Allyn & Bacon.

———. (1999). The environment as culture in developmental research. In S. L. Friedman & T. D. Wachs (Eds.), *Measuring environment across the life span* (pp. 279–323). Washington, DC: American Psychological Association.

Triandis, H. C. (2000). Cross-cultural versus cultural psychology: A synthesis? In A. L. Comunian & U. P. Gielen (Eds.), *International perspectives on human development* (pp. 81–95). Lengerich, Germany: Pabst Science.

Valsiner, J., & Lawrence, J. (1997). Human development in culture across the life span. In J. W. Berry, P. R. Dasen & T. S. Saraswathi (Eds.), *Handbook of cross-cultural psychology* (2nd ed., Vol. 2, pp. 69–106). Boston: Allyn & Bacon.

Weisner, T. S. (1997). The ecocultural project of human development: Why ethnography and its findings matter. *Ethos, 25,* 177–190.

Zevalkink, J. (1997). Attachment in Indonesia: The mother-child relationship in context. Unpublished Ph.D. diss., University of Nijmegen, Nijemgen, Netherlands.

Selected Bibliography

Uwe P. Gielen

This selected bibliography covers general introductions to the cross-cultural study of childhood and adolescence, handbooks, historically oriented studies, the major periods of the human life cycle, immigrant children, childrearing, and childhood and adolescence in various regions of the world. The bibliography emphasizes books rather than more specialized articles, which can be found in the respective chapters included in this volume.

GENERAL INTRODUCTIONS

Bjorklund, D. F., & Pellegrini, A. D. (2002). *The origins of human nature: Evolutionary developmental psychology*. Washington, DC: American Psychological Association.

Bril, B., Dasen, P. R., Sabatier, C., & Krewer, B. (Eds.). (1999). *Propos sur l'enfant et l'adolescent: Quels enfants pour quelles cultures?* [Essay on the child and the adolescent: What children for what cultures?] Paris: L'Harmattan.

Bril, B., & Lehalle, H. (1988). *Le développement psychologique est-il universel? Approaches interculturelles* [Is psychological development universal? Intercultural approaches]. Paris: Presses Universitaires de France.

Cole, M., & Cole, S. R. (2004). *The development of children* (5th ed.). New York: Scientific American Books.

Comunian, A. L., & Gielen, U. P. (Eds.). (2000). *International perspectives on human development*. Lengerich, Germany: Pabst Scientific.

Erikson, E. H. (1963). *Childhood and society* (2nd ed.). New York: Norton.

Gardiner, H. W., & Kosmitzki, C. (2004). *Lives across cultures: Cross-cultural human development* (3rd ed.). Boston: Allyn & Bacon.

Gielen, U. P., & Roopnarine, J. L. (Eds.). (in press). *Childhood and adolescence: Cross-cultural perspectives and applications*. Westport, CT: Praeger.

Greenfield, P. M., & Cocking, R. R. (Eds.). (1994). *Cross-cultural roots of minority child development*. Hillsdale, NJ: Erlbaum.

Greenfield, P., Keller, H., & Kagitçibasi, Ç. (Eds.). (in press). A new paradigm for developmental psychology. Mahwah, NJ: Erlbaum.

Kagitçibasi, Ç. (1996). *Family and human development across cultures: A view from the other side*. Mahwah, NJ: Erlbaum.

Keller, H., Poortinga, Y. H., & Schoelmerich, A. (Eds.). (2002). *Between biology and culture: Perspectives on ontogenetic development*. Cambridge: Cambridge University Press.

Munroe, R. L., & Munroe, R. H. (1975/1994). *Cross-cultural human development*. Prospect Heights, IL: Waveland Press.

Nsamenang, B. (1992). *Human development in cultural context. A third world perspective*. Newbury Park, CA: Sage.

Rogoff, B. (2003). *The cultural nature of human development*. New York: Oxford University Press.

Saraswathi, T. S. (Ed.). (2003). *Cross-cultural perspectives in human development: Theory, research, and practice*. Delhi: Sage.

Stigler, J. W., Shweder, R. A., & Herdt, G. (Eds.). (1990). *Cultural psychology: Essays on comparative human development*. Cambridge: Cambridge University Press.

Thomas, R. M. (1999). *Human development theories: Windows on culture*. Thousand Oaks, CA: Sage.

Toomela, A. (Ed.). (2003). *Cultural guidance in the development of the human mind*. Westport, CT: Praeger.

Trommsdorf, G. (Ed.). (1995). *Kindheit und Jugend in verschiedenen Kulturen: Entwicklung und Sozialisation in kulturvergleichender Sicht* [Childhood and youth in different cultures: Development and socialization in culture-comparative perspective]. Weinheim, Germany: Juventus.

Valsiner, J. (1989). *Child development in cultural context*. Toronto: Hogrefe and Huber.

———. (2000). *Culture and human development* (2nd ed.). London: Sage.

Wagner, D., & Stevenson, H. (Eds.). (1982). *Cultural perspectives on child development*. San Francisco: Freeman.

Werner, E. E. (1979). *Cross-cultural child development: A view from Planet Earth*. Monterey, CA: Brooks/Cole.

Whiting, B. B., & Edwards, C. P. (1988). *Children of different worlds: The formation of social behavior*. Cambridge, MA: Harvard University Press.

HANDBOOKS

Adler, L. L. (Ed.). (1993). *International handbook on gender roles*. Westport, CT: Greenwood.

Berry, J. W., Dasen, P. B., & Saraswathi, T. S. (1997). *Handbook of cross-cultural psychology* (2nd ed.), Vol. 2, *Basic processes and human development*. Boston: Allyn & Bacon.

Damon, W., & Eisenberg, N. (Eds.). (1998). *Handbook of child psychology* (5th ed.). New York: Wiley.

Laboratory of Comparative and Human Cognition (LCHC). (1983). Culture and development. In P. H. Mussen (Series Ed.) & W. Kessen (Vol. Ed.), *Handbook of child psychology*, Vol. 1, *History, theory, and methods* (pp. 295–356). New York: Wiley.

LeVine, R. A. (1970). *Cross-cultural study in child psychology.* In P. H. Mussen (Ed.), *Carmichael's manual of child psychology* (3rd ed., Vol. 2, pp. 559–610). New York: Wiley.

Mistry, J., & Saraswathi, T. S. (2003). The cultural context of child development. In R. M. Lerner, M. A. Easterbrooks, & J. Mistry (Eds.), *Handbook of psychology.* Vol. 6, *Developmental psychology* (pp. 267–291). New York: Wiley.

Munroe, R. H., Munroe, R. L., & Whiting, B. B. (Eds.). (1981). *Handbook of cross-cultural human development.* New York: Garland Press.

Rohner, R. P., & Khaleque, A. (2003). *Handbook for the study of parental acceptance and rejection.* Storrs, CT: Rohner Research Publications.

Shweder, R. A., Goodnow, J., Hatano, G., LeVine, R. A., Markus, H., & Miller P. (1998). The cultural psychology of development: One mind, many mentalities. In W. Damon (Series Ed.) and R. M. Lerner (Vol. Ed.), *Handbook of child development* (5th ed.), Vol. 1, *Theoretical models of human development* (pp. 865–937). New York: Wiley.

Suvannathat, C., Bhanthumnavin, D., Bhuapirom, L., & Keats, D. M. (Eds.). (1985). *Handbook of Asian child development and child rearing practices.* Bangkok: Behavioral Science Research Institute, Srinakharinwirot University.

Triandis, H. C., & Heron, A. (Eds.). (1981). *Handbook of cross-cultural psychology*, Vol. 4, *Developmental psychology.* Boston: Allyn & Bacon.

RELATED BOOKS

Bavin, E. L. (1995). Language acquisition in crosslinguistic perspective. *Annual Review of Anthropology, 24,* 373–396.

Berry, J. W. (1976). *Human ecology and cognitive style: Comparative studies in cultural and psychological adaptation.* New York: Sage/Halsted.

Best, D. L., & Ruther, N. (1994). Cross-cultural themes in developmental psychology: An examination of texts, handbooks, and reviews. *Journal of Cross-Cultural Psychology, 25,* 54–77.

Dasen, P. R. (Ed.). (1997). *Piagetian psychology: Cross-cultural contributions.* New York: Gardner Press.

Dennis, W. (1966). *Group values through children's drawings.* New York: Wiley.

Ember, C. R., & Ember, M. (Eds.). (1995). *Cross-cultural research for social science.* Englewood Cliffs, NJ: Prentice-Hall.

Gibson, K., Konner, M., & Lancaster, J. (Eds.). (1991). *The brain and behavioral development: Biosocial dimensions.* Hawthorne, NY: Aldine.

Gottlieb, G. (1992). *Individual development and evolution.* New York: Oxford University Press.

Hofstede, G. H. (2001). *Culture's consequences: Comparing values, behaviors, institutions, and organizations across nations* (2nd ed.). Thousand Oaks, CA: Sage.

Husén, T. (1967). *International study of achievement in mathematics: A comparison of twelve countries* (Vol. 1). New York: Wiley.

Johnson-Powell, G., Yamamoto, J., Wyatt, G. E., & Arroyo, W. (Eds.). (1997). *Trans-cultural child development: Psychological assessment and treatment*. New York: Wiley.

Keating, D., & Hertzman, C. (Eds.). (1999). *Developmental health and the wealth of nations: Social, biological, and educational dynamics*. New York: Guilford Press.

Lambert, W. E., & Klineberg, O. (1967). *Children's views of foreign peoples: A cross-national study*. New York: Appleton-Century-Crofts.

Luria, A. R. (1976). *Cognitive development: Its cultural and social foundations*. Cambridge, MA: Harvard University Press.

McClelland, D. C. (1961). *The achieving society*. Princeton: Van Nostrand.

Nieuwenhuys, O. (1994). *Children's lifeworlds: Gender, welfare, and labour in the developing world*. London: Routledge.

Nunes, T., Schliemann, A. D., & Carraher, D. W. (1993). *Street mathematics and school mathematics*. New York: Cambridge University Press.

Pereira, M. E., & Fairbanks, L. A. (Eds.). (1993). *Juvenile primates*. New York: Oxford University Press.

Roopnarine, J. L., & Gielen, U. P. (Eds.). (in press). *Families in global perspective*. Boston: Allyn & Bacon.

Roopnarine, J. L., Johnson J. E., & Hooper, F. H. (Eds.). (1994). *Children's play in diverse cultures*. Albany: State University of New York.

Rubin, K. H. (Ed.). (1998, July). Social and emotional development: A cross-cultural perspective. Special issue, *Developmental Psychology*.

Sabatier C., & Dasen, P. R. (Eds.). (2001). *Cultures, développement et education. Autres enfants, autres écoles* [Cultures, development, and education. Other children, other schools]. Paris: L'Harmattan.

Scheper-Hughes, N., & Sargent, C. (Eds.). (1998). *Small wars: The cultural politics of childhood*. Berkeley: University of California Press.

Schieffelin, B. B., & Ochs, E. (Eds.). (1986). *Language socialization across cultures*. Cambridge: Cambridge University Press.

Sharma, D., & Fischer, K. (Eds.). (1998). *Socioemotional development across cultures*. San Francisco: Jossey-Bass.

Smith, P. K., Morita, Y., Junger-Tas, J., Olweus, D., Catalano, R., & Slee, P. (1999). *The nature of school bullying: A cross-national perspective*. London: Routledge.

Super, C. M. (Ed.). (1987). *The role of culture in developmental disorder*. New York: Academic Press.

Super, C. M., & Harkness, S. (1986). The developmental niche: A conceptualization at the interface of child and culture. *International Journal of Behavioral Development*, 9, 545–570.

United Nations Children's Fund (UNICEF). (2004). The state of the world's children. New York: Oxford University Press. (Published yearly.)

United Nations Development Programme (UNDP). (2004). *Human development report 2004*. New York: Oxford University Press. (Published yearly.)

Valsiner, J. (1988). *Developmental psychology in the Soviet Union*. Bloomington: Indiana University Press.

Williams, J., & Best, D. (1990). *Sex and psyche: Gender and self viewed cross-culturally*. Newbury Park, CA: Sage.

Zinnecker, J., & Silbereisen, R. K. (Eds.). (1996). *Kindheit in Deutschland* [Childhood in Germany]. Weinheim, Germany: Juventa.

Zukow, P. G. (1989). *Sibling interactions across cultures: Theoretical and methodological issues.* New York: Springer-Verlag.

HISTORY OF CHILDHOOD AND ADOLESCENCE

Ariès, P. (1965). *Centuries of childhood: A social history of family life.* (Robert Baldick, Trans.). New York: Random House/Vintage Books.

Clement, P. F. (1997). *Growing pains: Children in the industrial age, 1850–1890.* New York: Twayne.

Cohen, A. R. (1999). *A history of children.* Westport, CT: Greenwood Press.

Cunningham, H. (1995). *Children and childhood in Western society since 1500.* London: Longman.

DeMause, L. (Ed.). (1975). *The history of childhood.* New York: Harper Torchbooks.

Fuchs, R. (1984). *Abandoned children: Foundlings and child welfare in nineteenth century France.* Albany: State University of New York Press.

Golden, M. (1990). *Children and childhood in classical Athens.* Baltimore: Johns Hopkins University Press.

Hawes, J., & Hiner, R. (Eds.). (1991). *Children in historical and comparative perspective.* Westport, CT: Greenwood.

Hiner, R., & Hawes, J. M. (Eds.). (1985). *Growing up in America: Children in historical perspective.* Urbana: University of Illinois Press.

Kett, J. (1977). *Rites of passage: Adolescence in America, 1790 to present.* New York: Basic Books.

Levi, G., & Schmitt, J. C. (Eds.). (1997). *A history of young people in the West* (Vols. 1–2). Cambridge, MA: Harvard University Press.

Wiedeman, T. (1989). *Adults and children in the Roman Empire.* New Haven: Yale University Press.

INFANCY

Artschwanger Kay, M. (Ed.). (1982). *Anthropology of human birth.* Philadelphia: Davis.

Blaffer Hrdy, S. (1999). *Mother nature: A history of mothers, infants, and natural selection.* New York: Pantheon.

Bloch, H., & Bornstein, M. A. (Eds.). (1994). *Francophone perspectives on early development.* Hillsdale, NJ: Erlbaum.

Chisholm, J. (1983). *Navajo infancy: An ethological study of child development.* New York: Aldine.

Field, T. M., Sostek, A. M., Vietze, P., & Leiderman, P. H. (Eds.). (1981). *Culture and early interactions.* Hillsdale, NJ: Erlbaum.

Fishbein, H. (1984). *The psychology of infancy and childhood: Evolutionary and cross-cultural perspectives.* Hillsdale, NJ: Erlbaum.

Freedman, D. G. (1974). *Human infancy: An evolutionary perspective.* Hillsdale, NJ: Erlbaum.

Gottlieb, A., & De-Loache, J. S. (Eds.). (2000). *A world of babies: Imagined childcare guides for seven societies*. Cambridge: Cambridge University Press.

Hausfater, G., & Hrdy, S. B. (Eds.). (1984). *Infanticide: Comparative and evolutionary perspectives*. New York: Aldine de Gruyter.

Hewlett, B. S. (1998). Diverse contexts of human infancy. In C. R. Ember & M. Ember (Eds.), *Cross-cultural research for social science* (Vol. 1, pp. 171–200). Upper Saddle River, NJ: Prentice-Hall.

Honig, A. S. (2000). Cross-cultural study of infants and toddlers. In A. L. Comunian & U. P. Gielen (Eds.), *International perspectives on human development* (pp. 275–308). Lengerich, Germany: Pabst Science.

IJzendoorn, M. H. van, & Sagi, A. (1999). Cross-cultural patterns of attachment. In J. Cassidy & P. R. Shaver (Eds.), *Handbook of attachment: Theory, research, and clinical applications* (pp. 713–734). New York: Guilford Press.

Leiderman, P. H., Tulkin, S., & Rosenfeld, A. (Eds.). (1977). *Culture and infancy: Variations in the human experience*. New York: Academic Press.

Nugent, J. K., Lester, B. M., & Brazelton, T. B. (Eds.). (1989). *The cultural context of infancy*. Norwood: Ablex.

Stuart-Macadam, P., & Dettwyler, K. A. (Eds.). (1995). *Breast-feeding: Biocultural perspectives*. New York: Aldine de Gruyter.

CHILDREN AROUND THE WORLD

Bronfenbrenner, U. (1970). *Two worlds of childhood: U.S. and U.S.S.R*. New York: Russell Sage.

deConinck-Smith, Sandin B., & Schrumpf, E. (Eds.). (1997). *Industrious children around the world*. Odense, Denmark: Odense University Press.

Göncü, R. (Ed.). (1999). *Children's engagement in the world: Sociocultural perspectives*. Cambridge: Cambridge University Press.

Jahoda, G., & Lewis, I. M. (Eds.). (1988). *Acquiring culture: Cross cultural studies in child development*. London: Croom Helm.

Mead, M., & Wolfenstein, M. (1955). *Childhood in contemporary cultures*. Chicago: University of Chicago Press.

Roopnarine, J. L., Johnson, J. E., & Hooper, F. H. (Eds.). (1994). *Children's play in diverse cultures*. Albany: State University of New York Press.

Seabrook, J. (2001). *Children of other worlds*. Sterling, VA: Pluto Press.

United Nations Children's Fund (UNICEF). (2004). *The state of the world's children*. Oxford: Oxford University Press. (Published yearly.)

Whiting, B. B., & Whiting, J. W. M. (1975). *Children of six cultures: A psycho-cultural analysis*. Cambridge, MA: Harvard University Press.

Young, M. E. (Ed.). (2002). *From early childhood development to human development: Investing in our children's future*. Washington, DC: World Bank.

IMMIGRANT AND MINORITY CHILDREN

Adler, L. L., & Gielen, U. P. (Eds.). (2003). *Migration: Immigration and emigration in international perspective*. Westport, CT: Greenwood Press.

Ahearn, F., & Athey, J. (Eds.). (1991). *Refugee children: Theory, research and service.* Baltimore: John Hopkins University Press.

Anwar, M. (1998). *Between cultures: Continuity and change in the lives of young Asians.* London: Routledge.

Berrol, S. C. (1995). *Growing up American: Immigrant children in America, then and now.* New York: Twayne.

Booth, A., Crouter, A. C., & Landale, V. (Eds.). (1997). *Immigration and the family: Research and policy on U.S. immigrants.* Mahwah, NJ: Erlbaum.

Brittain, C. (2002). *Transnational messages: Experiences of Chinese and Mexican immigrants in American schools.* New York: LFB Scholarly Publishing LLC.

Caplan, N., Whitmore, J. K., & Choy, M. H. (1991). *Children of the boat people: A study of educational success.* Ann Arbor: University of Michigan Press.

Child, I. L. (1943). *Italian or American? The second generation in conflict.* New Haven: Yale University Press.

Eldering, L., & Kloprogge, J. (Eds.). (1998). *Different cultures, same schools: Ethnic minority children in Europe.* Amsterdam: Swets and Zeiteinger.

Ghuman, P. A. S. (2003). *Double loyalties: South Asian adolescents in the West.* Cardiff, UK: University of Wales Press.

Gibson, M. A. (1989). *Accommodation without assimilation: Sikh immigrants in an American high school.* Ithaca, NY: Cornell University Press.

Gibson, M., & Ogbu, J. (Eds.). (1991). *Minority status and schooling: A comparative study of immigrant and involuntary minorities.* New York: Garland.

Greenfield, P. M., & Cocking, R. R. (Eds.). (1994). *Cross-cultural roots of minority child development.* Hillsdale, NJ: Erlbaum.

Harvard Education Review. (2001). *Special issue: Immigration and education, 71* (3), i–x, 345–648.

Hernandez, D. (Ed.). (1998). *Children of immigrants: Health, adjustment, and public assistance.* Washington, DC: National Academy Press.

Hill, S. A. (1999). *African American children: Socialization and development in families.* Thousand Oaks, CA: Sage.

Hostetler, J. A., & Huntington, G. E. (1971). *Children in Amish society: Socialization and community education.* Orlando, FL: Holt, Rinehart, & Winston.

McAdoo, H. P. (Ed.). (2002). *Black children: Social, educational, and parental environments* (2nd ed.). Thousand Oaks, CA: Sage.

Montero-Sieburth, M., & Villaruel, F. (Eds.). (1999). *Making invisible Latino adolescents visible: A critical approach to Latino diversity.* New York: Garland.

Parker, D. (1995). *Through different eyes: The cultural identities of young Chinese people in Britain.* Aldershot, UK: Avebury.

Phinney, J., & Rotherham, M. (Eds.). (1987). *Children's ethnic socialization: Pluralism and development.* Beverly Hills, CA: Sage.

Portes, A., & Rumbaut, R. G. (2001). *Legacies: The story of the immigrant second generation.* Berkeley: University of California Press.

Ross Leadbeater, B. J., & Way, N. (2001). *Growing up fast: Transitions to early adulthood of inner-city adolescent mothers.* Mahwah, NJ: Erlbaum.

Rumbaut, R., & Cornelius, W. A. (1995). *California's immigrant children: Theory, research, and implications for educational policy.* San Diego: Center for U.S.-Mexican Studies, University of California.

Rumbaut, R. G., & Portes, A. (Eds.). (2001). *Ethnicities: Children of immigrants in America.* Berkeley: University of California Press.

Suárez-Orozco, C., & Suárez-Orozco, M. M. (2001). *Children of immigration.* Cambridge, MA: Harvard University Press.

Suárez-Orozco, M. M., & Suárez-Orozco, C. (1995). *Transformations: Immigration, family life, and achievement motivation among Latino adolescents.* Stanford, CA: Stanford University Press.

Sung, B. L. (1987). *The adjustment experience of Chinese immigrant children in New York City.* Staten Island, NY: Center for Migration Studies.

Taylor, R. (Ed.). (1998). *Minority families in the United States: A multicultural perspective* (3rd ed.). Upper Saddle River, NJ: Prentice-Hall.

Taylor, R., Gibbs, J., & Huang, L. N. (1997). *Children of color: Psychological interventions with culturally diverse youth.* San Francisco: Jossey-Bass.

Tokuhama-Espinosa, T. (2000). *Raising multinational children: Foreign language acquisition and children.* Westport, CT: Greenwood.

Waters, M. (1999). *Black identities: West Indian immigrant dreams and American realities.* Cambridge, MA: Harvard University Press.

Wong, Y. F. L. (1992). *Education of Chinese children in Britain and the USA.* Clevedon, England: Multilingual Matters.

Zentella, A. C. (1997). *Growing up bilingual: Puerto Rican children in New York.* Oxford: Blackwell.

Zhou, M. (1997). Growing up American: The challenge confronting immigrant children and children of immigrants. *Annual Review of Sociology, 23,* 63–95.

Zhou, M., & Bankston, C. L. (1998). *Growing up American: How Vietnamese children adapt to life in the United States.* New York: Russell Sage.

CHILDREARING

Bornstein, M. H. (Ed.). (1991). *Cultural approaches to parenting.* Hillsdale, NJ: Erlbaum.

——. (Ed.). (2002). *Handbook of parenting* (2nd ed., 5 vols.). Mahwah, NJ: Erlbaum.

Bozett, F. W., & Hanson, S. M. H. (1991). *Fatherhood and families in cultural context.* New York: Springer.

Gottlieb, A., & DeLoach, J. S. (Eds.). (2000). *A world of babies: Imagined childcare guides for seven societies.* Cambridge: Cambridge University Press.

Harkness, S., & Super, C. M. (Eds.). (1996). *Parents' cultural belief systems: Their origins, expressions, and consequences.* New York: Guilford Press.

Hewlett, B. (Ed.). (1992). *Father-child relations: Cultural and biosocial contexts.* New York: Aldine de Gruyter.

Lamb, M. (Ed.). (1987). *The father's role: Cross-cultural perspectives.* Hillsdale, NJ: Erlbaum.

Lamb, M. E., Sternberg, K. J., Hwang, C. P., & Broberg, A. G. (Eds.). (1992). *Childcare in context: Cross-cultural perspectives.* Hillsdale, NJ: Erlbaum

LeVine, R. A., Miller, P. M., & West, M. M. (Eds.). (1988). *Parental behavior in diverse societies.* San Francisco: Jossey-Bass.

Levinson, D. (1989). *Family violence in cross-cultural perspective*. Newbury Park, CA: Sage.

Minturn, L., & Lambert, W. W. (1964). *Mothers of six cultures: Antecedents of child rearing*. New York: Wiley.

Rogoff, B. (1990). *Apprenticeship in thinking: Cognitive development in social context*. New York: Oxford University Press.

Rohner, R. P. (1975). *They love me, they love me not: Worldwide study of parental rejection*. New Haven: HRAF Press.

———. (1986). *The warmth dimension*. Beverly Hills, CA: Sage.

Roopnarine, J. L., & Carter, D. B. (Eds.). (1992). *Parent-child socialization in diverse cultures*. Norwood, NJ: Ablex.

Sigel, I. E., McGillicuddy-DeLisi, A., & Goodnow, J. J. (Eds.). (1992). *Parental belief systems: The psychological consequences for children* (2nd ed.). Hillsdale, NJ: Erlbaum.

Small, M. F. (2001). *Kids: How biology and culture shape the way we raise our children*. New York: Random House.

Trommsdorff, G. (Ed.). (1989). *Sozialisation im Kulturvergleich* [Socialization in cross-cultural comparison]. Stuttgart, Germany: F. Enke Vlg.

Whiting, B. B. (Ed.). (1963). *Six cultures: Studies of childrearing*. New York: Wiley.

ADOLESCENCE

Alsaker, F. D., & Flammer, A. (1999). *The adolescent experience: European and American adolescents in the 1990s*. Mahwah, NJ: Erlbaum.

Amit-Talai, V., & Wulff, H. (Eds.). (1995). *Youth cultures: A cross-cultural perspective* (2nd ed.). New York: Routledge.

Arnett, J. (2004). *Adolescence and emerging adulthood: A cultural approach* (2nd ed.). Upper Saddle River, NJ: Prentice-Hall.

Brown, B. B., Larson, R., & Saraswathi, T. S. (Eds.). (2002). *The world's youth: Adolescence in eight regions of the globe*. New York: Cambridge University Press.

Burbank, V. K. (1988). *Aboriginal adolescence: Maidenhood in an Australian community*. New Brunswick, NJ: Rutgers University Press.

Chisholm, L., Buchner, P., Kruger, H. H., & Du Bois-Reymond, M. (Eds.). (1995). *Growing up in Europe: Contemporary theories in childhood and youth studies*. New York: Walter de Gruyter.

Condon, R. G. (1987). *Inuit youth: Growth and change in the Canadian Arctic*. New Brunswick, NJ: Rutgers University Press.

Davis, S. S., & Davis, D. A. (1989). *Adolescence in a Moroccan town*. New Brunswick, NJ: Rutgers University Press.

Eliade, M. (1975). *Rites and symbols of initiation*. New York: Harper & Row.

Fuchs, E. (Ed.). (1976). *Youth in a changing world: Cross-cultural perspectives on adolescence*. The Hague: Mouton.

Gibbons, J. L., & Gielen, U. P. (Eds.). (2000). Adolescence in international and cross-cultural perspective. Special issue, *International Journal of Group Tensions, 29* (1–2).

Gibbons, J. L., & Stiles, D. A. (2004). *Thoughts of youth: An international perspective on adolescents' ideal person*. Greenwich, CT: Information Age.

Gibson-Cline, J. (1996). *Adolescence from crisis to coping: A thirteen nation study*. Oxford: Butterworth-Heinemann.

Gillespie, J. M., & Allport, G. W. (1955). *Youth's outlook on the future: A cross-national study*. Garden City, NY: Doubleday.

Gilmore, D. (1990). *Manhood in the making: Cultural concepts of masculinity*. New Haven: Yale University Press.

Hollos, M., & Leis, P. E. (1989). *Becoming Nigerian in Ijo society*. New Brunswick, NJ: Rutgers University Press.

Hurrelmann, K. (Ed.). (1994). *International handbook of adolescence*. Westport, CT: Greenwood.

Hurrelmann, K., & Engel, U. (Eds.). (1989). *The social world of adolescents: International perspectives*. Berlin: Walter de Gruyter.

Junger-Tas, J., Terlow, G. W., & Klein, M. W. (1994). *Delinquent behavior among young people in the Western world*. New York: Kugler.

Kahane, R., with Rapoport, T. (1997). *The origins of postmodern youth: Informal youth movements in a comparative perspective*. Berlin: Walter de Gruyter.

Kett, J. (1977). *Rites of passage: Adolescence in America 1790 to present*. New York: Basic Books.

LeTendre, G. K., & Rohlen, T. P. (2002). *Learning to be an adolescent: Growing up in U.S. and Japanese middle schools*. New Haven: Yale University Press.

Levi, G., & Schmitt, J. C. (Eds.). (1997). *A history of young people in the West* (Vols. 1–2). Cambridge, MA: Harvard University Press.

Loughery, J. (1995). *Into the widening world: International coming-of-age stories*. New York: Persea Books.

Mahdi, L. C., Foster, S., & Little, M. (Eds.). (1987). *Betwixt and between: Patterns of masculine and feminine initiation*. LaSalle, IL: Open Court.

Nurmi, J. E. (Ed.). (1998). *Adolescents, culture, and conflicts: Growing up in contemporary Europe*. New York: Garland.

Offer, D., Ostrov, E., Howard, K. I., & Atkinson, R. (1988). *The teenage world: Adolescents' self-image in ten countries*. New York: Plenum Medical.

Raffaelli, M., & Larson, R. (Eds.), *Homeless and working youth around the world: Exploring developmental issues*. San Francisco: Jossey-Bass.

Schlegel, A., & Barry III, H. (1991). *Adolescence: An anthropological inquiry*. New York: Free Press.

Scott, R., & Scott, W. A. (1998). *Adjustment of adolescents: Cross-cultural similarities and differences*. London: Routledge.

Weisfeld, G. (1999). *Evolutionary principles of human adolescence*. New York: Basic Books.

Yates, M., & Youniss, J. (Eds.). (1999). *Roots of civic identity: International perspectives on community service and activism in youth*. Cambridge: Cambridge University Press.

Young, H. B., & Ferguson, L. R. (1981). *Puberty to manhood in Italy and America*. New York: Academic Press.

AGING AND DYING

Counts, D. R., & Counts, D. A. (Eds.). (1991). *Coping with the final tragedy: Cultural variation in dying and grieving*. Amityville, NY: Baywood.

Dickenson, D., & Johnson, M. (Eds.). (1993). *Death, dying, and bereavement*. London: Sage.

Frazier, C. L., & Glascock, A. P. (2001). Aging and old age in cross-cultural perspective. In L. L. Adler & U. P. Gielen (Eds.), *Cross-cultural topics in psychology* (2nd ed., pp. 115–128). Westport, CT: Greenwood Press.

Fry, C. L. (1980). *Aging in culture and society: Comparative viewpoints and strategies*. New York: J. F. Bergin.

———. (1996). Age, aging, and culture. In R. H. Binstork & L. K. George (Eds.), *Handbook of aging and the social sciences* (4th ed., pp. 117–136). New York: Academic Press.

Gielen, U. P., & Laungani, P. (1999). International perspectives on death and bereavement. Special issue, *International Journal of Group Tensions, 28* (1–2).

Holmes, E. R., & Holmes, L. D. (1995). *Other cultures, elder years* (2nd ed.). Thousand Oaks, CA: Sage.

Huntington, R. (1991). *Celebrations of death: The anthropology of mortuary ritual*. Cambridge: Cambridge University Press.

Irish, D. P., Lundquist, K. S., & Nelson, V. J. (1993). *Ethnic variations in dying, death, and grief: Diversity in universality*. London: Taylor & Francis.

Keith, J., Fry, C., Glascock, A. P., Ikels, C., Dickerson-Putnam, J., Harpending, H. C., & Draper, P. (1994). *The aging experience: Diversity and commonality across cultures*. Thousand Oaks, CA: Sage.

Lehr, U., Seiler, E., & Thomas, H. (2000). Aging in a cross-cultural perspective. In A. L. Comunian & U. Gielen (Eds.), *International perspectives on human development* (pp. 571–589). Lengerich, Germany: Pabst.

Parkes, C. M., Laungani, P., & Young, W. (1997). *Death and bereavement across cultures*. London: Routledge.

Secretan, T. (1995). *Going into darkness: Fantastic coffins from Africa*. London: Thames & Hudson.

Simmons, L. (1945). *The role of the aged in primitive society*. New Haven: Yale University Press.

Sokolovsky, J. (Ed.). (1990). *The cultural context of aging: Worldwide perspectives*. New York: Bergin and Garvey.

THE AMERICAS

Aptekar, L. (1988). *Street children of Cali*. Durham, NC: Duke University Press.

Briggs, J. L. (1998). *Inuit morality play: The emotional education of a three-year-old*. New Haven: Yale University Press.

Condon, R. G. (1988). *Inuit youths: Growth and change in the Canadian Arctic*. New Brunswick, NJ: Rutgers University Press.

Hecht, T. (1998). *At home in the street: Street children of northeast Brazil*. New York: Cambridge University Press.

Henry, J., & Zunia, H. (1944). *Doll play of Pilaga Indian Children: An experimental and field analysis of the behavior of Pilaga Indian Children*. Research monograph no. 4. New York: American Orthopsychiatric Association.

Hill, K., & Hurtado, A. M. (1996). *Ache life history: The ecology and demography of a foraging people*. New York: Aldine de Gruyter.

Holtzman, W. H., Diaz-Guerrero, R., & Swartz, J. D. (1975). *Personality development in two cultures: A cross-cultural longitudinal study of school children in Mexico and the United States*. Austin: University of Texas.

Landy, D. (1959). *Tropical childhood: Cultural transmission and learning in a rural Puerto Rican Village*. Chapel Hill: University of North Carolina Press.

Roopnarine, J. L., & Brown, J. (Eds.). (1997). *Caribbean families: Diversity among ethnic groups*. Norwood, NJ: Ablex.

Scheper-Hughes, N. (1992). *Death without weeping: The violence of everyday life in Brazil*. Berkeley: University of California Press.

NEAR AND MIDDLE EAST, NORTH AFRICA

Ahmed, R. A., & Gielen, U. P. (Eds.). (1998). *Psychology in the Arab countries*. Menoufia, Egypt: Menoufia University Press.

Ammar, H. (1996). *Growing up in an Egyptian village*. New York: Octagon Books.

Davis, S. S., & Davis, D. A. (1989). *Adolescence in a Moroccan town: Making social sense*. New Brunswick, NJ: Rutgers University Press.

Fernea, E. W. (Ed.). (1995). *Children in the Muslim Middle East*. Austin: University of Texas Press.

Friedl, E. (1997). *Children of Deh Koh: Young life in an Iranian village*. Syracuse: University of Syracuse Press.

Hobbs, J. J. (1989). *Bedouin life in the Egyptian wilderness*. Austin: University of Texas Press.

Nicolaisen, J., & Nicolaisen, I. (1997). *The pastoral Tuareg*. Copenhagen: Rhodes.

Prothro, E. T. (1962). *Childrearing in the Lebanon*. Cambridge, MA: Harvard University Press.

Rabin, A. I. (1965). *Growing up in the kibbutz*. New York: Springer.

Spiro, M. E. (1958). *Children of the kibbutz*. Cambridge, MA: Harvard University Press.

SUB-SAHARAN AFRICA

Ainsworth, M. D. (1967). *Infancy in Uganda: Infant care and the growth of love*. Baltimore: John Hopkins University Press.

Beckwith, C., & Fisher A. (1999). *African ceremonies* (Vols. 1–2). New York: Abrams.

Dasen, P. R. (1984). The cross-cultural study of intelligence: Piaget and the Baoulé. *International Journal of Psychology, 19*, 407–434.

Erny, P. (1973). *Childhood and cosmos: The social psychology of the black African child*. Washington, DC: Black Orpheus Press.

———. (1981). *The child and his environment in black Africa: An essay on traditional education*. New York: Oxford University Press.

Fortes, M. (1938). *Social and psychological aspects of education in Taleland*. Supplement to *Africa, 2* (4).

Gay, J., & Cole, M. (1967). *The new mathematics and an old culture: A study of learning among the Kapelle of Liberia*. New York: Holt, Rinehart, & Winston.

Hewlett, B. S. (1991). *Intimate fathers: The nature and context of Aka Pygmy paternal infant care*. Ann Arbor: University of Michigan Press.

Hollos, M., & Leis, P. E. (1989). *Becoming Nigerian in Ijo society.* New Brunswick, NJ: Rutgers University Press.

Kaye, B. (1962). *Bringing children up in Ghana.* London: Allen & Unwin.

Kilbride, P. L., & Kilbride, J. C. (1990). *Changing family life in East Africa: Women and children at risk.* University Park: Pennsylvania State University Press.

Kilbride, P. L., Suda, S., & Njeru, E. (2000). *Street children in Kenya: Voices of children in search of a childhood.* Westport, CT: Greenwood.

Lancy, D. F. (1996). *Playing on the mother ground: Cultural routines for children's development.* New York: Guilford Press.

LeVine, R. A., Dixon S., LeVine, S., Richman, A., Leiderman, P. H., Keefer, C. H., & Brazelton, T. B. (1994). *Child care and culture: Lessons from Africa.* Cambridge: Cambridge University Press.

Rabain, J. (1979). *L'enfant du lignage: Du sevrage à la classe d'âge chez les Wolof du Sénégal* [The child of the lineage: From weaning to age classification among the Wolof of Senegal]. Paris: Payot.

Read, M. (1960/1968). *Children of their fathers: Growing up among the Ngoni of Malawi.* New York: Holt, Rinehart, & Winston.

Serpell, R. (1993). *The significance of schooling: Life-journeys in an African society.* Cambridge: Cambridge University Press.

INDIAN SUBCONTINENT

Berland, J. C. (1982). *No five fingers are alike.* Cambridge, MA: Harvard University Press.

Burra, N. B. (1995). *Born to work: Child labour in India.* New Delhi: Oxford University Press.

Kakar, S. (1981). *The inner world: A psychoanalytic study of childhood and society in India* (2nd ed.). Delhi: Oxford University Press.

———. (1998). *The Indian psyche* (Vols. 1–2). New Delhi: Oxford University Press/ Penguin Books.

Kurtz, S. (1992). *All the mothers are one.* New Delhi: Discovery.

Rohner, R. P., & Chaki-Sircar, M. (1988). *Women and children in a Bengali village.* Hanover, NH: University Press of New England.

Saraswathi, T. S. (Ed.). (1999). *Culture, socialization, and human development: Theory, research, and applications in India.* New Delhi: Sage.

Saraswathi, T. S., & Dutta, R. (1987). *Developmental psychology in India.* Delhi: Sage.

———. (1988). *Invisible boundaries: Grooming for adult roles.* New Delhi: Northern Book Centre.

Seymour, S. (1999). *Women, family, and childcare in India.* New York: Cambridge University Press.

Sharma, D. (Ed.). (2003). *Childhood, family, and sociopolitical change in India: Reinterpreting the inner world.* Delhi: Sage.

Sharma, D., & Gielen, U. P. (2000, Winter). Childhood and sociocultural change in India: A reinterpretation of Sudhir Kakar's work. Special issue, *International Journal of Group Tensions, 29* (3–4).

Sharma, N. (1996). *Identity of the adolescent girl.* New Delhi: Discovery.

Viramma, J. R., & Racine, J. L. (1997). *Viramma: Life of an untouchable.* (W. Hobson, Trans.). New York: Verso/UNESCO.

SOUTH SEAS AND SOUTHEAST ASIA

Brown, G. (1910). *Melanesians and Polynesians: Their life-histories described and compared.* London: Macmillan.

Bruch, H. B. (1990). *Growing up agreeably: Bonerate childhood observed.* Honolulu: University of Hawaii Press.

Burbank, V. (1988). *Aboriginal adolescence: Maidenhood in an Australian Aboriginal community.* New Brunswick, NJ: Rutgers University Press.

Côté, J. E. (1994). *Adolescent storm and stress. An evaluation of the Mead/Freeman controversy.* Hillsdale, NJ: Erlbaum.

Freeman, D. (1983). *Margaret Mead and Samoa: The making and unmaking of an anthropological myth.* Cambridge, MA: Harvard University Press.

Guthrie, G. M., & Jacobs, P. J. (1966). *Child rearing and personality development in the Philippines.* University Park: Pennsylvania State University Press.

Hamilton, A. (1981). *Nature and nurture: Aboriginal child-rearing in north-central Arnhem Land.* Canberra: Australian Institute of Aboriginal Studies.

Herdt, G. (1987). *Guardians of the flutes* (2nd ed.). New York: Columbia University Press.

Herdt, G., & Leavitt, S. (Eds.). (1998). *Adolescence in Pacific island societies.* Pittsburgh: University of Pittsburgh Press.

Hollan, D. W., & Wellenkamp, J. C. (1996). *The thread of life: Toraja reflections on the life cycle.* Honolulu: University of Hawaii Press.

Marshall, L. B. (Ed.). (1981). *Siblingship in Oceania: Studies in the meaning of kin relations.* Ann Arbor: University of Michigan Press.

———. (Ed.). (1985). *Infant care and feeding in the South Pacific.* New York: Gordon & Breach.

Mead, M. (1928). *Coming of age in Samoa.* New York: Morrow.

———. (1930). *Growing up in New Guinea: A comparative study of primitive education.* New York: Morrow.

Mead, M., & MacGregor, F. C. (1951). *Growth and culture: A photographic study of Balinese Childhood.* New York: Putnam.

Mershon, K. E. (1971). *Seven plus seven: Mysterious life rituals in Bali.* New York: Vantage Press.

Morton, H. (1996). *Becoming Tongan: An ethnography of childhood.* Honolulu: University of Hawaii Press.

Nuckolls, C. W. (1993). *Siblings in South Asia: Brothers and sisters in cultural context.* New York: Guilford Press.

Ochs, E. (1988). *Culture and language development: Language acquisition and socialization in a Samoan village.* Cambridge: Cambridge University Press.

Ritchie, J., & Ritchie, J. (1979). *Growing up in Polynesia.* Sydney: Allen & Unwin.

Suvannathat, C., Bhanthumnavin, D. Bhuapirom, L., & Keats, D. M. (Eds.). (1985). *Handbook of Asian child development and child rearing practices.* Bangkok: Behavioral Science Research Institute, Srinakharinwirot University.

Williams, T. R. (1969). *A Borneo childhood.* Oxford: Blackwell.

EAST ASIA

Behnke Kinney, A. (Ed.). (1995). *Chinese views of childhood.* Honolulu: University of Hawaii Press.

Bond, M. H. (Ed.). (1996). *The handbook of Chinese psychology.* Hong Kong: Oxford University Press.

Formanek, S., & Linhart, S. (Eds.). (1992). *Japanese biographies: Life histories, life cycles, life stages.* Vienna: Austrian Academy of Science.

Goodman, R. (1990). *Japan's "international youth": The emergence of a new class of school children.* Oxford: Oxford University Press.

Ho, D. Y. F. (1986). Chinese patterns of socialization. In M. Bond (Ed.), *The psychology of the Chinese people* (pp. 1–37). Hong Kong: Oxford University Press.

Kessen, W. (Ed.). (1975). *Childhood in China.* New Haven: Yale University Press.

Lau, S. (Ed.). (1997). *Growing up the Chinese way: Chinese child and adolescent development.* Hong Kong: Chinese University Press.

Palmore, E. G., & Maeda, D. (1985). *The honorable elders revisited* (2nd ed.). Durham, NC: Duke University Press.

Path, D. W. (1980). *Long engagements: Maturity in modern Japan.* Stanford, CA: Stanford University Press.

Peak, L. (1991). *Learning to go to school in Japan: The transition from home to preschool life.* Berkeley: University of California Press.

Shwalb, D. W., Imaizumi, N., & Nakazawa, J. (1987). The modern Japanese father: Roles and problems in a changing society. In M. E. Lamb (Ed.), *The father's role: Cross-cultural perspectives* (pp. 247–269). Hillsdale, NJ: Erlbaum.

Shwalb, D. W., & Shwalb, B. J. (Eds.). (1996). *Japanese childrearing: Two generations of scholarship.* New York: Guilford Press.

Stevens, H. W., Azuma, H., & Hakuta, K. (Eds.). (1986). *Child development and education in Japan.* New York: Freeman.

Stevenson, H. W., & Stigler, J. W. (1992). *The learning gap: Why our schools are failing and what we can learn from Japanese and Chinese education.* New York: Summit Books.

Tobin, J. T., Wu, D. Y. H., & Davidson, D. H. (1989). *Preschool in three cultures: Japan, China, and the United States.* New Haven: Yale University Press.

Wagatsuma, H., & DeVos, G. A. (1984). *Heritage of endurance: Family patterns and delinquency formation in urban Japan.* Berkeley: University of California Press.

White, M. (1993). *The material child: Coming of age in Japan and America.* New York: Free Press.

Index

About the Editors and Contributors

THOMAS M. ACHENBACH is professor of psychiatry and psychology and director of the Center for Children, Youth, and Families at the University of Vermont. Before moving to the University of Vermont, he was an associate professor of psychology at Yale University and a research psychologist at the National Institute of Mental Health. Dr. Achenbach has been a German Government Fellow at the University of Heidelberg and a Social Science Research Council Senior Faculty Fellow at Jean Piaget's Centre d'Epistémologie Génétique at the University of Geneva. He chaired the American Psychological Association's Task Force on Classification of Children's Behavior and served on the American Psychiatric Association's Task Force to Revise DSM-III. Dr. Achenbach is the recipient of the Distinguished Contribution Award of the American Psychological Association's Section on Child Clinical Psychology and the author of over 200 publications. His current research focuses on standardized assessment of psychopathology and adaptive functioning across cultures and across the life span.

LEWIS APTEKAR is a professor of counselor education at San Jose State University. His academic awards include two Fulbright scholarships (Colombia and Swaziland), and the Kellogg/Partners of the Americas Fellowship in International Development. He was also a United Nations Representative for the International Year of the Disabled in South America. He has done research and intervention with the Transpersonal Psychosocial Organization at Addis Ababa University in Ethiopia. His books include *Street Children of Cali* (1988) and *Environmental Disasters in Global Perspective* (1994). He has published over fifty chapters and articles in scientific journals and has been affiliated with the Universidad del Valle, Colombia, Institute of African Studies, University of Nairobi, University of Swaziland, Addis Ababa University, Johns Hopkins University, and the Free University of the Netherlands. He is the current president of the Society for Cross-Cultural Research.

JEFFREY JENSEN ARNETT is an independent scholar affiliated with the Department of Human Development at the University of Maryland. He is the author of a book on heavy metal music fans, *Metalheads: Heavy Metal Music and Adolescent Alienation* (1996), and the textbook *Adolescence and Emerging Adulthood: A Cultural Approach* (2004). In recent years his research and writing have focused on emerging adulthood, the age period from eighteen through the mid-twenties, characterized by exploration and instability for young people in industrialized societies. He is the chairman of the Special Interest Group on Emerging Adulthood sponsored by the Society for Research on Adolescence.

DEBORAH L. BEST is professor and chairwoman of psychology, Wake Forest University. She is past president of the International Association for Cross-Cultural Psychology, having served on the executive board for ten years, and is associate editor of the *Journal of Cross-Cultural Psychology*. She has published a number of books, articles, and chapters on the development of gender stereotypes in the United States and cross-nationally, on memory development in children and older adults, and on health education with adolescents. Her research has been supported by the NIH, the Andrus Foundation, the American Cancer Society, and the AOL Time Warner Foundation.

MARC H. BORNSTEIN is senior investigator and head of child and family research at the National Institute of Child Health and Human Development. Bornstein was a Guggenheim Foundation Fellow and received an RCDA from the NICHD, the Ford Cross-Cultural Research Award from the HRAF, the McCandless Young Scientist Award from the APA, the U.S. PHS Superior Service Award from the NIH, and the Arnold Gesell Prize from the Theodor Hellbrügge Foundation. Bornstein has held faculty positions at Princeton University and New York University as well as visiting academic appointments in Munich, London, Paris, New York, and Tokyo. Bornstein is coauthor of *Development in Infancy* (four editions) and general editor of *The Crosscurrents in Contemporary Psychology Series* (ten volumes). He also edited the *Handbook of Parenting* (Vols. 1–4, two editions), and he coedited *Developmental Psychology: An Advanced Textbook* (four editions) as well as four other volumes. Bornstein is editor of *Child Development* and *Parenting: Science and Practice*.

PAULINE F. BYNOE is assistant professor of special education, Brooklyn College, City University of New York. She received her Ed.D. from Columbia University. Her research interests include schooling and policies, Caribbean immigrant children and schooling, and curriculum and instruction as they impact on children with special needs. She has conducted a multiyear federal demonstration model to train culturally and linguistically diverse teachers for urban settings.

XINYIN CHEN received his academic training in China and Canada. He is currently a professor in the Department of Psychology, University of Western Ontario. He has received a William T. Grant Scholars Award and several other academic awards. His research interest is mainly in children and adolescents' socioemotional functioning (e.g., shyness-inhibition, aggression, and social competence), peer groups and networks, and parenting, with a focus on cross-cultural issues. He has been conducting, with his international collaborators, several large-scale, longitudinal projects in Canada, China, Brazil, India, Italy, and South Africa. His empirical articles have been published in developmental journals such as *International Journal of Behavioral Development, Child Development,* and *Developmental Psychology.*

OKSANA CHUMACHENKO obtained her M.A. degree in social-organizational psychology at Teachers College, Columbia University. As a result of her involvement in the diverse activities of the Institute for International and Cross-Cultural Psychology at St. Francis College, her current interests include cross-cultural management research, organizational anthropology, and shamanism.

HILLARY N. FOUTS is a postdoctoral fellow at the National Institute of Child Health and Human Development, Section on Social and Emotional Development. She has conducted research among the Bofi foragers and farmers in the Central African Republic. Her research focuses on social and emotional development, parent-child relations in small-scale societies, and the social, emotional, and biological contexts of weaning in early childhood. Her current interests include parent-offspring reproductive conflicts in early childhood, maternal caregiving transitions during pregnancy and weaning, infant care in different cultural and socioeconomic contexts, and caregiver sensitivity in early childhood.

ANDREW J. FULIGNI is associate professor in the Departments of Psychiatry and Psychology at the University of California, Los Angeles, after previously serving as an associate professor at the Department of Psychology at New York University. His research focuses on the family relationships and academic adjustment of adolescents from a variety of cultural groups, with a particular focus on the children of immigrant families. This work has been funded by a FIRST award from the NICHD and a Faculty Scholars Award from the William T. Grant Foundation. Fuligni was recently selected as a recipient of the APA Division 7 Boyd McCandless Award for Early Career Contribution to Developmental Psychology. He has also served on the editorial boards of the *Journal of Research on Adolescence* and *Child Development.*

HARRY W. GARDINER is professor emeritus at the University of Wisconsin, La Crosse, where he designed and taught courses in cross-cultural psychology, child development, humor in education, and international studies for twenty-seven years. He continues to teach the Orientation to Study Abroad course, as he has for the past eighteen years. He has engaged in training, teaching, and research in Europe, Asia, and the United States and has traveled to more than sixty countries. Dr. Gardiner is a past president of the Society for Cross-Cultural Research and editor of the teaching forum in the *Cross-Cultural Psychology Bulletin*. His most recent book (2004), coauthored with Corinne Kosmitzki, is *Lives Across Cultures: Cross-Cultural Human Development* (3rd ed.).

JUDITH L. GIBBONS, a professor of psychology at Saint Louis University, is a past president of the Society for Cross-Cultural Research and a fellow of the American Psychological Association. At Saint Louis University, where she offers courses in adolescent development, the psychology of women, and cross-cultural psychology, she won the university-wide teaching award. With Deborah Stiles, she is the author of *The Thoughts of Youth: An International Perspective on Adolescents' Ideal Person*. She has been doing research in Guatemala for over fifteen years and is currently studying child and adolescent development in indigenous Mayan communities in Guatemala.

UWE P. GIELEN is professor of psychology and director of the Institute for International and Cross-Cultural Psychology at St. Francis College, New York City. He is a past president of the Society for Cross-Cultural Research and of the International Council of Psychologists as well as a past chairman of the Psychology Section of the New York Academy of Sciences. He has been the editor of both *World Psychology* and the *International Journal of Group Tensions*. His areas of interest include moral development, international and cross-cultural psychology, and Tibetan Buddhism. He is editor, coeditor, or coauthor of fourteen books, including *International Perspectives on Human Development*, *Cross-Cultural Topics in Psychology* (2nd ed.), *Psychology in the Arab Countries*, *Families in Global Perspective*, and *Handbook of Culture, Therapy, and Healing*.

O. MAURICE HAYNES has been a data analyst in the Child and Family Research Section of the National Institute of Child Health and Human Development since 1991. He received his Ph.D. in comparative psychology from Wayne State University in 1985.

GISELA JIA received her B.A. in English literature (1988) and M.A. in linguistics (1991) from Beijing University, China, and her Ph.D. in cognitive and developmental psychology (1998) from New York University. She has been an assistant professor of psychology at Lehman College, City University of New York, since 1998. Her research interests include first- and second-language acquisition, and the linguistic, social, and psychological adjustments of immigrant children.

VIOLET KASPAR is a developmental psychologist and assistant professor with the Department of Psychiatry, University of Toronto. She is also a scientist with the Centre for Addiction and Mental Health–Clarke Site, a WHO Centre of Excellence. Her research examines determinants of children's mental health and adaptation, including personal risk factors and contextual processes through which conditions of trauma exposure, social stress, and material deprivation are manifested as physical or mental pathology in racial or ethnic minorities.

ROBERT A. LeVINE is an anthropologist who has been studying childhood and parenthood in different cultural settings since 1955. He is Roy E. Larsen Professor of Education and Human Development, Emeritus, at Harvard University, and has recently been teaching at the University of Hong Kong. His chapter in this book is based on research in a Gusii community in Kenya, conducted with his wife, Sarah E. LeVine, pediatrician Suzanne Dixon, and a team of other child development researchers. A selection of LeVine's articles from 1960 to 1996 will be published as a monograph of the Comparative Education Research Centre of the University of Hong Kong, titled *Socializing Children: Comparative Studies of Parents, Learning, and Educational Change*.

ASHLEY E. MAYNARD is assistant professor of psychology at the University of Hawaii. She received her Ph.D. from UCLA in 1999. Her primary research interests are in the areas of sibling socialization, the impact of the daily routine on development, and cultural learning environments, both in and out of school. She has done research with the Zinacantec Maya in Chiapas, Mexico, with families in Los Angeles, and in Hawaii. She has received awards for her research from the New York Academy of Sciences (James McKeen Cattell Award) and the APA Division 7.

KATHLEEN PAINTER has been a research psychologist at the Child and Family Research Section Laboratory at the National Institutes of Child Health and Human Development since 1987. She received an M.A. degree from George Mason University, Fairfax, Virginia, in 1985.

LILIANA PASCUAL is a sociologist. She was a guest research scientist at the National Institute of Child Health and Human Development from 1990 to 1994. Currently, she is an associate professor at the University of Buenos Aires, Argentina, and a senior research scientist at Buenos Aires City's Education Secretariat. Her research interests are in the areas of health and educational sociology.

JAIPAUL ROOPNARINE is professor of child and family studies at Syracuse University. His research interests include father-child relationships across cultures, early childhood education in global perspective, and Caribbean immigrant families and schooling. His books include *Caribbean Families: Diversity Among Ethnic Groups; Conceptual, Social-Cognitive, and Contextual Issues in the Fields of Play; Approaches to Early Childhood Education;* and *Families in Global Perspective*.

T. S. SARASWATHI retired as senior professor in human development and family studies at the Maharaja Sayajirao University of Baroda, India. Her areas of research interest include adolescence, socialization, and moral development, with special focus on cross-cultural perspectives. She is a coeditor of the 1997 *Handbook of Cross-Cultural Psychology* and editor of the recently published volume *Cross-Cultural Perspectives in Human Development: Theory, Research, and Applications*.

RONALD SINGH is currently in the Law Program of the University of London. He received his master's degree in urban studies from Hunter College, City University of New York. He is a former editor of the community newspaper *The Caribbean Journal*. His research interests include politics in the Caribbean and immigrant families and their political participation in the new country.

DANIEL A. WAGNER is a professor of education and director of the National Center on Adult Literacy at the University of Pennsylvania. He is also director of the International Literacy Institute, cosponsored by UNESCO and the University of Pennsylvania. Dr. Wagner has extensive experience in national and international educational issues. He has recently published the following books: *Literacy: Developing the Future* (first published in 1992, now in six languages), *What Makes Workers Learn: The Role of Incentives in Workplace Education and Training* (1994), *Adult Basic Skills: Innovations in Measurement and Policy Analysis* (1997), *International Perspectives on the School-to-Work Transition* (1999), *The Future of Literacy in a Changing World* (1999), and *Literacy: An International Handbook* (1999).